I0483242

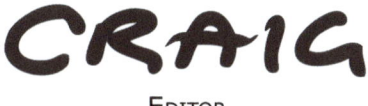

EDITOR

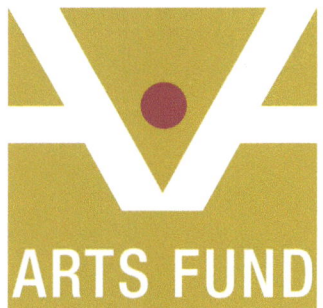

region of waterloo

ARTS FUND

*Si monumentum requiris circumspice.*

CRAIG MUSSELMAN WOULD LIKE TO THANK THE REGION OF WATERLOO ARTS FUND (WWW.ARTSFUND.CA) FOR THEIR GENEROUS GRANT. THIS BOOK WOULD NOT EXIST WITHOUT THEIR SUPPORT. FOR LINKS TO PURCHASE THE BOOK OR SUBMIT ART TO THE NEXT VOLUME PLEASE VISIT:

**TALENTNEXTDOOR.COM**

IF YOU ARE AN ARTIST LOOKING TO BE PUBLISHED OR WOULD LIKE TO FIND OUT ABOUT CRAIG'S OTHER BOOKS: PLEASE VISIT

**CRAIGMUSSELMAN.COM**

TO SEE IF I HAVE AM MAKING A BOOK IN A GENRE THAT WOULD INTEREST YOU OR HIRE ME.

"TALENT NEXT DOOR - KITCHENER WATERLOO & AREA VOLUME 2" LAYOUT AND DESIGN © 2011 CRAIG MUSSELMAN ISBN 978-0-9877895-1-8. ART USED WITH PERMISSION FROM THE WONDERFUL ARTISTS IN THE COMMUNITY WHO OTHERWISE RETAIN © COPYRIGHT OF THEIR RESPECTIVE WORKS. GREAT EFFORTS WERE MADE TO ENSURE THE ACCURACY OF THE CONTENT OF THIS COMPILATION, SO CRAIG MUSSELMAN REGRETS ANY ERRORS, BUT MUST DISCLAIM ANY LIABILITY RESULTING FROM OMISSIONS OR COMMISIONS THEREOF.

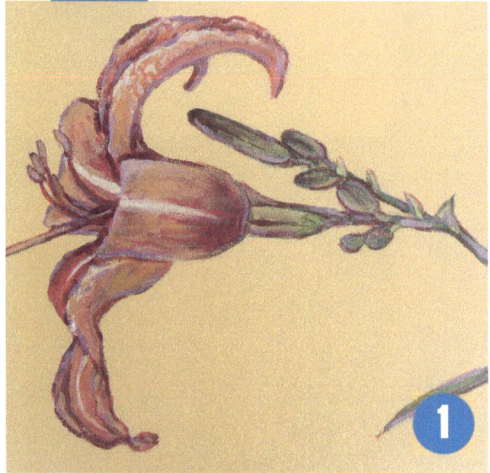

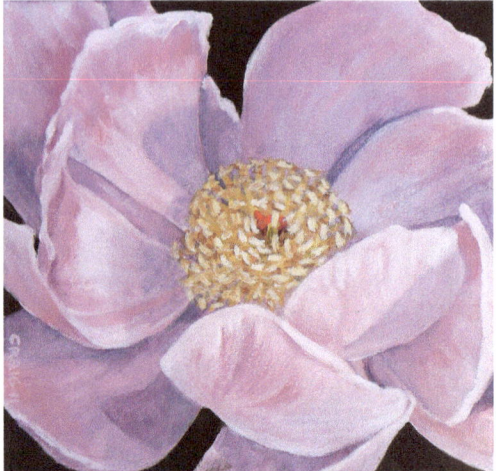

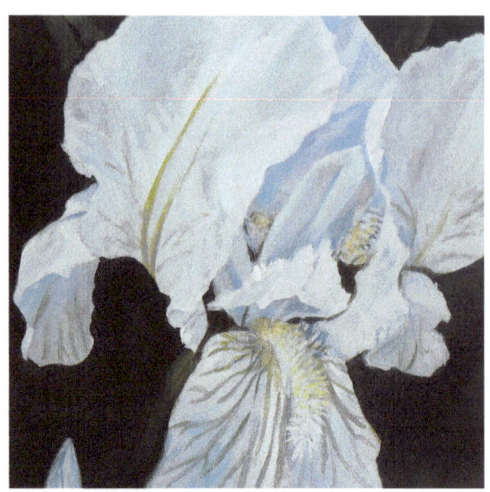

**1** **Lily, Peony, Iris** 12x12" each. Acrylic on Canvas.

**2** **Celestial Prophesy** Photomanipulation from scratch. Credit: Sxc.hu.

**3** **Pinball Machine 2.** Hyperreal construction/photomanipulation from scratch using own photos.

# CRAIG MUSSELMAN

**LOCATION:** Waterloo
**WEB:** CraigMusselman.com, NightmareInShiningArmour.com MachinesAndMagic.com, TalentNextDoor.com, Steampunkart.ca, RealisticArt.org, ShootItFor.me
**EMAIL:** TalentNextDoorBook@gmail.com, Solipsism@innocent.com, MachinesAndMagic@gmail.com

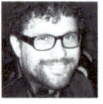

Editor - Craig Musselman is an internationally award winning Artist and Graphic Designer, specializing in elaborate digital photomontage works of art, as well, acrylic painting, and prop & costume design. He has been featured in Advanced Photoshop Magazine, ImagineFX Magazine, as well as co-authored a textbook on creative uses of Photoshop. His most recent book "Machines and Magic", features 91 Fantasy Sci Fi aritsts from around the world available 2011. He is also the founder and author of the TalentNextDoor.com series of books on local arts. Look for other books coming soon through his collection of websites: SteampunkArt.ca, RealisticArt.org, ShootItFor.me (his photo stock site) or CraigMusselman.com for the latest news and emails to submit to, or inquire about the books. For more about THIS book and helpful links visit: TalentNextDoor.com . Craig was born in 1970 & lives in Waterloo, with his longtime partner. Just look for his famous pink bicycle helmet.

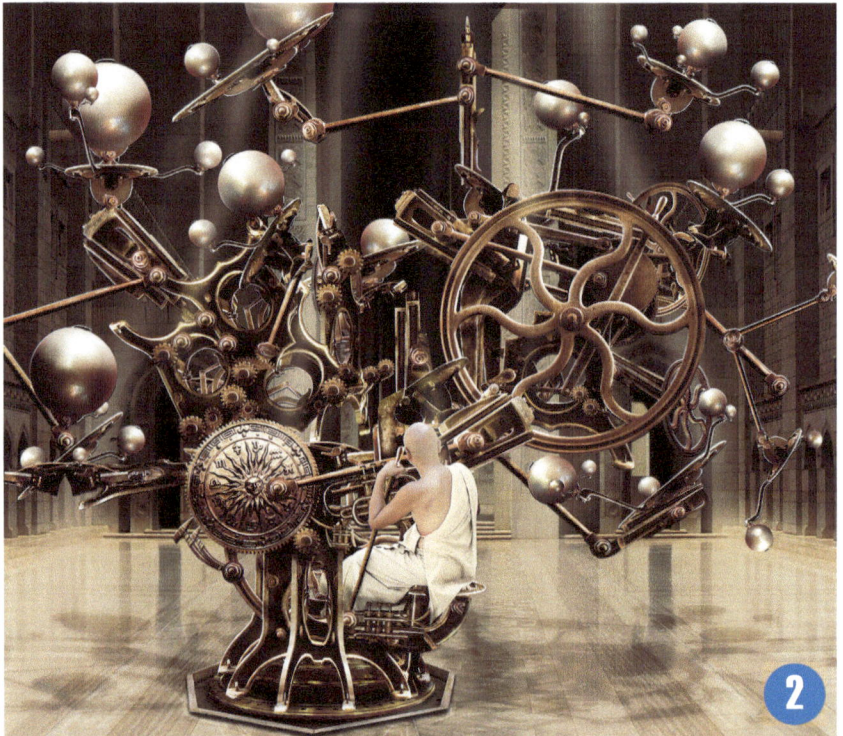

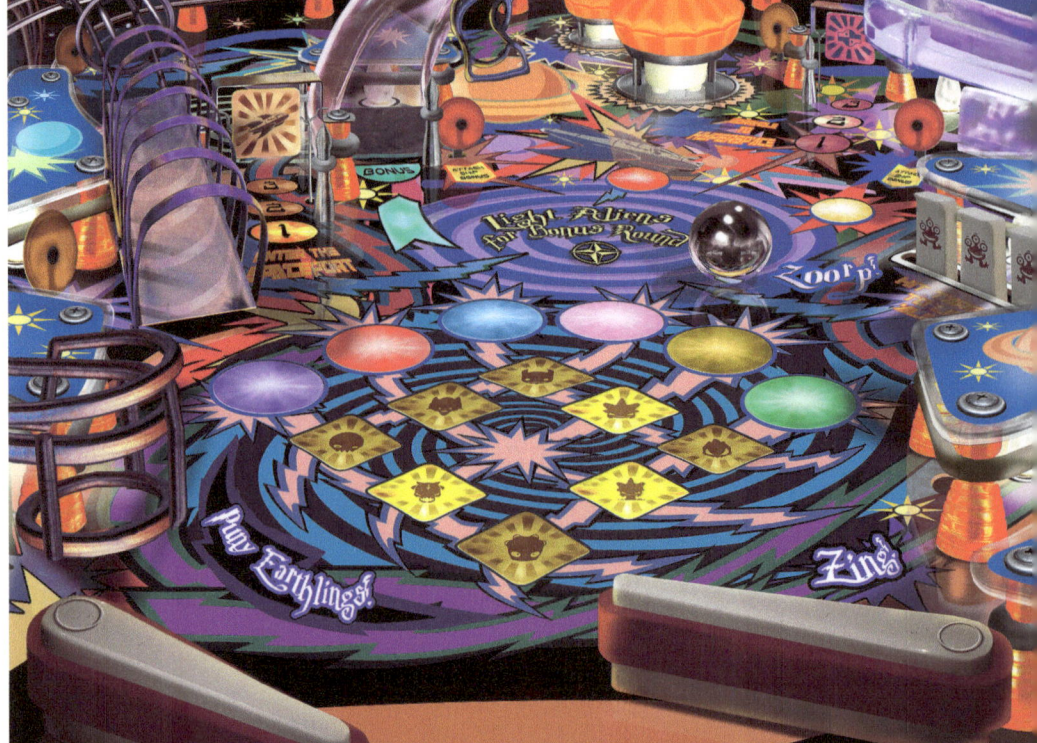

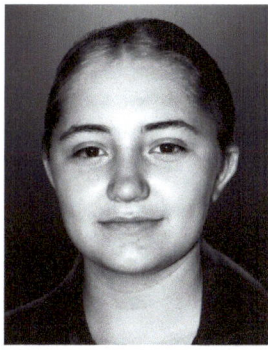 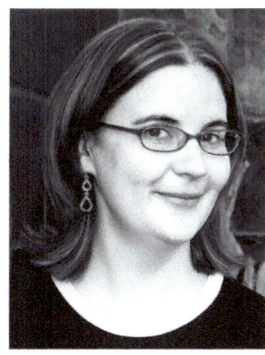 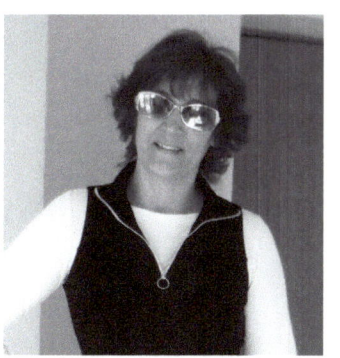 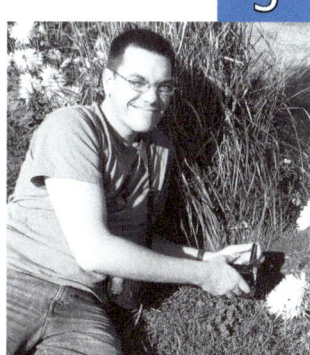

Last year I undertook an amazing project - without regard to social squabbling and politics, funding, or contacts, I set out to recruit every artist in the KW area and put them in one showcase art book. The result was Talent Next Door Vol 1. It was so much fun I decided to do it again - and on the strength of book 1 - received a grant from the Region of Waterloo Arts Fund to help out. Volume 2 is what you see here: a lot of new faces, all new artwork - and bigger and better! Well over 100 artists living in and around KW - all in one place!

All works (submitted before the deadline) were judged independently by four international artists (above from left): Zlatka Subotičanec (already a superstar in her teens), Ona Loots (one of the only two people I will freely admit can Photoshop better than I can), Elena Bissinger (whose persistence allowed me to discover her amazing body of work), and of course my partner, muse and art critic - Joël Larose who puts up with me and the craziness at the deadline. I would like to thank the judges for a very difficult task. They were handed over 400 pieces of art and told to "Just Pick the Best 5" - like that was possible. From that, they were to choose their favourite overall. The next 8 pages show a small sample of their own work with a list of their choices.

After taking in the works featured here, it is my hope that you use the listings on each page the website, to contact the artists, praise them, and find out how you can see (and BUY!) more of their work and invite them to exhibit in upcoming gallery shows. Everyone is also encouraged to submit their own work to the growing gallery on the TalentNextDoor.com website. If you are not in the book, there may be a next time. Feel free to email me at TalentNextDoor@gmail.com and join the facebook page (see the website) for updates.

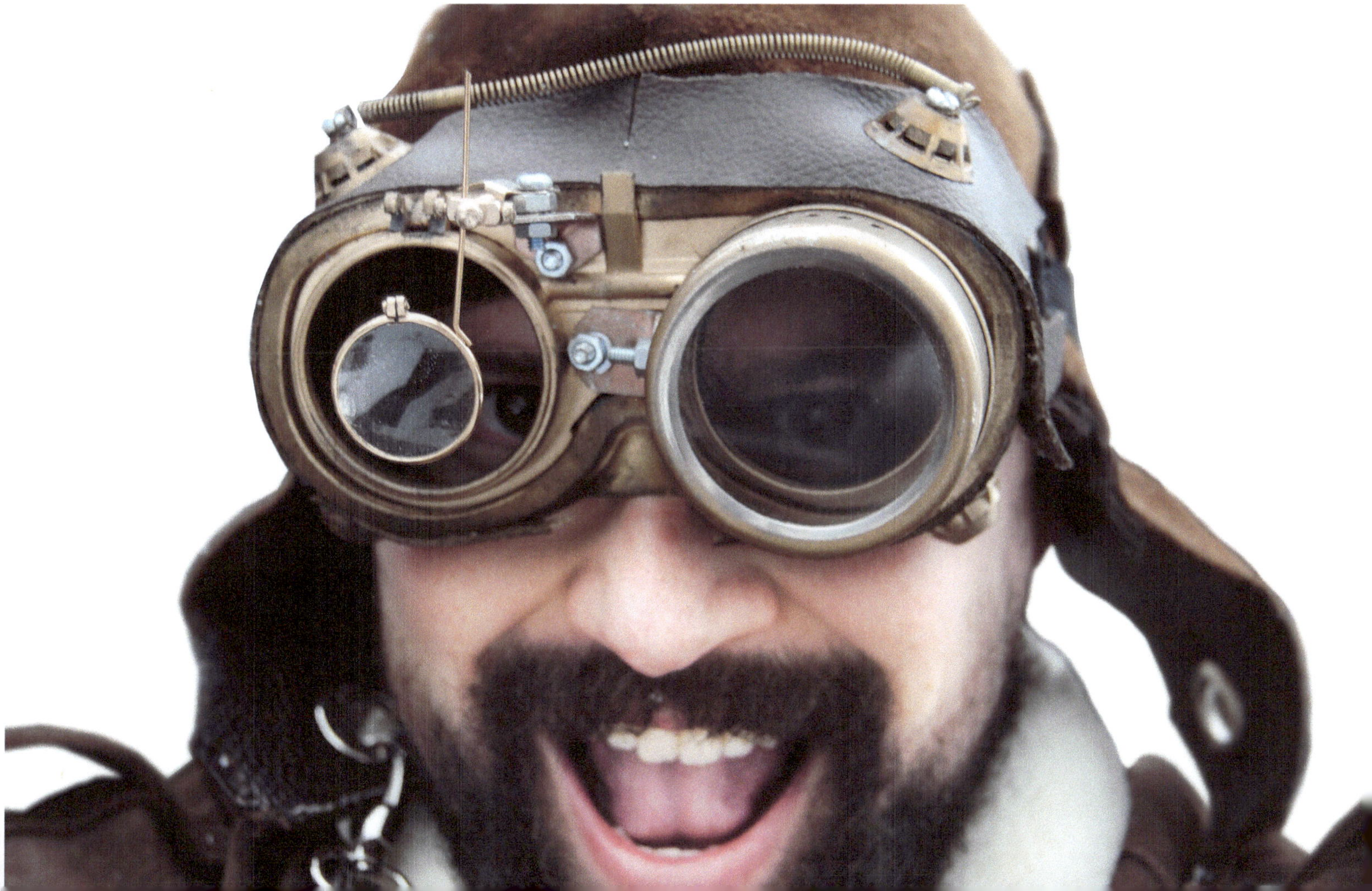

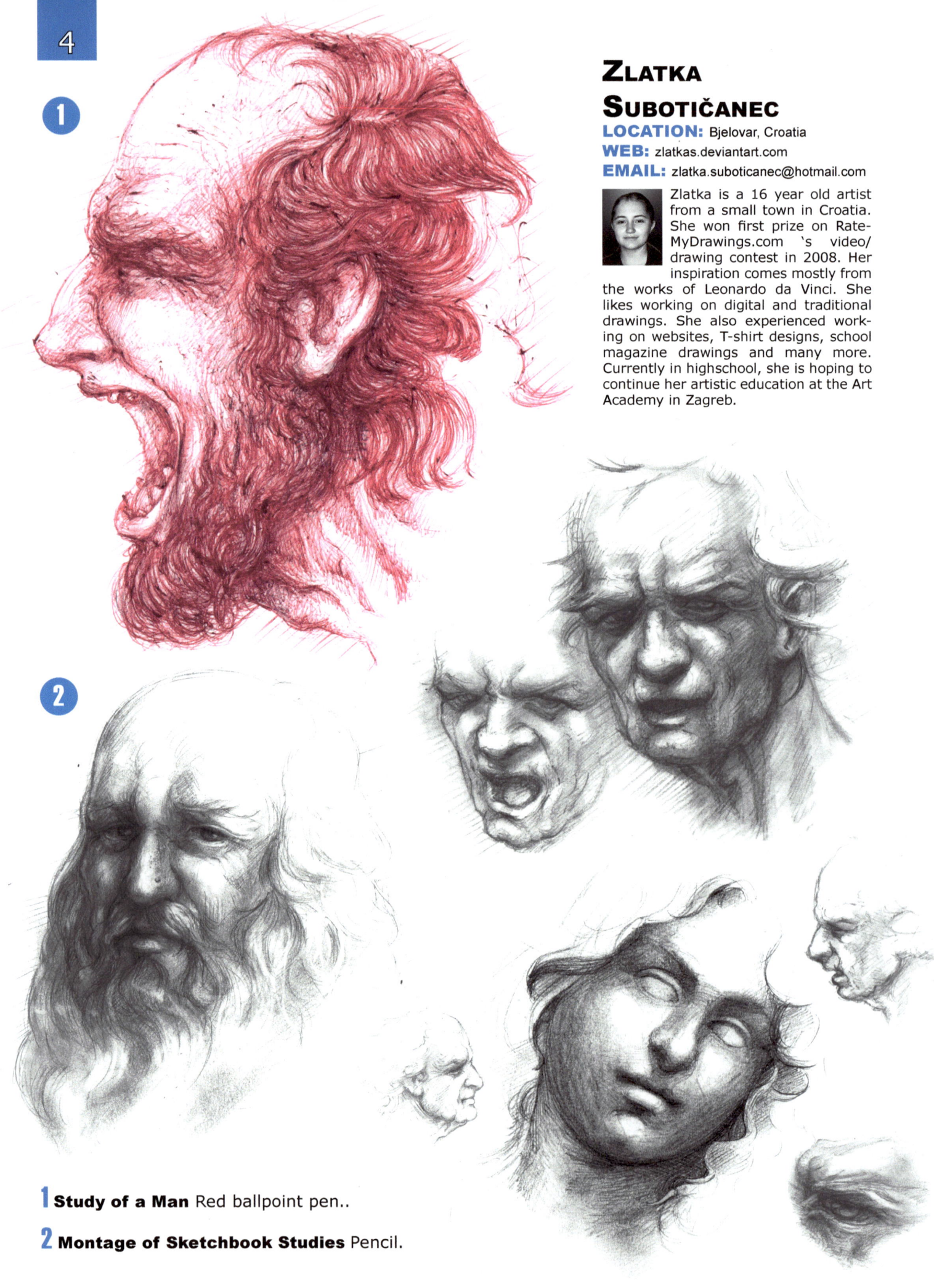

1

# ZLATKA SUBOTIČANEC

**LOCATION:** Bjelovar, Croatia
**WEB:** zlatkas.deviantart.com
**EMAIL:** zlatka.suboticanec@hotmail.com

Zlatka is a 16 year old artist from a small town in Croatia. She won first prize on Rate-MyDrawings.com 's video/drawing contest in 2008. Her inspiration comes mostly from the works of Leonardo da Vinci. She likes working on digital and traditional drawings. She also experienced working on websites, T-shirt designs, school magazine drawings and many more. Currently in highschool, she is hoping to continue her artistic education at the Art Academy in Zagreb.

2

**1 Study of a Man** Red ballpoint pen..

**2 Montage of Sketchbook Studies** Pencil.

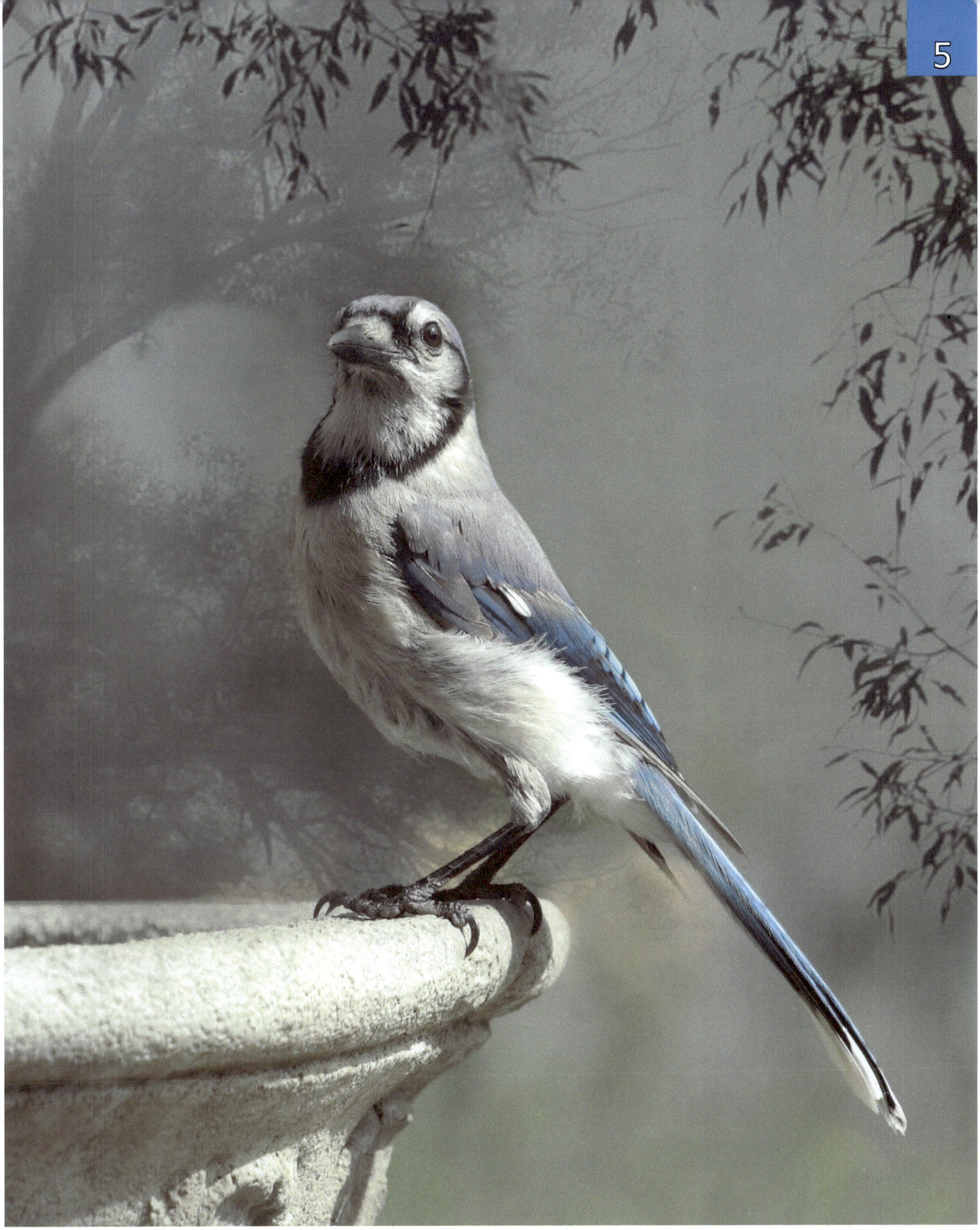

**JAN PILLER** "WINGS IN MY DREAMS"

ZLATKA's SHORT LIST

**JAN PILLER** "WINGS IN MY DREAMS"
▶ **Albert Casson** "SUN KISSED"
▶ **Jacob Bian** "BEYOND III
▶ **Mark Rehkopf** "TOONED UP"
▶ **Jan Piller** "SEAFOOD DELIGHT"

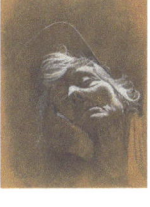 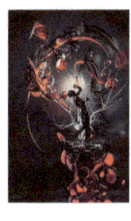 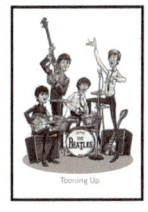 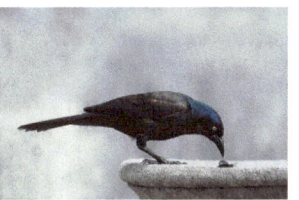

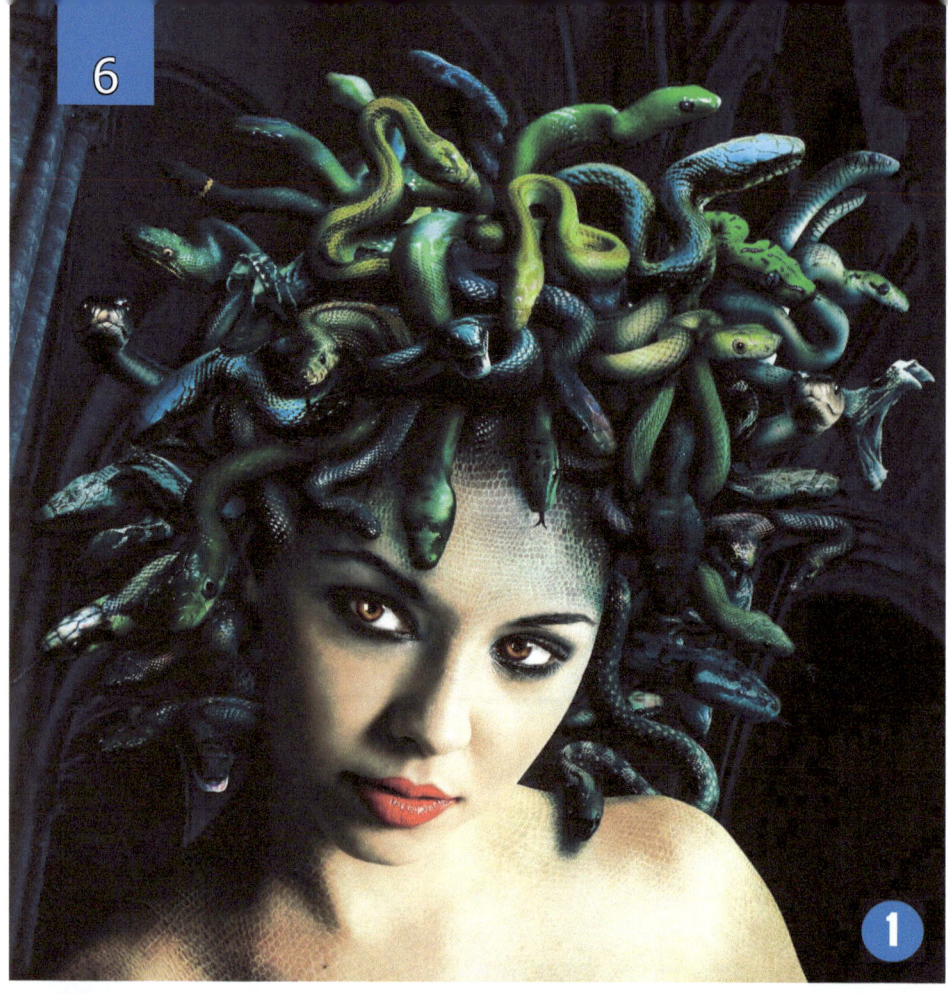

**1**

# ONA LOOTS

**LOCATION:** Pretoria, South Africa
**WEB:** Onanymous.daportfolio.com
**EMAIL:** Onymous@gmail.com

Ona Loots aka Onanymous, is a web designer and illustrator from Pretoria, South Africa. Her amazing photomanipulations have been a major force to contend with in online competitions since starting in 2005. She works mostly in digital mediums, but thinks it sometimes just feels good to get your hands dirty, even though she says she does miss her undo button.

**1** **Medusa** Photoshop. Photo Credit: sxc.hu, istockphoto.

**2** **Casandra** Photoshop. Photo Credit: sxc.hu, istockphoto.

**3** **Elemental Magic** Photoshop. Photo Credit: sxc.hu, Marcus Ranum.

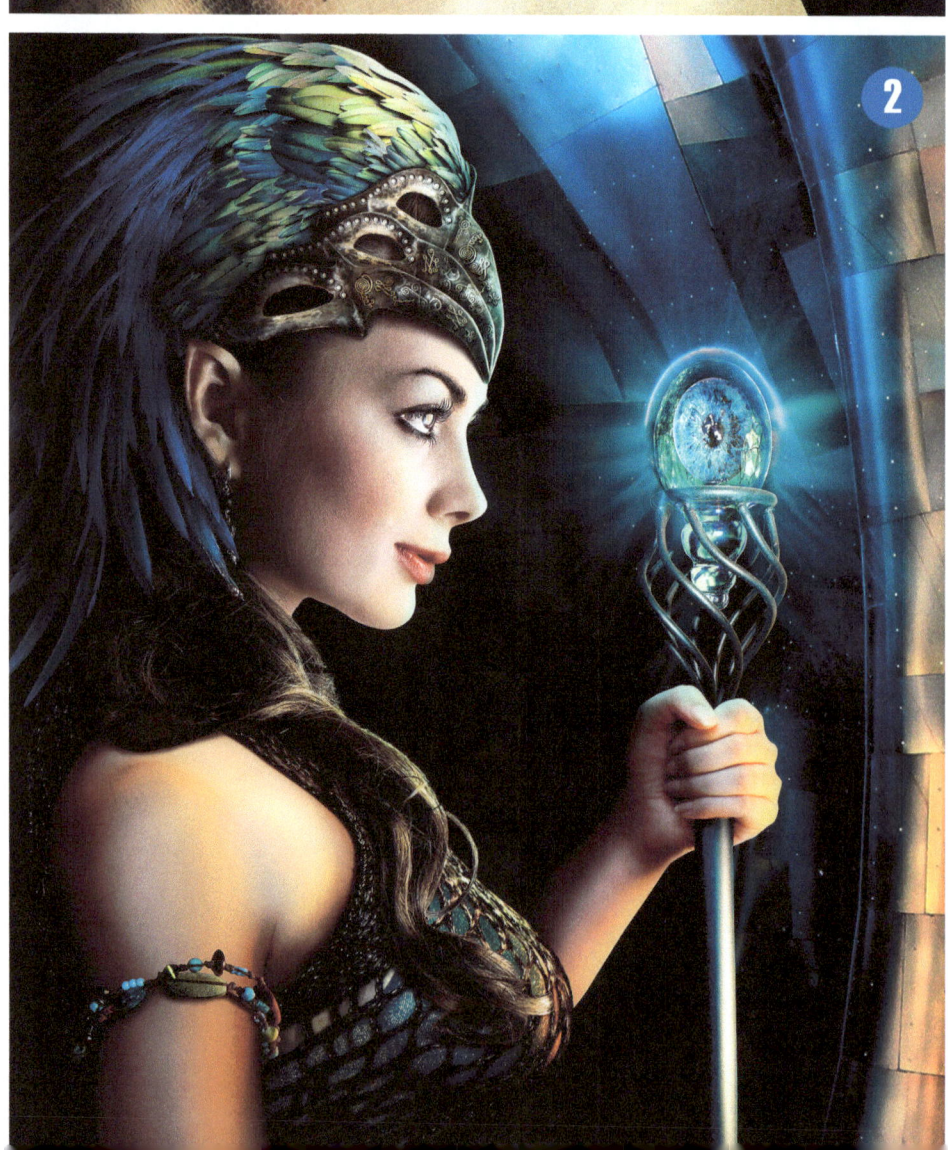

**2**

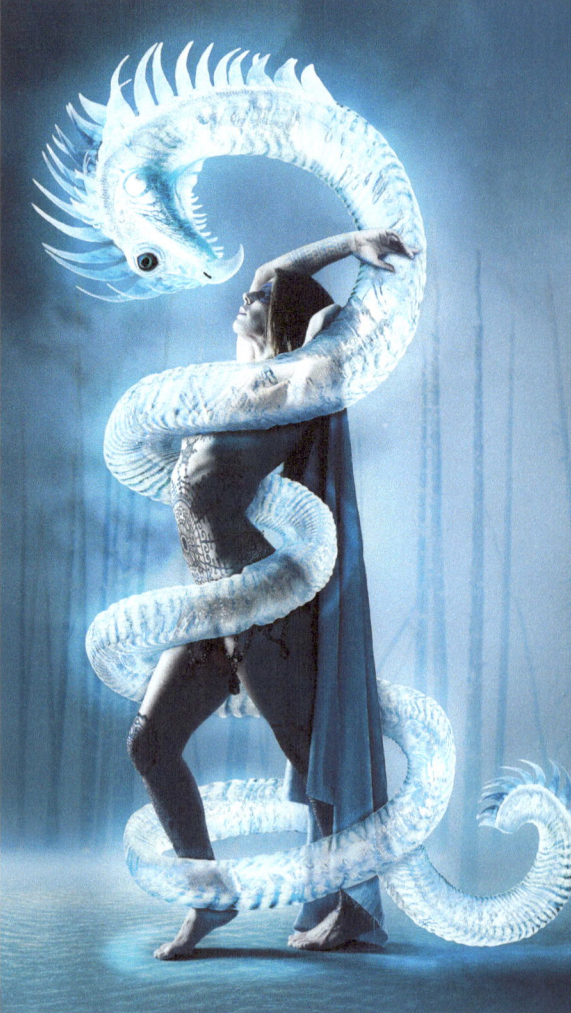

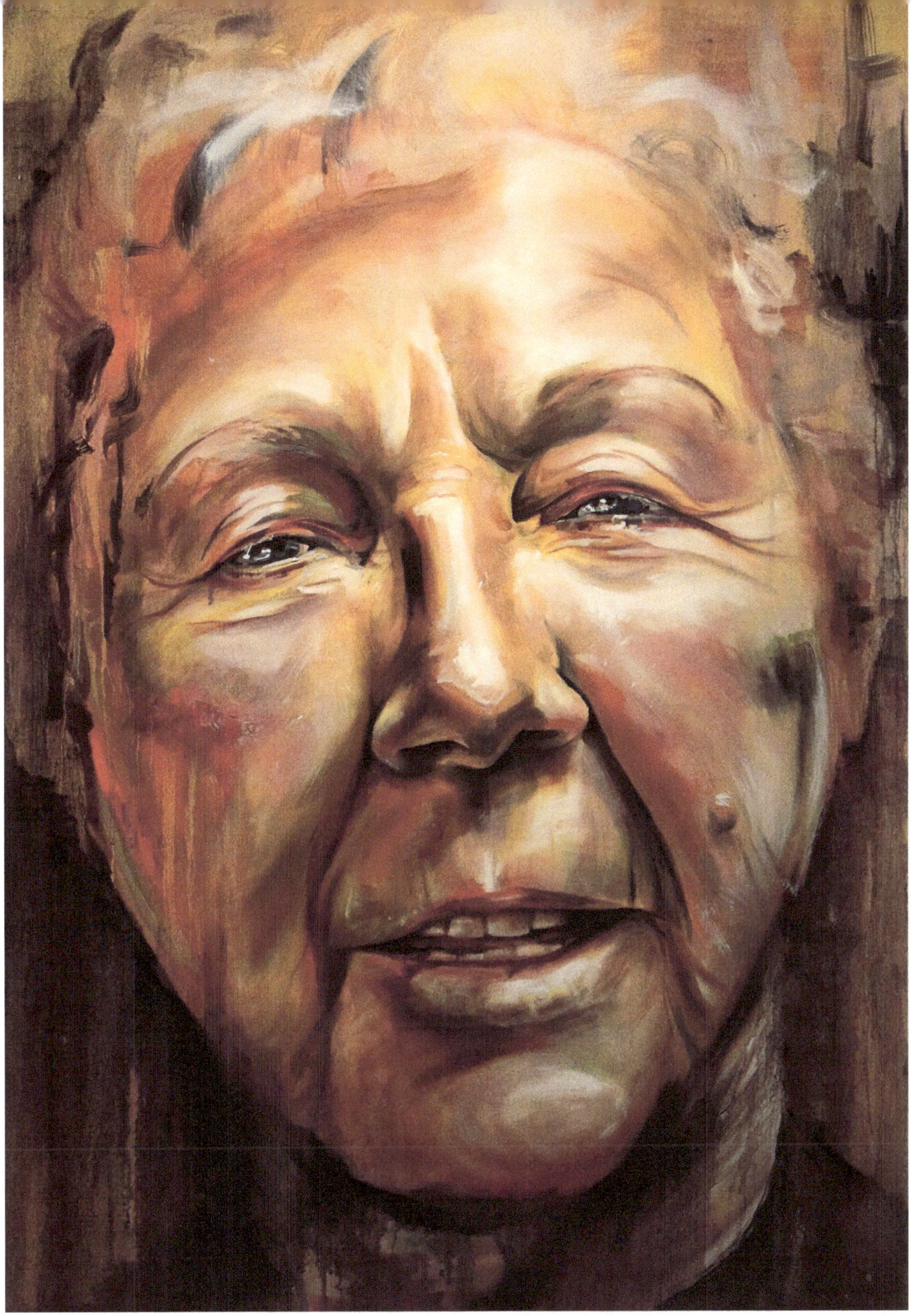

KIRSTIN PAULY "SELF PORTRAIT (OMA)"

ONA's SHORT LIST

**KIRSTIN PAULY** "SELF PORTRAIT (OMA)"
▶ **Steven Tippin** "ABOUT"
▶ **Shirley Al** "DANCER"
▶ **Alexis Tyrala** "PORTRAIT STUDY"
▶ **Albert Casson** "SUN KISSED"

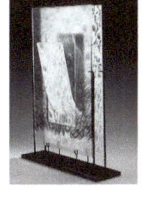 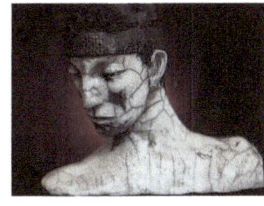 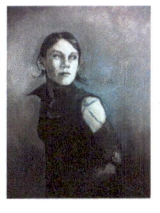 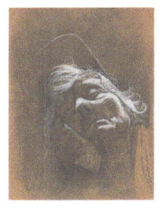

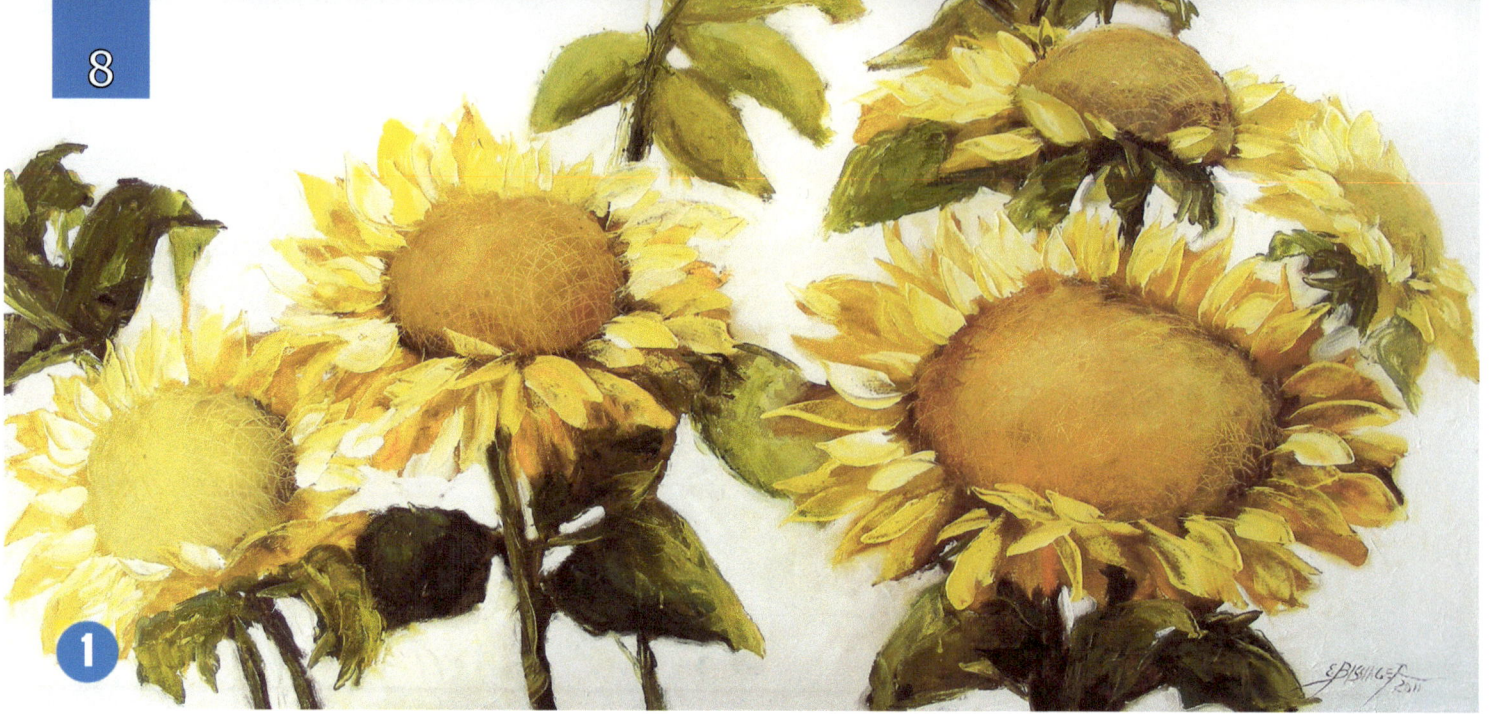

**1** **Trei Dorinte** (Three Wishes)
100x50cm Oil on canvas.

**2** **Tolba** (Santa's Bag)
130x70cm Oil on canvas.

**3** **Carnavalul de la Venetia**
(Carnival in Venice) 60x60 cm
Oil on Canvas.

# ELENA BISSINGER

**LOCATION:** Romania
**WEB:** http://ElenaBissinger.weebly.com
**EMAIL:** Aditonilena@yahoo.com

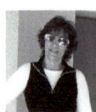

I am an artist from Romania. My father encouraged me to paint & I attended the University of Visual Arts in Oradea. In my artistic record gathered more than 2,000 works in oil on canvas. They are in private collections around the world: USA ,EUROPE. I participated in many international art events. In camp we got international creative award "Golden Brush". I appeared in International Dictionary of Artists 2011 & "International Contemporary Artists" vol.2 by ICA PUBLISHING. Art for me is a source of positive energy. Painting helped me get over a very tough challenge in 2008 when I was diagnosed with cervical cancer. I just expected to paint again and I am happy that I am now well.

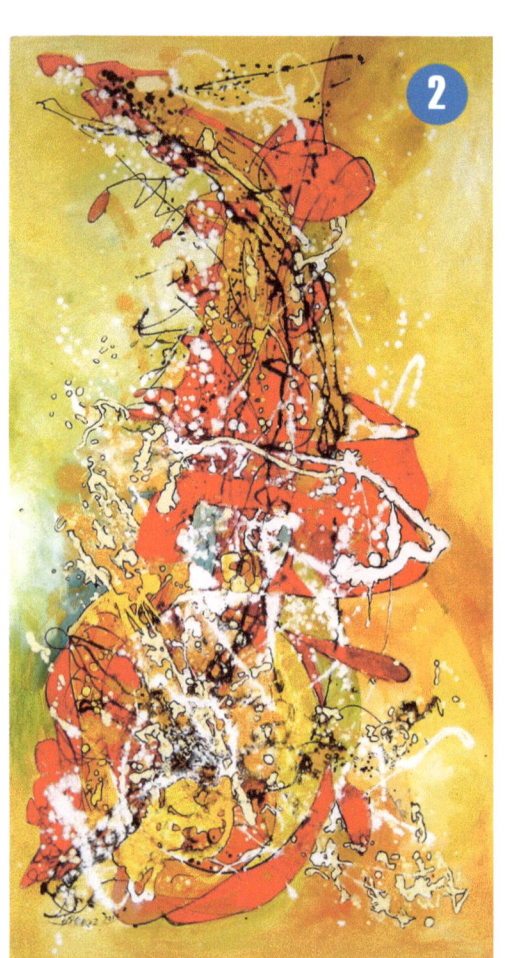

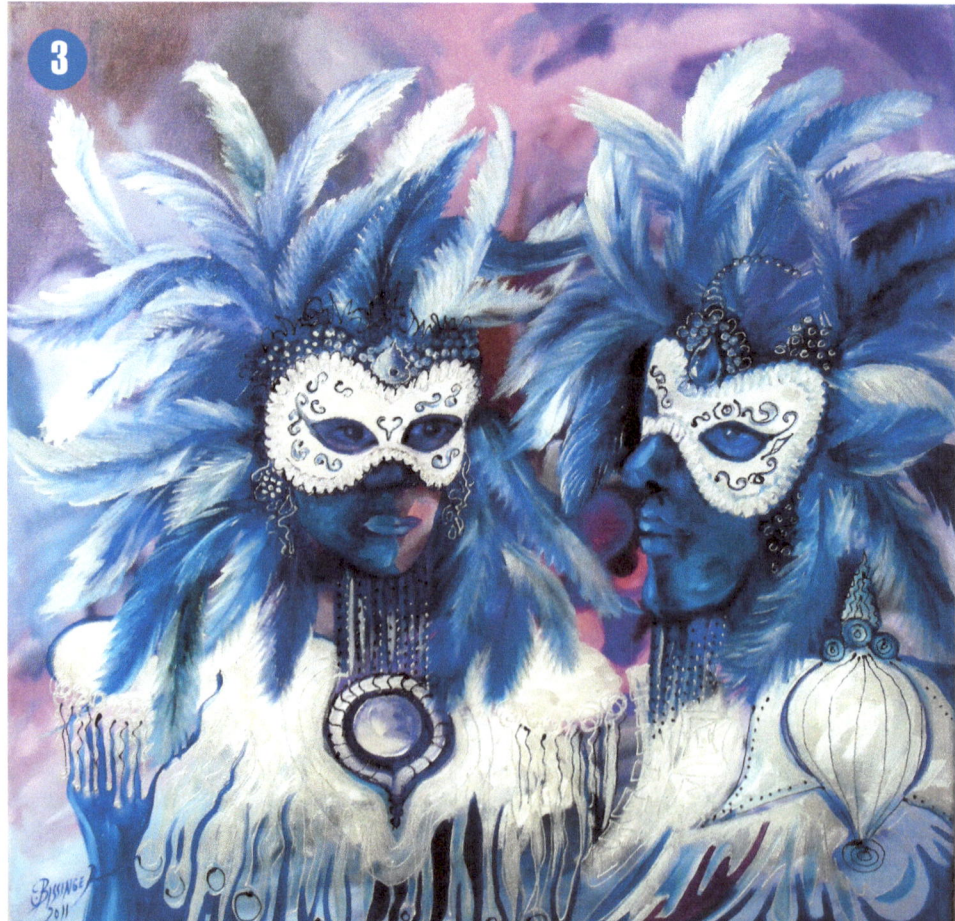

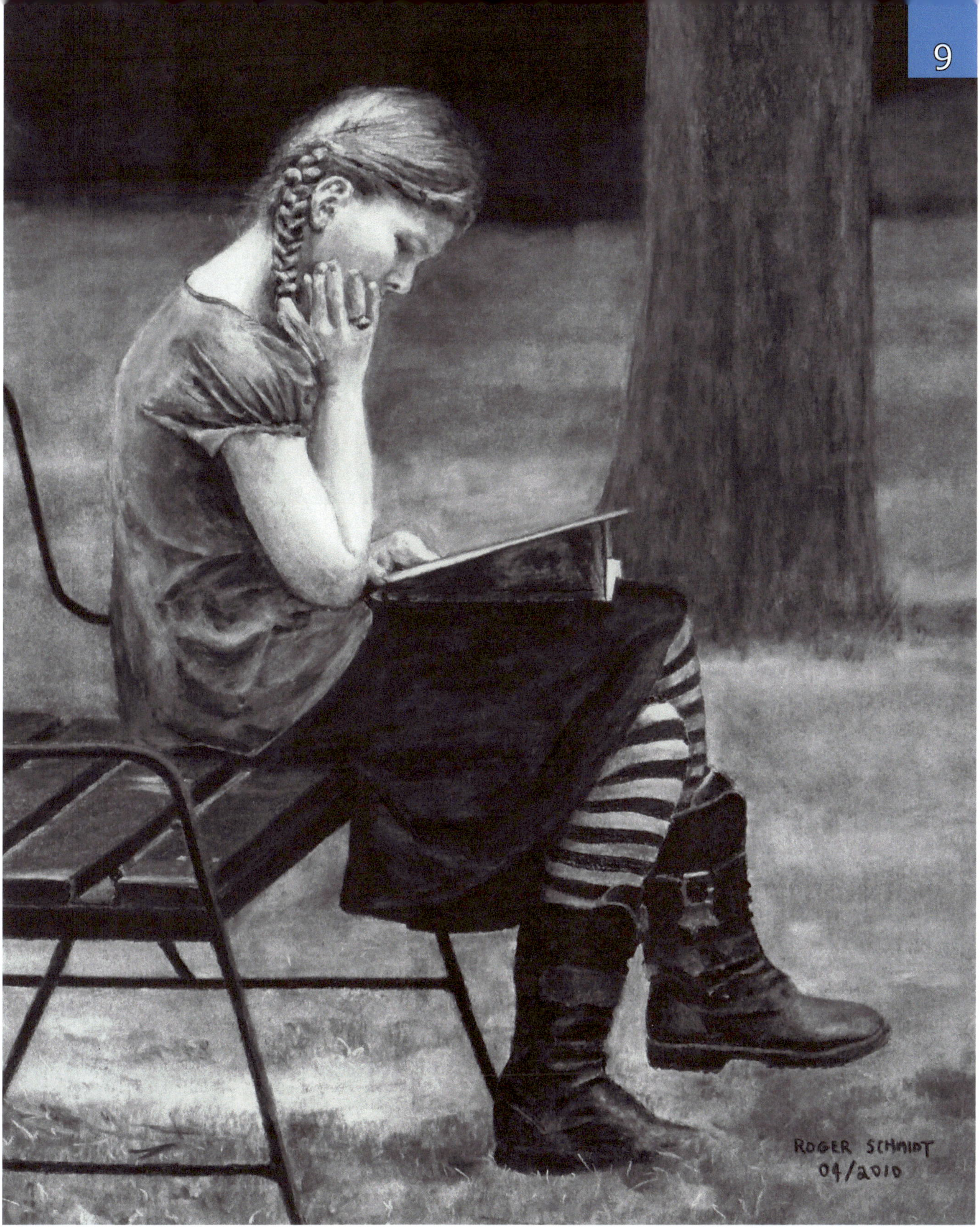

ROGER SCHMIDT
04/2010

ELENA'S SHORT LIST

**ROGER SCHMIDT** "STRATFORD PARK READER"

**ROGER SCHMIDT** "STRATFORD PARK READER"
▶ **Adele Figliomeni** "FACE YOUR OPPONENT"
▶ **Cathy Pascoe** "REFLECTIONS AND REFRACTIONS"
▶ **Sanela Dizdar** "OWEN SOUND BEACH"
▶ **Jan Piller** "WINGS IN MY DREAMS"

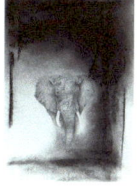
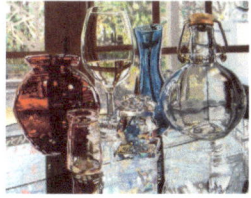
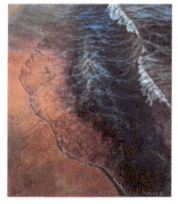
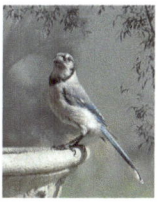

# JOËL LAROSE

**LOCATION:** Waterloo
**EMAIL:** Joel.larose@gmail.com

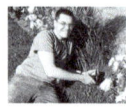 Joël Larose is the partner and muse of the editor who listens calmly to all his frustrations about publishing, and more importantly helps with decisions when late nights have taken their toll. He is a blackbelt martial artist, programs computers, and has extensive knowlege of Tarot symbolism, Astrology and ancient Japan. He is currently exploring the world of photography.

**1 We Are Not Amused** Photo.

**2 Coloured Minority** Photo.

**3 Look At Me!** Photo.

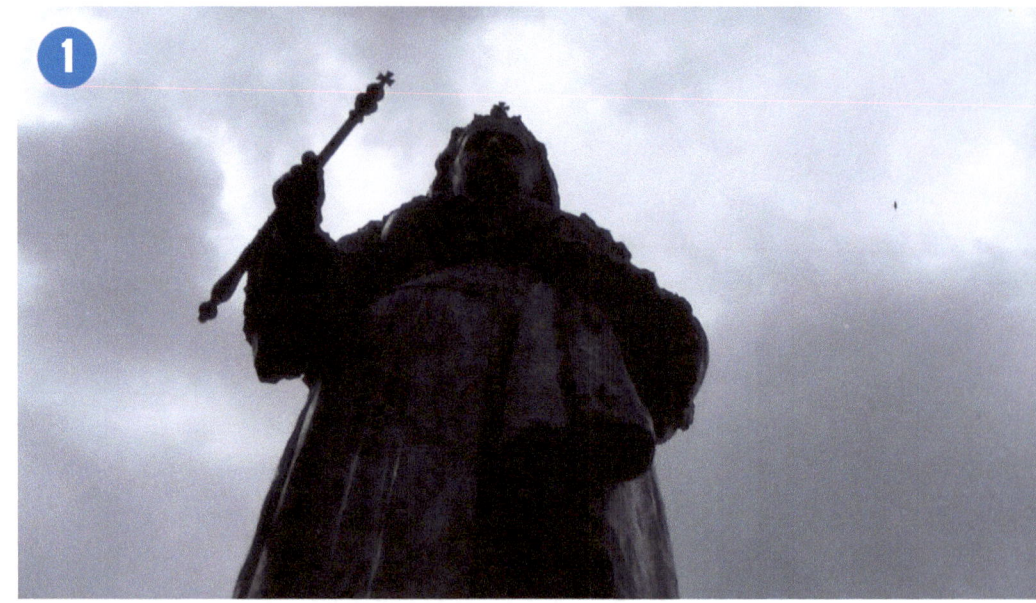

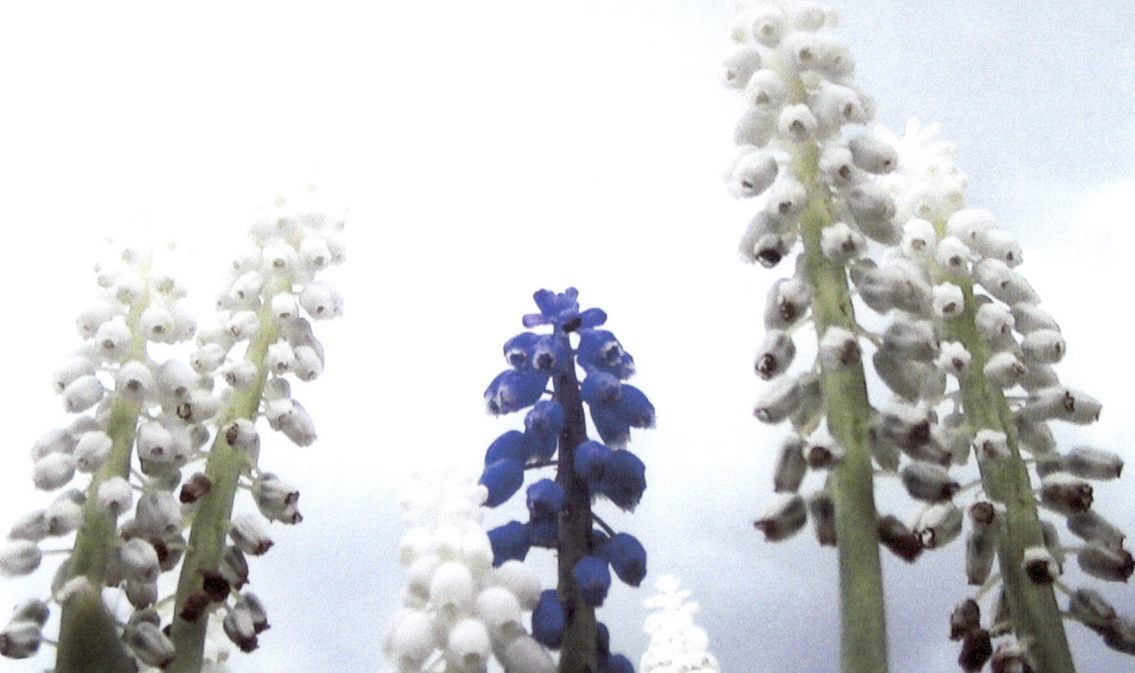

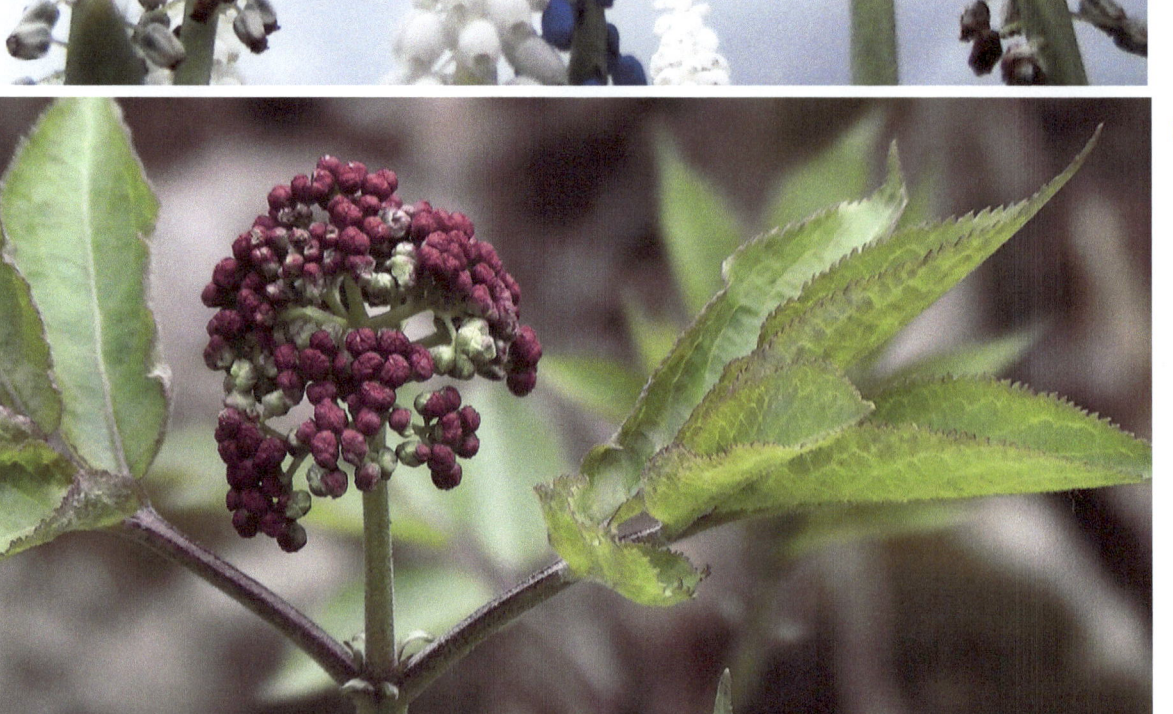

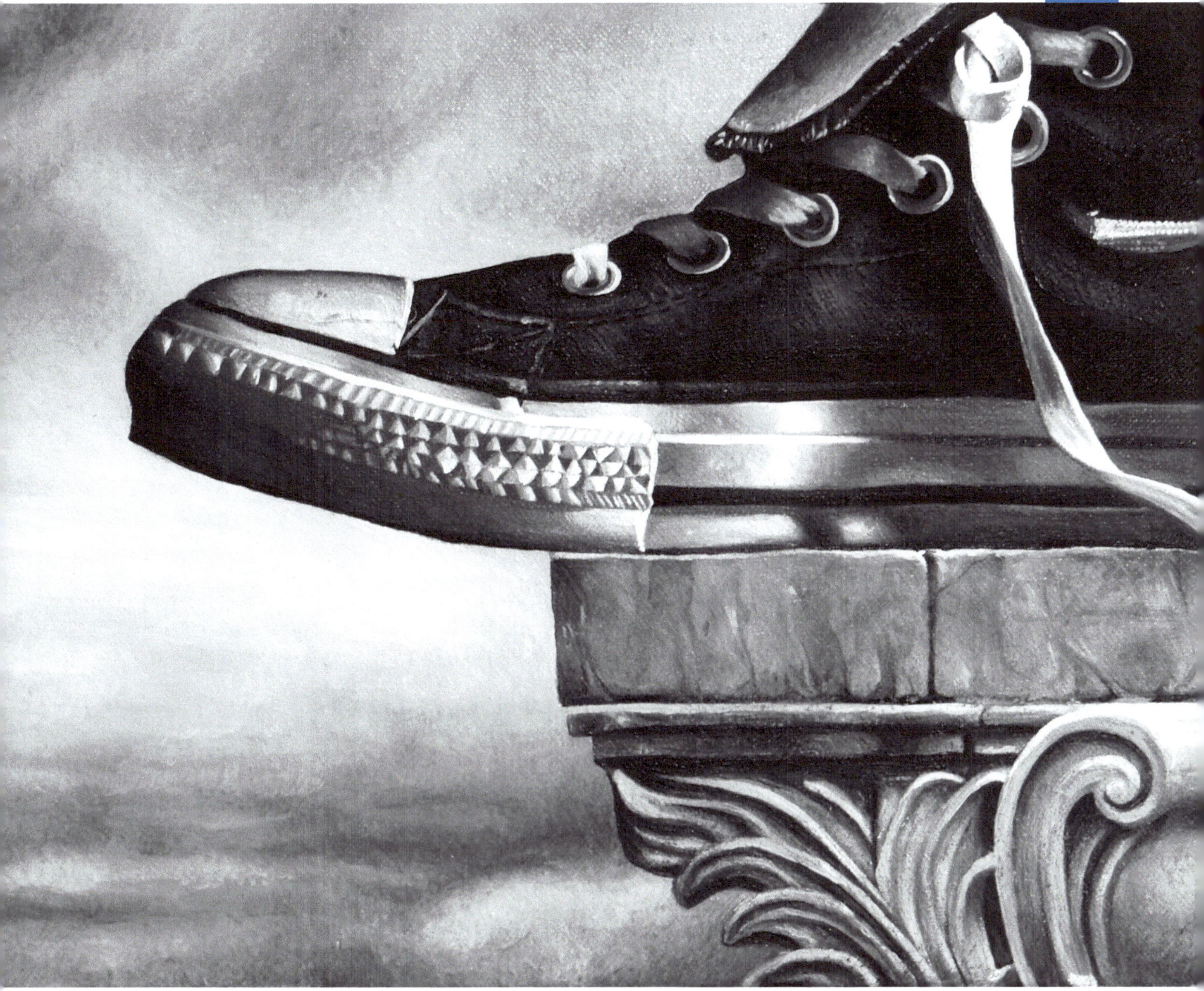

**BRENT SCHREIBER** "Yes or No"

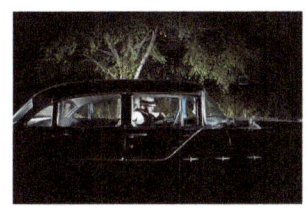 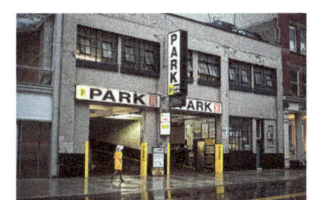 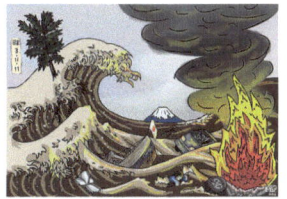 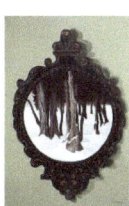

JOËL's short list

**BRENT SCHREIBER** "Yes or No"
▶ **Conan Stark** "No Need To Get Funny When You Can Get Lost"
▶ **Danny Bailey** "Yellow Park"
▶ **Margaret Gissing** "Great Wave Over Japan"
▶ **Murray Dekeyser** "Mirrorscape"

# ROGER SCHMIDT

**LOCATION:** Stanley Park, Kitchener
**WEB:** rogerschmidt.blogspot.com
**EMAIL:** rog.schmidt@rogers.com

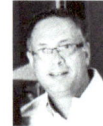

Roger Schmidt was born in 1961, and raised in the Laurention Hills of Quebec. In his youth, he loved to draw and paint, but by his late teens, music (guitar playing) took over, and remained his primary creative outlet. He now resides in Kitchener, with his wife and two young adult daughters, and recently, began drawing and painting once again. He is excited about rediscovering this past joy, and has resolved to work hard at improving his skills as an artist.

**1 Moments of Uncertainty** 11 x 14 Charcoal and white chalk on toned paper board. From a photo of my niece getting ready for her sister's wedding and un-sure of her dress.

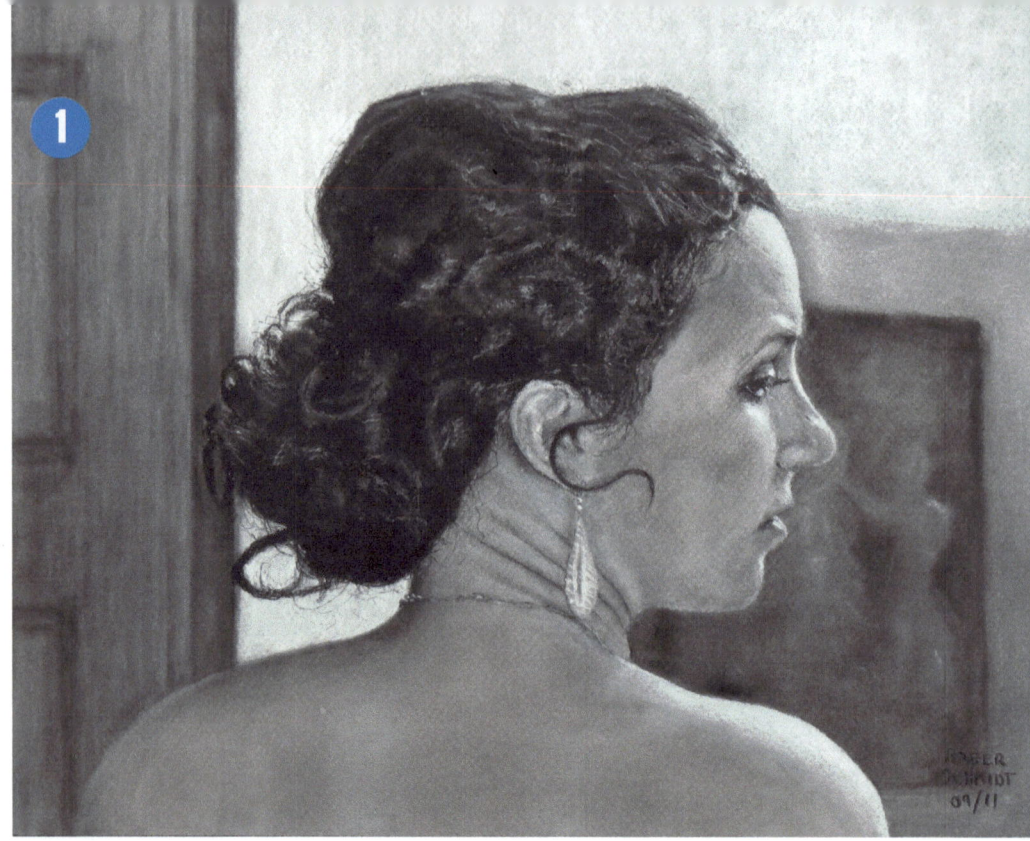

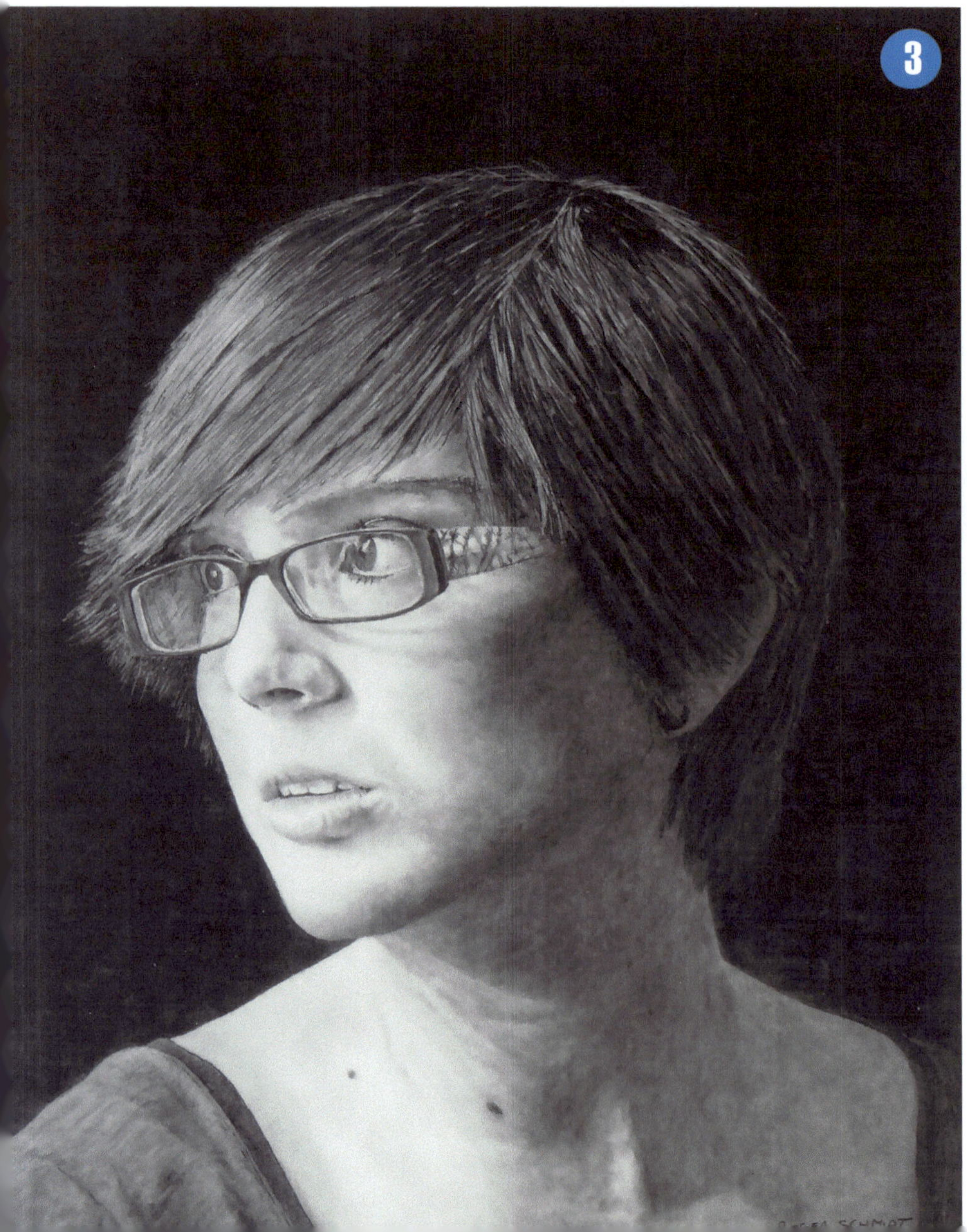

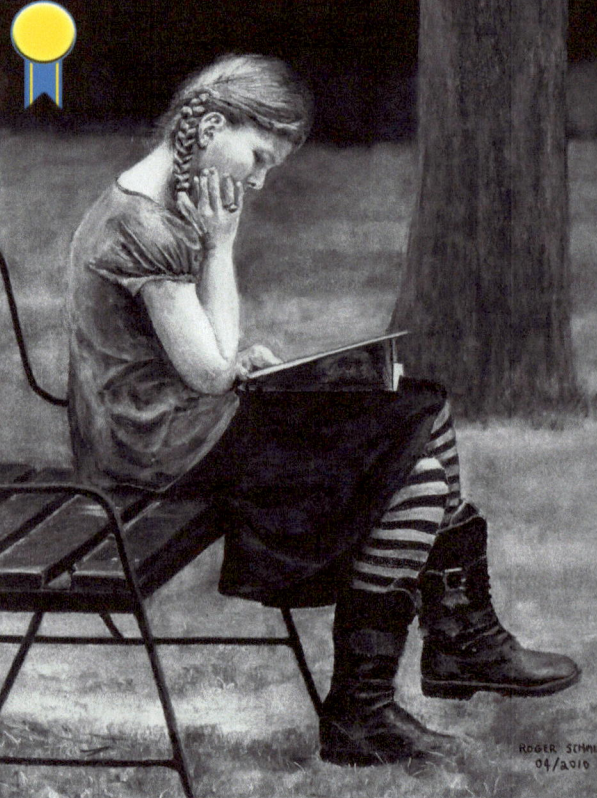

**2 Stratford Park Reader** 11x14" Charcoal and white chalk on pa-per - Drawn from a photograph I snapped of an unknown per-son, while visiting the "Art in the Park" event in Stratford.

**3 Emma** 14 x 20" Graphite on paper. A portrait of my daughter, Emma.

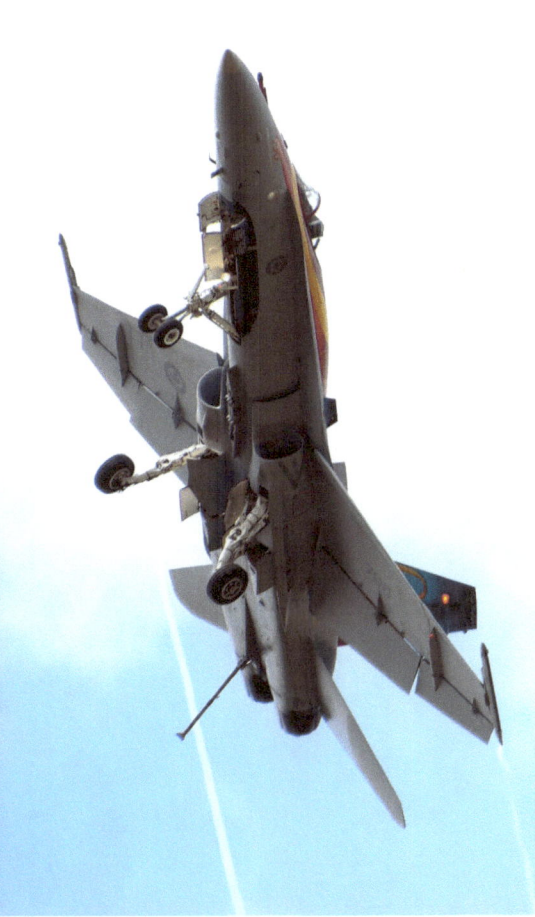

**1 Flyby** (Detail) Photo.

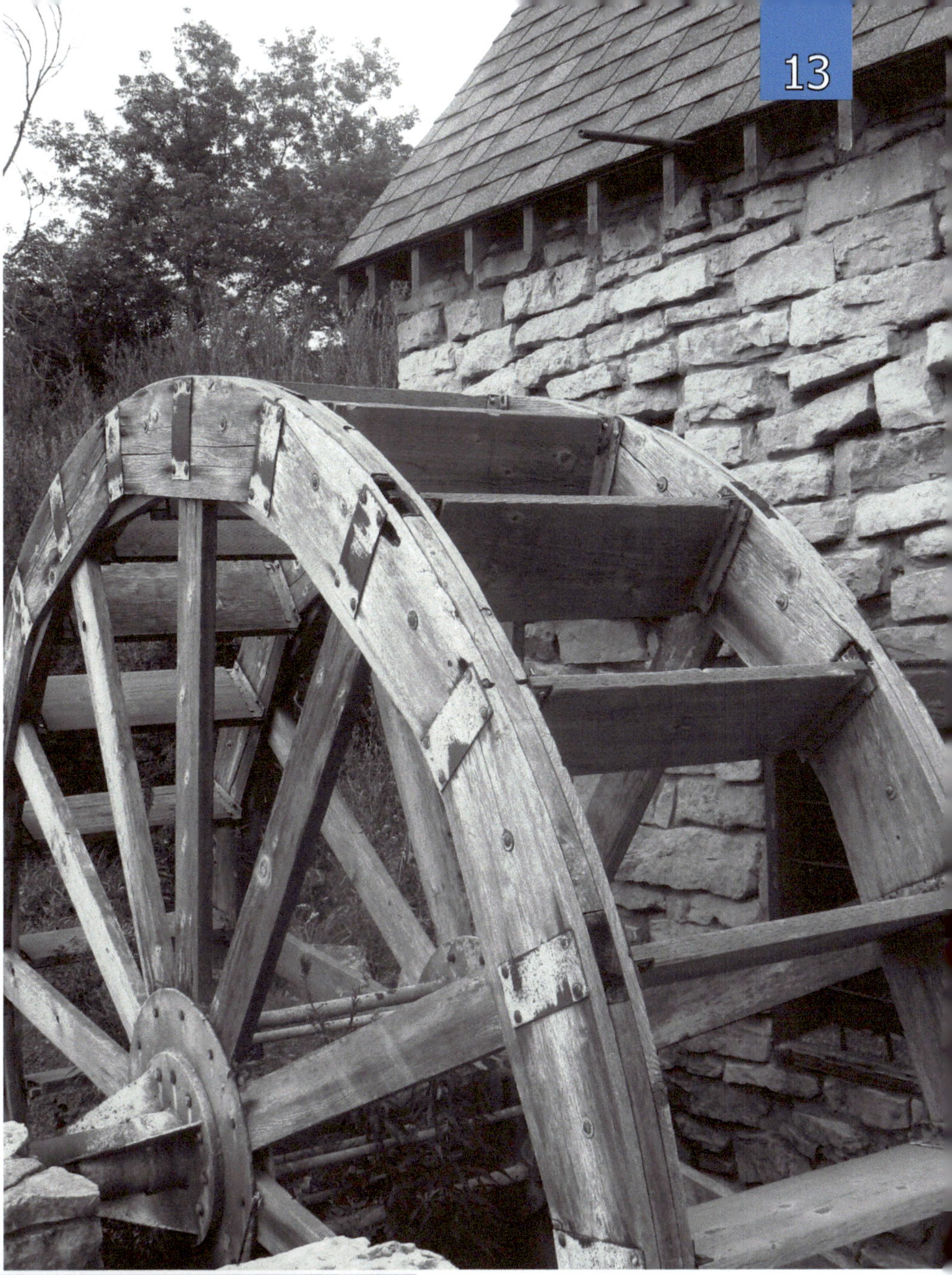

# ALEX POMINVILLE

**LOCATION:** Waterloo

**WEB:**
http://pominvillephotography.showitsite.com

**EMAIL:** pominvillephotography@gmail.com

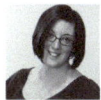 Alex started her business, Pominville Photography, in January 2010. Her photographs have been published and used in auctions for charity events. She enjoys photographing families, weddings, and large gatherings but she also has a passion for photographing the beauty in any situation. Alex finds inspiration and support through her children; Keean and Scarlett, and through her husband; Donald.

**2 Waterwheel** Photo.

**3 Sweet Rain Drops** Photo.

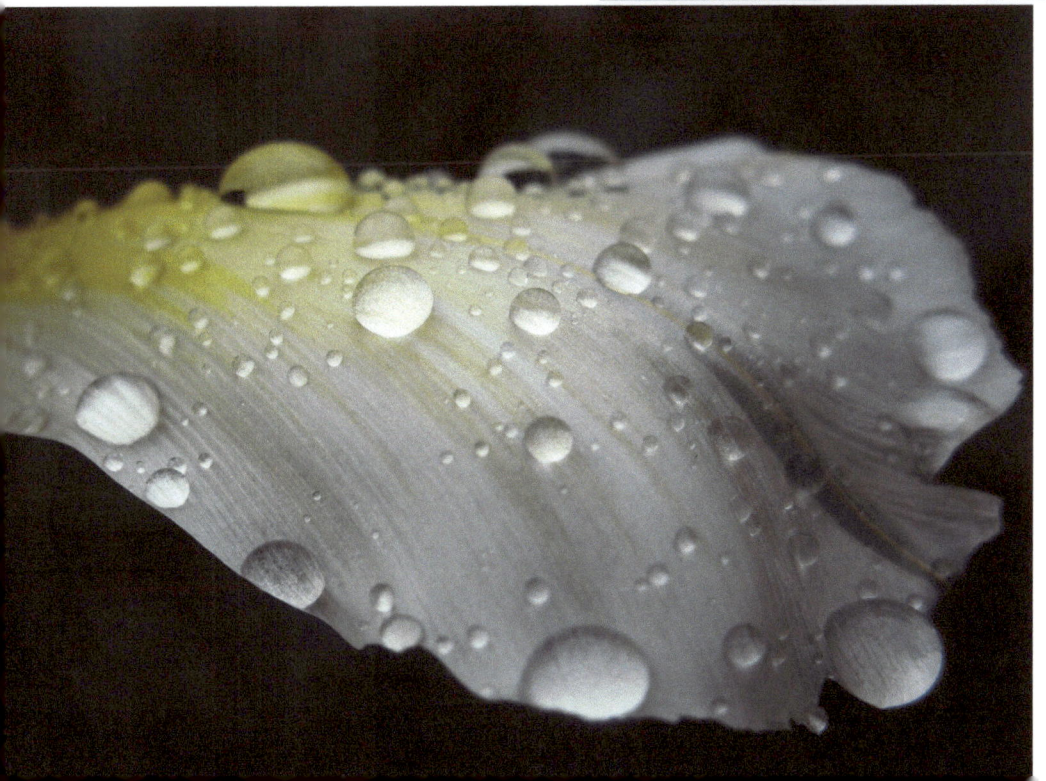

**1 A Northern Vision** 36x36"
Acrylic on canvas.

## NIK HARRON
**LOCATION:** Kitchener
**WEB:** nikharron.com
**EMAIL:** nik@nikharron.com

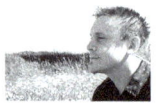

Originally born in Belfast, Ireland, nik harron (who likes his name uncapitalized) immigrated to Canada in 1981 and has recently chosen to make his home in Kitchener. His creative work spans several disciplines, but has focused in recent years on the Canadian landscape. His heavily textural approach to painting bridges the gap between traditional painting and sculpture, thematically exploring the surface of the world as a mirror to the inner landscape.

**2 Field, Full of Promise**
24x24" Acrylic on wood panel.

**3 Sunset Abstract** 24x24"
Acrylic and glass on canvas.

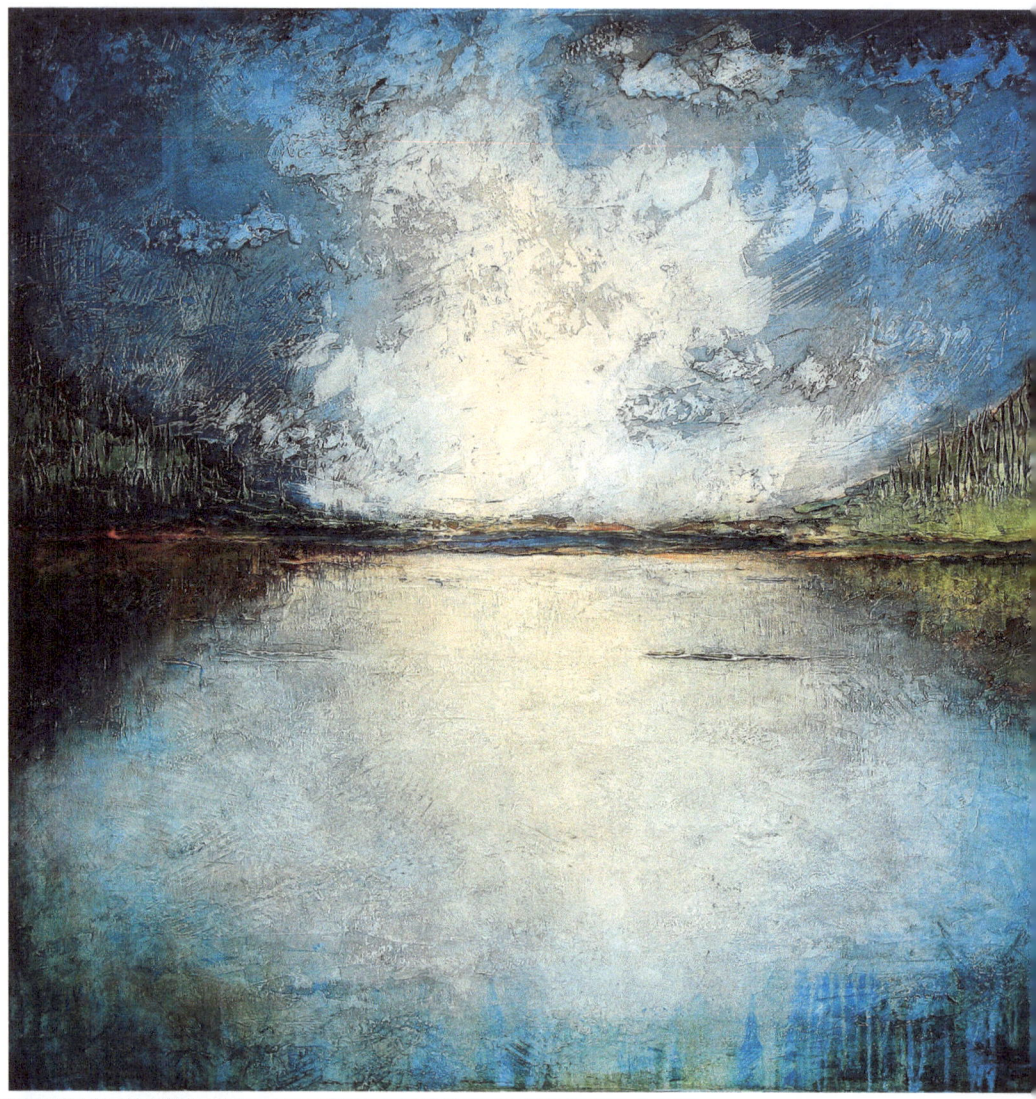

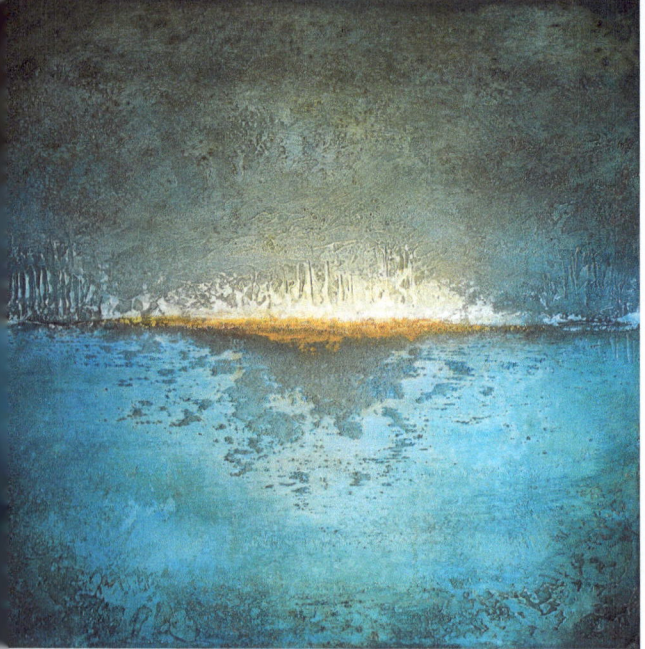

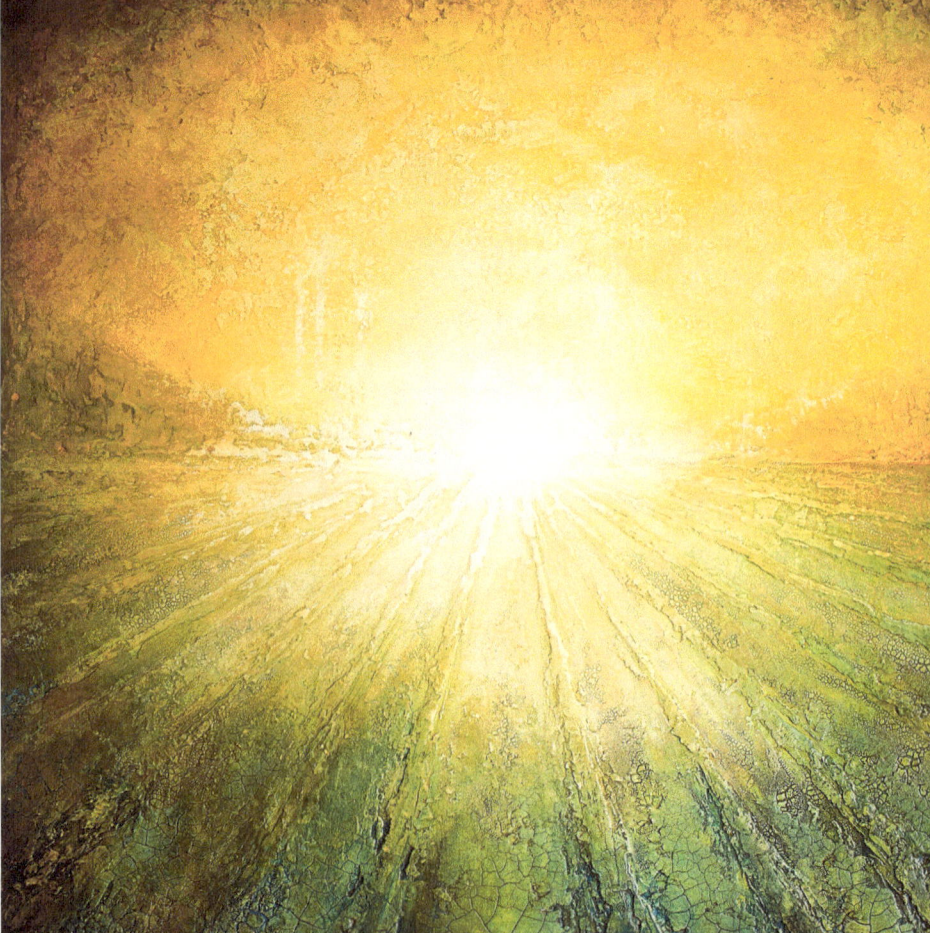

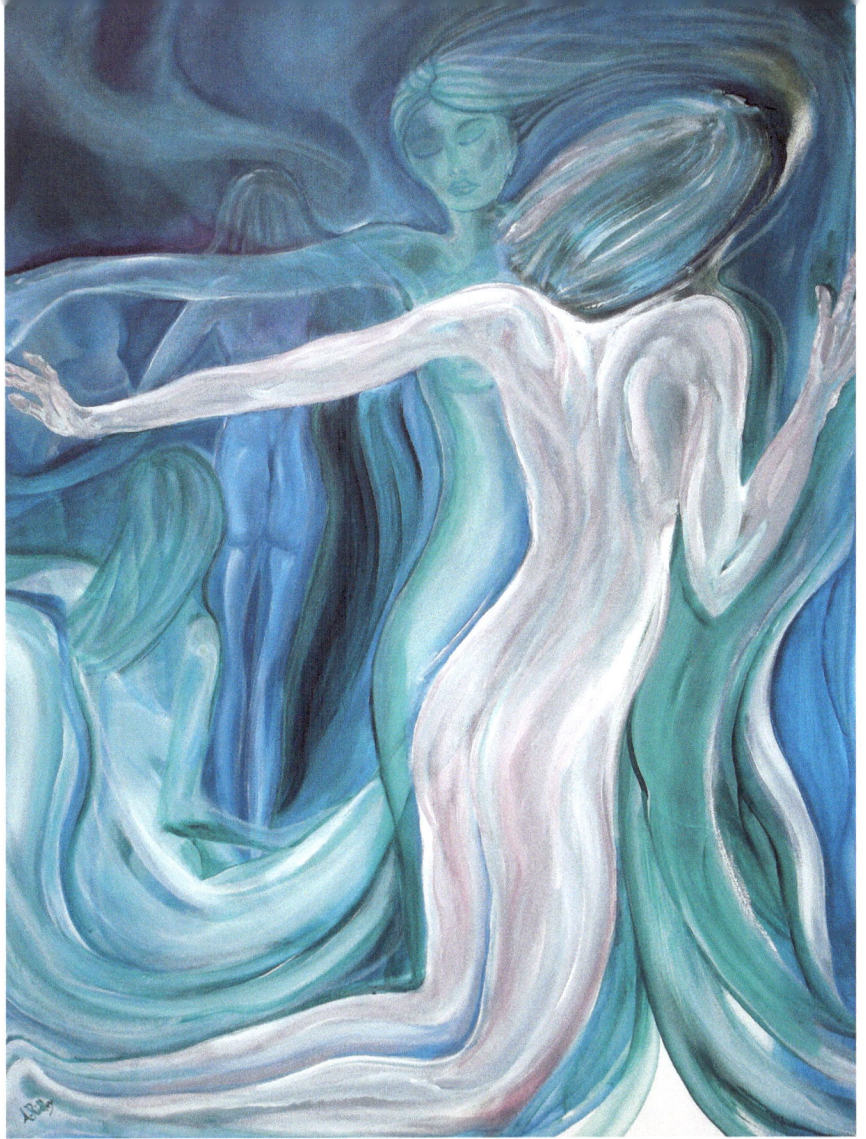

**1**

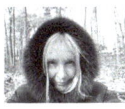

**1** **Sleepwalkers** 48x36" Acrylic on Canvas.

# AILEEN RIDLEY
**LOCATION:** Breithaupt Park, Waterloo
**WEB:** (N/A)
**EMAIL:** aridley@golden.net

Aileen was born in Coventry, England where she studied and practiced art, before immigrating to Canada . She continues her lifetime passion for creating art in her Waterloo studio in Breithaupt Woods. Surrounded by trees, birds, plants, wild animals and an occasional human, her unpredictable and voracious imagination conjures up myriad figurative and impressionistic works in acrylics, oils and clay.

**2** **Summer's Wrath** 54x36" Acrylic on Canvas.

**3** **Siblings** 12x12x14" Unfired white clay.

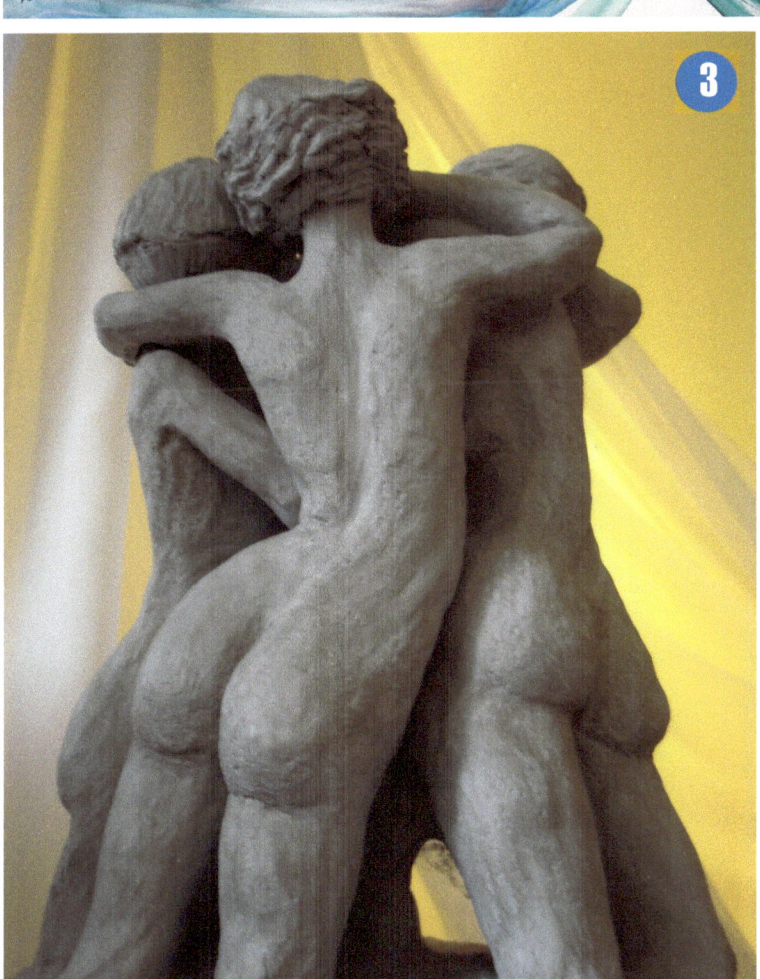

**3**

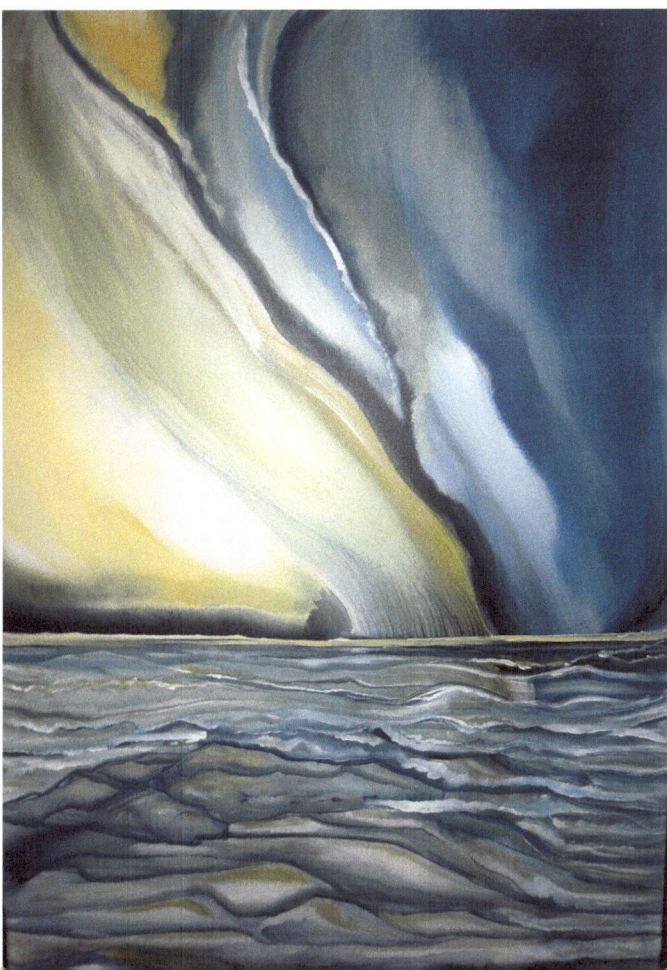

# AMY FERRARI

**LOCATION:** Waterloo / Studio: Kitchener
**WEB:** amyferrariart.com
**EMAIL:** amyfcar@aol.com

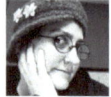

Amy is always distracted and fascinated by shapes, colors, and patterns she finds in everything. Design School and 20+ years of painting has resulted in a unique curvaceous style and an intuitive, transformative technique. Ferrari currently teaches two workshops in acrylics at the Button Factory in Waterloo.

**1 Summer Meadow Dance**
24x24" Acrylic on canvas.

**2 Limitless Afternoon Dreams**
36x30" Acrylic on canvas.

**3 Kakabeka River Dance**
40x60" Acrylic on canvas.

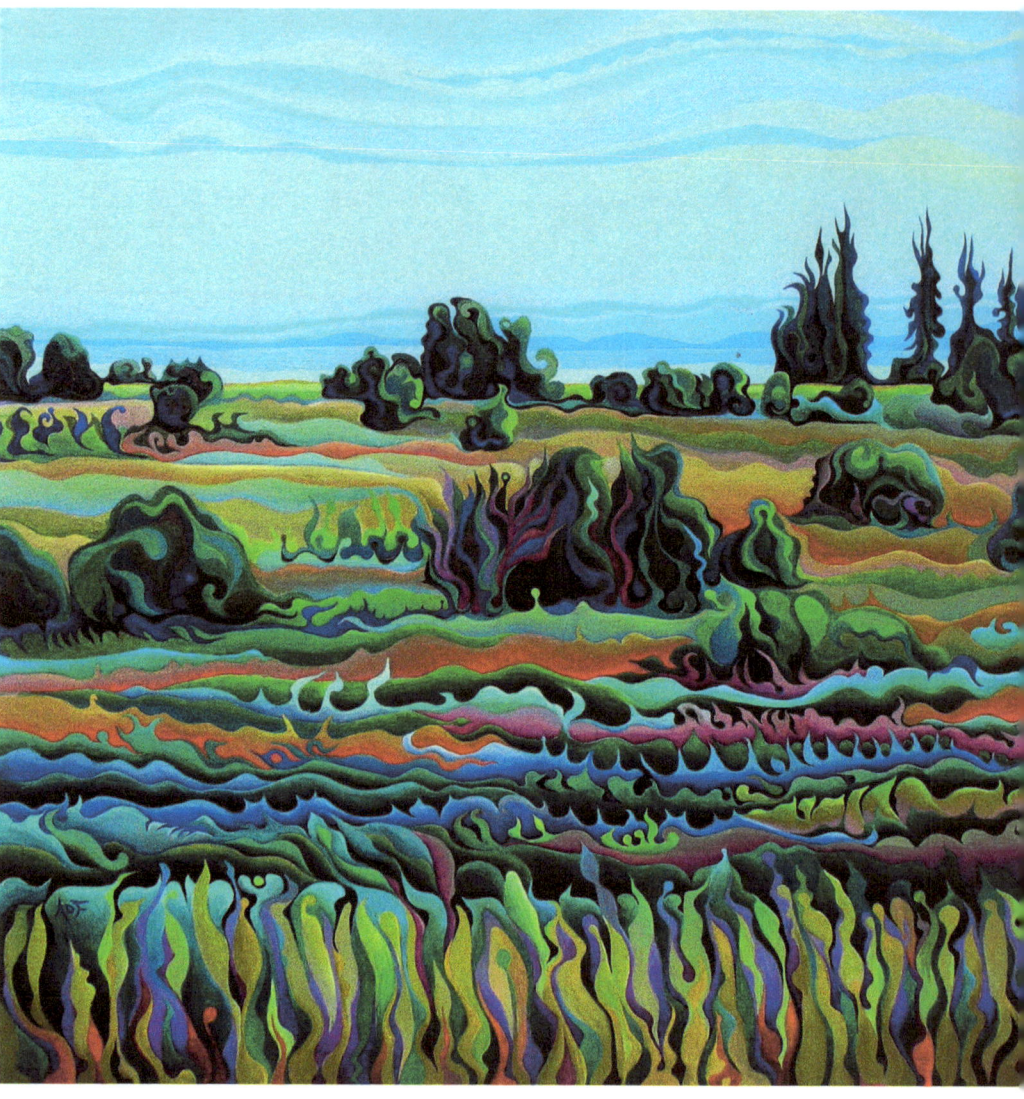

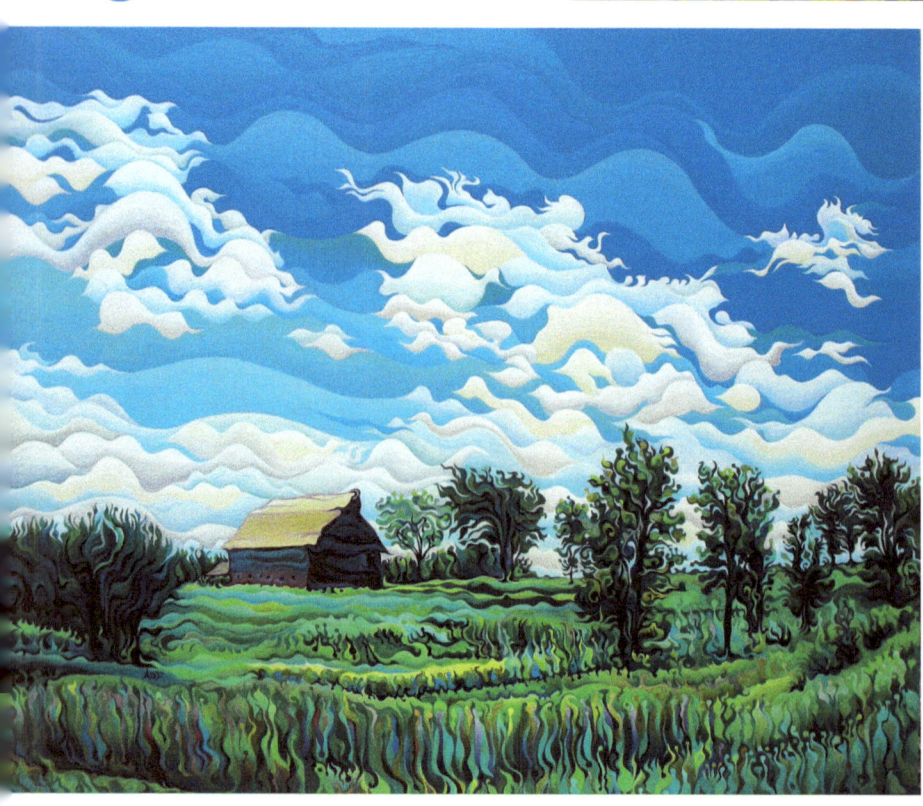

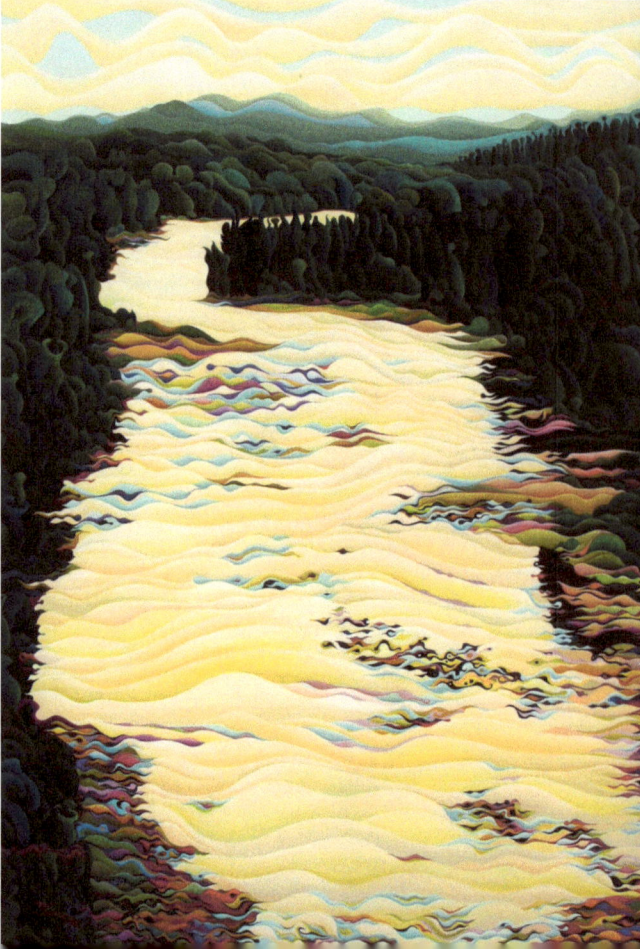

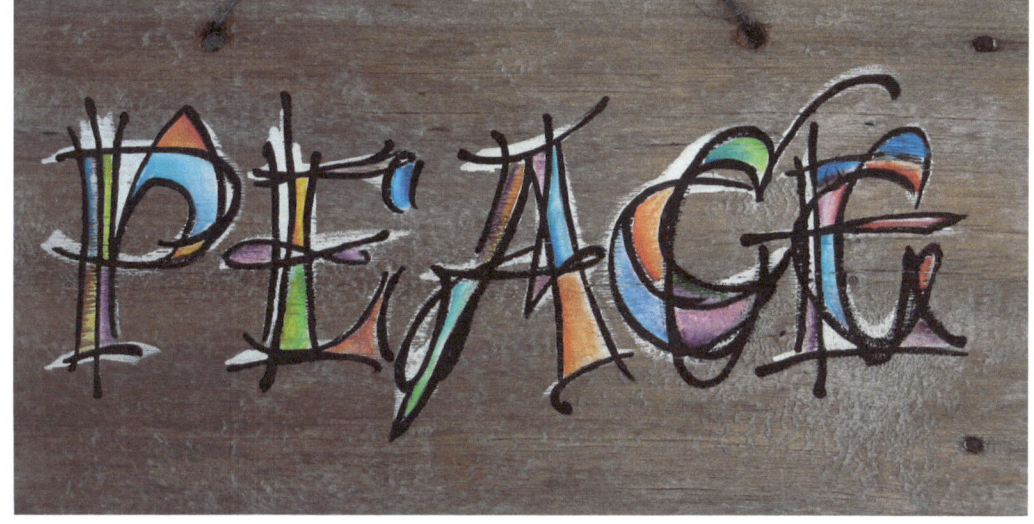

**1** **Peace** 14x30"

**2** **All Is Well** 8x8"

**3** **Ask** 9x19"

# CHERYL WEBER GOOD

**1**

**LOCATION:** Baden

**WEB:** writehand.ca

**EMAIL:** cheryl@writehand.ca

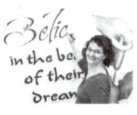

Cheryl Weber Good is a freelance calligraphy artist with a passion for quotes unleashed through art. Her hand lettering artwork has a wide range of uses including commissions for weddings, institutions, and home décor. Her classes focus on finding the unique vibrancy of the student, teaching through experimentation and fun. She's interested in mental health, and does workshops linking art and inner restoration.

**2**

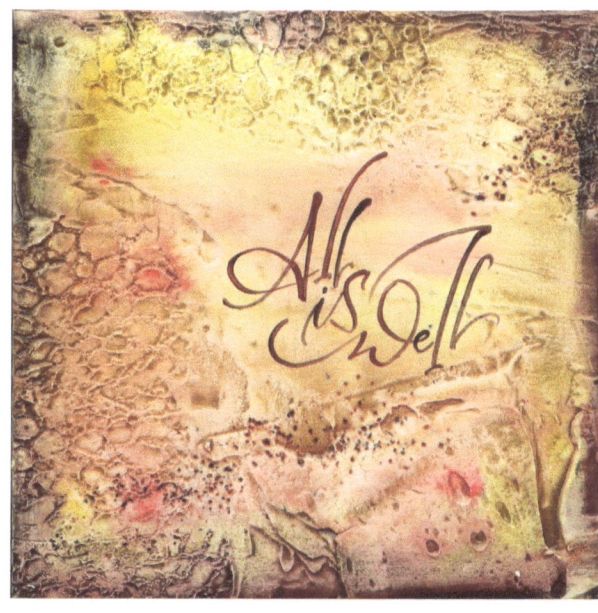

**3**

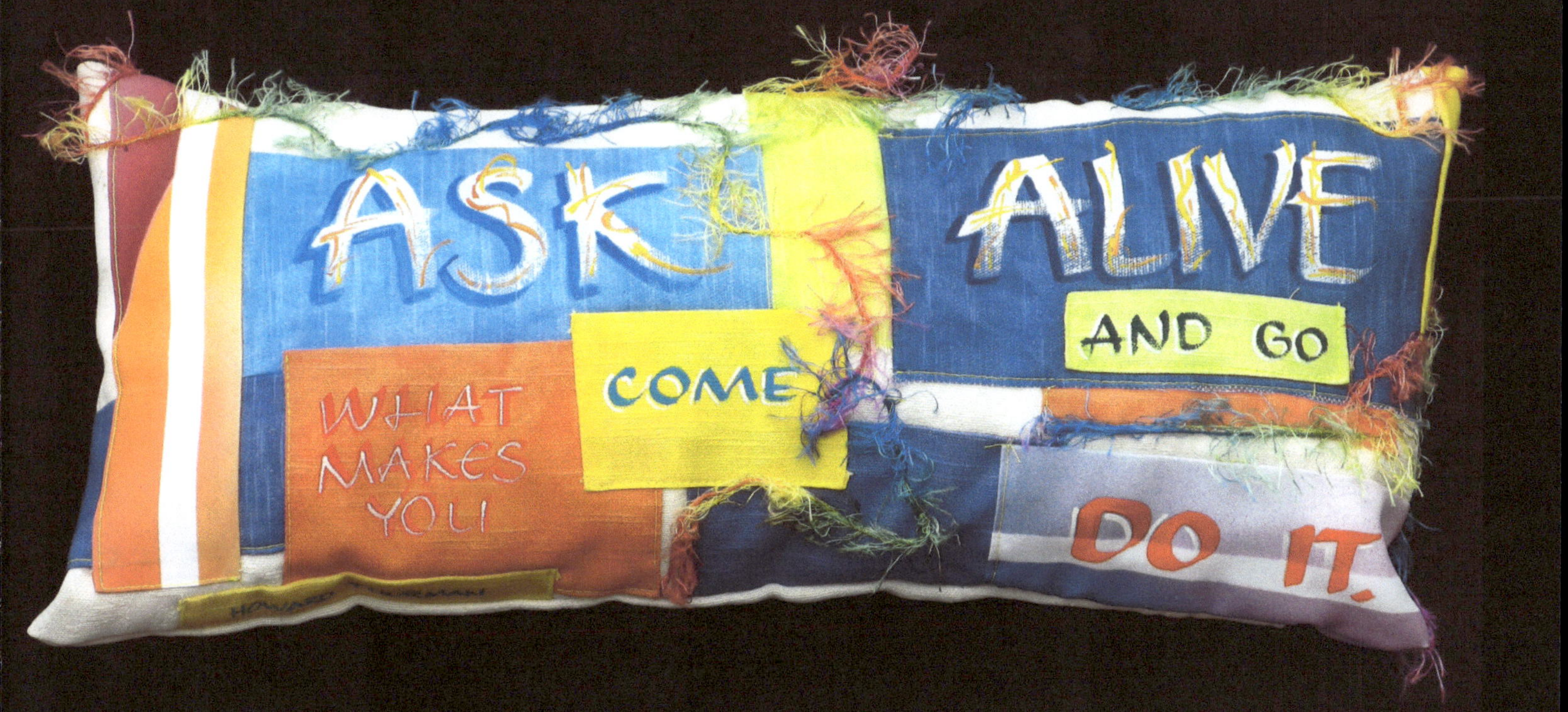

# KIRSTIN PAULY

**LOCATION:** Waterloo
**WEB:** kirstinpauly.tumblr.com
**EMAIL:** kirstin.pauly@gmail.com

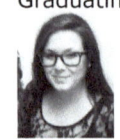 Graduating April 2012 from Honours Fine Arts at the University of Waterloo, Kirstin will be continuing life as an artist while traveling, pursuing other educational opportunities, and hopes to proceed to Grad School in the future. For now her work consists of mostly painting and ink drawings, with vibrant colour palettes and subtle distortions of her portrayed subjects; the feeling of a bare naked display of the individual is evident.

**1** **Asychronicity 1** 3x4' Oil on Canvas.Capturing awkwardness and ambiguity, my Asychronicity series depicts my subjects in very playful and whimsical way, influenced by Fantastical and Surrealist art.

**2** **Self Portrait (Oma)** 3.5x5', Oil on Canvas. This portrait of my Oma was a very introspective process; I looked to evoke psychological characteristics in subtle ways, coupled with a painterly, gestural way a  of handling oils.

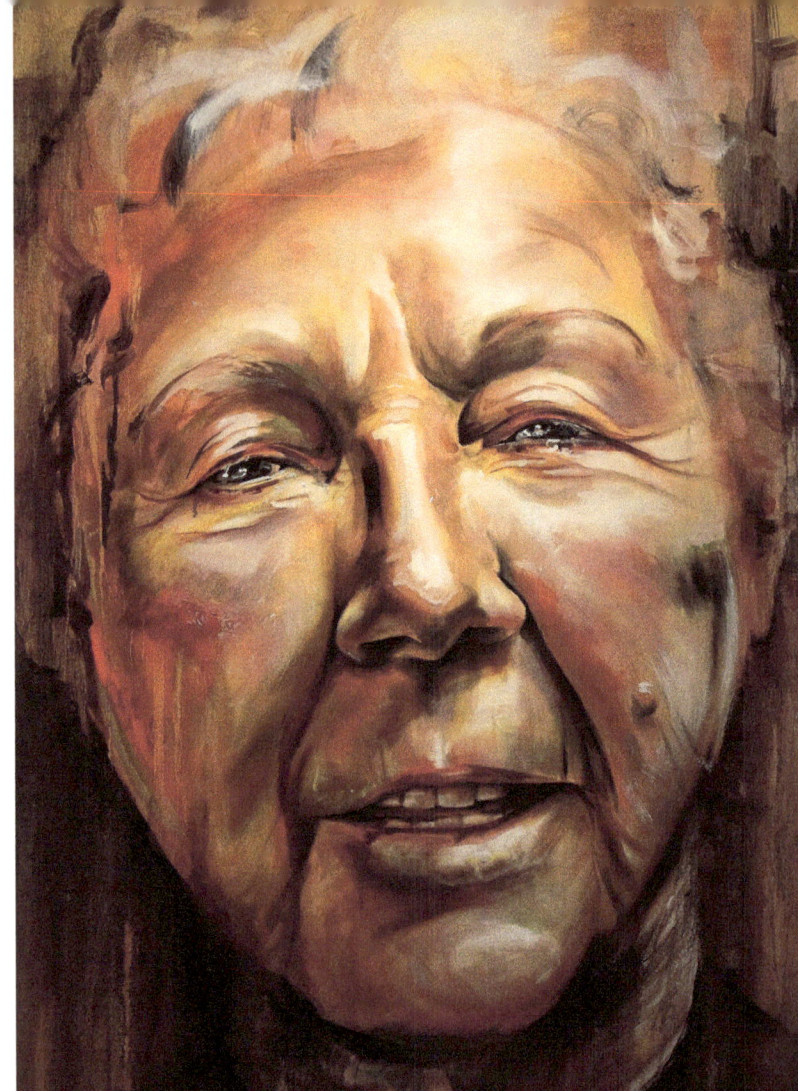

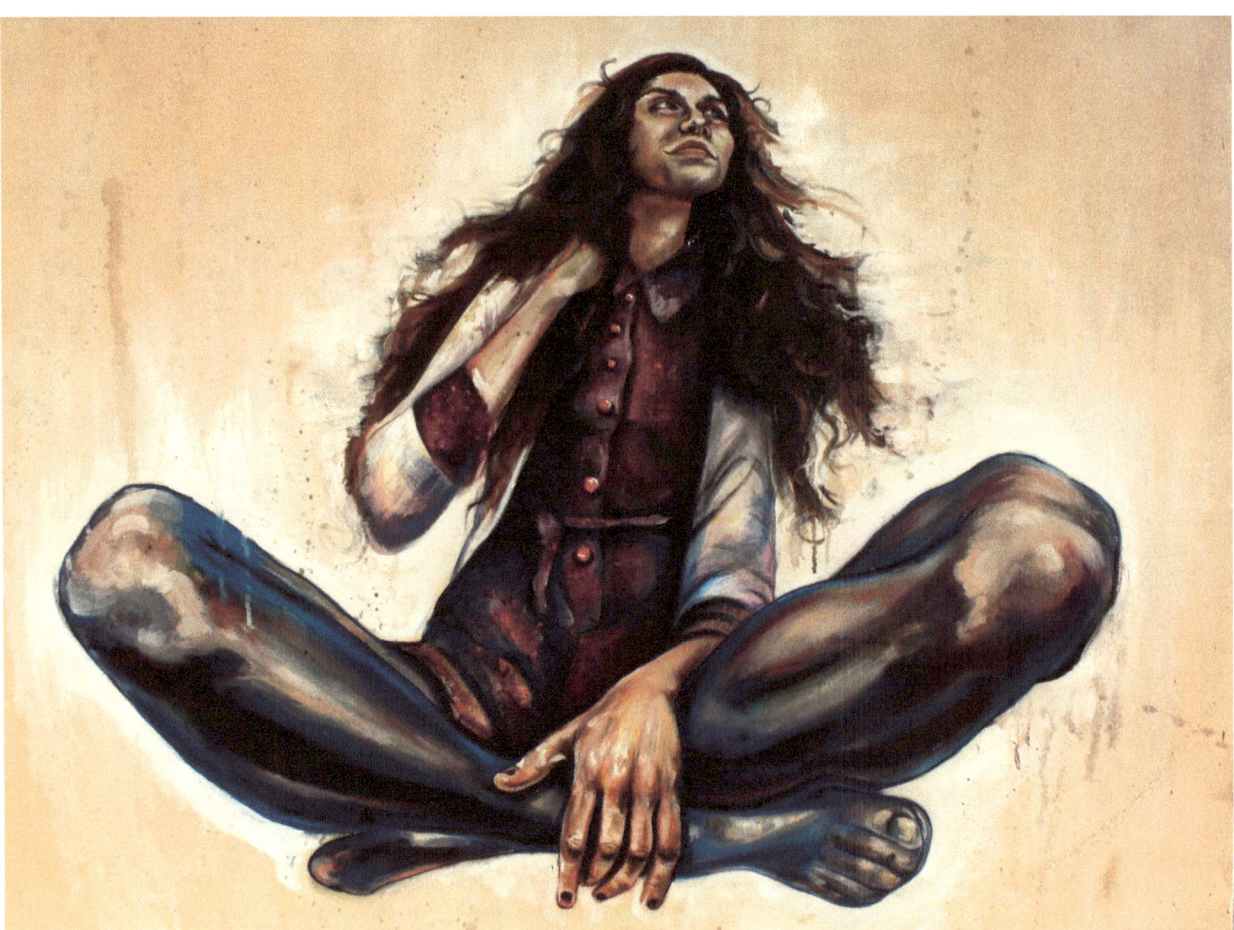

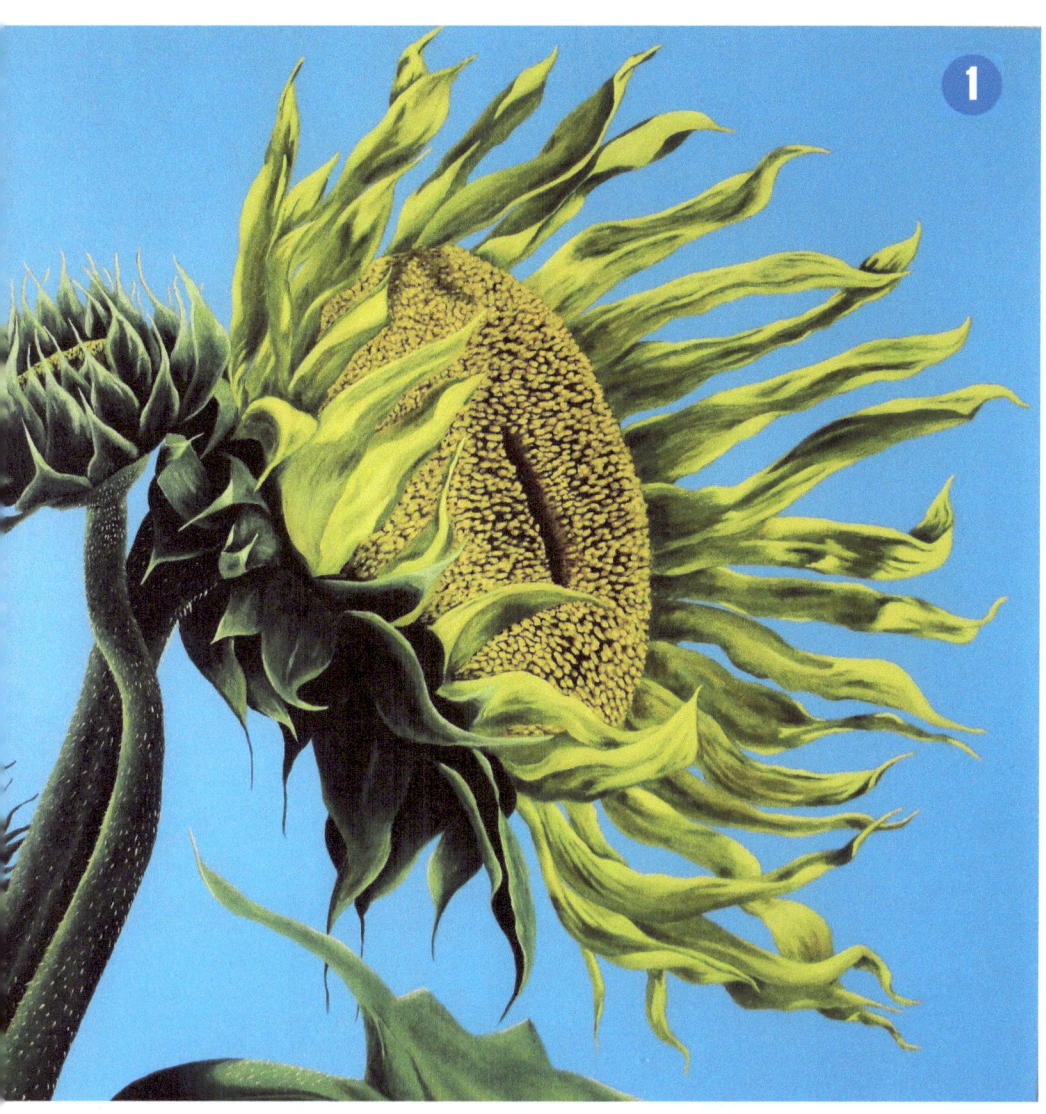
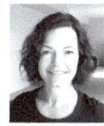

# CHRISTINA PREECE

**LOCATION:** Kitchener
**WEB:** christinapreece.com
**EMAIL:** cpreece.artmail@gmail.com

Christina paints landscape paintings and finds inspiration from the scenery and farm-land in the Southern Ontario area. She also enjoys drawing still life scenes in graphite. She received a BFA from Waterloo and a BA from Western. She currently divides her time between caring for her family, reading, exercising, gardening and painting.

**1 Sunswept** 24×24" Acrylic on canvas.

**2 Grand River Trail** 22×22" Oil on canvas.

**3 Summer Presence** 18×18" Oil on canvas.

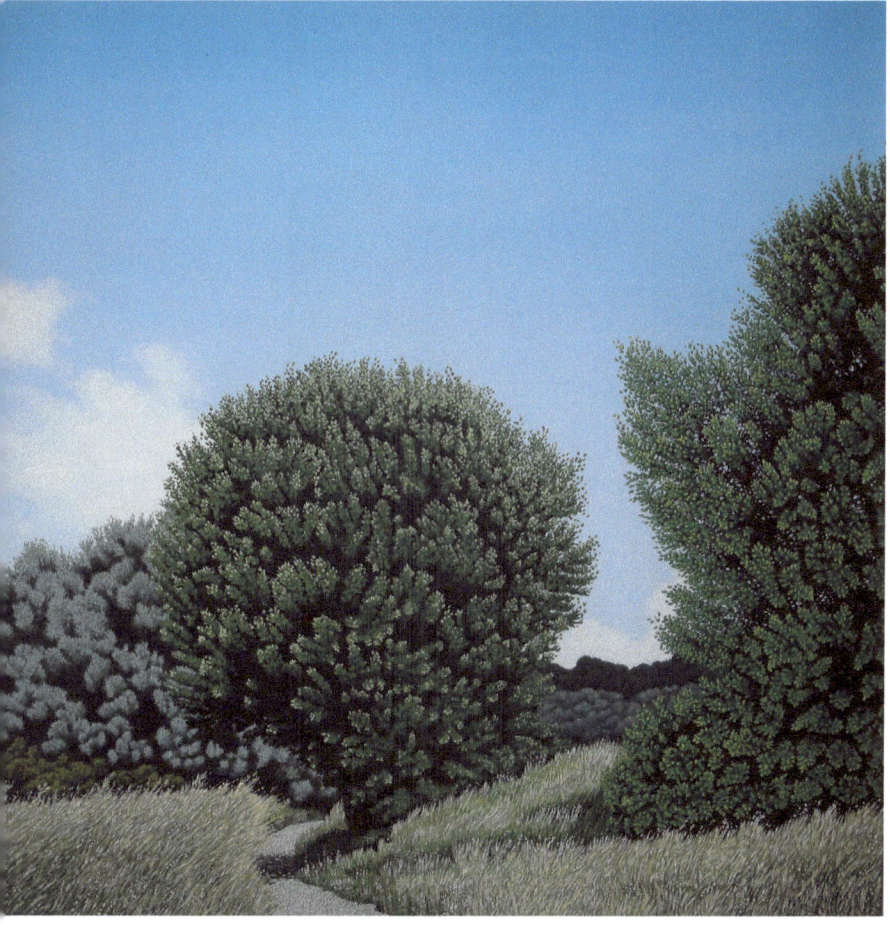
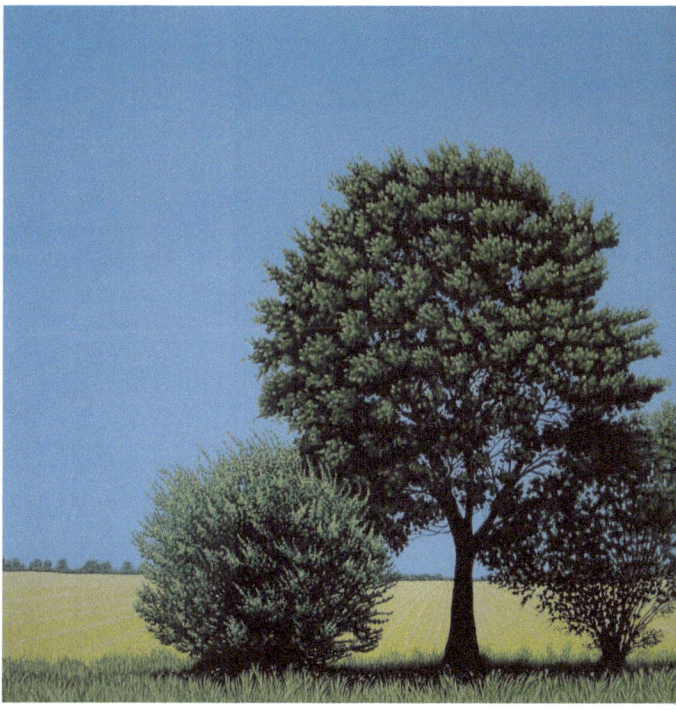

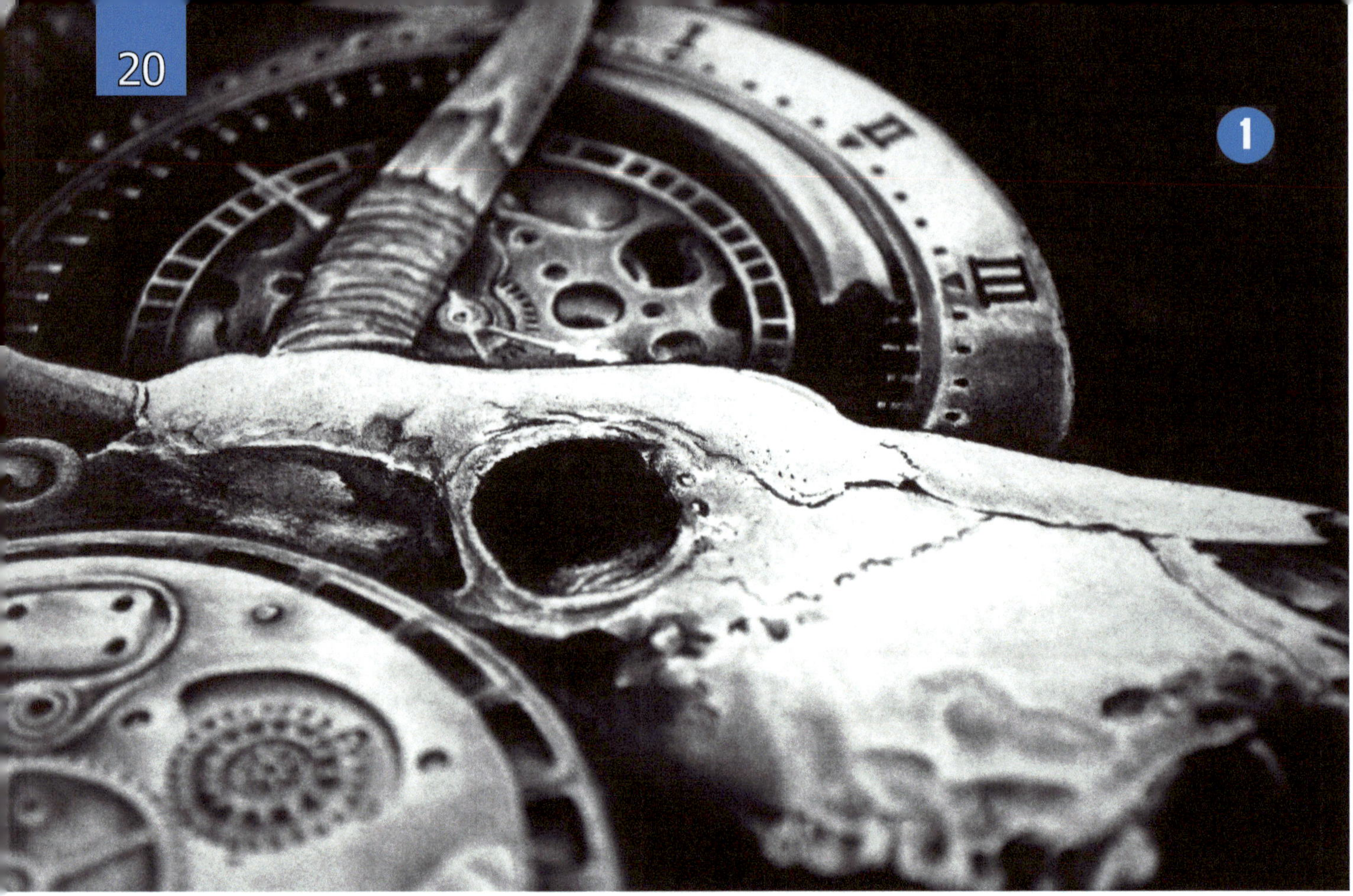

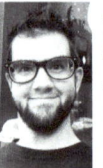

**1**

**1** **Like Clockwork** 9x14" Pencil on paper.

**2** **American Goddess** 10x16" Pencil on paper.

**3** **A Dapper Gentlefly** 6x9.5" Pencil on paper.

# CHRIS WINTERSON

**LOCATION:** Waterloo

**WEB:** www.facebook.com/pages/ Chris-Winterson-Art/102656573145677

**EMAIL:** chriswintersontattoos@hotmail.com

After graduating from the arts program at the University of Waterloo, Chris pursued tattoo apprenticeships in Guelph, Kitchener, and Waterloo - finally getting his start in 2010. Now working at Berlin Tattoo in Kitchener, he is thrilled to be able to make a living off his drawings and tattoos. Anyone interested in getting tattooed can see examples of his work on facebook group 'Chris Winterson Art'

**2**

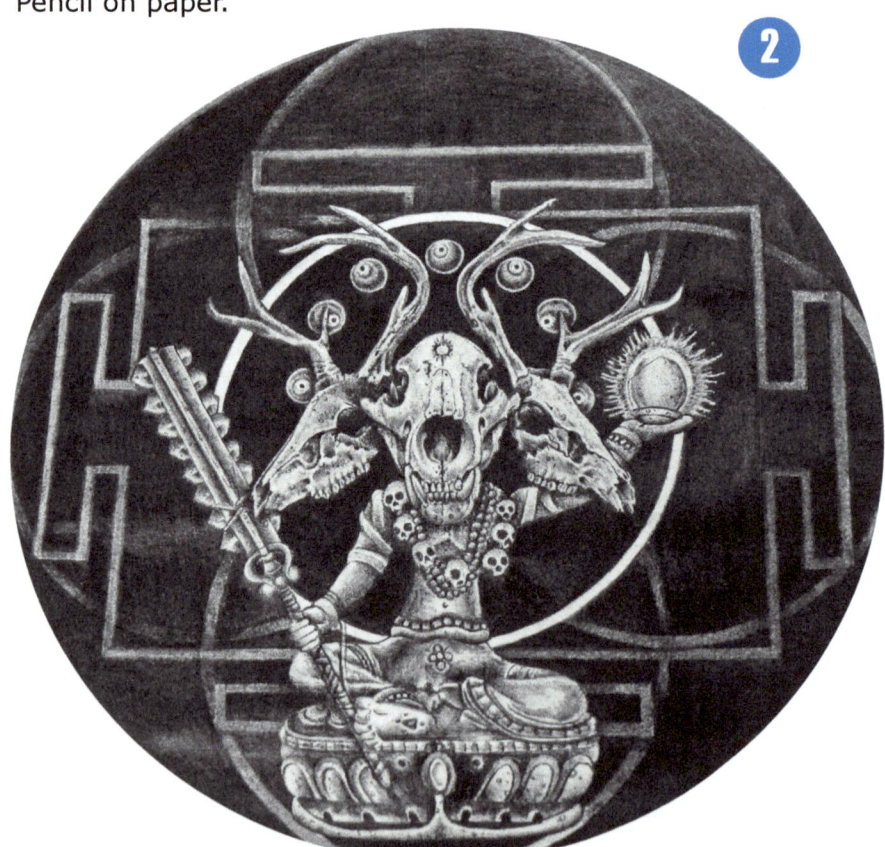

**3**

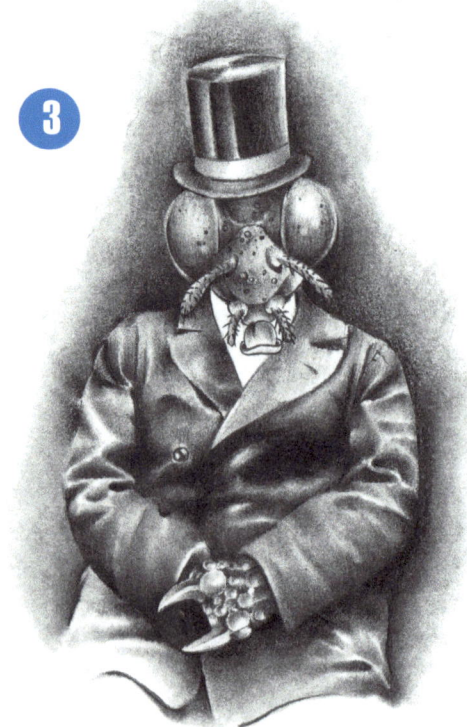

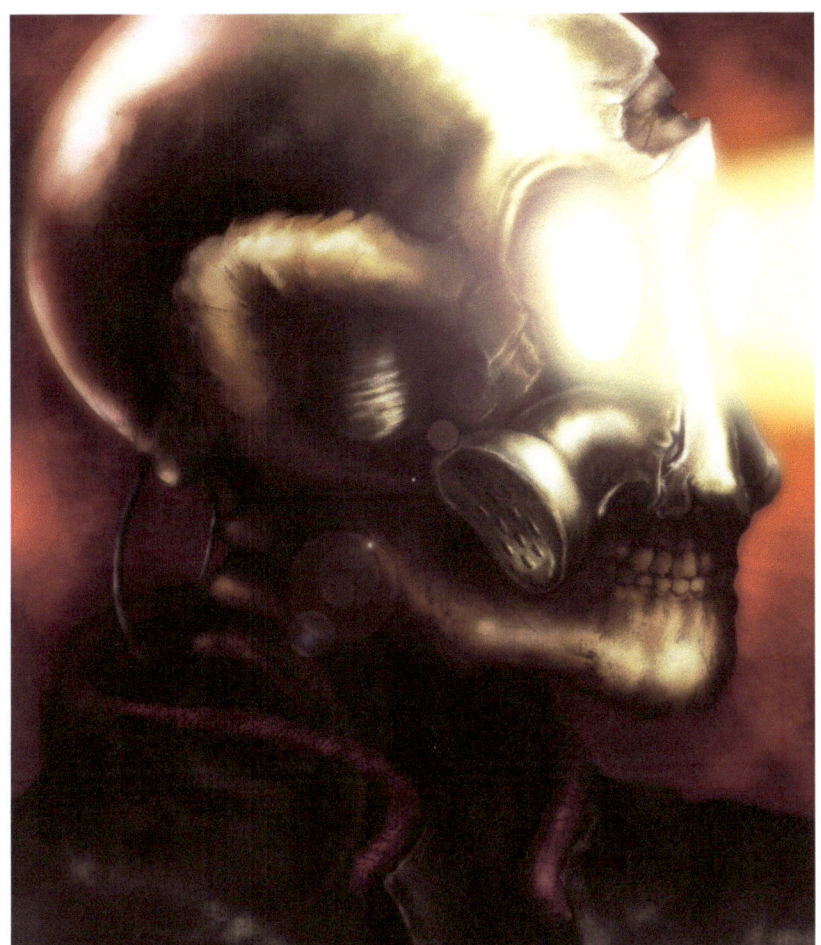

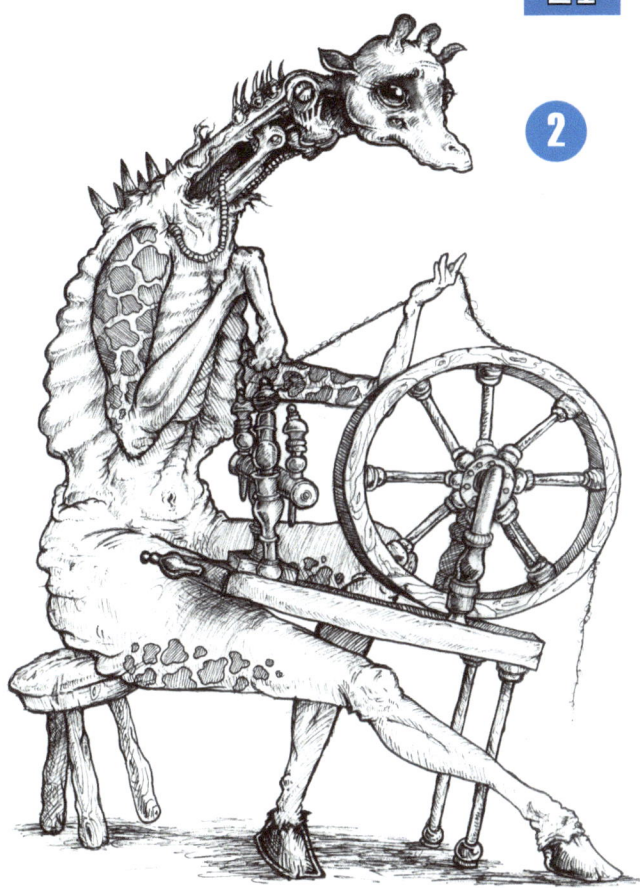

# PETER TUCKER ①

**LOCATION:** Kitchener
**WEB:** WoeAndFauna.com
**EMAIL:** contact@WoeAndFauna.com

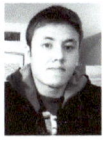 Peter Tucker originates from a tiny island off the coast of Massachusetts, and through wild cosmic chance he arrived where he always wanted to be - Canada. His work is inspired by brain surgery he underwent where he became fascinated with the human subconscious, memories, and emotions. He's currently working on two series; "Phantasmagoria" based on haunting dream-like imagery, and the "Woe & Fauna" series based on him mixing people's favorite animal with an emotion that best represents their spirit, making each piece personal and collaborative. He works in traditional pen and ink.

**1 Thought Police** 8×9.5" Digital Illustration. This illustration was based on the Classic Novel, 1984 by George Orwell.

**2 Longing** 6×9" Traditional Pen & Ink Illustration. Part of the Woe & Fauna Series.

**3 Mending** 11×14" Traditional Pen & Ink Illustration. Part of the Woe & Fauna Series

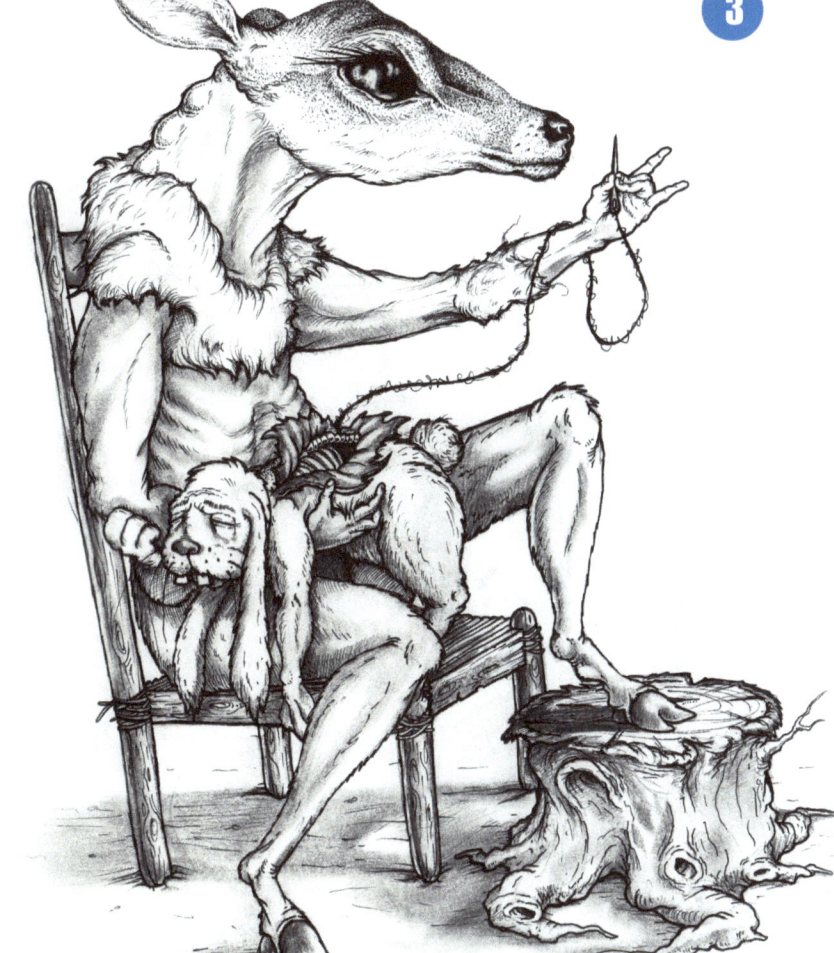

# CONAN STARK

**LOCATION:** Waterloo
**WEB:** ConanStark.com
**EMAIL:** photography@conanstark.com

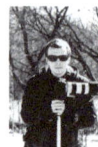

Conan Stark attended the University of Waterloo obtaining a B.F.A. (2002) and later a B.E.D. (2003) from the University of Western Ontario. He is currently working as a practicing artist in the region and teaches art at Cameron Heights C.I. He was born in Northern Ontario growing up in a low tech atmosphere and moved to the region in the mid 1980s, where he was exposed to a new world of suburban pop culture. This contrast presents itself in the themes and production of his work through his fascination with both traditional and contemporary art practices. His photographs are based on a range of subjects including: portraits, architecture, landscapes and photo reportage, captured using a range of film and digital cameras.

**1** **Get Out of My Kingdom (detail)** 13x19" Photograph.

**2** **No Need To Get Funny When You Can Get Lost** 13x19" Photograph

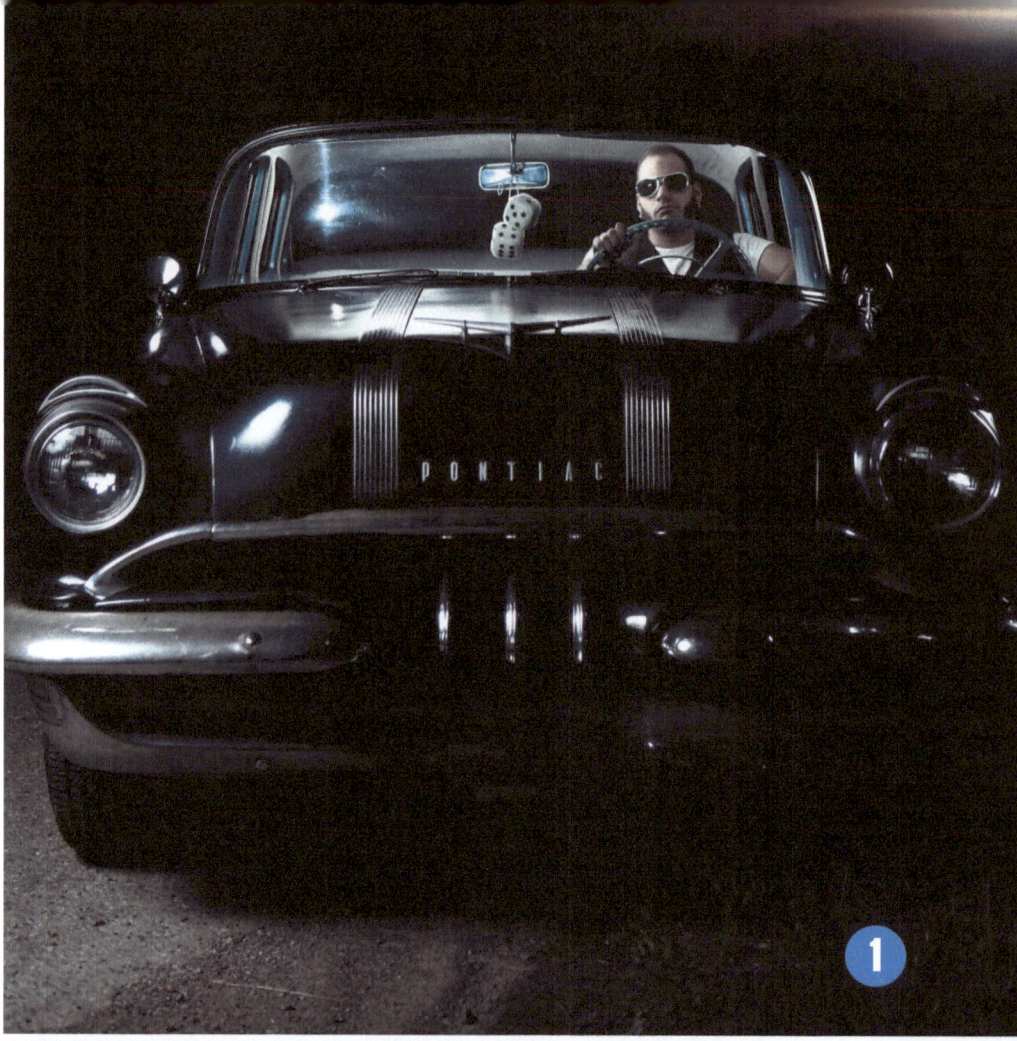

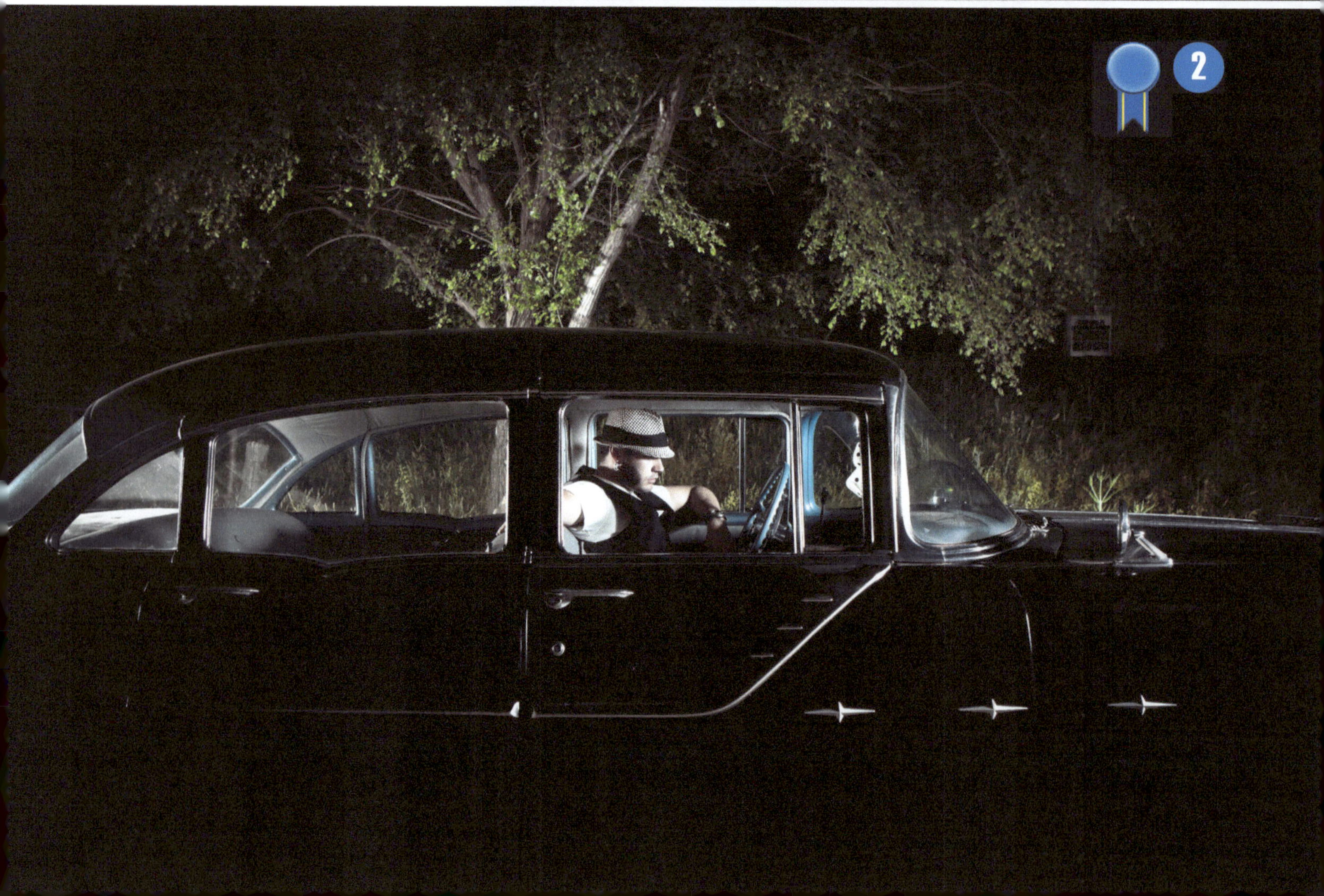

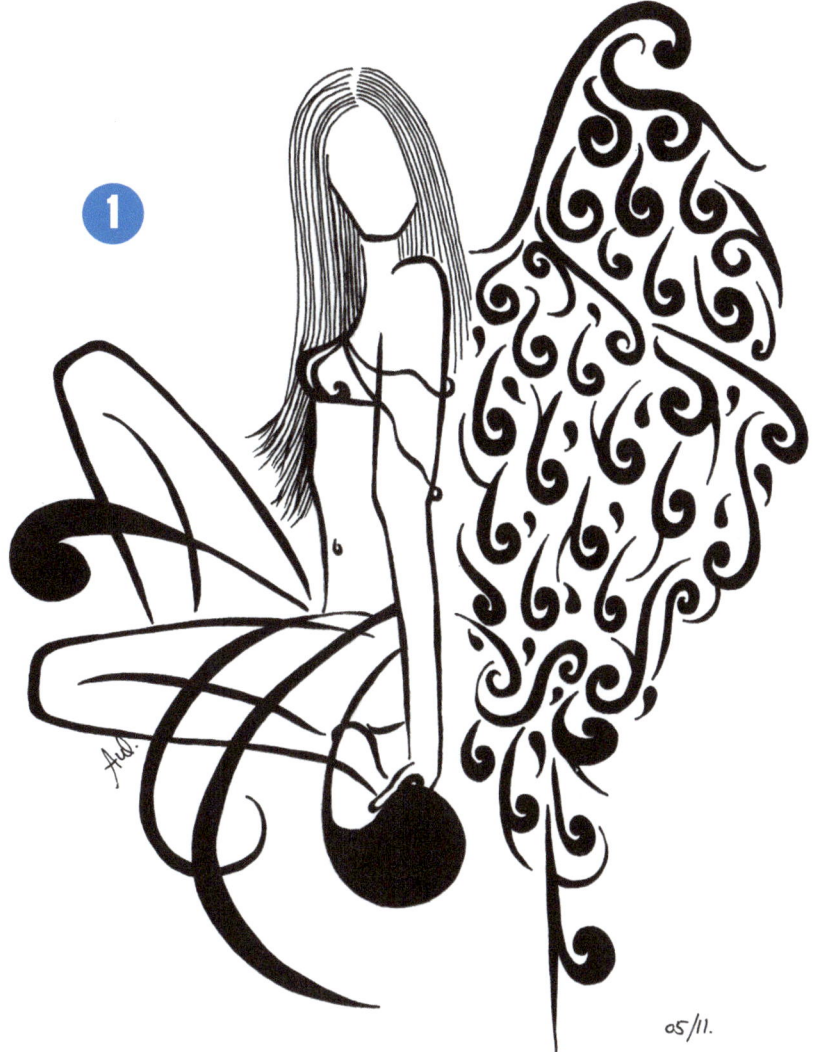

# ANGELA WERSTINE

**LOCATION:** St. Jacobs
**WEB:** www.facebook.com/Artist.Angela.Werstine
**EMAIL:** angela.werstine@live.com

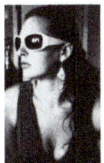

Angela Werstine's ink on paper work is sensual, erotic, beautiful, simple and elegant. Her drawings are evocative pieces that highlight the hips, legs, breasts and essential curves, and it makes sense that female beauty is the focus considering that Angela is a woman who is now able to celebrate her own body in a brand new way. Angela embellishes, accessorizes and infuses each piece with her own style and energy that perfectly reflects her new and lighter self. She uses as many lines as she sees fit, while celebrating the strength and beauty of the female body and spirit.

**1 Butterfly Kisses** 24x26" Ink on paper.

**2 Atlantic** 24x26" Ink on paper.

**3 Metis Pride** 24x26" Ink on paper.

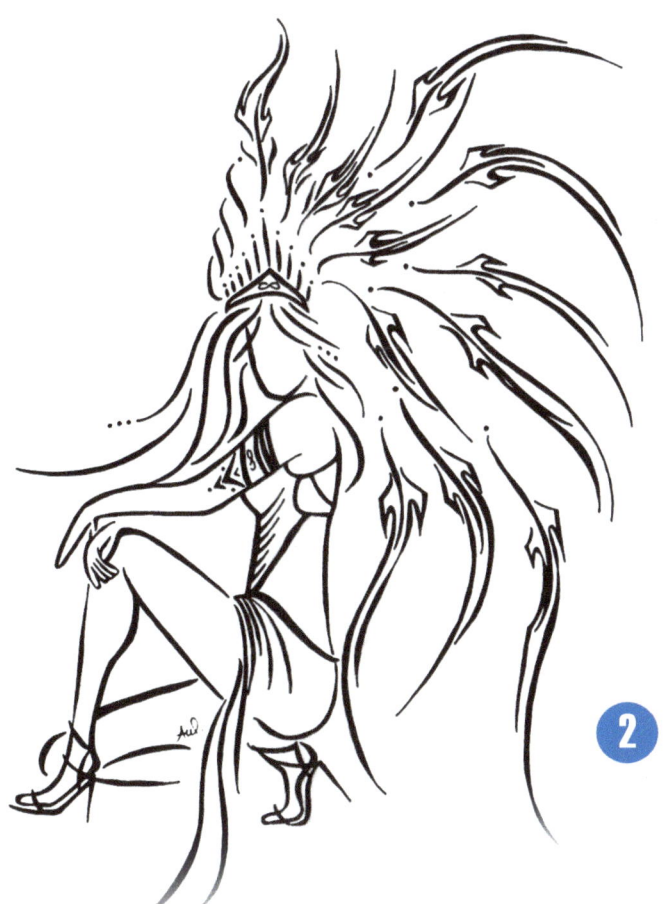

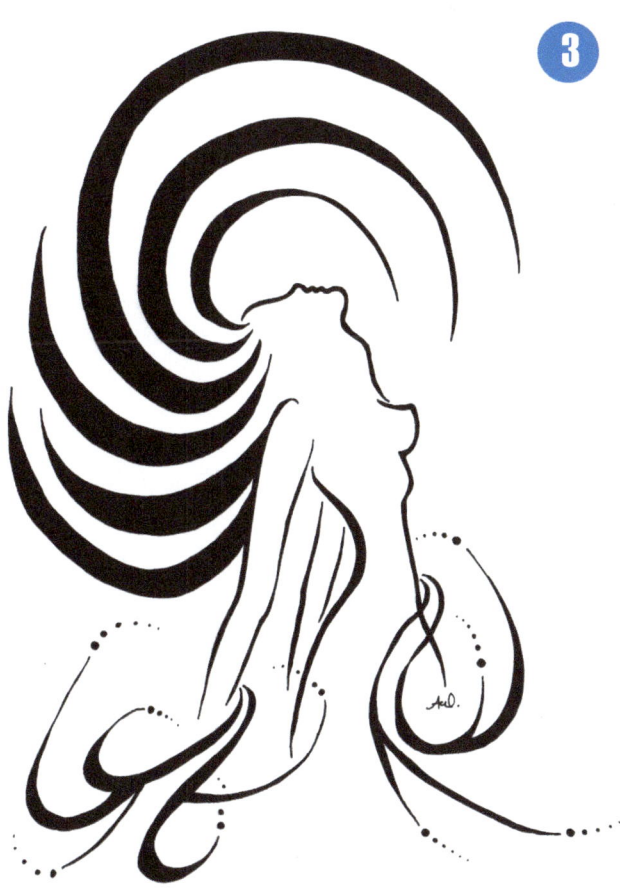

05/11.

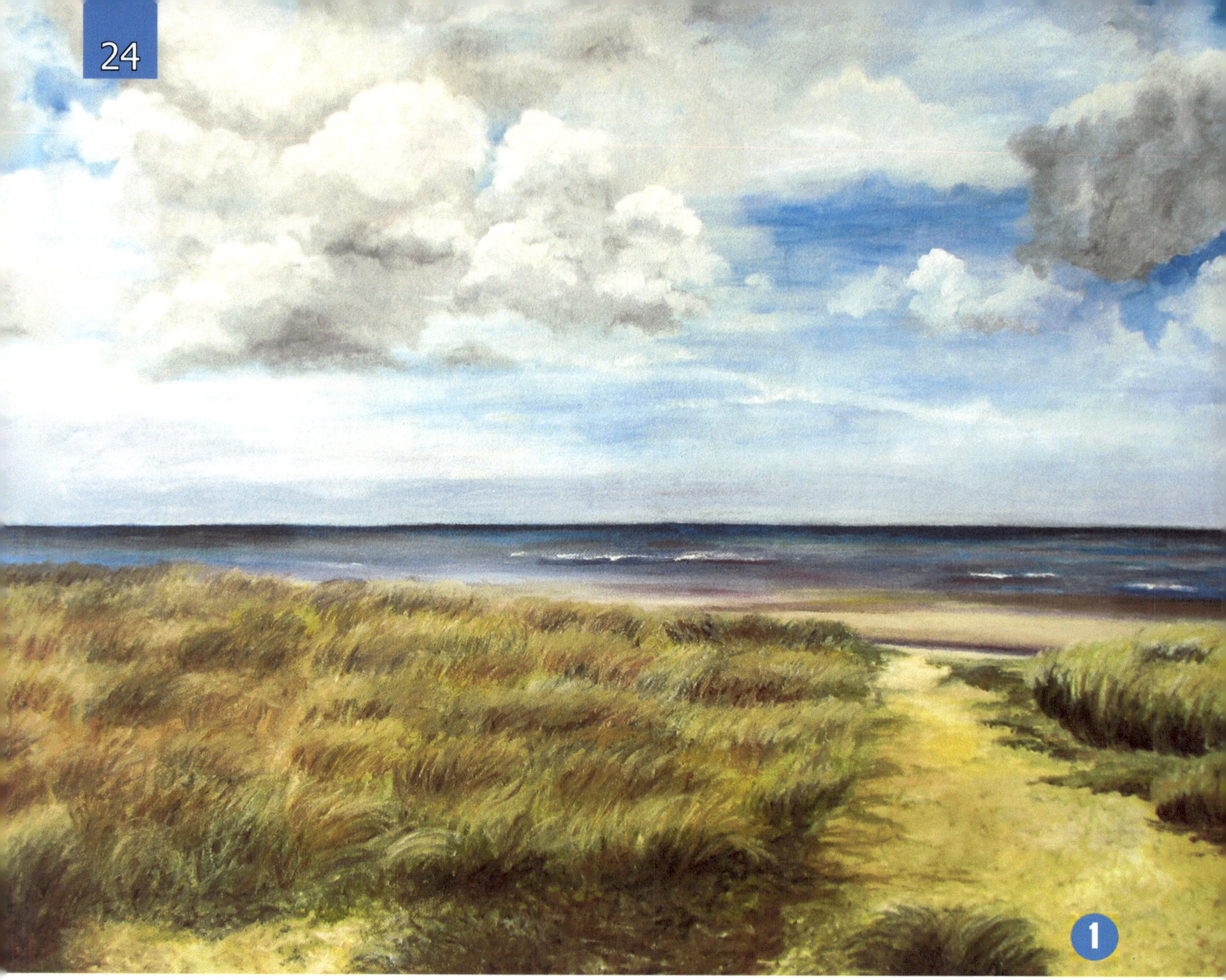

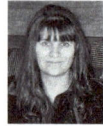

# MARCELA VEDINAS

**LOCATION:** Elmira
**WEB:** N/A
**EMAIL:** tec35no@yahoo.ca

Marcela paints with traditional oils on canvas "conventional oils have a preserving nature to them". This parallels most of Marcela's subject matter of accustomed landscapes and time honored sceneries. Her technique is to first photograph a scene and then transform the image into oil painting. "I try not to change anything from the photo, so it is essential I take a suitable picture". Marcela continually practices her craft and hopes to fulfill her desire to be an appreciated artist in her community.

**1 Lake Huron** 19×25" Oil on canvas.

**2 Wild Lilies** 20×24" Oil on canvas.

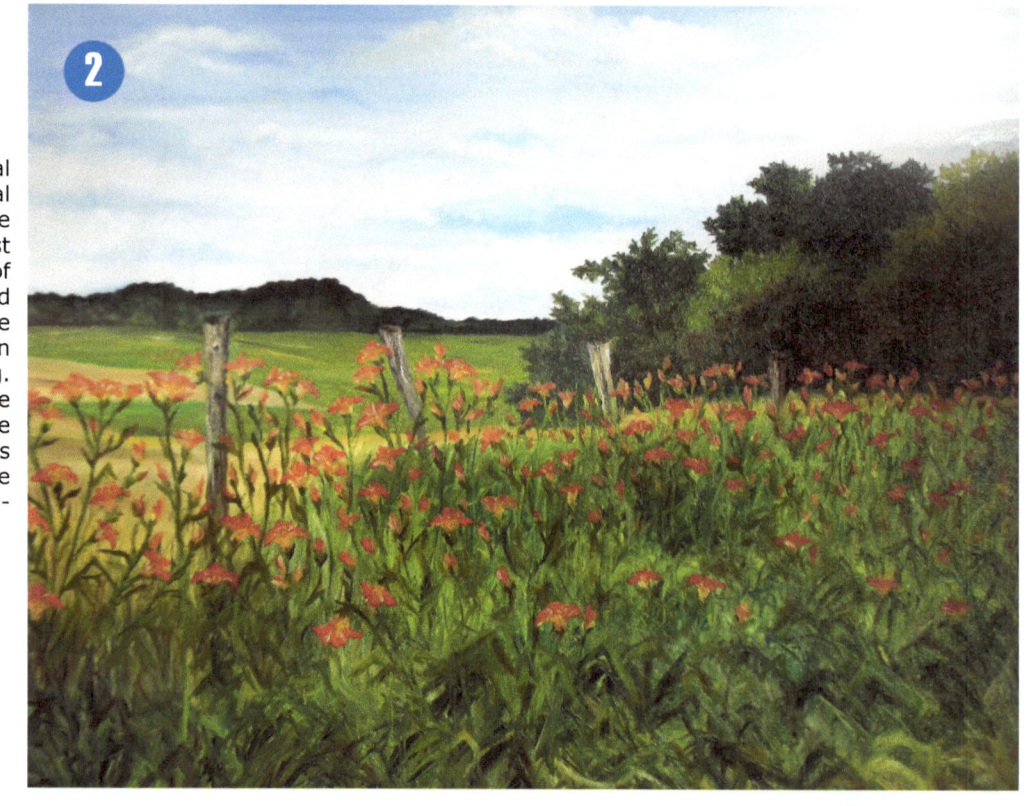

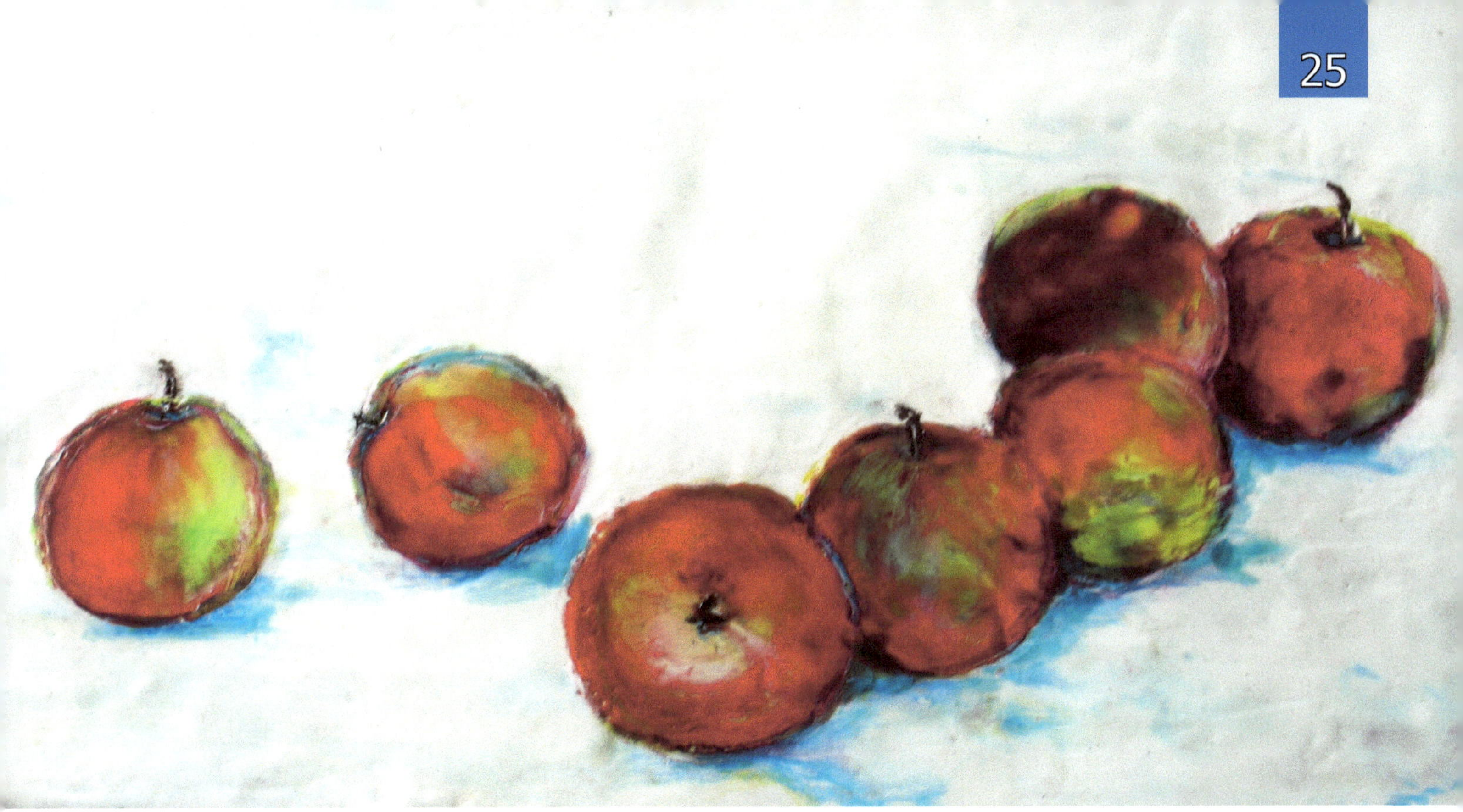

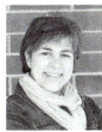

# ANNA KOOT

**LOCATION:** St. Marys
**WEB:** annakoot.com
**EMAIL:** gekoot@quadro.net

**1** **Apple Still Life** 12x24" Encaustic on wood panel.

**2** **Chat Line** 8x20" Watercolour.

Anna has always loved being creative. Everything from 'pom-pom' tissue flowers as a kid to anything she can get her hands on today. She began decorative painting in 1991, soon teaching in local shops and around her kitchen table. She continues to teach today in her home studio. Focusing on watercolour, she had the opportunity to illustrate 2 children's books. Henry & Harriet (grief) and Beaver Tales (Alzheimers).

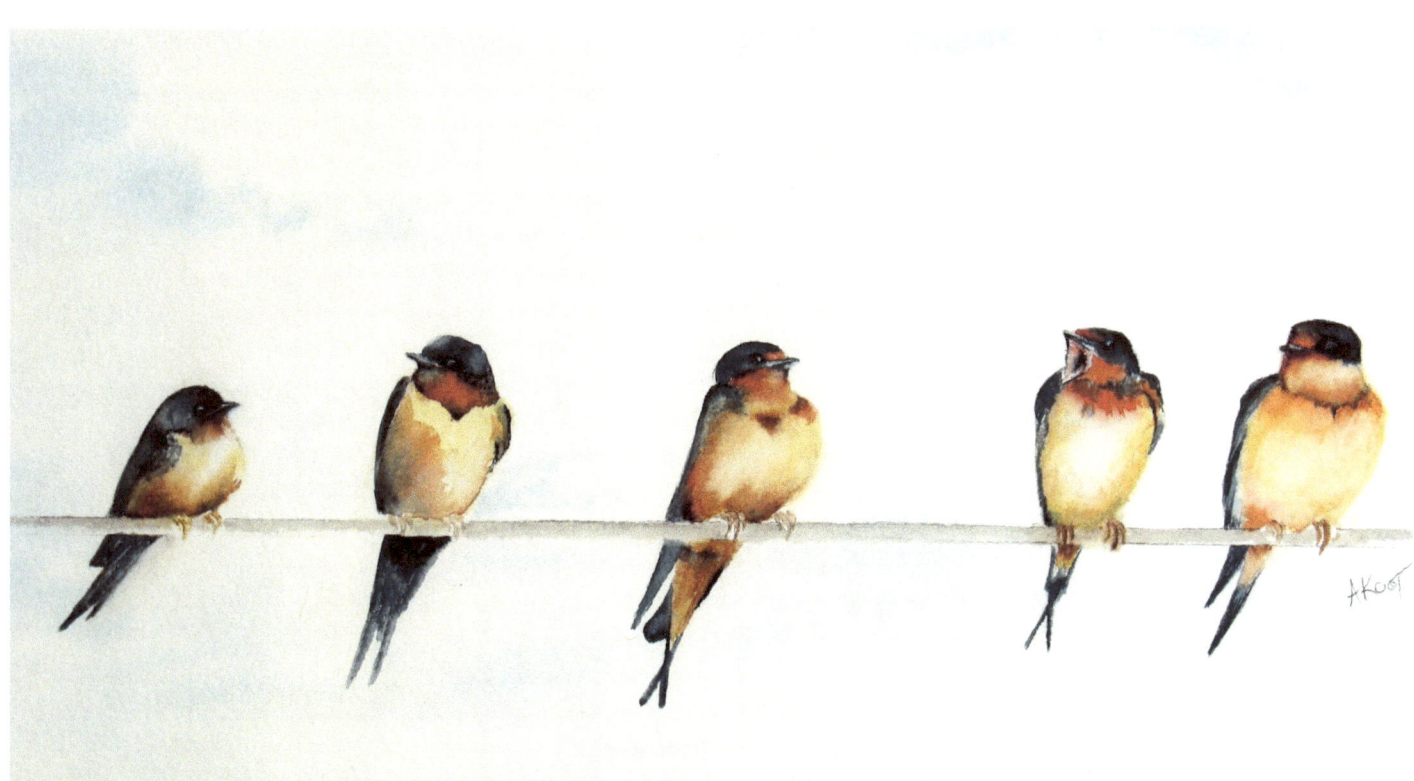

**1** **You Blinked First** 22x15"
Graphite/Charcoal. If eyes could
speak, would I be friend or foe?

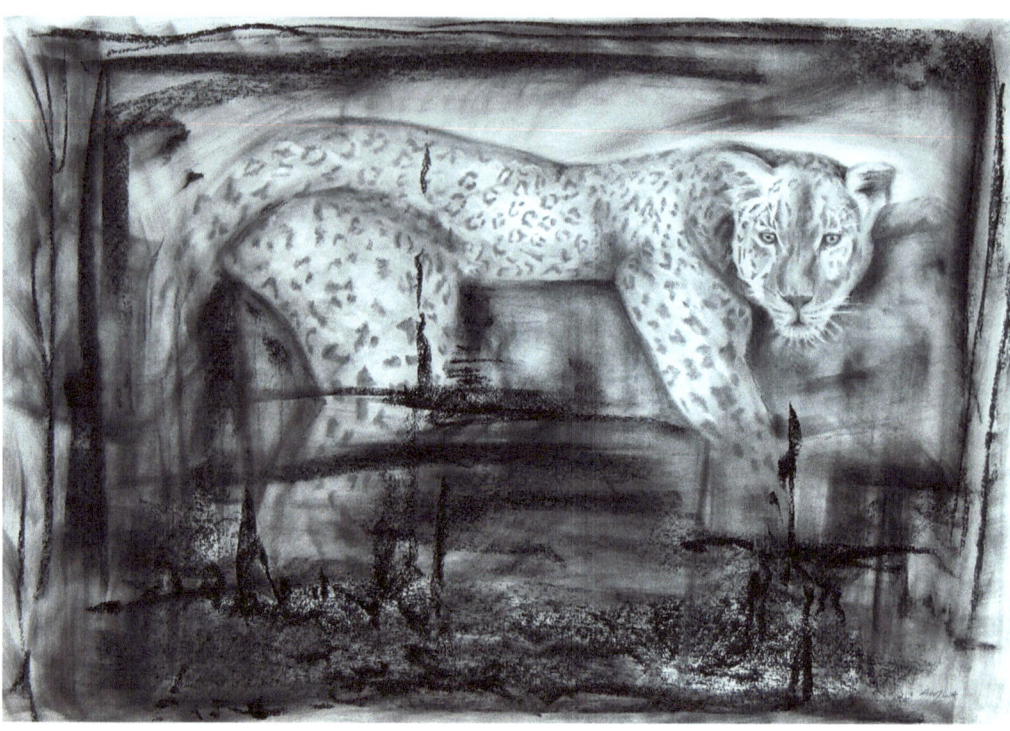

**2** **Face Your Opponent** 15x22"
Graphite/Charcoal. Be strong,
stand your ground and face your
opponent head on.

**3** **King Lear** 22x15" Graphite/
Charcoal. The essence of power
and strength.

# ADELE FIGLIOMENI

**LOCATION:** Shakespeare
**WEB:** AdeleFigliomeni.com:
**EMAIL:** AdelinasGallery@rogers.com

Growing up my father would say:"You'll always find a fork in the road and I will try to
guide you to the right. At times you might go
astray to the left, but I will try to push you
back to the right." I guess after listening to
this old proverb so many times, I chose a career that
allowed me to design the roads in which I and others
would travel. After 15 years of designing roads as a
Civil Engineering Technologist and years of traveling to
the right, I'm going to take some chances and make a
couple of left turns. In May 2005, I opened Adelina's
Studio & Gallery in Shakespeare, Ontario. And now my
works are in private collections across Canada, USA,
and Europe. My passion to create continues to evolve.
I describe my new graphite paintings as a matrix of
realism and abstract fusion.

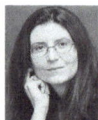

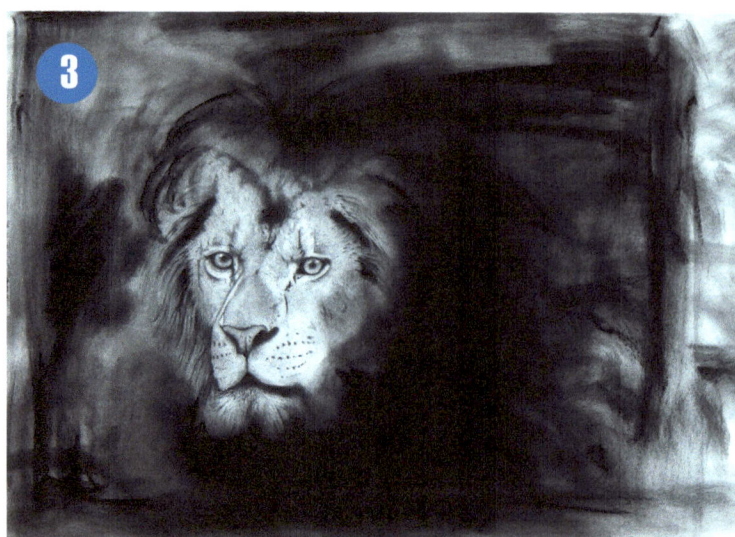

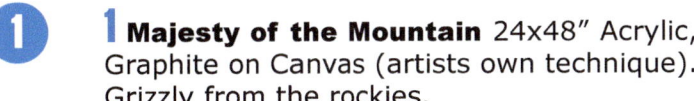

**1 Majesty of the Mountain** 24x48" Acrylic, Graphite on Canvas (artists own technique). Grizzly from the rockies.

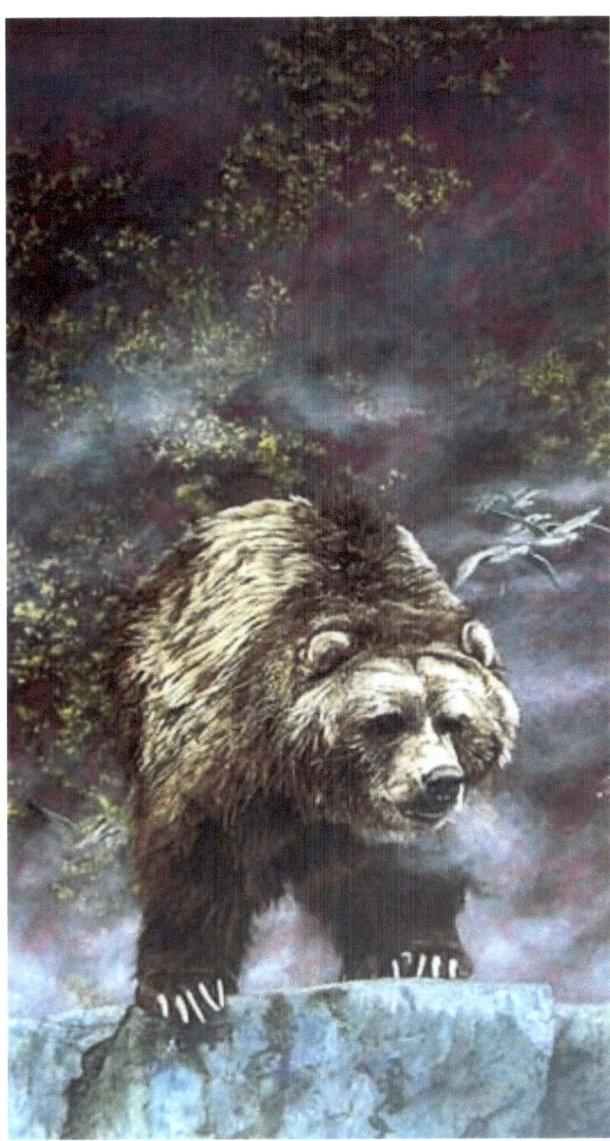

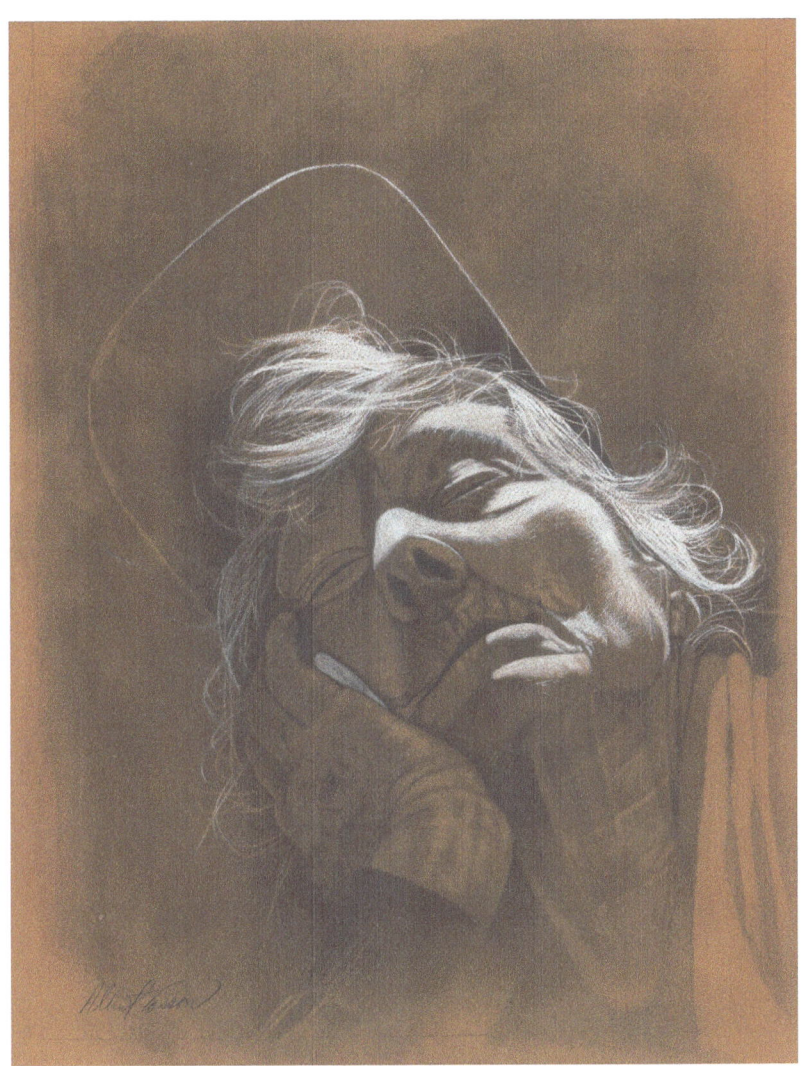

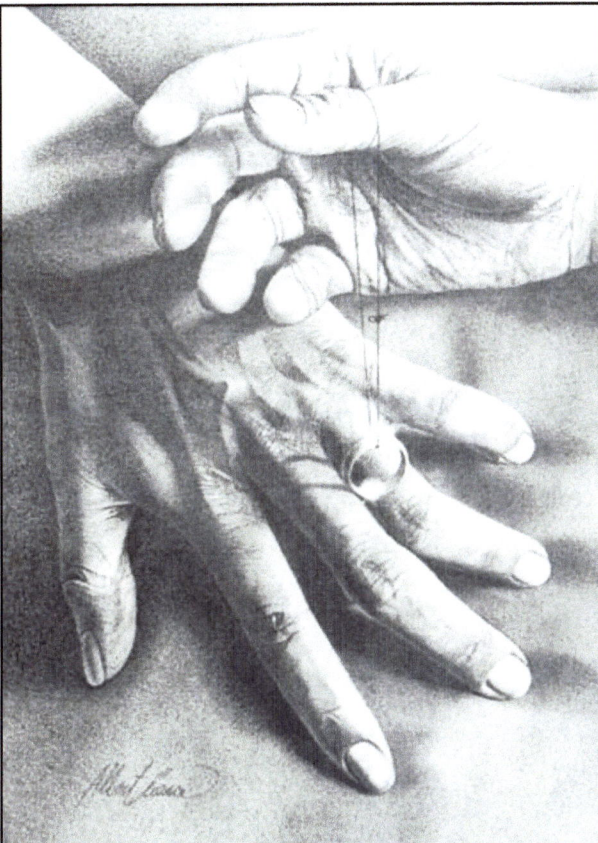

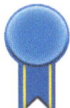 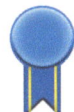 

# ALBERT CASSON
**LOCATION:** Kitchener
**WEB:** albertcasson.com
**EMAIL:** casson25@rogers.com

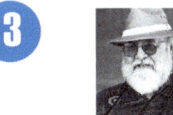 Albert is a graduate of the Ontario College of Art in Toronto. Artist of the year in Barrie and the Wye Marsh. Inducted into the Walk of Fame in Milton, Ontario. Commissioned by Kodak Canada, Calgary Zoo, Vancouver Aquarium, Winnipeg Zoo, Molson Indy in Toronto, R.M.S Segwun in Gravenhurst, Panasonic Canada, Royal City Realty in Guelph etc. Albert now resides in Kitchener, Ontario.

**2 Sun Kissed** 16x20" Black and White Conte on Coloured Paper. An old woman rests while the sun kisses her face.

**3 The Promise** 15x20" Graphite Pencil on Canvas. Our marriage is as fragile as The Promise made (symbolized by the ring hung by a fragile string).

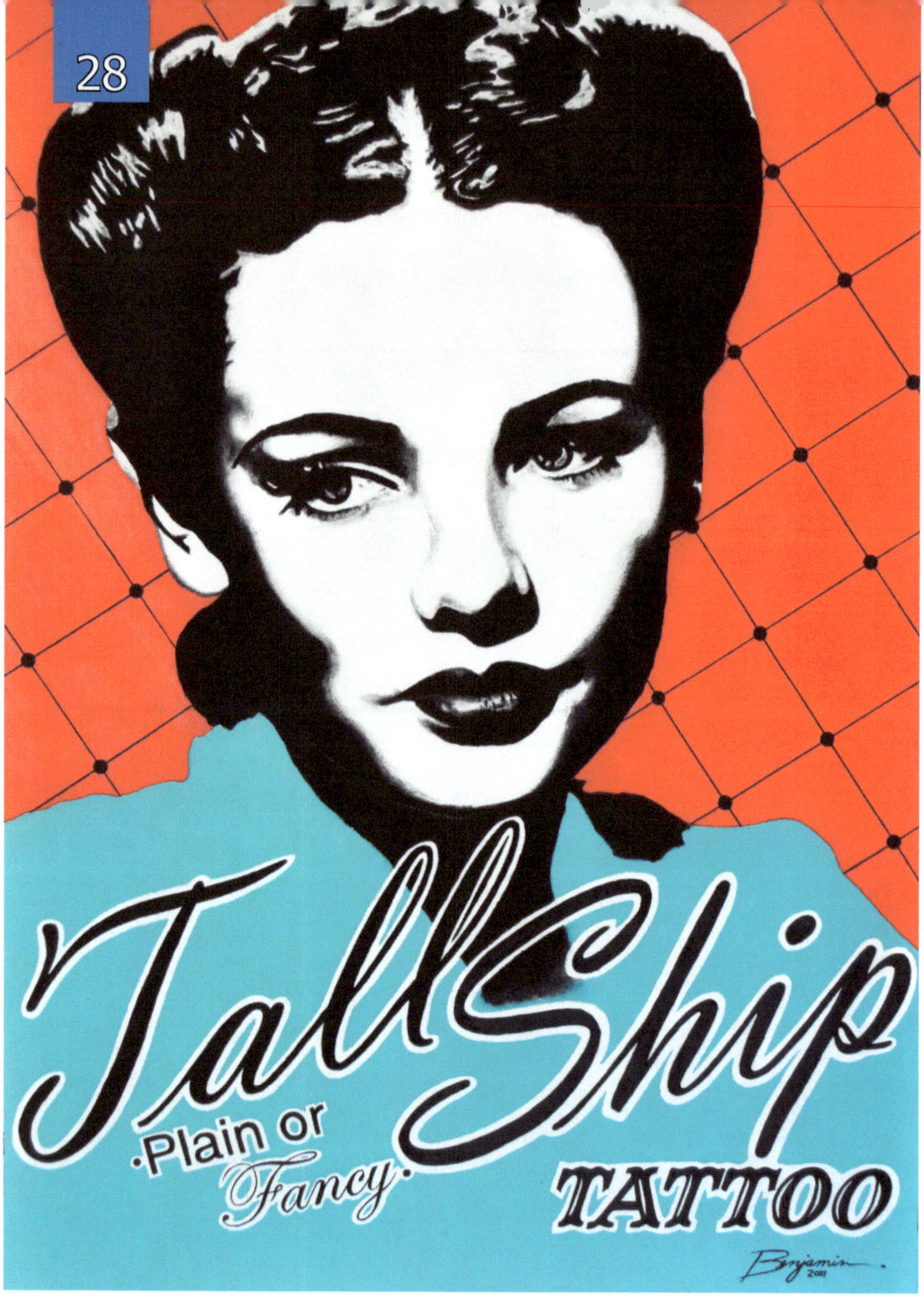

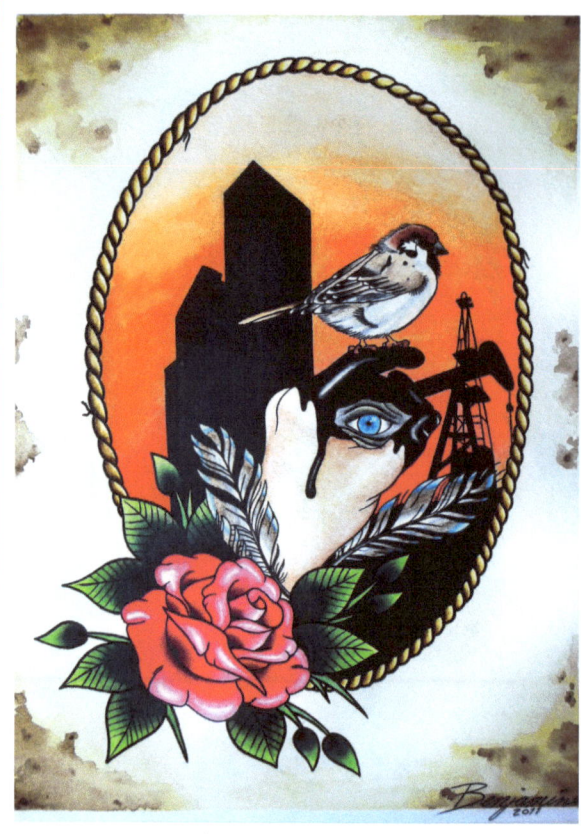

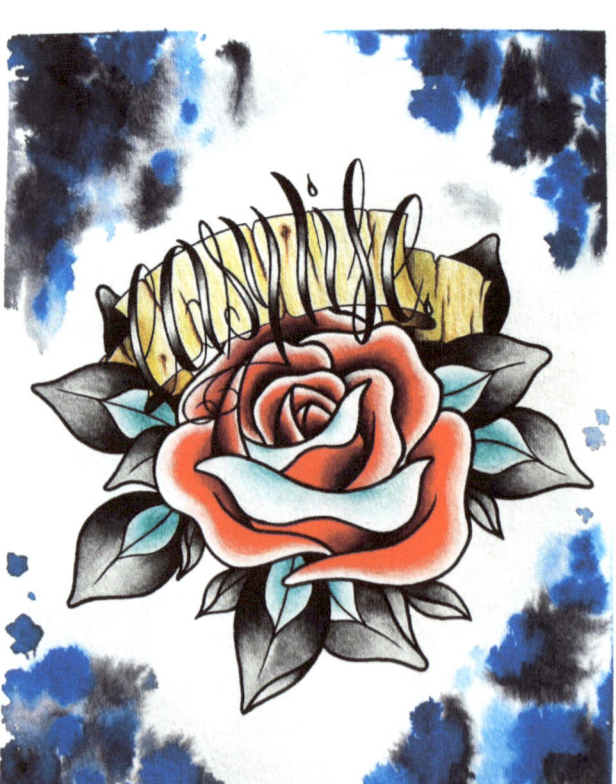

**1** **Vivien Leigh** 16x21" Charcoal, Prismacolour Markers, Pencil Crayon. Prints available, commissions accepted.

**2** **Sparrow** 10x14" Watercolour.

# BEN DOT

**LOCATION:** Tall Ship Tattoo - Waterloo
**WEB:** facebook.com/easylifetattoos
**EMAIL:** bendottattoos@gmail.com

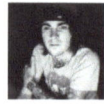 My name is Ben and I am currently tattooing out of Tall Ship Tattoo in Waterloo - apprenticing under Jeremy Zettler. I have been working at Tall Ship Tattoo for over a year now and developing my skills as a tattooer and an artist. I love everything involving nature and have a passion to see the world as I tattoo. I have prints available upon request and happily take on commission work!

**3** **Easy Life** Rose 8x10"

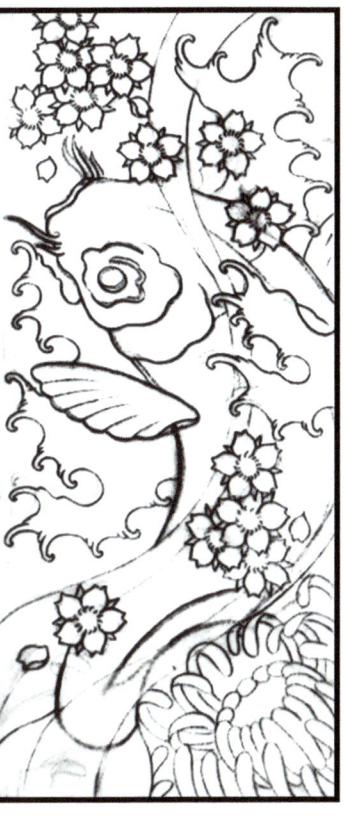
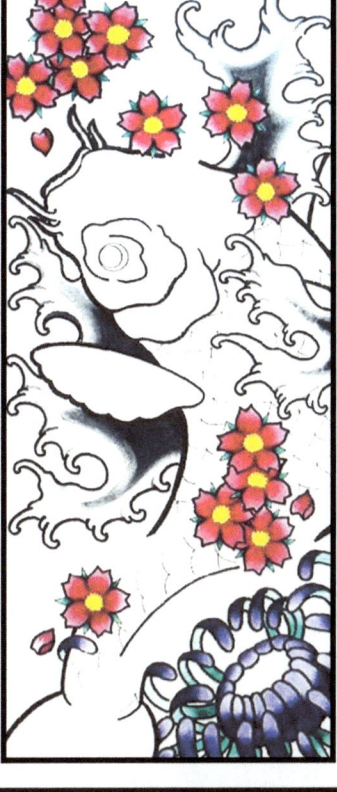
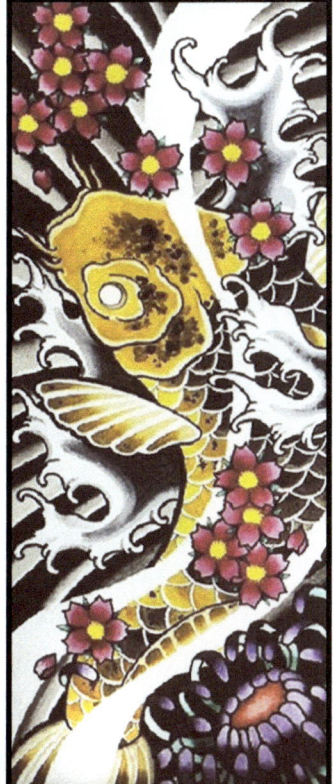

# TALL SHIP TATTOO (JEREMY ZETTLER)

**LOCATION:**
2 King St S.Uptown Waterloo
**WEB:** TallShipTattoo.blogspot.com
**EMAIL:** TallShipTattoo@hotmail.com

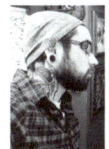

I'm a tattooer and owner of Tall Ship Tattoo uptown Waterloo. Very into antiques and oddities, weaponry, taxidermy tattooing and painting. I've been painting and drawing for about 20 years, pretty much since I can remember. Love doing watercolor and charcoal.

**1**

**1 Japanese Koi** 8x24" Watercolor.

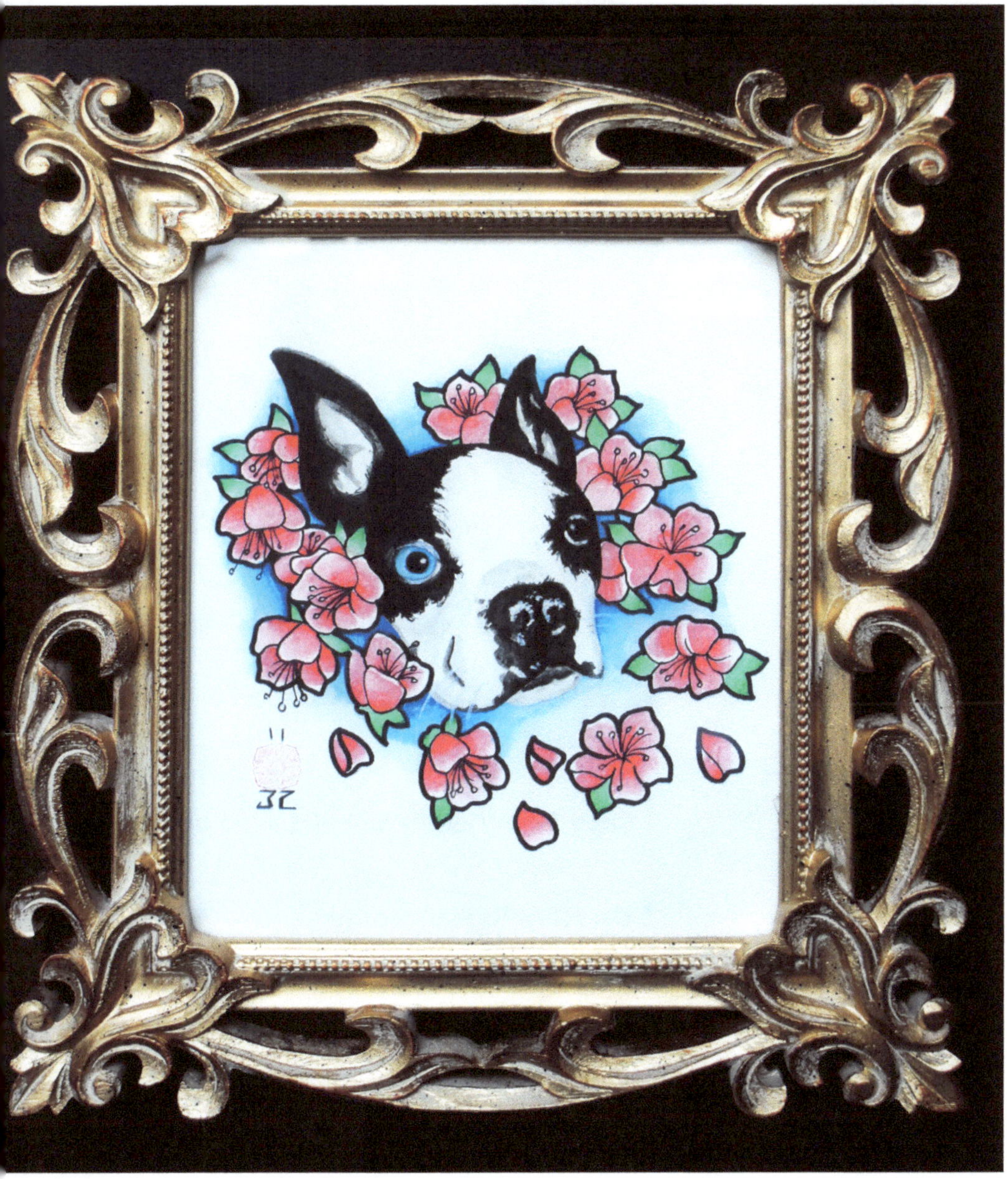

**2**

**2 Audge Podge** 12x8" Watercolor.

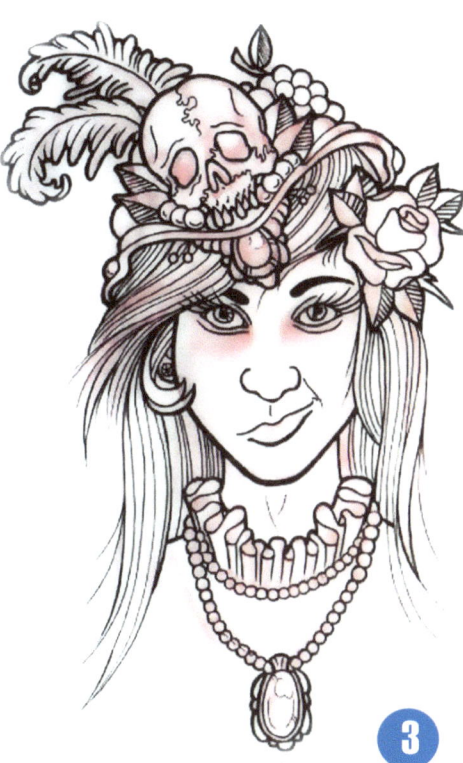

**3**

**3 Percy** 6x10" Liner marker and pencil crayon on tracing paper.

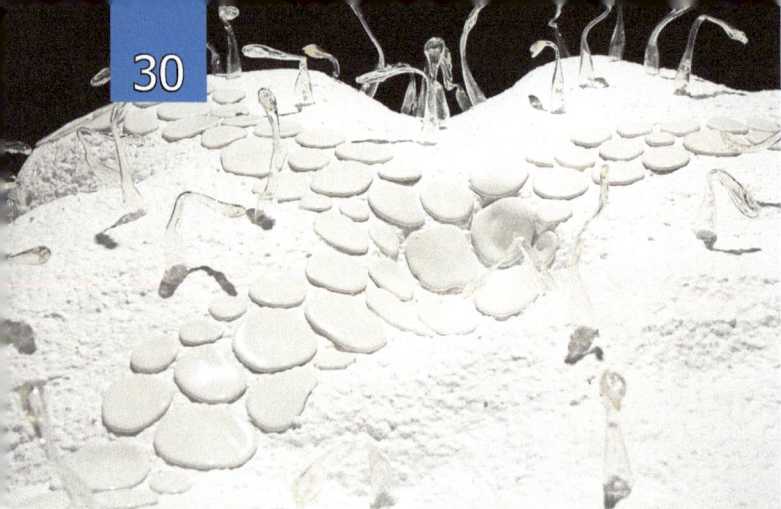

# CHRISTOPHER KORROCK-ABILLY

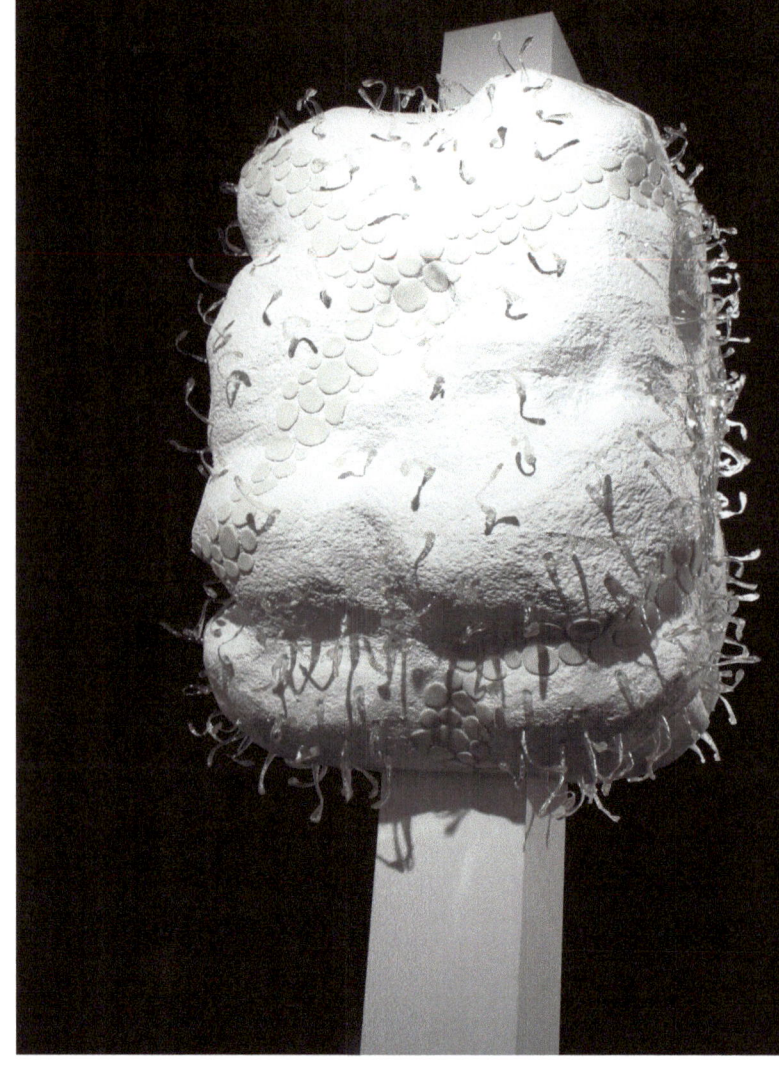

**1**

**LOCATION:** Kitchener
**WEB:** N/A
**EMAIL:** diablo_master005@hotmail.com

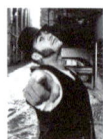

I like to create everything my mind can come up with. My art usually consist of things from painting, drawing, clay, sculpture and soft sculpture. It always has a bit of abnormality to my work usually combining objects together to create something new. Most of my influence is from the idea of Frankenstein's monster and Dr. Frankenstein himself. I went to study fine art at University of Waterloo and it was the best decision my mentor and I decided.

**3**

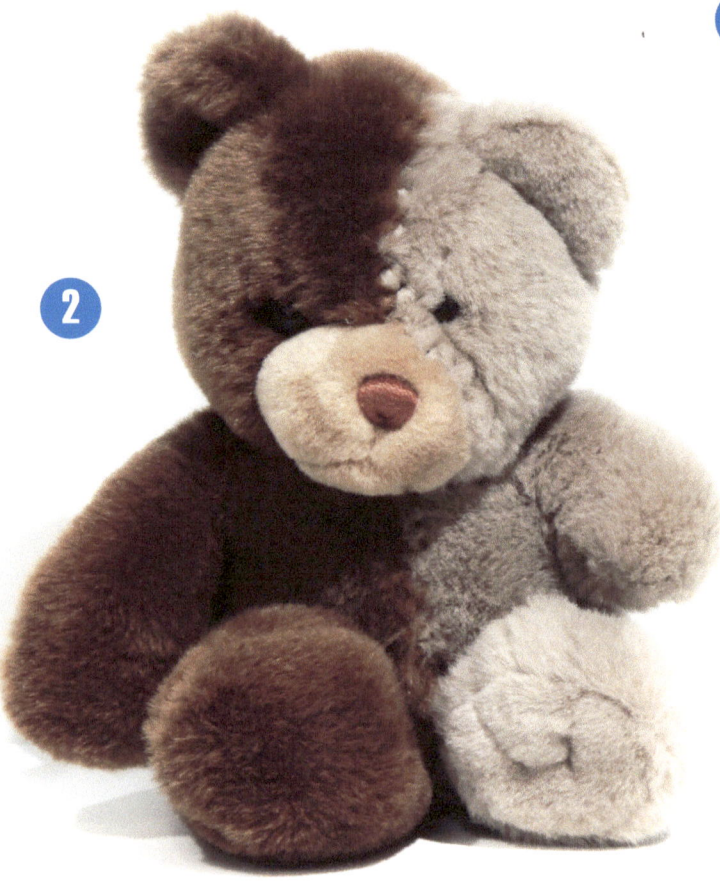

**2**

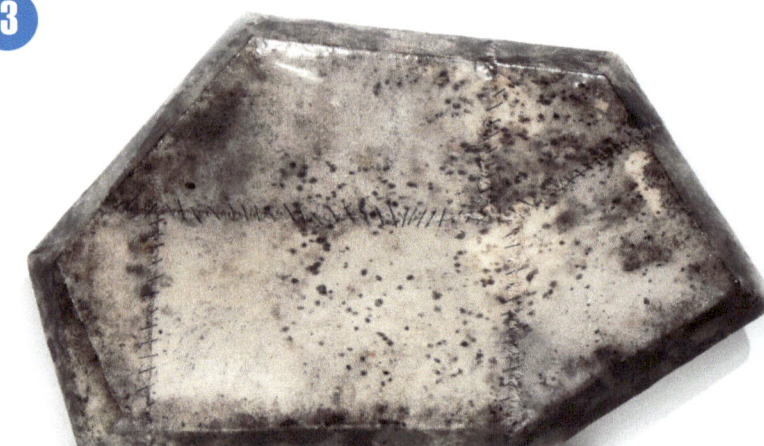

**1** **Cata** (with detail) 5x4x4' Mixed media.

**2** **Dr. Hide** 8x5x5" Stuffed animals and thread.

**3** **11 21 2010** 12x15" Canvas and mold.

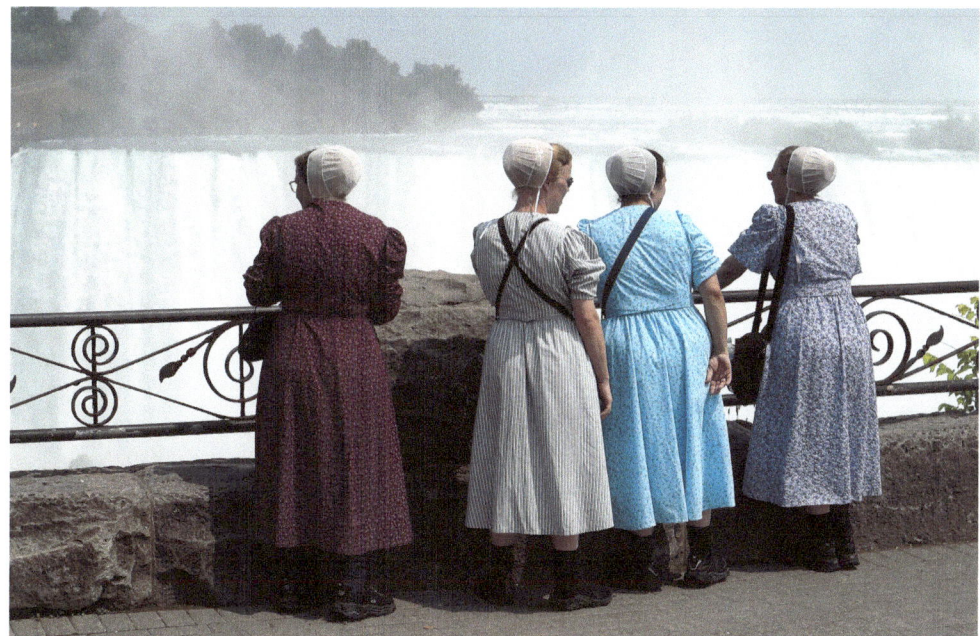

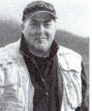

# DANNY BAILEY

**LOCATION:** Kitchener
**WEB:** wix.com/djdannyray/danny-bailey
**EMAIL:** ShootingTheWorld@rogers.com

Danny Bailey is a professional videographer photographer that has documented images and stories from over 44 countries worldwide. His image "Maids of the Mist" was chosen as the "Viewer Choice Runner Up" in a 2011 LIFE Magazine competition themed "Together." He has just recently celebrated his first gallery show with Silicon W in Kitchener displaying his collection of "Bengali Dyes ."Danny studied Broadcasting at Conestoga College and has promoted his craft on camera with over 50 on-air features with CTV in Canada.

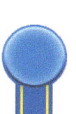

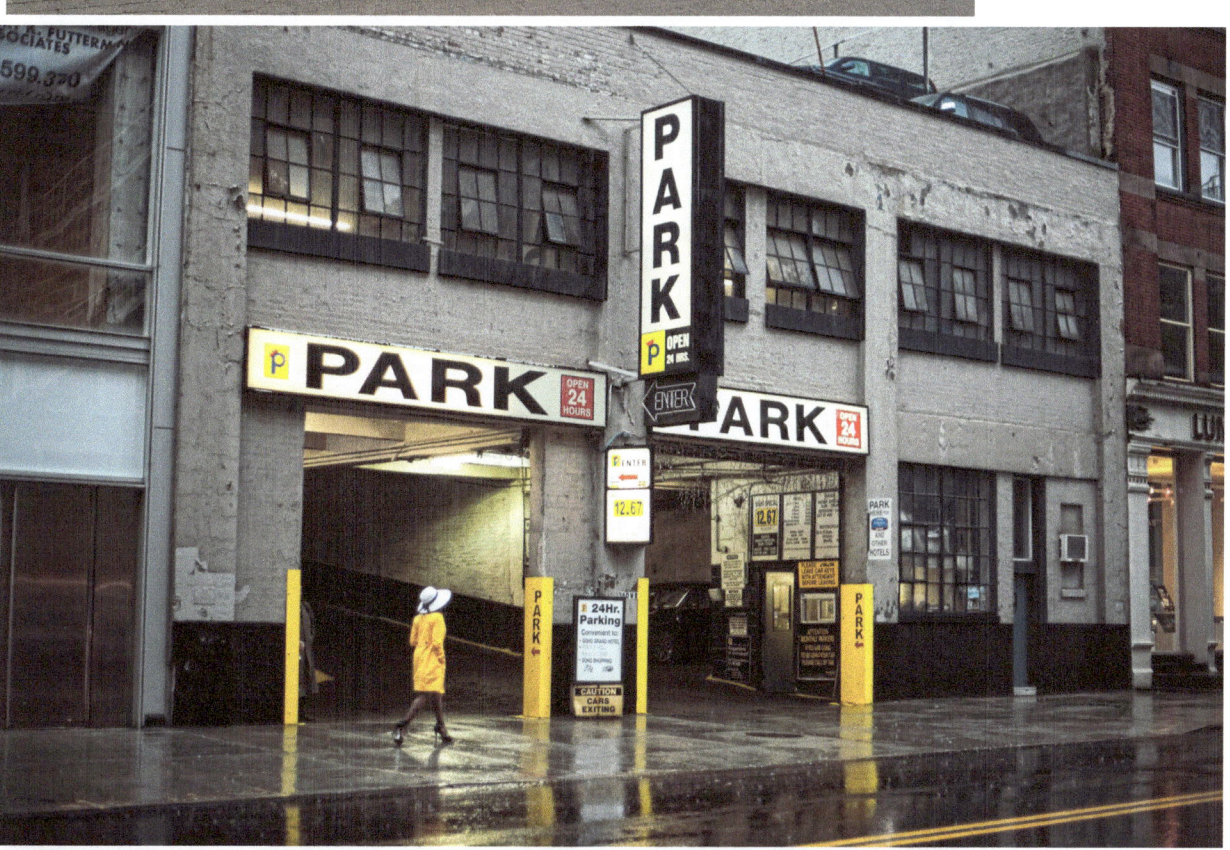

**1 Maids of the Mist** Photograph.

**2 Yellow Park** Photograph.

**3 NY Couple** Photograph.

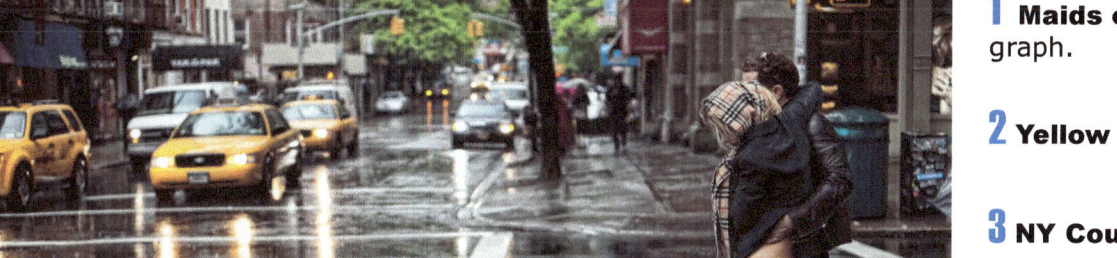

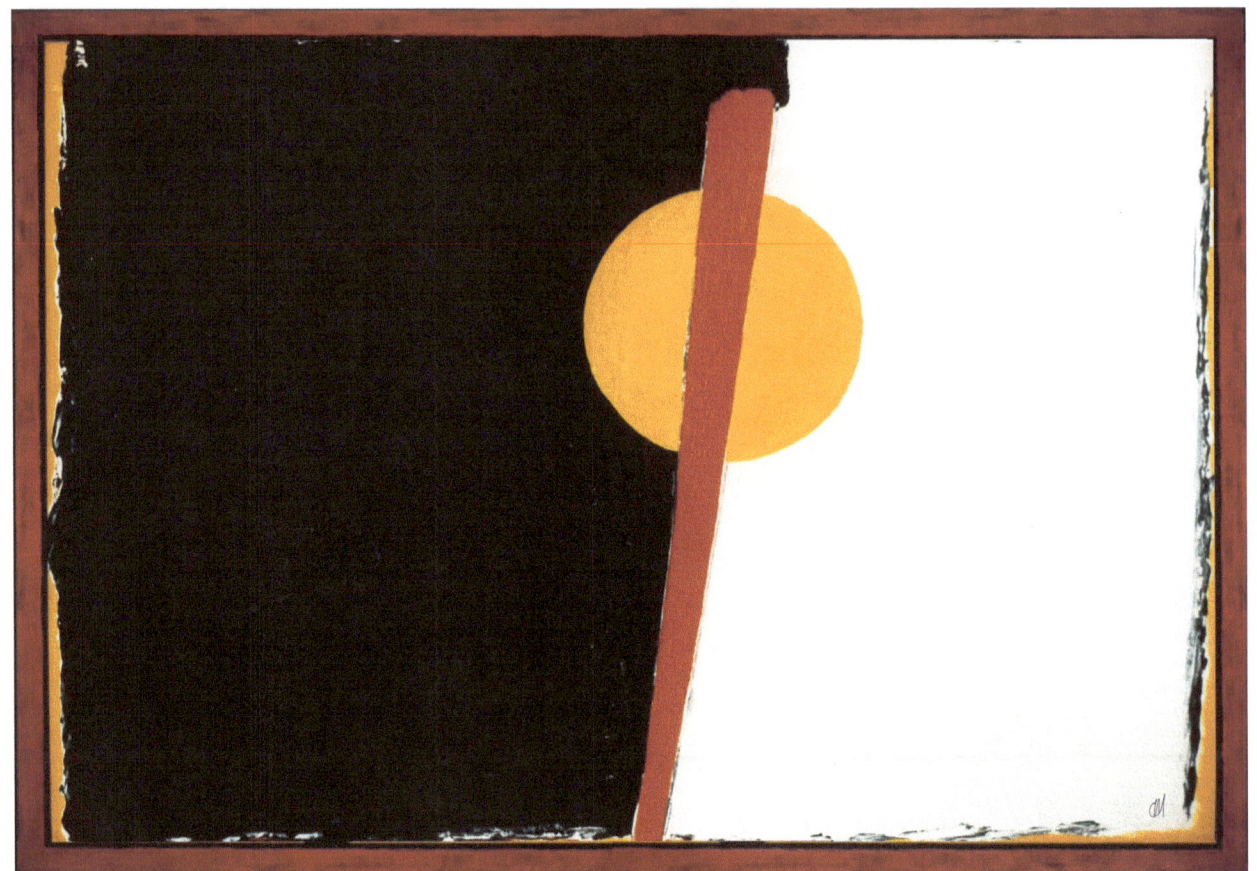

**1**

# CAROLINE DE GRUCHY

**LOCATION:** Kitchener
**WEB:** crvisuals.com
**EMAIL:** caroline@crvisuals.com

Caroline is a writer / artist / creative freelancer who works in a variety of media in the real and virtual world.

**2 Abstract** 9x12" Mixed media on board.

**1 Direct Communication**
22x30" Acrylic on paper.

**3 1930** 16x20" Oil on board.

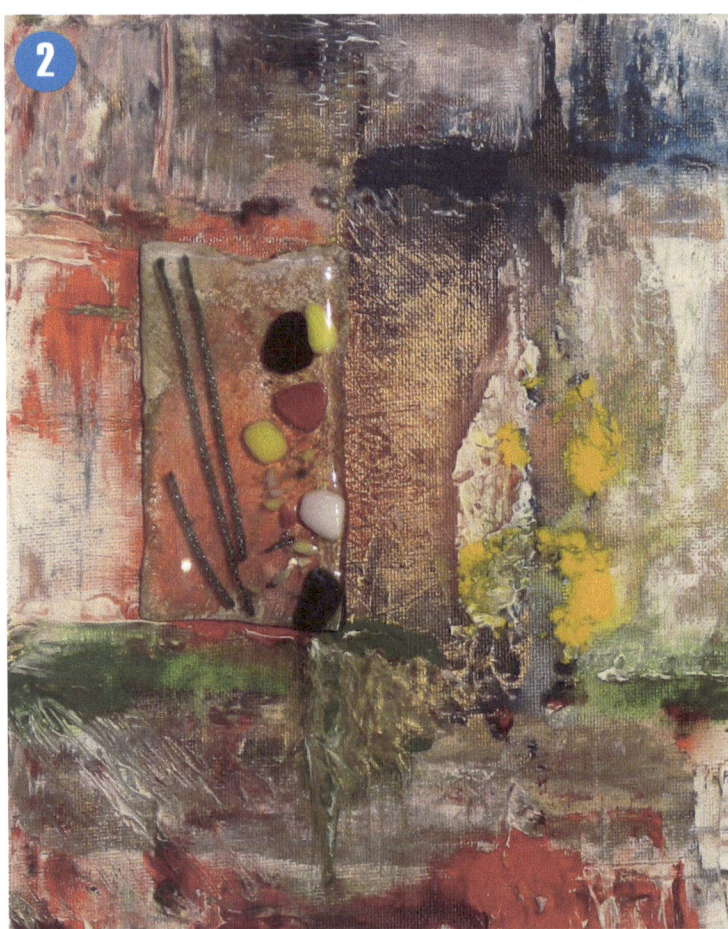

**2**

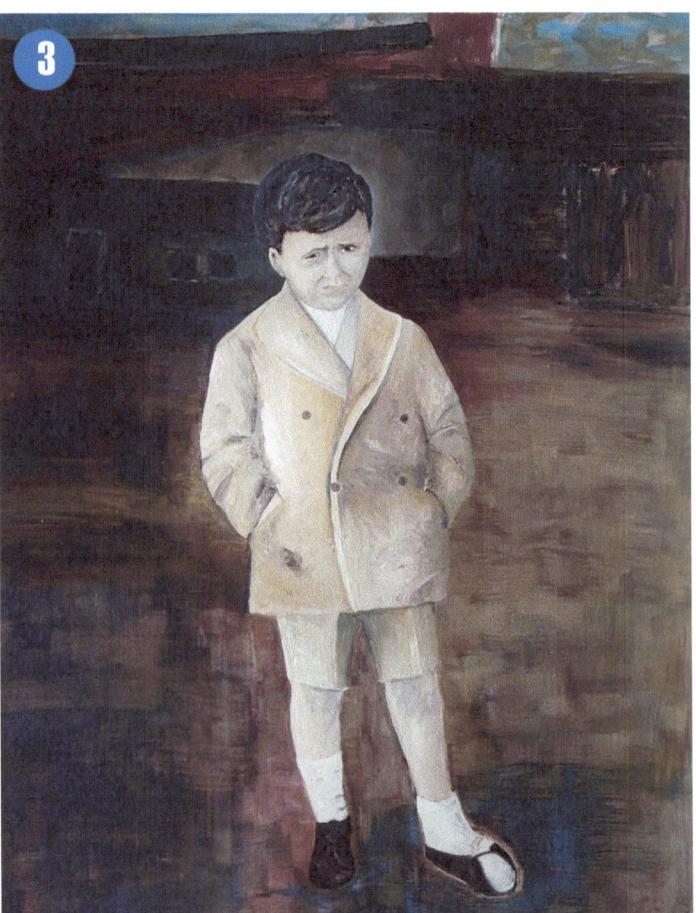

**3**

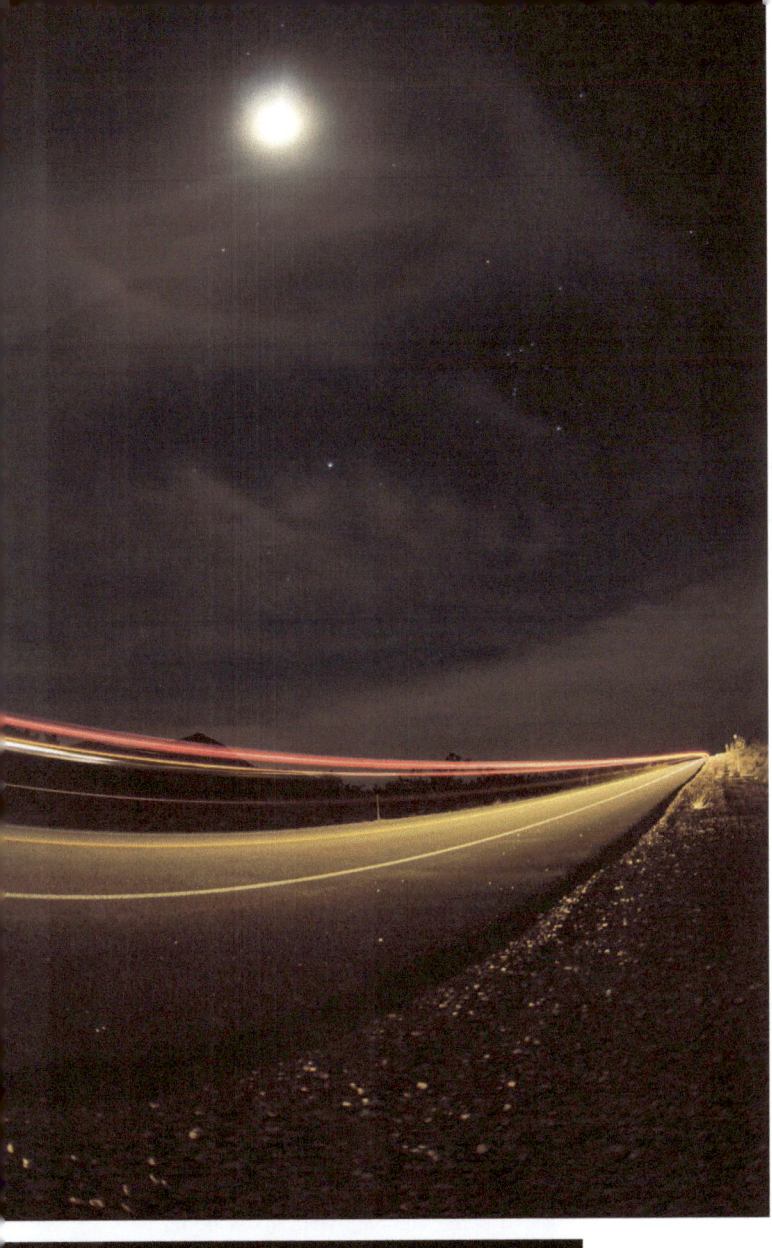

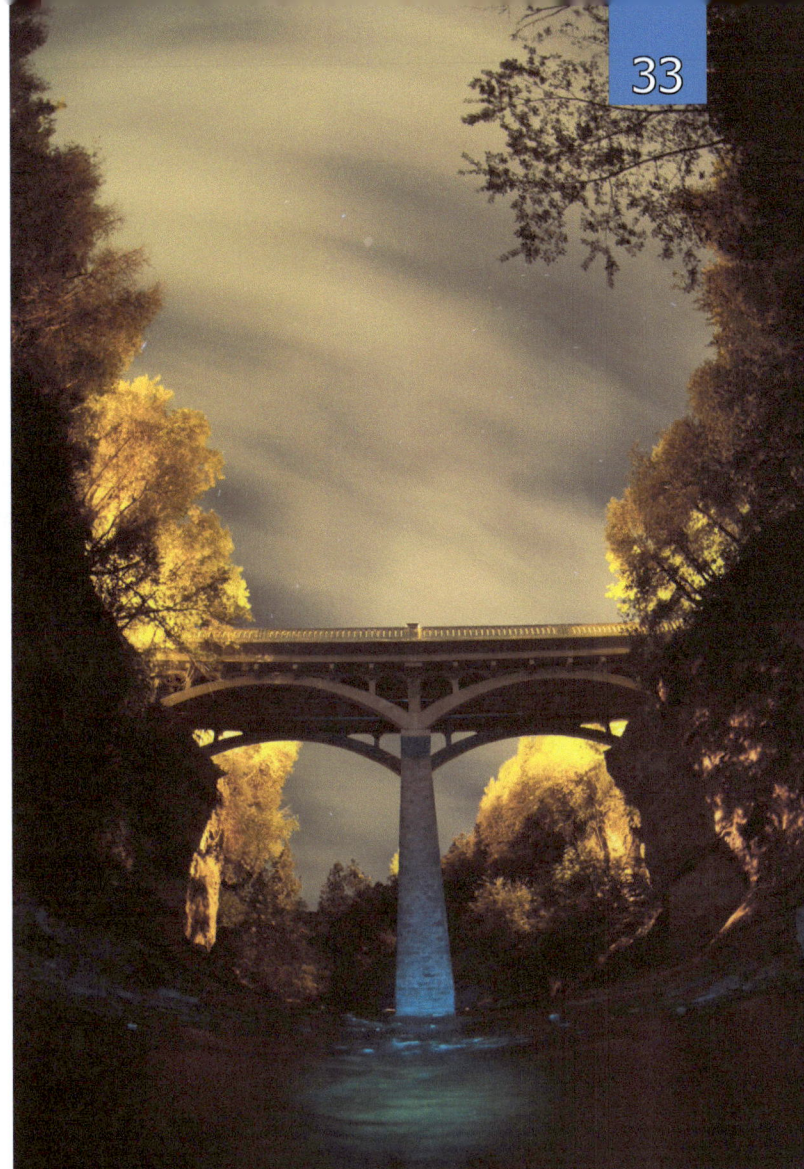

**1**

**2**

**1** **Lost In Space** 13×19" Digital Print. 30 second exposure on the outskirts of the Grand Canyon.

**2** **Bridge to Rivendell** 13×19" Digital Print. 4.5 minute exposure with diffused light painting, using a flashlight, of the bridge.

**3**

**3** **Window on Our World** (detail) 13×19" Digital Print. 20 minute exposure with diffused light painting, using a lantern, around trees and rocks to create depth.

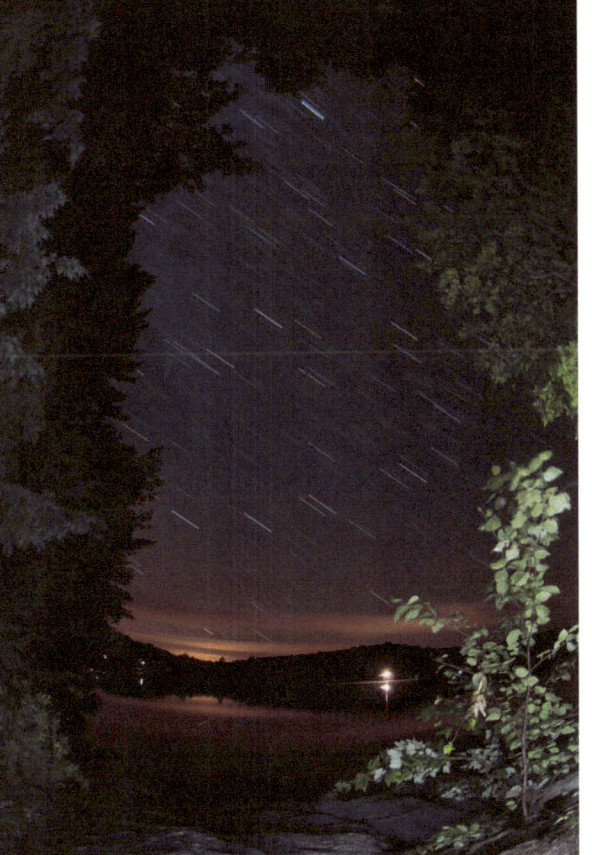

# ZAVEN TITIZIAN

**LOCATION:** Kitchener
**WEB:** Flickr.com/photos/64753128@N06
**EMAIL:** ZavenTitizian@gmail.com

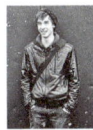

Zaven was born in Kitchener, Ontario, in 1993. The art of photography started for Zaven through the creative and highly art-based sub-culture of skateboarding. His passion and curiosity for skateboarding, art and science has lead to experimentation of super wide angle, night and long exposure photographs. Zaven takes a purist approach to his photography by not applying any editing or photo manipulation, save slightly straightening a crooked photo taken in the dark. He plans to pursue science and art as a career by getting accepted into the architecture program at the University of Waterloo.

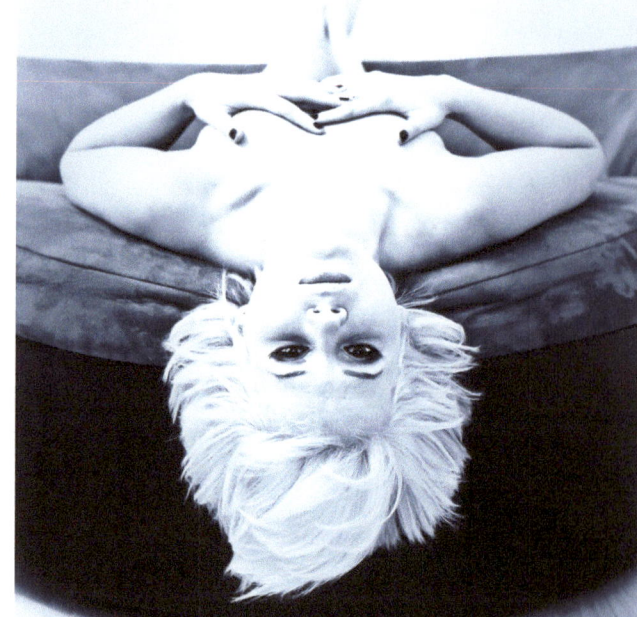

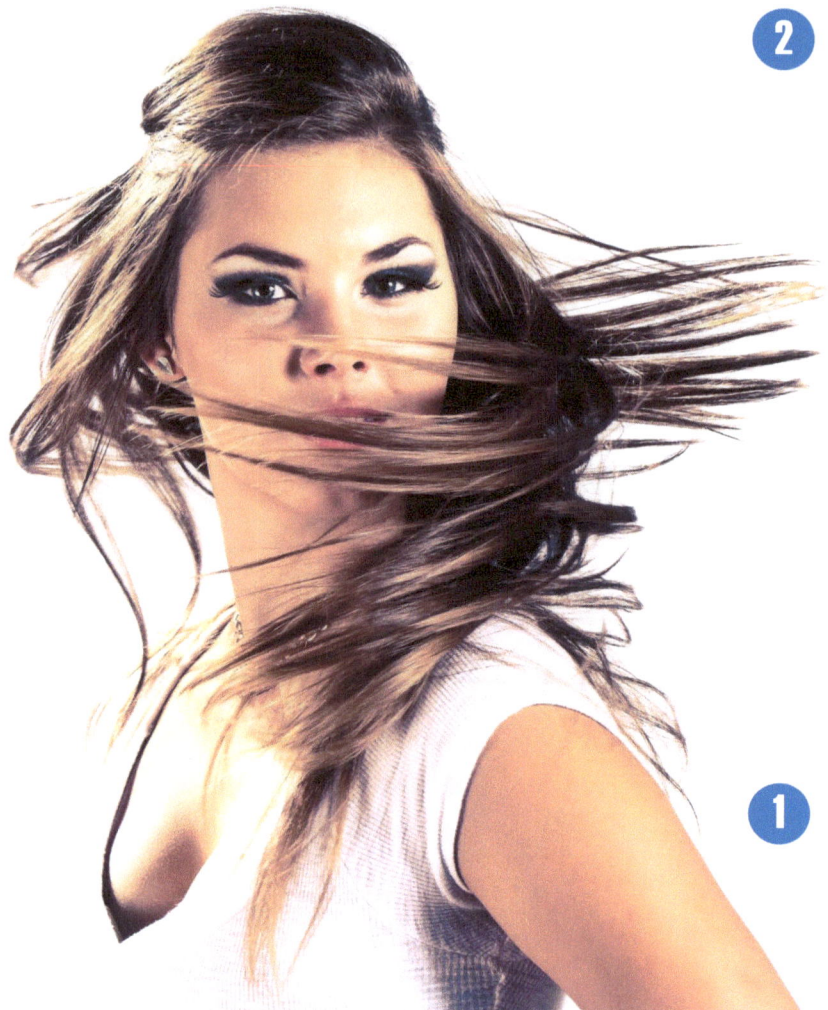

## ANDY WRIGHT

**LOCATION:** Kitchener
**WEB:** pointandshootimagery.com
**EMAIL:** andy@pointandshootimagery.com

Originally from England, Andy is a passionate photographer with love of unique portraiture. His portfolio includes models, events and the Arts. An ability to capture the emotional power of theater productions with a photojournalistic twist has created some stunning work in his portfolio. He has had numerous pieces used in music magazines and a few CD's featuring his artwork as well. He really enjoys working with unusual lighting and being unconventional, and has a very quirky sense of humour.

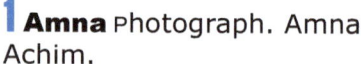
**1 Amna** Photograph. Amna Achim.

**2 Oh No She Isn't** Photograph. Fully clothed picture of Christine Astles.

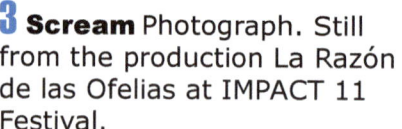
**3 Scream** Photograph. Still from the production La Razón de las Ofelias at IMPACT 11 Festival.

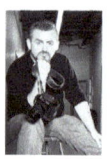

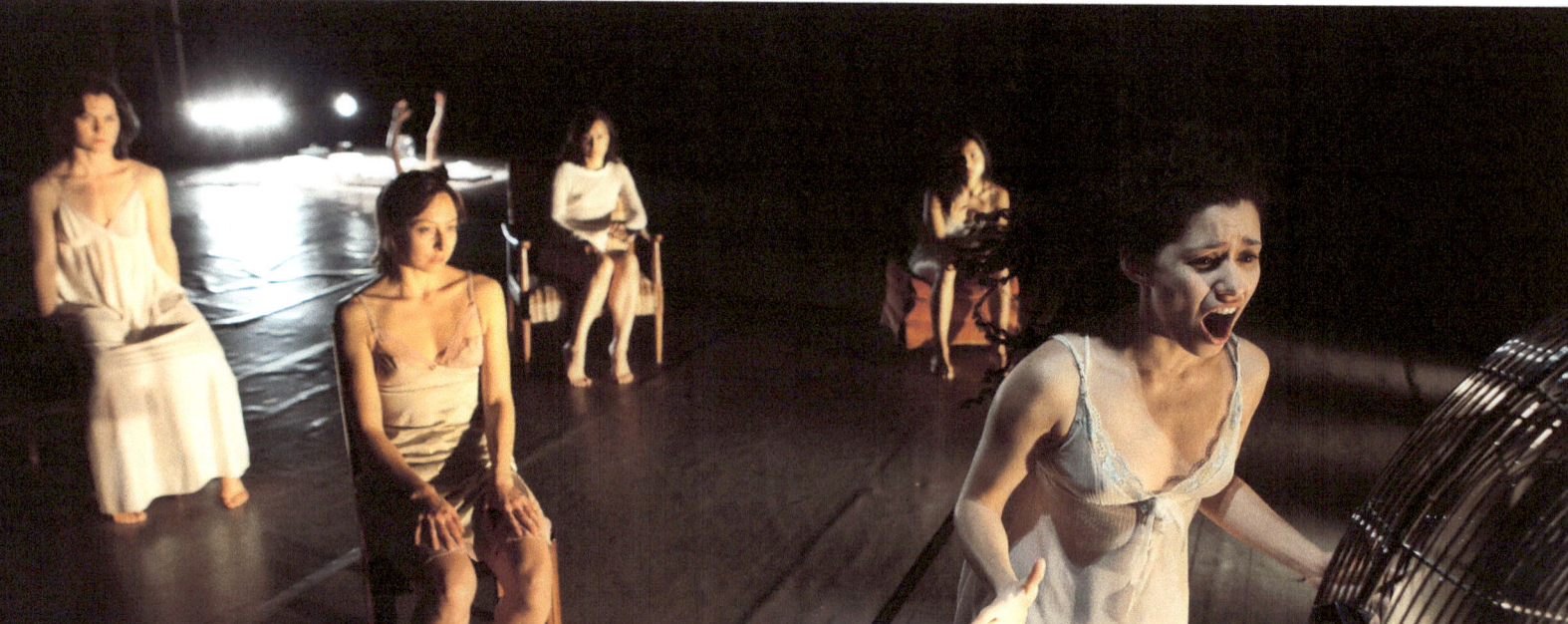

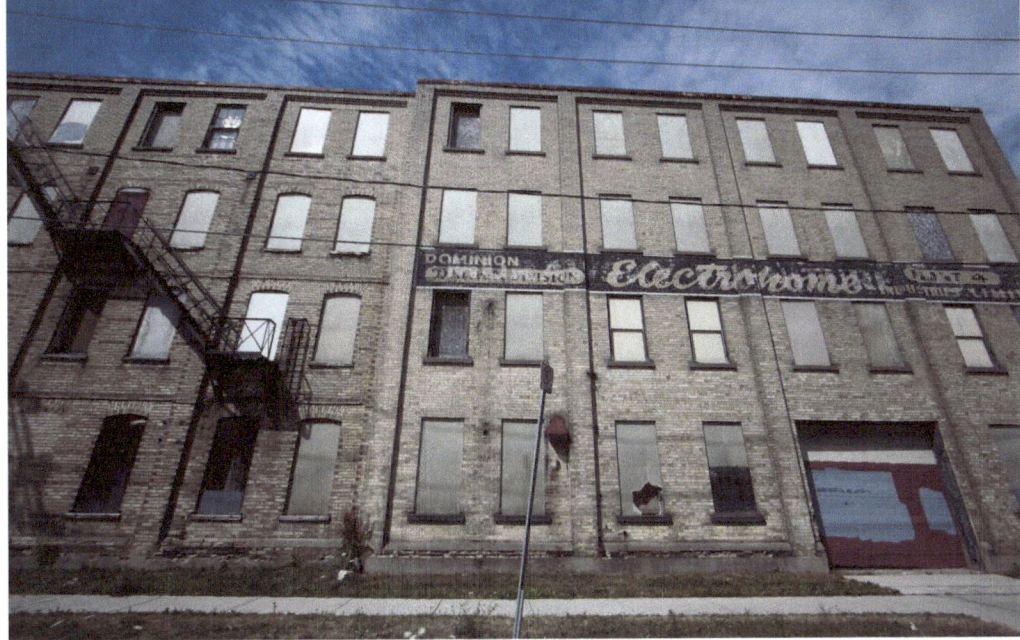

## BRIAN DOUGLAS

**LOCATION:** Kitchener
**WEB:** bdouglasphotography.com
**EMAIL:** brian@bdouglasphotography.com

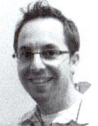 Brian Douglas is an experienced photographer and artist who thrives on finding new, creative forms of visual expression. Brian's photographs depict nature and still life in their most raw and honest forms, finding beauty in harsh surroundings, tranquility in the everyday. Each piece is a poem in itself, exhibiting a depth and a fullness that captures the viewer's imagination and heart.

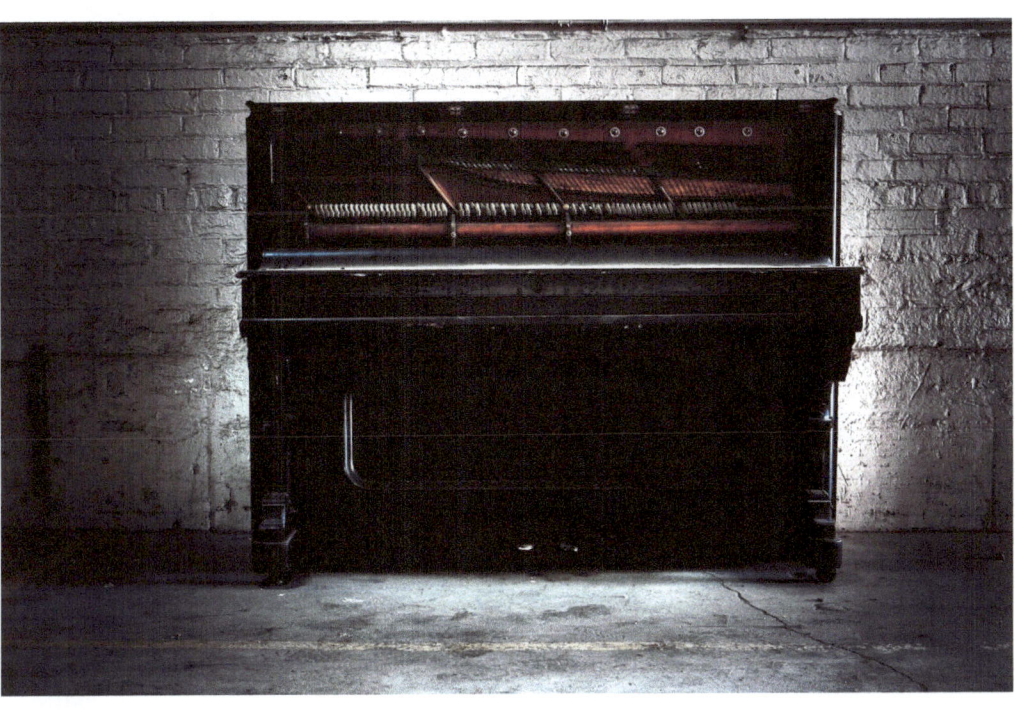

**1 Dominion Electrohome** Photograph.

**2 Moraine Lake, BC** Photograph.

**3 And We Danced Through the Night** Photograph.

# SARA GEIDLINGER

**LOCATION:** Clair Hills, Waterloo
**WEB:** sarageidlinger.com
**EMAIL:** sara@sarageidlinger.com

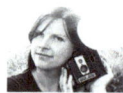

Living and working in KW, Sara is a photographer who feels that this city is her backdrop.

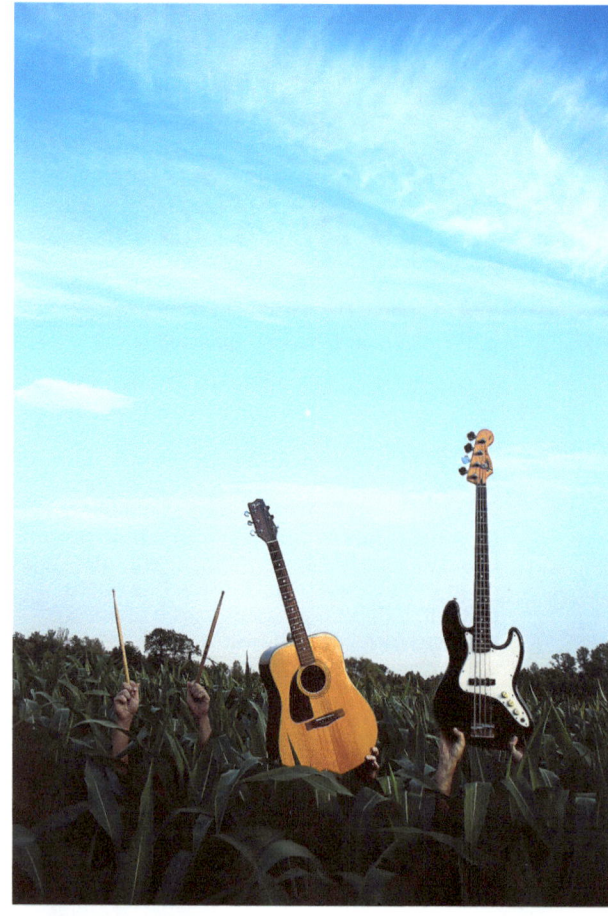

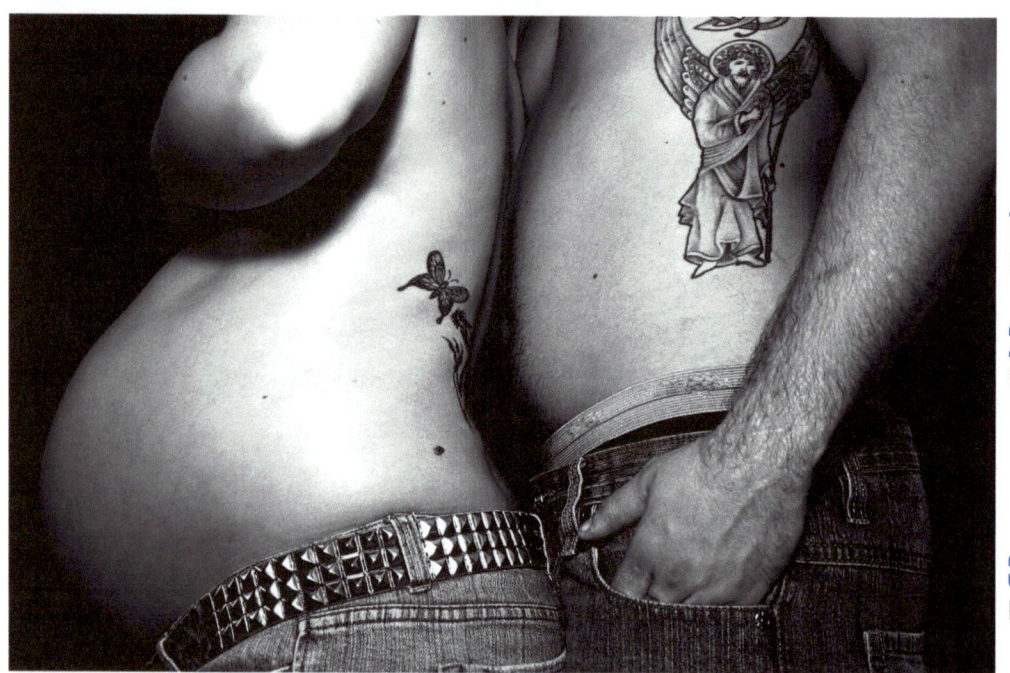

**1** **Heal the Rift, New Dundee**
Photograph.

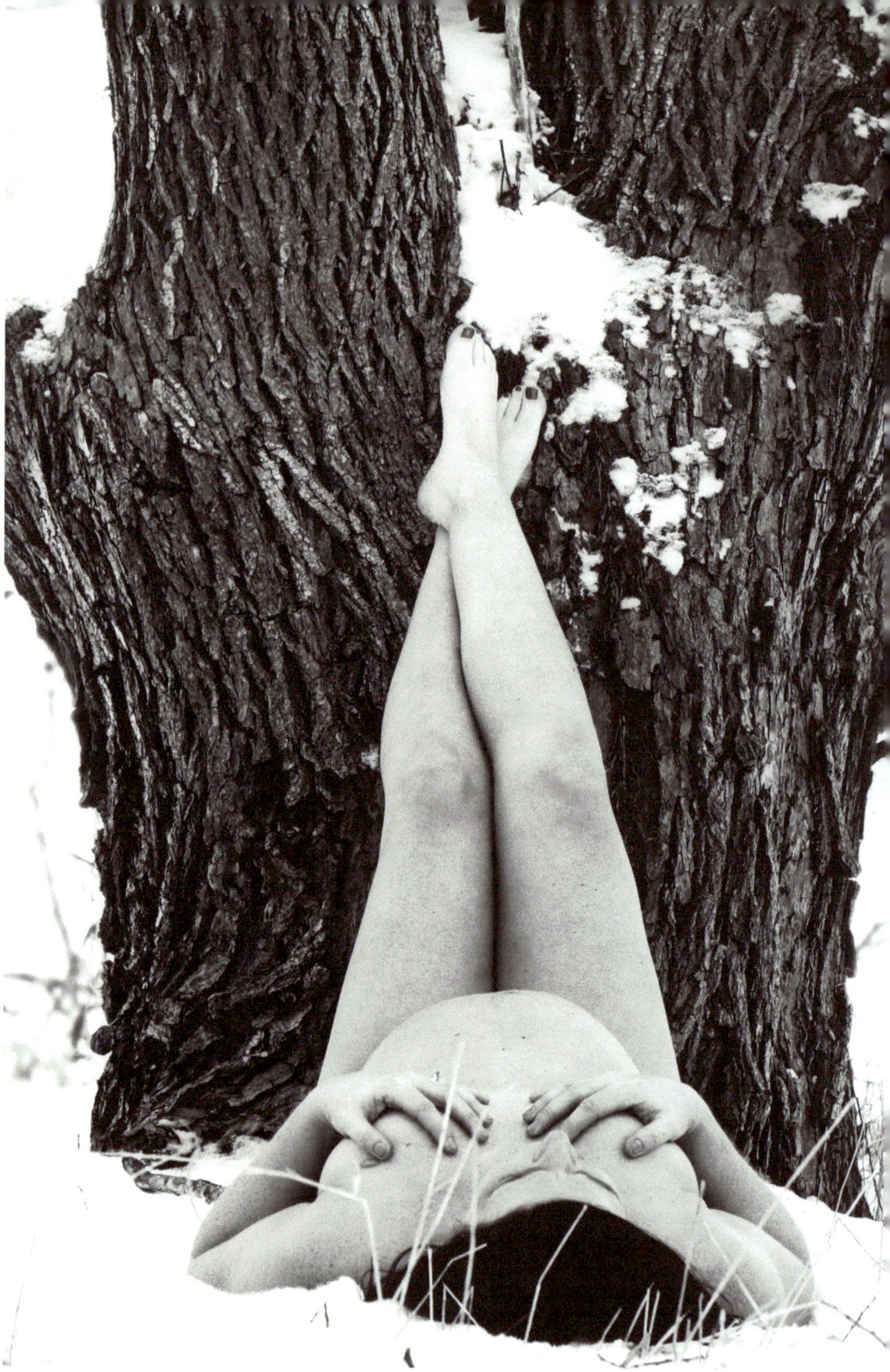

**2** **Winter Walk, Waterloo**
Photograph.

**3** **Expecting Ella, Waterloo**
Photograph.

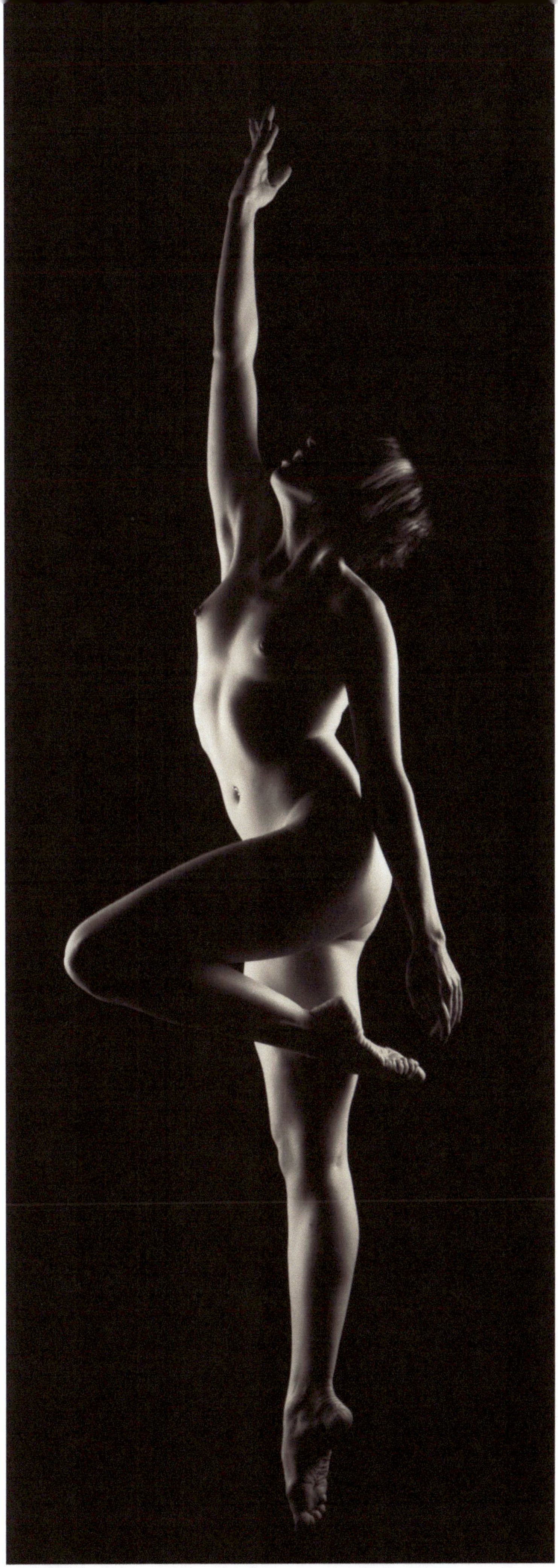

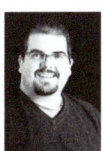

# ALEX WILSON

**LOCATION:** Waterloo
**WEB:** AlexWilsonPhoto.com
**EMAIL:** Alex@alexwilsonphoto.com

Alex loves working with professional and amateur models alike to create artistic nudes. Minimalistic and often ambiguous, most of his figure work tries to honest yet secretive, intimate yet anonymous, and naked yet obscured. Near-abstract bodyscapes images engage the viewer while celebrating the human form. Alex is currently working on a follow-up to his most recent book, "Figure: Volume 1".

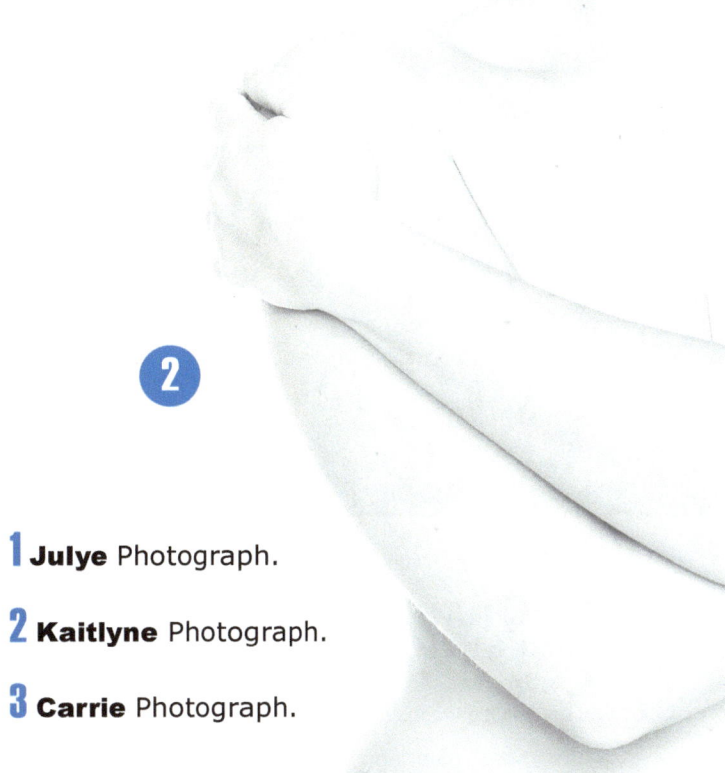

**1 Julye** Photograph.

**2 Kaitlyne** Photograph.

**3 Carrie** Photograph.

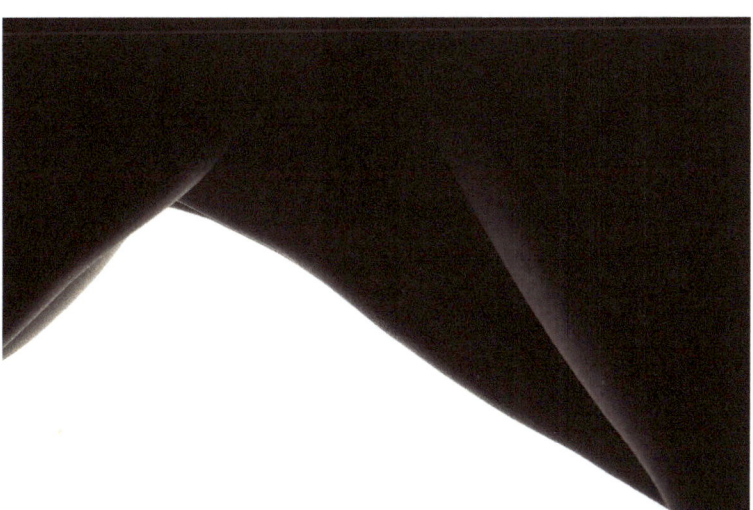

**1 Self Portrait** 30x20" Acrylic on canvas.

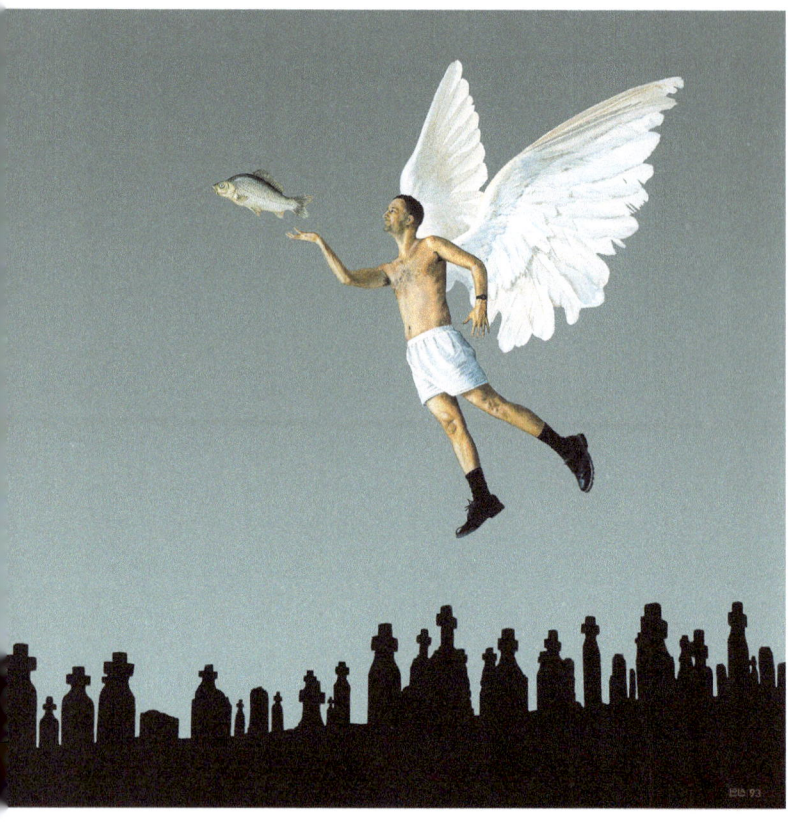

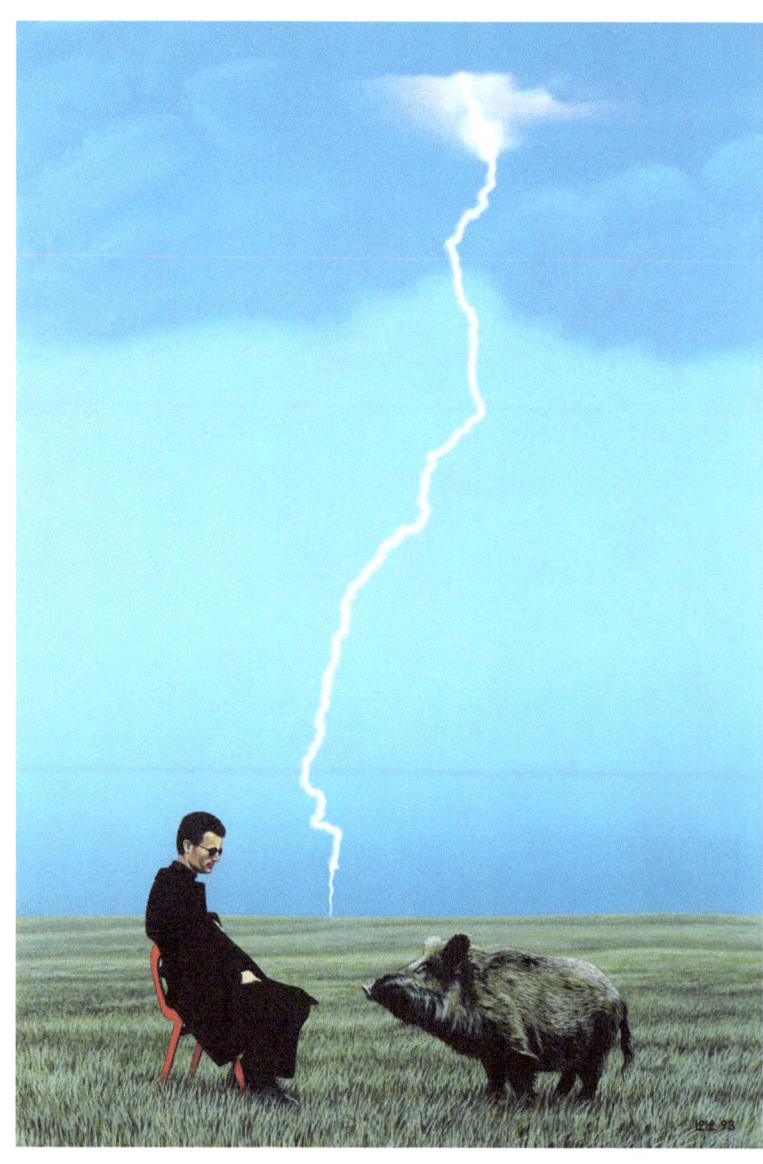

# IGOR DRAGOSLAVIC

**LOCATION:** Waterloo
**WEB:** leaddog.ca
**EMAIL:** igor@leaddog.ca

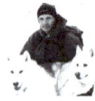 These paintings were created in the early nineties; with people in mind that Igor left behind in the war-torn Yugoslavia. Waterloo became Igor's much beloved new home. However, with the urban sprawl steadily chipping away the nature in the Waterloo Region, Igor increasingly often finds himself longing for the vast tundra and sea ice spaces in the Canadian Arctic.

**2 Divided** 24x36" Acrylic on canvas.

**3 Should I Stay Or Should I Go?** 36x36" Acrylic on canvas.

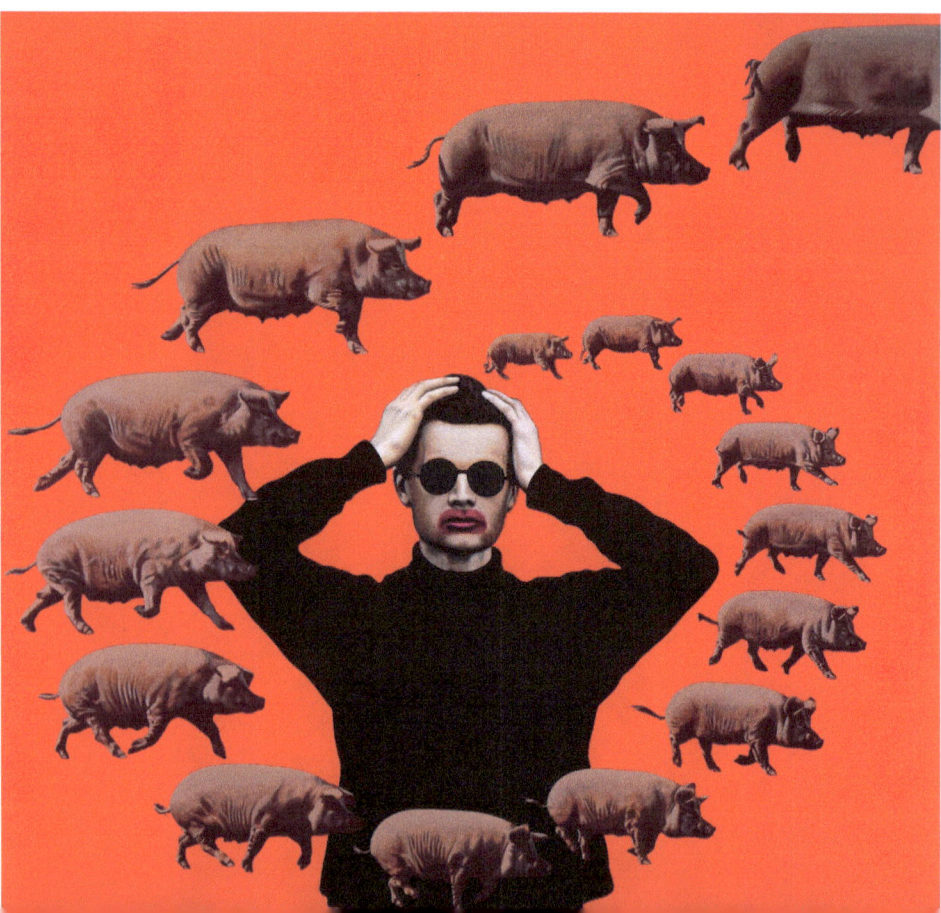

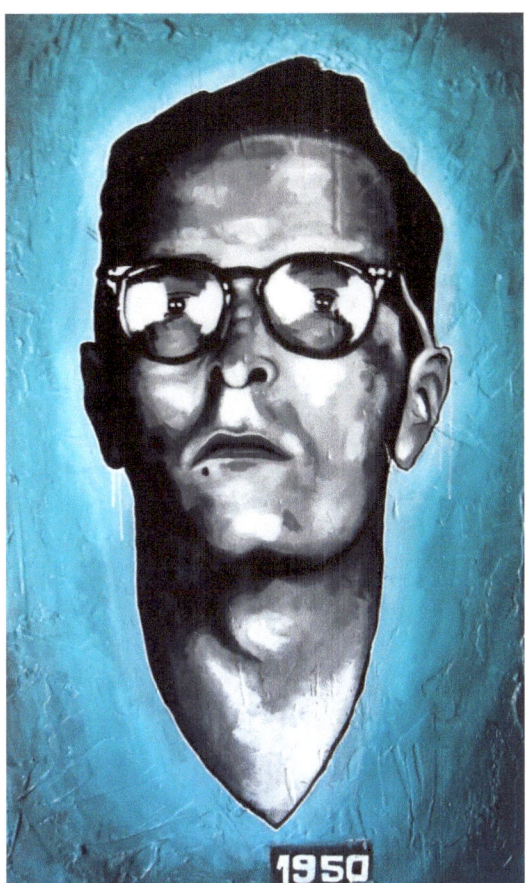

1 **Original Guilty** 24x42″ Acrylic on canvas.

2 **TKO** 24x48″ Acrylic and spray paint on canvas.

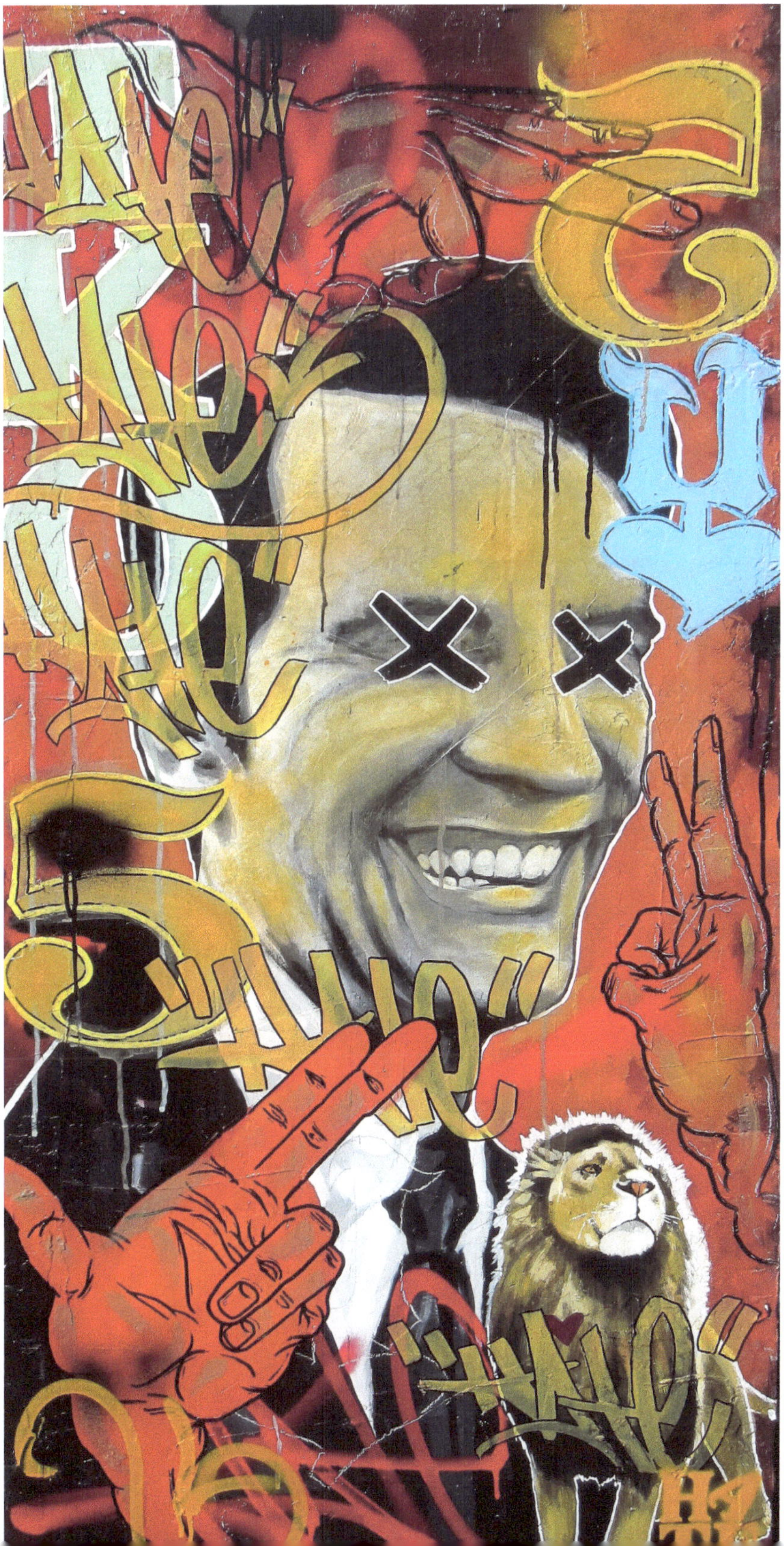

# CHRIS AUSTIN

**LOCATION:** Downtown Kitchener
**WEB:** Chrisaustinart.blogspot.com
**EMAIL:** Flausty03@hotmail.com

I am a self taught painter and life long resident of Kitchener, Ontario. My work is a celebration of beauty with an urban twist. Painting is a passion that stimulates and enlivens me

3 **Number 9** 24x48″ Acrylic on canvas.

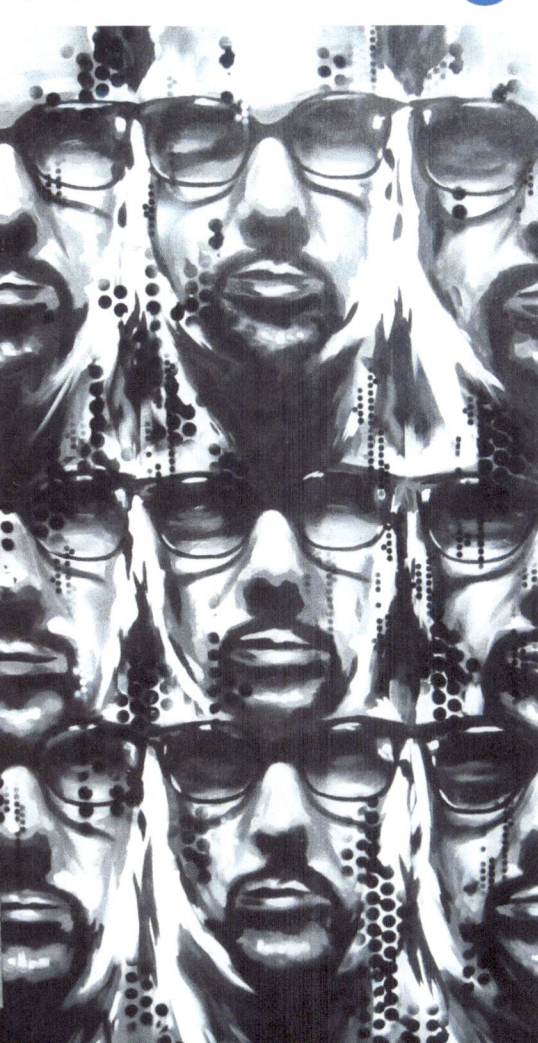

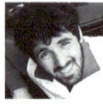

# COREY WAURECHEN

**LOCATION:** Waterloo
**WEB:** CoreyCanvas.com
**EMAIL:** Corey@coreycanvas.com

Bio: Corey is a self-taught printmaker. For his inspiration he looks to 19th century literary sources, creating book covers and illustrations for his favourite novels and short stories. With his work Corey hopes to inspire the modern reader to pick up the "classics," as well as some other under-appreciated, but equally fantastic books.

**1** **The Time Machine** 5x 7" Linocut.

**2** **The Devil-Fish** 3.5x5" Linocut.

**3** **The Jewel of the Seven Stars** 5x7" Linocut.

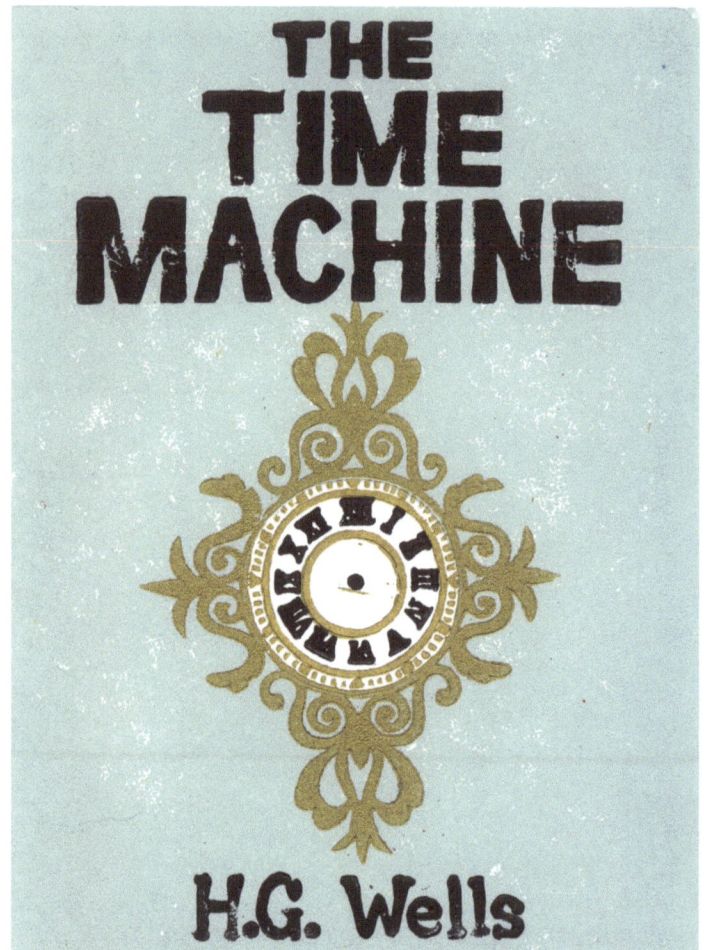

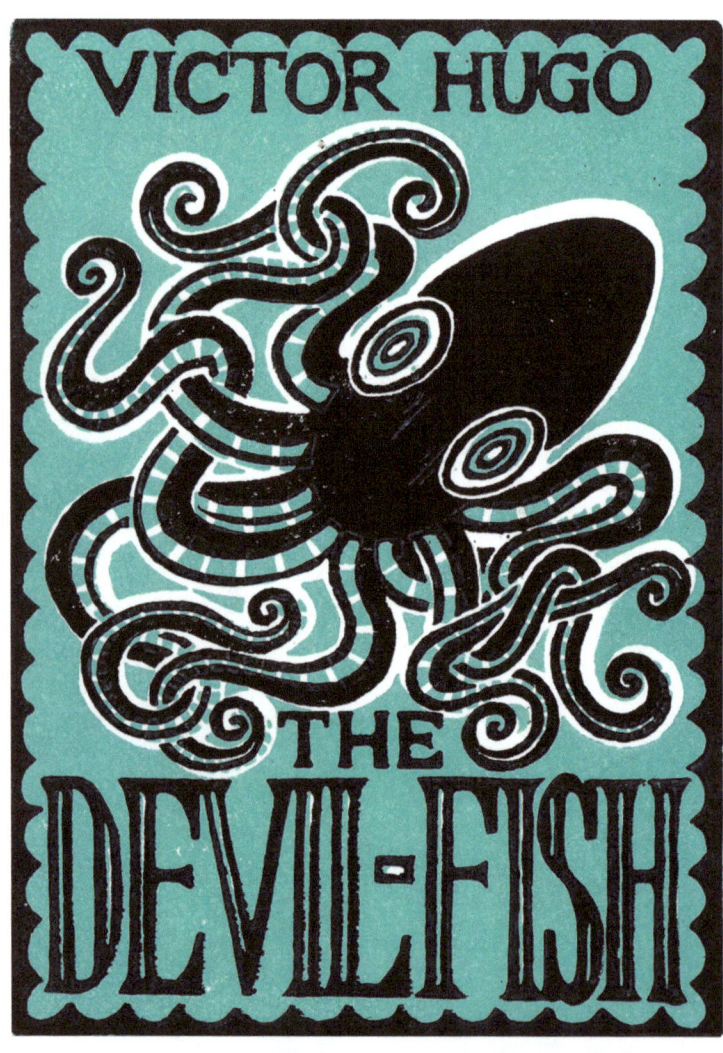

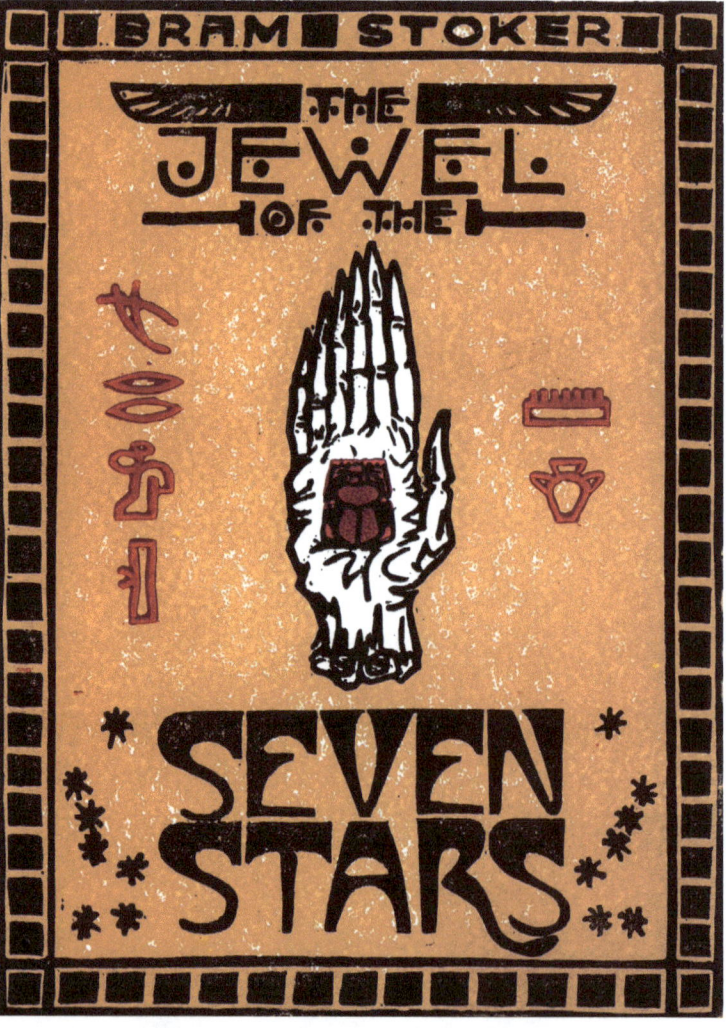

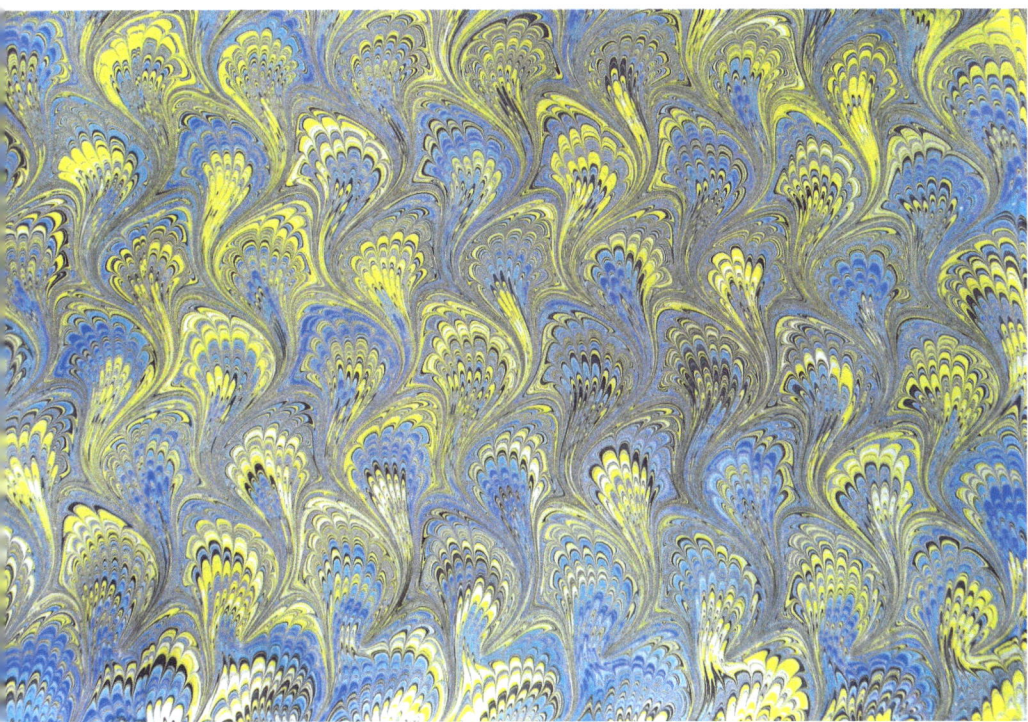

# KEVIN MARTIN

**LOCATION:** New Dundee
**WEB:** Papertrail.ca
**EMAIL:** Info@papertrail.ca

Kevin has taught himself marbling over the past 16 years, having found that it is a good fit with his wife's hand papermaking. Together they run the Papertrail, where they sell papermaking, marbling, and bookbinding supplies and teach basic classes in these crafts. He is also interested in letterpress and type casting, both of which also satisfy his need for tinkering in old machinery and preserving the knowledge of old trades.

**1 Untitled** 12x18" Acrylic marbling on handmade paper, bouquet design

**2 Untitled** 18x24" Acrylic marbling on machine-made paper, stone pattern.

**3 Untitled** 18x24" Acrylic marbling on machine-made paper, free-form design.

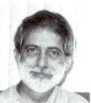

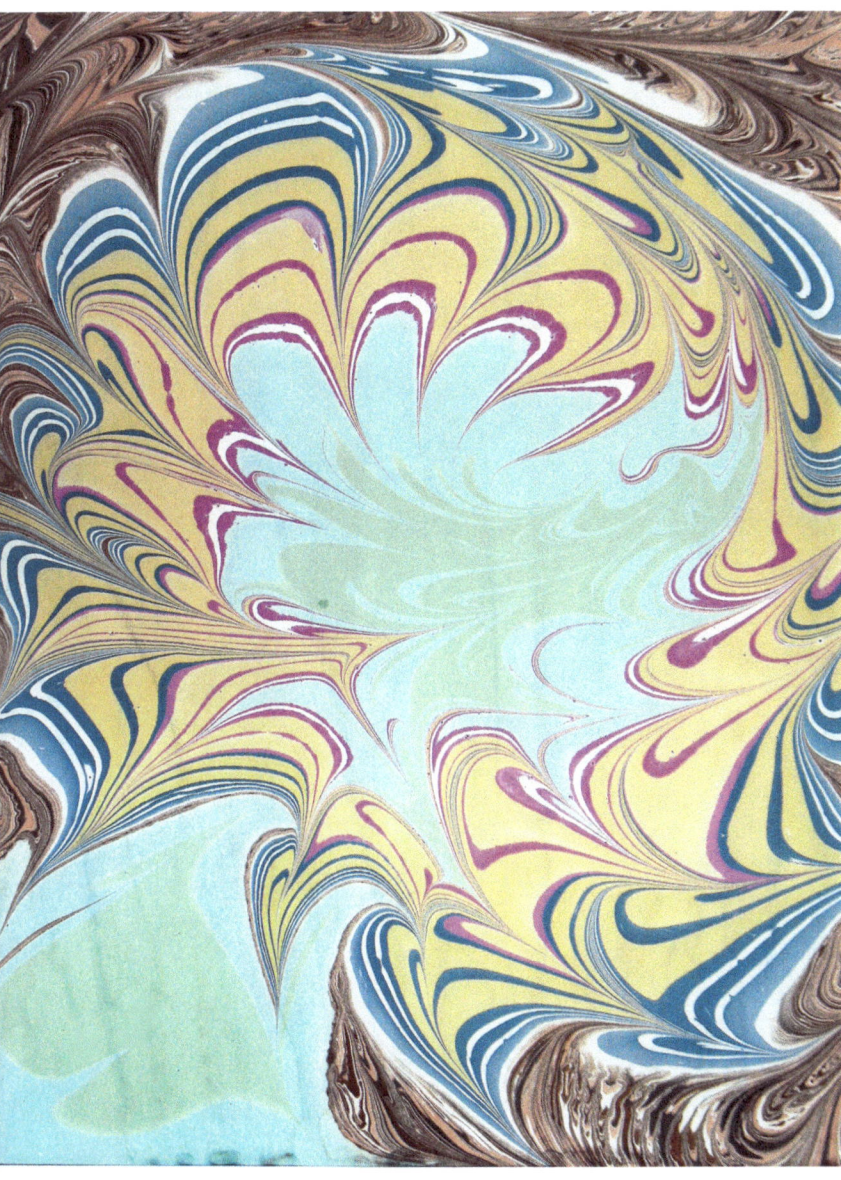

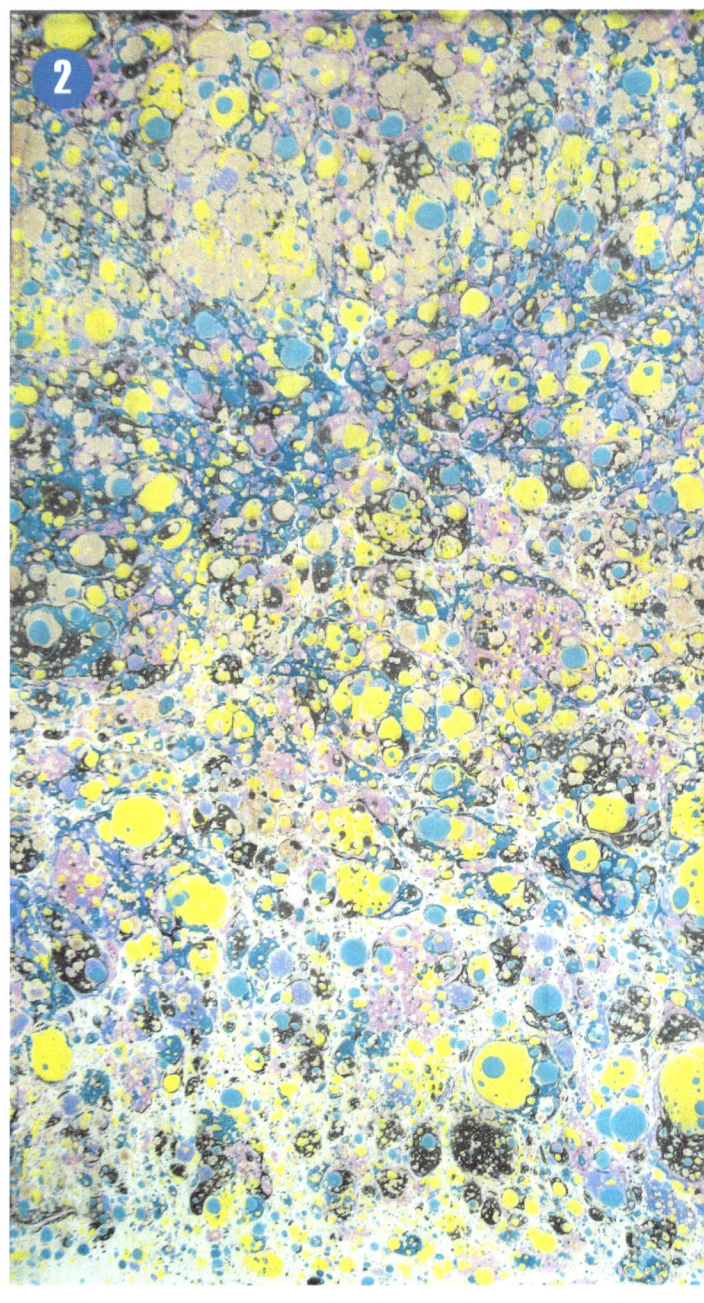

**1** **Break Time** 30x16" Post-processed photograph. From inside the confines of a mid-20th century factory, we sense the cold and bleak reality of a worker's point of view.

**2** **Persistence** 30x22" Pochoir painting. This piece employs pleasant and muted imagery to project an optimistic view of nature's persistence in spite of an overwhelming onslaught of concrete and asphalt.

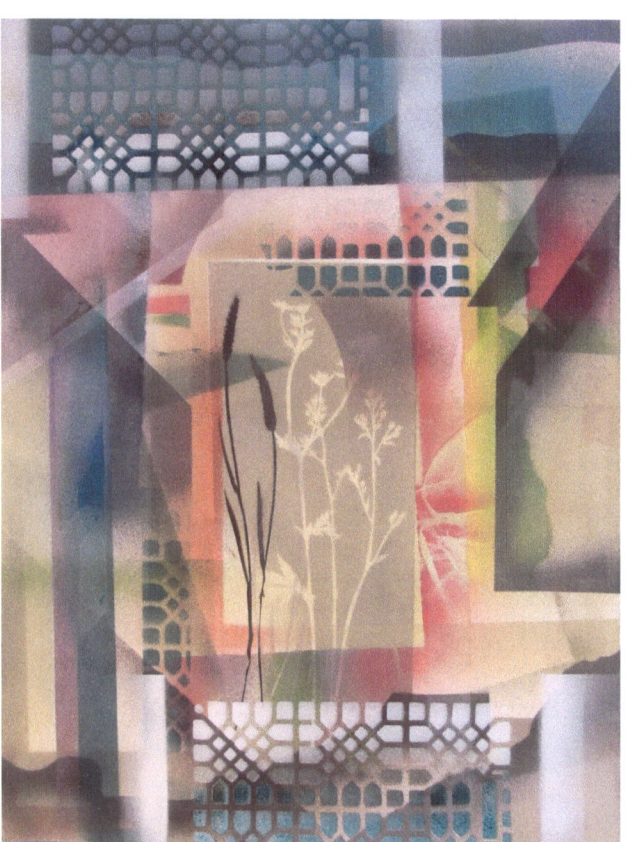

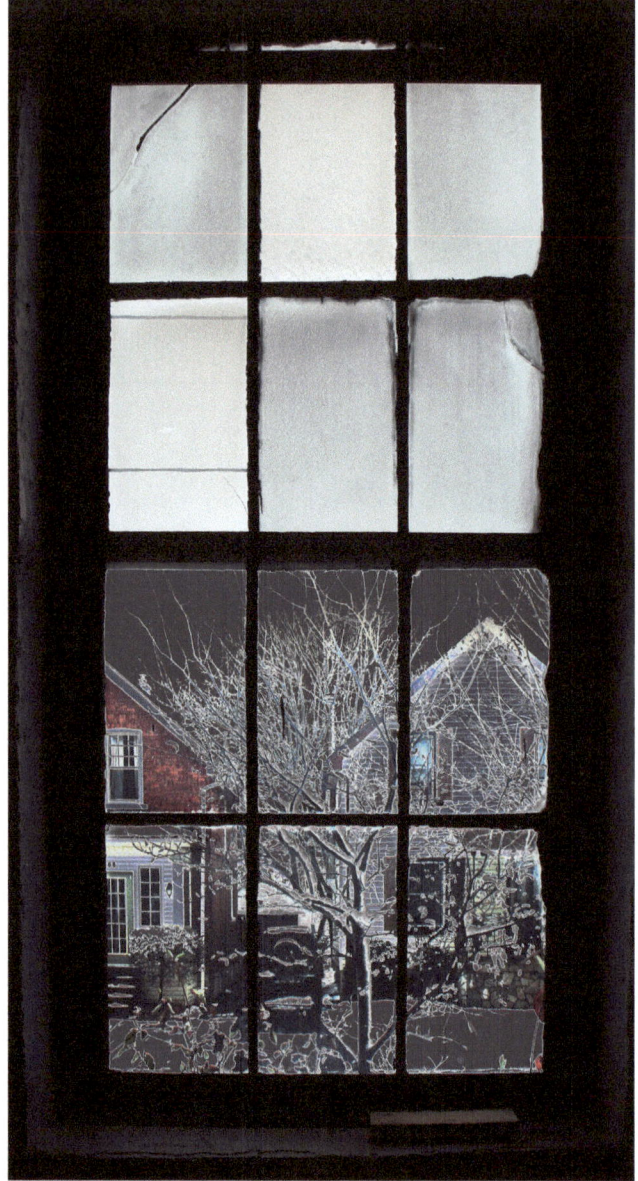

**3** **Autumn Notes** 9x12" Mixed media monoprint. An image rich with autumn colours, evoking warmth, comfort and security, centers around the hearth with its promise of a cornucopia of emotional pleasure.

# Gloria Kagawa

**LOCATION:** New Hamburg
**WEB:** GloriaKagawa.com
**EMAIL:** Gloria@gloriakagawa.com

Gloria specializes in printmaking; she also paints and enjoys working with photography and Japanese calligraphy at her farmhouse studio. Her images often incorporate architectural elements, transparent layers and reflections, which she uses as a context to comment on the human condition. Gloria graduated with an Honours degree in fine arts at the University of Waterloo and her works are in a number of public and private collections.

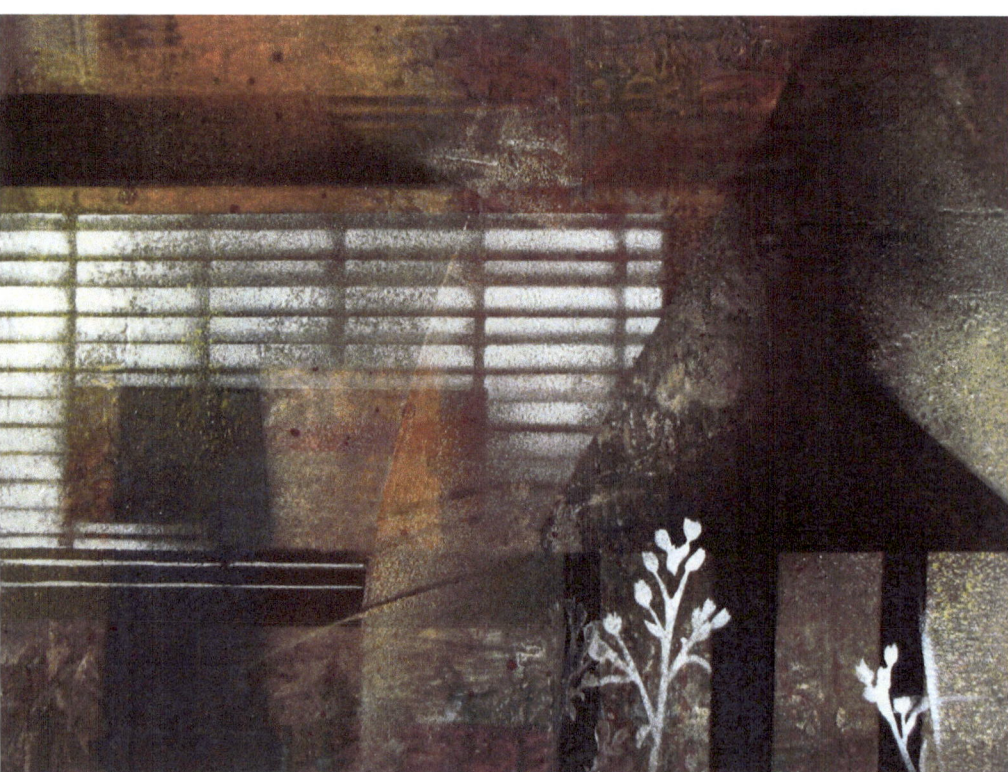

# JAN
# BENTLEY-FOGOLIN

**LOCATION:** Kitchener
**WEB:** polarpottery.com
**EMAIL:** polarpotter@gmail.com

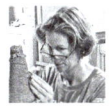

Jan, a potter for almost 30 years gets her energy and inspiration from nature. She learned her technical skills in George Brown College's Commercial Ceramics program. Along with Jan's animal creations she also devotes many months to creating one of a kind Victorian Santa figures for the Christmas season. Jan gives private lessons in hand-built and wheel thrown pottery at her Polar Pottery Studio in Kitchener.

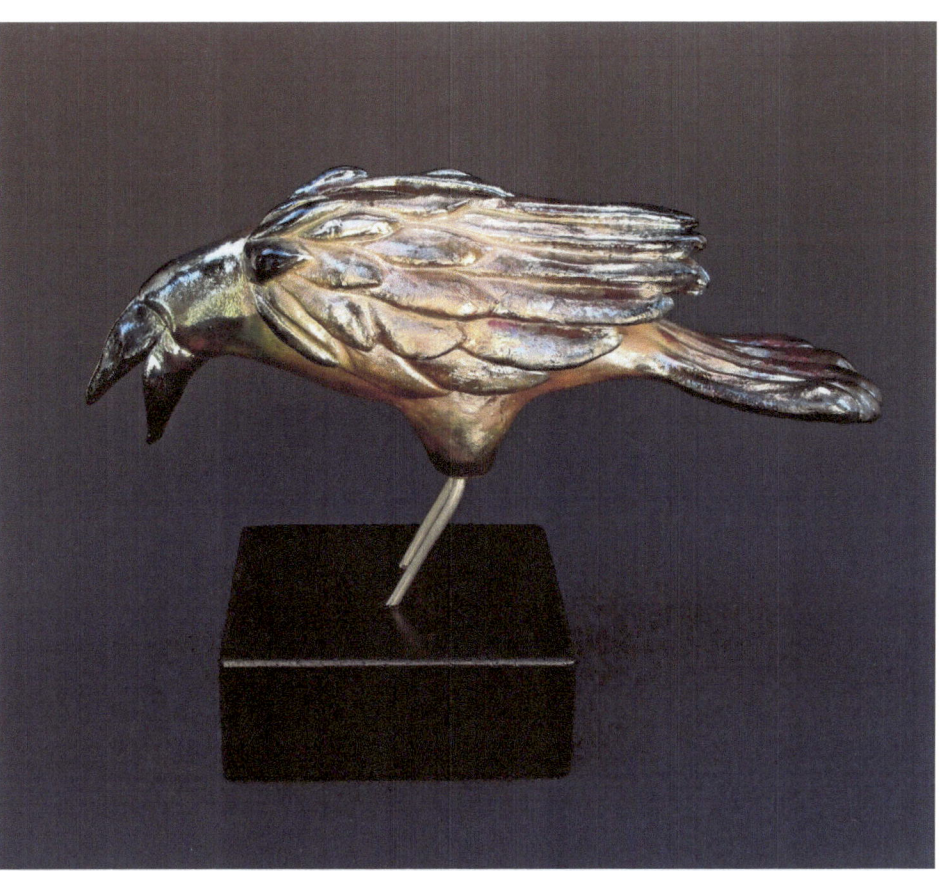

**1 Crow** 12x25cm Raku Clay.

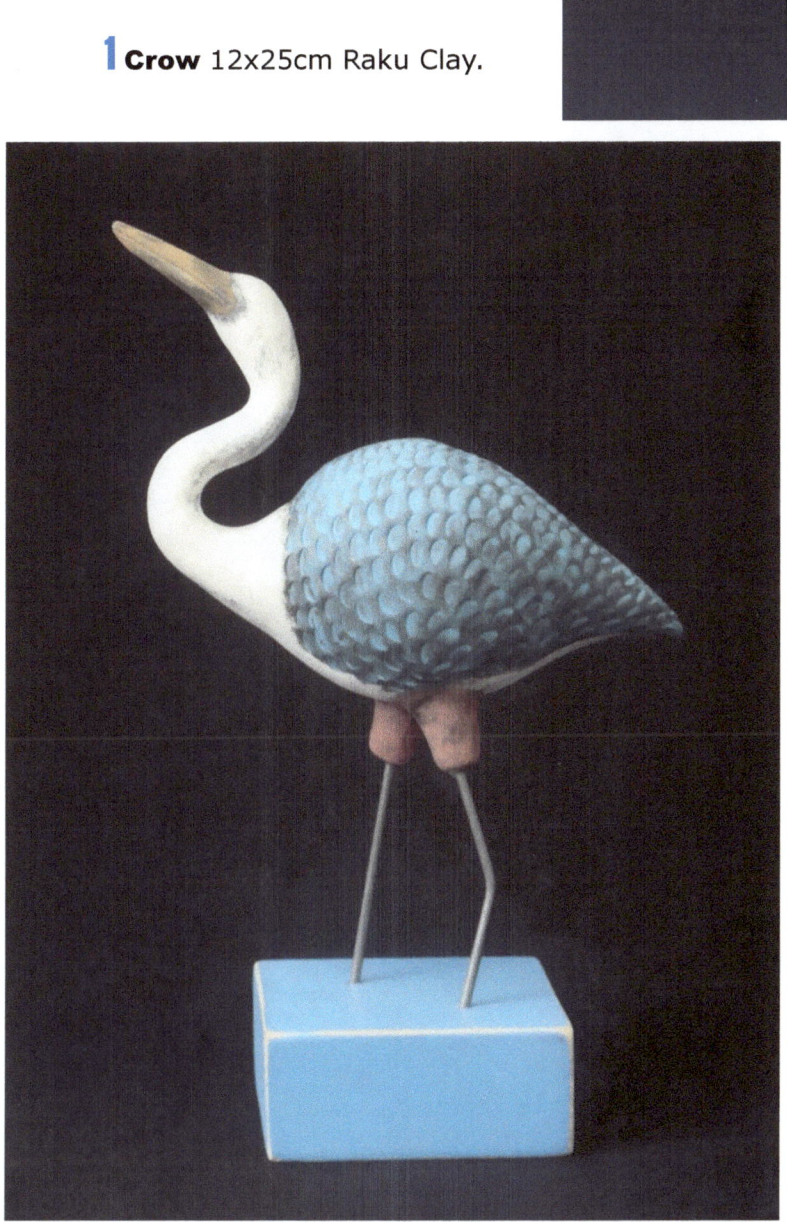

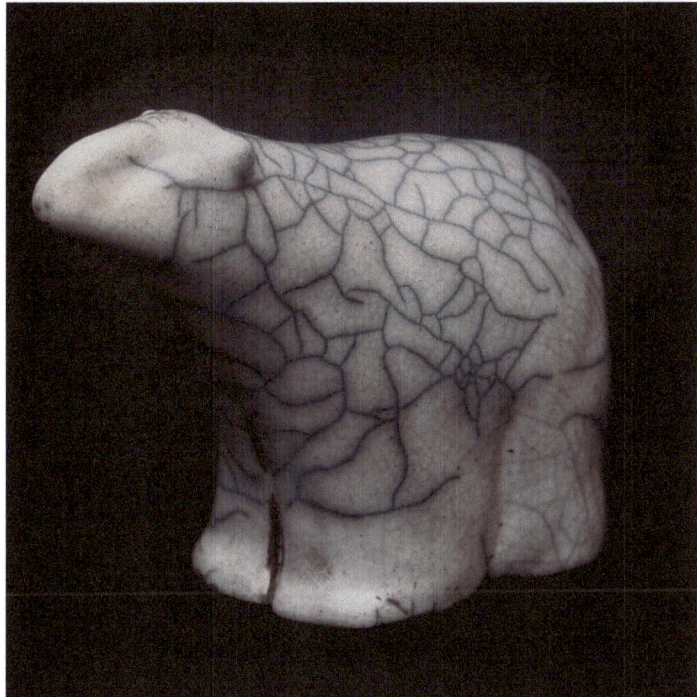

**2 Heron** 21x25cm Cone 6 Porcelain.

**3 Polar Bear** 11x9cm Raku Clay.

**1** **Bougainvillea** 20x16" Acrylic on canvas.

**2** **Stream Through Forest** 18x24" Acrylic on canvas.

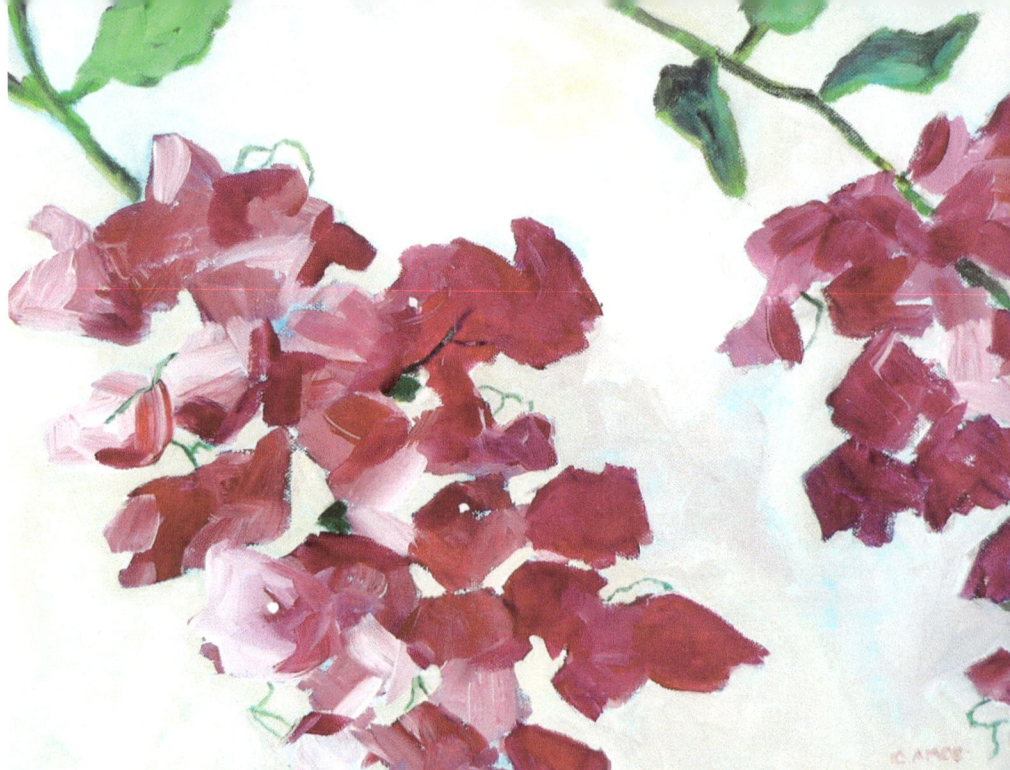

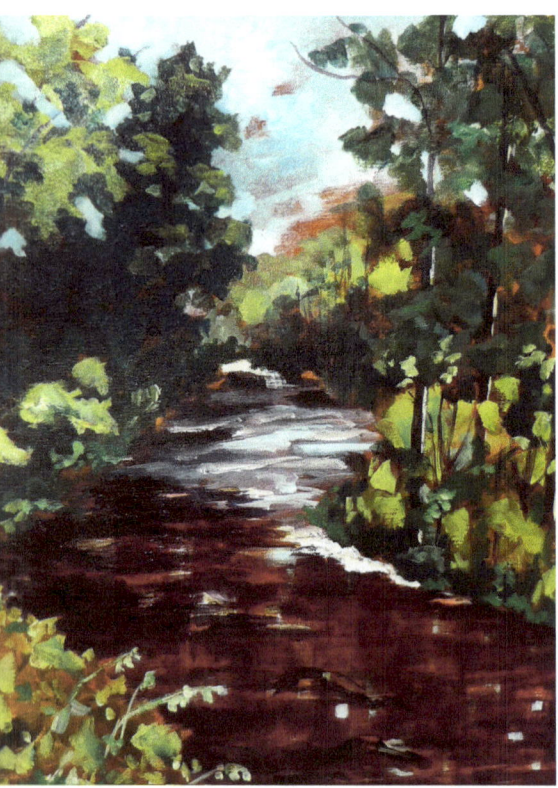

**3** **Pink Chair With Flowers** 22x28" Acrylic on canvas.

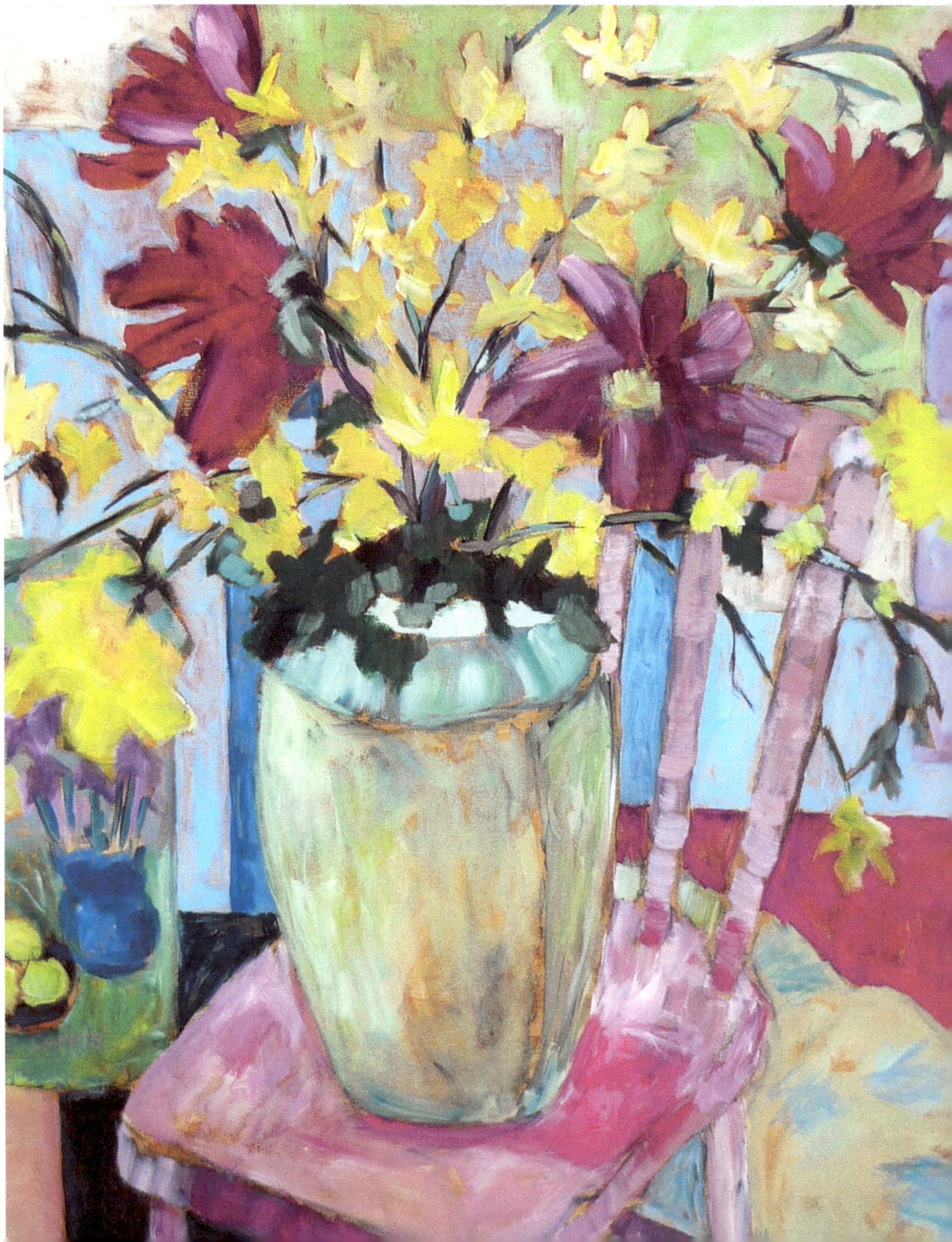

# CATHY AMOS

**LOCATION:** Waterloo
**WEB:** (Under Construction)
**EMAIL:** Gonepainting@hotmail.com

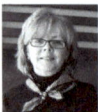

I took my first watercolour course in 2001 and never looked back. I've taken classes and workshops with exceptional instructors and progressed into the exciting world of acrylic painting in 2007. I feel very privileged to be able to pick up a paintbrush and decide what my subject will be and how I will interpret it on canvas. I love colour and the whole creative process!

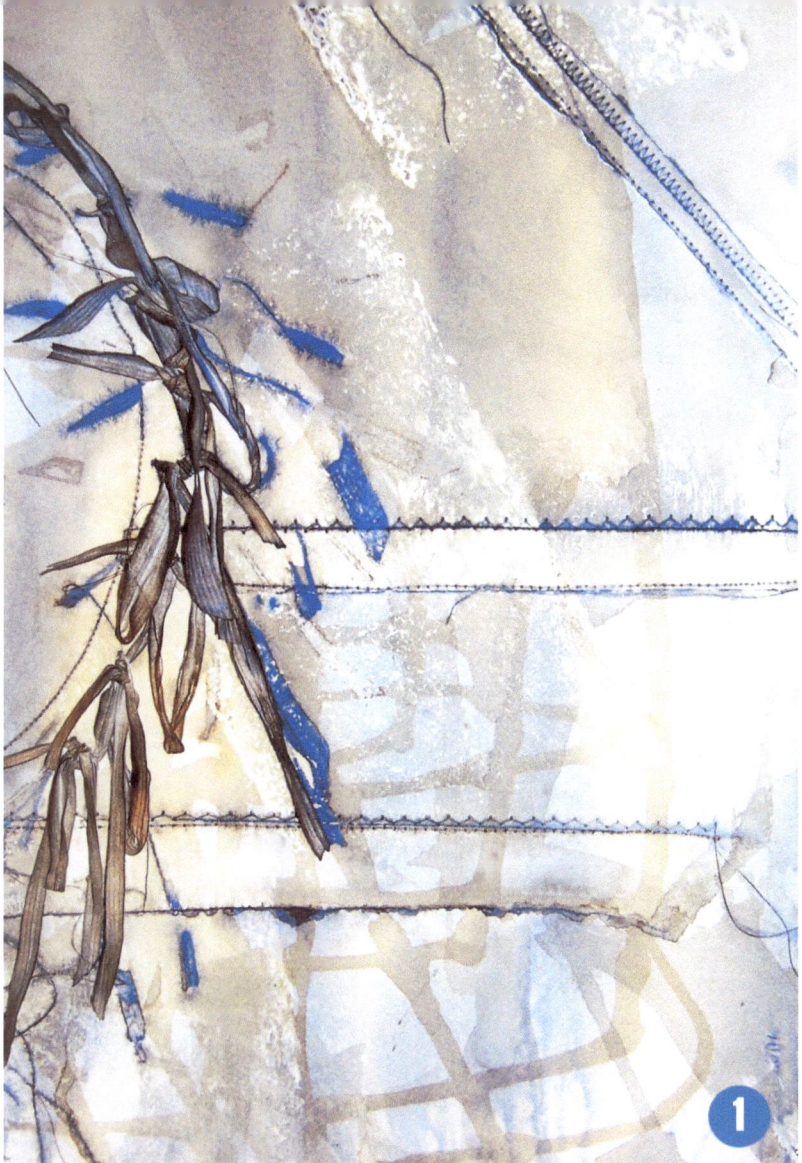

# DIANE EASTHAM

**LOCATION:** Columbia Forest, Waterloo
**WEB:** dianeeastham.com
**EMAIL:** deastham@sympatico.ca

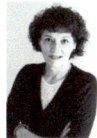

Diane is an award-winning multi-media artist, photographer, writer, teacher and creativity coach. She likes to stitch paper for texture and paint it with acrylics for intense colour. She finishes these pieces with words, fibres, old computer bits...whatever comes to hand. She is inspired by the work of the string theorists at the Perimeter Institute in Waterloo. Diane has written a book about creativity and all the wonderful challenges it has to offer.

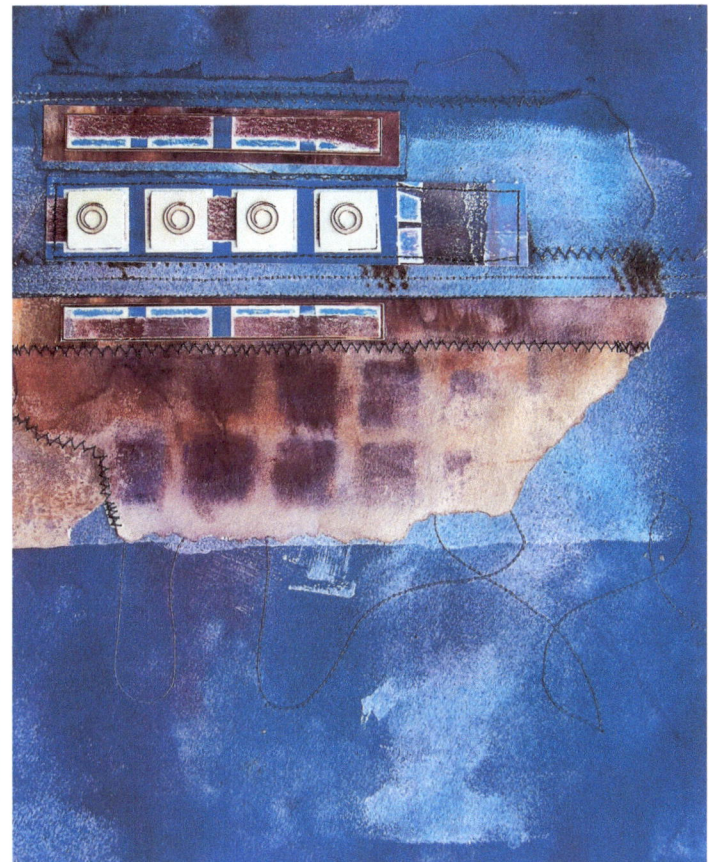

**1 String Theory: Knots in the String** 17x 22" 140 lb Watercolour paper, Golden fluid acrylics, silk fibre and sewing machine stitching.

**2 String Theory: Music of the Spheres** 19x22" 140 lb Watercolour paper, Golden fluid acrylics, string, metals, sewing machine stitching and collage.

**3 String Theory Blues** 19x22" 140 lb Watercolour paper, Golden fluid acrylics, string, metals, sewing machine stitching and paper collage.

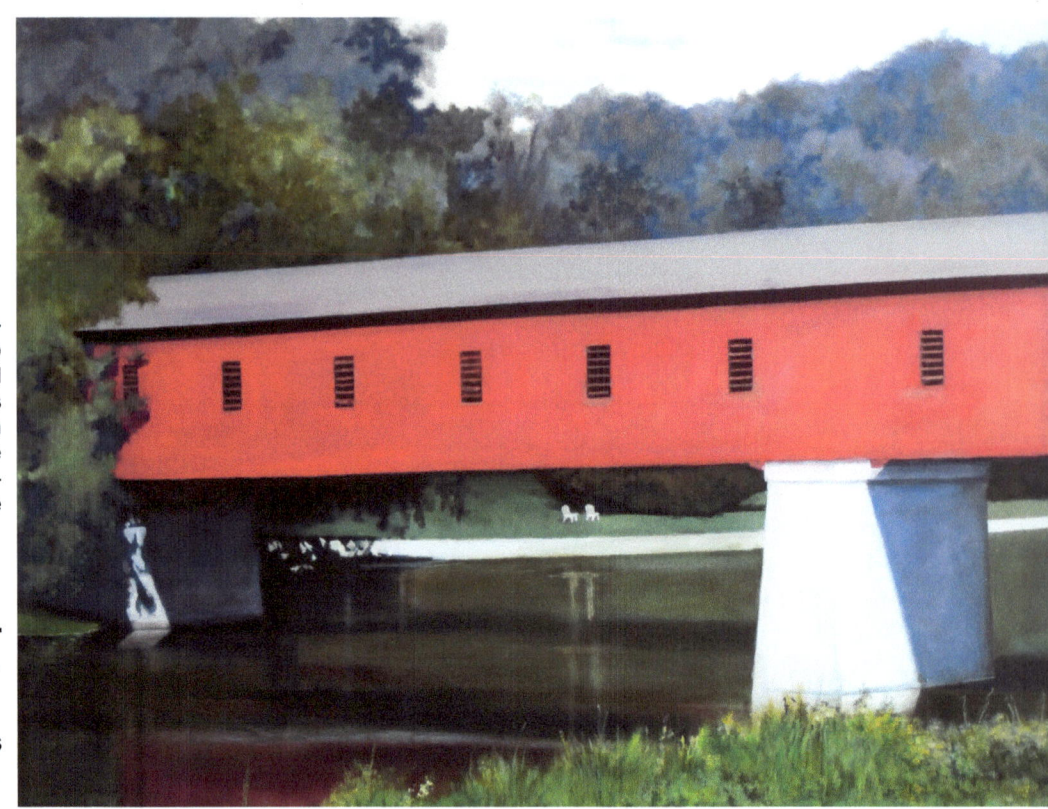

# TERRY TORRA

**LOCATION:** Kitchener
**WEB:** Artbyttorra.com
**EMAIL:** ttttorra@hotmail.com

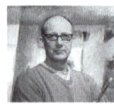

Terry is an accomplished landscape painter born in Ontario and in love with it's powerful natural elements. They serve as a source for his many series on this subject which highlights colour, texture and subtle gradations. He has explored various styles and currently paints in his own style named "Post Post Modern Realism"

**1 Covered Bridge at West Montrose** 30x40" Acrylic on canvas.

**2 Crow Over North Dumphries Field** 30x36" Acrylic on canvas.

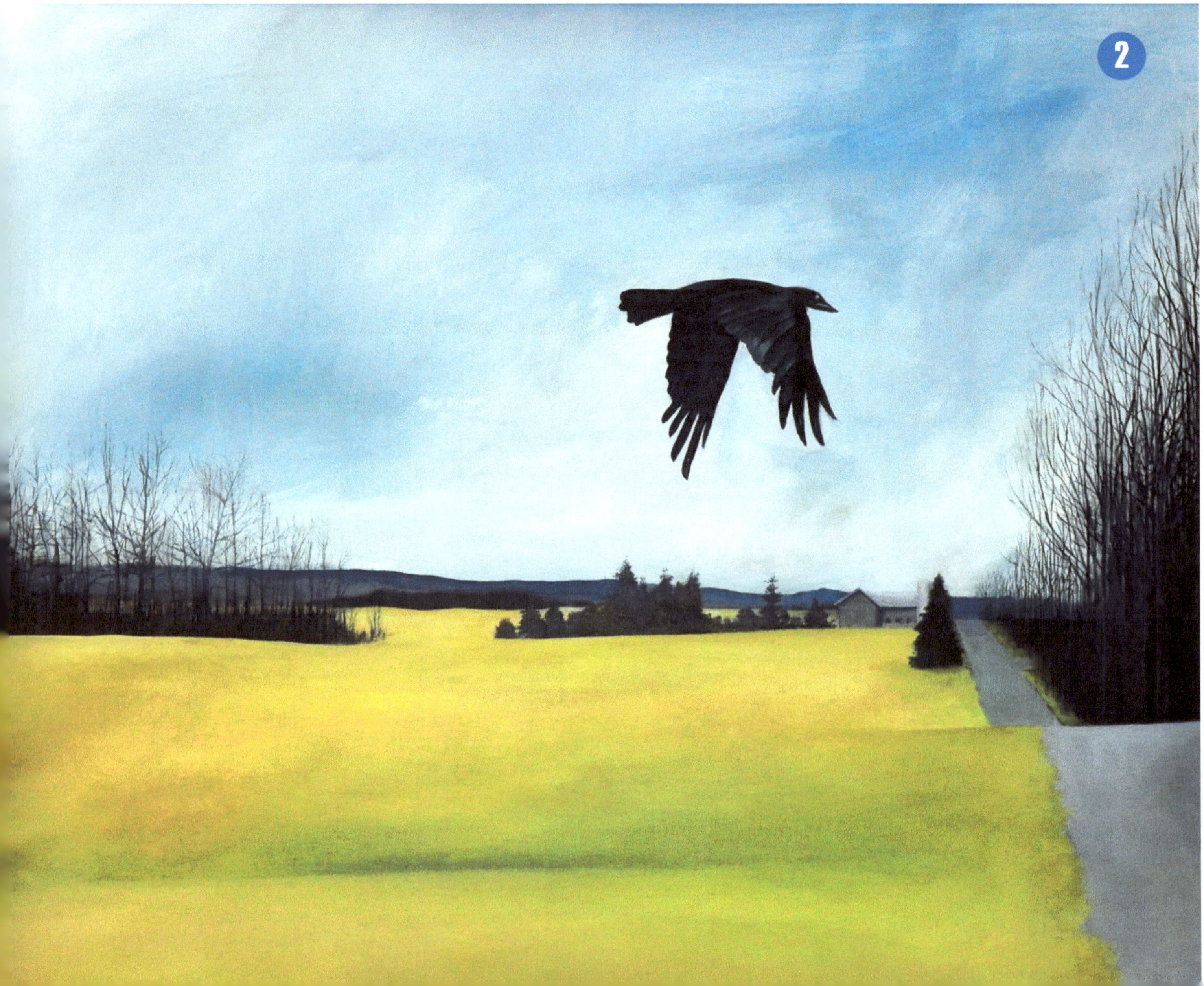

# ELAINE COWAN

**LOCATION:** Waterloo
**WEB:** UptownGalleryWaterloo.com
**EMAIL:** Etcartist@rogers.com

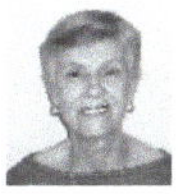

Elaine was born and raised in the Kitchener/Waterloo area. She has studied under a number of well-known artists including Zolton Szabo, Devona Paquette , Art Cunanan and Bea Hogan. Some of her private works are in Florida, California and Japan. She is a member of the COAA, Waterloo Community Arts Centre andUptown Gallery.

**1 White Blossoms** Acrylic on yupo paper. Her love of colour is evident in this vibrant painting.

**2 Garden Gate** Acrylic on yupo paper. After a few loosely dropped colours on yupo paper, that looked like flowers, this painting of the Garden Gate emerged.

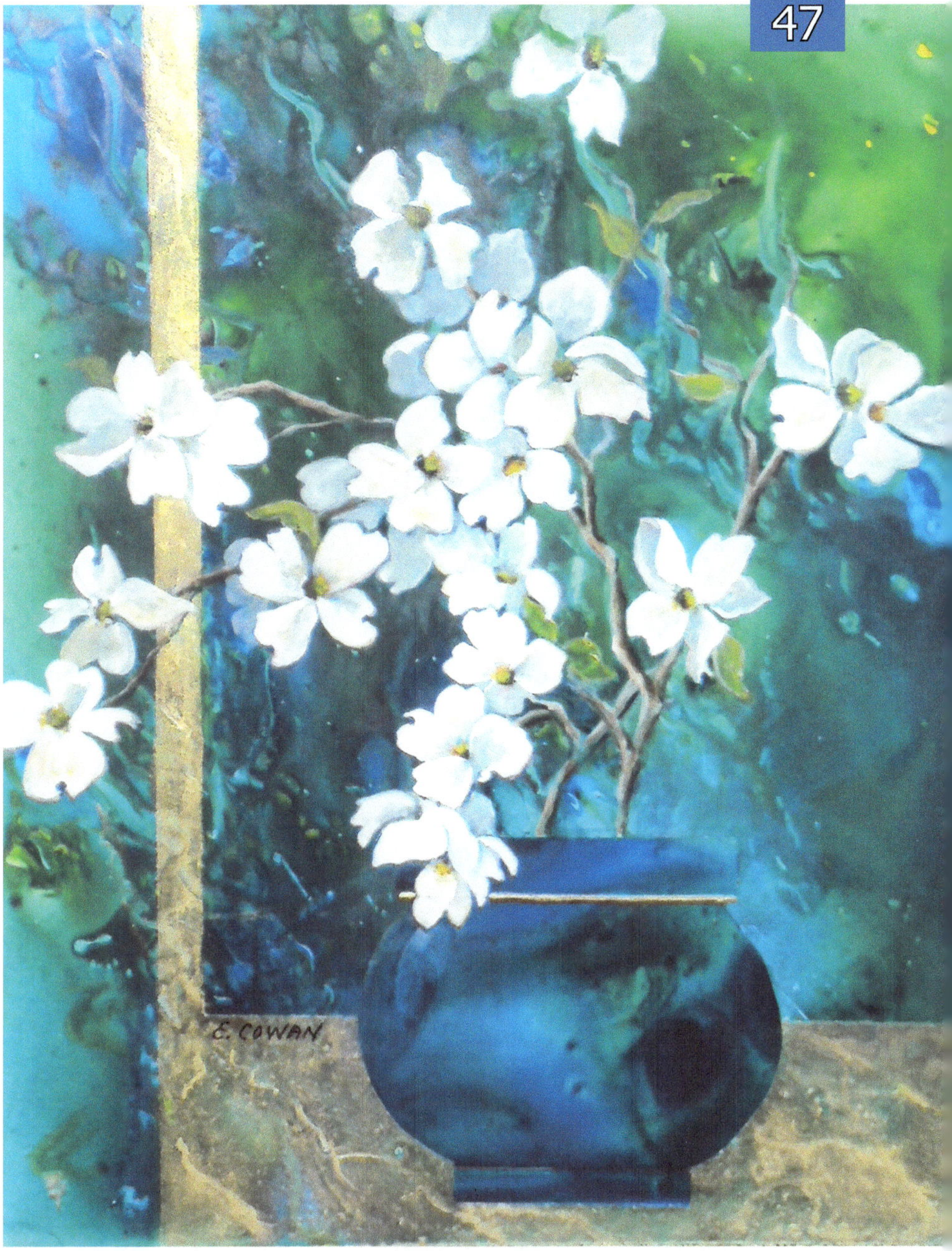

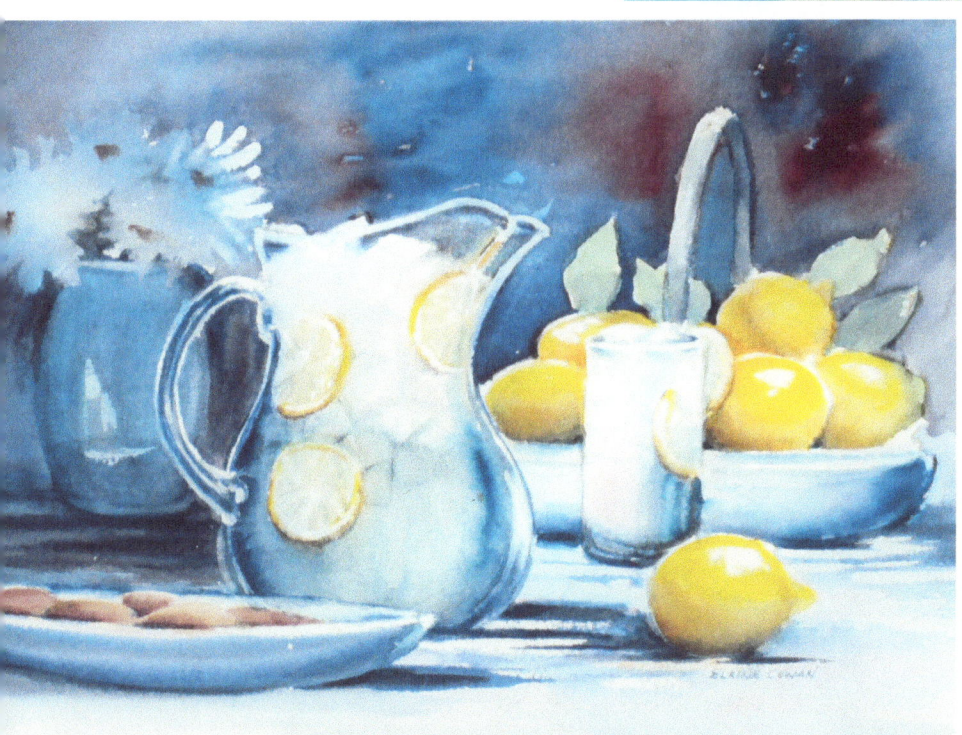

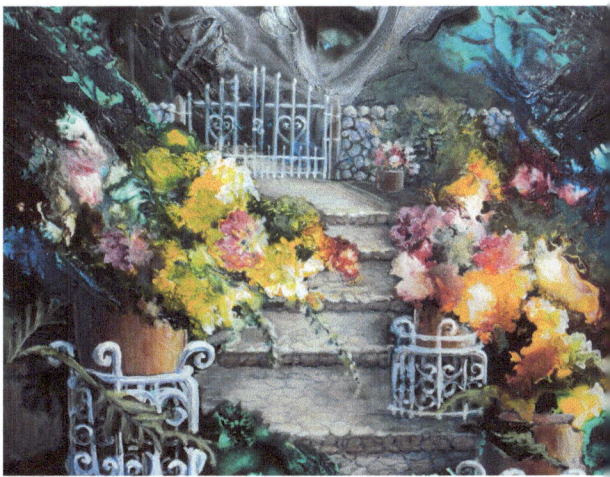

**3 Lemonade** Watercolour.

# RUBY KINGSBURY

**LOCATION:** Kitchener
**WEB:** (N/A)
**EMAIL:** Rgkingsbury@gmail.com

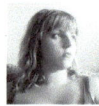

Ruby has lived in Kitchener her entire life. She studied Fine Arts at the University of Waterloo and primarily focuses on using oil on canvas. I reference local imagery in my artistic practice by focusing on reconstituting images of the past to reflect the present.

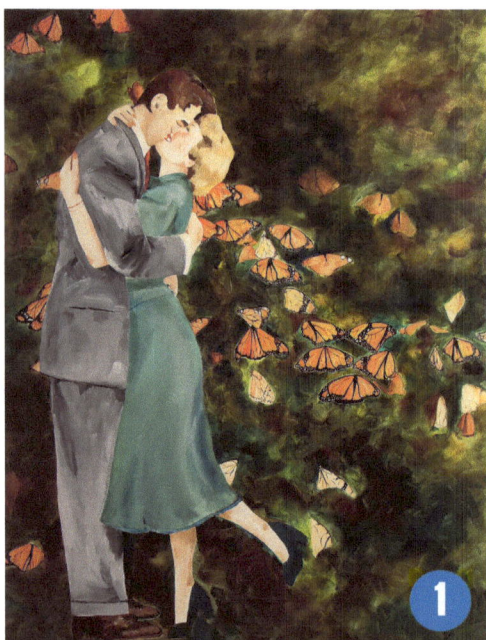

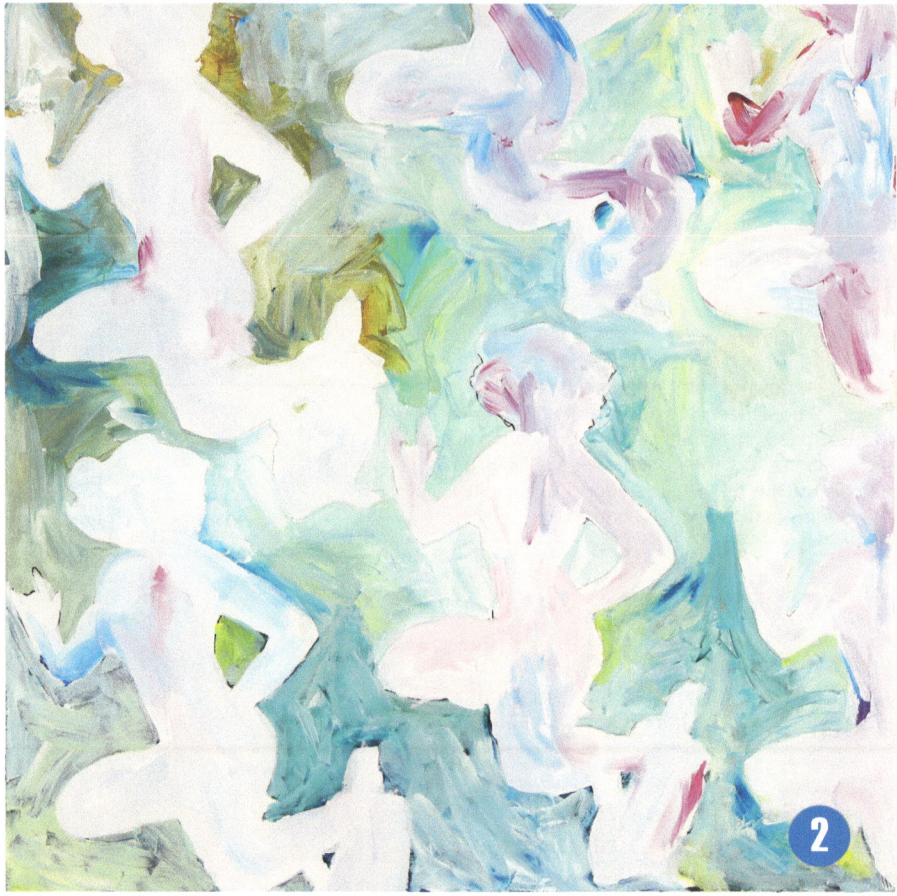

**1** **The Kiss** 36×42″ Oil on Masonite Board.

**2** **Beach** 16×16″ Acrylic on Masonite Board.

**3** **The March** 24×36″ Oil on Canvas.

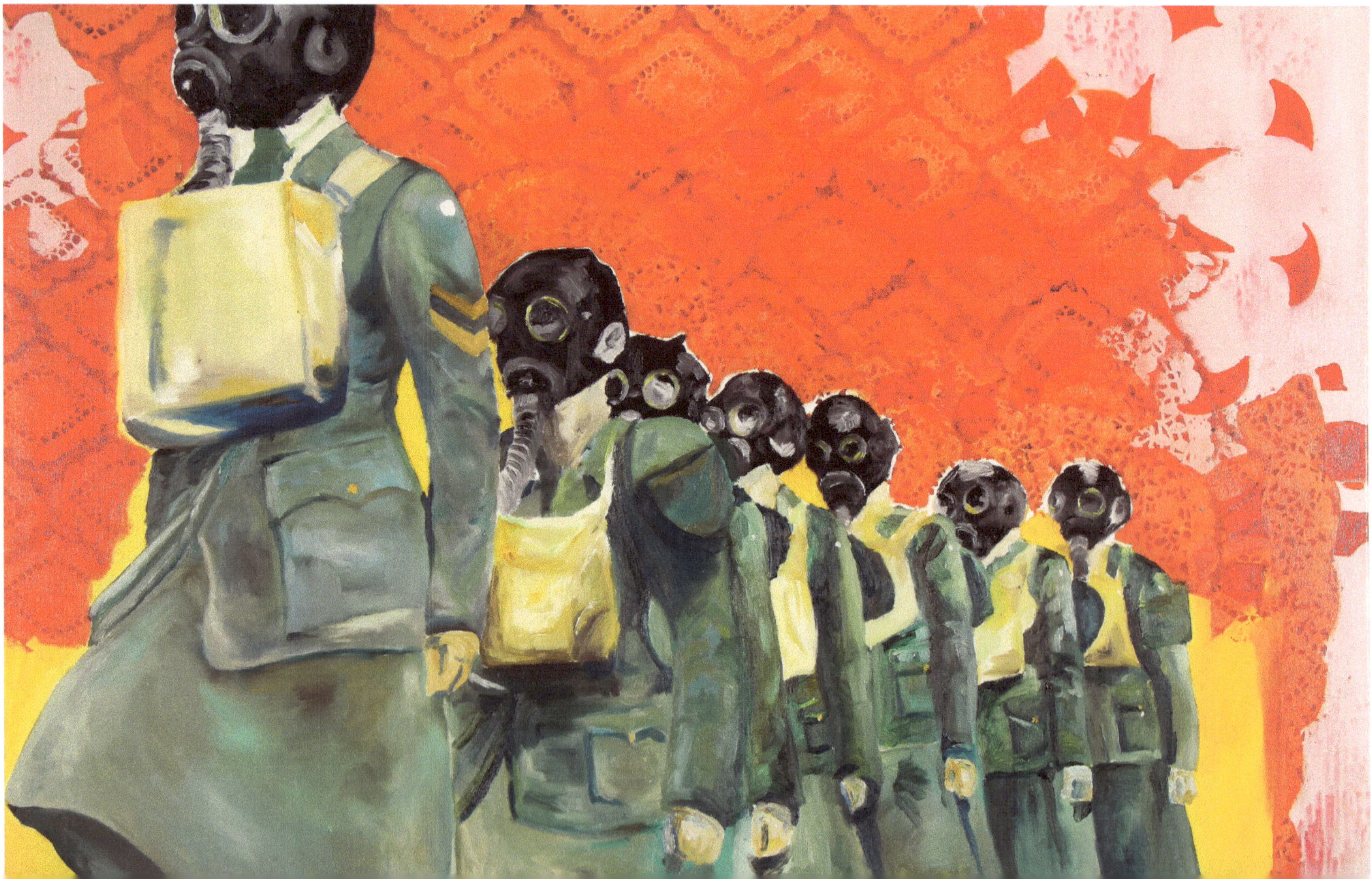

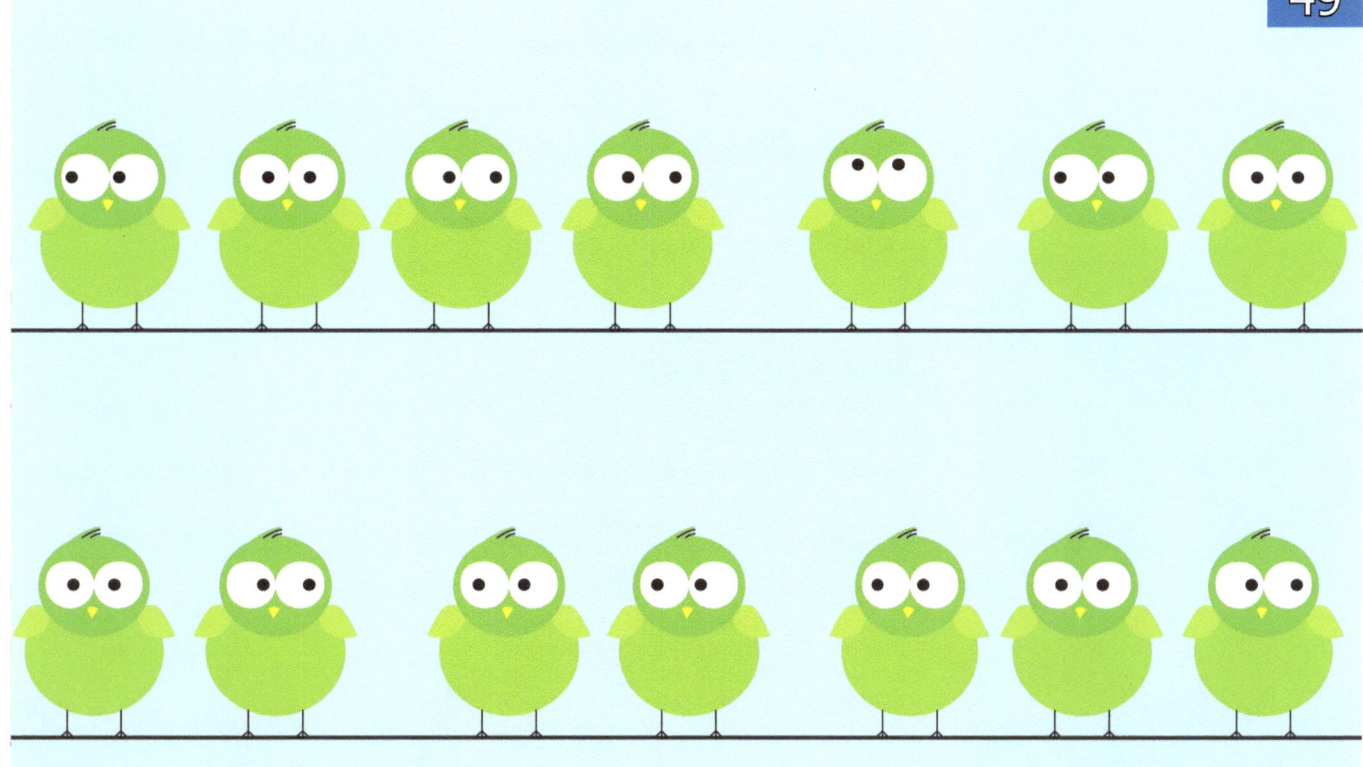

## JULES HALL

**LOCATION:** Kitchener
**WEB:** Greengiraffedesign.ca
**EMAIL:** Jules@greengiraffedesign.ca

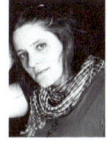
Jules is a graphic designer, painter and photographer in Kitchener. She loves to work digitally or get her hands messy with acrylic paint on canvas. She is finishing a diploma in graphic design from Conestoga College. Her quirky sense of humour and love of colour seem to sneak into all the work she does.

**1 Birds on a Wire** Digital Illustration. These little fellow are part of a series of patterns I illustrated.

**2 Giraffe** 5×7" Acrylic on canvas. Giraffes are nature's most ridiculous animal. What's not to love?

**3 Emerald Snake** 5×7" Photograph.

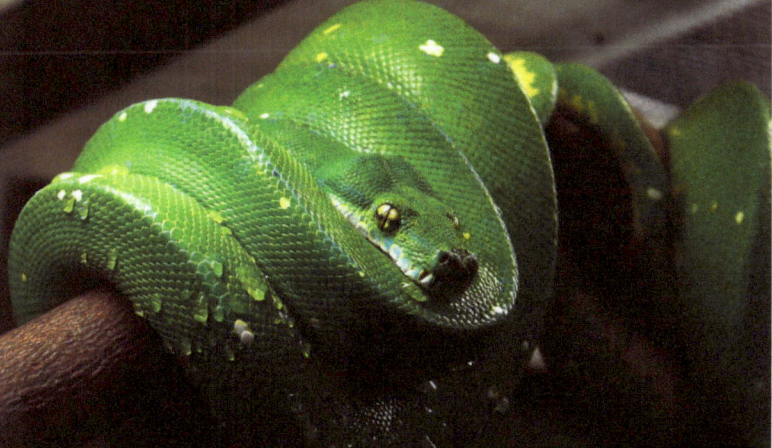

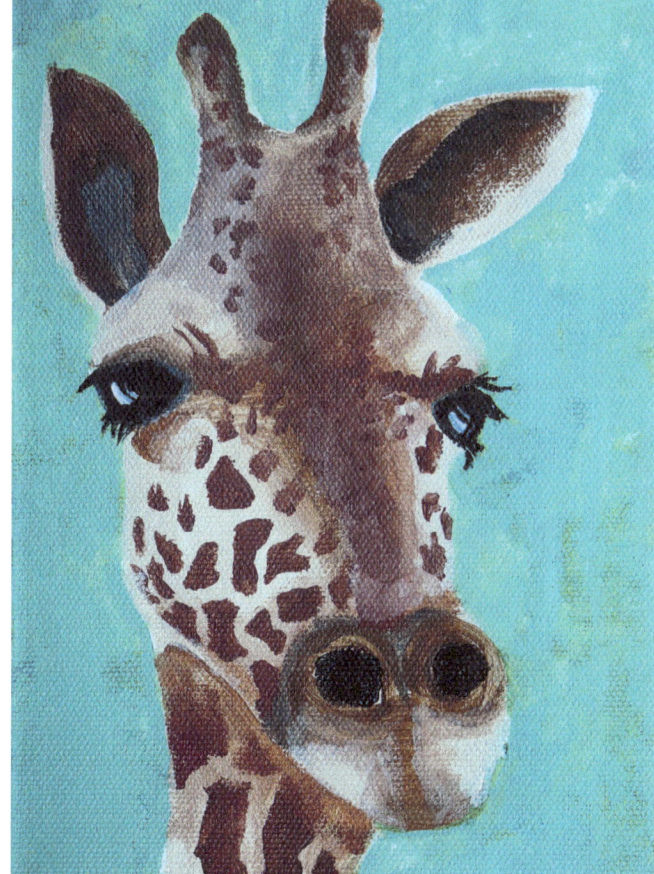

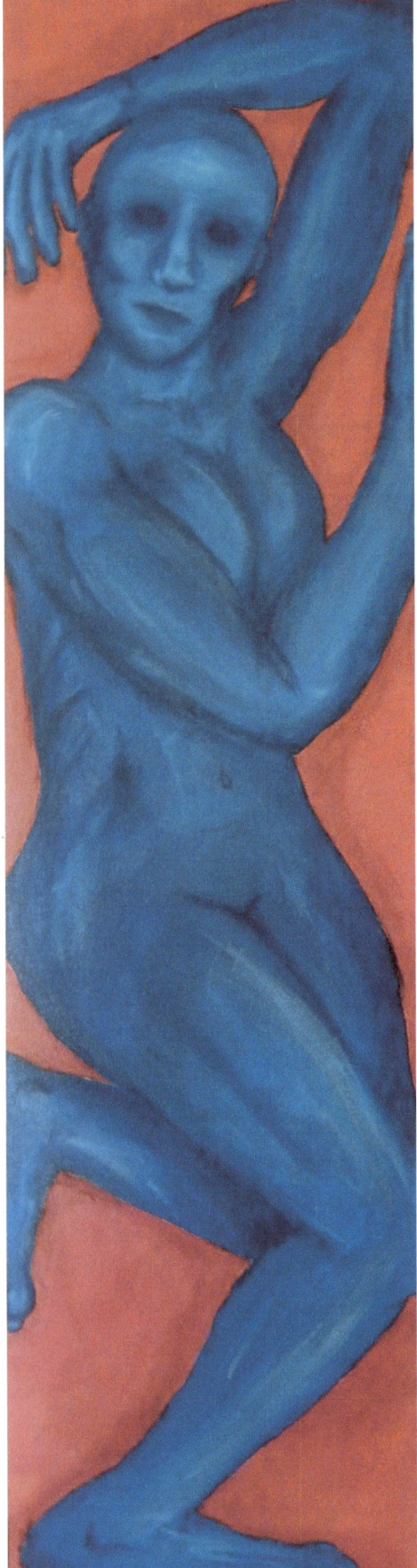

**1 Caged** 12x42" Acrylic on canvas.

**2 Hope** 16x20" Acrylic on canvas.

**3 Rise** 23x36" Acrylic on canvas.

# JEN HAZZARD

**LOCATION:** Kitchener
**WEB:** (N/A)
**EMAIL:** Jenhazzard@gmail.com

Jen is a graduate of Wilfrid Laurier University who fell in love with (and in) Waterloo, and is invested in the community of Kitchener-Waterloo. She paints with acrylics and loves to get creative through fine art, acting & writing. You can find her in the community teaching about global issues and she uses her artwork to express her thoughts around these topics.

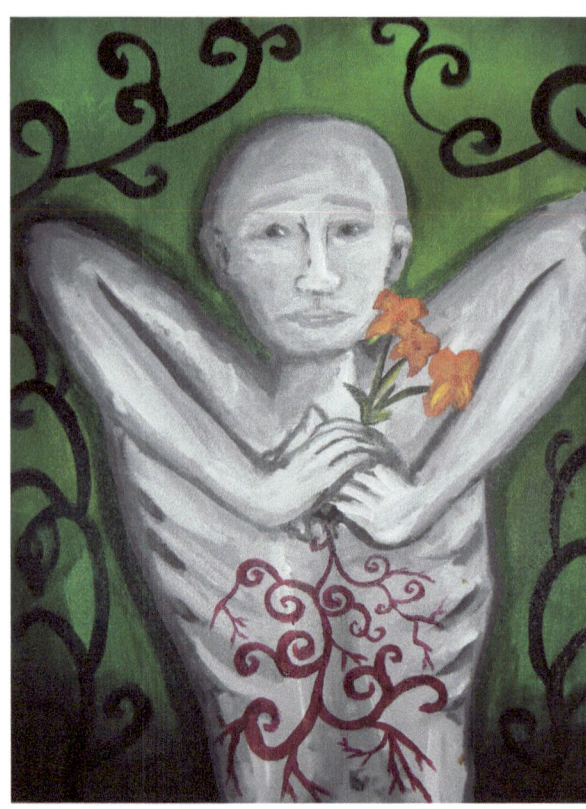

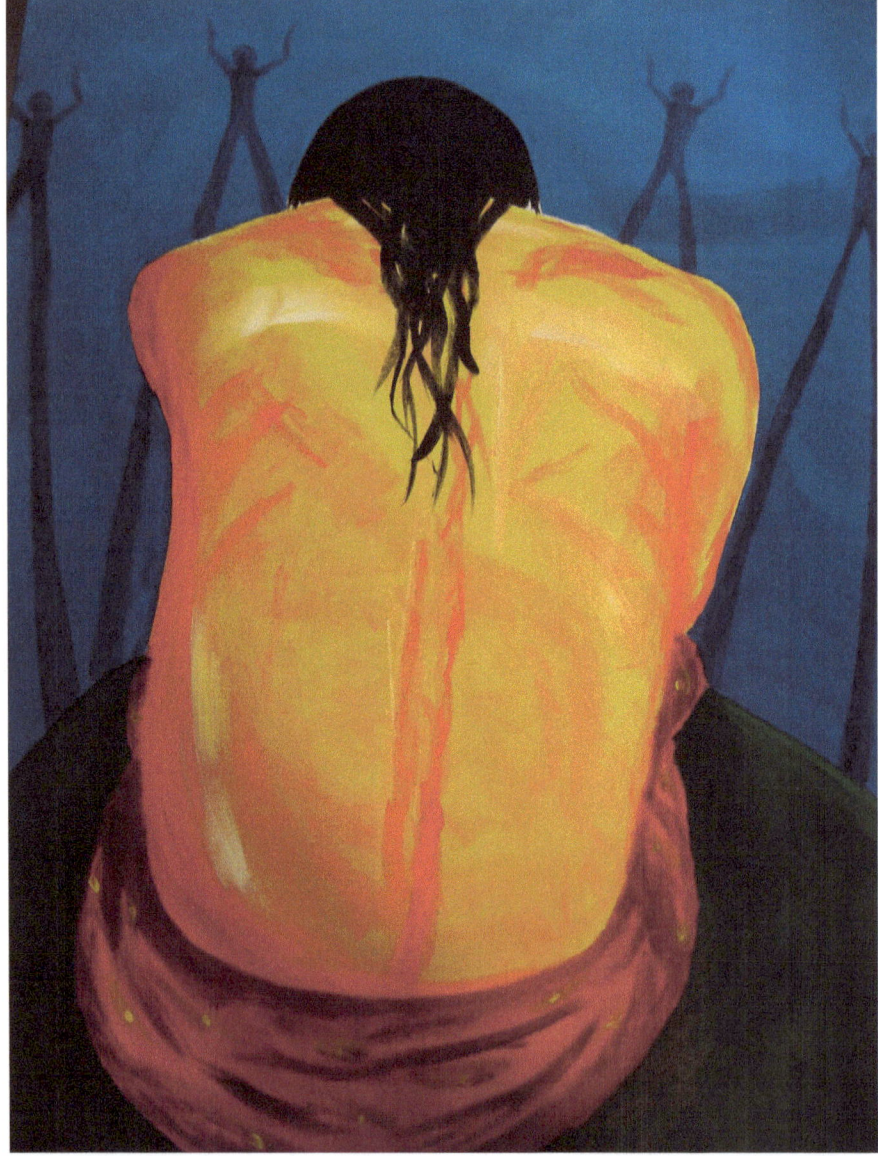

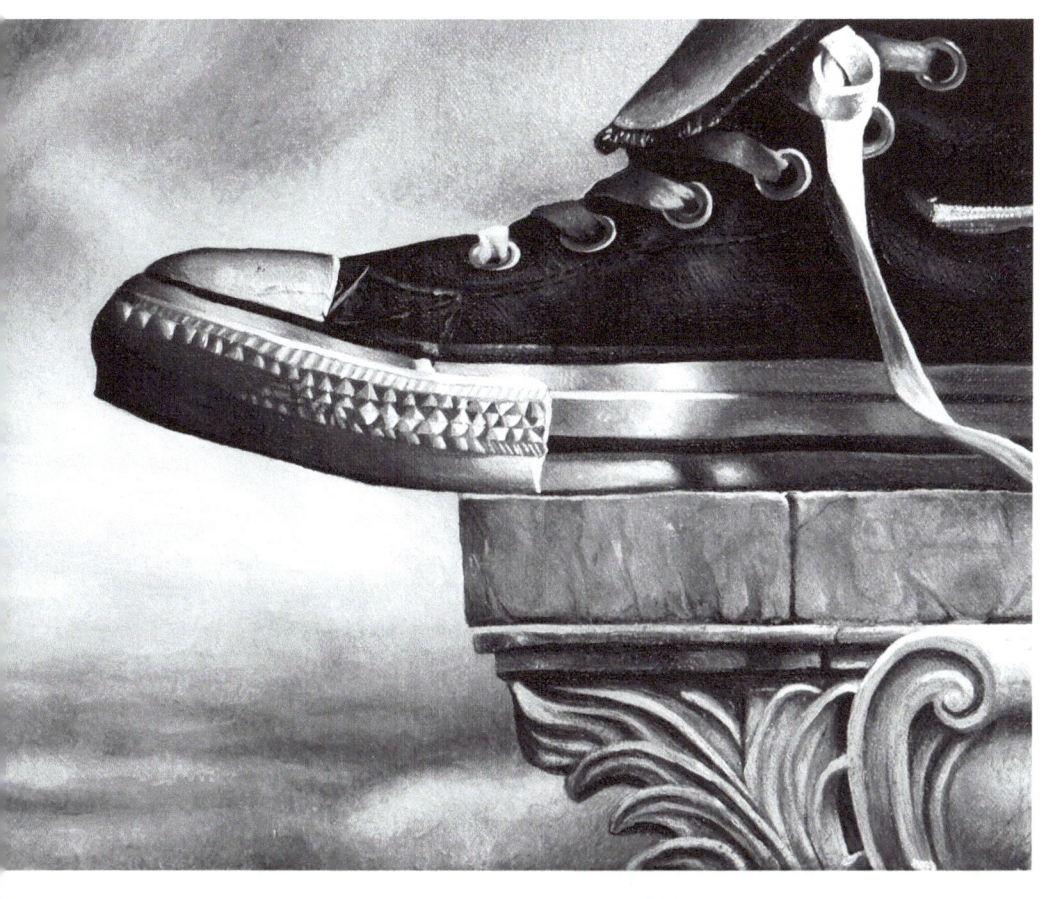

**1** **Yes Or No** 14x11" Acrylic on Canvas.

**2** **Listen** 12x12" Acrylic on Canvas.

**3** **Trudge** 12x12" Acrylic on Canvas.

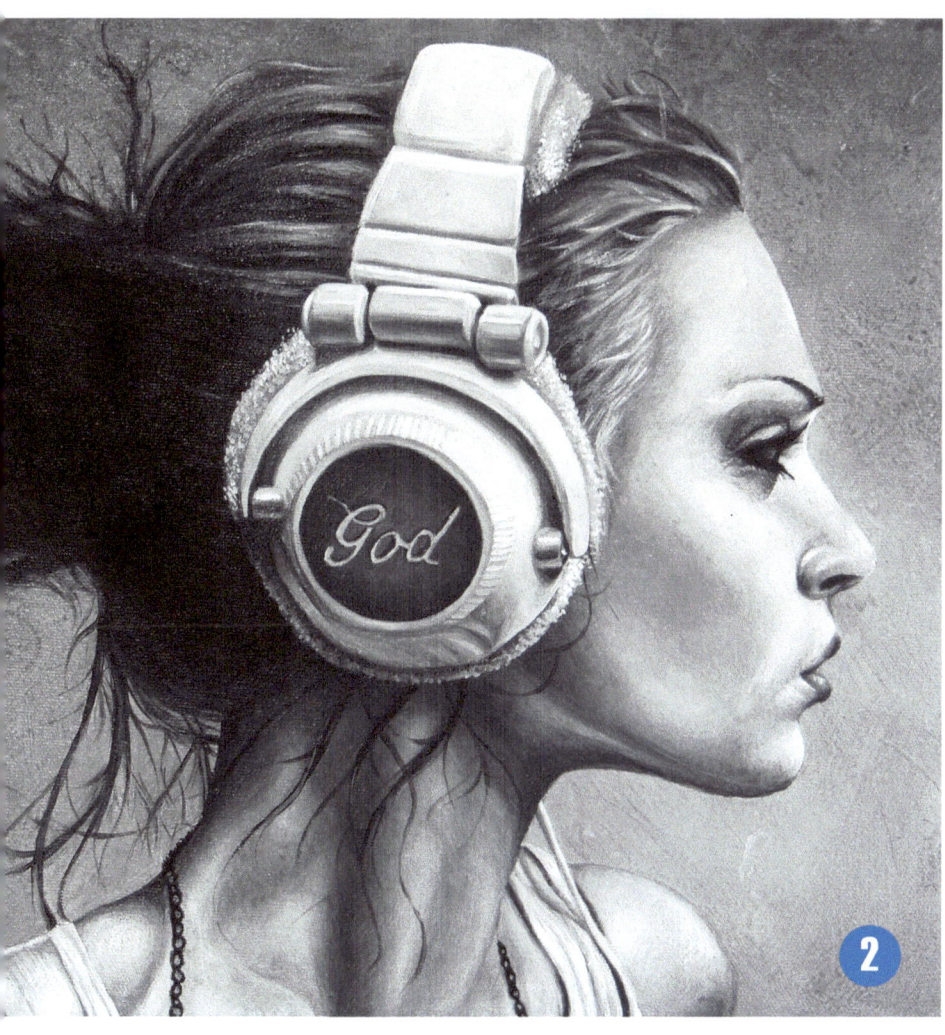

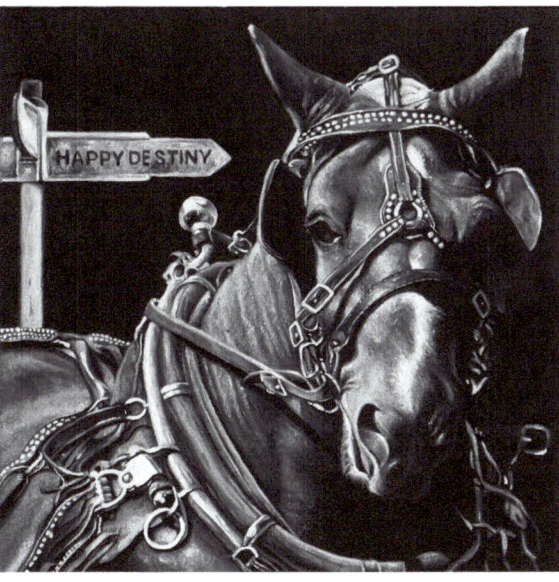

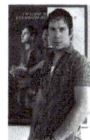

# BRENT SCHREIBER
**LOCATION:** Elmira
**WEB:** BrentSchreiber.com
**EMAIL:** Info@brentschreiber.com

Brent Schreiber is an Artist located in Elmira, Ontario. His personal work focuses on large scale figurative paintings. Combining traditional painting, design and narrative themes, Brent's work strives to connect the emotional to the physical. His work is held in both Private and Public Collections in the United States and Canada.

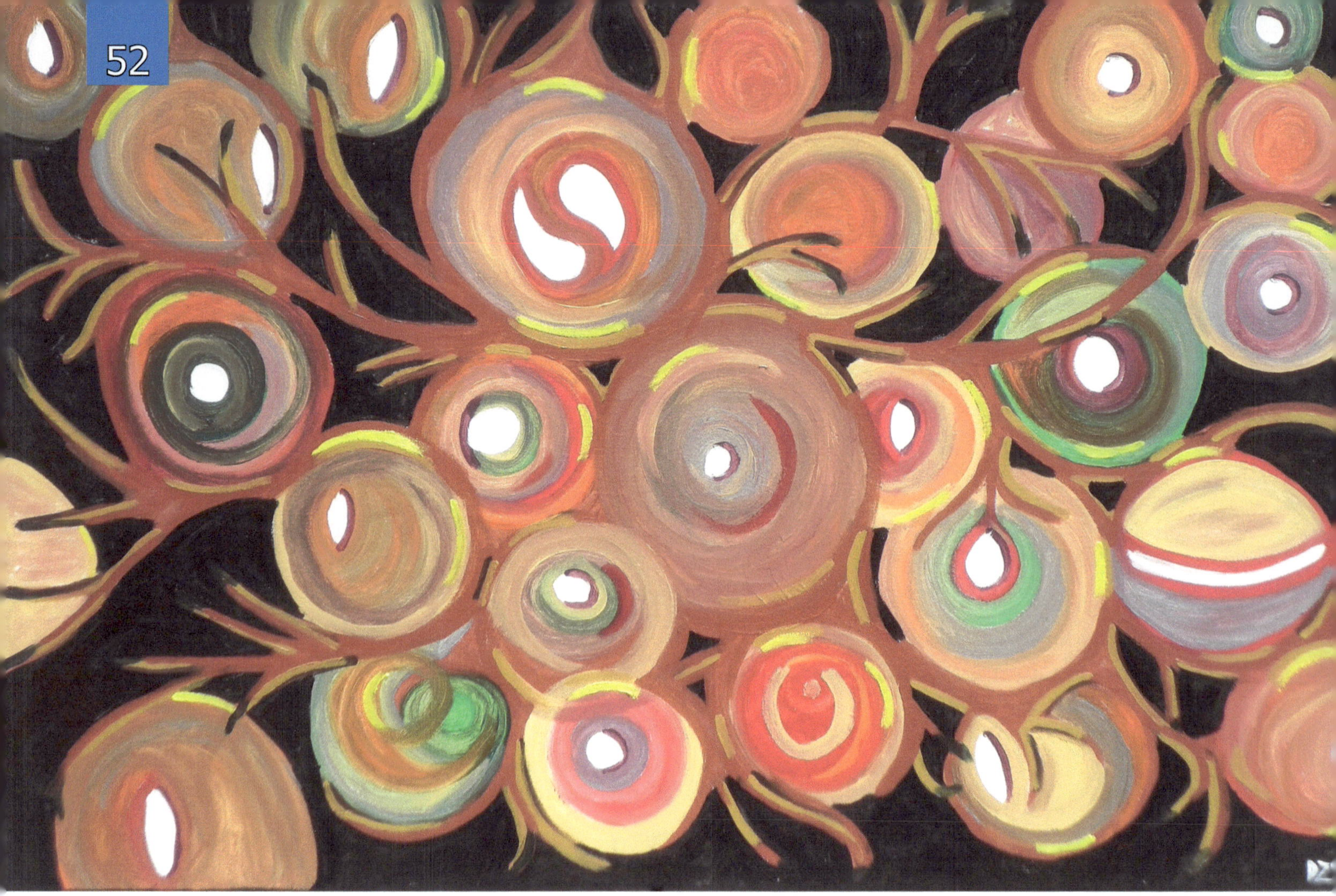

**1**

**1 Bulb** 3x2' Acrylic on canvas. The growth of nothing into everything.

**2 Proton** 3x2' Acrylic on canvas. The relese of energy in a whirlwind of sadness.

# DAN ZYBALA

**LOCATION:** Waterloo
**WEB:** Flickr.com/photos/danzybala
Artallies.com/artiststore/browse/58-dan-zybala?sef=hc
**EMAIL:** Dzybala-cc@conestogac.on.ca

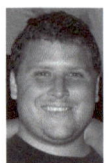

Dan Zybala is a self-taught artist exploring the many sides of creation in an art world of so many possibilities. In the future the abstraction of modern day appeals will enlighten my thoughts on the way I imagine art in my own mind. To me my paintings are a work of art proving the reality of what exists outside the square.

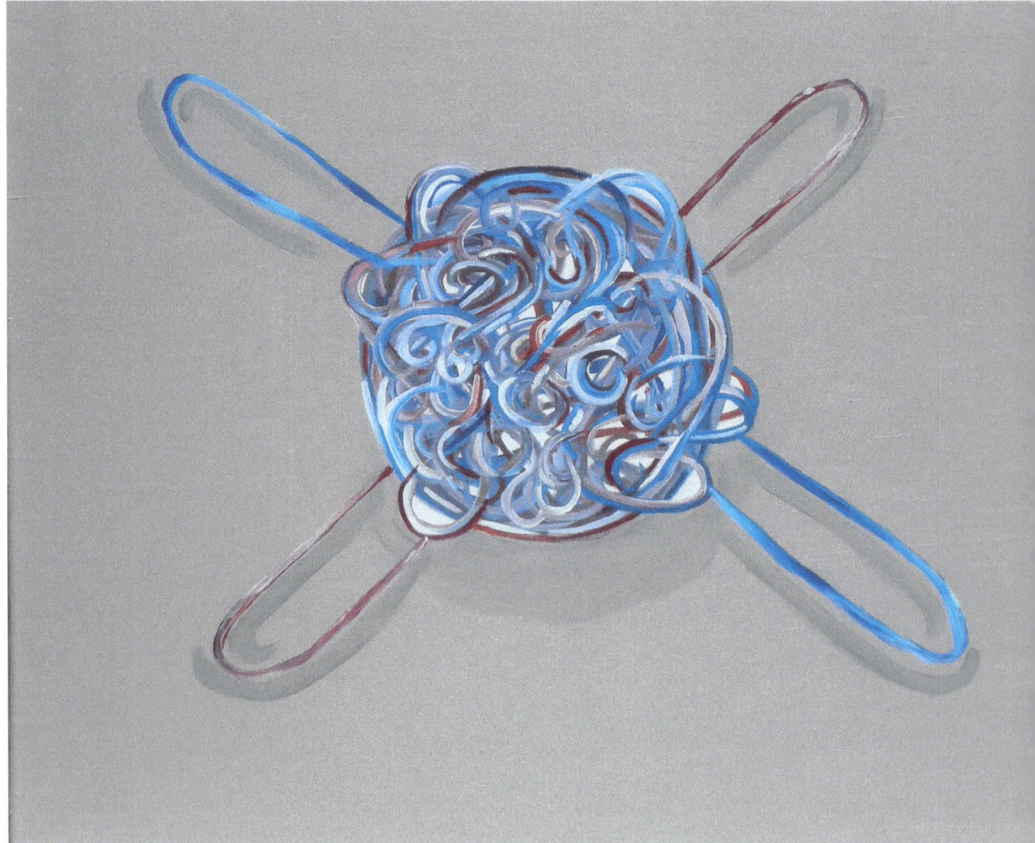

**2**

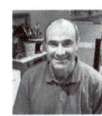

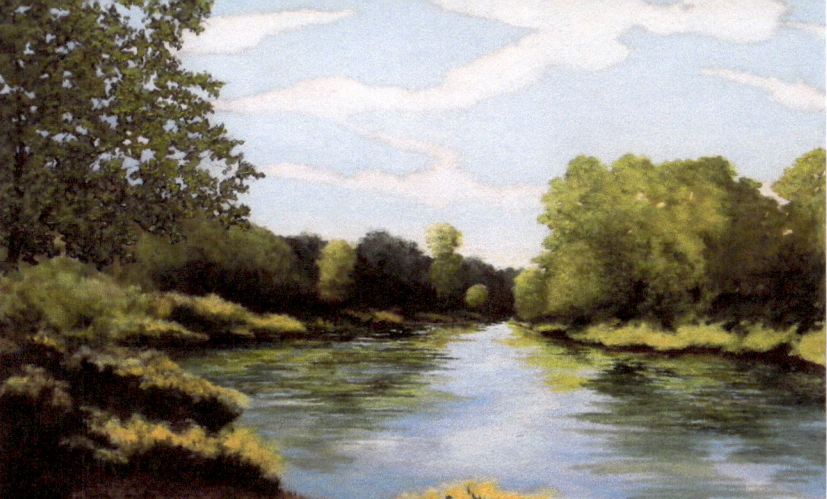

# JASON FALLAISE

**LOCATION:** Waterloo
**WEB:** (N/A)
**EMAIL:** Jfallaise@rogers.com

I am a high school teacher with the Waterloo Region District School Board. I obtained a Fine Art degree from the University of Guelph in 1985. I create paintings in watercolour and acrylic and enjoy working with the qualities each medium provides. My paintings have been purchased through Gallery on the Grand, Edissi Fine Arts and in major fundraising events such as Swing in the Park, Grand River Hospital Silent Auction and the Brain Injury Society Art Auction. Presently I am selling my work privately and I am also accepting commissions.

**1 Grand River Late August** 18x24" Acrylic on canvas.

**2 View Out A Window** 22x30" Sienna watercolour.

**3 Amsterdam Pit Stop** 22x30" Watercolour.

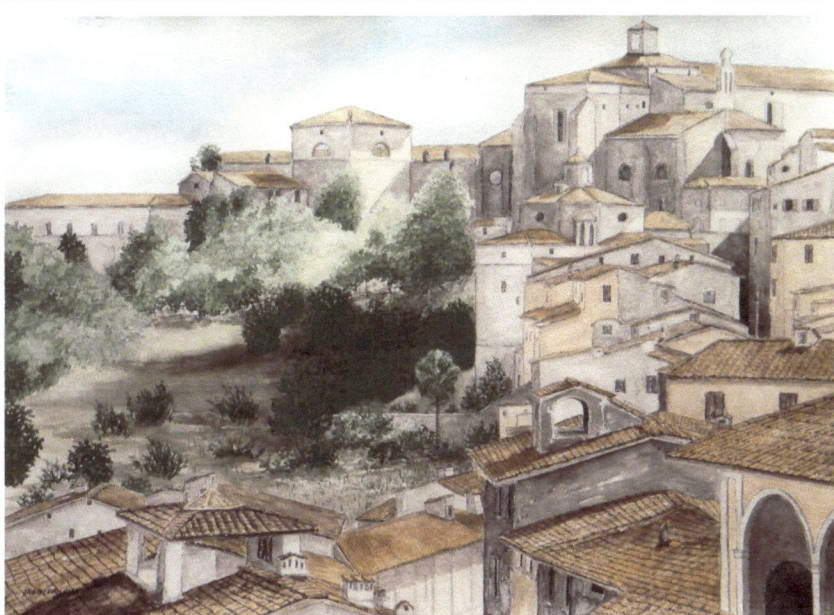

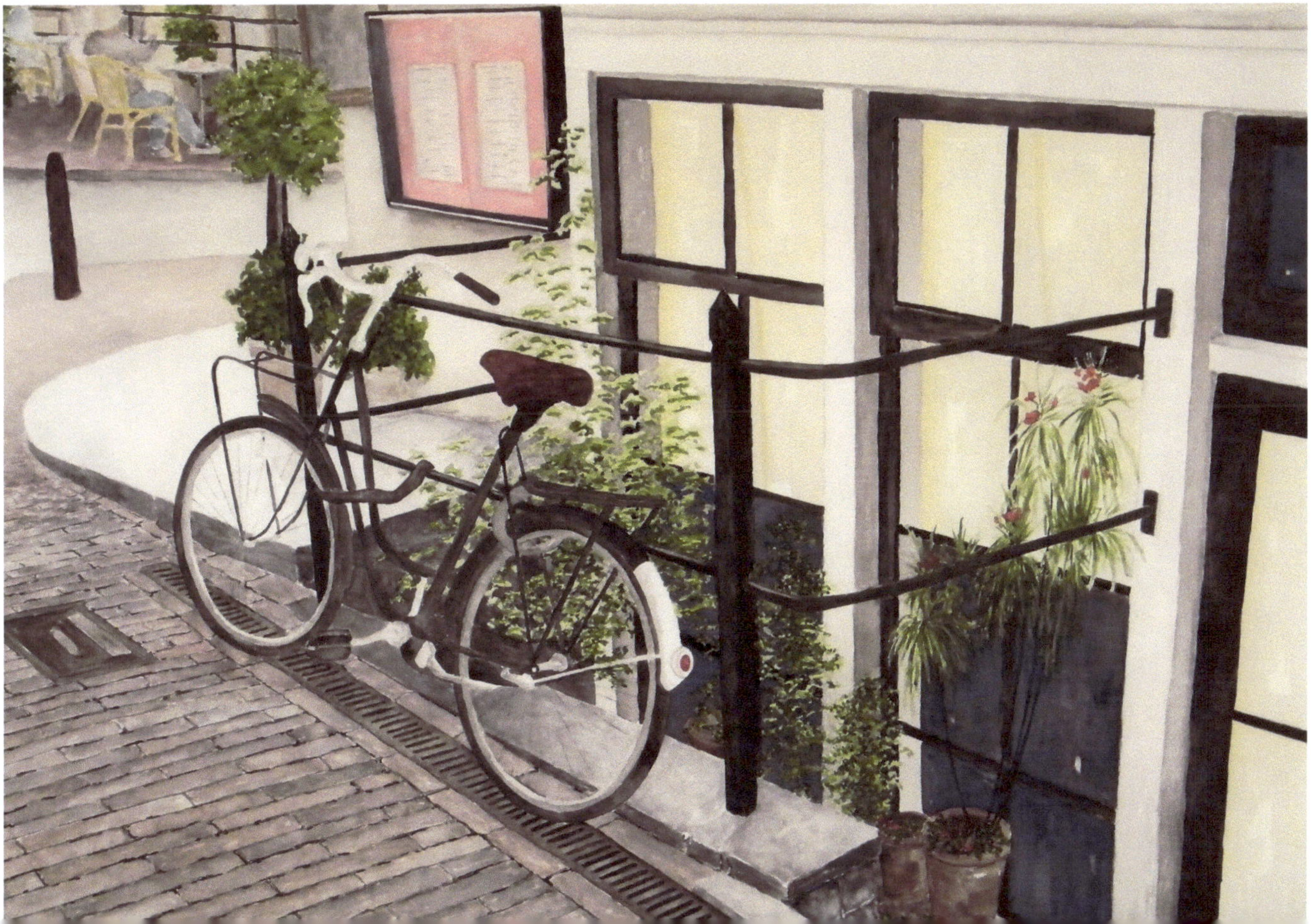

**1** **Dead Friend** 13x12" Hand drawn and inked then digitally colored.

**2** **Sled Slayers** 8.5x10" Hand drawn and inked then digitally colored.

**3** **Inner Demons** 17.5x12" Pencil, ink, and oil free pastels done on cardboard.

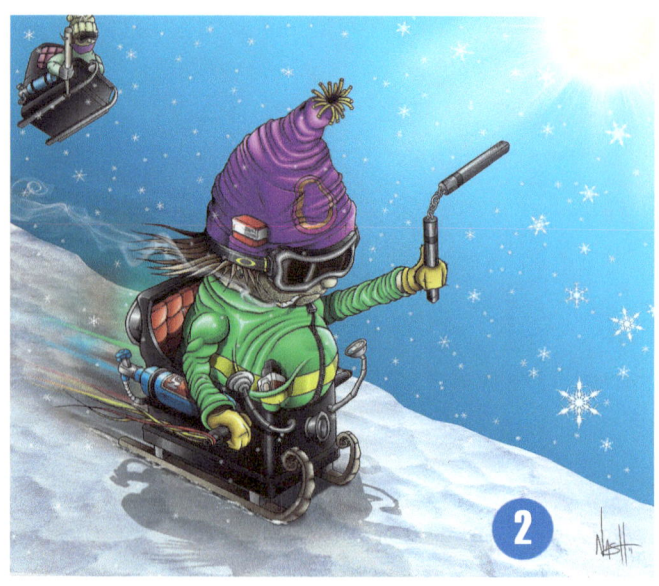

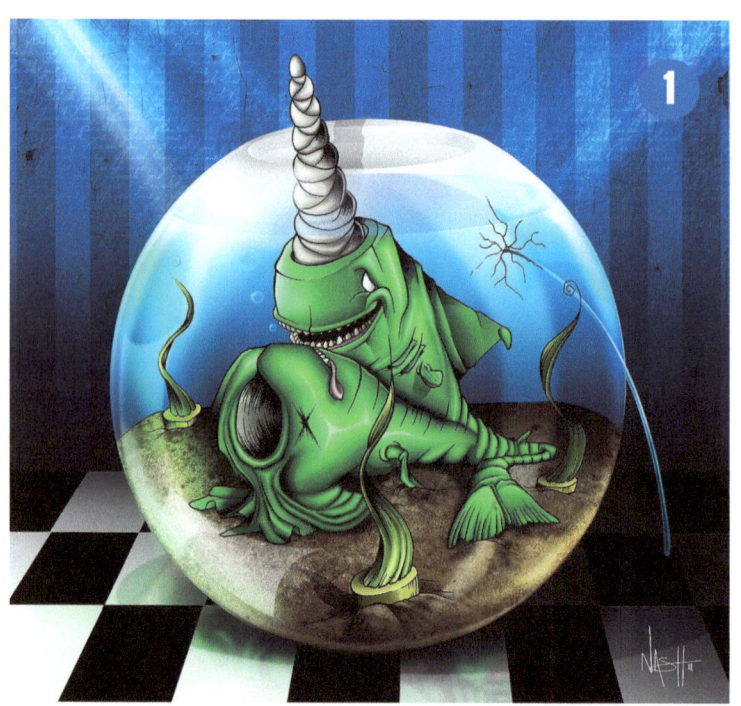

# DAN NASH GOTTFRIED

**LOCATION:** Waterloo
**WEB:** CyberAudioOnline.com
**EMAIL:** Dang@cyberaudioonline.com

Dan is an artist and recent 2011 Design Edge Canada graphic design award winner. He thrives when he can tap into his creative energy and pull out something that has a positive effect. To relish in the moment of creation through hard work and passion sparks a feeling like no other. His art is felt from within which allows for the creation of edgy, original and thought provoking pieces.

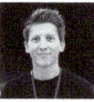

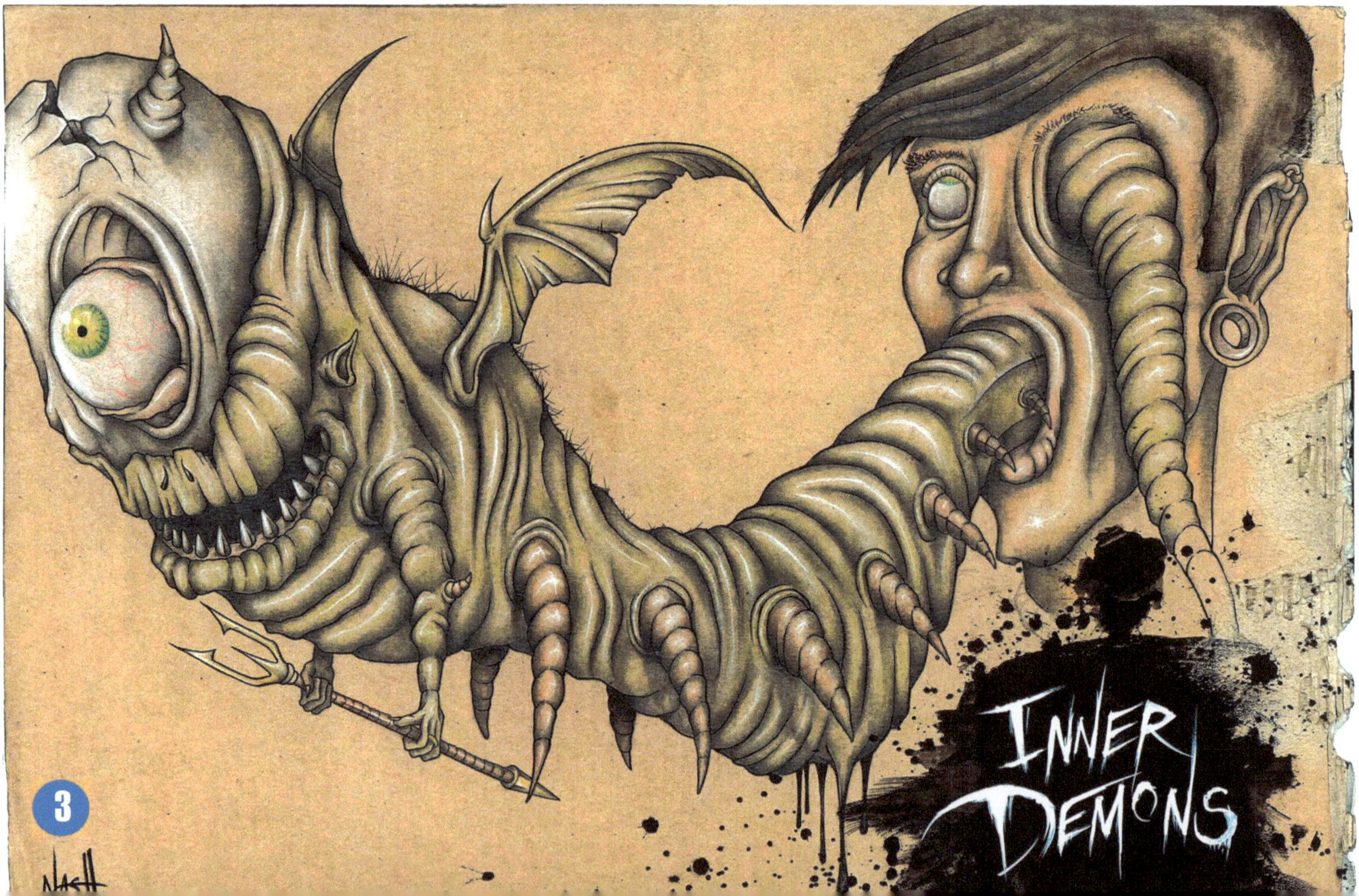

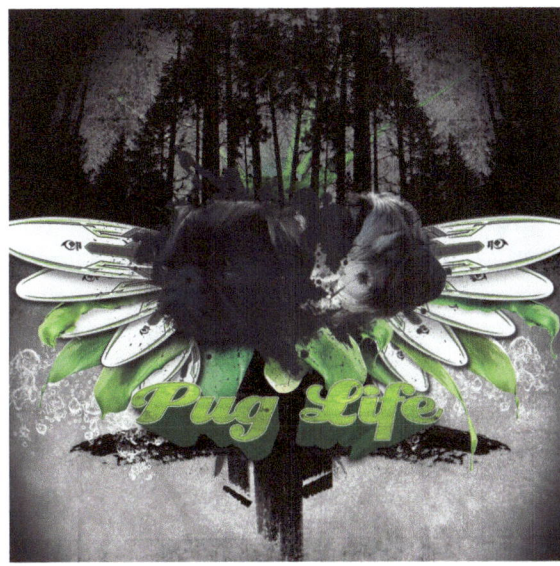

**1** **Pug Life** 19.75x19.75" Digital Art. Inspired by the greatest surfing pug I know.

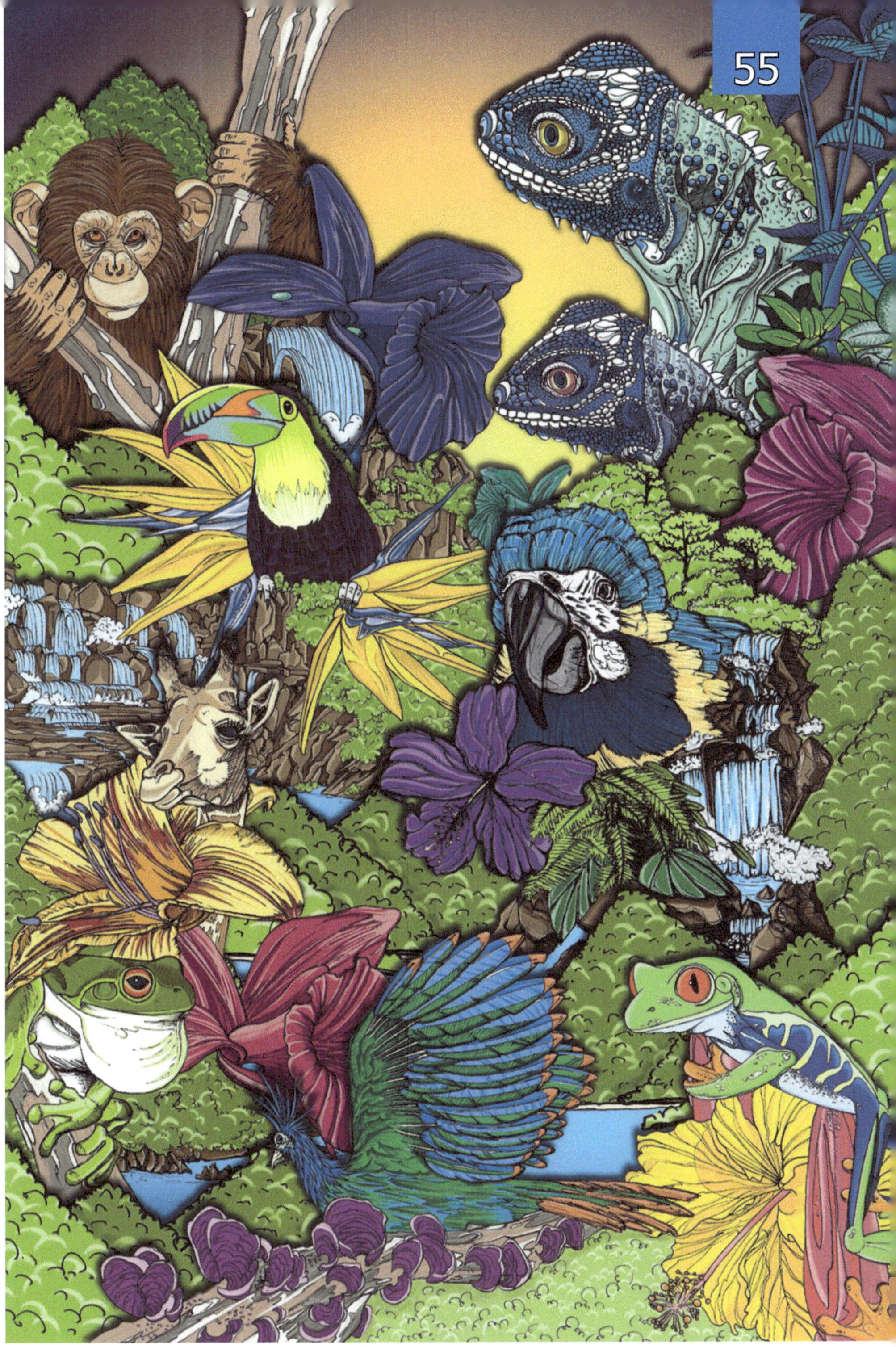

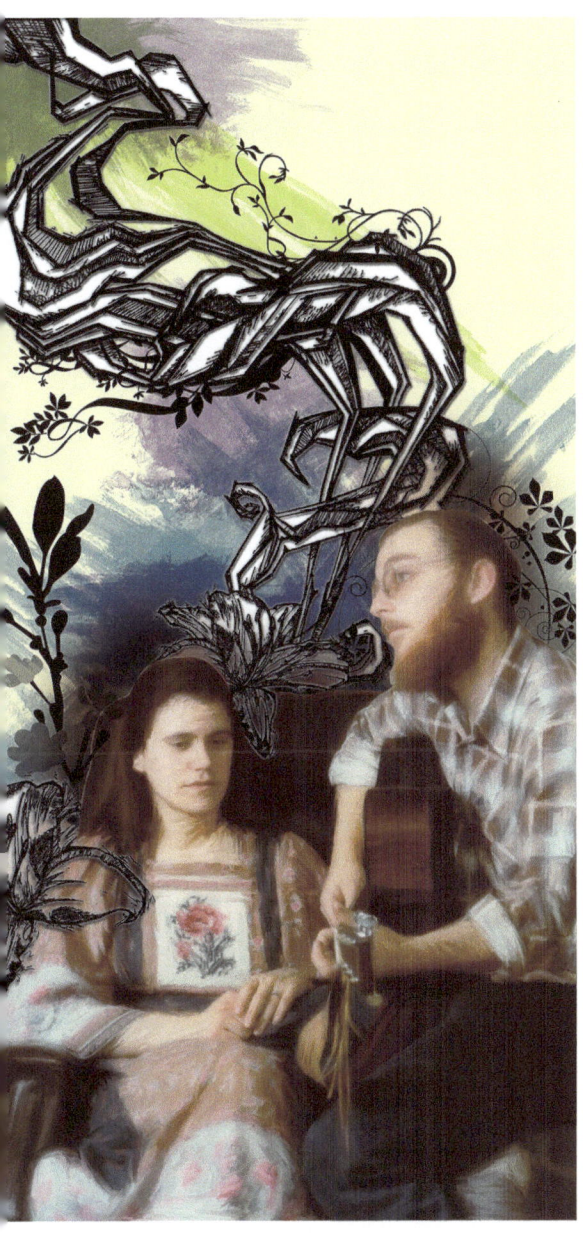

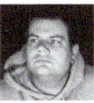

**2** **Rain Forest Mural** 24x36" Digital Art. Fundraiser for autistic kids.

**3** **Portrait Of My Parents** 13.5x27" Digital Art. Hand drawn sketches and digital painting.

# GABE GRIFFITHS

**LOCATION:** Kitchener
**WEB:** Be.net/gabegriffiths
**EMAIL:** Griffiths.gabe@gmail.com

Colour is almost always my starting point for any piece I make. I like to stand out and make a statement by playing with complimentary colour schemes, and vibrant pops of contrasting elements. A lot of my work stems from my imagination. I like to think of floating cities built out of words and letters, where there are no rules and nature is king. Most of my inspiration comes from urban art and graffiti. Typography and Illustration are my jam!

# KERRY L. ROSS

**LOCATION:** Kitchener-Waterloo
**WEB:** KLRartist.ca
**EMAIL:** Keleross@netscape.net

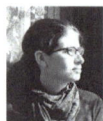

Kerry Ross achieved a Bachelor of Fine Arts (Calgary) in 1995. Today, it is the faces and ideas she encounters on her travels that deeply colour her art. Unconcerned with extraneous detail, Kerry's paintings focus the mind, isolating the image for the purpose of contemplation. This allows space for the unregulated responses of the viewer's eye. The result is that concepts about modernity, femininity and beauty become one with the image!

**1 Cherish the Day** 17x21.5" Watercolour and ink on 140Lb cold press watercolour paper.

**2 The Perils and the Power of Looking** 17x23.5" Watercolour, conte and ink on 140Lb cold press watercolour paper.

**3 The Garden Closes At Sunset** 9.5x14" Watercolor and ink on 140Lb cold press watercolour paper.

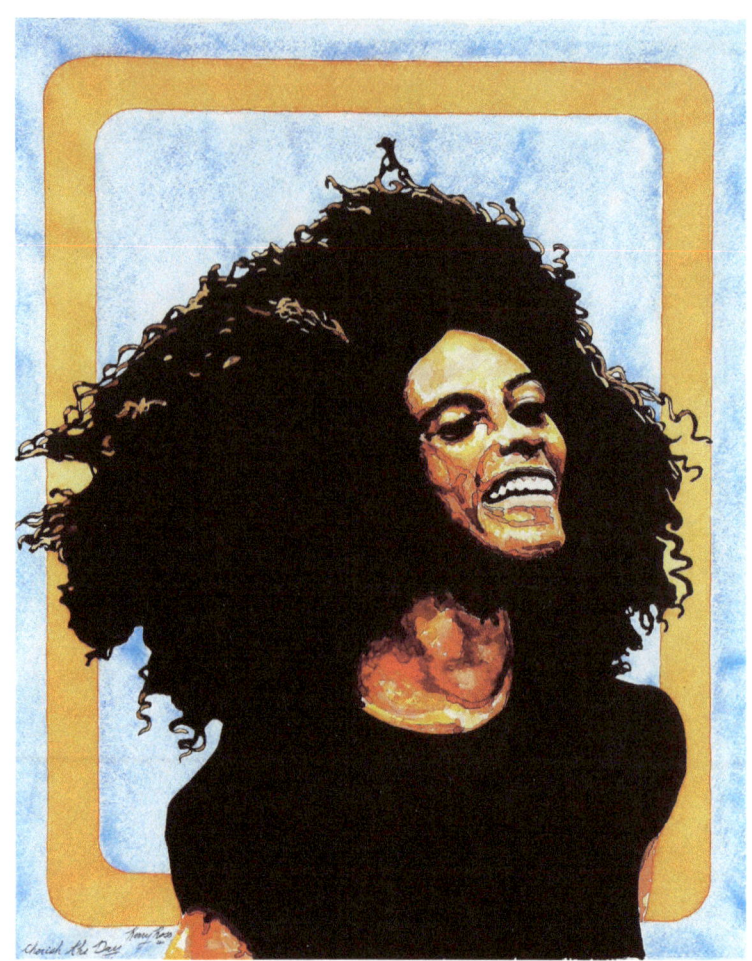

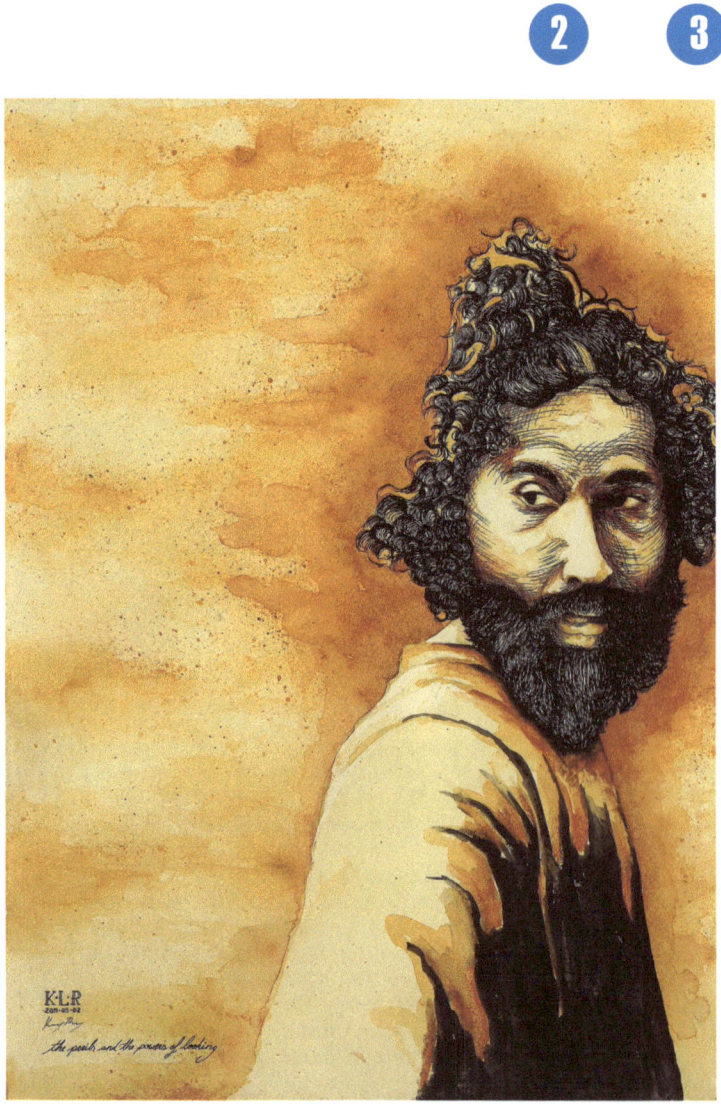

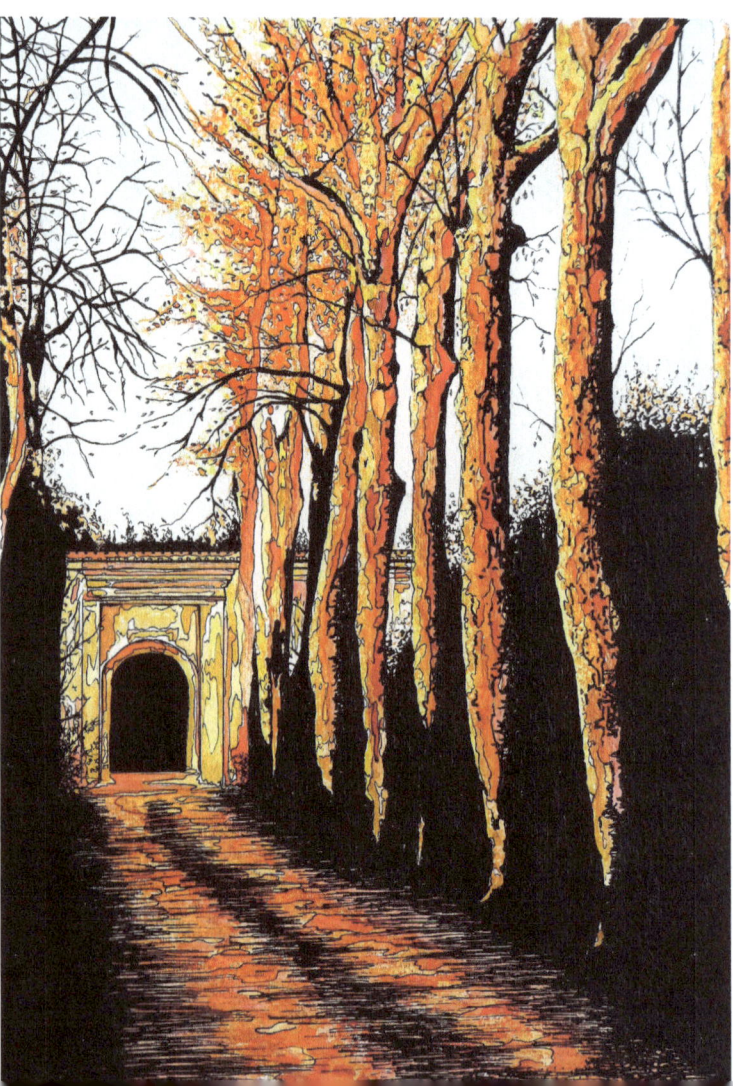

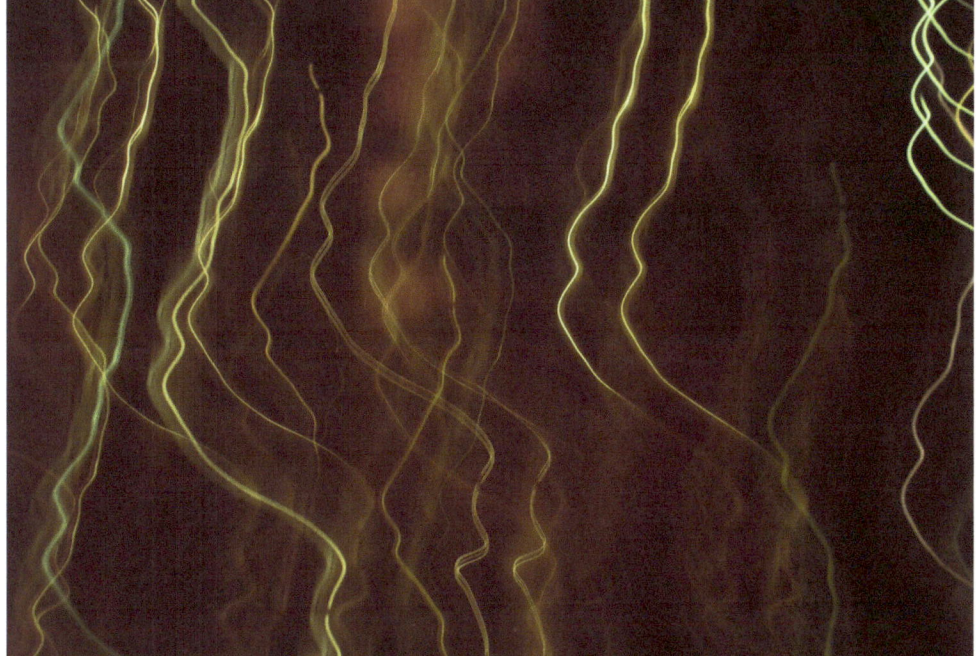

# J. RYAN BROOKS

**LOCATION:** Toronto / Zuckerloft Studio
**WEB:** (N/A)
**EMAIL:** john.ryan.brooks@gmail.com

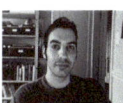

Ryan has been a member of Zuckerloft Studio in Kitchener for 4 years now and it continues to be a very rewarding and creative environment. Currently living in Toronto, Ryan works in the event industry designing show installations and dreaming of a day when the artists will rise up and conquer the world in a perfectly juxtapositioned manner of course.

**1 Nerve Centre** 7.5×11" Photography. Long exposure, completely unaltered.

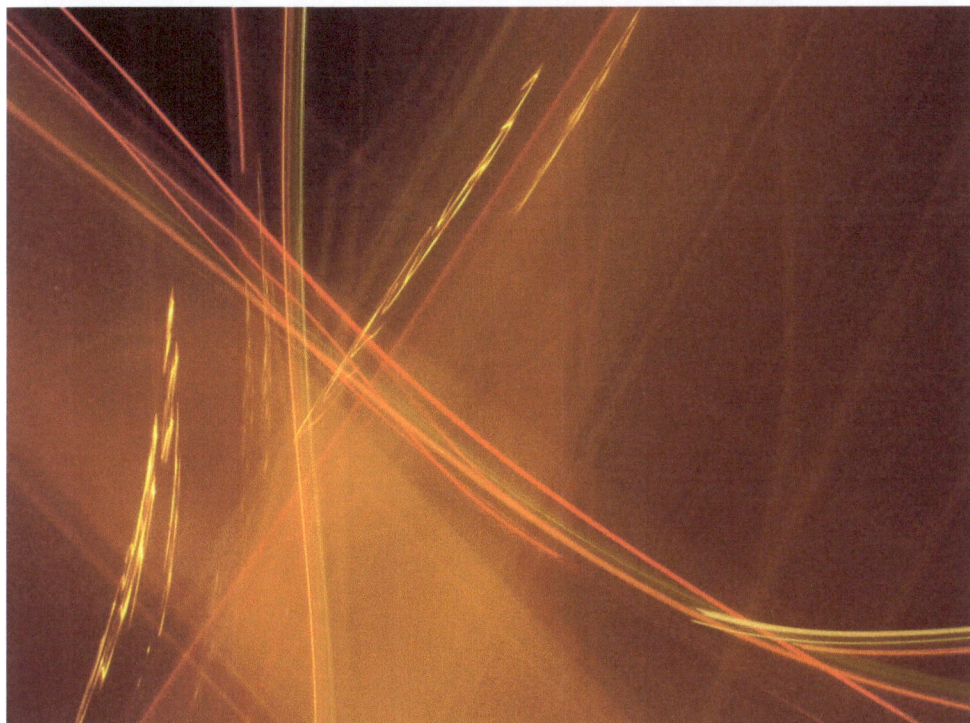

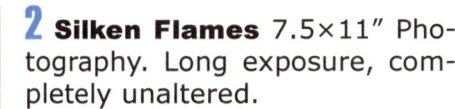 **Silken Flames** 7.5×11" Photography. Long exposure, completely unaltered.

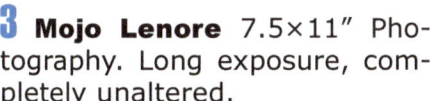 **Mojo Lenore** 7.5×11" Photography. Long exposure, completely unaltered.

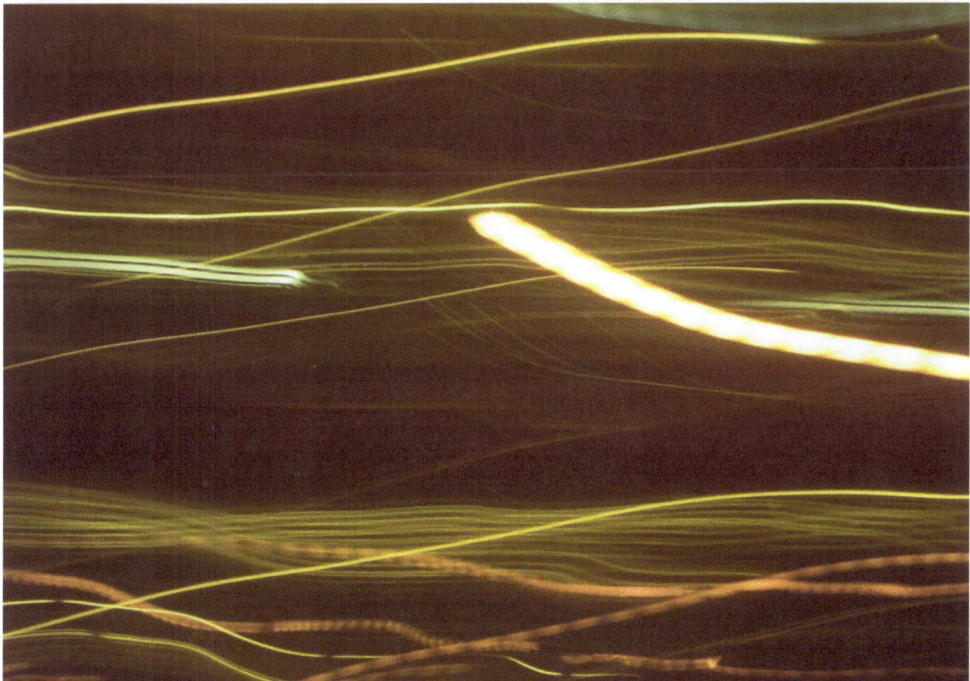

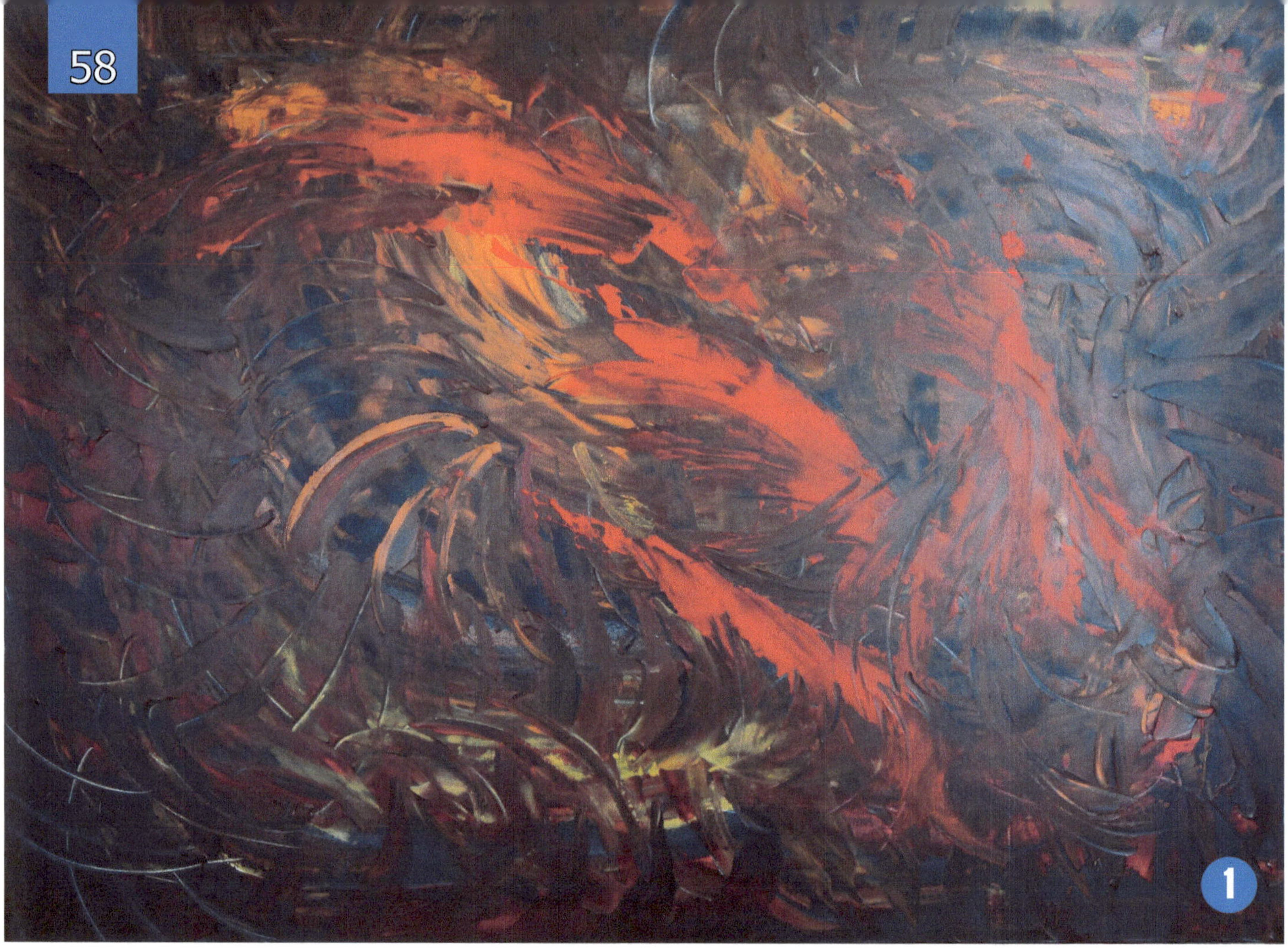

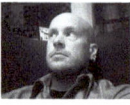

1 **Belligerent Red Dragon** 36X48" Acrylic on gallery-stretched canvas.

# D. H. McKee

**LOCATION:** Kitchener
**WEB:** Zuckerloft.com
**EMAIL:** Art@zuckerloft.com

D. H. McKee is a contemporary abstract artist and photographer. He was born in London, Ontario, went to school in Toronto, and lives in Kitchener-Waterloo. He has spent the last decade learning the artist's trade and making connections in the arts community while maintaining a career in the high-tech sector.

2 **Speed Razor** 36X48" Acrylic on gallery-stretched canvas.

3 **The Projects** 36X36" Acrylic on gallery-stretched canvas.

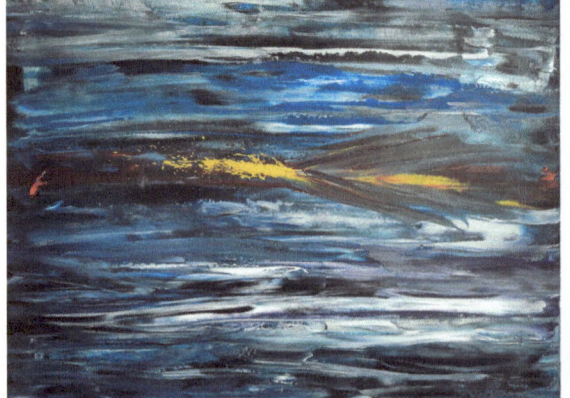

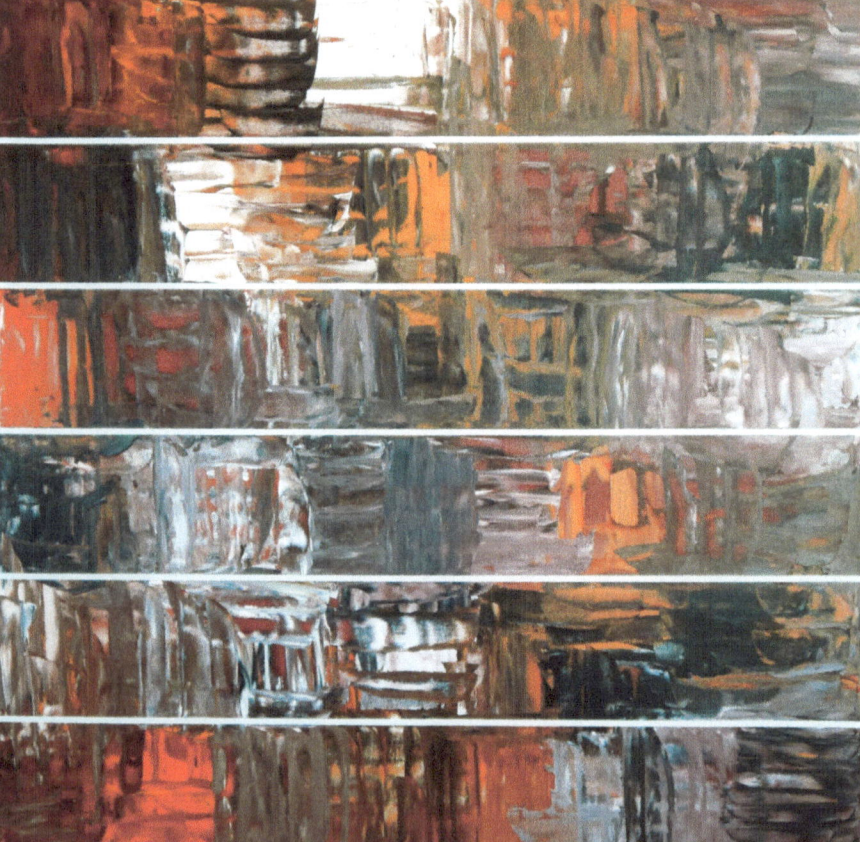

# TODD MANUEL

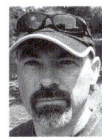

**LOCATION:** Kitchener
**WEB:** (N/A)
**EMAIL:** Tdm@rogers.com

Todd is a Kitchener area artist who moved from his native Newfoundland to Ontario in 1999. For over 20 years, Todd's creative and artistic energies have been largely utilized in the commercial art field working for various sign companies. Todd also had a mural painting business and has most recently focused on pursuing painting fulltime.

**1** **Teatime II** 14x18" Oil on canvas. 2010.

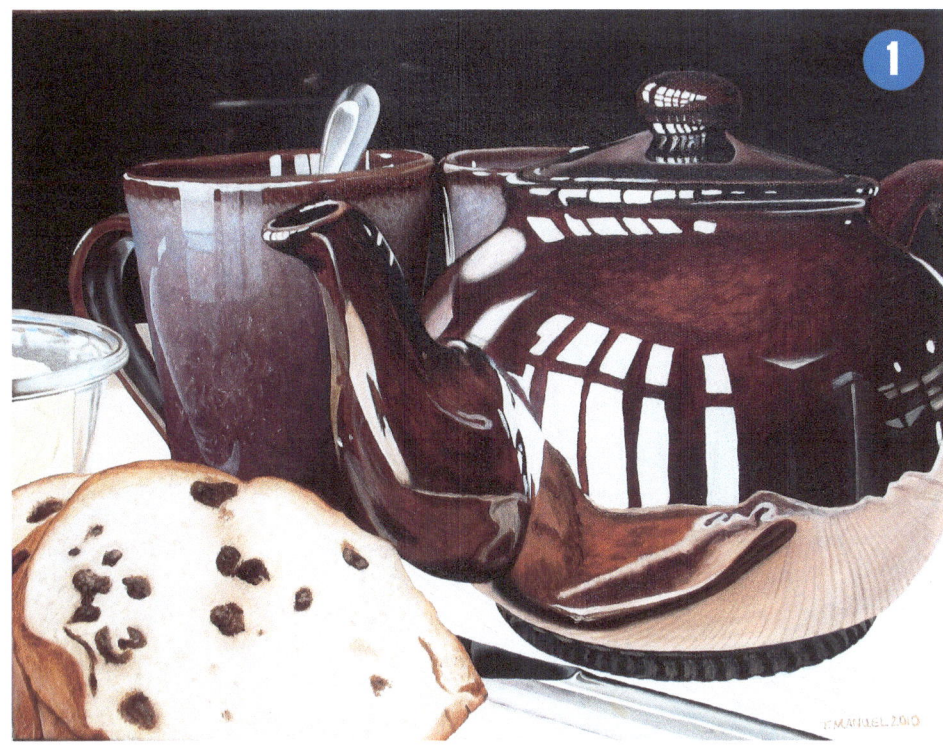

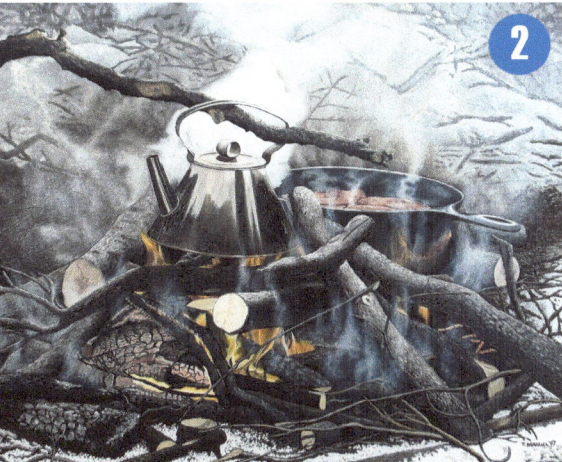

**2** **Bologna Fire** 16x20" Oil on canvas. 1997.

**3** **Jello Jars** 24x30" Oil on canvas 2011.

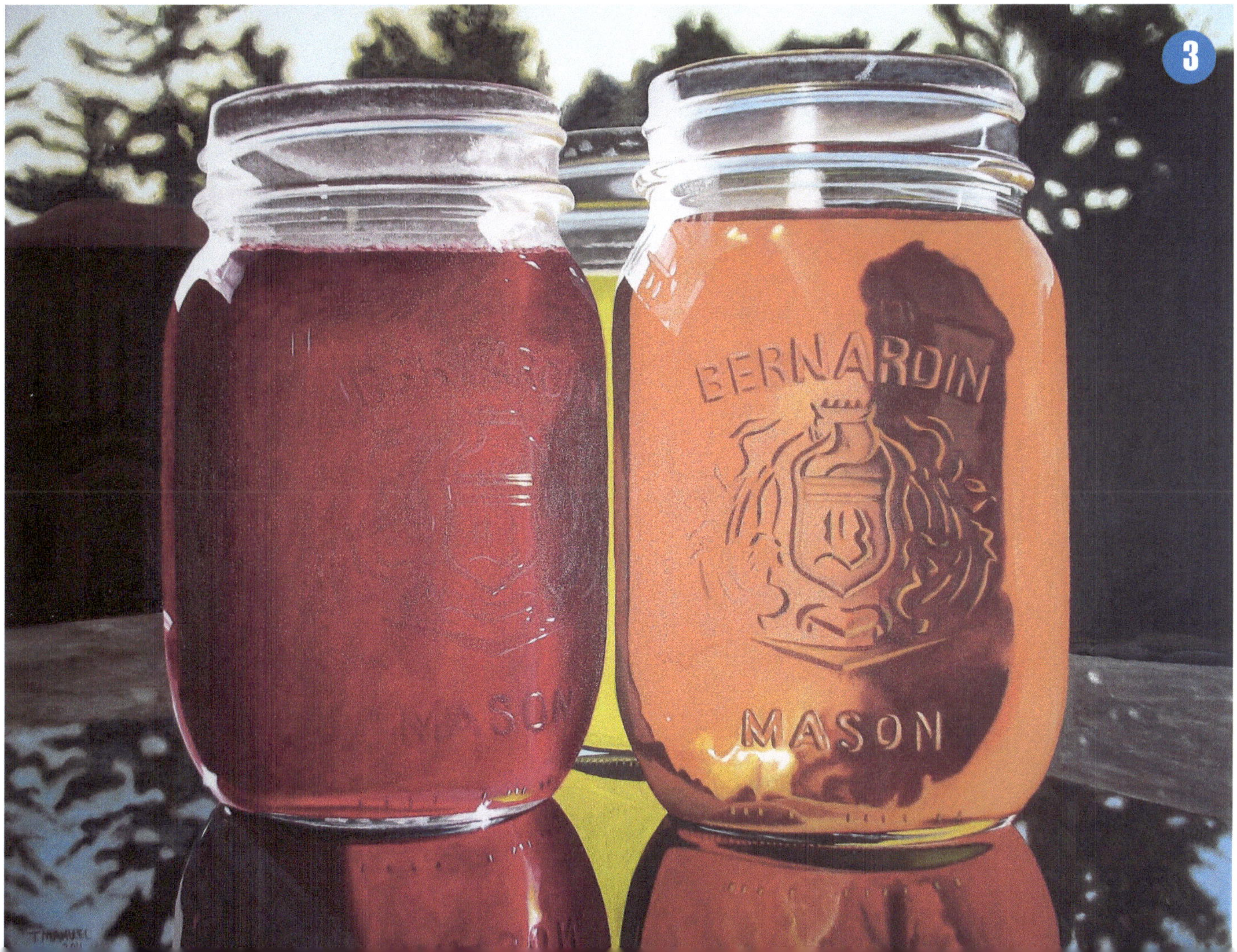

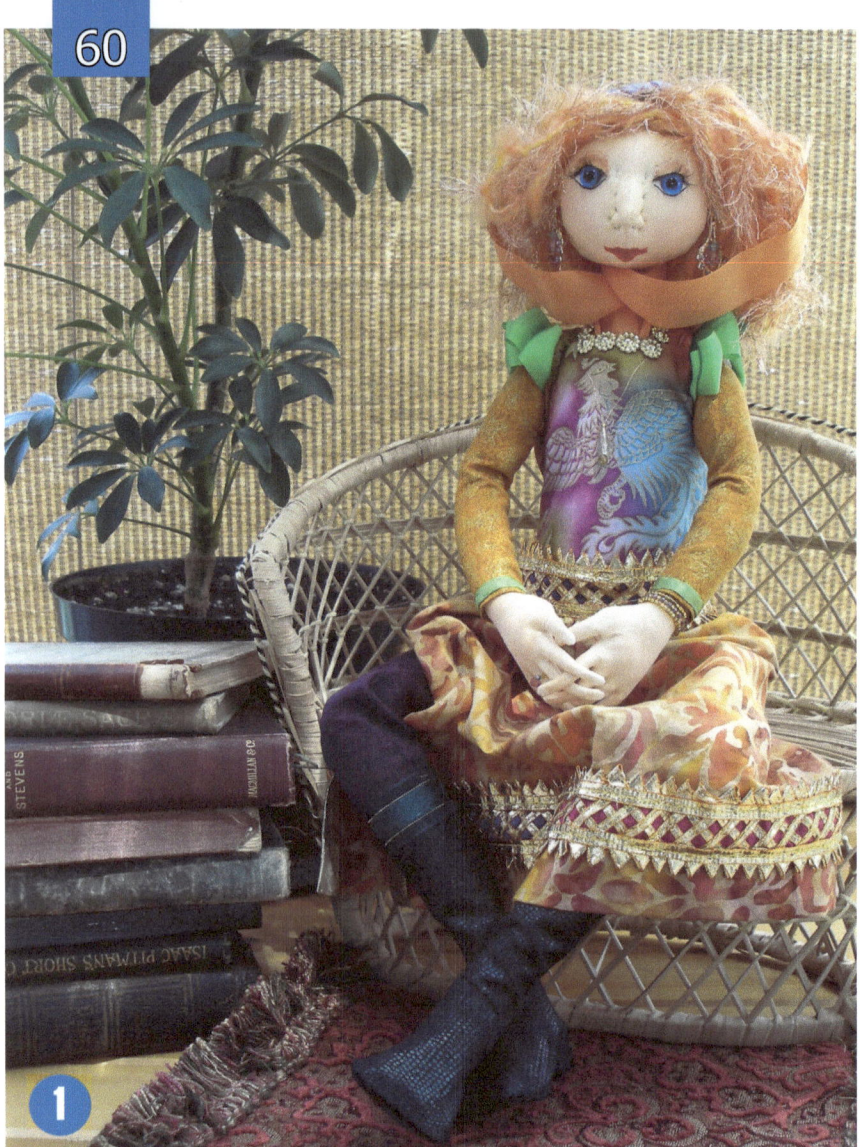

**1 Fanny Fanita** An articulated soft sculpted cloth doll. She has glass eyes and real eyelashes. She is brightly attired with soft leather boots and purple hat. Her shoulder frills and scarf are silk and she is wearing her favorite beaded earrings, bracelet and ring.

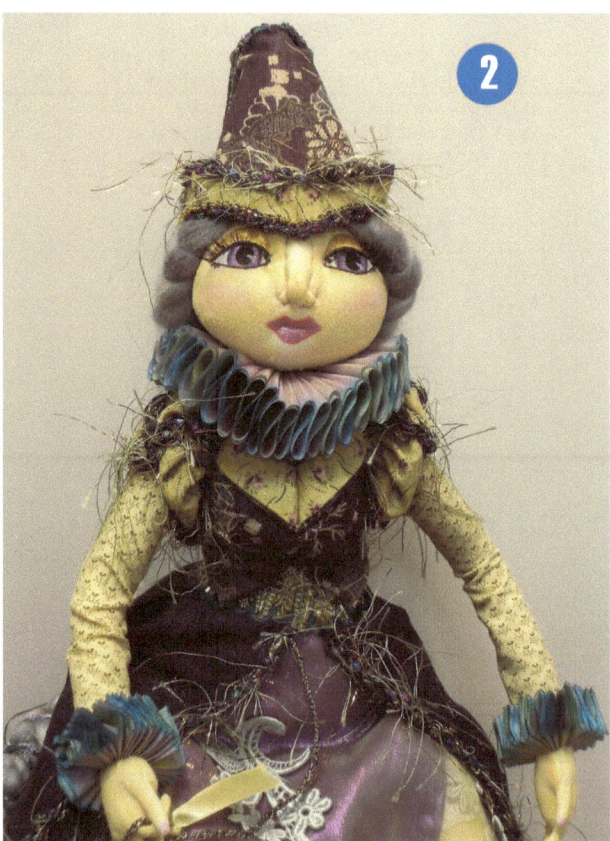

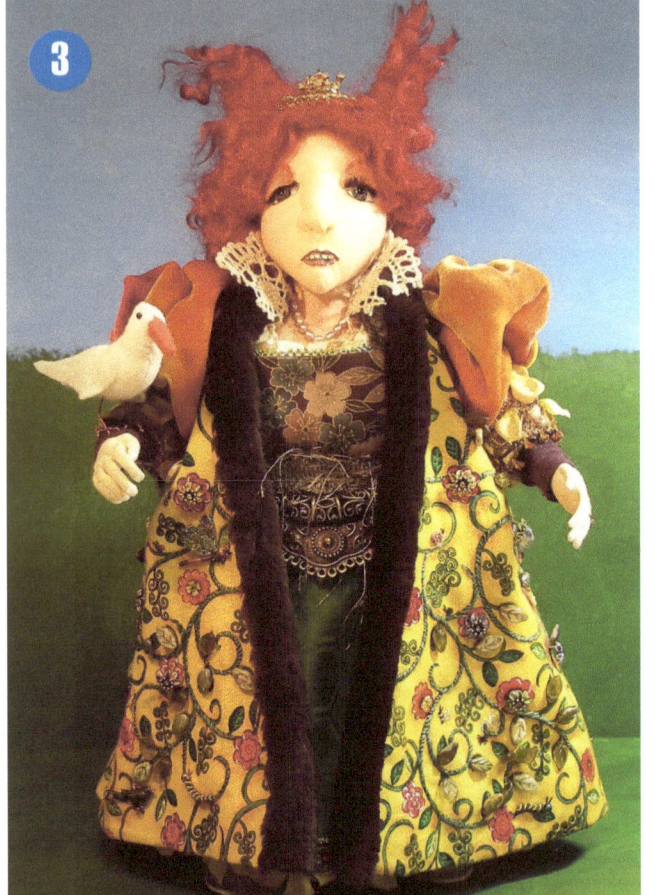

## JACQUELINE RULA

**LOCATION:** Waterloo
**WEB:** Circleworks.net
**EMAIL:** Jax@circleworks.net

 An Award Winning Doll Artist Jacqueline aka Jax has been published is several magazines like Art Doll Quarterly and Doll Collector Magazine. "Doll Art is a multi-media art form that can be expressed in many ways but, for me, cloth is always at the core."

**2 Esmina** An articulated doll with moveable arms and legs and bendable fingers. She is a soft sculpted cloth doll inspired by the Victorian Style. Her ruff and cuffs are silk ribbon, her outfit and hat are Japanese cotton and her hair is silk roving.

**3 Gertrude Groan Countess of Gormenghast** A soft sculpted cloth doll inspired by a character from a trilogy of books by Mervin Peake; Titus Groan, Gormenghast and Titus Alone. Gertrude is seen here with her good friend Master Chalk, a white Roark. Her coat is covered in stump embroidery and beaded insects and trimmed in "fur" with velvet sleeve puffs. Her skirt is silk and hemmed with flower petals and her hair is felted wool roving.

# JOHN RULA

**LOCATION:** Waterloo
**WEB:** Circleworks.net
**EMAIL:** Rula@circleworks.net

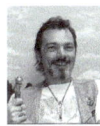

John Rula is a multi-faceted artist who paints, makes assemblages and works in jewellery design. "Through my work I strive to create a sense that enlightens and inspires the viewer to imagine something fantastic and wonderful. I believe the purpose of art is to move the spirit and instill a positive experience."

**1 Landscape** 40x30" Acrylic on Canvas. From the "Cubemorphic" series. 2007.

**2 Spring Blizzard Sigh** 36x48" Acrylic on Canvas. From the "Out of the Dark" series. 2011.

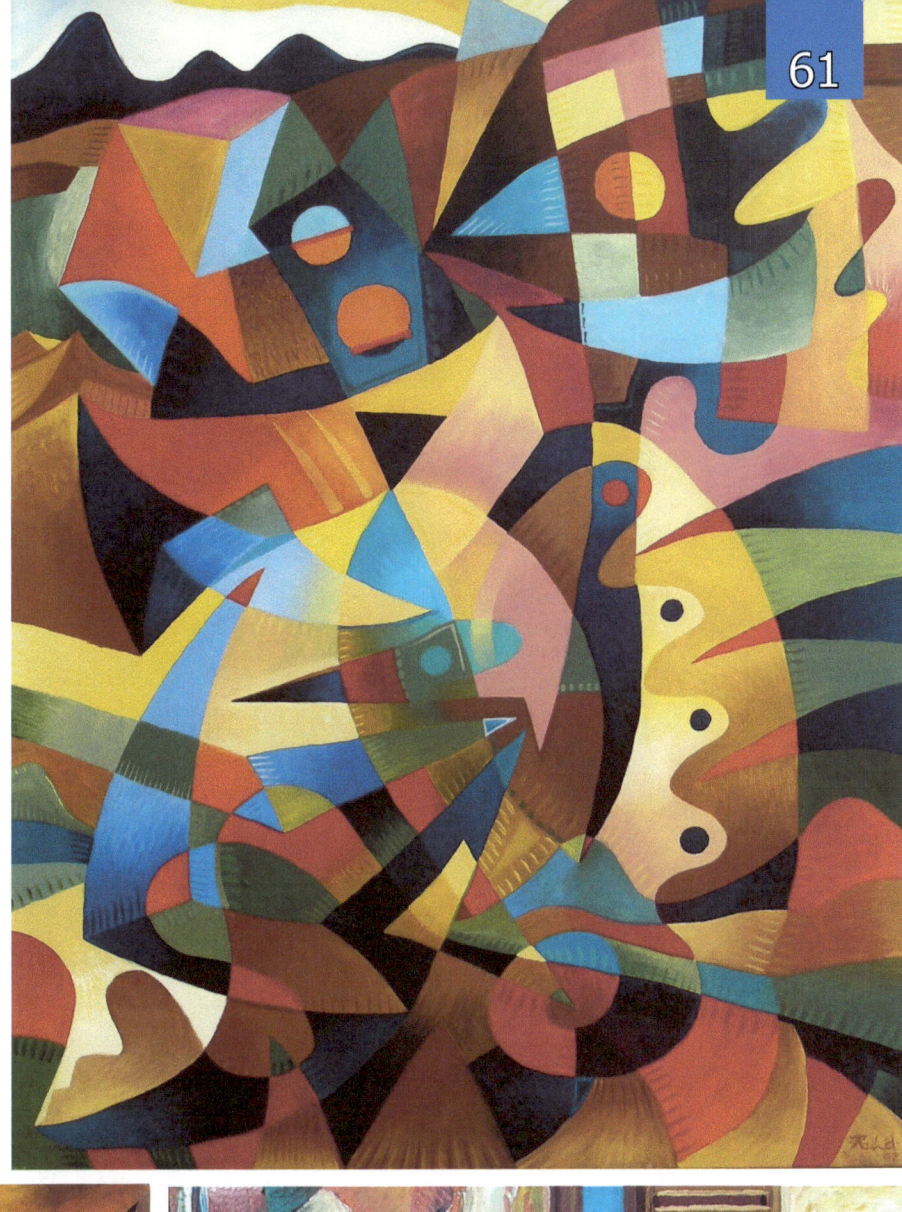

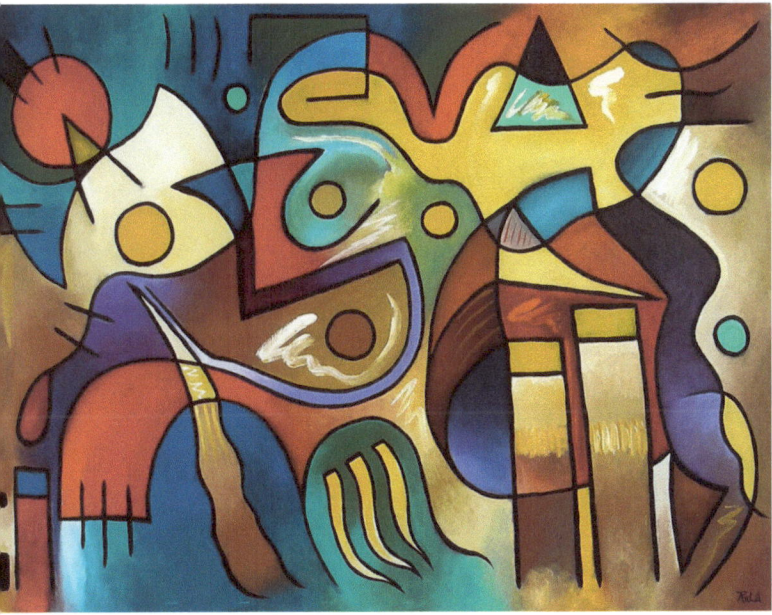

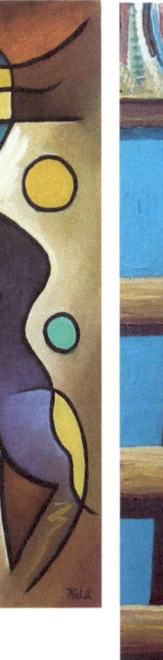

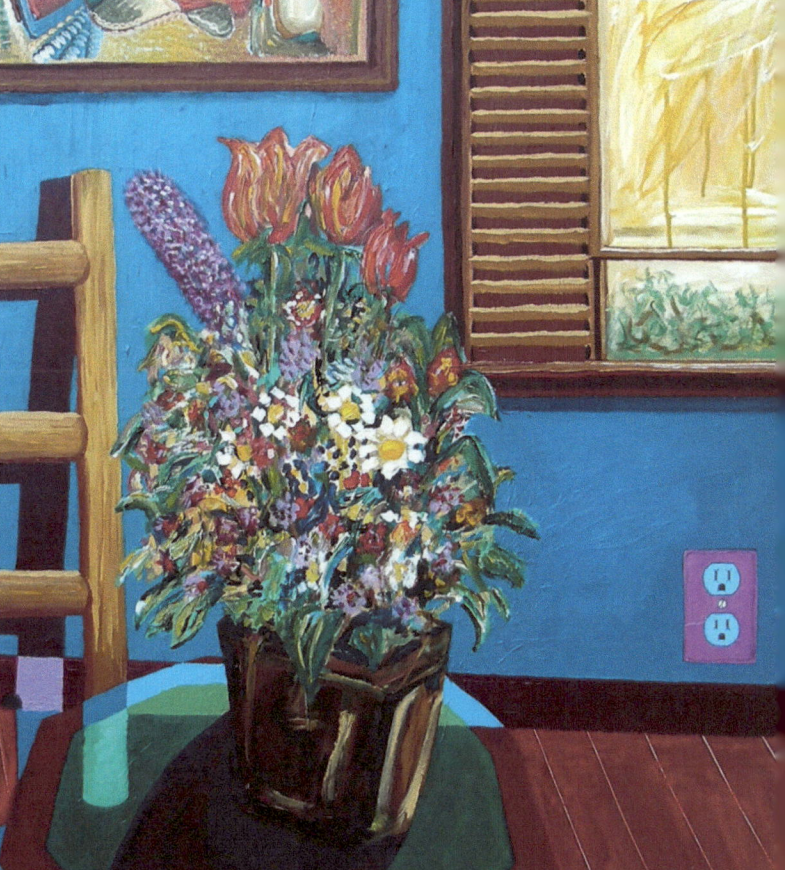

**3 Still Life with Flowers** 36x30" Acrylic on Canvas. From the "Flower Extravaganza" series. 2009.

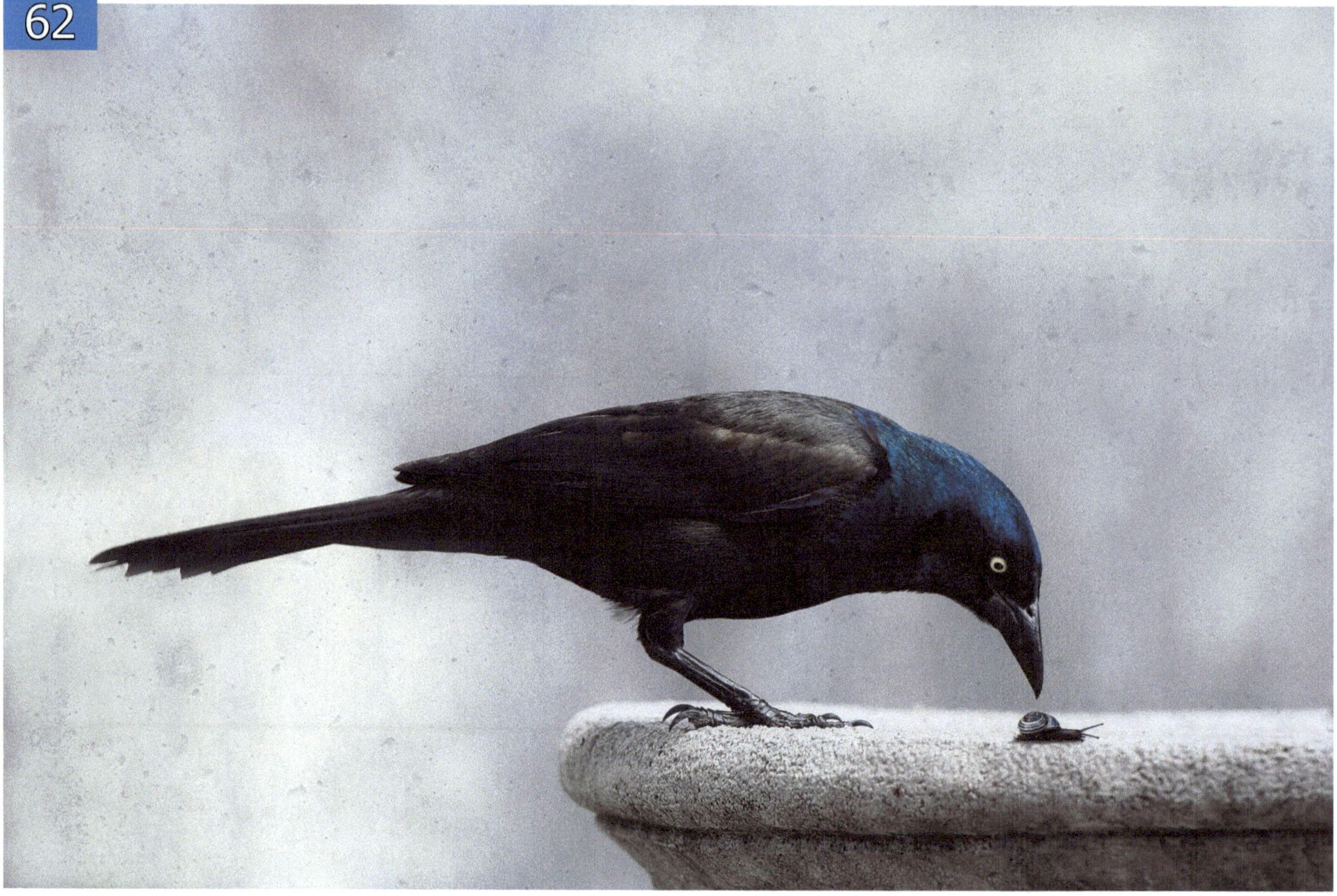

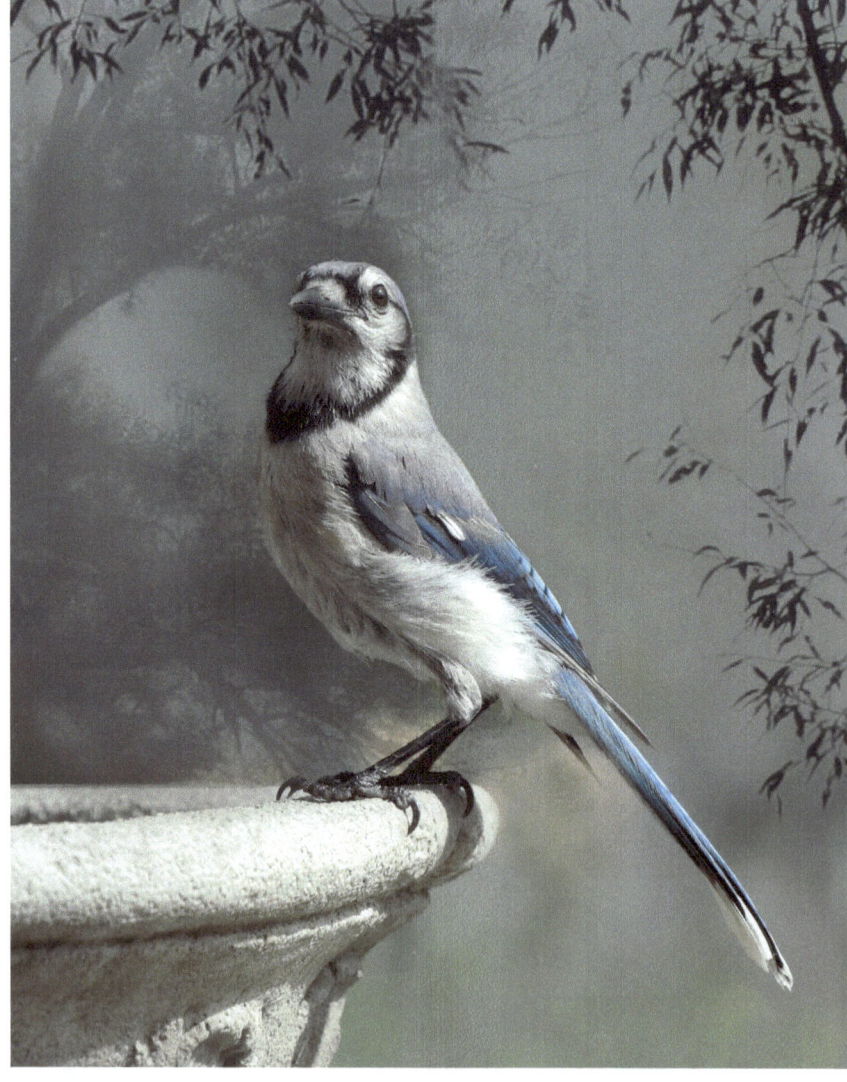

1 **Seafood Delight** Photo.

2 **Dance of the Migration** Photo.

3 **Wings in My Dreams** Photo.

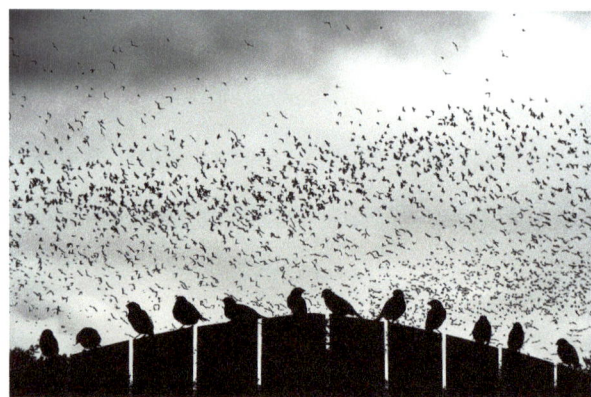

# JAN PILLER

**LOCATION:** Plattsville
**WEB:** Jan-Piller.ArtistWebsites.com
**EMAIL:** ppiller@rogers.com

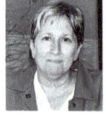 She calls herself a Hobby Photographer, but Jan has twice seen her work printed in juried publications, has a large canvas hanging in the Australian Parliament and is privileged to name Massachusetts Institute of Technology (Visual Arts Program) as one of the many organizations that have purchased her art. While she's honored at this interest in her work, her greatest goal is that someday she will be the kind of person her dog thinks she is.

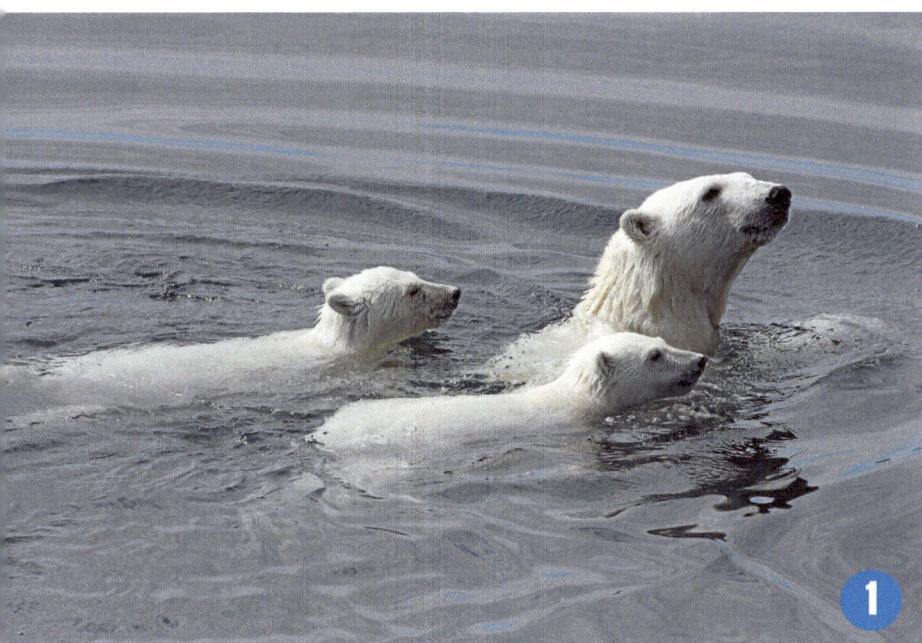

1

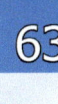

2

## JEAN WELLER

**LOCATION:** Waterloo
**WEB:**
Uptowngallerywaterloo.com/artists/JWeller/Main.html
**EMAIL:** JandJ.weller@sympatico.ca

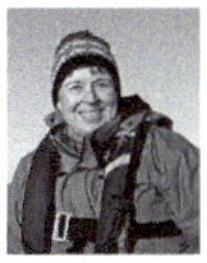

Jean's lifelong interest in photography began in childhood with a Kodak Brownie camera, and continued as she honed her photography skills. In later years she has been fortunate to combine her love of photography with her love of travel. Jean has traveled to many countries – one of her travel highlights includes following the Silk Road from China to Central Asia and Iran. She has also visited Africa, India, Nepal, South East Asia, South America, New Zealand, Iceland and Antarctica. From 2005 to 2010, Jean has spent summers in the Canadian Arctic and has been guest photographer for Cruise North Expeditions for 4 of those years. In this capacity she has photographed Arctic animals, people and northern landscapes. The resulting pictures have been purchased by tour companies and published in their brochures. Jean is an accredited Toronto Photography Judge and has judged at photographic competitions. Jean's framed prints and cards are for sale at the Uptown Gallery, Waterloo Town Square.

**1** Swimming Bears     **2** Chinstrap Penguin     **3** Iceberg In The High Arctic     Photographs

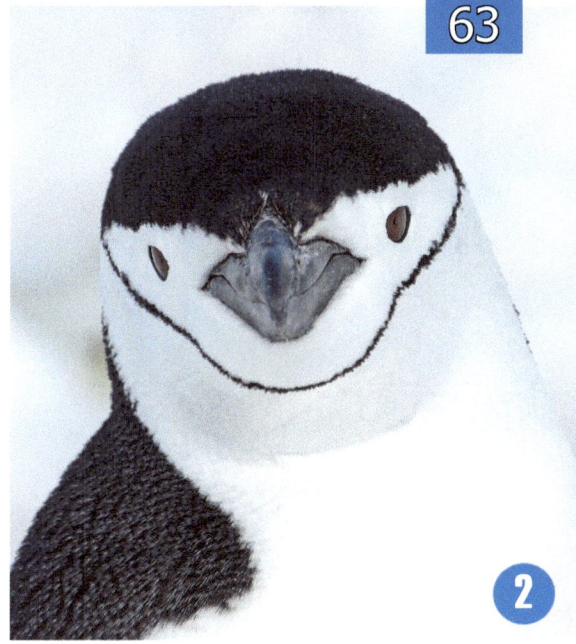

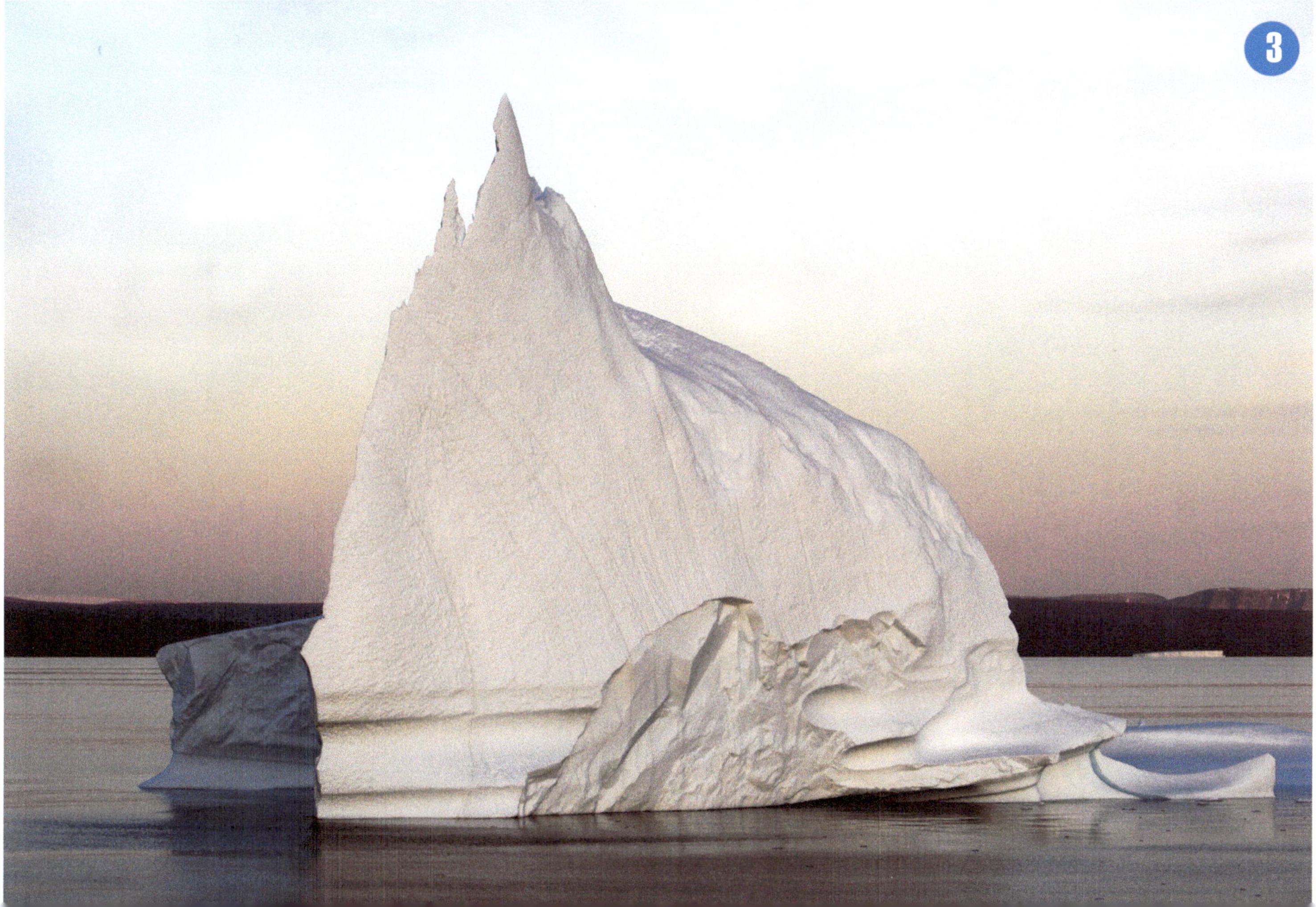

3

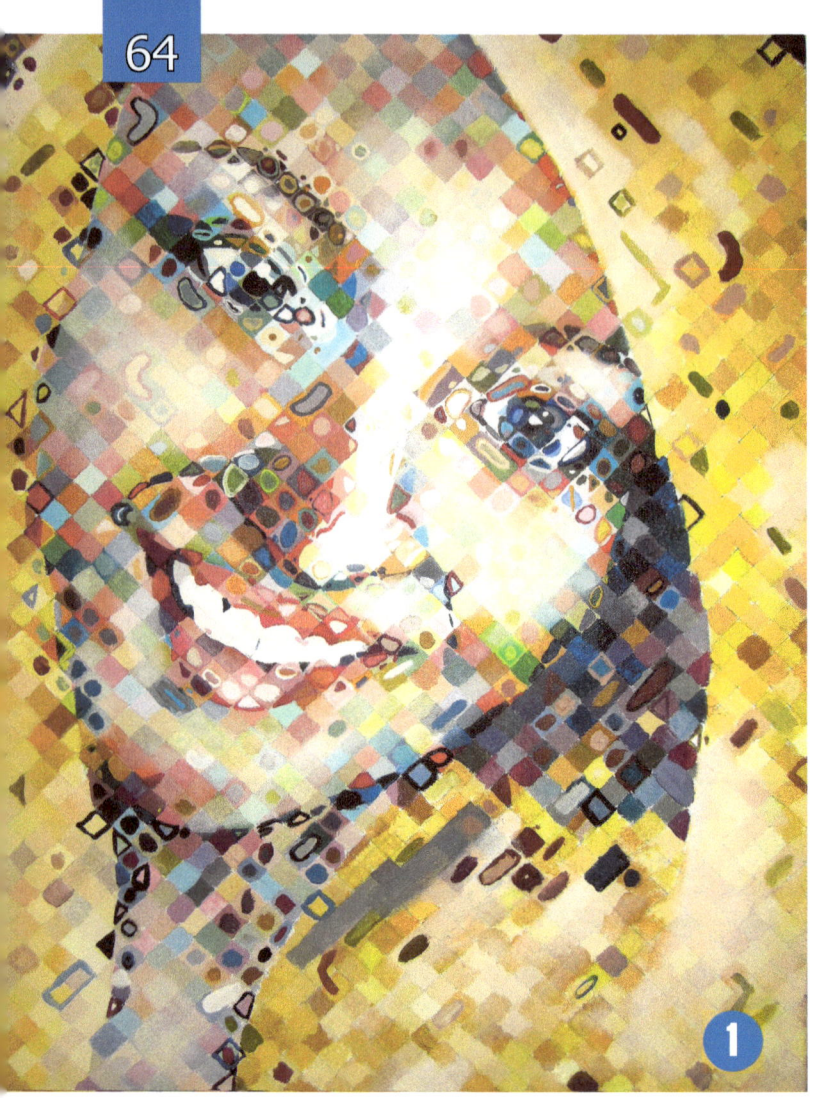

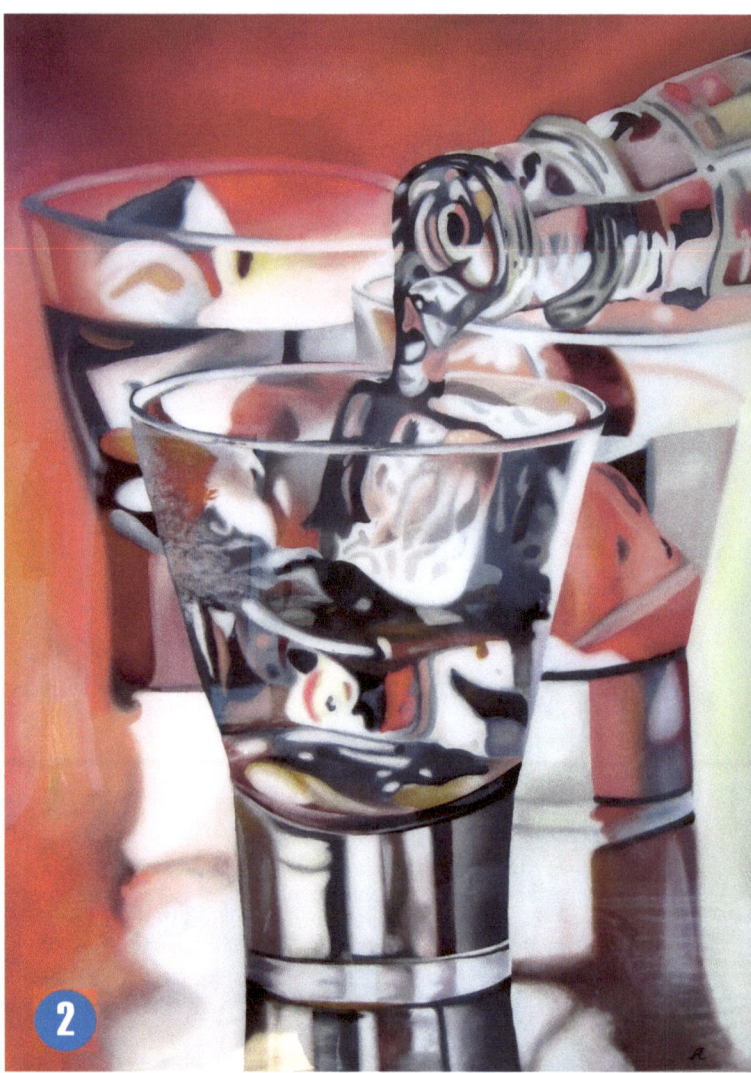

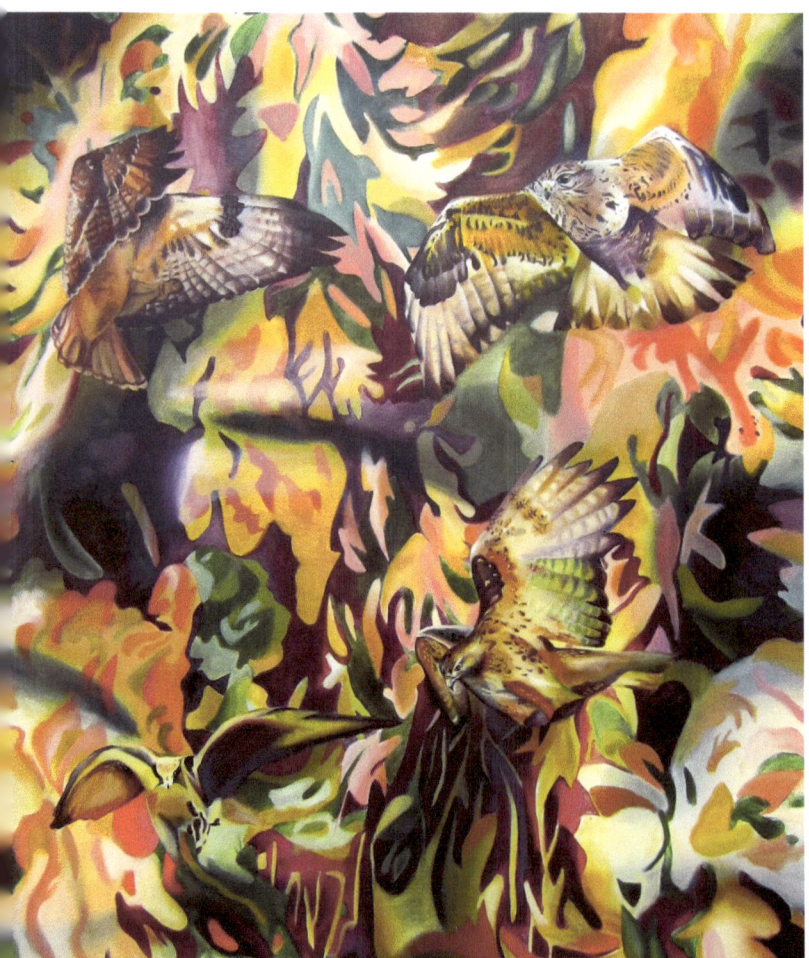

# ALISHIA ELLIS

**LOCATION:** Waterloo
**WEB:** (N/A)
**EMAIL:** Ellis.Alishia@gmail.com

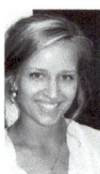

Alishia is a passionate artist with a love for paint. She is a Fine Art student studying at the University of Waterloo. Her investigations primarily deal with the totality of mental processes including the subconscious. The imagery found within Alishia's paintings are derived from her free-association writings. Her fascination with the art community has led her to exhibit her work in local galleries as well become the co-curator of the Artery Gallery.

**1 Self Portrait** 1x2' Acrylic on canvas.

**2 Shot Glass** 3x4' Acrylic on canvas with resin.

**3 Five Hawks** 4x5' Oil on canvas.

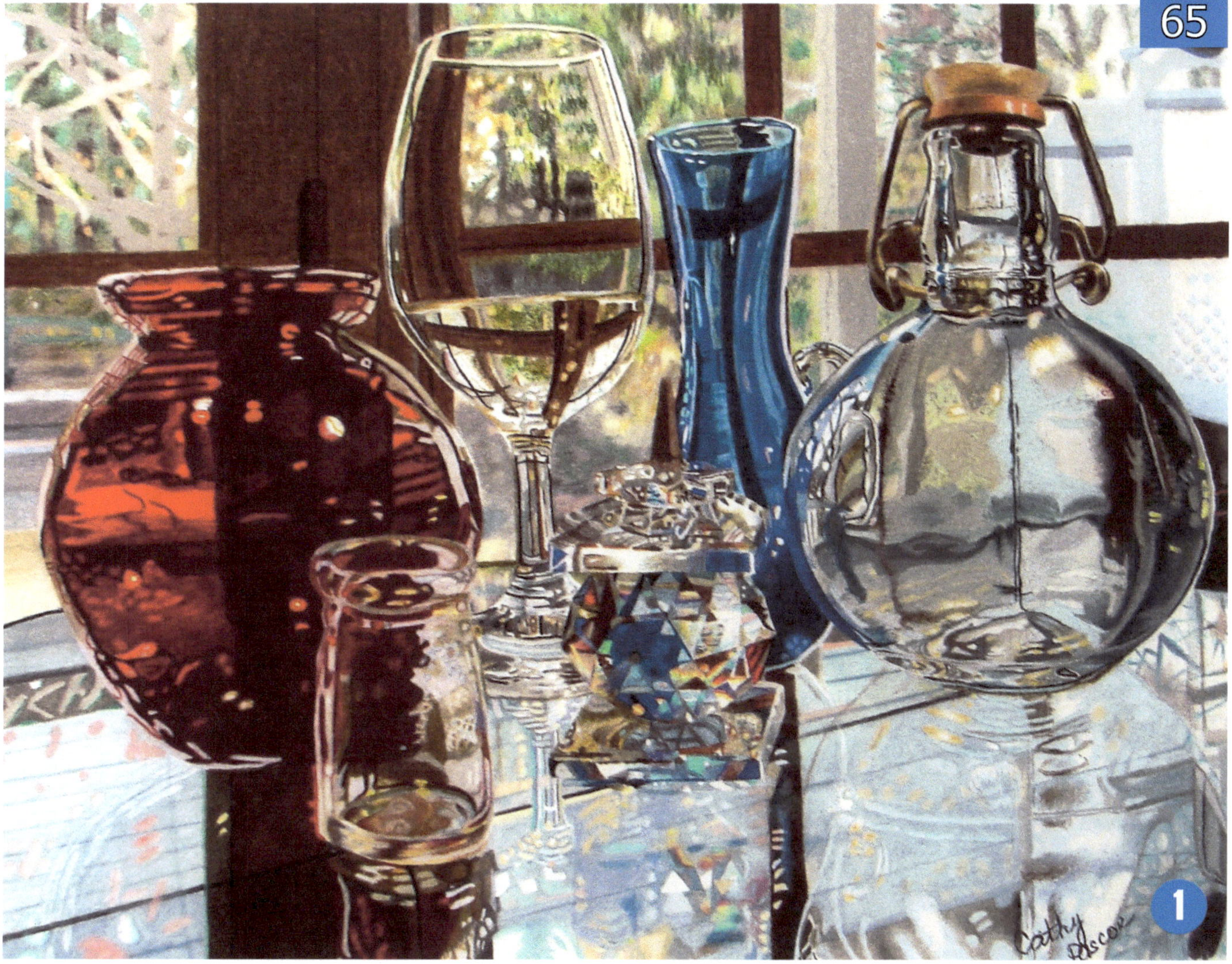

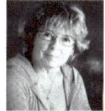

1 **Reflections and Refractions** 8x10" Coloured pencil.

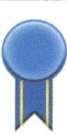

# CATHY PASCOE

**LOCATION:** Waterloo
**WEB:**
facebook.com/profile.php?id=100000636171631
**EMAIL:** cathypascoe@live.ca

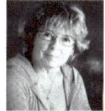

Cathy has her BA in French and German and her BEd. As a teacher, she has worked with all grades of elementary children over thirty years. As a student she studied with David Blackwood for four years to learn the process of etching using copper plates. Her art work is exhibited at Quest Art Gallery, Waterloo Uptown Gallery, Voila Institute and the Centre for International Governance Innovation. She is on staff at seven different art galleries in Ontario as an art instructor for children & adults.

2 **Safety** 8x10" Coloured pencil.   3 **Posted** 8x10" Coloured pencil.

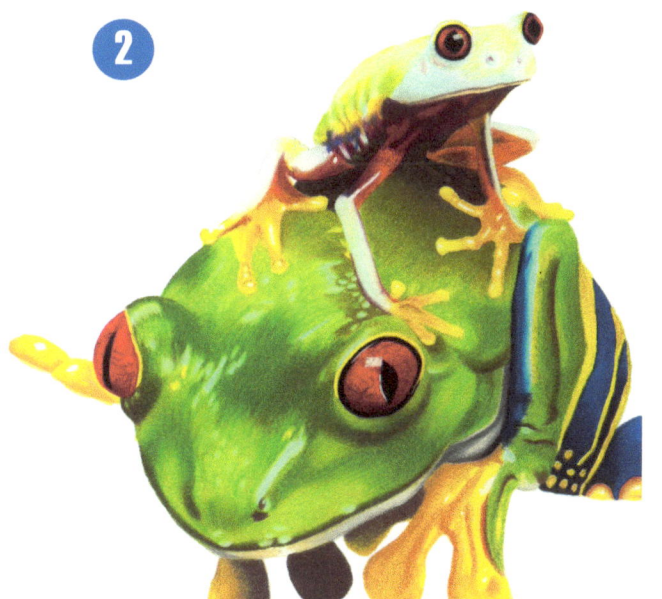

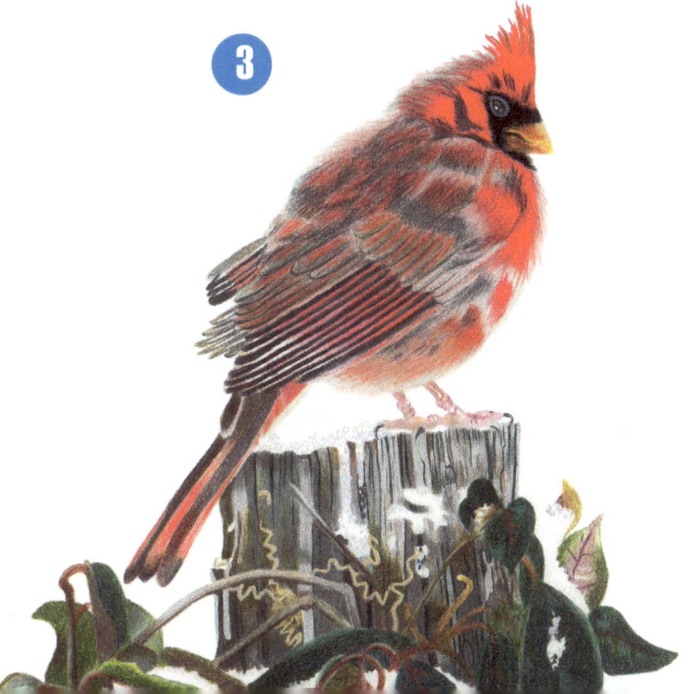

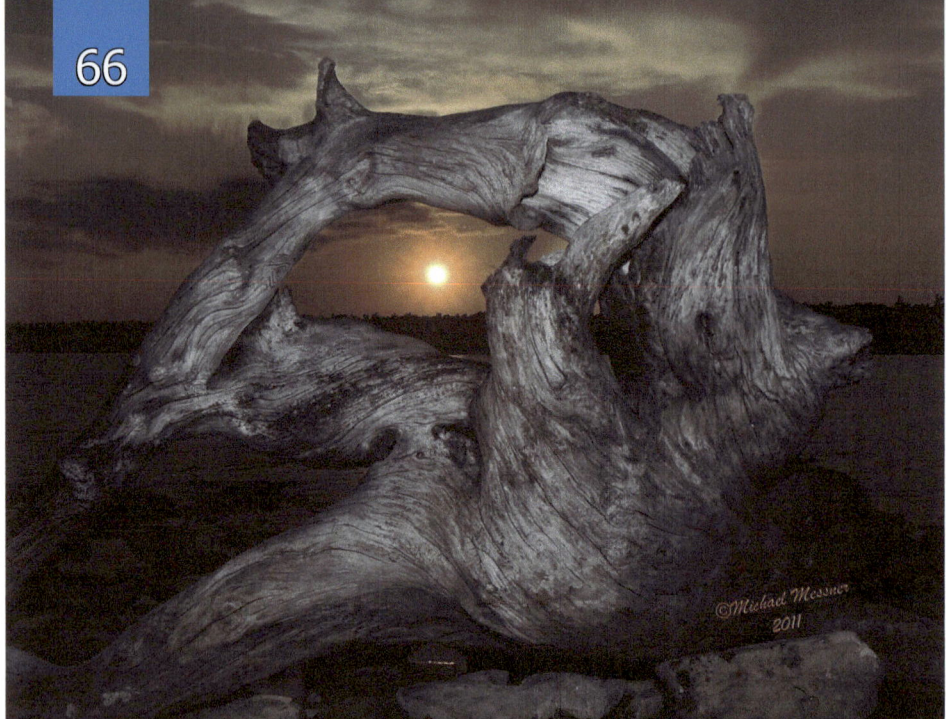

**1 Driftwood Sunset** Available on canvas or fine art photographic paper.

**2 The Shed** Photograph on canvas, also available as archival photograph for Art Decor.

# MICHAEL MESSNER

**LOCATION:** Kitchener
**WEB:** Artistic-Photo.com
**EMAIL:** Info@artistic-photo.com

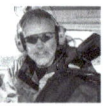 Michael Messner is a Professional Photographer based in Kitchener Ontario. He has traveled across Canada, taking beautiful photographs of our country. Magazines and calendar companies such as Hallmark Calendars regularly featured Michael's breathtaking scenic images. In recent years Messner has traveled to Ireland and the American Deserts where he has sought out and captured the most amazing mystical images for the discerning Art Collectors. Messner works with professional cameras and prints images using only archival media, pigments and acid free framing techniques.

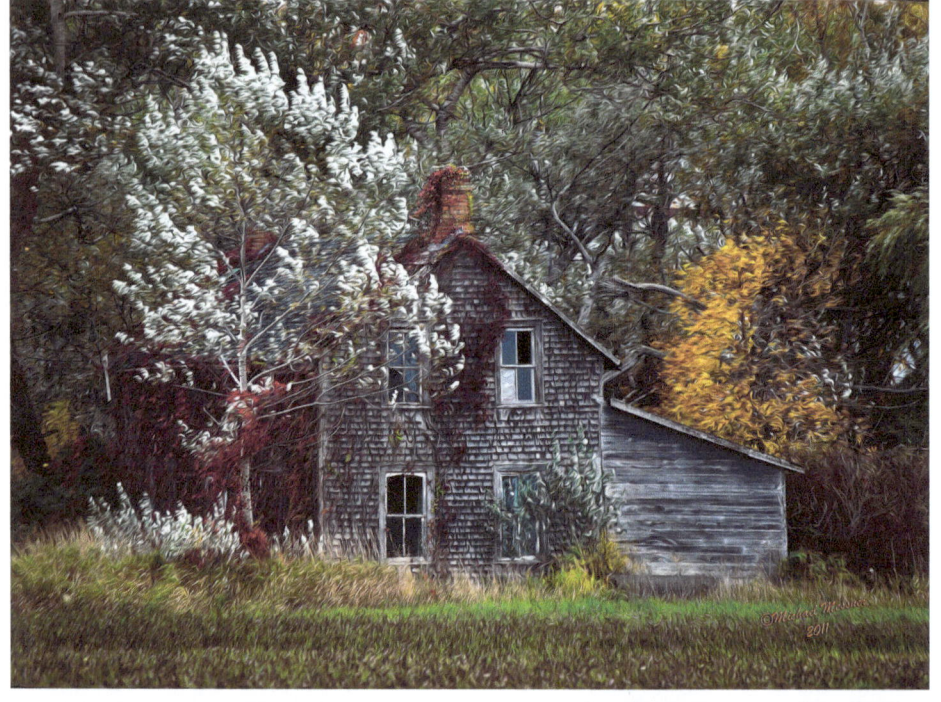

**3 The Farm** Fine Art print on archival paper.

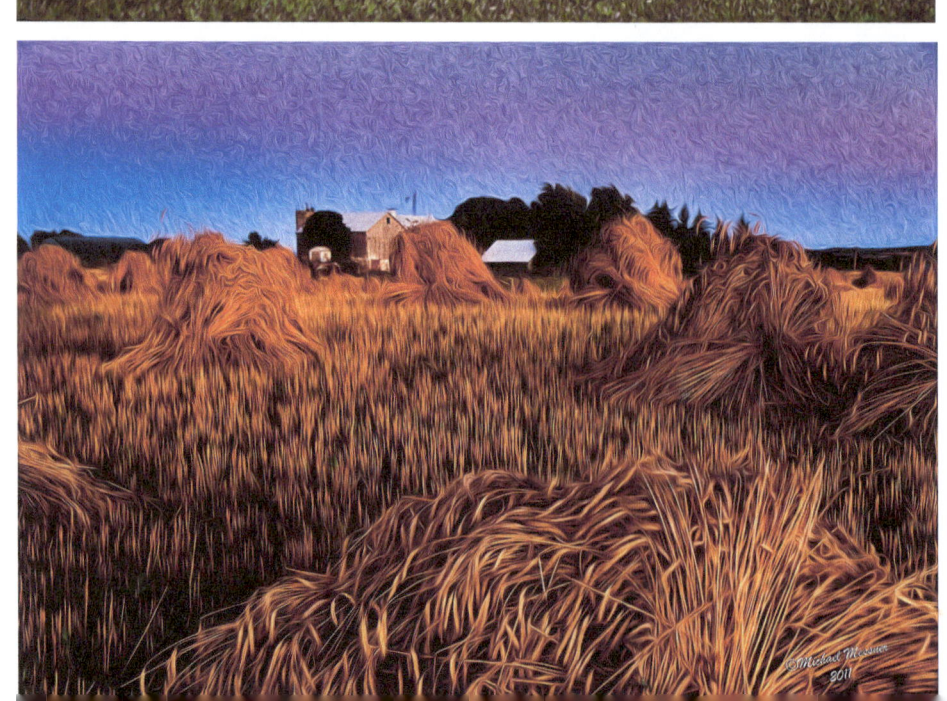

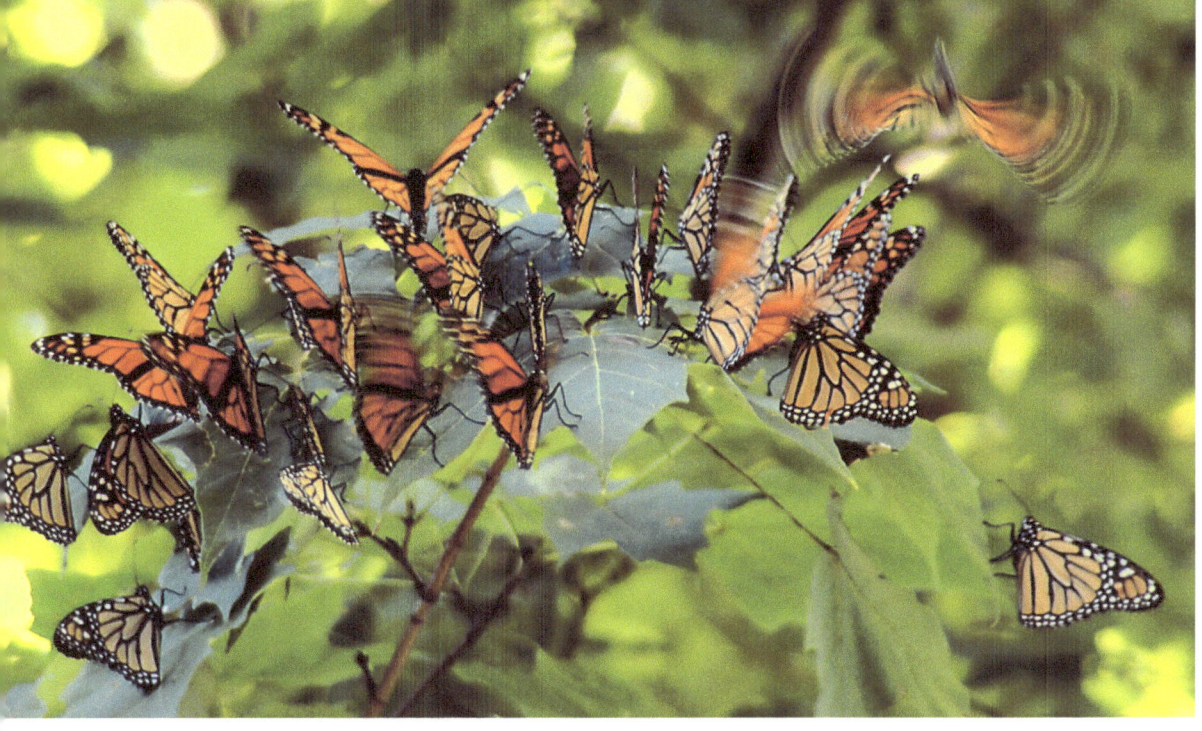

# PATRICK WEY

**LOCATION:** Petersburg
**WEB:** PatrickWey.com
**EMAIL:** imedia@patrickwey.com

Patrick Wey's 35 year photographic career was celebrated by Canada's national television network. The CBC broadcast Patrick's surreal photo-animated study of a Cree ceremonial leader, "Urban Elder". This was followed by the airing of their documentary profile of Patrick's career, entitled, "A Path of His Own". Patrick Wey is internationally regarded as a fine art photographer. His work extends into commercial areas, including documentary, industrial and editorial photography. He is also a Video Producer of both commercial & artistic films

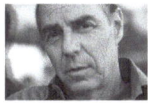

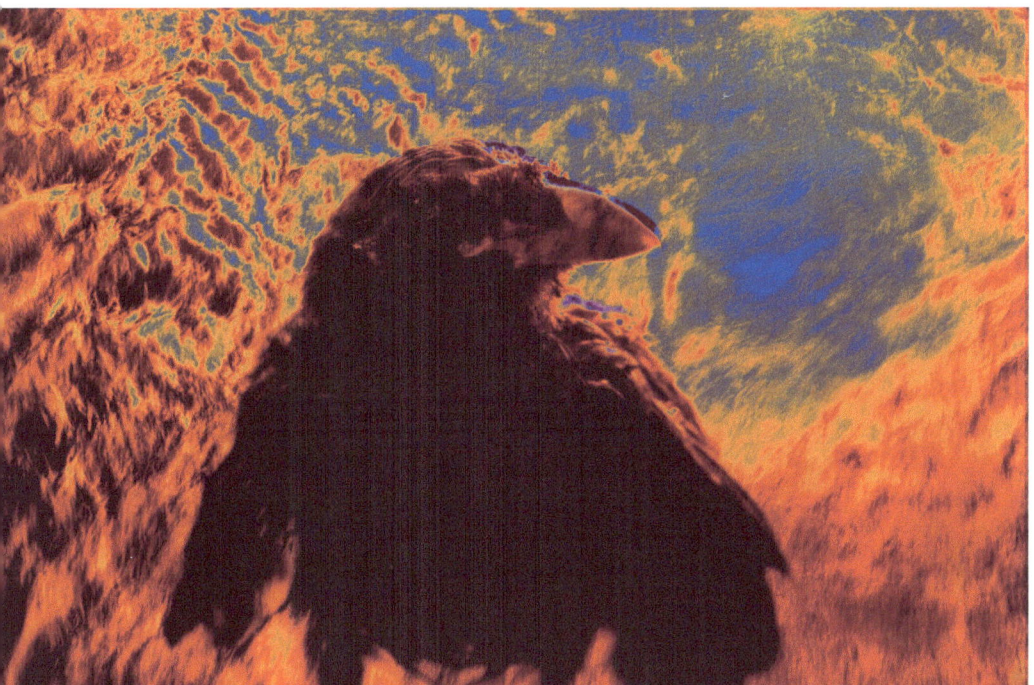

**1 Monarchs On Route Heading South** Photograph Slightly Manipulated.

**2 Rosseta in Dreamtime** Photograph Manipulated.

**3 Eve and Her Apples** Photograph Manipulated.

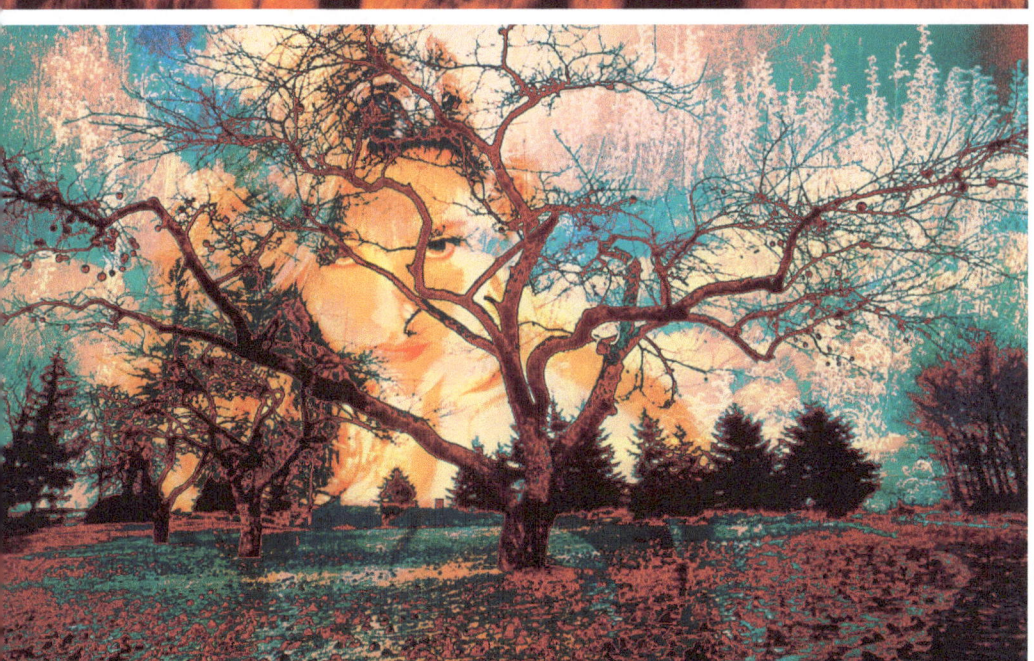

68

# RICHARD ELSWORTHY

**LOCATION:** Erbsville
**WEB:** (N/A)
**EMAIL:** RichardElsworthy@bellnet.ca

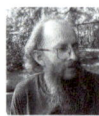

I almost grew up somwhere else living in a number of places in Canada till going to highschool in Galt and then of to the U of W for Math and Physics ending with a BSc which enabled me to do woodworking and have many other interests that are rewarding in a non-monetary way.

**1 Triceratops** Cherrywood cut side grain. Waterbase ink on plain paper.

**2 Stegosaurus** Cherrywood cut side grain. Waterbase ink on plain paper.

**3 Trex** Cherrywood cut side grain (above) Waterbase ink on plain paper (below).

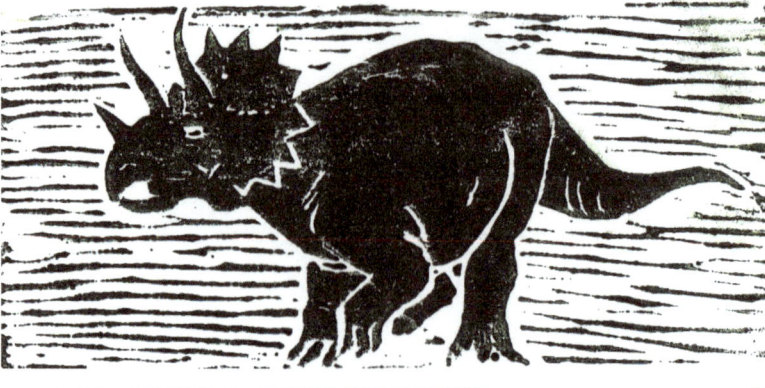

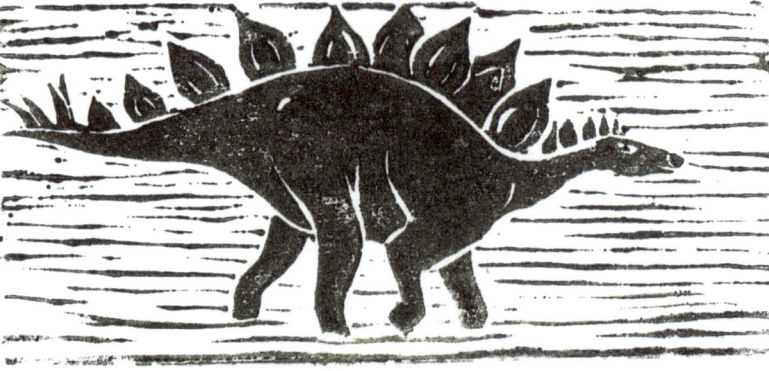

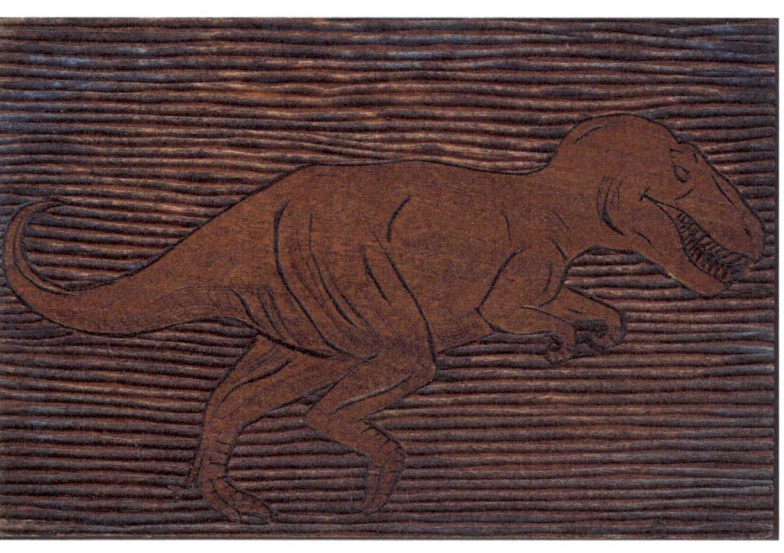

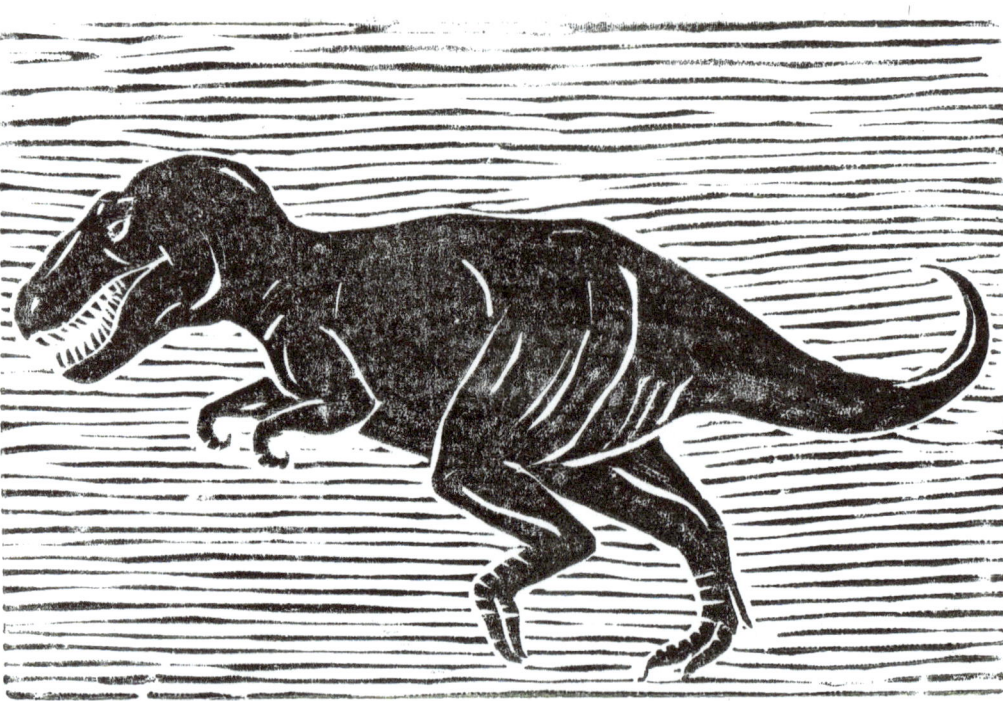

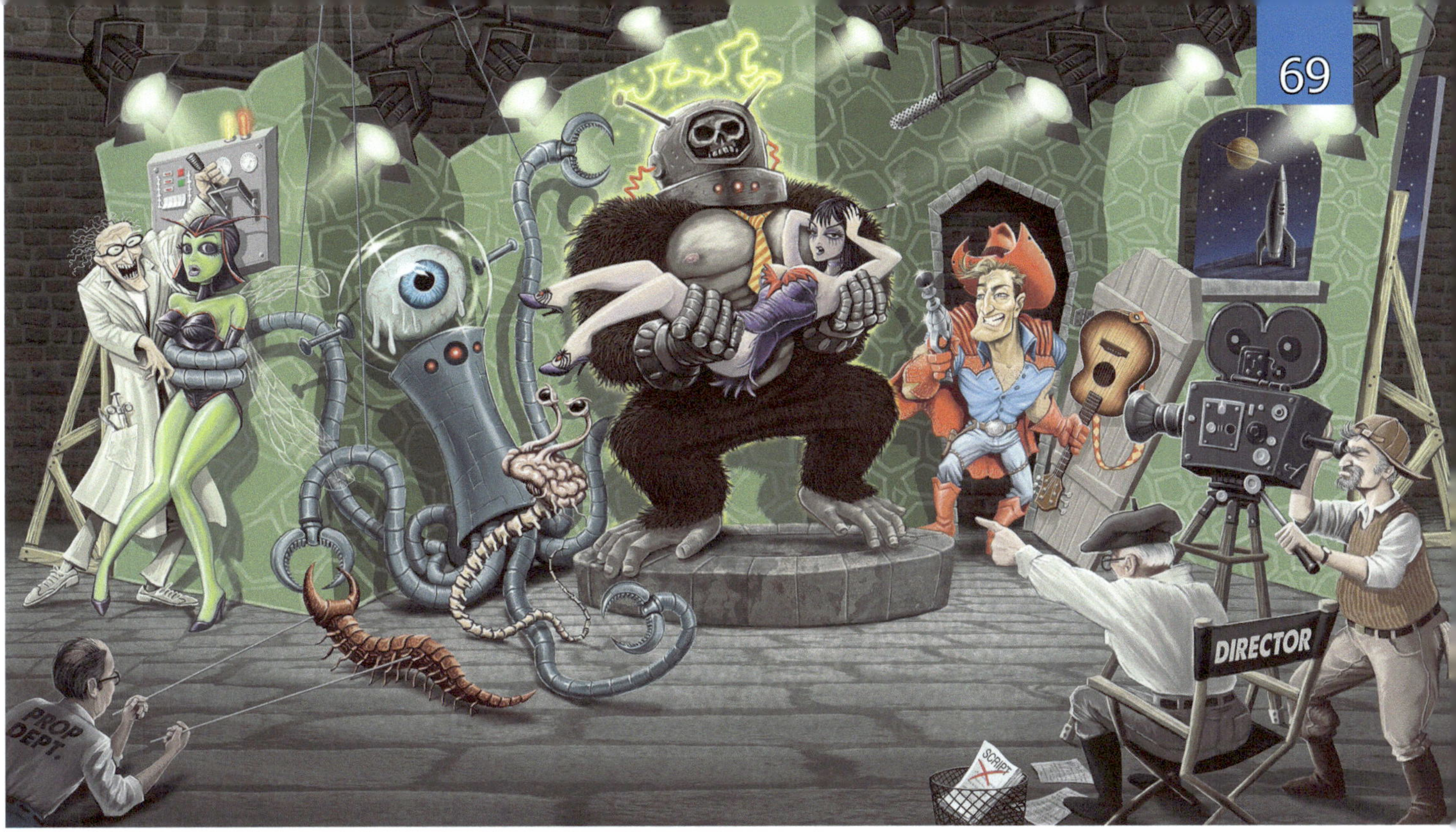

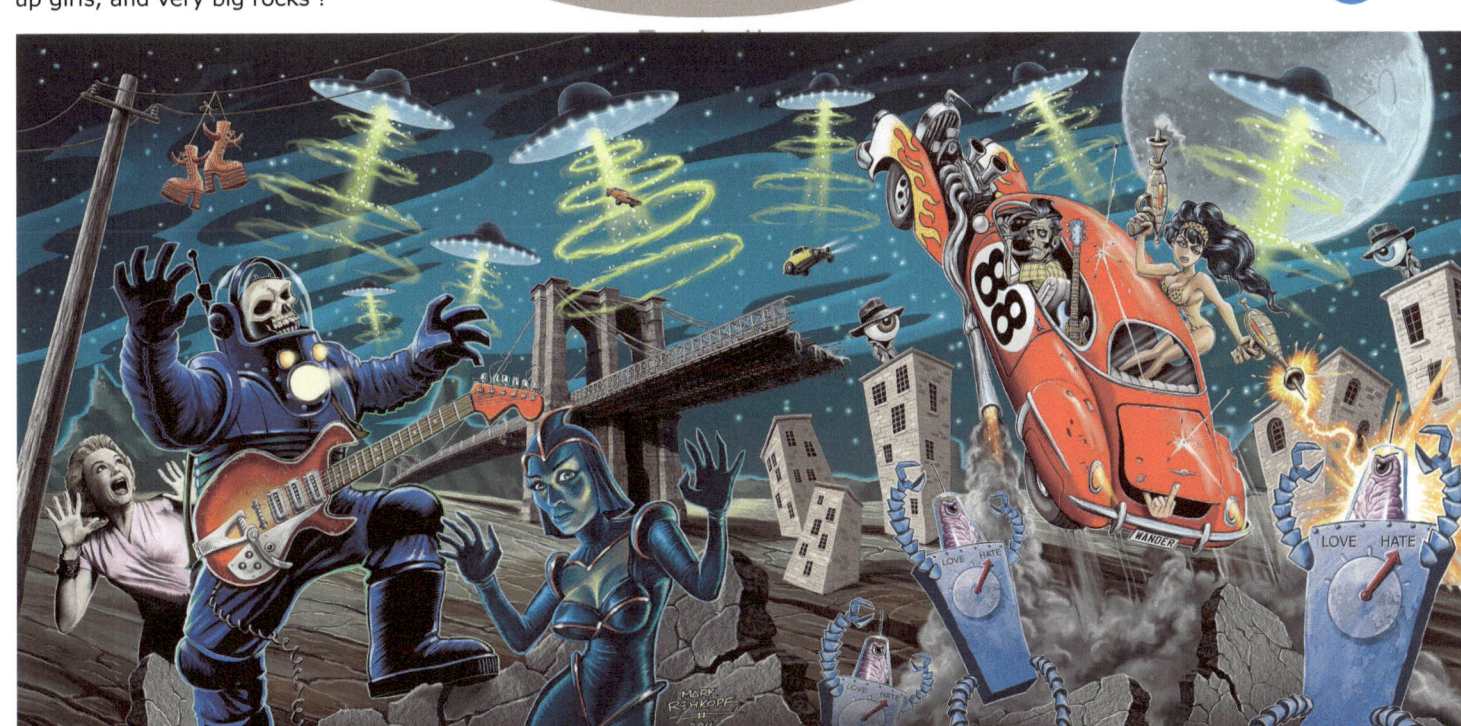

# Mark Rehkopf

**LOCATION:** St. Jacobs
**WEB:** AdventureVisual.com
**EMAIL:** Mark@adventurevisual.com

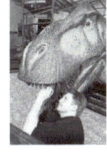

Mark Rehkopf is a diverse freelance artist with over twenty years experience. He works in realism, abstract, comic and cartoon, and all the various stages in between. He as spent the last ten years sculpting life-sized dinosaur exhibits for natural history museums worldwide. Today he concentrates on painting and illustrating for public companies and private collectors. Mark has a penchant for painting wildlife, retro pop art, science-fiction, fantasy, dinosaurs, pin-up girls, and very big rocks !

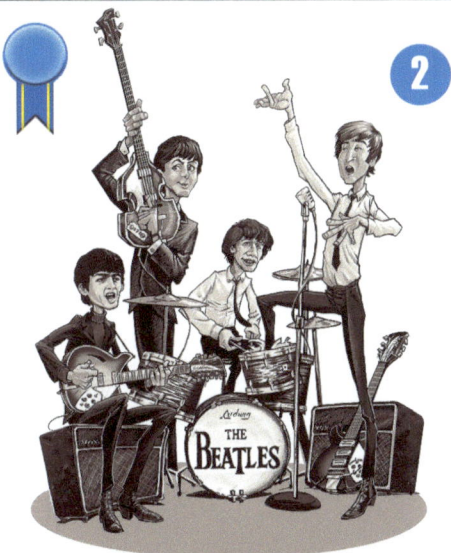

**1** **B Movie Action** Digital.

**2** **Tooned Up** Digital.

**3** **Public Display of Infection** Digital.

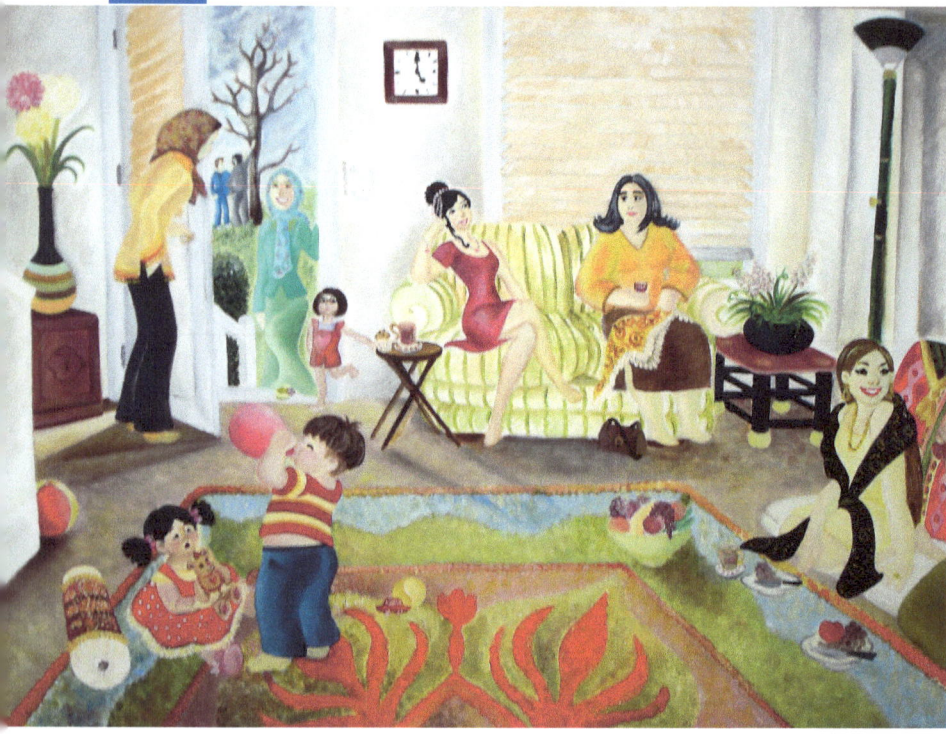

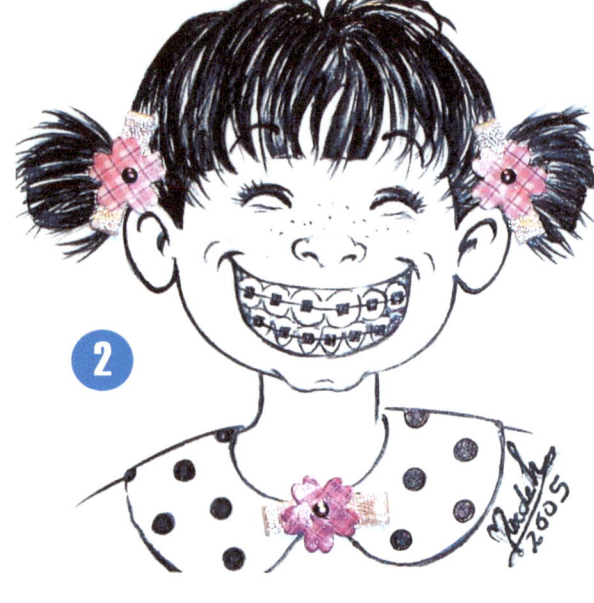

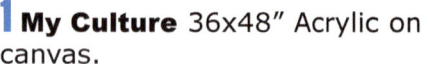

**1** **My Culture** 36x48" Acrylic on canvas.

**2** **Big Smile!** 3x3" Pen sketch.

**3** **Untitled** 36x48" Acrylic on canvas.

# MAEDEH ASHRAFIZADEH

**LOCATION:** Waterloo
**WEB:** Maedeh.ca
**EMAIL:** Email.maedeh@gmail.com

Maedeh is a freelance artist with a passion for animation and cartooning. She has a degree in Fine Arts from the University of Waterloo and has taken some Digital Imaging courses at Conestoga College as well. Other than drawing comics and illustrating for children's books, Maedeh also enjoys painting and craft making. She finds graphic design an interesting program to combine with her hand-made artworks.

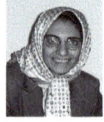

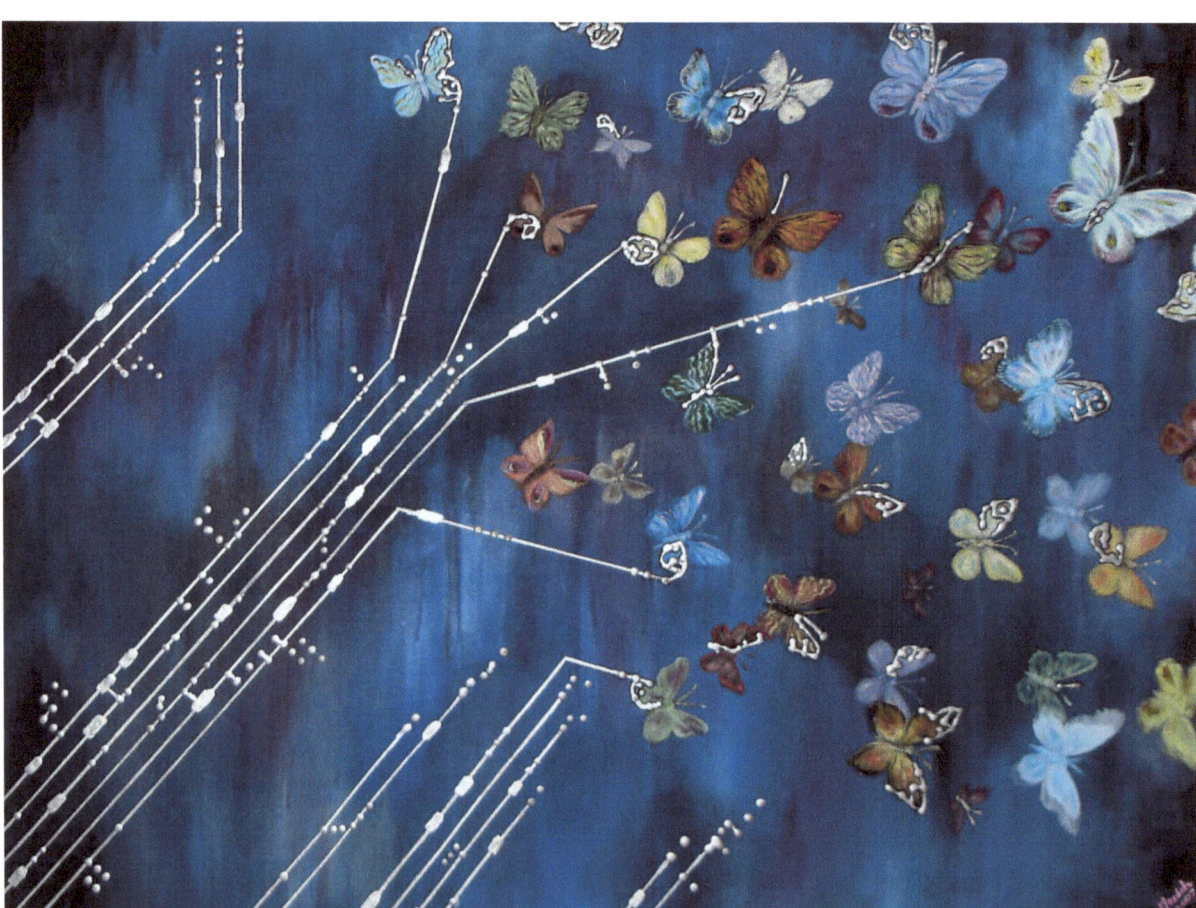

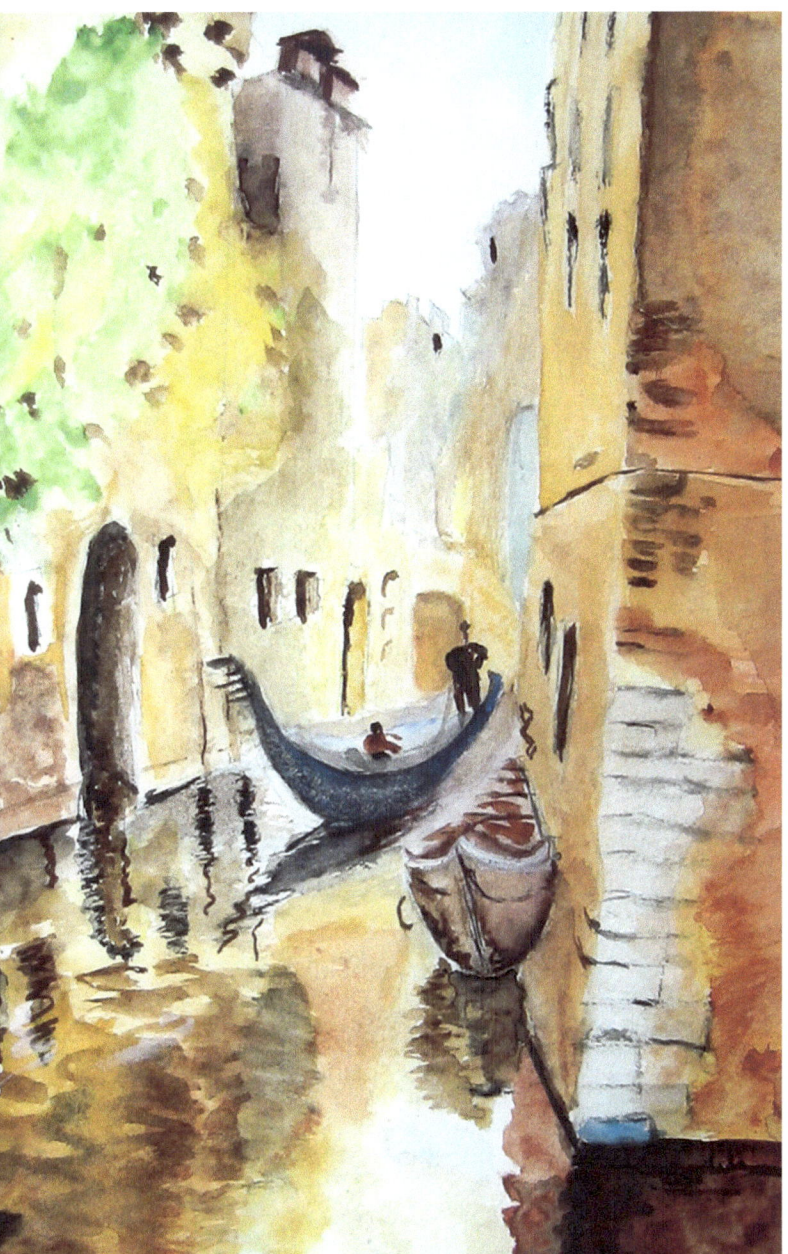

# LAILA SHOUCKRY

**LOCATION:** Waterloo
**WEB:** Flickr.com/photos/lailagallery/
**EMAIL:** Laila.shouckry@live.com

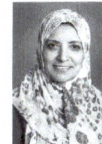

Laila Shouckry was born in Egypt but spent much of her life in Dubai. She currently resides in Waterloo. She achieved her B.Sc. in Electrical Engineering. Later on, she completed courses in Arts and Crafts at the Women's Association of the United Arab Emirates. She participated in various exhibitions and events in United Arab Emirates. She has a multitude of artistic talents in various sectors, including: oil painting, water color painting, graphic drawing, ceramic crafting, silk and glass painting, and glass etching.

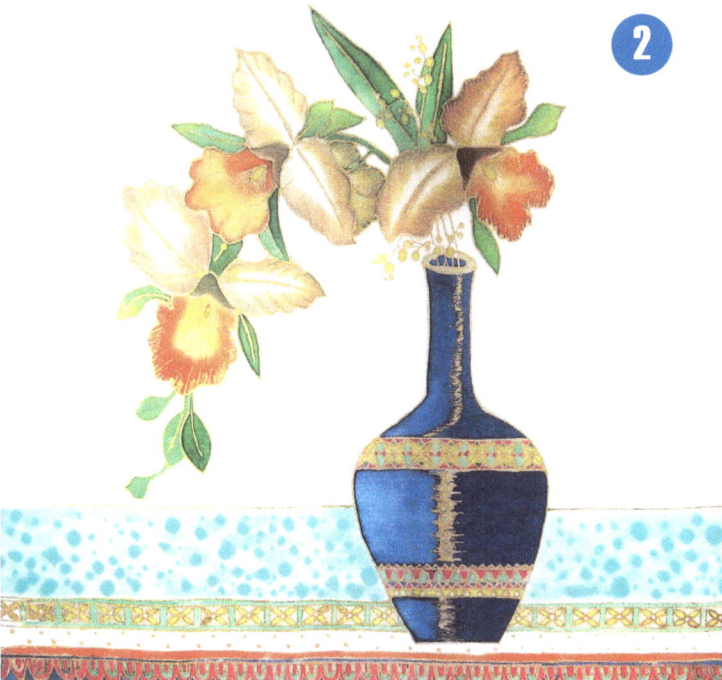

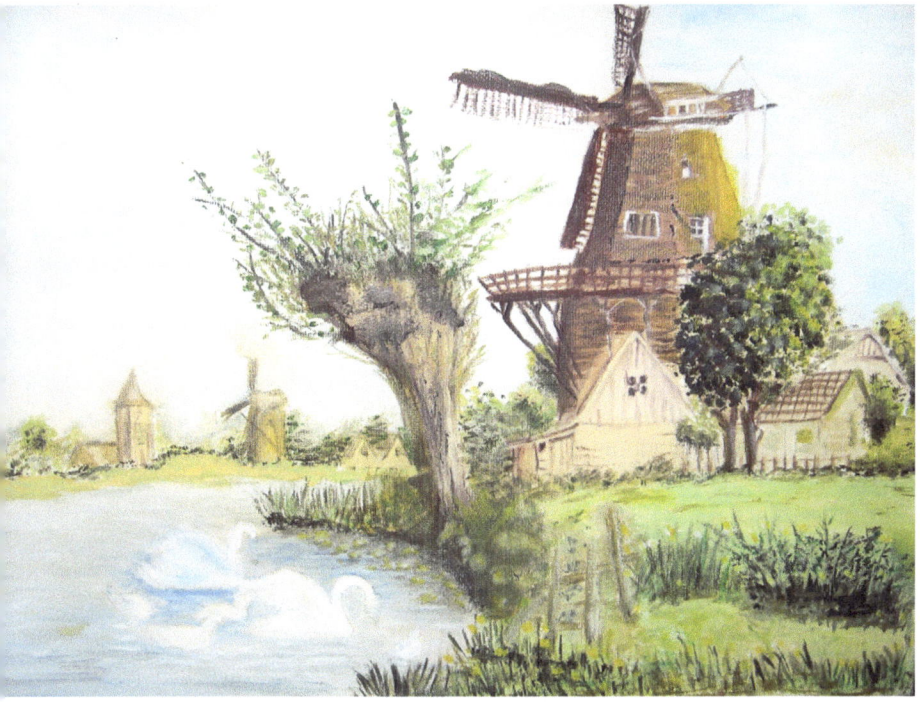

**1 The Life on the River** Water colour.

**2 Blue Pot** Water-based silk colors on silk.

**3 Wind Mills** Oil on wood.

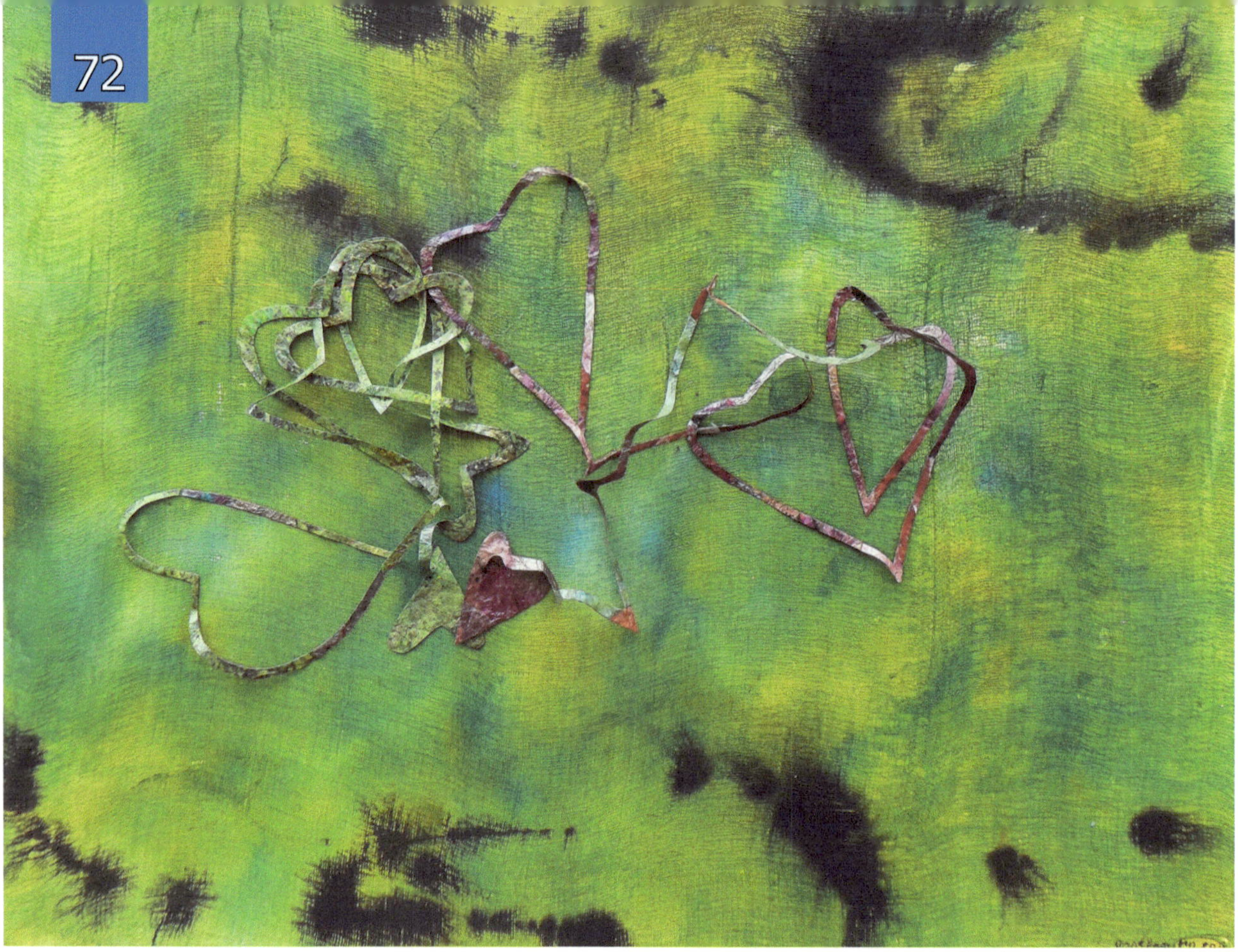

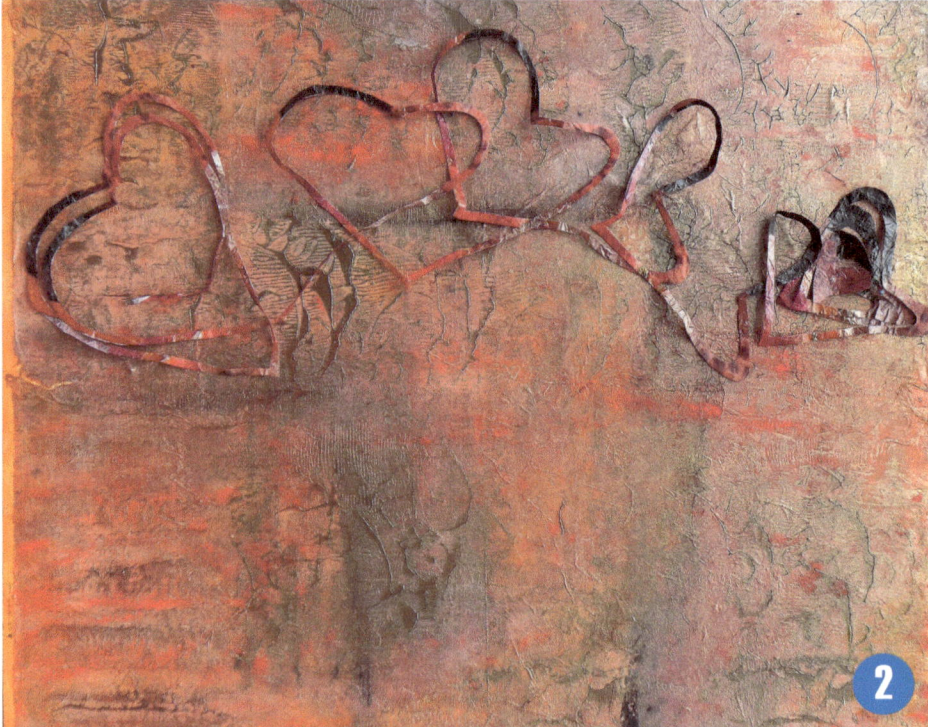

**1 Heart Art** 20x28" Mixed media green.

**2 Heart Art** 20x28" Mixed media red.

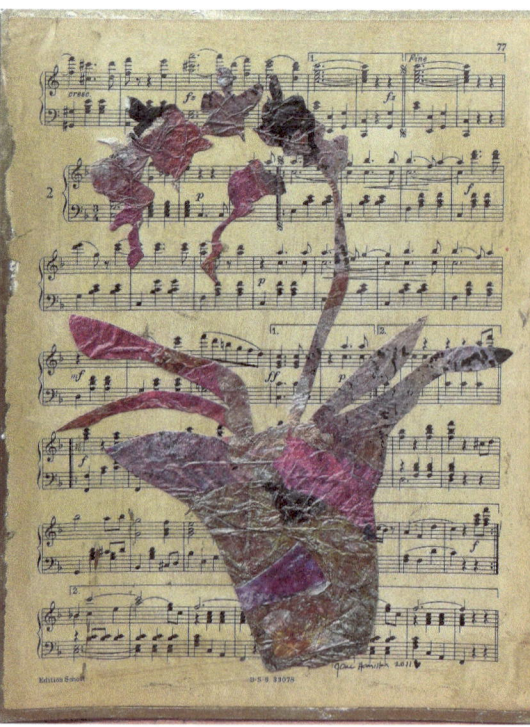

# JANE HAMILTON

**LOCATION:** Waterloo, Old Westmount
**WEB:** janehamilton.ca
**EMAIL:** janeyoung@rogers.com

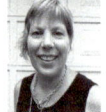

**3 Orchid** 11x17" Mixed media.

Heart Art is a new series by artist Jane Hamilton. It was born from the sudden loss of her 16 year old daughter in 2010. Through this series, Jane has sought to captre and then express her eternal connection to Carly. The textured backgrounds represent life's textured quality and the concentric hearts symbolize pure love and eternal life. All proceeds from this work are donated.

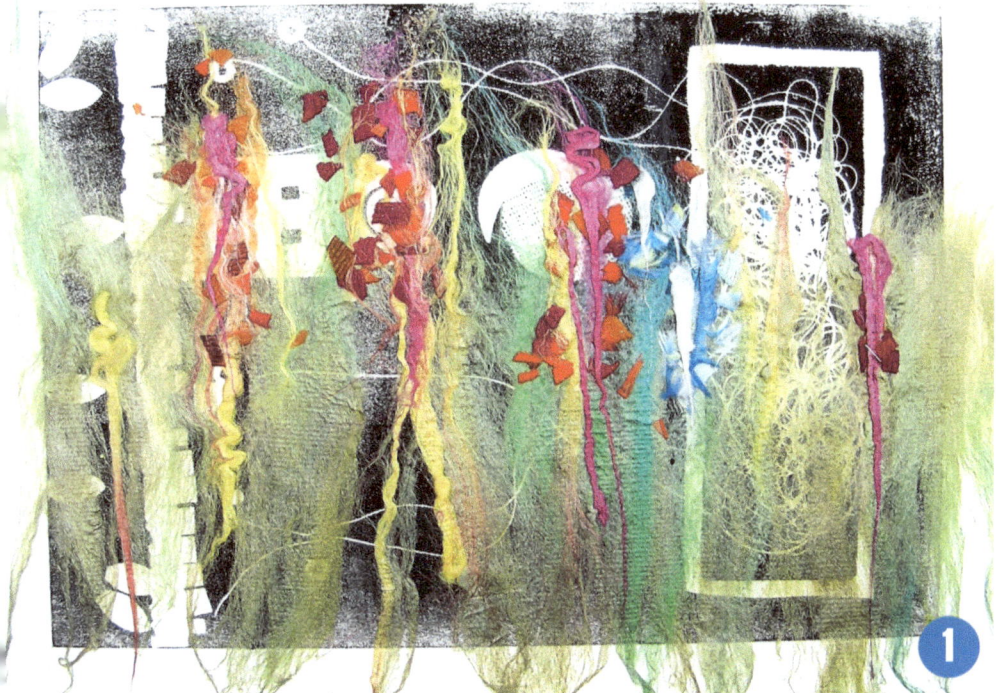

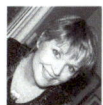

# FRANCES A GREGORY

**LOCATION:** St. Jacobs
**WEB:** FrancesGregory.net
**EMAIL:** Fagregory@rogers.com

Frances is an award winning painter and printmaker who loves experimenting with new materials and mediums. Recently she has been experimenting with silk fusion and collage. Her style is most often representational using either realism or abstraction. She appreciates the natural environment for it's creator-directed order and beauty. She takes her inspiration from nature's moods and the power of light to transform an ordinary subject into something exciting, tender or even mystical.

**2 Windows To My Soul** 15×28"
Printing inks on paper.

**3 Natural Vibrations** 20×26"
Silk filaments, wood, gold leaf and printing inks on paper.

**1 A Seasonless Garden** 16×20"
Silk filaments, fibers and printing inks on paper.

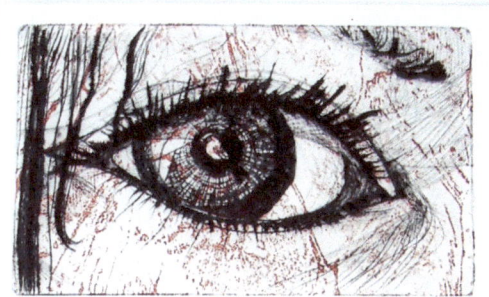

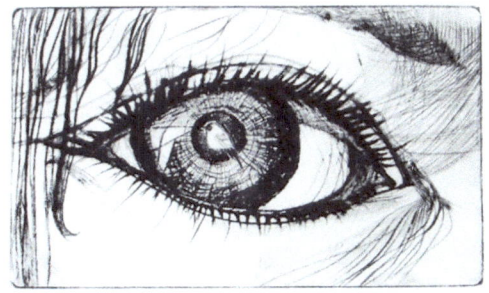

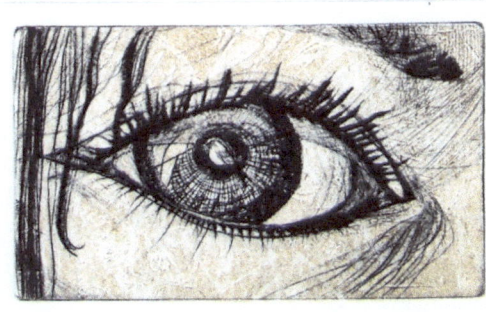

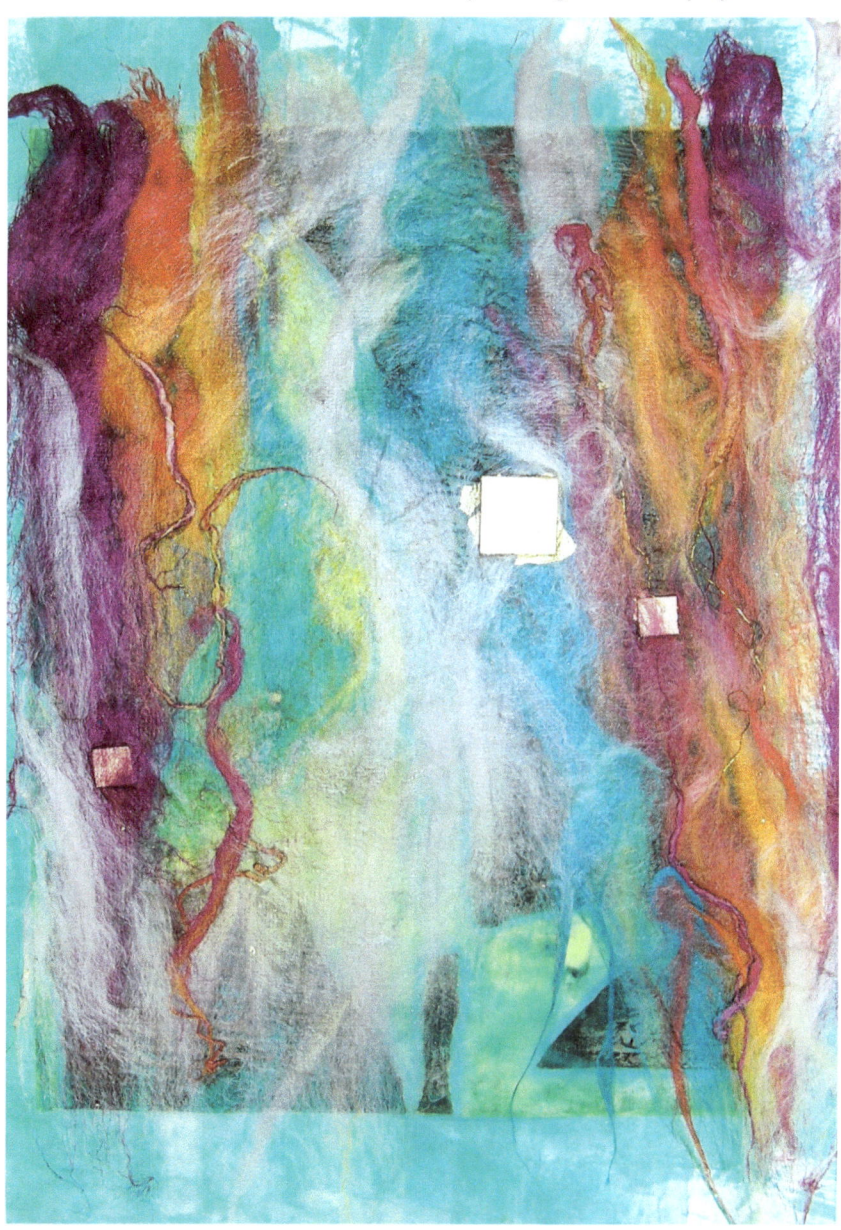

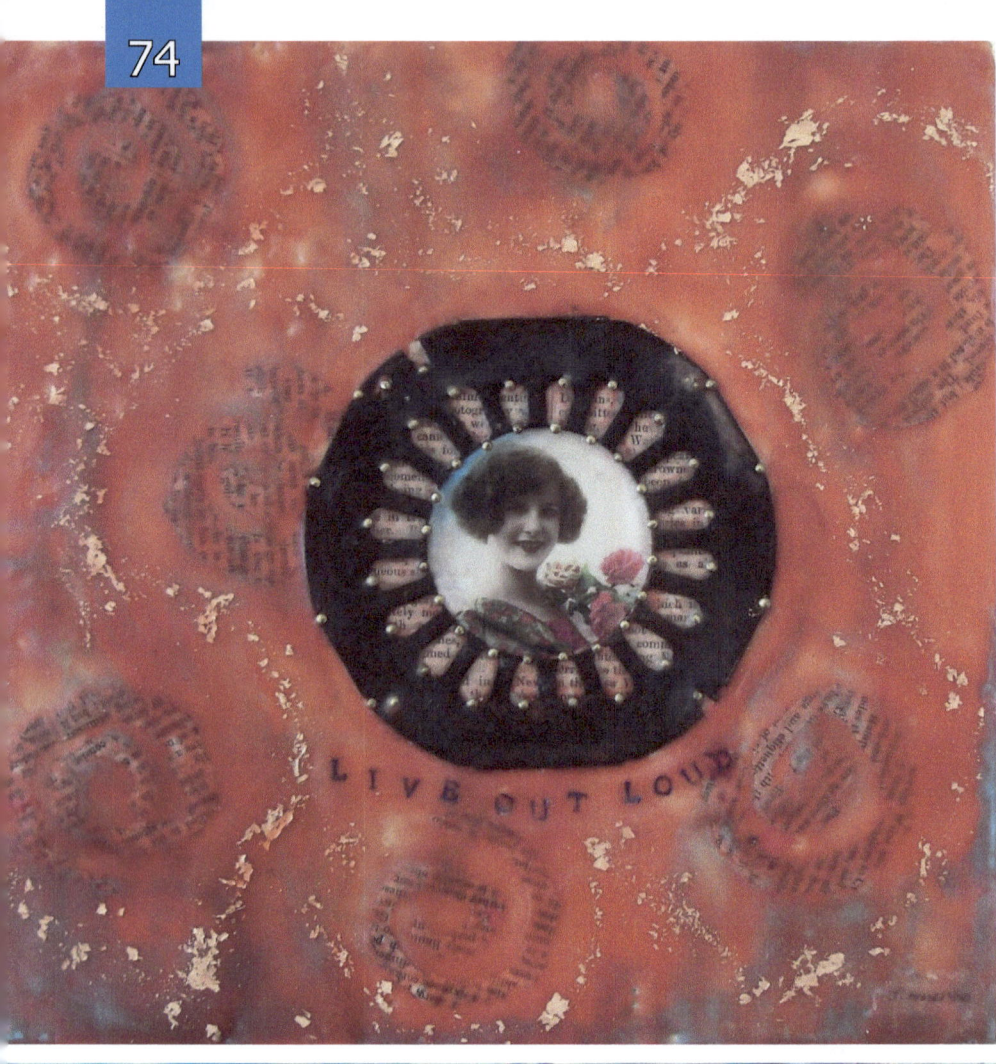

# JAKKI ANNERINO

**LOCATION:** Kitchener
**WEB:** Flickr.com/photos/jakkila
**EMAIL:** annerino_jakki@rogers.com

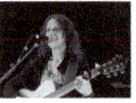

Jakki is an encaustic and mixed media artist as well as a singer/songwriter. Jakki explores mystery, memory and whimsy in her encaustic pieces. She likes to use vintage image transfers as well as organics and found objects to help convey these ideas. Jakki was a featured artist on Kitchener City Hall's Digital Cube Gallery in August, 2011.

**1 Live Out Loud** 9x9" Encaustic.

**2 Dream Prelude #1** 9x9" Encaustic.

**3 If Only** 9x9" Encaustic.

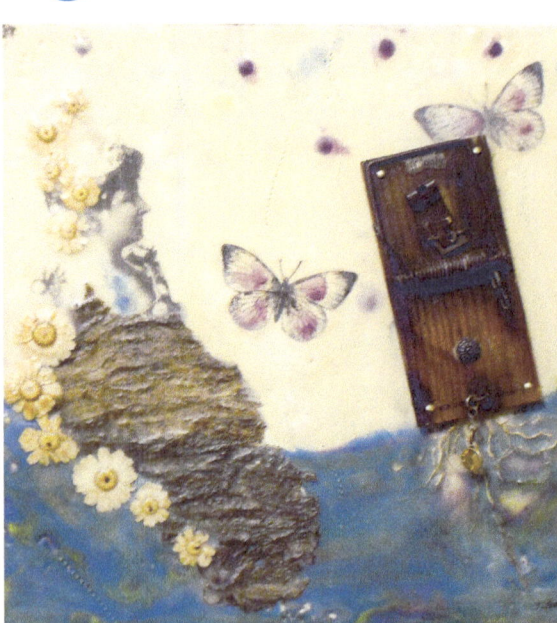

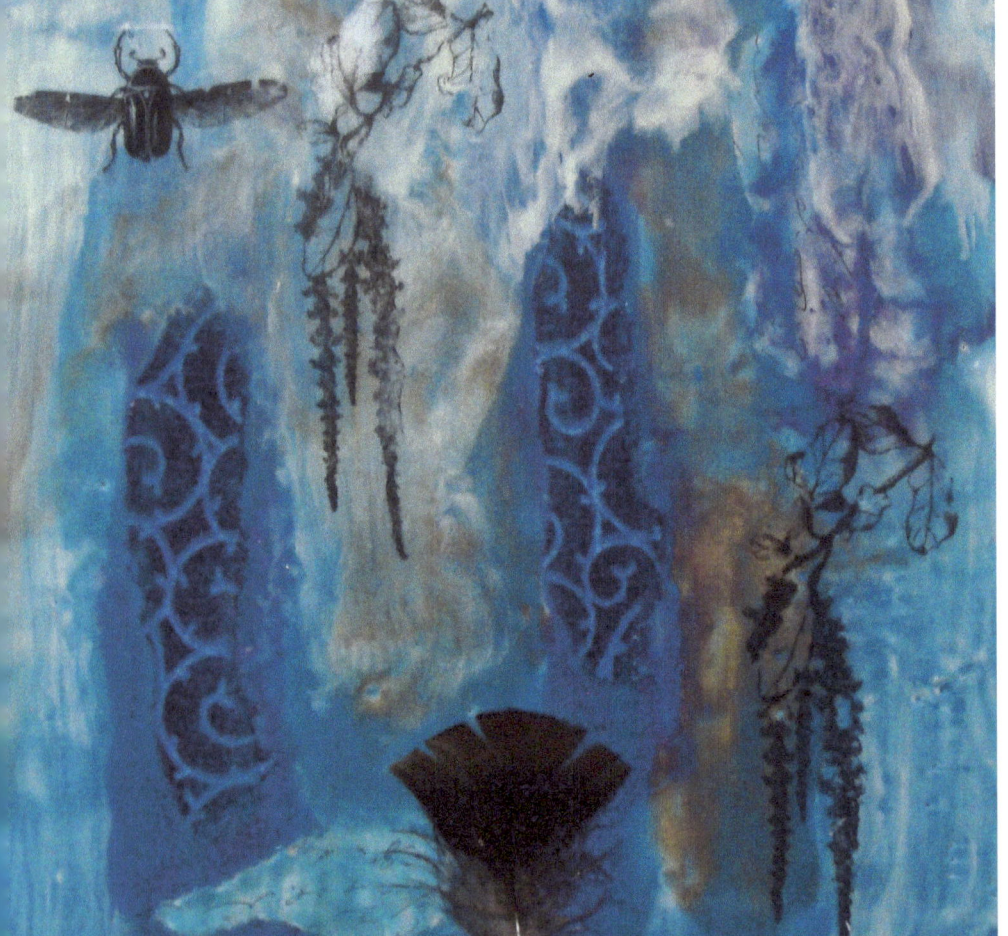

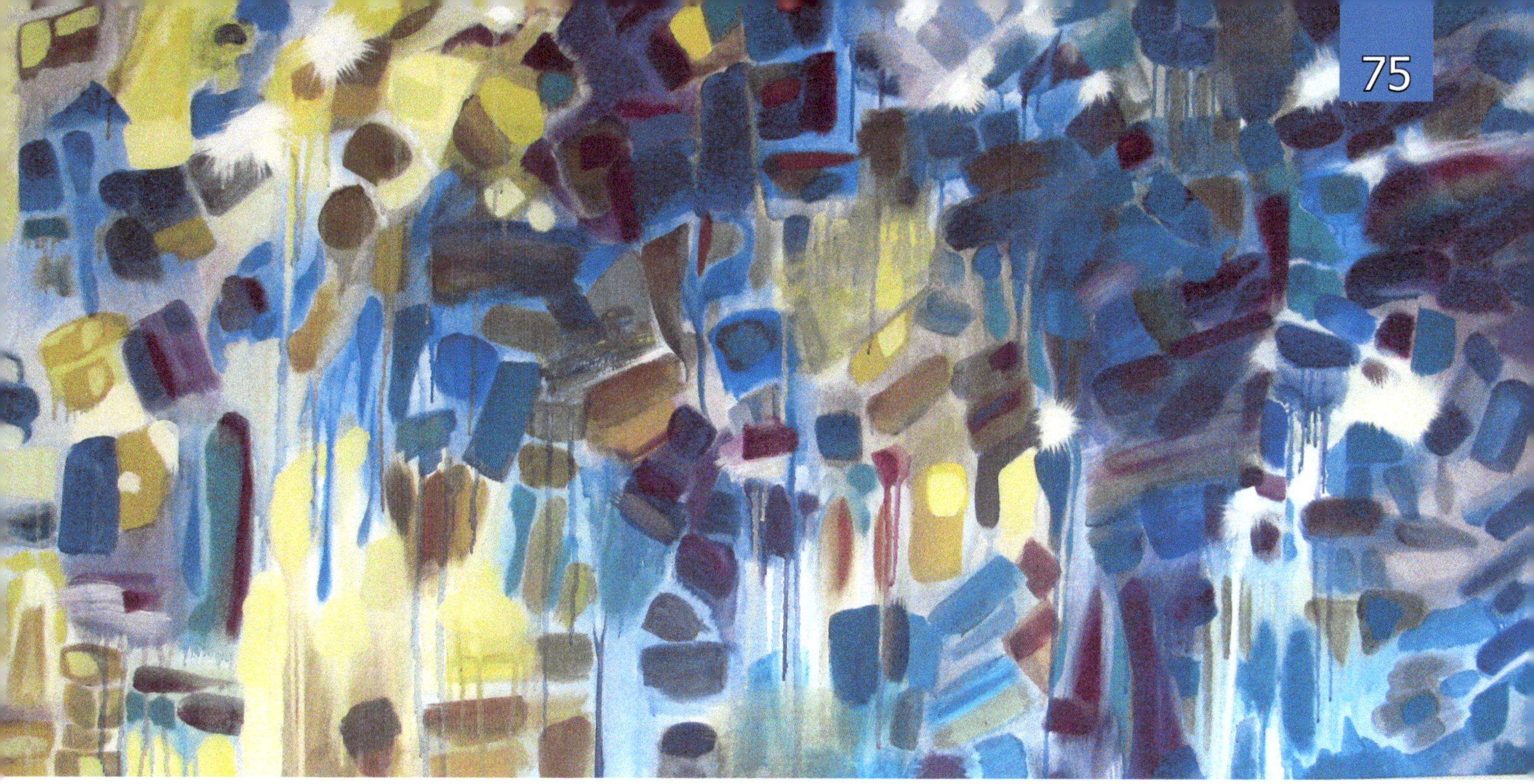

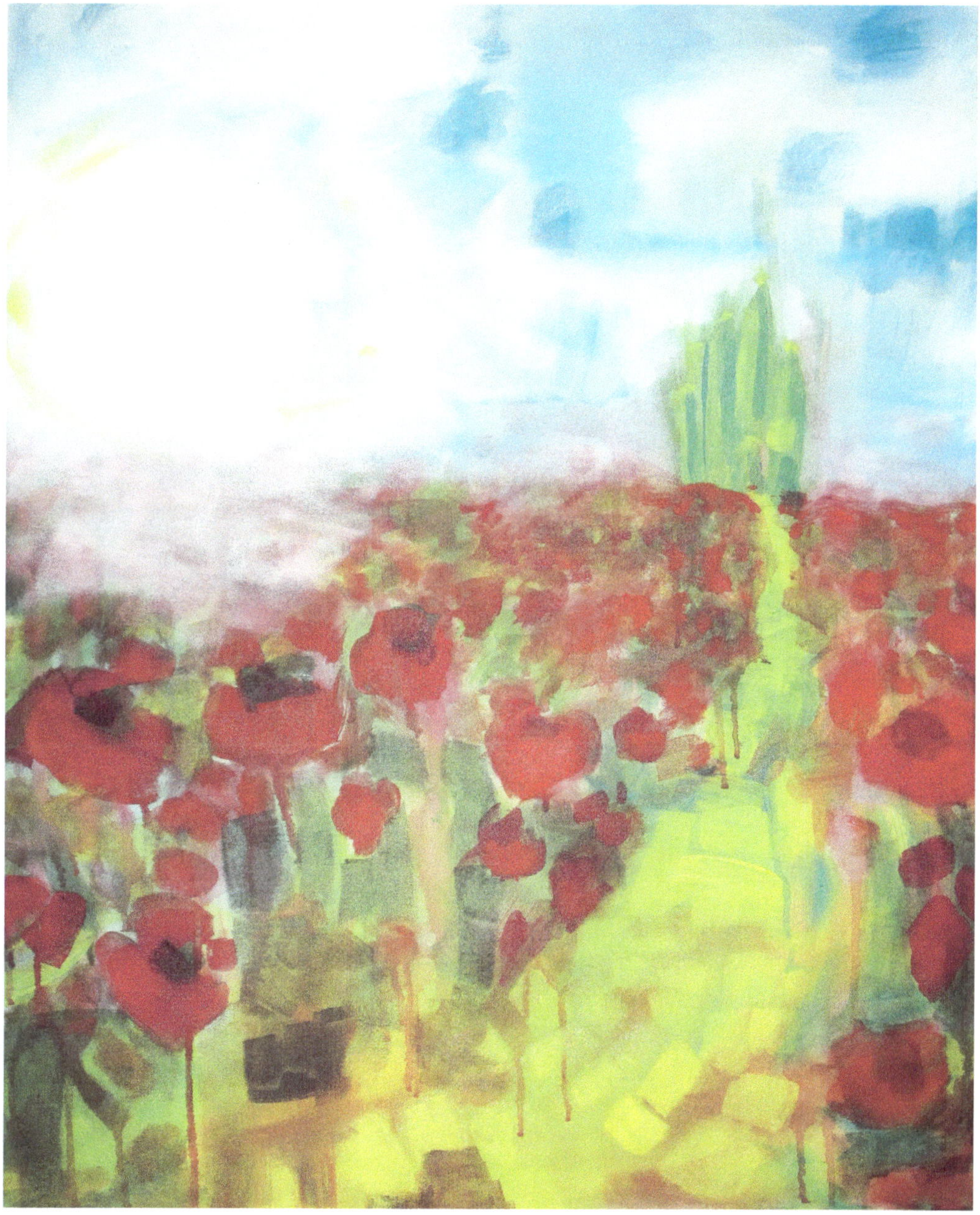

# DIANA ERB

**LOCATION:** Kitchener
**WEB:** DianaErb.ca
SightAndSoundstudios.ca
**EMAIL:** Hullodiana@gmail.com

Diana Erb was born and raised in Kitchener, Ontario. She studied Fine Art at the Ontario College of Art and Design and at Concordia University in Montreal. She received her BFA--major in Art Education—with distinction in 2011. Diana's paintings are largely autobiographical and explore universal splendors and sorrows of human life. Diana lives in New Hamburg, Ontario where she and her husband run a visual art and music studio, Sight & Sound Studios. They offer educational programming in the arts for all ages and abilities.

**1 A Dark Cloud** 24x48" Acrylic on Canvas. This painting is a comment on personal growth and change. A dark time can also bring a positive and bright future.

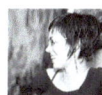

**2 Emerald City** 24x30" Acrylic on Canvas. Using the archetypal pop culture imagery from the film, Wizard of Oz, this painting is an expression of the collective experience of the quest for "something more".

# BARRY DANIELS

**LOCATION:** Westmount KW
**WEB:** SandbarStudios.ca
**EMAIL:** BDaniels_atlarge@hotmail.com

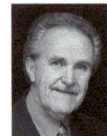 Visualizing and releasing artistic forms that are hidden within a wide variety of wood has been a challenge and a passion for Barry for many years. His love of wood and innate sense of artistic form and balance, along with years of developing master turning skills, enable him to create collectible pieces that are both pleasing to the eye and sensuous to the touch. Each turning, be it an artistic piece or a cremation urn, is truly unique and one-of-a-kind.

**1** **Delicate Nature** With a fine, silky, unfinished surface, this 'stand-alone' piece (probably Maple) draws the eye to a blossom of sensuous, natural canvas, exhibiting spalt lines and lovely pink-hued graining.

**2** **King Bolete** 9 ½" Tall. This stately vase , turned from a Beech limb, contrasts honey-blond wood with the stark black lines of spalting (dormant fungus colonies). Its downward-flowing rim is reminiscent of the shapes of the many fungi in our Canadian woodlands.

**3** **Reprieved** This closed, natural-edged piece was rescued from a fifteen-year-old stack of abandoned firewood. From a fruitwood tree, it exhibits the ravages of time...weathered stains and cracks, yet stands proudly as a finished and valuable piece of art.

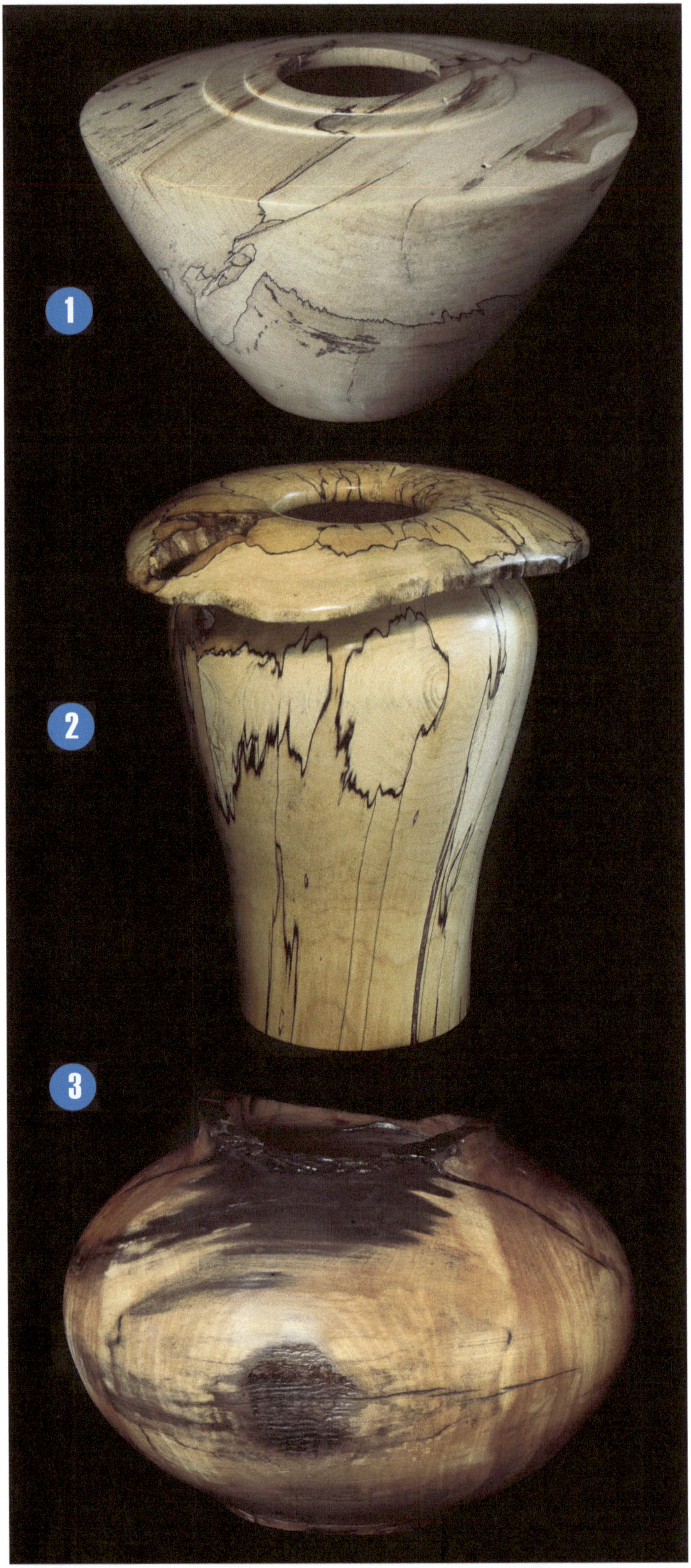

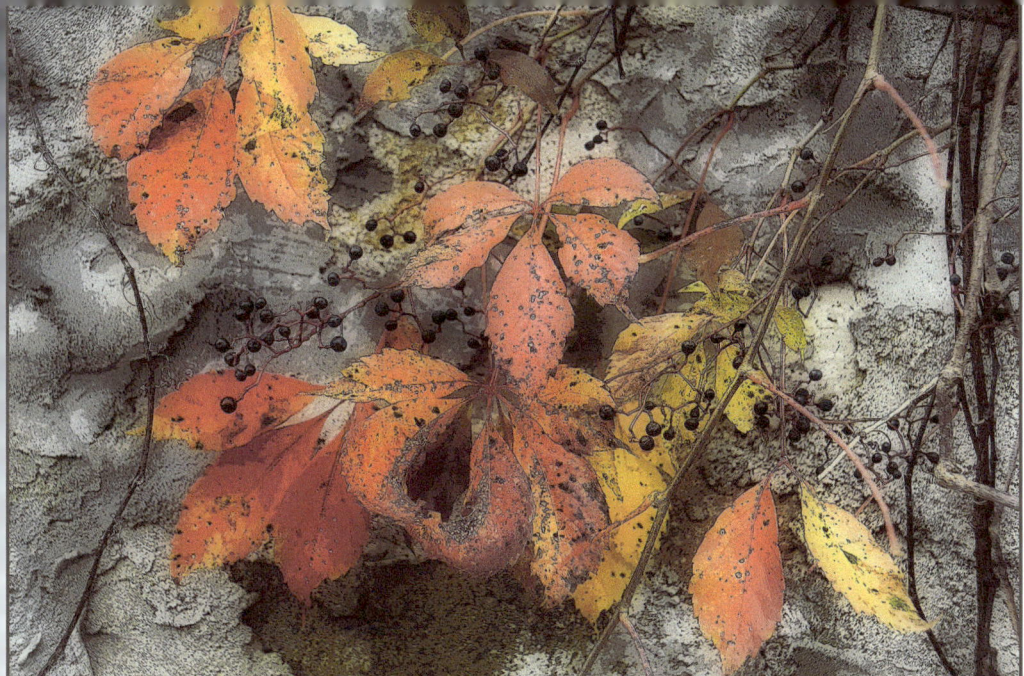

# SANDRA ROEMER

**LOCATION:** Westmount, KW
**WEB:** SandbarStudios.ca
**EMAIL:** HelloSandbar@yahoo.ca

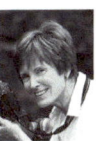

Photography has been Sandra's passion since childhood when she aquired her first camera. Capturing the essence of a subject or scene is her challenge. The greatest plus for Sandra is that in the search for exceptional photographs, new places call to be explored and time is reserved for quiet observation of nature and people. Awards include the 2010 first prize in CBC 's David Suzuki Nature Contest, first in Nature in the 2010 GTCCC (Greater Toronto Camera Clubs) contest, and 'Photographer of the Year' in 2009 and in 2010 at GRIPS Camera Club.

**1 Vines on Wall** This display of autumn was captured during a stroll through the town of Elora. The final effect was accomplished with creative post-processing of the photograph.

**2 Great Egret Posing** At the onset of a hike along Anhinga Trail in Florida's Everglades, this Great Egret took pause from its routine hunt. The fog and the early rays of sunrise set the stage for an ethereal scene.

**3 Solitude** While touring a country road near Doon, this solitary tree called to be photographed. The fog and delicate hues of sunrise added a soft & sensuous feel to the landscape.

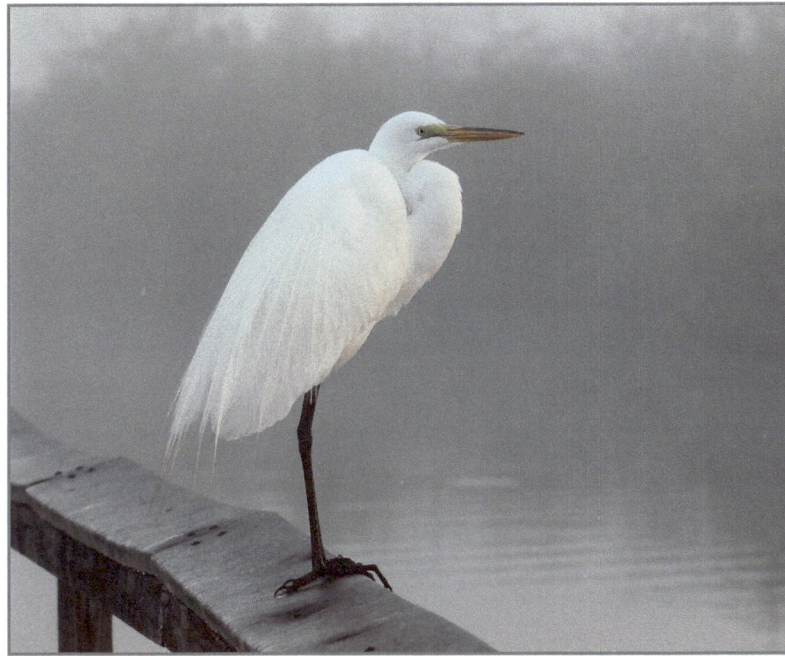

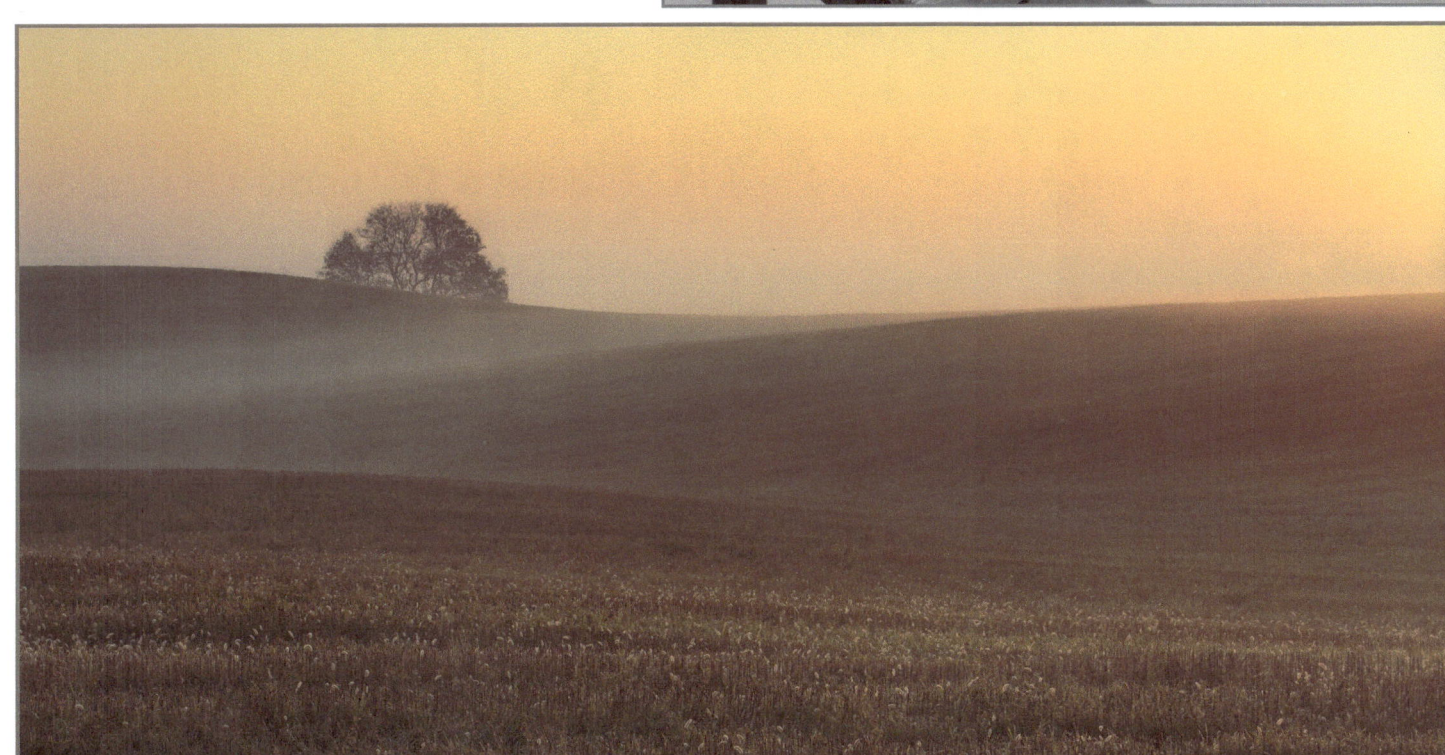

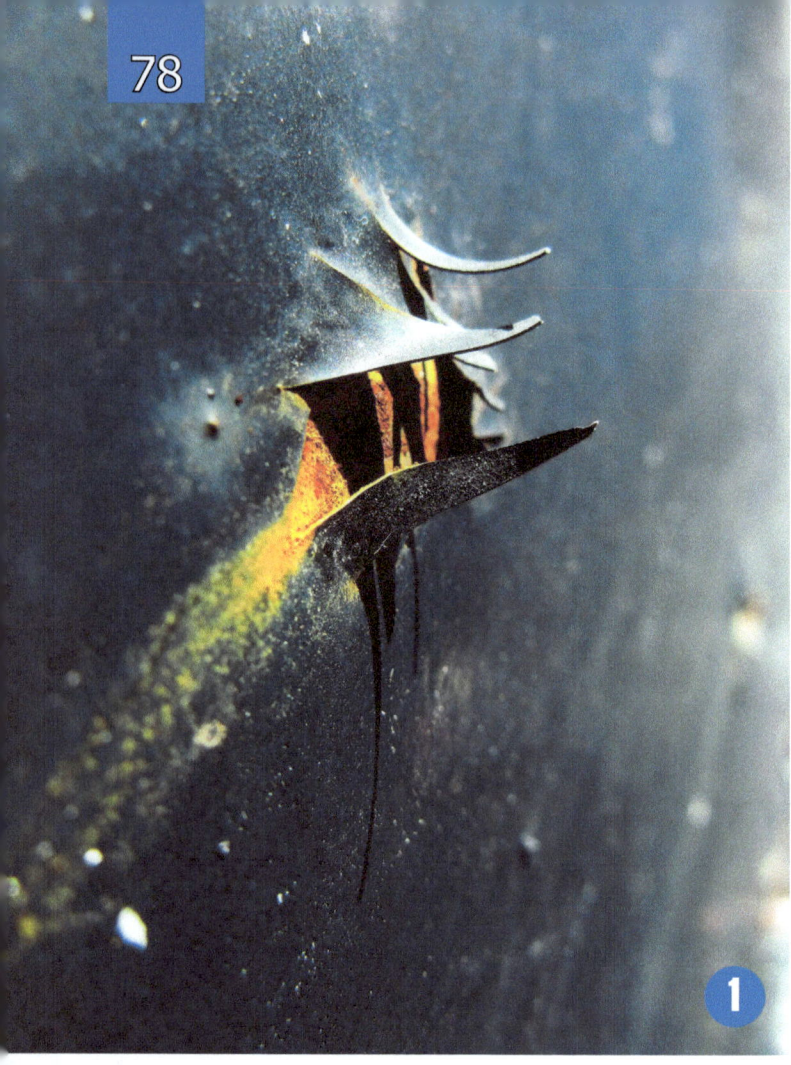

**1**

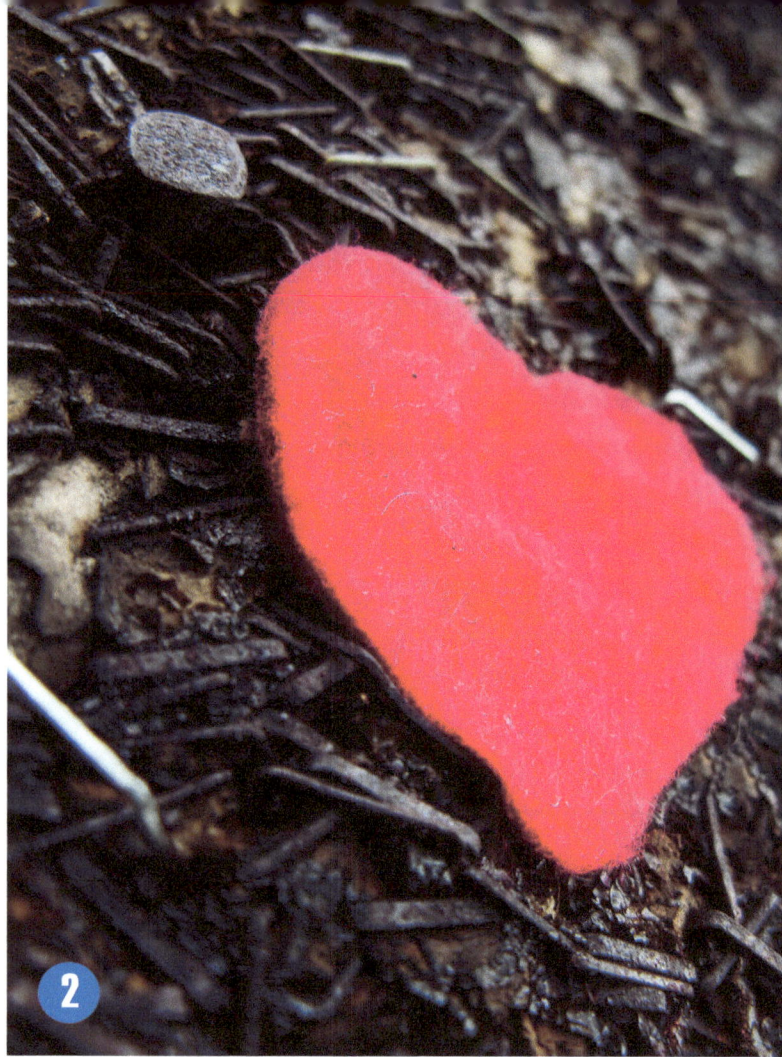

**2**

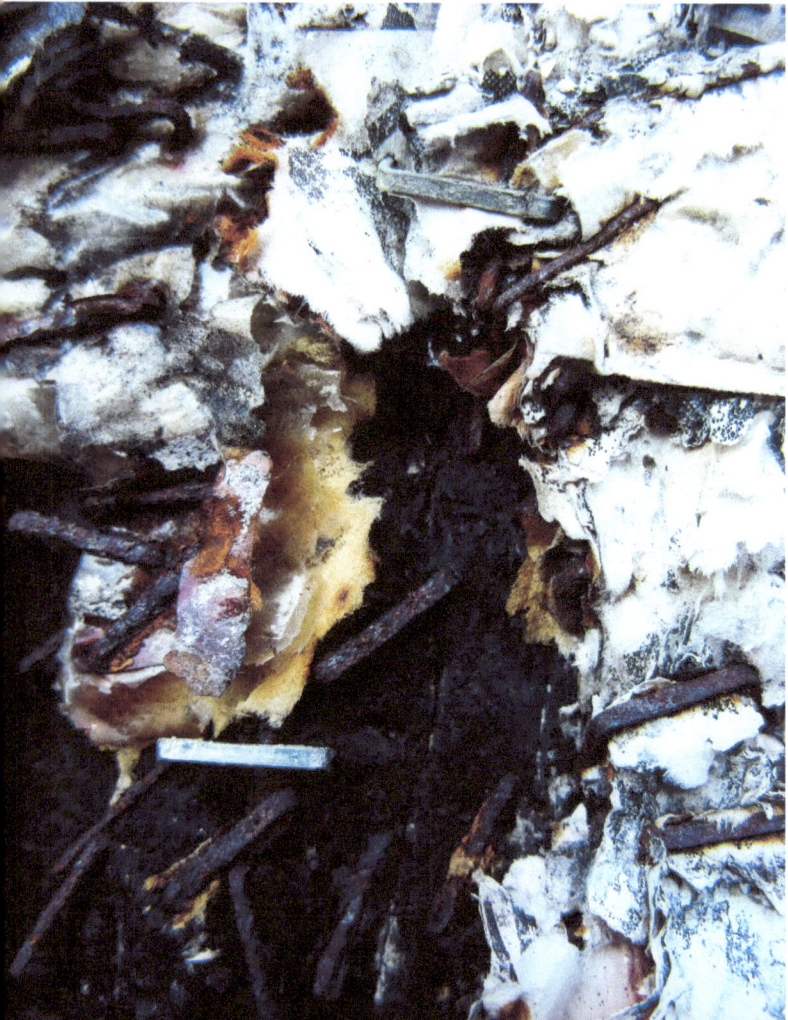

**1** **Leaden Bloom** Photograph.

**2** **Heart in the Wrong Place** Photograph.

**3** **In Sheep's Clothing** Photograph.

# JARED DAVISON

**LOCATION:** Waterloo
**WEB:** Davisonphotography.com
**EMAIL:** Jared.Davison.Photography@gmail.com

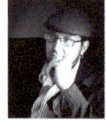 A founding member of the foto-RE collective, Jared's photographic sleuthing has been a subject of ongoing interest in the arts community. He has held exhibitions in KW, Cambridge and Toronto and his work has appeared in The Tannery District, The KW Art Gallery, The WalterFedy Architectural firm and the City of Waterloo Museum. Having a fondness for industrial archaeology, Jared has been documenting the forlorn sights in regional heritage factories such as RMS, The Breithaupt Block and The Waterloo Water Works. As a member of the Waterloo Community Arts Center and the KW Arts Awards, Jared supports a thriving aesthetic culture in the region of Waterloo.

# PIETER ZANTINGE

**LOCATION:** Kitchener
**WEB:** (N/A)
**EMAIL:** PieterZantinge@yahoo.ca

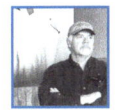 Originally from Holland, Pieter now calls Kitchener his home, where he is an active member in the local music and arts scene. The idea for painting the musicians came first. His and photography is a tool that Pieter uses as an extension of his memory. Playing with photographic effects generates ideas that he then implements in his paintings (i.e. black and white, altering exposures etc.). Regarding the paintings themselves, Pieter sees them as a simple homage to the musicians who have let him into their world and their lives, and his challenge is to draw out their personalities and passion.

**1** **Chantuese** 22x30 " Watercolour.

**2** **Ivory Icon** 11x15" Watercolour.

**3** **He Plays Blues** 22x 30" Watercolour.

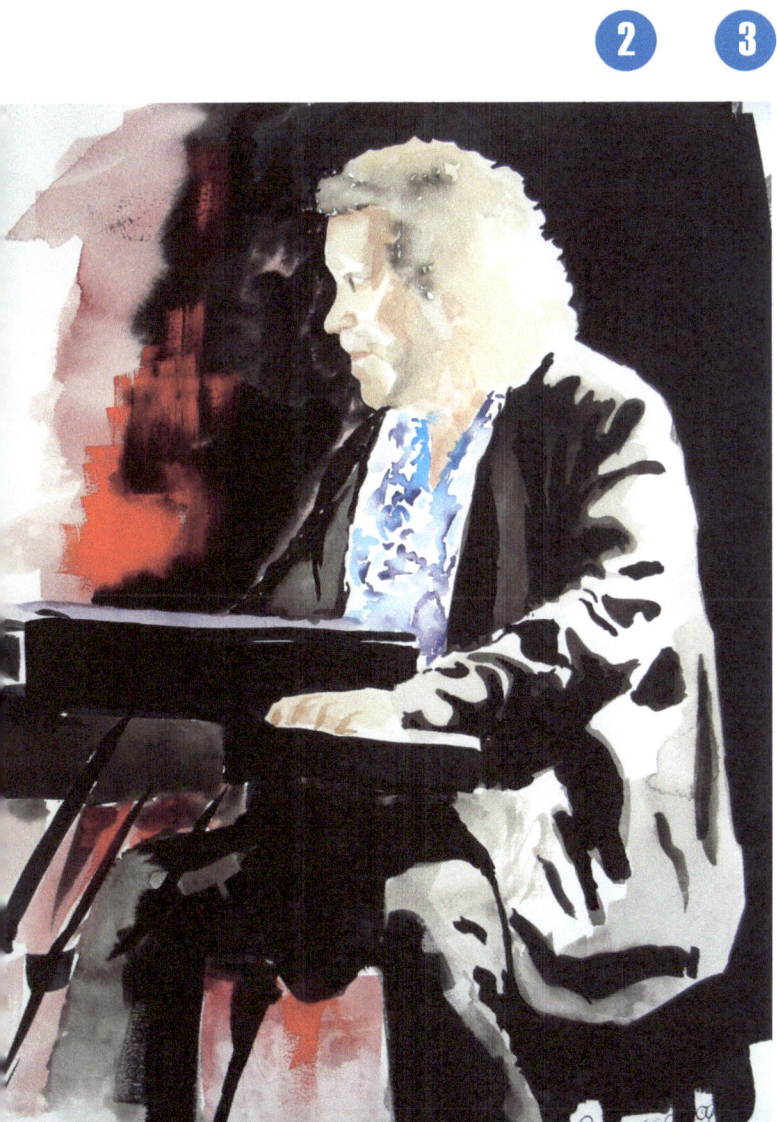

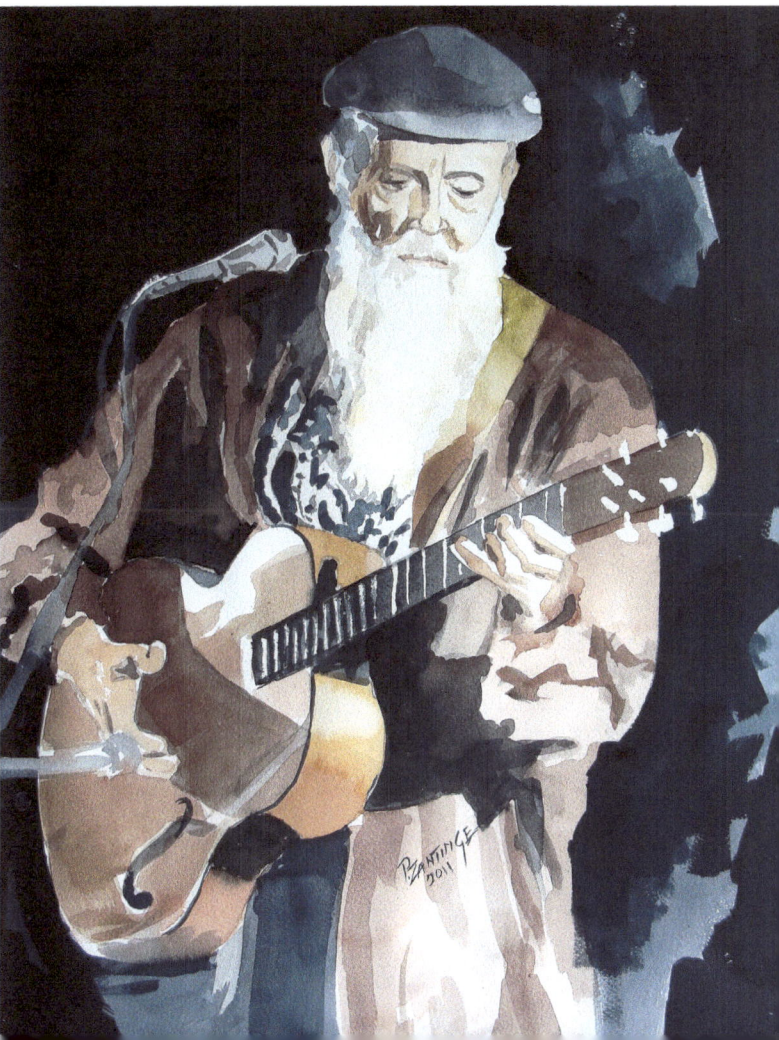

# CARMEN PETERS

**LOCATION:** Kitchener
**WEB:** Carmiepeters.com
**EMAIL:** Carmen.E.Peters@gmail.com

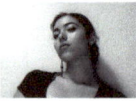

Carmen Peters is a recent graduate of the University of Waterloo. She completed an Honours Bachelors of Arts, Fine Arts Studio and Art History programs. While artistic expression has always been a part of her life, it was during her time at Waterloo where she began to explore and express her lifelong passion of science, in particular, physics and astronomy. She strives to fuse her scientific and artistic passions by her paintbrush.

**1** **Ascension** 14x18" Oil on Canvas.

**2** **Can You See It?** 10x12" Oil on Panel.

**3** **Finding My Desire** 4x5" Oil on Canvas.

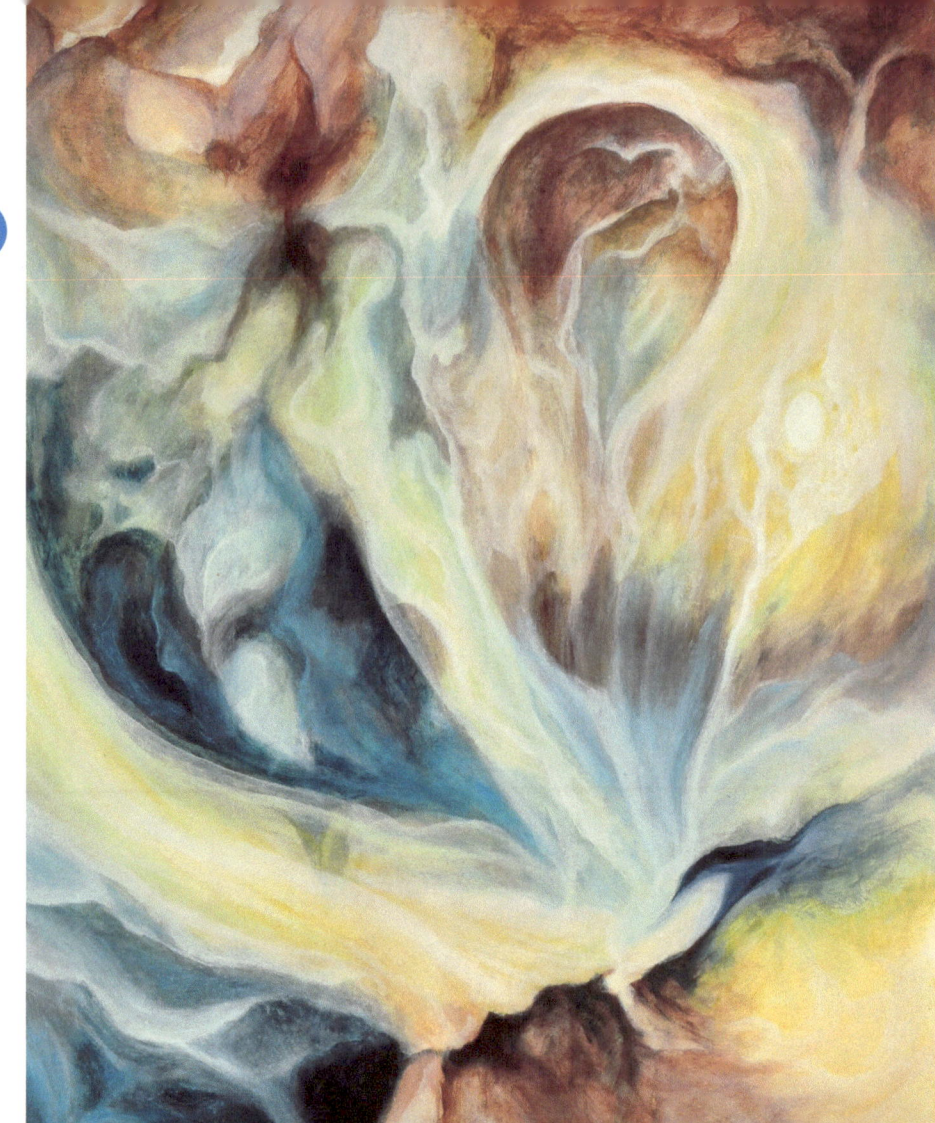

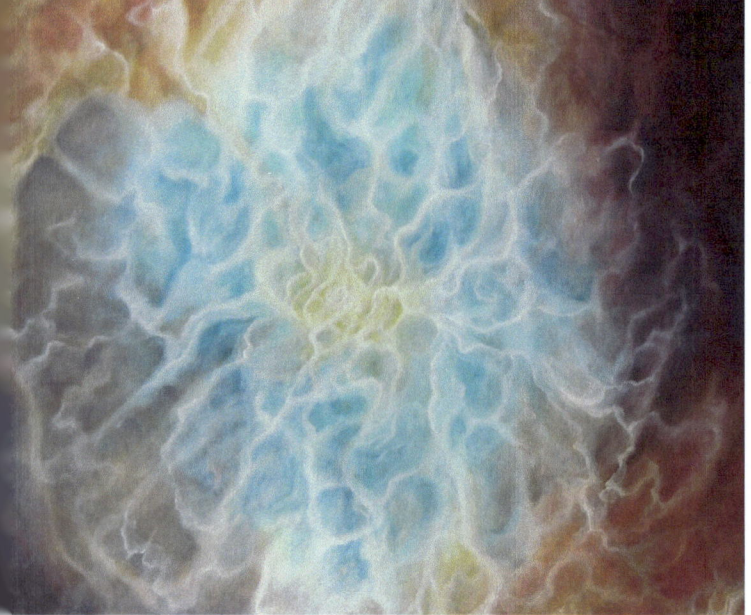

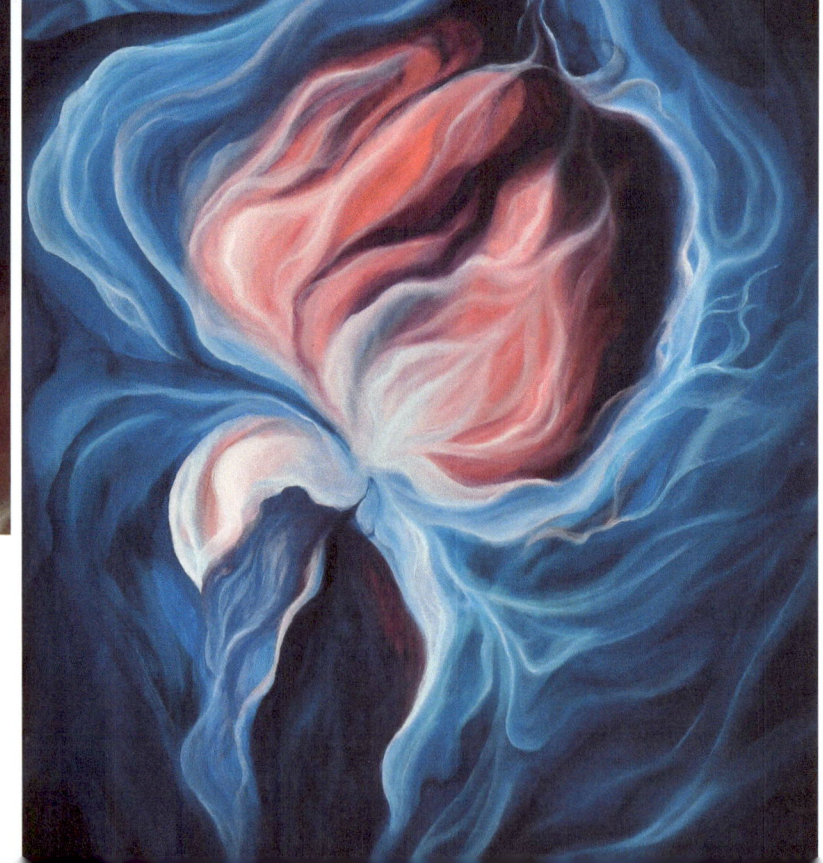

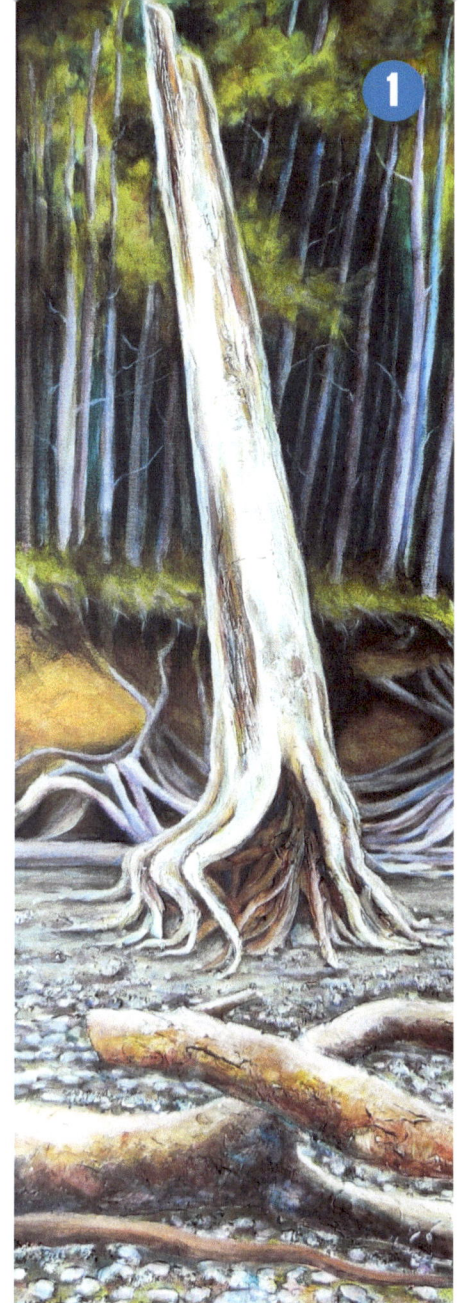

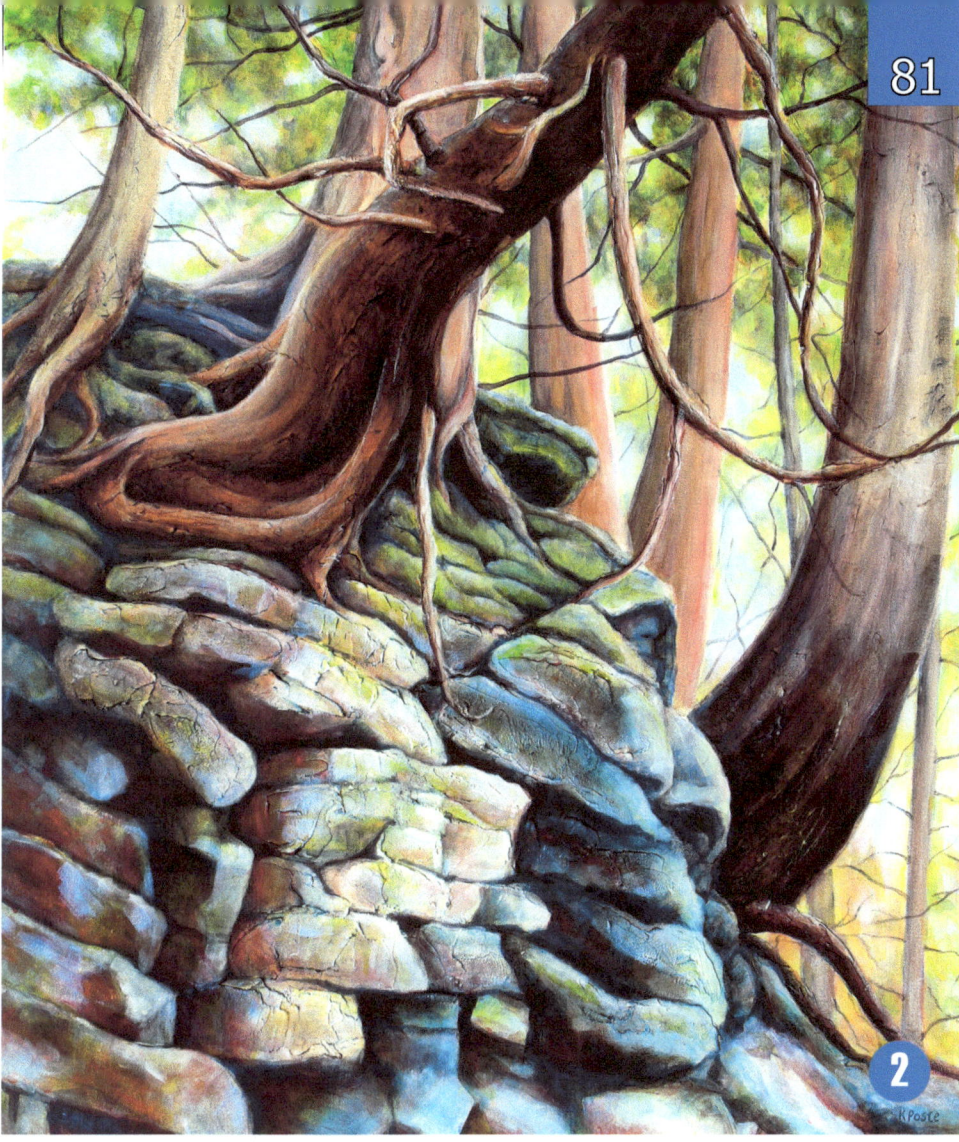

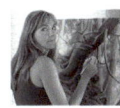

**1** **Ghost Log** 40x16" Acrylic on canvas.

**3** **Crawling** 30×40" Acrylic on canvas.

**2** **Tree Ledge** 36×30" Acrylic on canvas.

# KATHLEEN POSTE

**LOCATION:** Waterloo
**WEB:** (N/A)
**EMAIL:** Kathleen_p@sympatico.ca

Kathleen Poste is a self-taught artist who has drawn and painted all of her life. Without formal art training, she has developed her own techniques and styles. As a registered nurse with over 20 years experience and currently working as an emergency nurse, she has realized that life can be fragile and sometimes short. This realization has inspired her to invigorate her dreams to be an artist. Her current work is focused on nature and the forces of life. Painted with acrylics built up of glazes and finite textures to create depth and mood. Exploration of unique composition and the play of light and dark to create a distinct character to the canvas. Use of strong rich colour to create mood. Stylized impressionism with emphasis on the textural detail. Influences include Emily Carr, Georgia O'Keefe and the Group of Seven's rugged landscapes.

# ALEXIS TYRALA

**LOCATION:** Kitchener
**WEB:** AlexisTyrala.com
**EMAIL:** Contact@alexistyrala.com

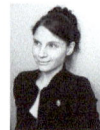

Painter and clerk at the art store "State of the Art Supplies" 84 King St N Waterloo. I started studying portrait painting in 2010 with Jon Tobin. My focus is on developing skills for realistic painting to complement my background in illustration. I paint in acrylic, starting with a monotone palette to build up light and shadow. For subject matter, I am intrigued by dark themes, sci-fi, the female form, and the macabre.

**1 Portrait Study** 24x30" Acrylic on board. From a series of self portraits.

**2 Skull** 18x24" Charcoal on Tiziano paper.

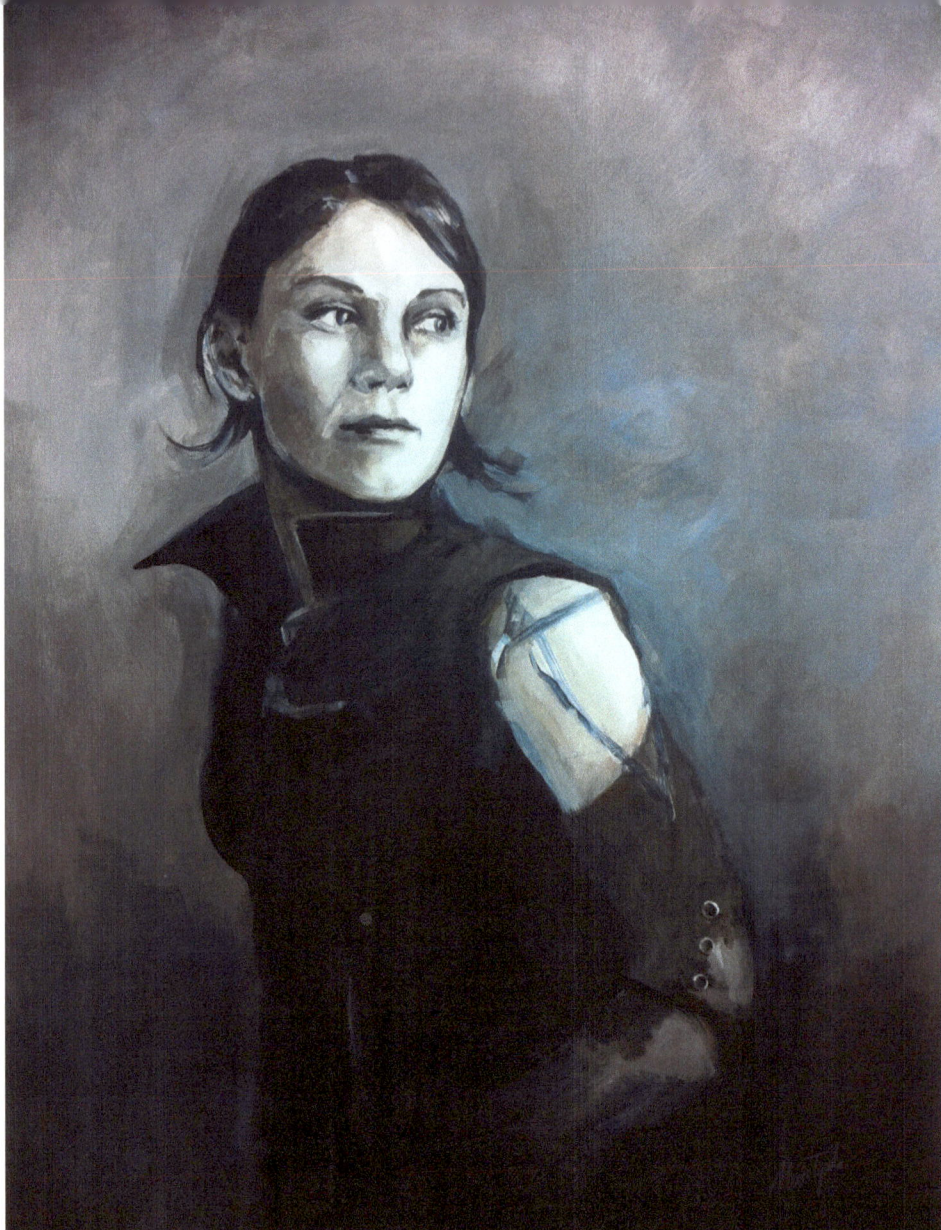

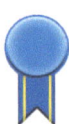

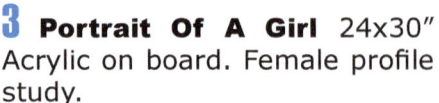

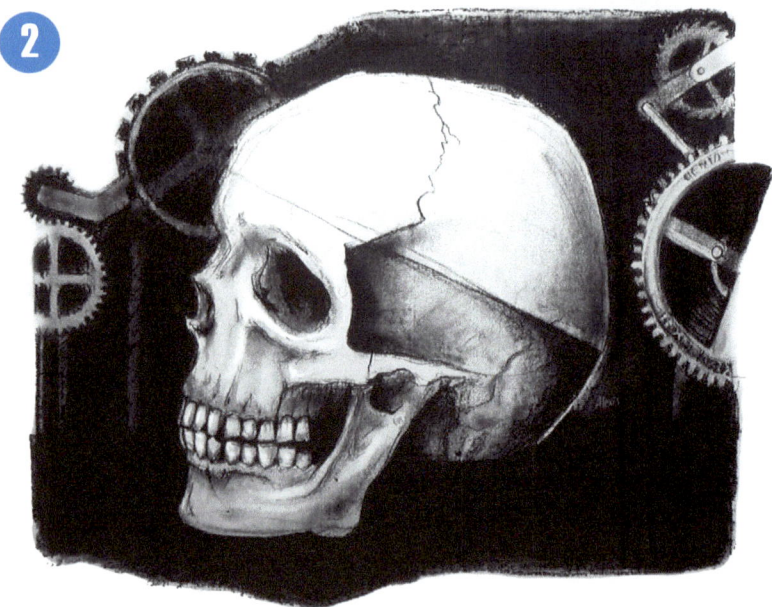

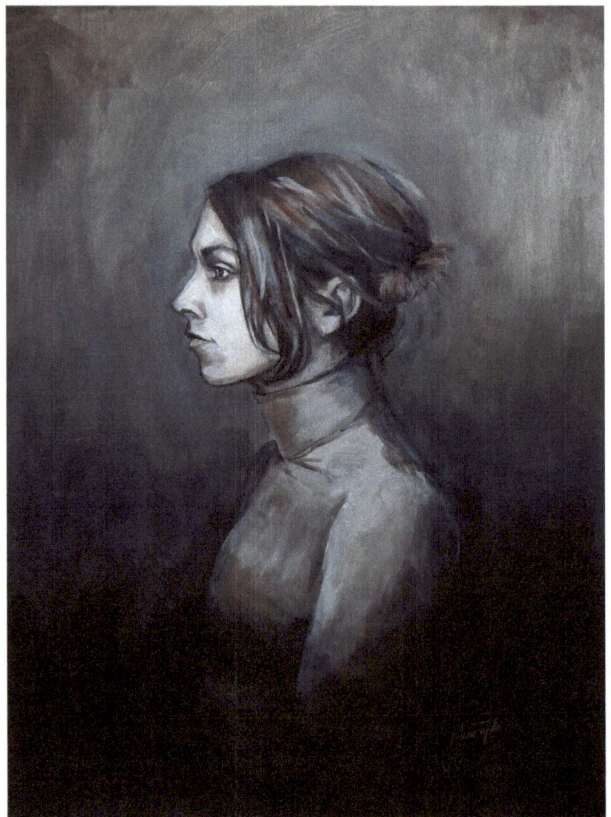

**3 Portrait Of A Girl** 24x30" Acrylic on board. Female profile study.

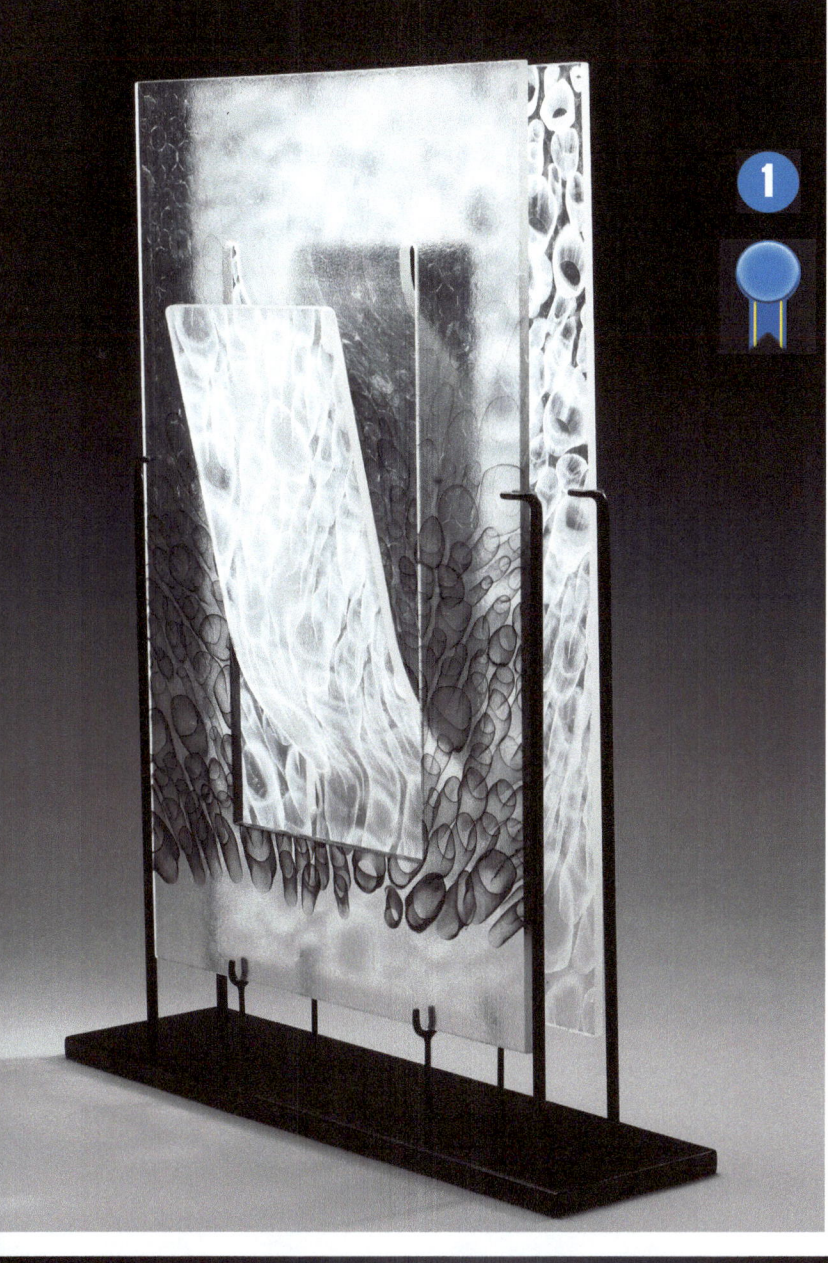

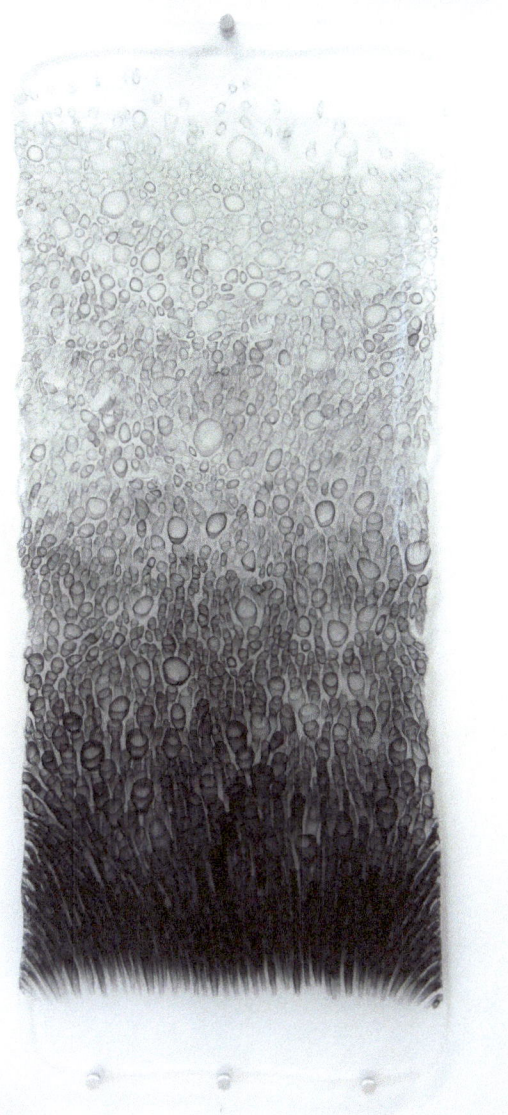

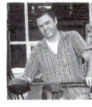

# STEVEN TIPPIN

**LOCATION:** Wellesley
**WEB:** StevenTippin.com
**EMAIL:** Steve.Tippin@gmail.com

Steven Tippin is a glass artist living and working in Wellesley, Ontario. He is currently the Vice President and the Ontario representative for the Glass Art Association of Canada. Tippin received his Undergraduate Bachelor degree in Printmaking and Sculpture from the University of Guelph and went on to study glass at Sheridan College where he tried to incorporate his seemingly bipolar mindset of printmaker and sculptor. He recently graduated from the MFA glass program at the Rochester Institute of Technology.

**1 About** 22x16x4.5" Water jet cut, fused and slumped glass.

**2 Tidal** 50x21x¼" Fused glass.

**3 Separation** 19.5x17.5x5" Cut and polished fused glass.

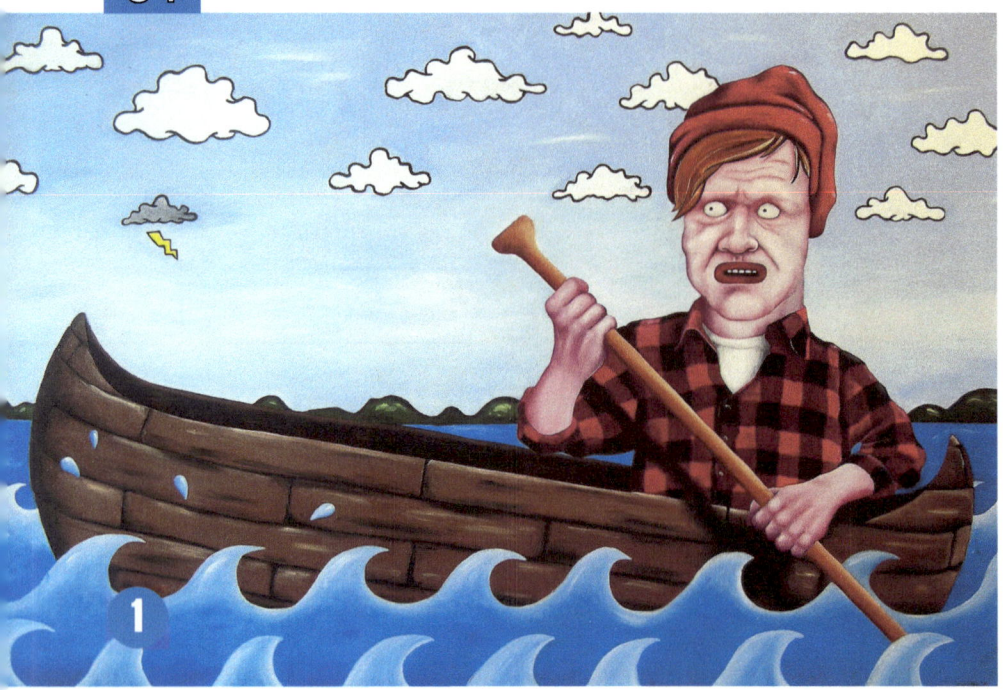

1

# LEIGH COONEY

**LOCATION:** Stratford
**WEB:** LeighCooney.com
**EMAIL:** LeighCooney@hotmail.com

Leigh Cooney is a globally collected, Irish born Canadian "pop-folk" artist. Leigh has no formal training in the arts, preferring to experiment on the canvas. Despite being self-taught, Leigh's paintings are in dozens of private collections and galleries all over the world. Leigh's subjects vary from writers to soldiers, and from satirical to whimsical, but the majority of his work focuses on the psychological in a light-hearted way.

**1** **Tom Thomson, Canoe Lake 1917** 24x30" Oil on canvas.

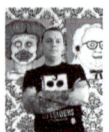

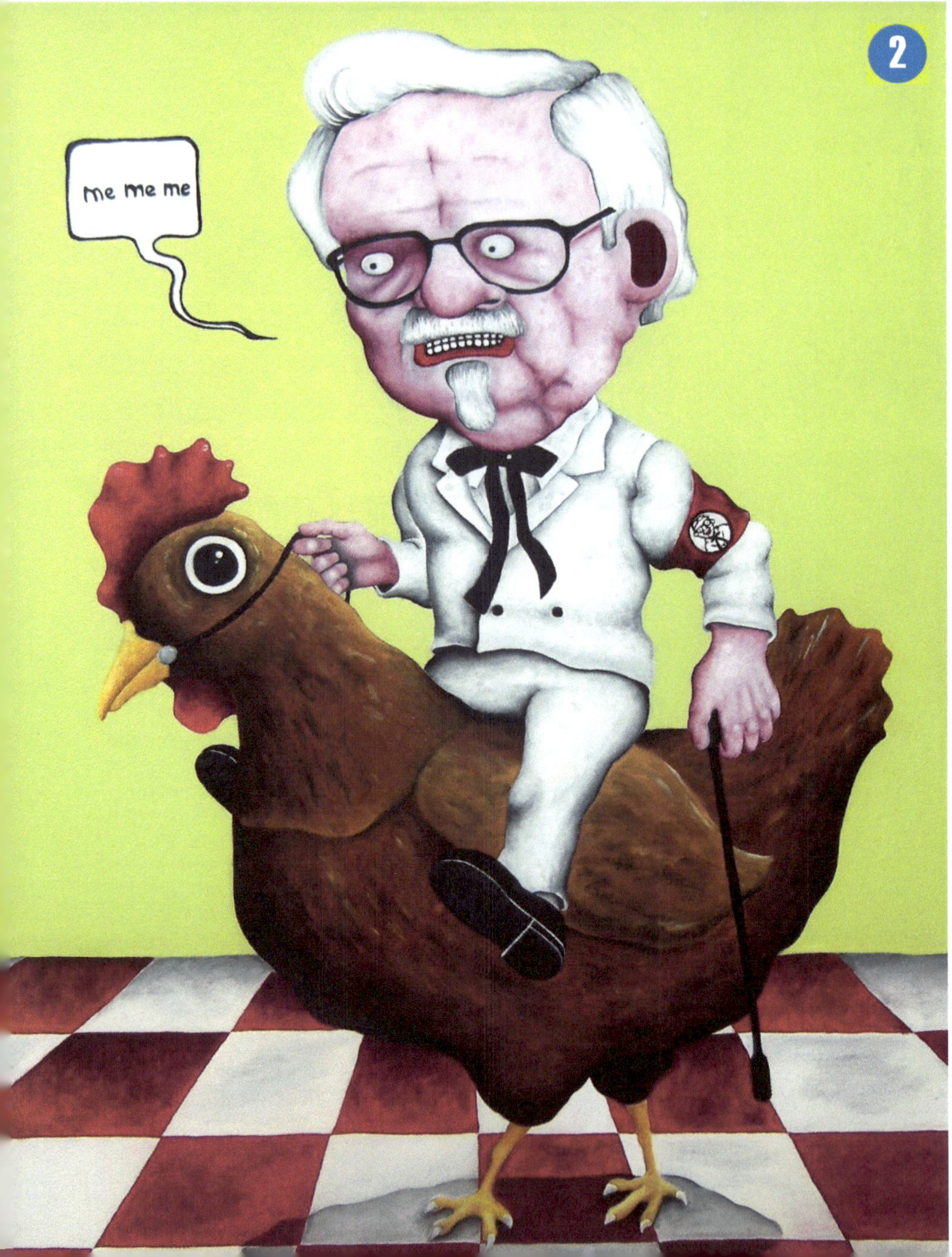

2

me me me

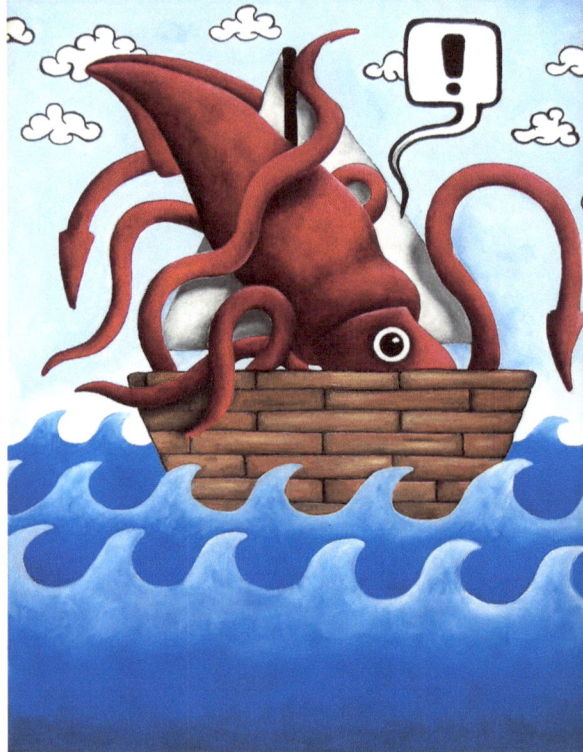

3

**2** **Chexploitation** 16x20" Oil on Canvas.

**3** **Portrait of the Artist as a Giant Squid** 11x14" Oil on Canvas.

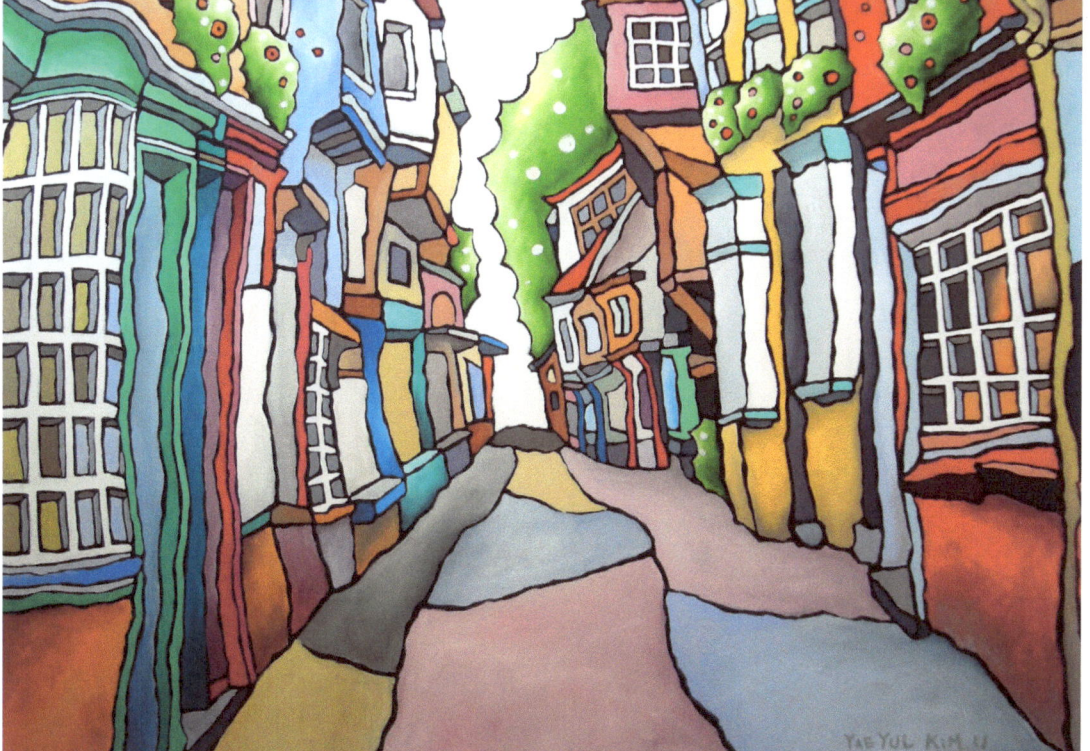

# YAEYUL KIM

**LOCATION:** Waterloo
**WEB:** Yaeyul.com
**EMAIL:** Yaeyul@yahoo.ca

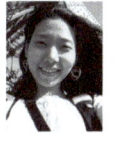

After graduating from University of Waterloo, majoring in Fine arts studio, Yaeyul has been working as a freelance artist in Waterloo, Ontario. She won C. J. Mills Printmaking Award in 2008. Her ideas come from daily thoughts, memories and experiences. She enjoys exploring ideas and developing new techniques for each theme. I have often discovered that the places from my memories are different in reality. My sweet memories become brighter and more beautiful while forms become uncertain and lose details. I revisit my places through my brush strokes from my memories on canvas.

**1 Place 006** 48x36" Oil on canvas.

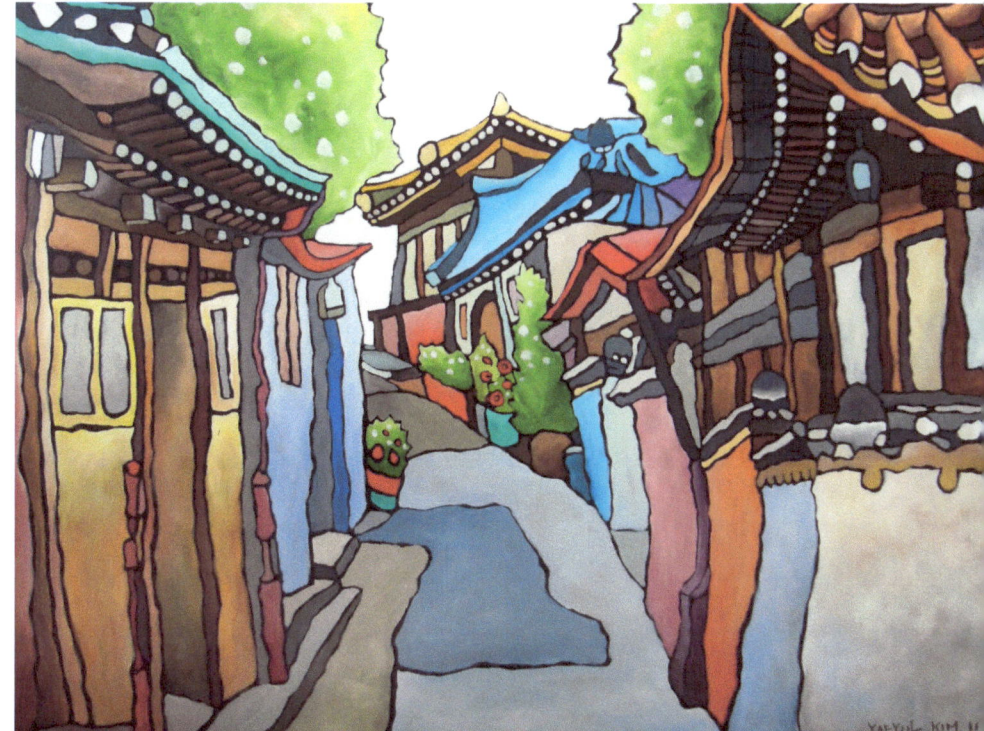

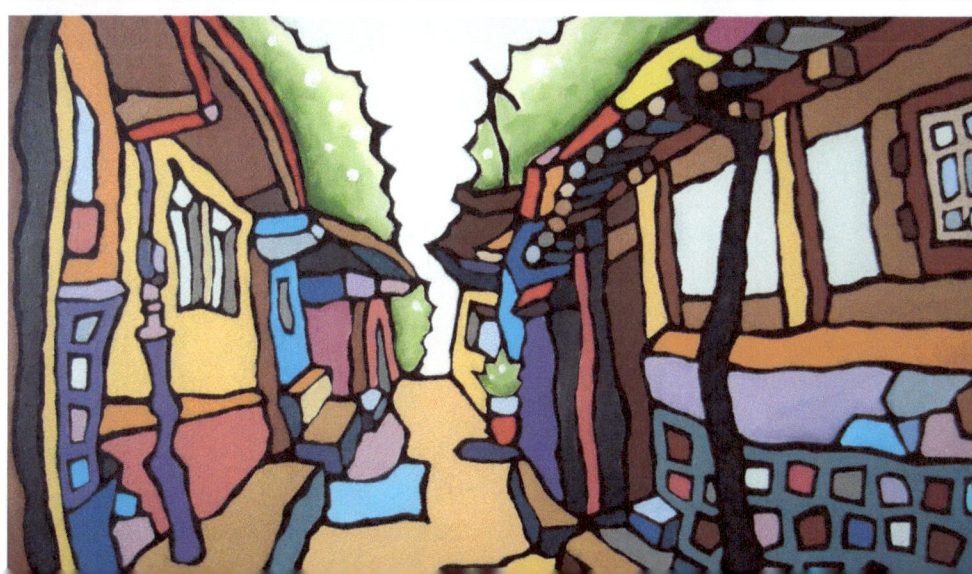

**2 Place 005** 48x36" Oil on canvas.

**3 Place 041** 30x18" Oil on canvas.

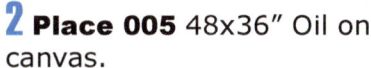

# MICHELLE SALTER

**LOCATION:** Stratford
**WEB:** www.michellesalter.ca
**EMAIL:** michelle@michellesalter.ca

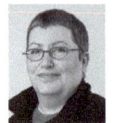

Michelle Salter paints with fire. She works in encaustic – the heat fusing of many layers of beeswax medium. Her work is influenced by her interest in nature and the environment as well as an appreciation of the abstract form. She loves the challenge of interpreting iconic Canadian seascapes in a new way. Salter is a graduate of the University of Waterloo with a B.A. in Fine Arts – Studio. Her work is collected throughout Canada and represented in many private and public collections.

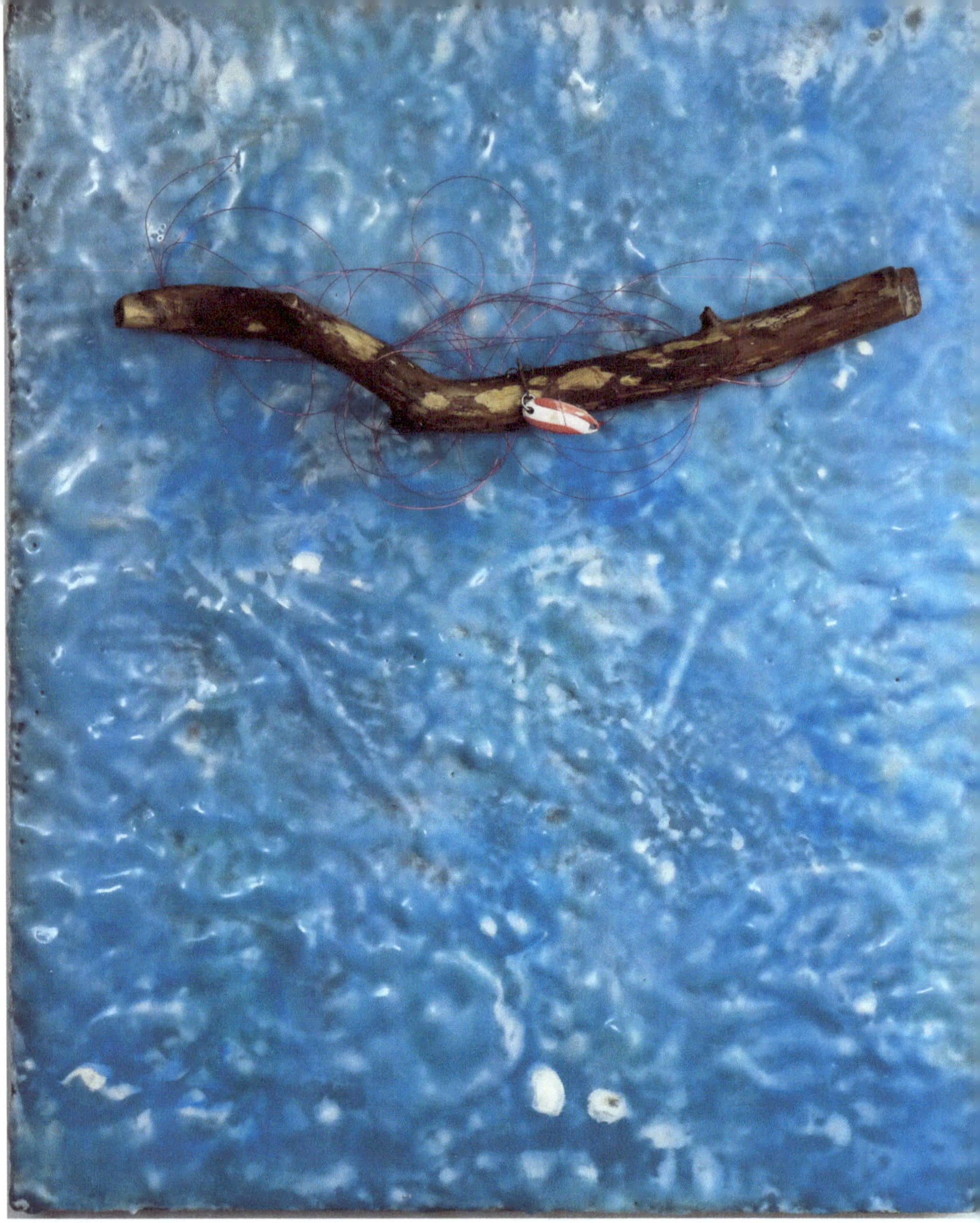

**1 Avon River Memories** 20x16" Encaustic, fishing lure, line and branch on birch panel 2011. When my sons were small, my husband and I would take them fishing for chub or shiners - anything that would bite, but their most common catch was a branch.

**2 Georgian Bay Granite #1** 12x12" Encaustic on birch panel 2011. Standing on the lichen covered granite along the shoreline of Georgian Bay.

**3 Georgian Bay** 12x12" Encaustic on birch panel 2011. This piece was inspired by watching the whirl-a-gig beetles skimming the waters of Georgian Bay.

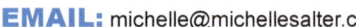

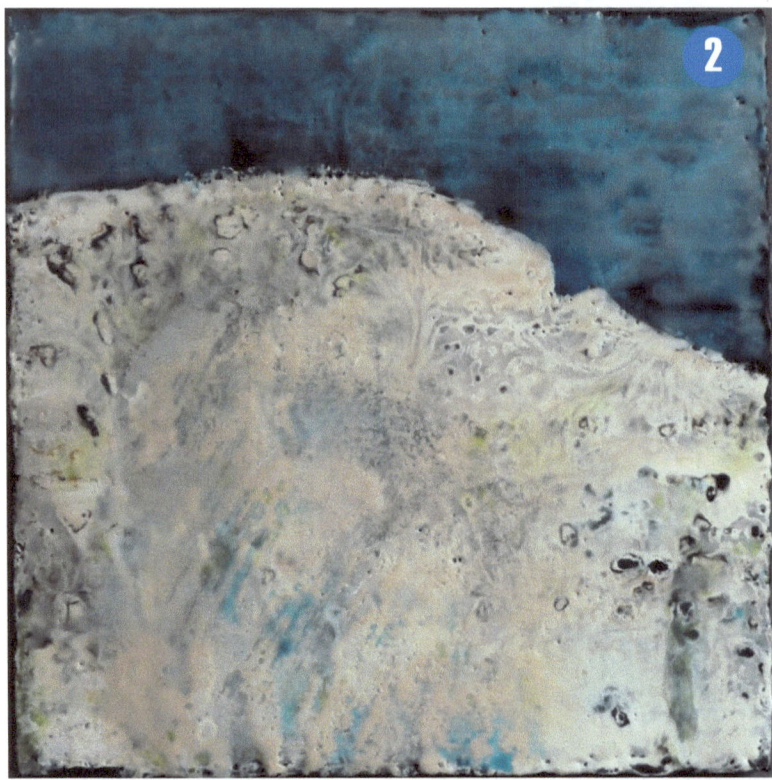

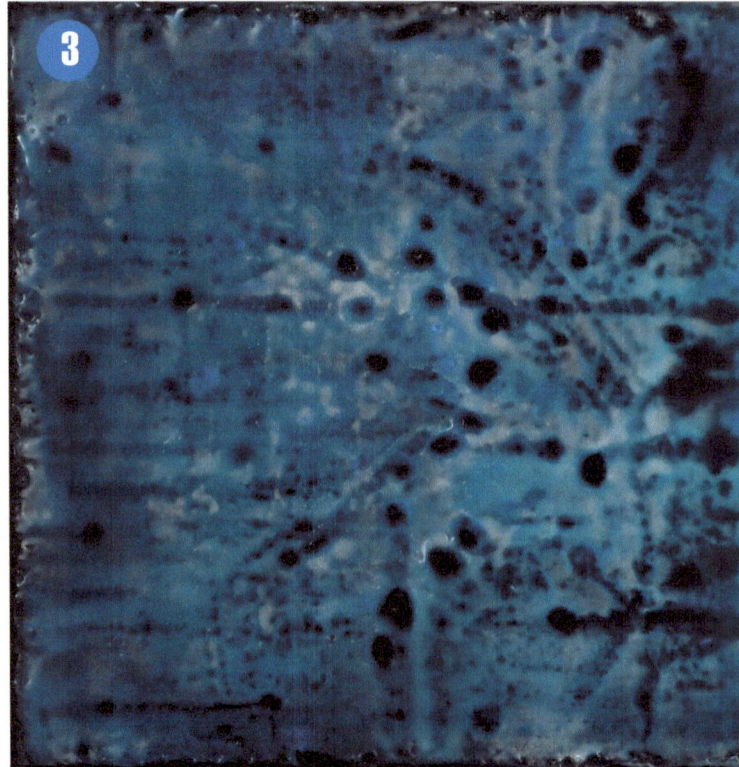

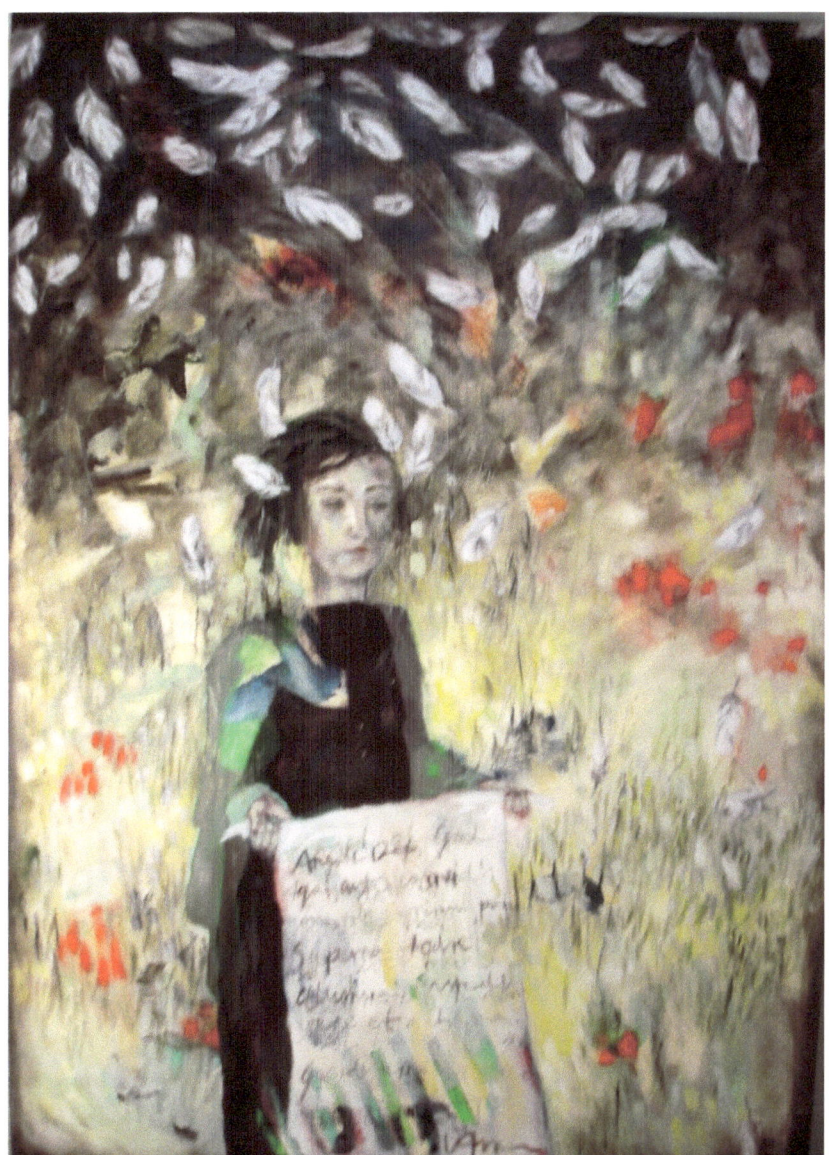

# KAROLINE VARIN-JARKOWSKI

**LOCATION:** Kitchener
**WEB:** KarolineVarin.com
**EMAIL:** Kvarin@yahoo.com

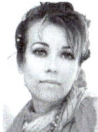

Karoline has a Bachelor of Fine Arts from the University of Waterloo and specializes in oil painting and altered books reflecting on the transience of life. She works with clients on commissions and teaches at the Kitchener Waterloo Art Gallery. Karoline is represented locally by Paula White-Diamond Gallery and by galleries in Oakville, Toronto and Ottawa. Her book work is in the National Collection of Polish Contemporary Book Art of the Museum of Lodz, Poland.

**1** **Angele Dei** 42x60" Oil and wax on canvas.

**2** **Guardian Angels III and IV** 9x27"each. Oil and wax on board.

**3** **The Bride** 27.5x27.5" Oil and wax on board.

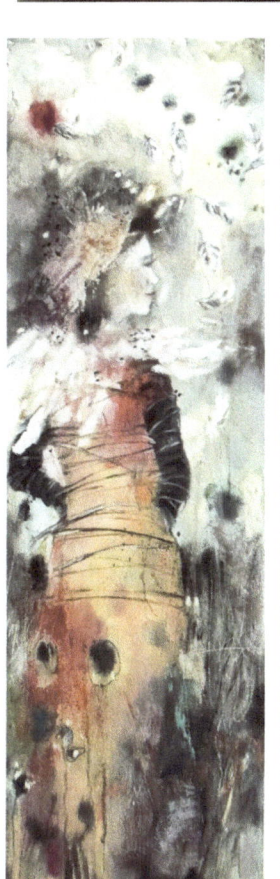 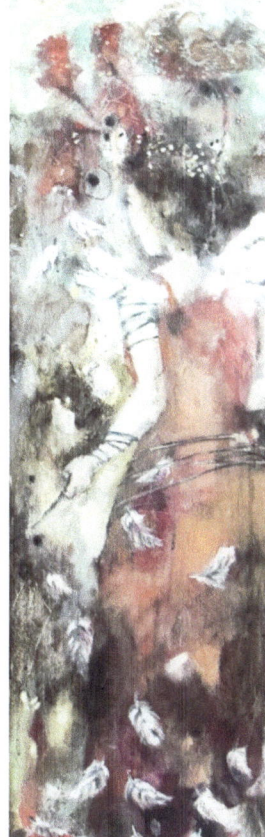

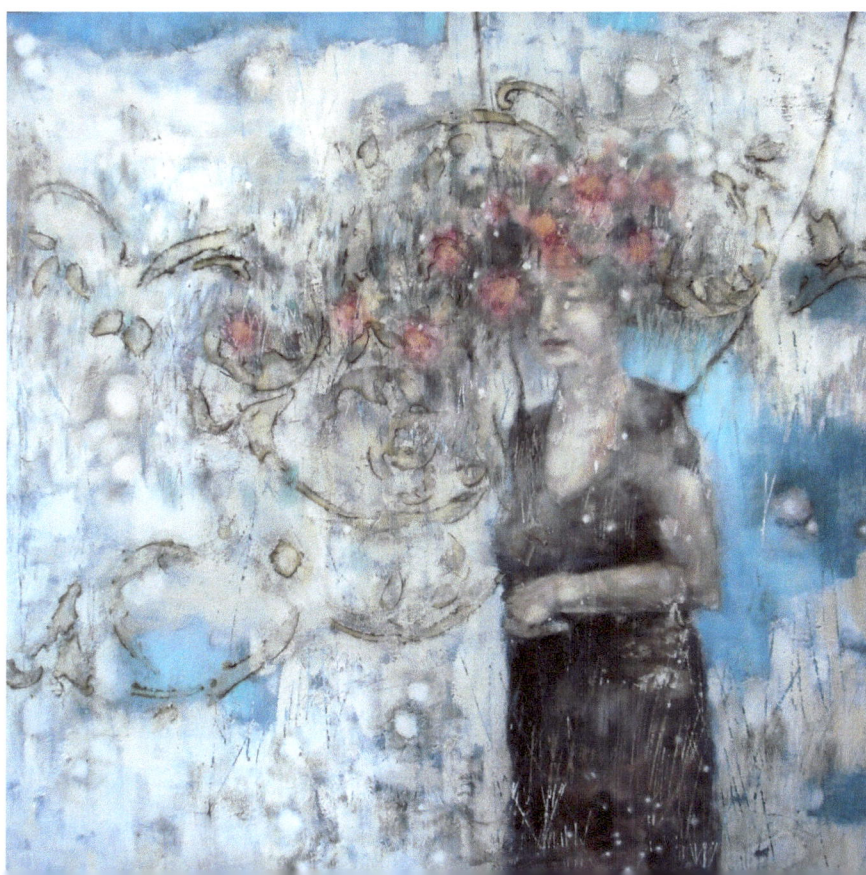

**1 Transformation of Joy-Butterfly Maiden** 5x7" Mixed Media. Number 1 in the Goddess Series.

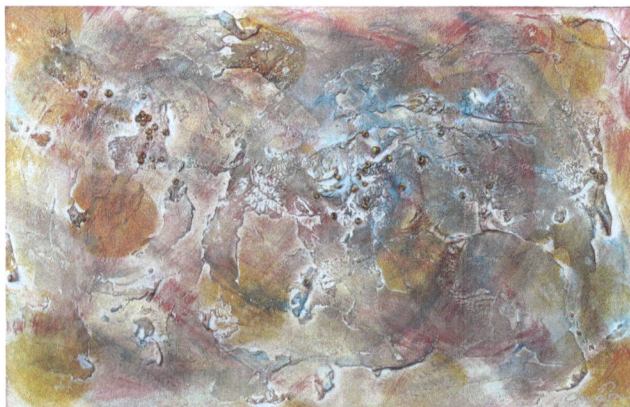

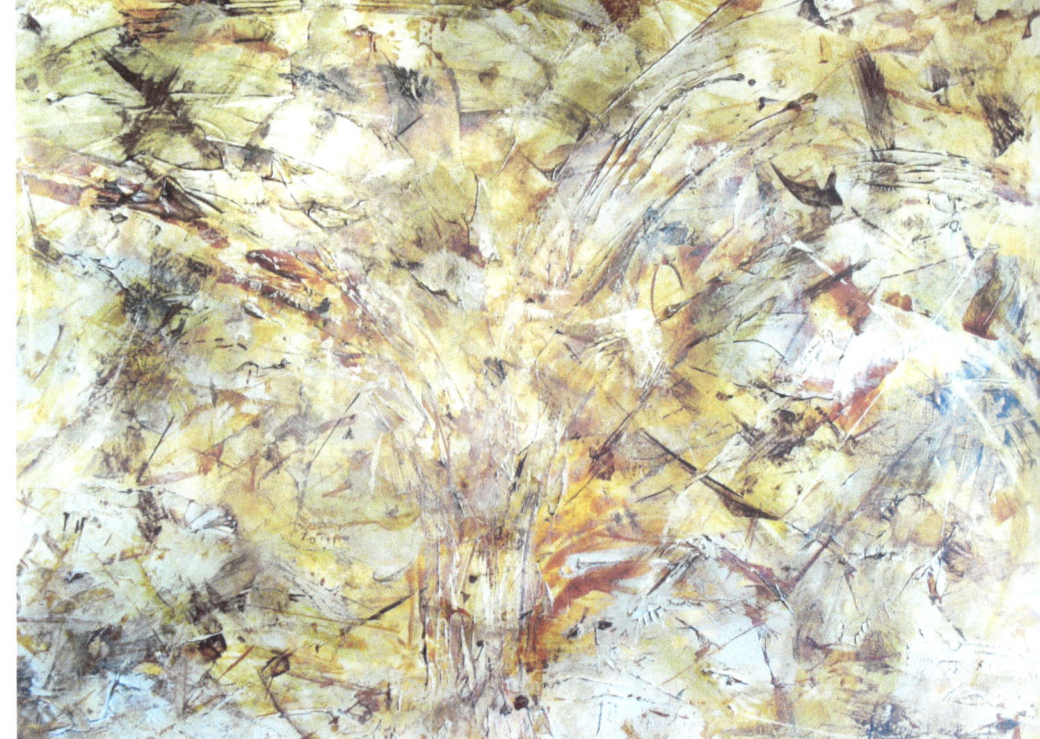

# JOY ROSS

**LOCATION:** Waterloo
**WEB:** (N/A)
**EMAIL:** JoyLoveOne@hotmail.com

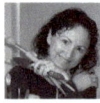

Joy Ross uses mixed media techniques and a varied colour pallet to explore altered realities that invoke stillness and beauty. She studied Illustration at Sheridan College and Fine Arts at the University of Waterloo. After studying collage with Jane Geard she finally understood what she could do with her paper obsession!

**2 Zeus' Pearls** 6"x9" Mixed Media. Zeus joined me in the studio for this one, and showed me how he created the Universe. Interesting afternoon!

**3 Tree of Life** 20x27" Mixed Media.

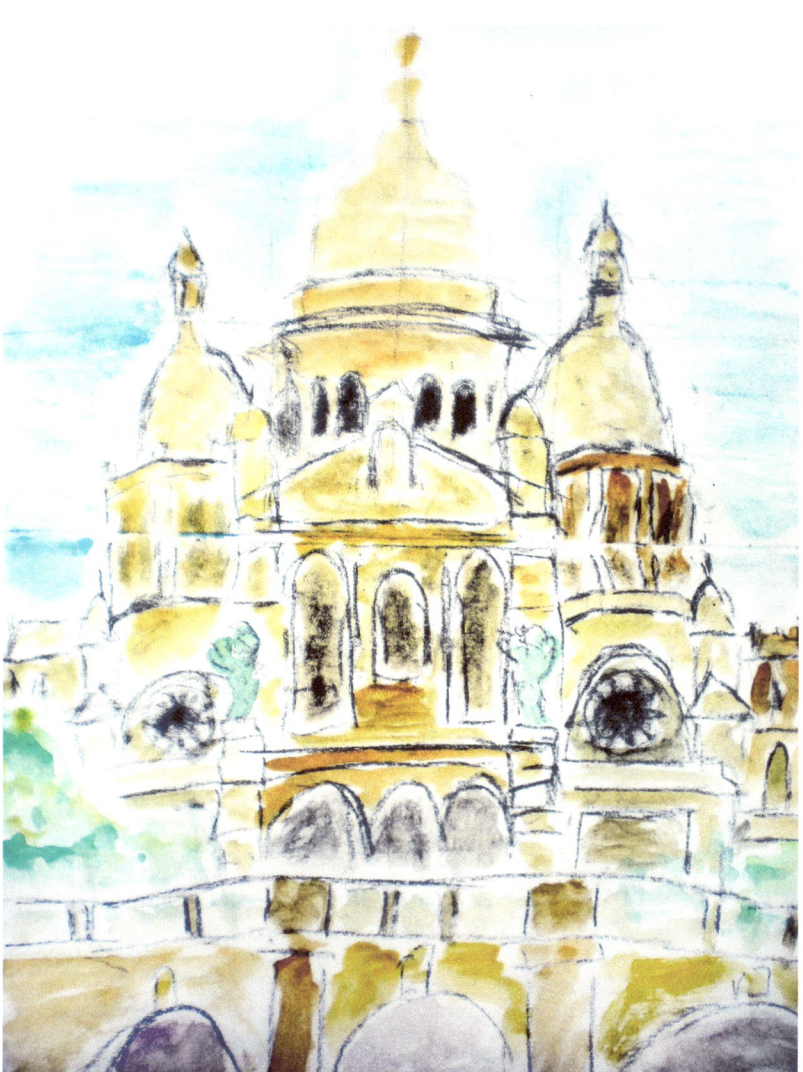

# JOAN ANG

**LOCATION:** Waterloo
**WEB:** Wix.com/joanlikecreature/home
**EMAIL:** Joanlikecreature@gmail.com

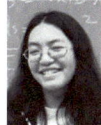

Joan is an engineering student at the University of Waterloo. She wanders from place to place and documents the transience of her life with drawings, paintings, writings and pictures. She also enjoys singing, knitting and learning languages.

**1** **Sacre Coeur, Paris** Watercolours and charcoal.

**2** **Entwined** 9x12" Oil on canvas.

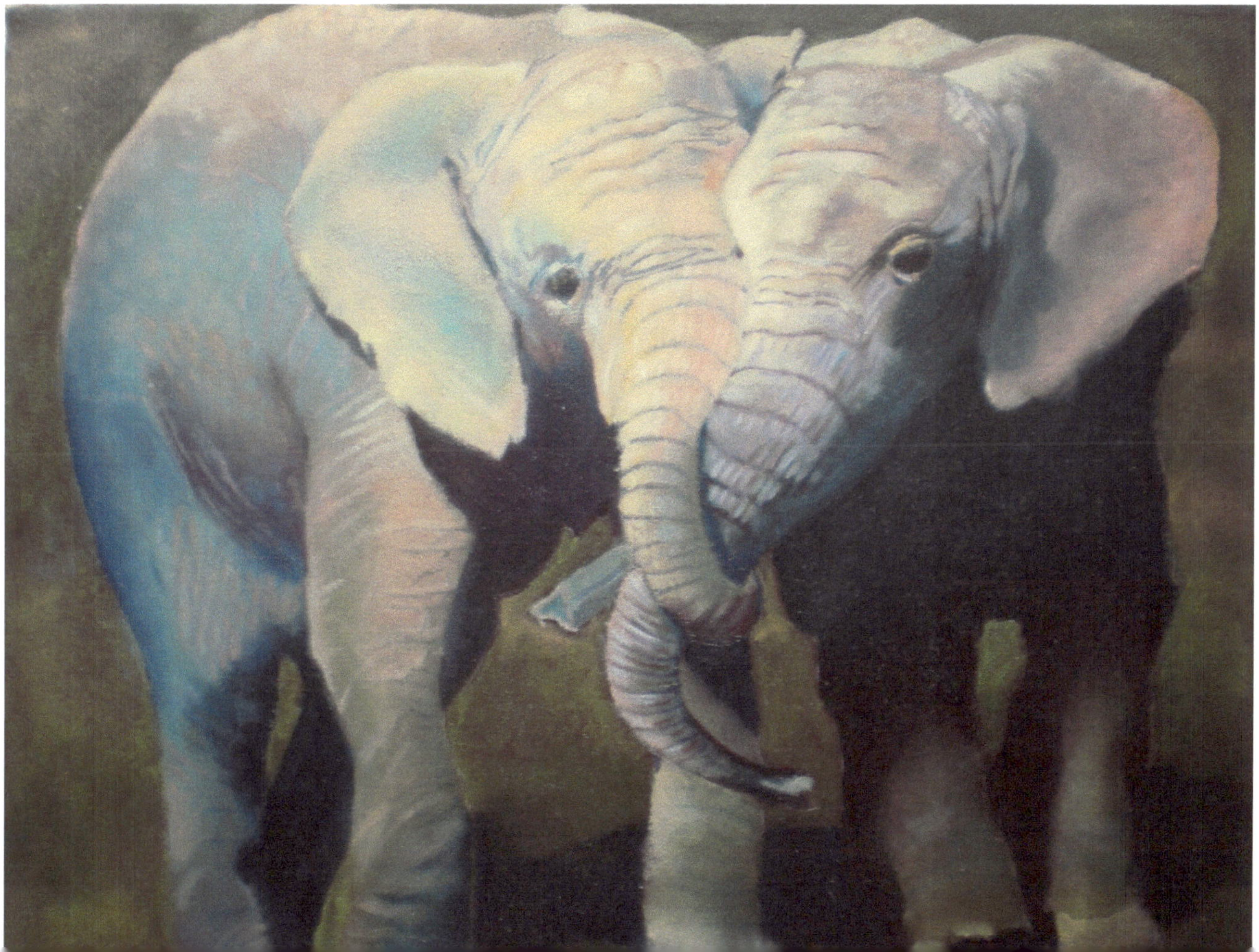

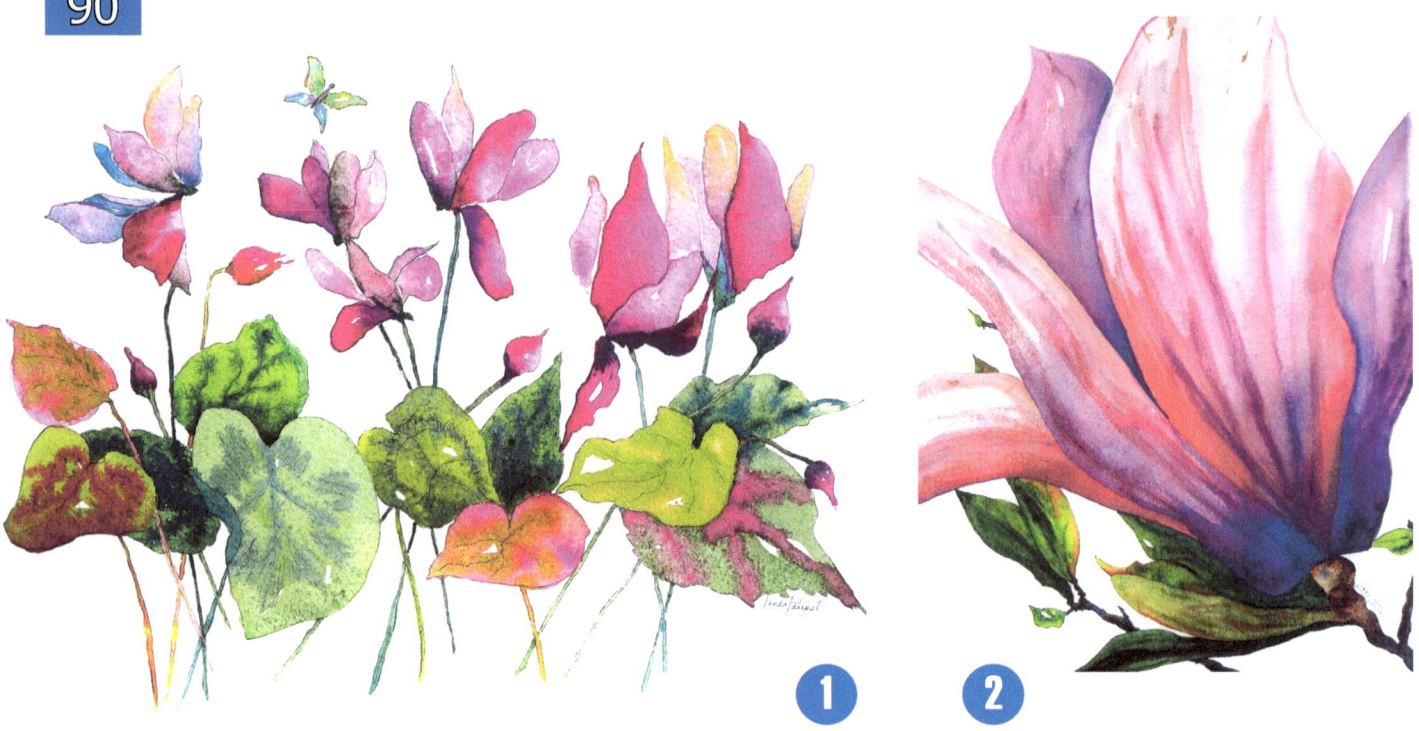

**1 Cyclamen** Ink & Watercolour on Paper.

**2 Magnolia Blossom** 11x15" Ink & Watercolour on Paper.

**3 Amaryllis** 14x20" Ink & Watercolour on paper.

# LINDA PAUPST

**LOCATION:** Waterloo
**WEB:** Krop.com/lindapaupst
Petalsnpens.blogspot.com
**EMAIL:** Lrpaupst@rogers.com

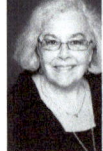

Linda's love of florals stem from her roots in her parents' flower shop, nursery, garden center & greenhouses in North Bay, Ontario. Of her work others have said - Artist Peter Etril Snyder: "excellent work, beautifully and elegantly drawn and well-placed int he space". Scott C "..you capture the strength, beauty..and fragility of flowers - here today gone tomorrow". Wendy Tupling Harris: ".. outstanding, refreshing, inspiring, moving". Linda's work is available from York Nursery of Kitchener, Blossoms Flowers of Burlington, and Ellen Lily, of Queen St. E Toronto.

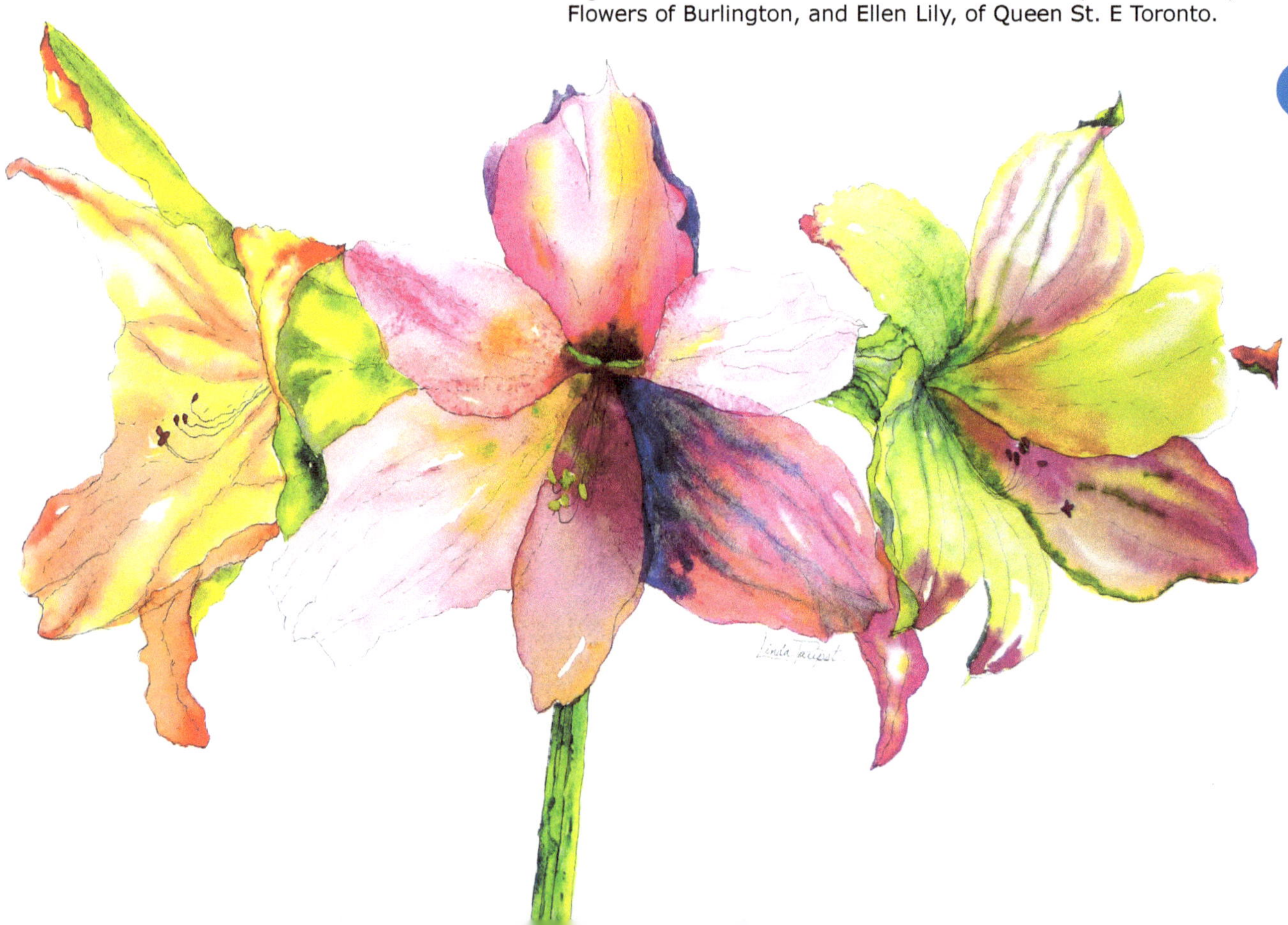

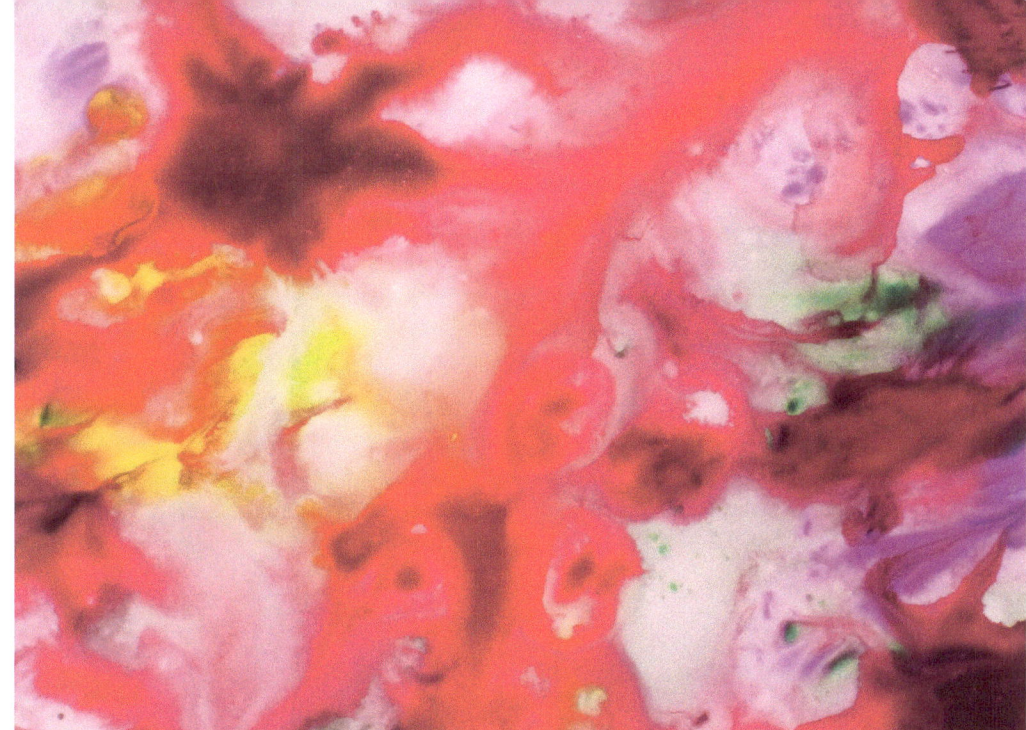

# WILMA VANDERLEEUW

**LOCATION:** Waterloo
**WEB:** (N/A)
**EMAIL:** WilmaVanderleeuw@gmail.com

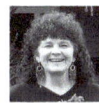

Wilma Vanderleeuw is a local Waterloo artist. She normally use a variety of media and subjects, but is always game to try somethig new. This year she is focusing on abstracted colours and shapes, and is working on a large series of small paintings in acrylic. They range in size from 4" by 4" and up to 6" by 7" She hopes this will lead to executing a number of much larger works in the end.

**1 Untitled** 4x7" acrylic.

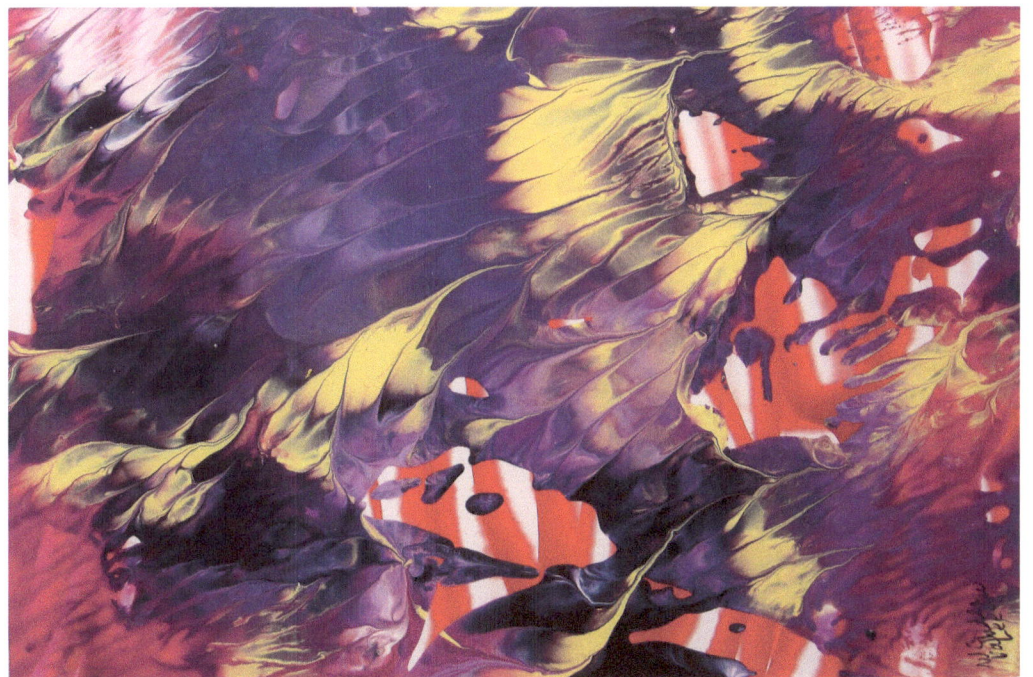

**2 Untitled** 4x7" acrylic.

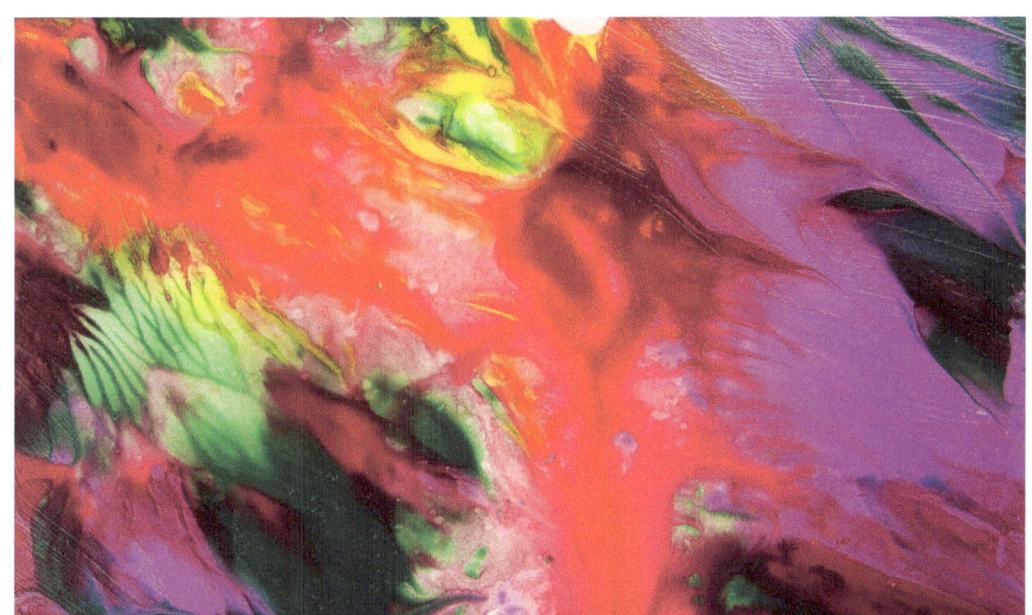

**3 Untitled** 4x7" acrylic.

# JEFFREY CHAN

**LOCATION:** Waterloo/Toronto
**WEB:** JeffreyChanArt.com
**EMAIL:** Jeff@JeffreyChanArt.com

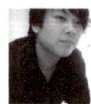

Jeffrey Chan is a Rock n' Roll fanatic who divides his time between Hong Kong, Toronto and Waterloo. He received his BFA Honours Studio Specialization from the University of Waterloo. Jeffrey draws his main inspiration from the current trends, music cultures, and all things Rock n' Roll. His style is a blended mixture of the past and present street-art culture, with his own artistic approach. A unique style composed from his painterly techniques through the extensive use of palette knives; and, the incorporation of aerosol stenciling and layering techniques of the growing street-art community. His choice of painting medium includes: Oil, Acrylic, Ink and Aerosol Spray. Through this style Jeffrey is able to create studio paintings fixated with the elements of the street art culture. Currently, Jeffrey is continuing his artistic career through the domains of painting, printmaking, and photography.

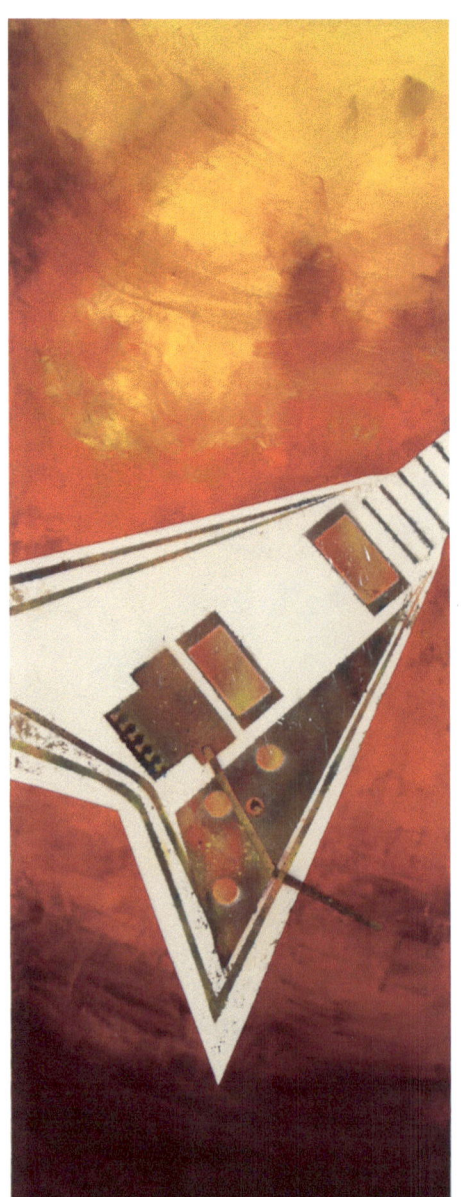

**1** **Guitar Rig #1: 6505** Oil, acrylic, aerosol on canvas.

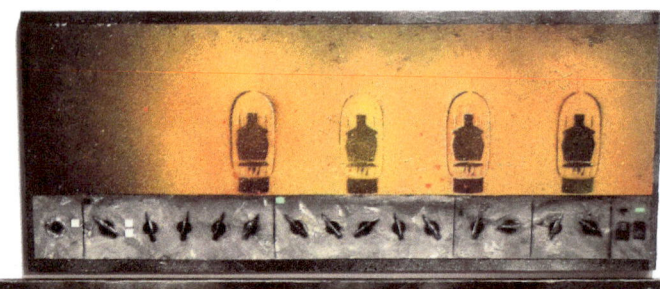

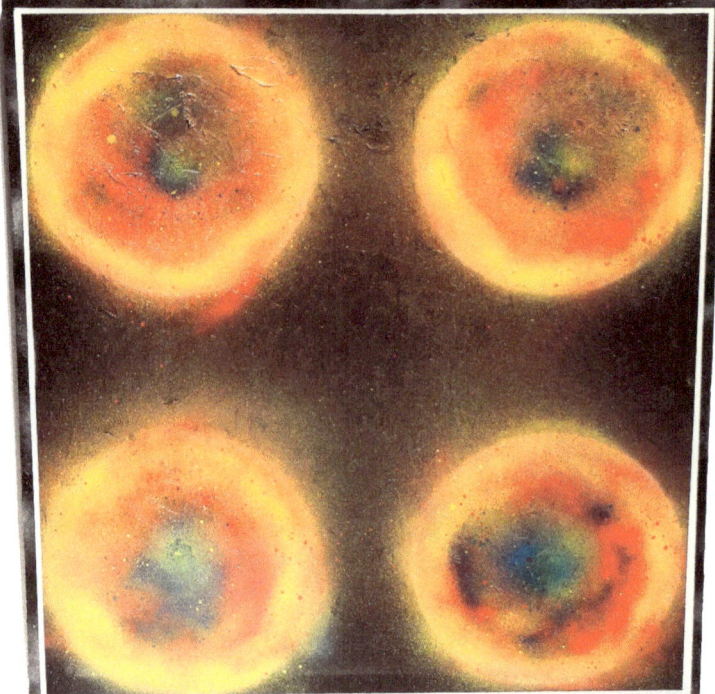

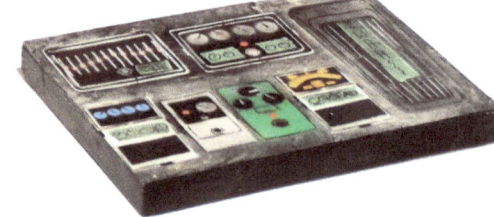

**2** **Guitar Series: Rhoads** 5.5x2.5' Oil, acrylic, aerosol on canvas.

**3** **Guitar Rig #1-3: Pedal Boards** Oil, acrylic, aerosol on canvas.

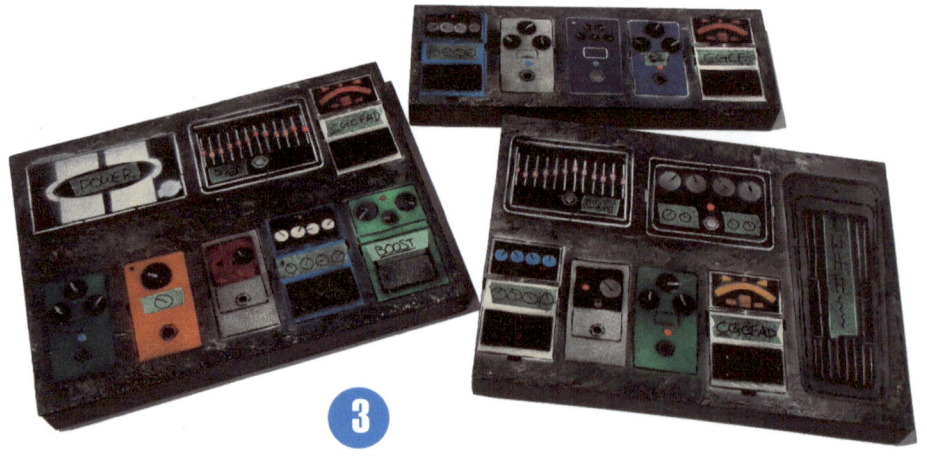

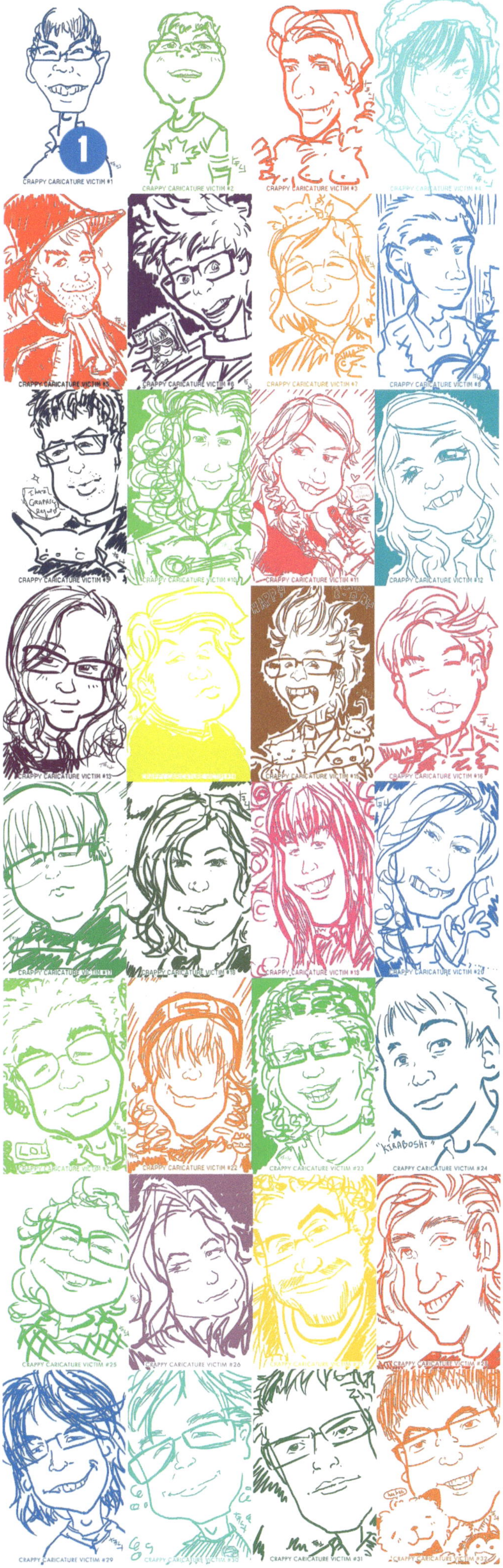

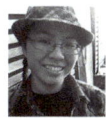

# ALCINA WONG

**LOCATION:** Waterloo (Earth)
**WEB:** Awsketchblog.wordpress.com
Kaitou-al.deviantart.com
**EMAIL:** White_kaitou@hotmail.com

Alcina (aka Jackpanda, Kaitou-al, K-AL) was born in the Toronto area with a passion for art, graphics, comics, animation, and basically any kind of story-telling medium. Currently studying at the University of Waterloo, she drifts between co-op, school, extra-curriculars, drawing...and more drawing.

**1 Crappy Caricature Project** Drawing caricatures of my Friends on Facebook. Photoshop and wacom tablet.

**2 White Sun** White sun, blue sky, field of red. Photoshop and wacom tablet.

**3 Smoking Gun** Traditional mixed media, pen ,pastel, coloured pencil, marker.

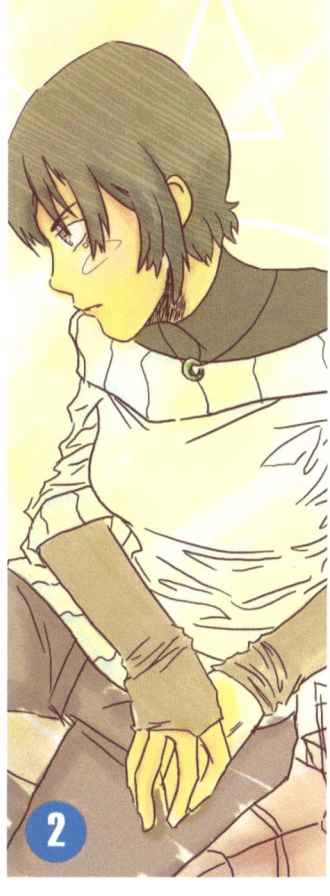

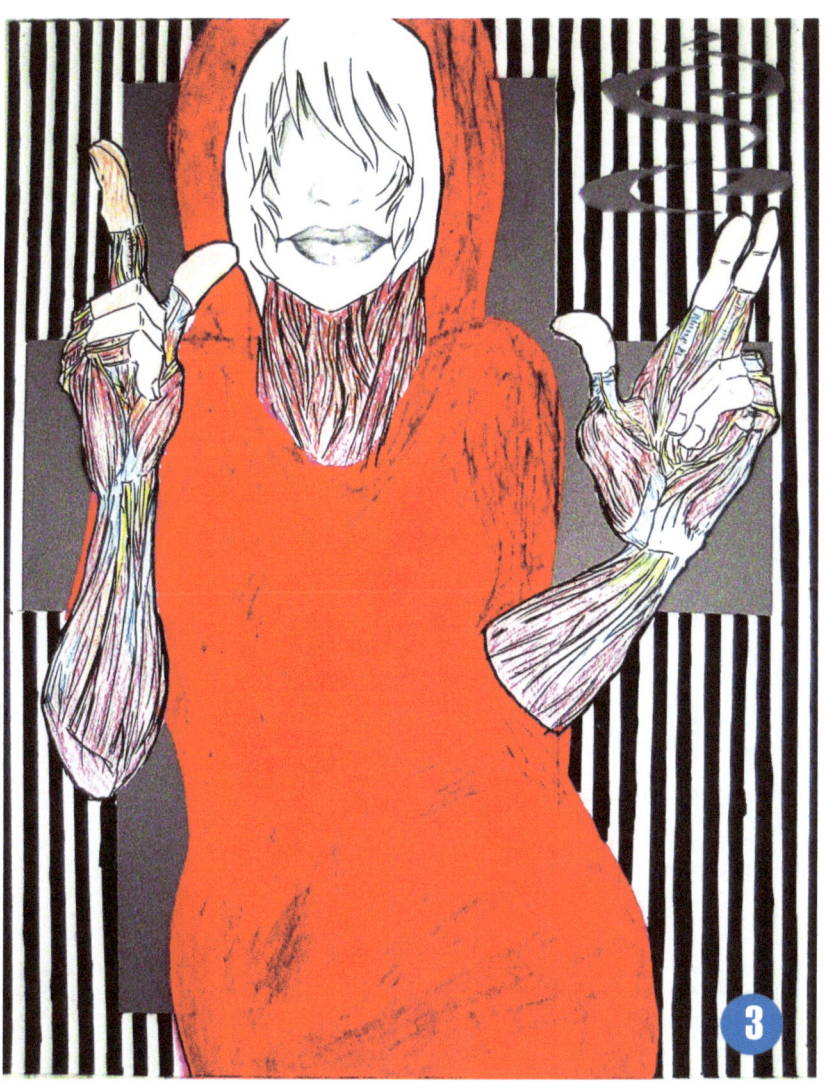

**1 Music Man** 18x24" Mixed Media on canvas. My musical grandson, Kieran.

**2 Nave's** Lily 18x24" Acrylic on canvas. Stargazer Lily from my garden.

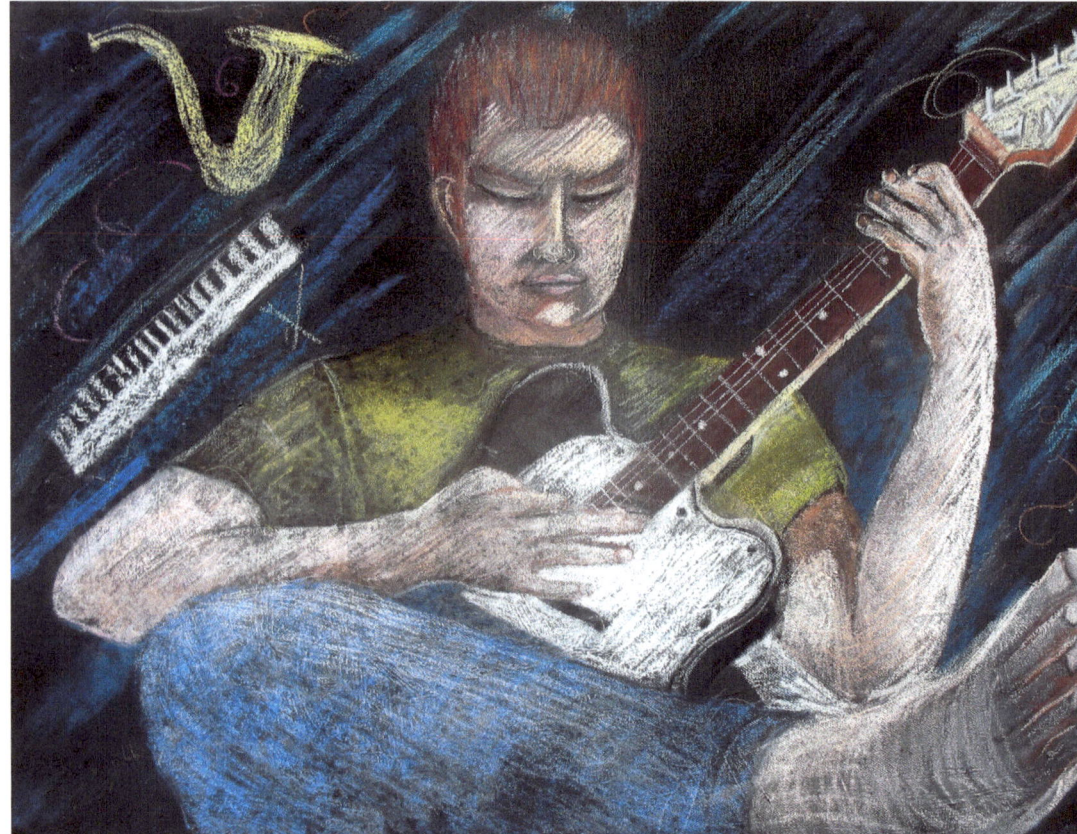

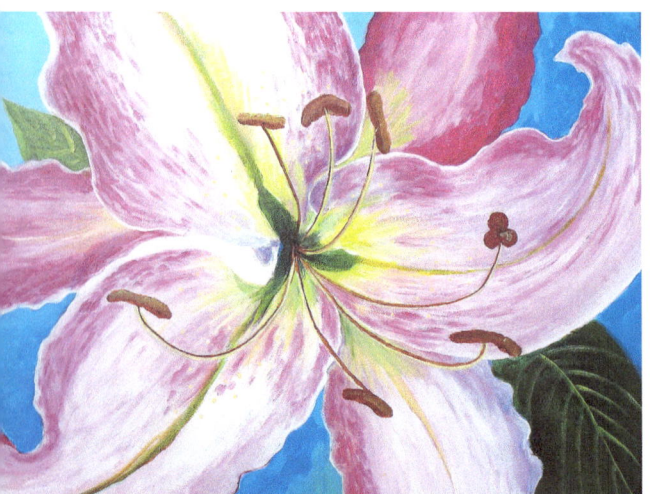

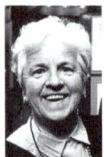

# DIANE TYRRELL

**LOCATION:** Waterloo
**WEB:** (N/A)
**EMAIL:** Diane.Tyrrell@yahoo.com

Diane Tyrrell has been an artist since she was a child and has taught hundreds of children and seniors to paint and draw. Although skilled in ceramics, pottery, printmaking, pastels and textiles (quilt making), painting in oils or acrylics is her first love. Currently excited about painting Byzantine Icons, she also enjoys painting landscapes, portraits of those she loves, and beauty from her garden.

**3 Down the Bohreen** 20x24" Oil on canvas. Memories of Ireland.

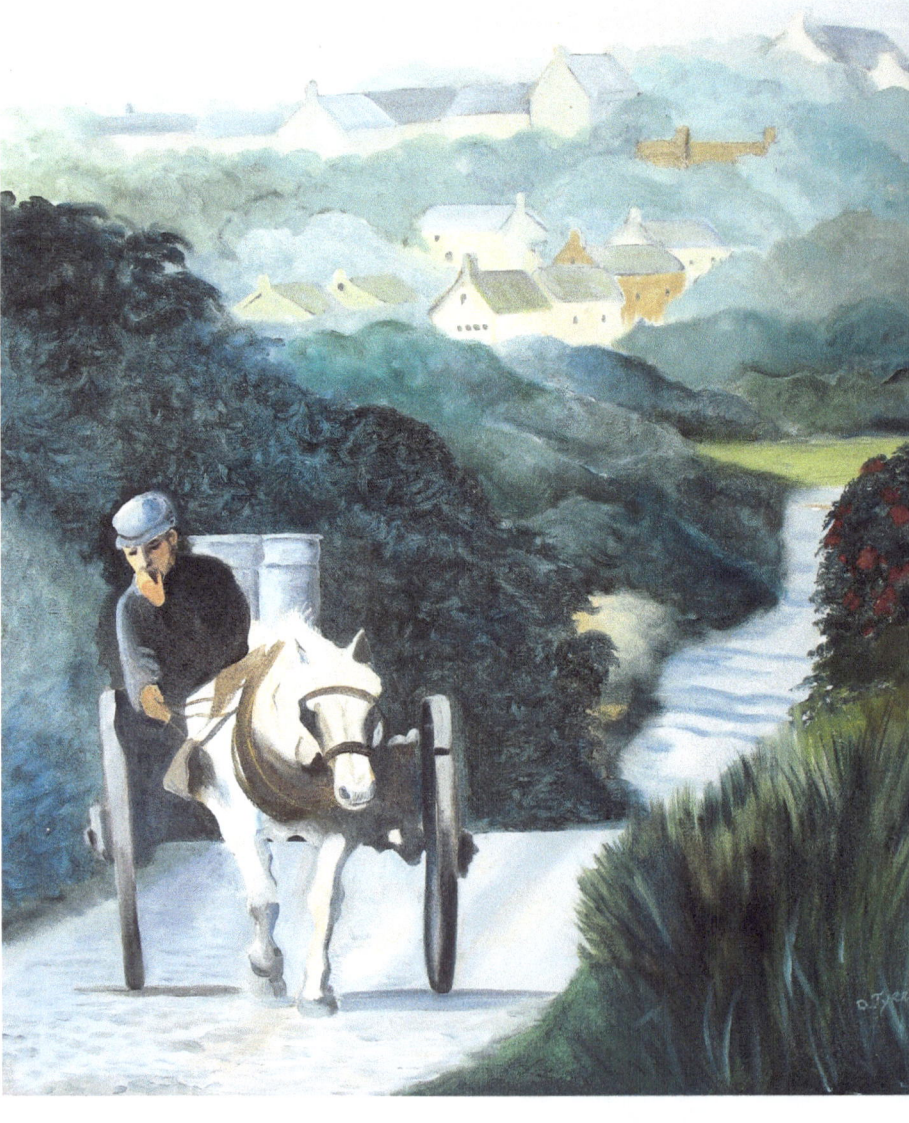

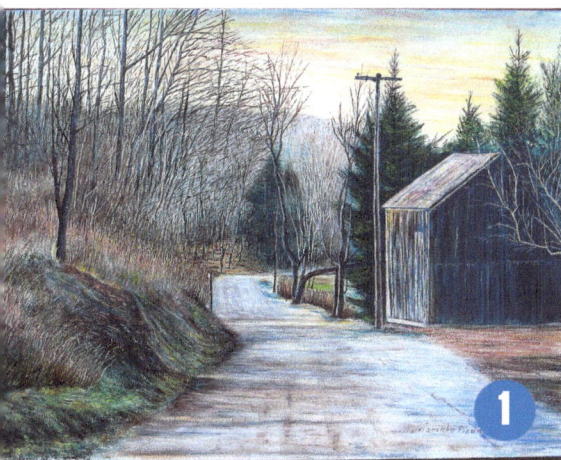

**1** **Barn in the Fall** 24x18" Oil on canvas. Painted in 2009.

# MARINKO PIPUNIC

**LOCATION:** Kitchener

**WEB:** Marinkoart.com

**EMAIL:** Marinko@marinkoart.com

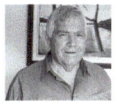

Marinko Pipunic was born and raised in Croatia and has since lived in the Netherlands and Alberta before settling in Kitchener. Marinko creates his art at his home studio in Kitchener and mainly focuses on landscape oil paintings. He has been an artist for over 40 years.

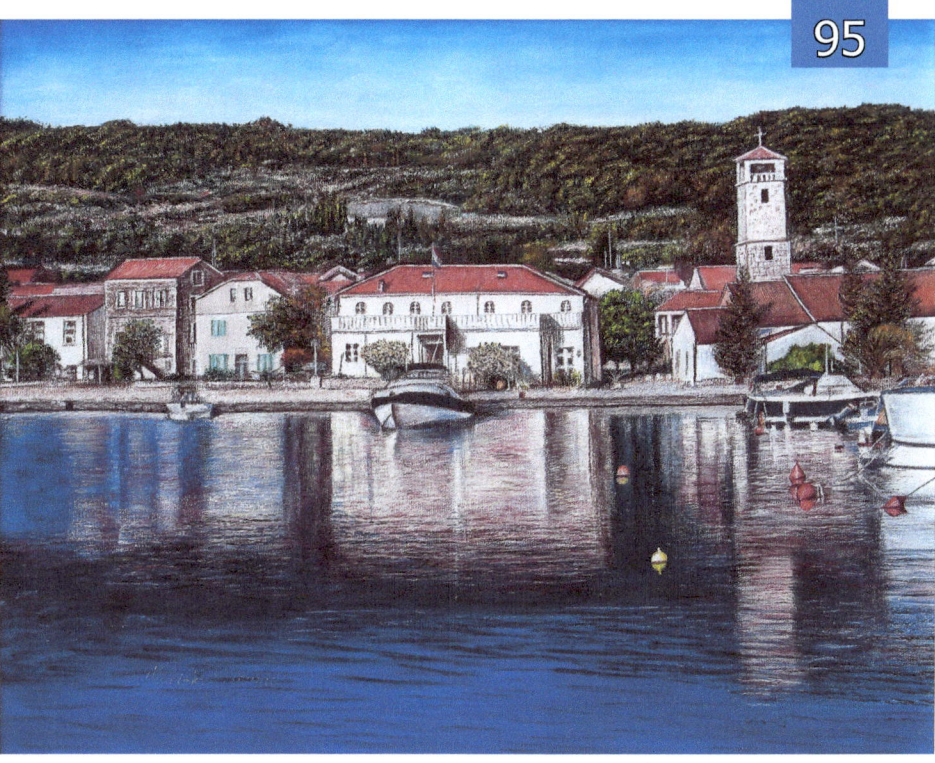

**2** **Island of Iz, Croatia** 24x18" Oil on canvas. Painted in 2010.

**3** **Gros Morne, Newfoundland** 24x18" Oil on canvas. Painted in 2010.

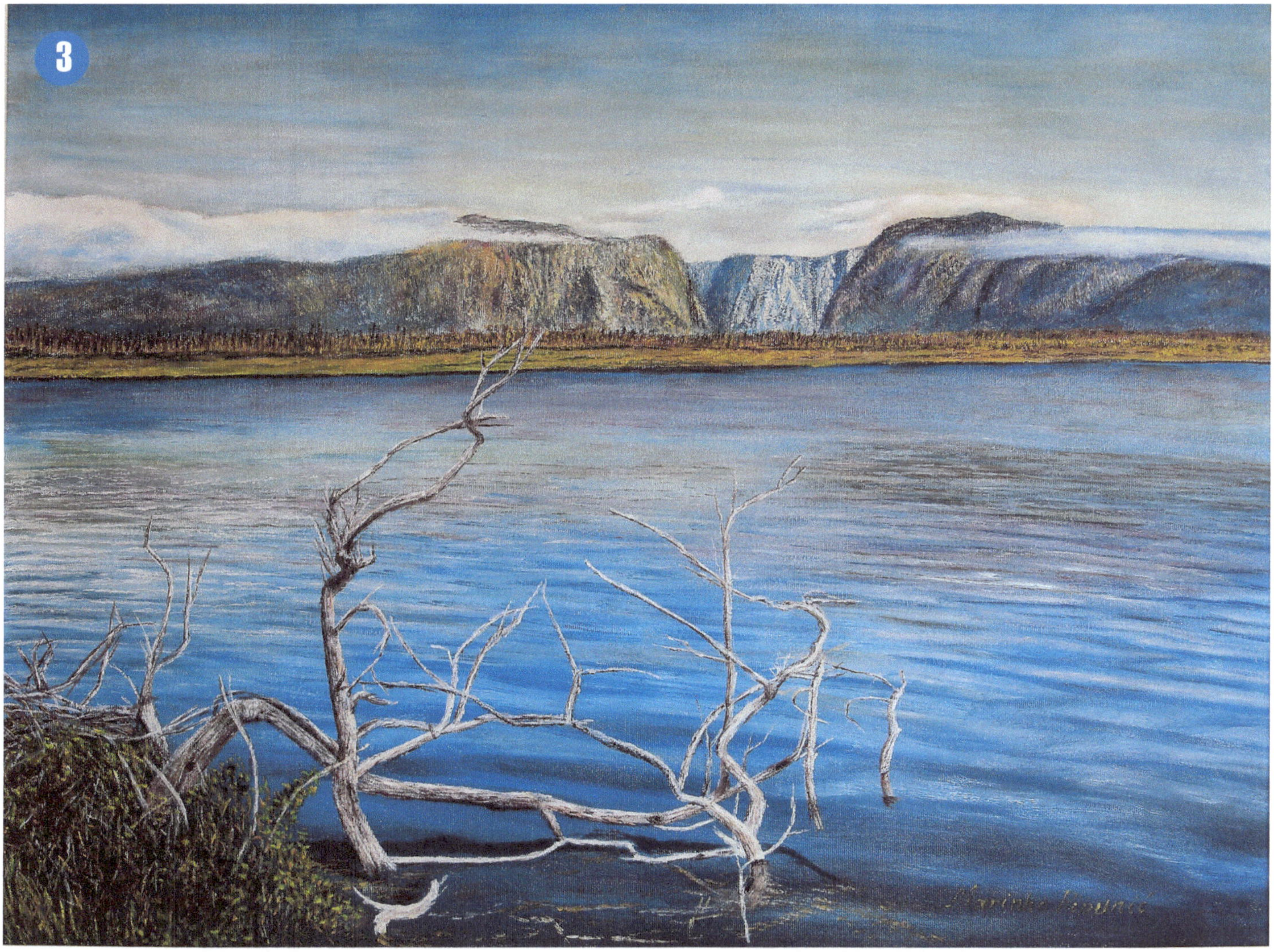

# NICLIN MCNEICE

**LOCATION:** Kitchener
**WEB:** StormmeKinkade.deviantart.com
**EMAIL:** Stormme@tcbs.net

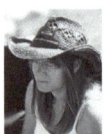

Niclin is an eclectic self taught traditional artist that does a variety of art in a variety of different styles [mostly pencil and pencil crayons with a dash of watercolors]. She is a huge fan of fantasy work, and animals [mostly cats and Rottweiler's.] She is always expanding her boundaries as an artist, looking for new and creative means of expressing her imagination and the world around her.

**1 Celtic Cross** 7x7" Indian Ink on white paper. I saw a piece of this image and I just had to make it a whole circle.

**2 Fairy of the Waning Quarter** 9x12" Pencil crayon on black paper – Part of the Fairies of the Moon series.

**3 Fairy of the Full Moon** 9x12" Pencil crayon on black paper – Part of the Fairies of the Moon series.

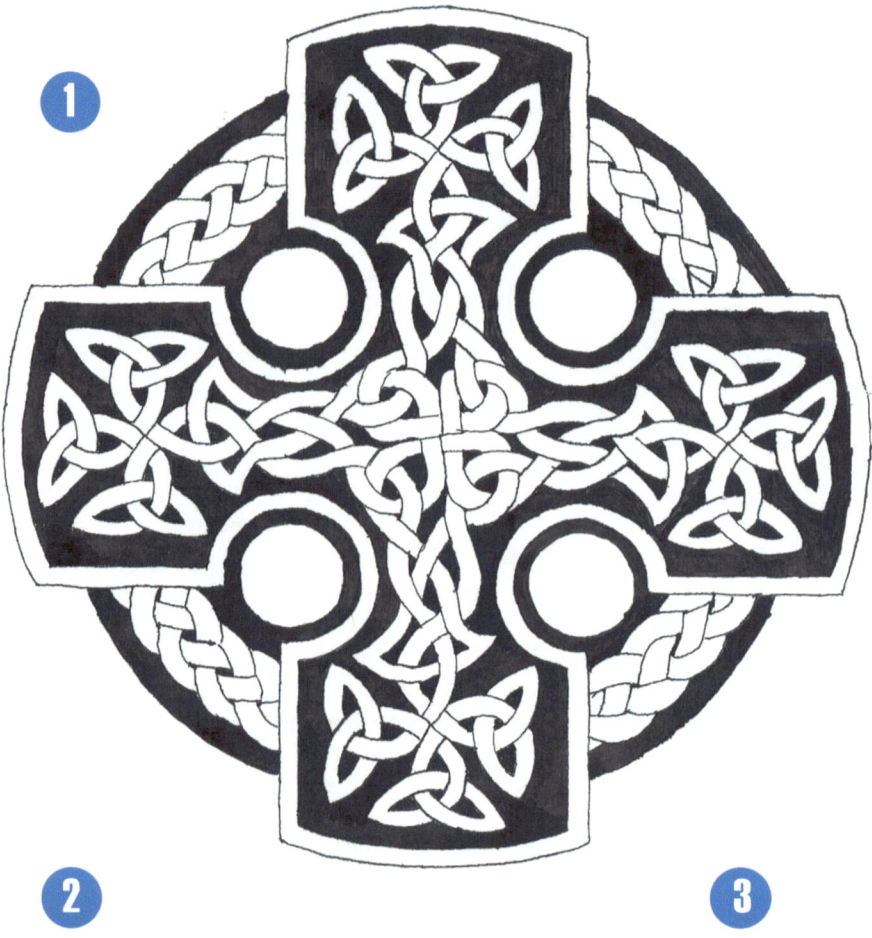

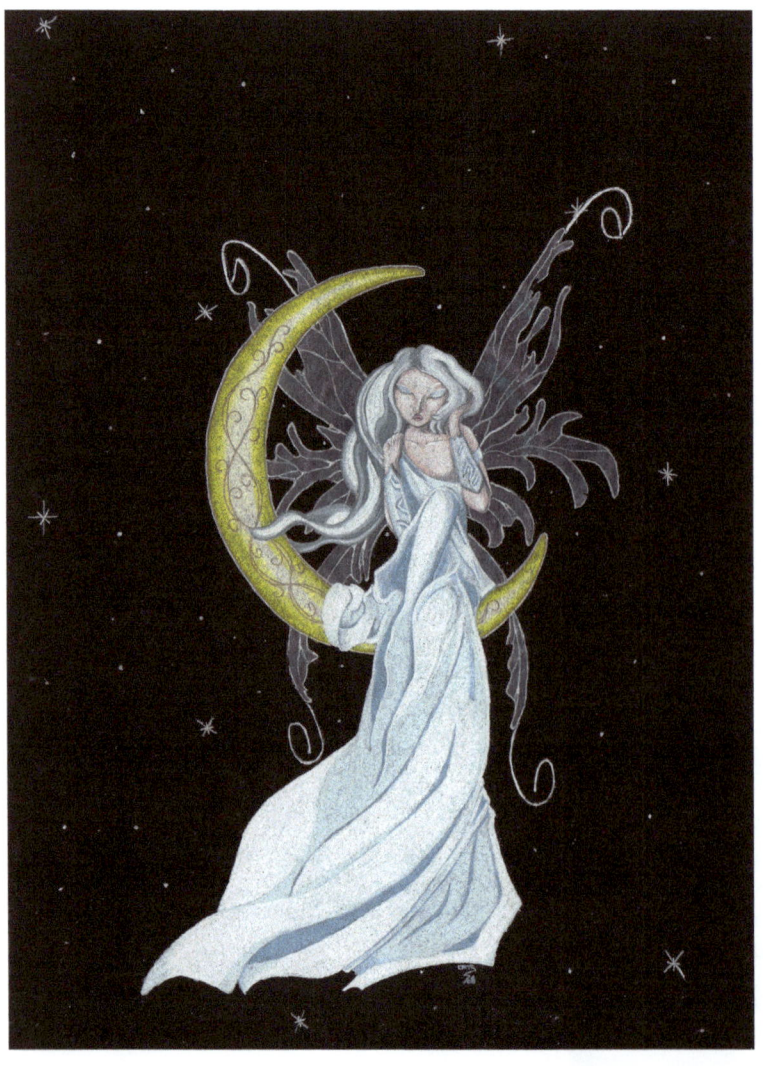

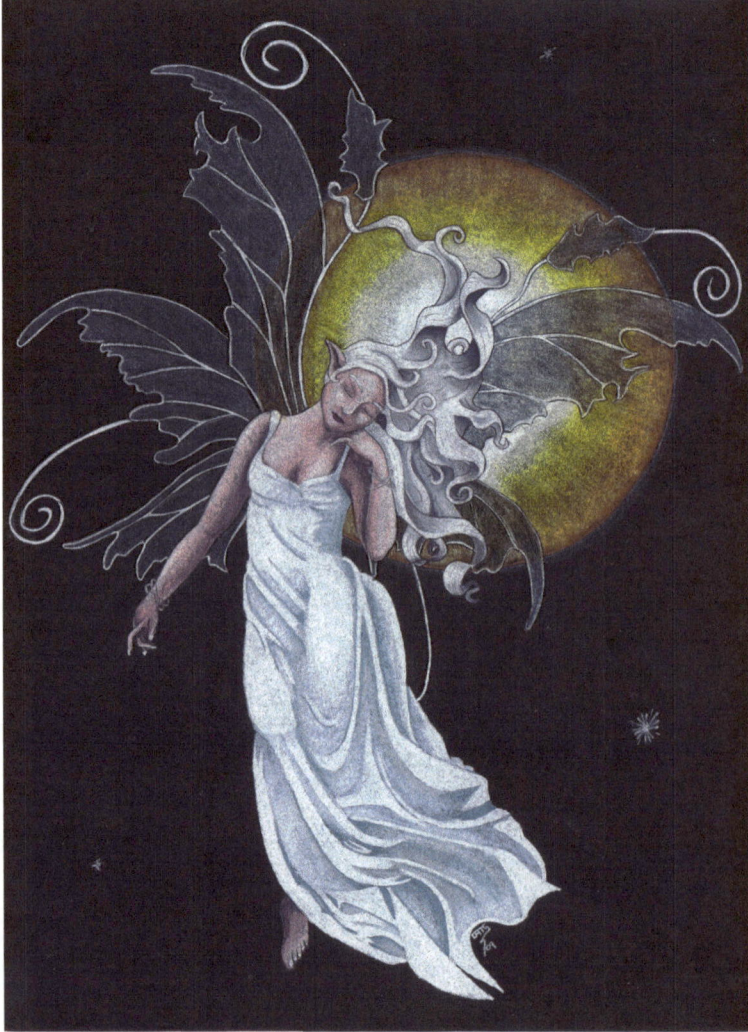

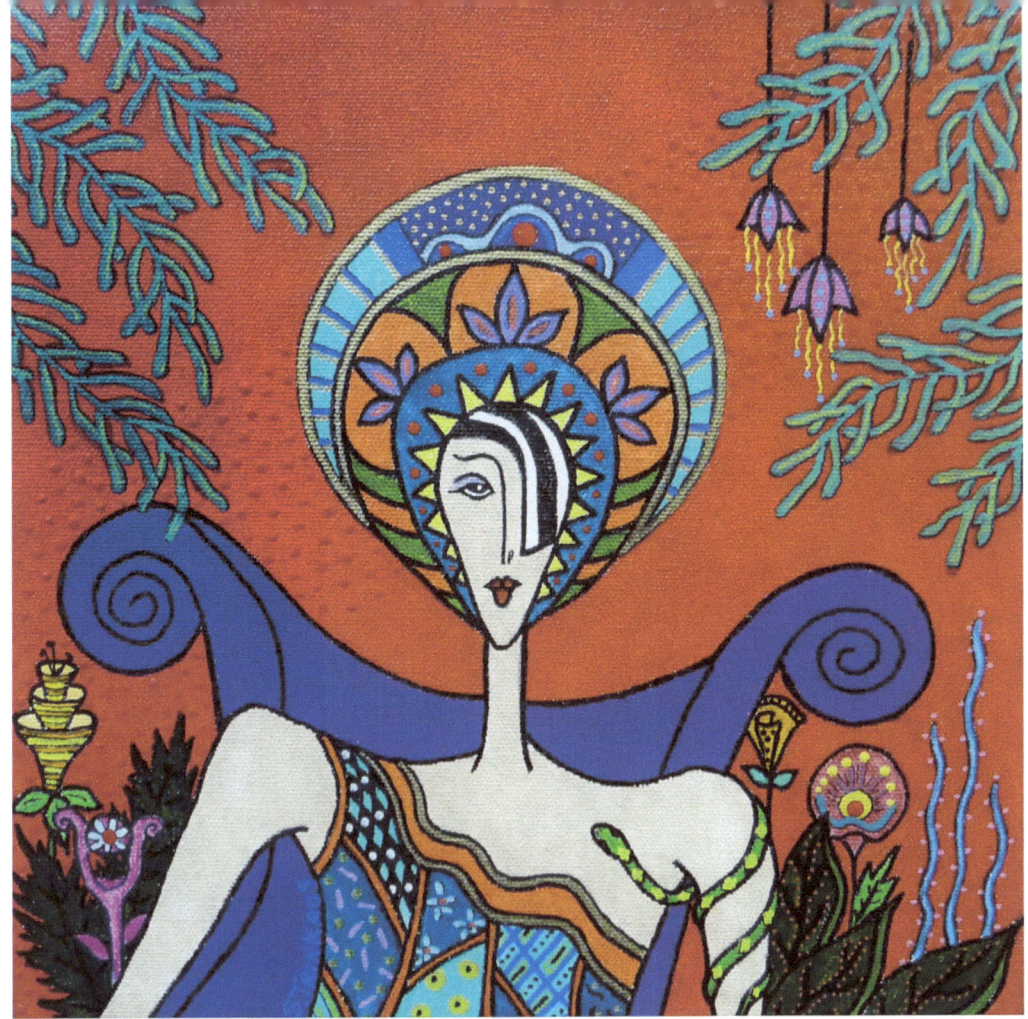

**1** **The Floral Princess** 10x10"
Acrylic.

# SHEILA TRINKAUS

**LOCATION:** Kitchener
**WEB:** STrinkaus.com
**EMAIL:** SheilaTrinkaus@hotmail.com

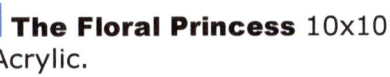
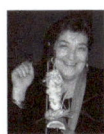

Throughout my life as an artist, I have had the opportunity to be educated, work and experiment in a wide variety of artistic areas such as silversmithing, pottery, stained glass, silk screening, silk painting and print making but the draw back to painting has always been strong and consistent. I enjoy working in a variety of mediums but acrylic seems to be my preferred. I am inspired by the inner feelings and emotions of the human animal and the intriguing world of reptiles and insects. Natures creativity amazes me.

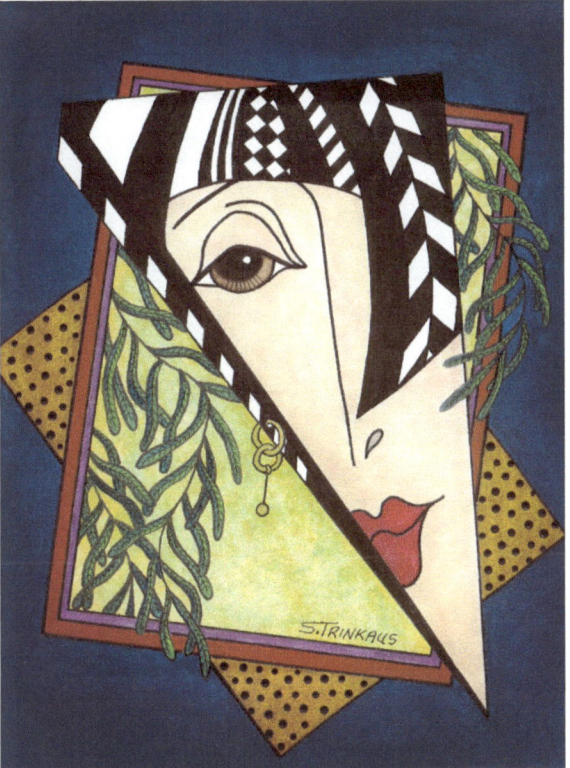

**2** **Triangular Face** 7x10"
Acrylic.

**3** **Kimono Clad** 15x79" Acrylic
on Wood.

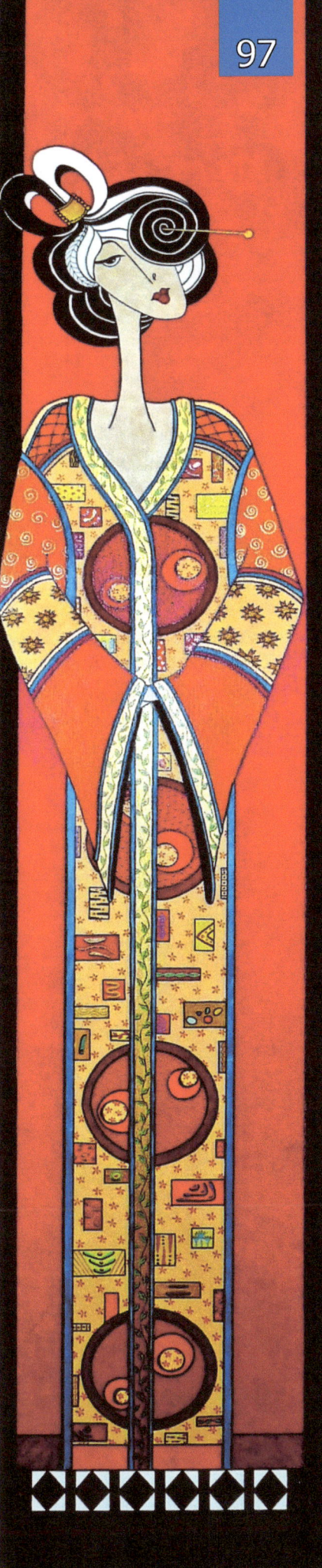

# RAFLAR

**LOCATION:** Westwood Estates
**WEB:** Raflar.com
**EMAIL:** Info@raflar.com

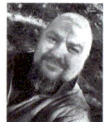

Ralf Wall, or as most know him, Raflar, is a landscape artist. He loves to wander through the Ontario wilderness and paint the scenery using watercolours or pen & ink. Using Kitchener as his home base, he travels from the shores of Lake Huron to the wooded lakes of the Algonquin Highlands to find inspiration.

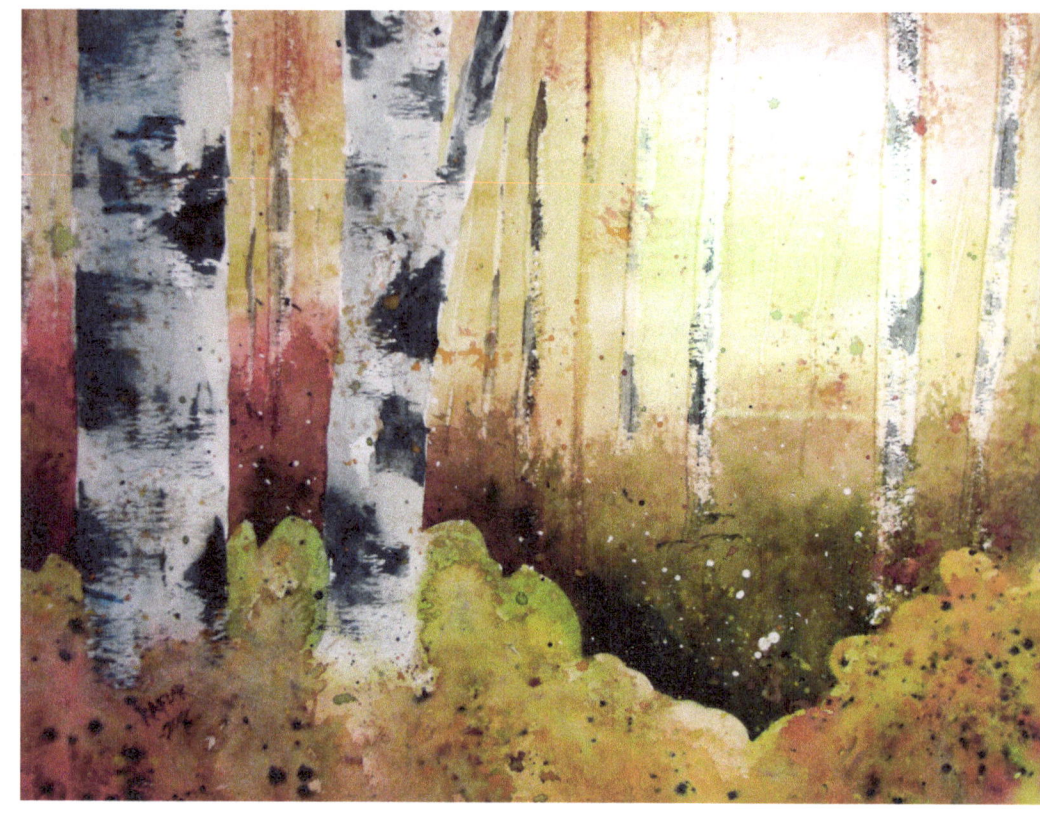

**1 Sunburst Through Trees 1**
12x16" Watercolour on paper.

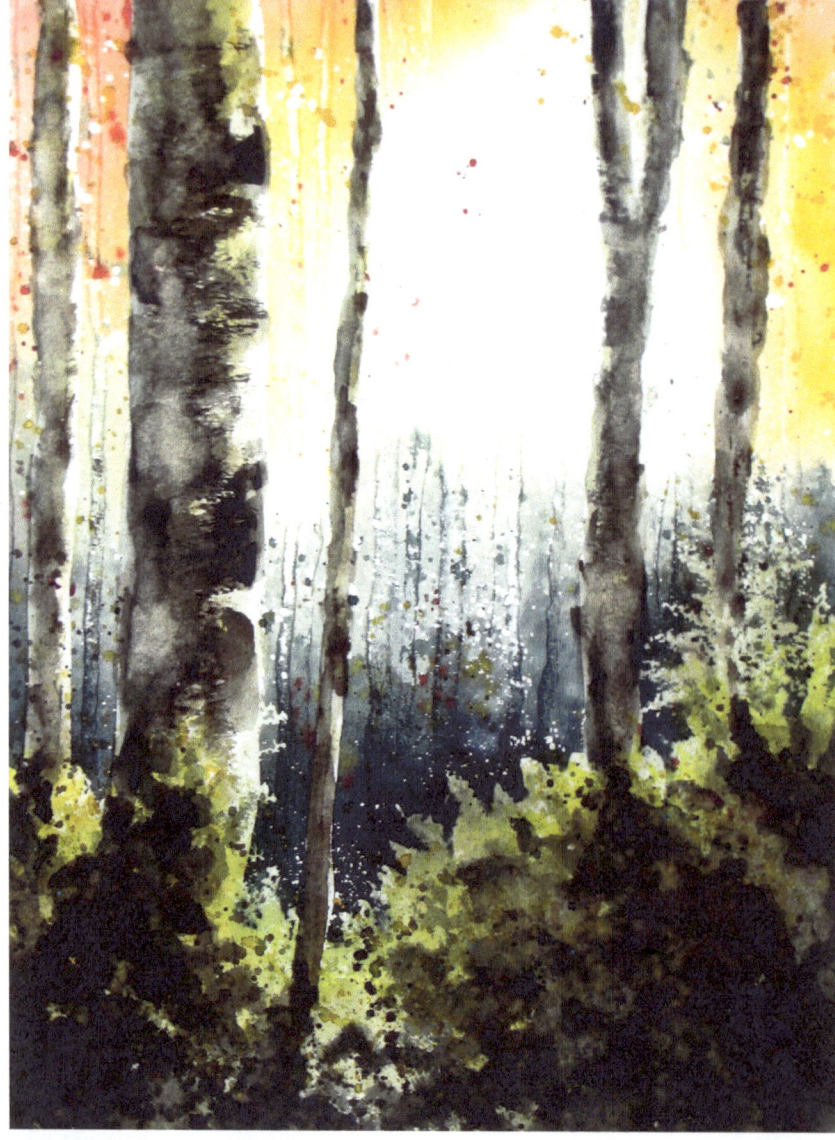

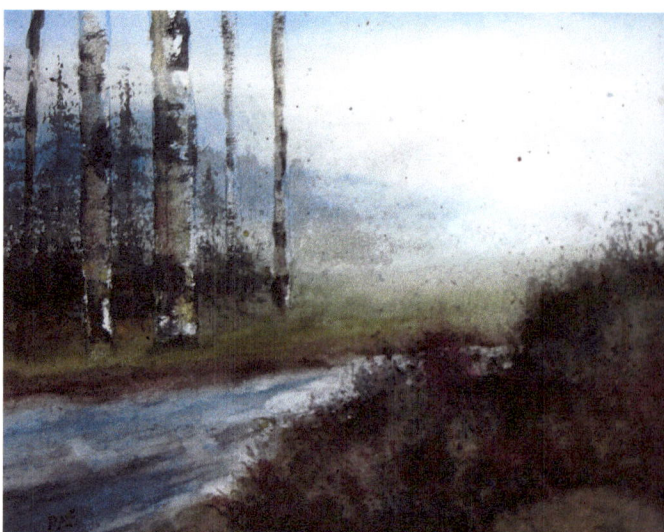

**2 Misty Lake** 12x16"
Watercolour on paper.

**3 Kitara's Woods** 12x16"
Watercolour on paper.

# JANET MAIN

**LOCATION:** Kitchener
**WEB:** janetmain.com
**EMAIL:** janet@janetmain.com

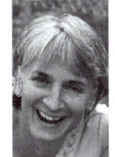

Janet grew up in Kitchener and has travelled extensively across Canada. The flow, subtlety and flexibility of watercolours serve her well in expressing her responses to the beauty of nature. She has been painting for five years, has held local, solo shows, and has contributed paintings to community shows in the Kitchener and Walkerton/Paisley/Elmwood areas. She has won several awards in juried art shows. Janet enjoys her involvement with KWSA and has benefitted much by sharing ideas with other artists.

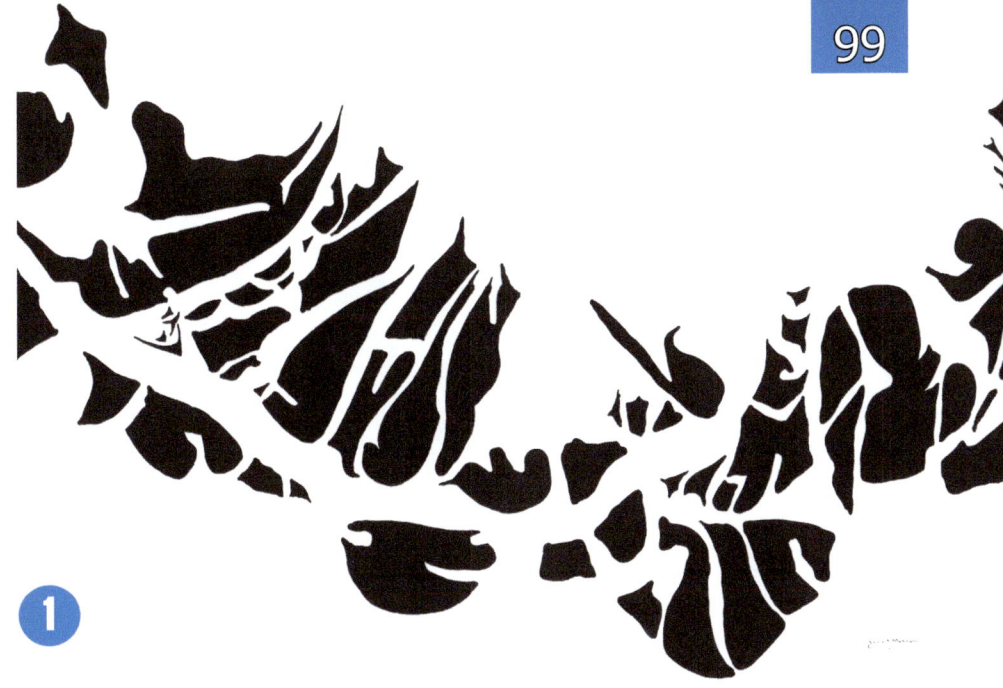

**1 Winter's Necklace** 30X22" Watercolour on Arches. Inspired by dark melt-waters of a stream flowing beneath snow-covered grasses and limbs.

**2 McClure's Mill, Chesley ON** 22x15" Watercolour on hot-press paper. Old mills and bank barns are part of Janet's heritage and she finds herself drawn to them as subjects.

**3 Graced by Light** 21x13.5" Watercolour on Arches. Morning scene near Lake Louise. Gleams of light through fog enliven evergreen branches.

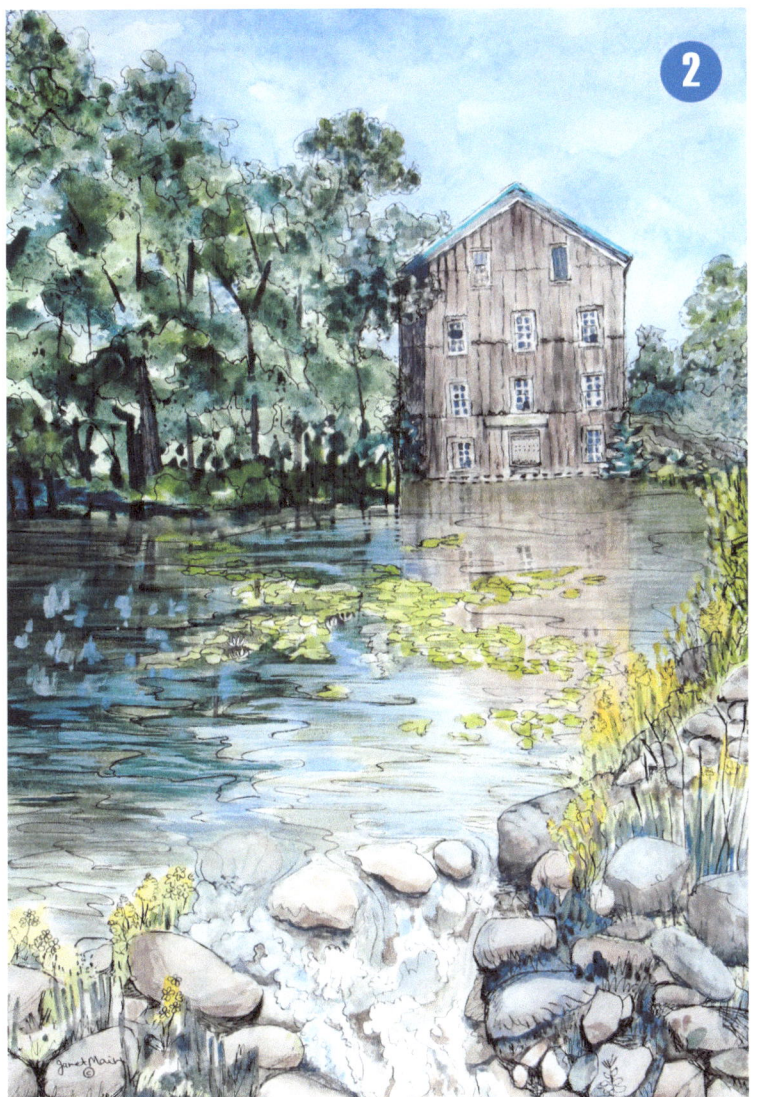

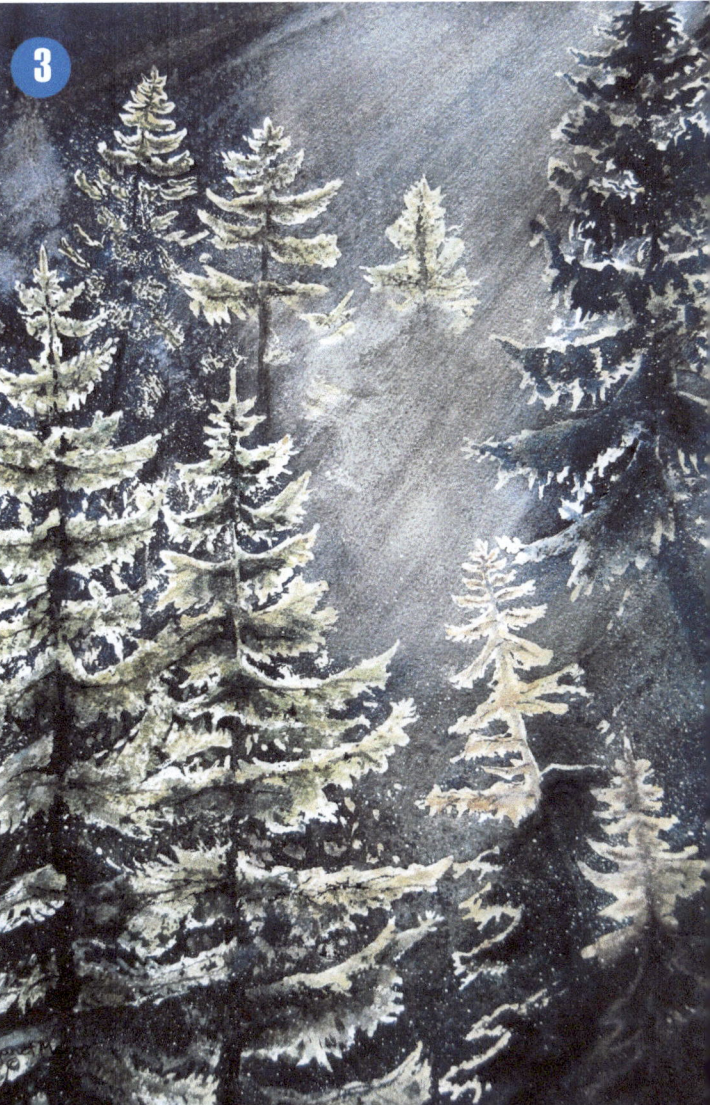

# KRISTINE BUNKER

**LOCATION:** Waterloo/Orillia
**WEB:** (N/A)
**EMAIL:** Kabunker@uwaterloo.ca

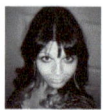

Kristine Bunker was born and raised in Orillia, Ontario. Her life has always had an aspect of art to it, starting with classes as a child, to volunteering in art classes at her local high school, and finally to her completion of her Honours Fine Arts degree at the University of Waterloo. Kristine has always had a passion for the grotesque, and her art is designed to repulse the viewer while evoking uncomfortable physical reactions due to the oozing and insidious portrayals of the body.

**1 Creep** Lifesize. Flexiwax and acrylic paint. I wanted to portray the feeling of a hand rising from the depths and crawling towards the viewer.

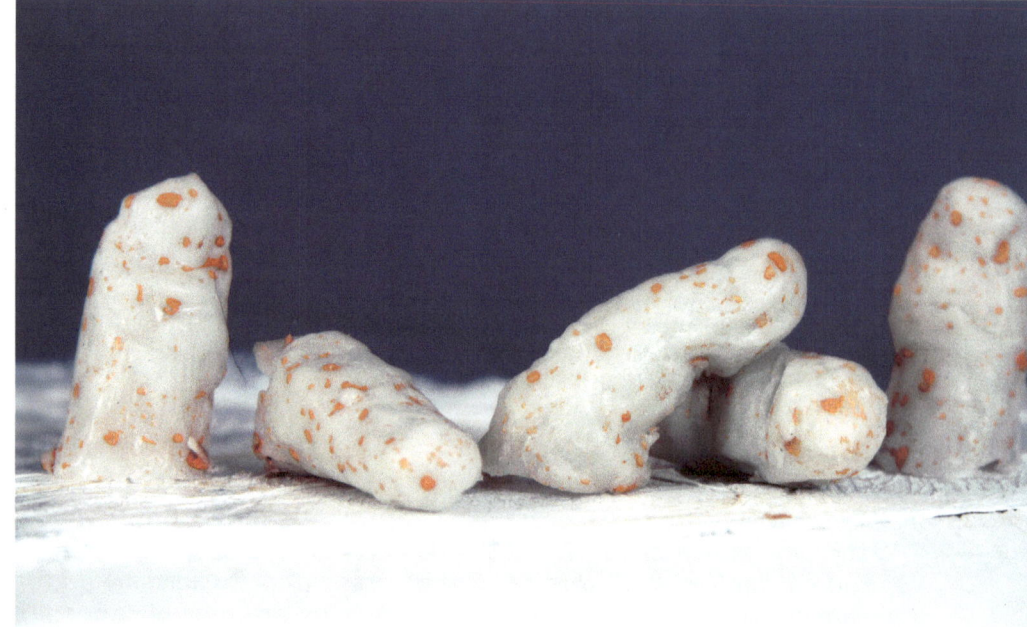

**2 Split** 2.5x2.5' Acyrlic paint, styrofoam, plastic wrap, drywall compound, varathane. The layers of material in this piece evoke the sense of split skin, inducing discomfort in the viewer due to the recognition of an open wound.

**3 Fester** 2x2' Acrylic paint, Styrofoam, plastic wrap. I have always had a passion for pimples and the impurities of skin. This works purpose is to create a physical impulse in the viewer to want to pick.

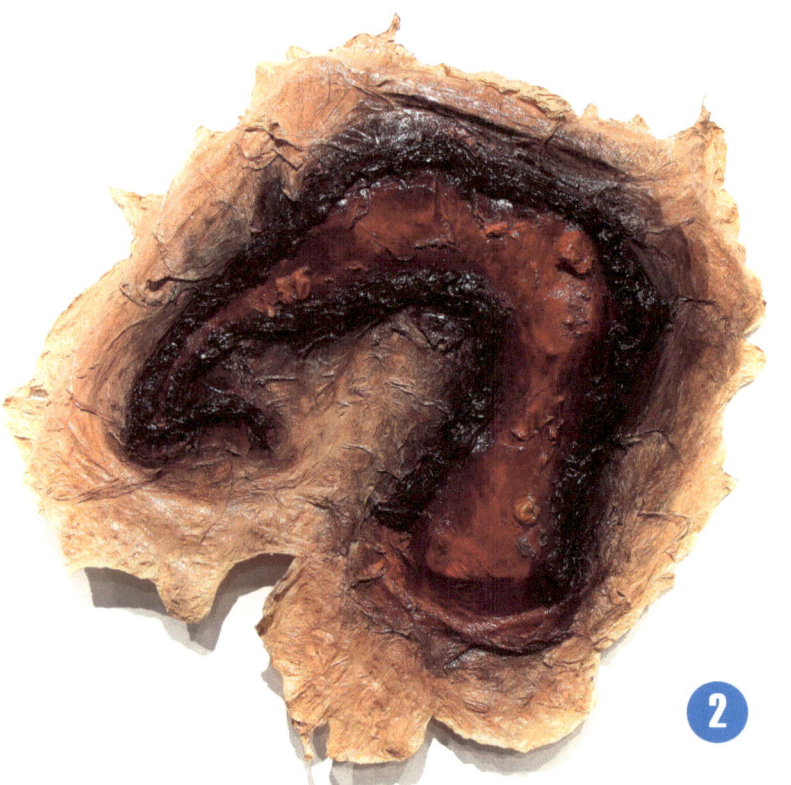

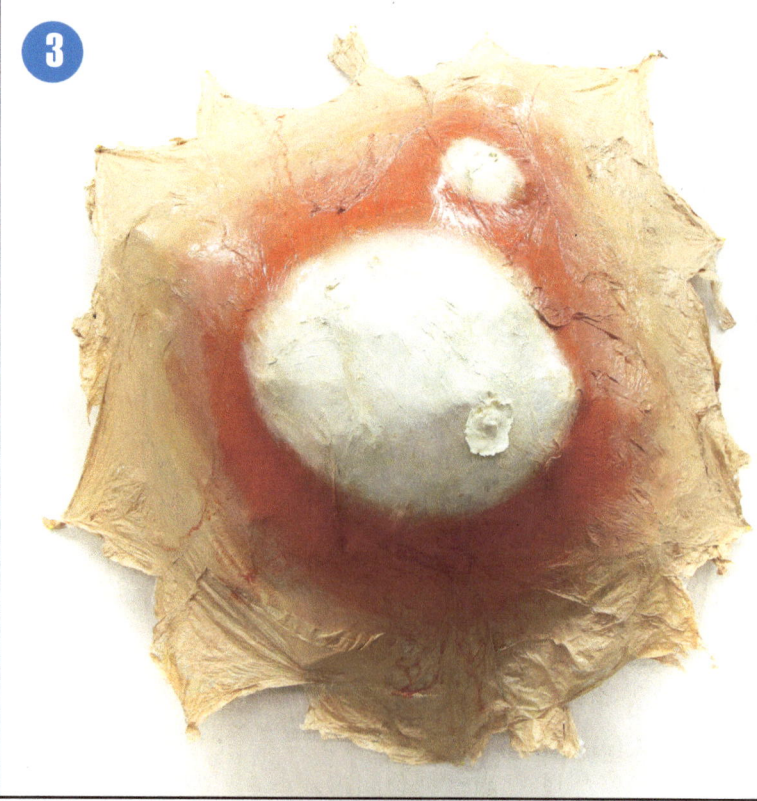

# JAMIE QUINN

**LOCATION:** Waterloo
**WEB:** (N/A)
**EMAIL:** QuinnJamieLynn@gmail.com

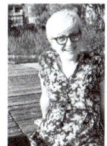

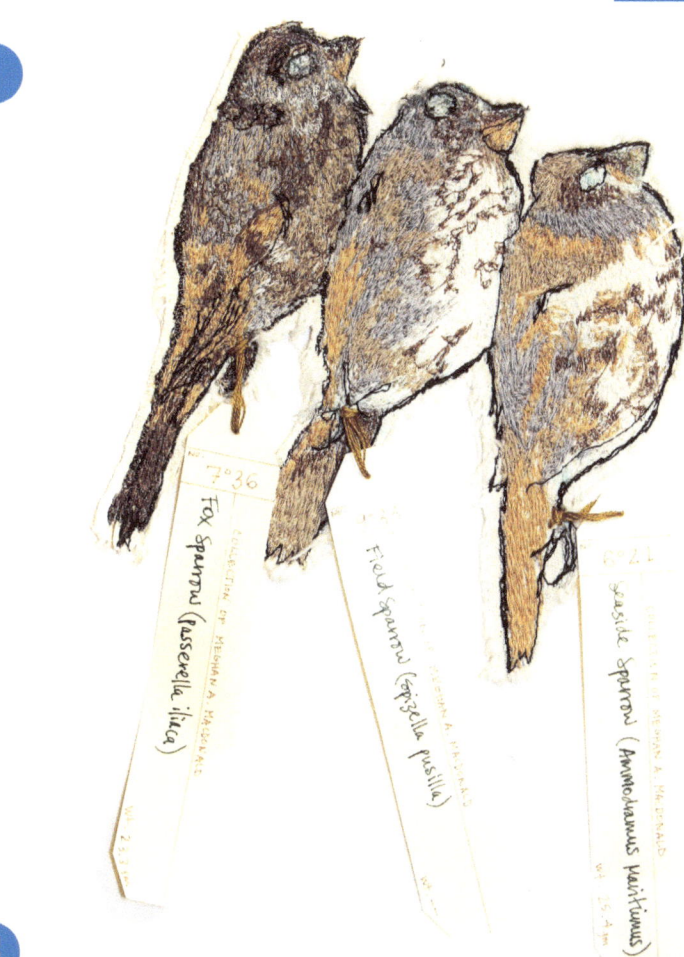

A graduate of Sheridan College's Crafts and Design program, Jamie Quinn specialized in Textiles and was awarded the J.V. O'Brien award for Outstanding Body of Work in her 2010 graduating class. She continued her education in printmaking at the Nova Scotia College of Art and Design in 2011. Time-honoured techniques such as stitching, embroidery and quilting are the foundation of Jamie's art, striving to create a connection between residual and contemporary styles with a distinct pronunciation of traditional women's work. Items imbued with a history are of particular interest, reflecting their romanticism and nostalgia with an intuitive approach to her practice.

**1 Dead Sparrows** Each bird 3x7". Machine embroidery.

**2 Tight Rope** 10x14" India ink and collage.

**3 Carnival Strippers** 5 frames, ranging from 3" to 8" diameter. Acetate collage

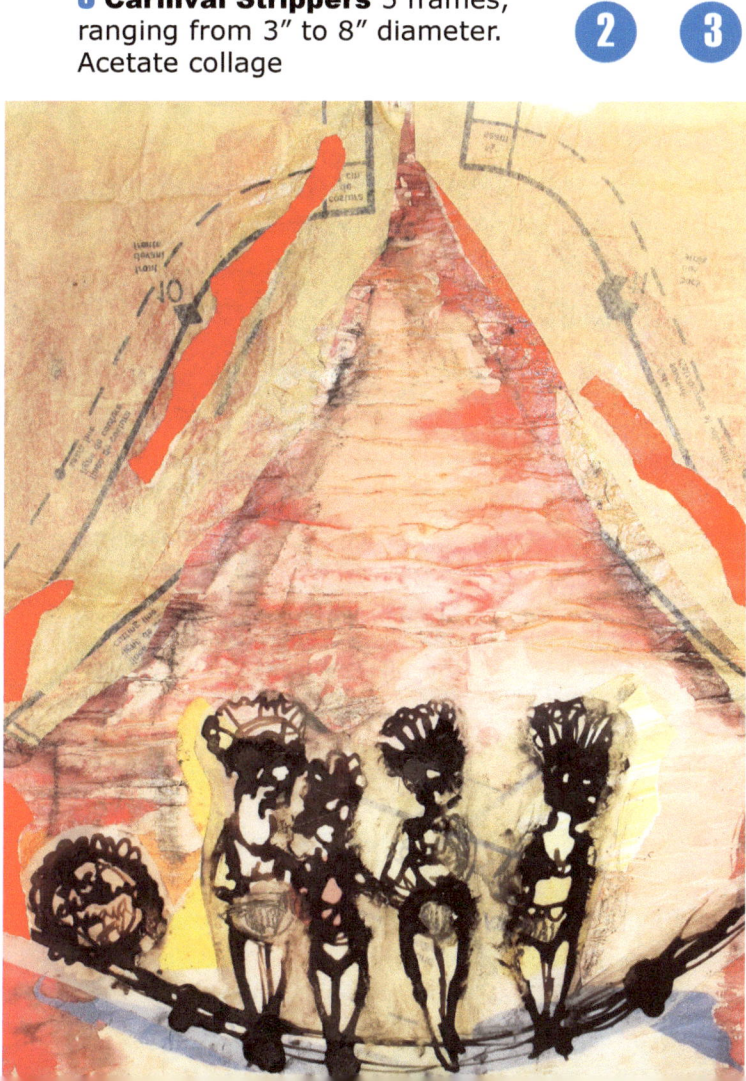

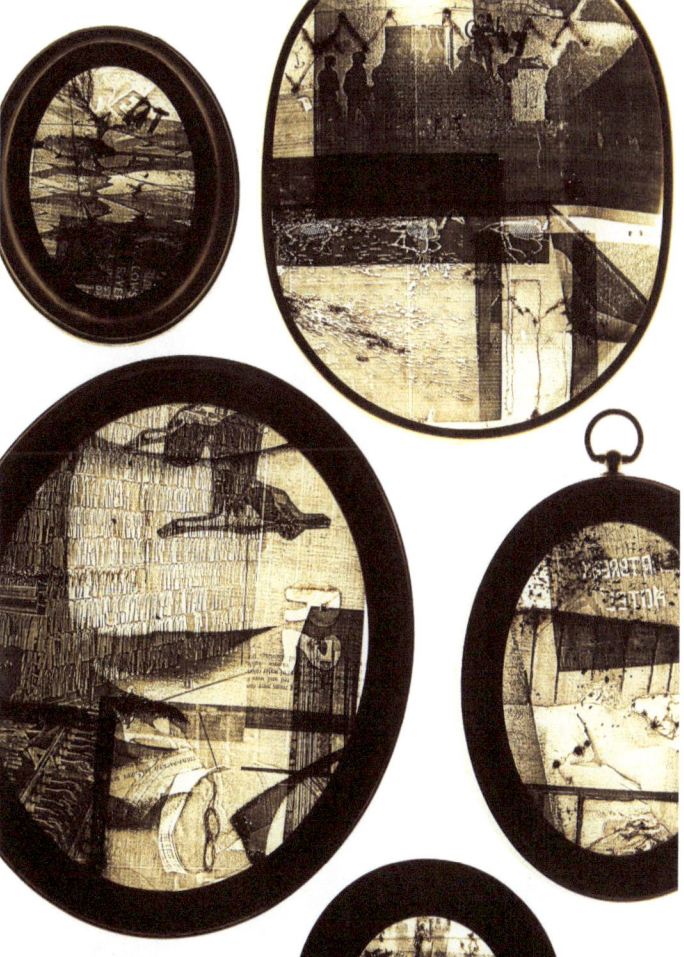

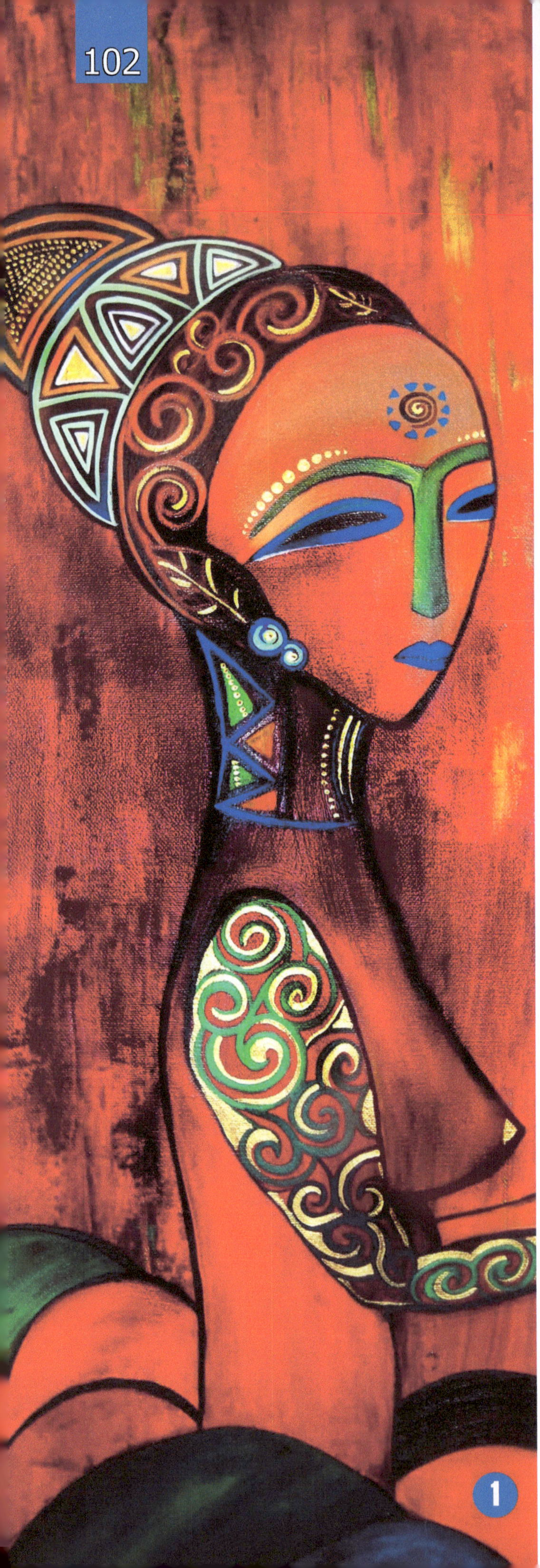

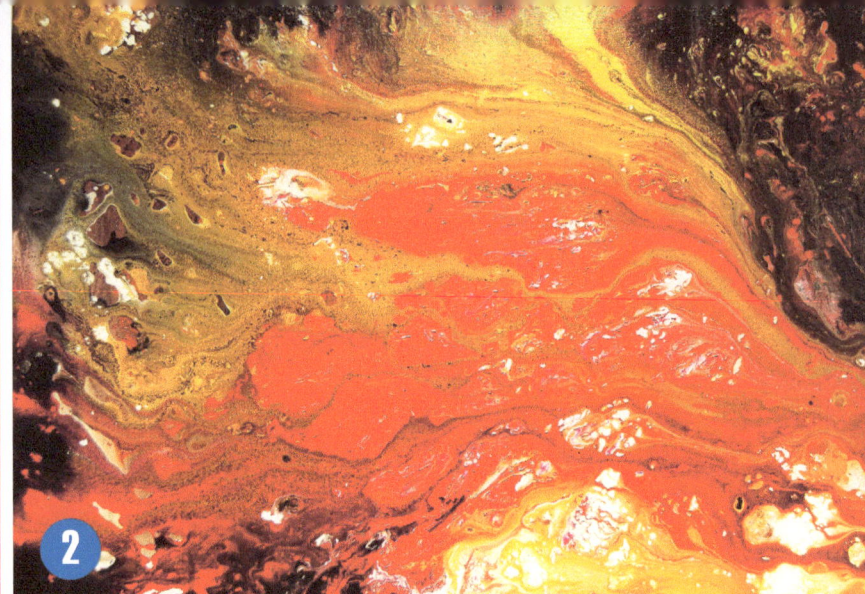

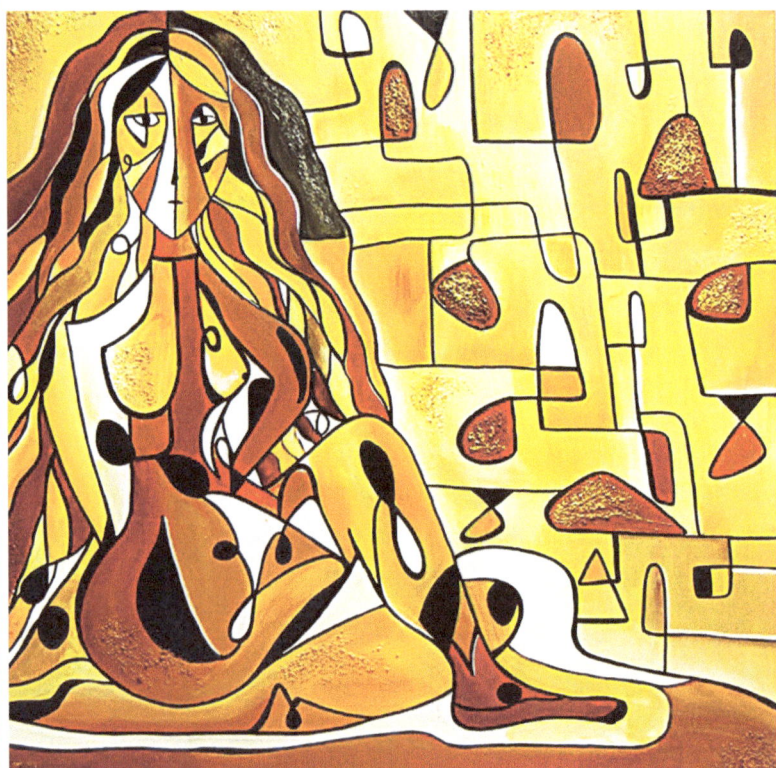

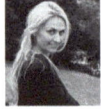

# LEANNE SAWCHUK

**LOCATION:** Waterloo
**WEB:** ArtByLeanneSawchuk.com
**EMAIL:** Leannesawchuk@gmail.com

Leanne is a self-representing artist from Waterloo whose primary medium of choice is acrylic. Leanne went to York University and studied both Visual Arts and Psychology. Art has always been a re-occurring symbol in her life where she uses it not only to bring joy to herself, but also to others. She looks as art as being a tool that can also be used to heal others, something that is evident in the time she spends as an Art Therapist. Art has been her outlet not only for creative energy but has served as a form of medicine over the years.

**1 If I Were You** 24x8" Acrylic on canvas.

**2 The Fire Within** 16×20" Acrylic on canvas.

**3 Pieces of Me** 24×24" Acrylic on canvas.

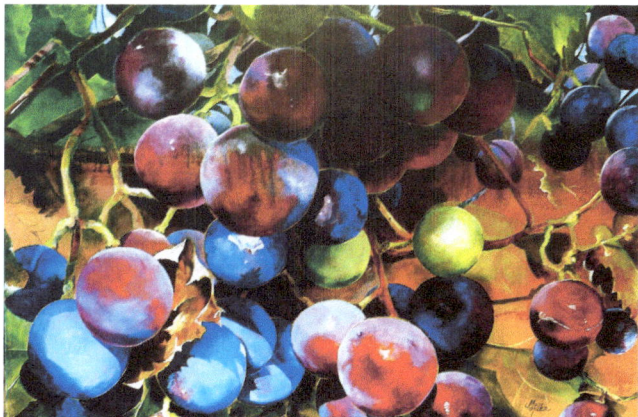

# MARY LOU HILLER 1

**LOCATION:** Waterloo
**WEB:** DiversityArtists.ca
**EMAIL:** MaryLouHiller@rogers.com

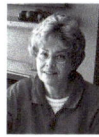

Once retired from a career as an arts educator/administrator Mary Lou embarked on her "second life" as a painter. Studies and travels with respected artists in Canada, the U.S. and abroad have informed the subject matter and techniques of her award-winning work. Moving freely between watercolour and acrylic media she interprets her themes realistically or expressionistically with a particular love for vibrant colour, evocative light and implied storyline. Her work can be viewed at Up-Town Gallery (Waterloo), Gallery M (Cambridge) or on the website: diversityartists.ca

**1 No Two the Same** 24x36" Acrylic on canvas.

**2 Barong Performance, Bali** 39x31" framed. Mixed acrylic.

**3 Of Cats and Carpet Bags** 26x38" Acrylic.

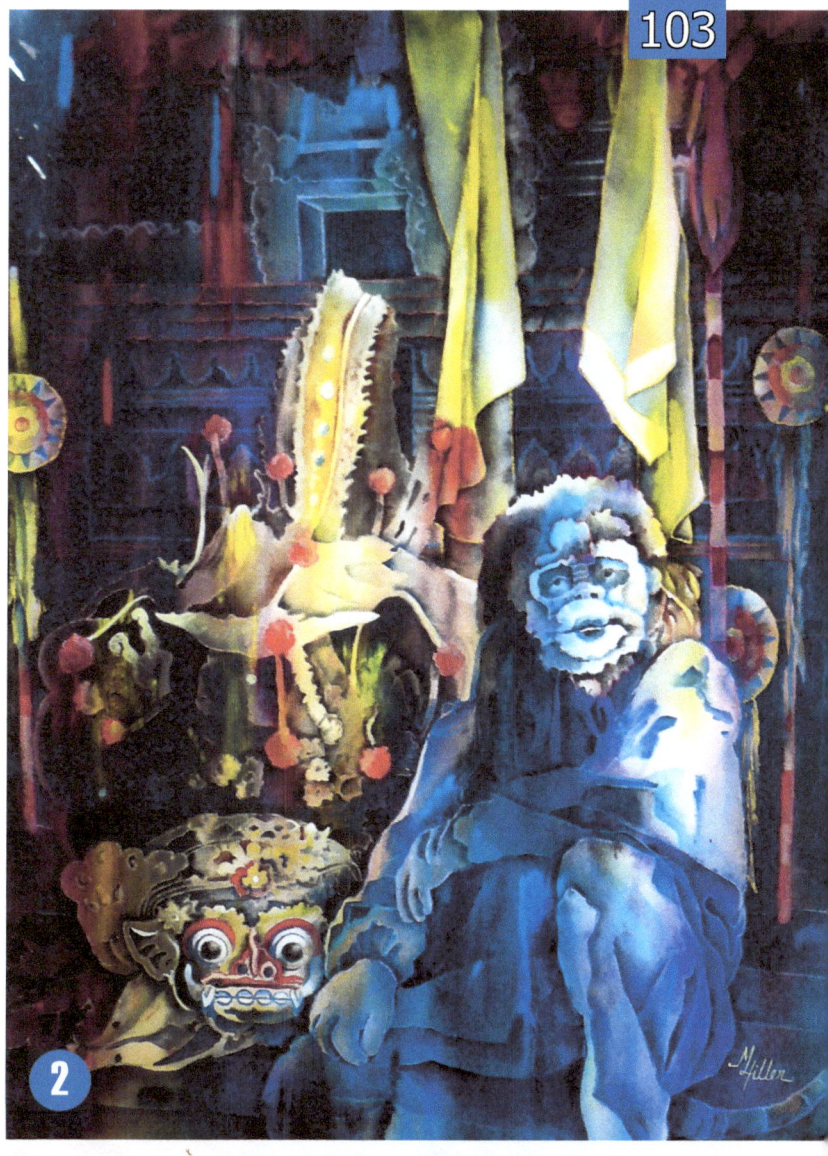

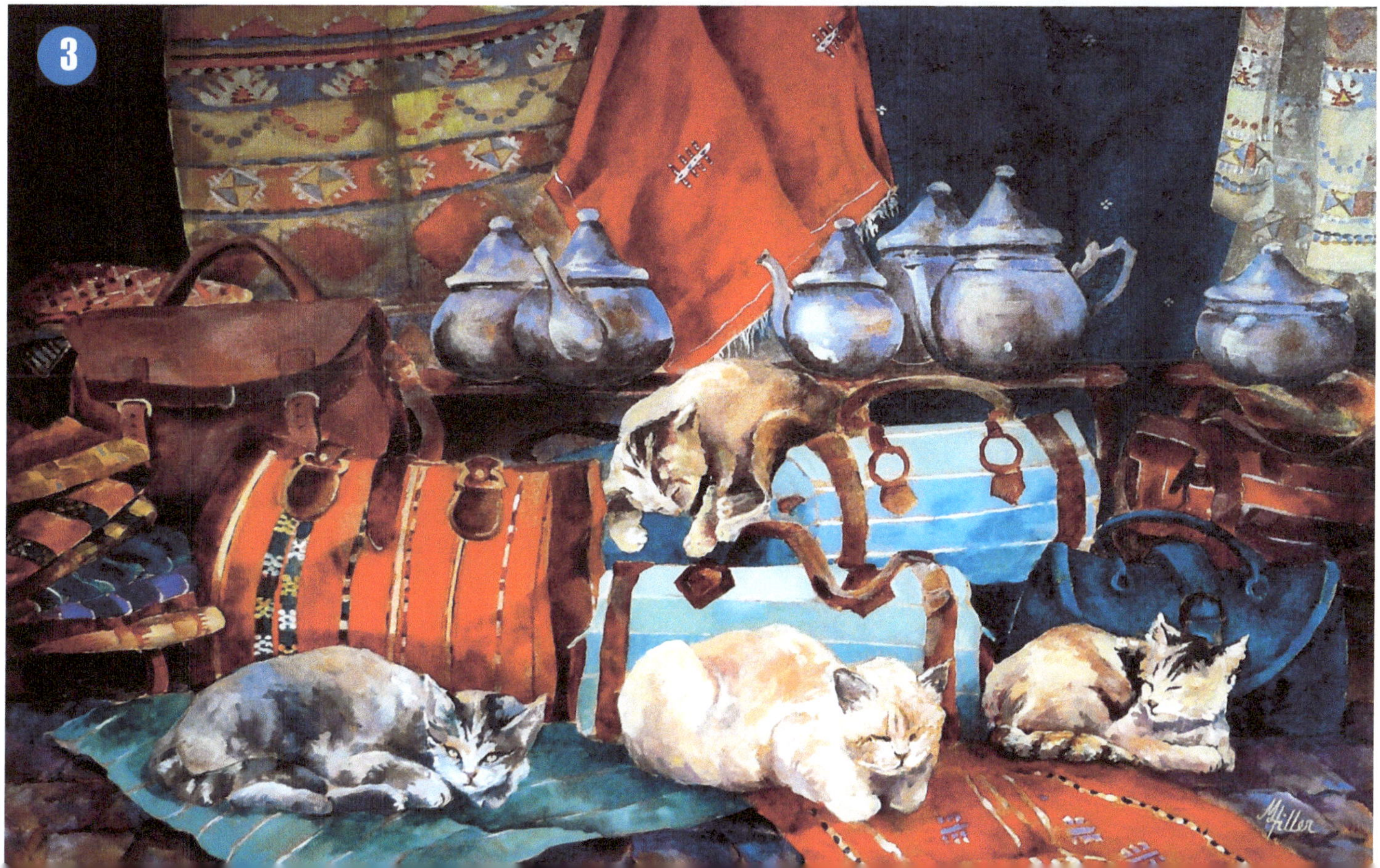

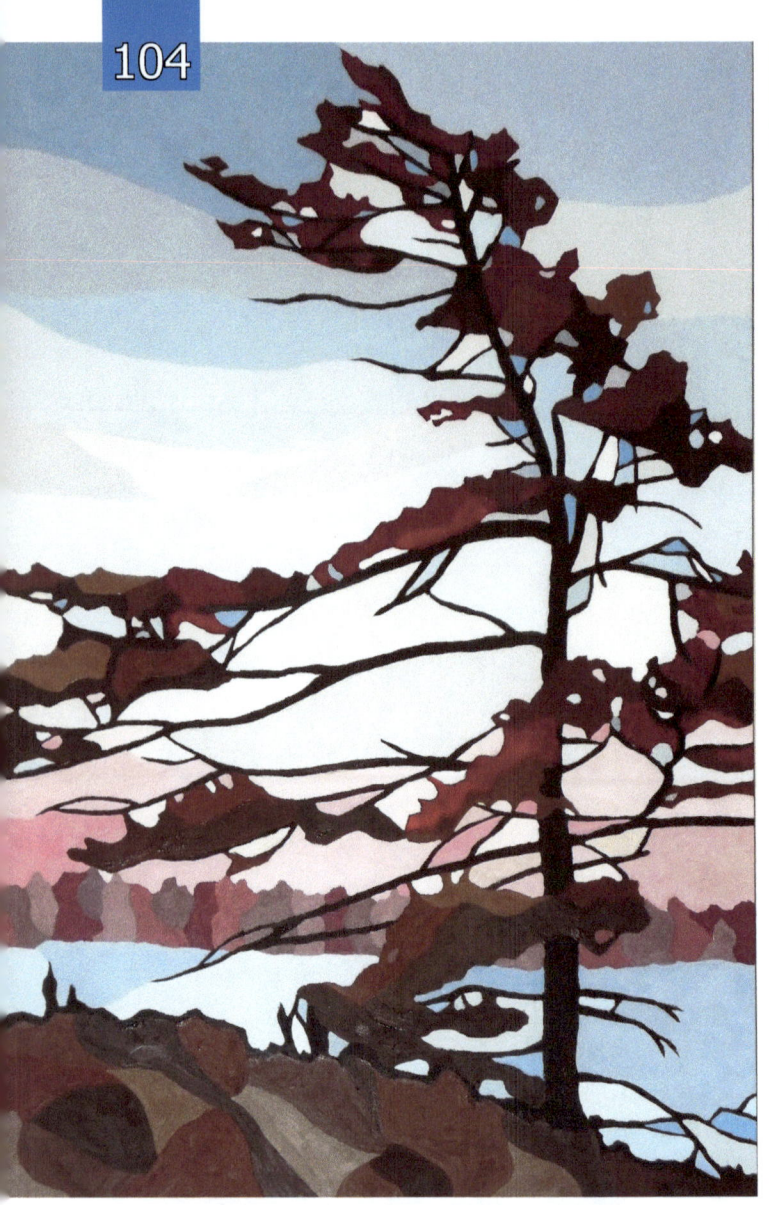

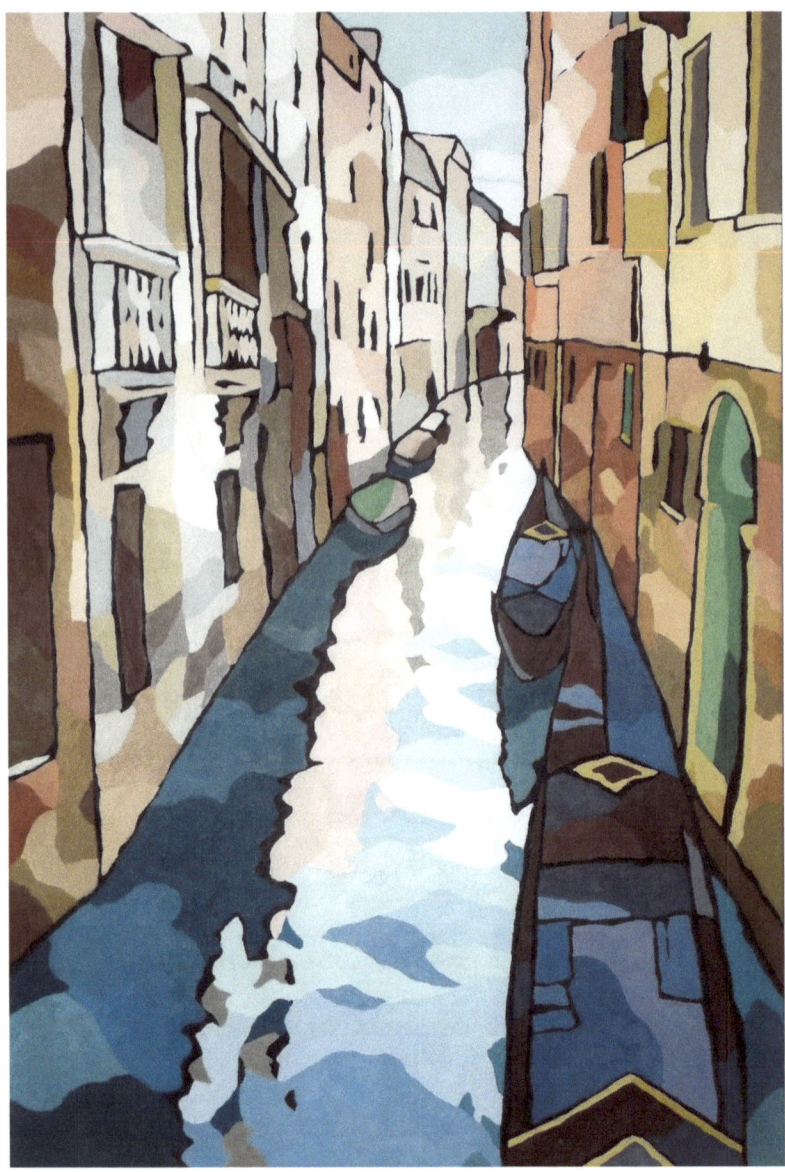

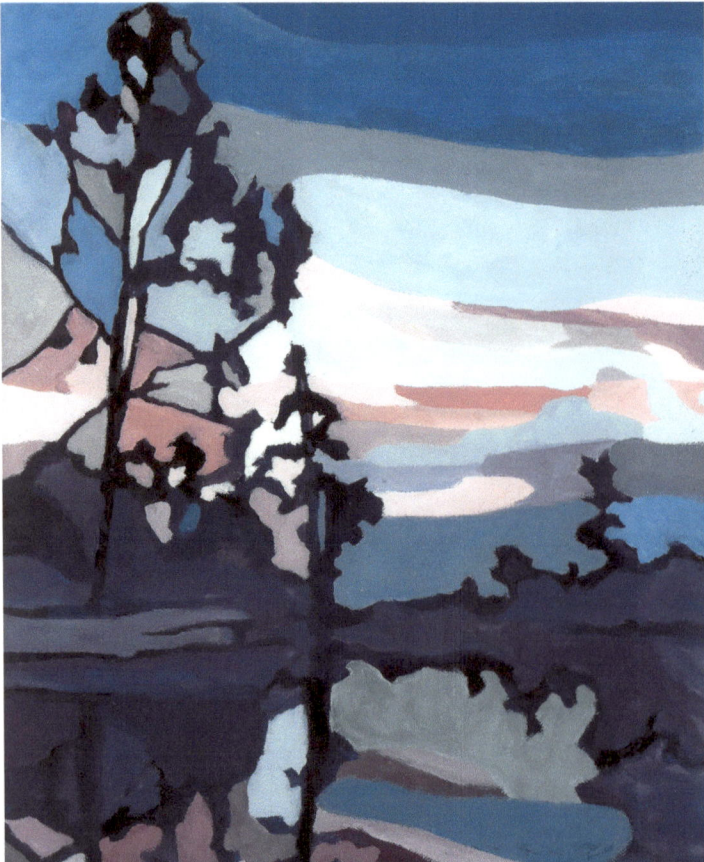

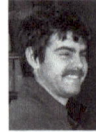

# JONATHAN MUNZ

**LOCATION:** Waterloo
**WEB:** search 'Paint by Munzy' on Facebook
**EMAIL:** Paintbymunzy@gmail.com

Jonathan Munz grew up just outside Waterloo in a small town and early on learned to enjoy sketching and painting. After going to college for graphic design he continued to love working with more classical mediums portraying the world through a variety of styles with oils on canvas.

**1 Cottage Tree** 24×36" Oil on canvas.

**2 Venice Street** 24x36" Oil on canvas.

**3 Bataliba Village** 14×18" Oil on canvas.

# SANELA DIZDAR

**LOCATION:** Kitchener
**WEB:** SanelaArt.com
**EMAIL:** Sanela.art@gmail.com

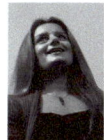

Sanela Dizdar is an artist and Graphic Designer. A constant self-challenger with her favorite tools of expression: graphics tablet, pastel, acrylic, oil and pencil/graphite. Her two challenges in art are painting water as alive and exploring human emotions. Sanela teaches drawing classes in Up-Town Gallery, Waterloo. Come and join her.

**1 Owen Sound Beach** 36x30" Acrylic on canvas.

**2 The Power of Positive Thought** 30x30" Acrylic on canvas.

**3 Part of the Face** 16x24" Pencil on canvas.

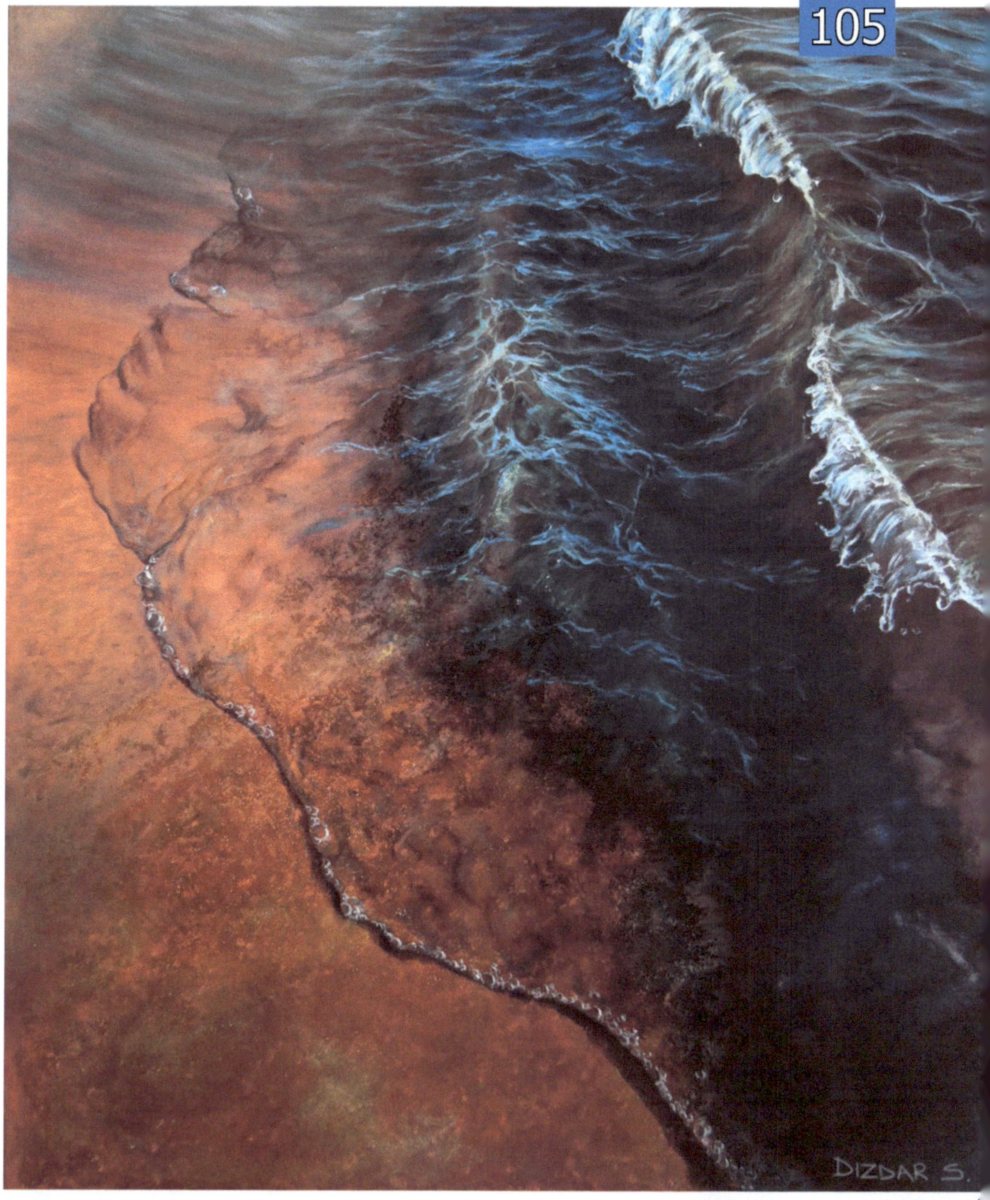

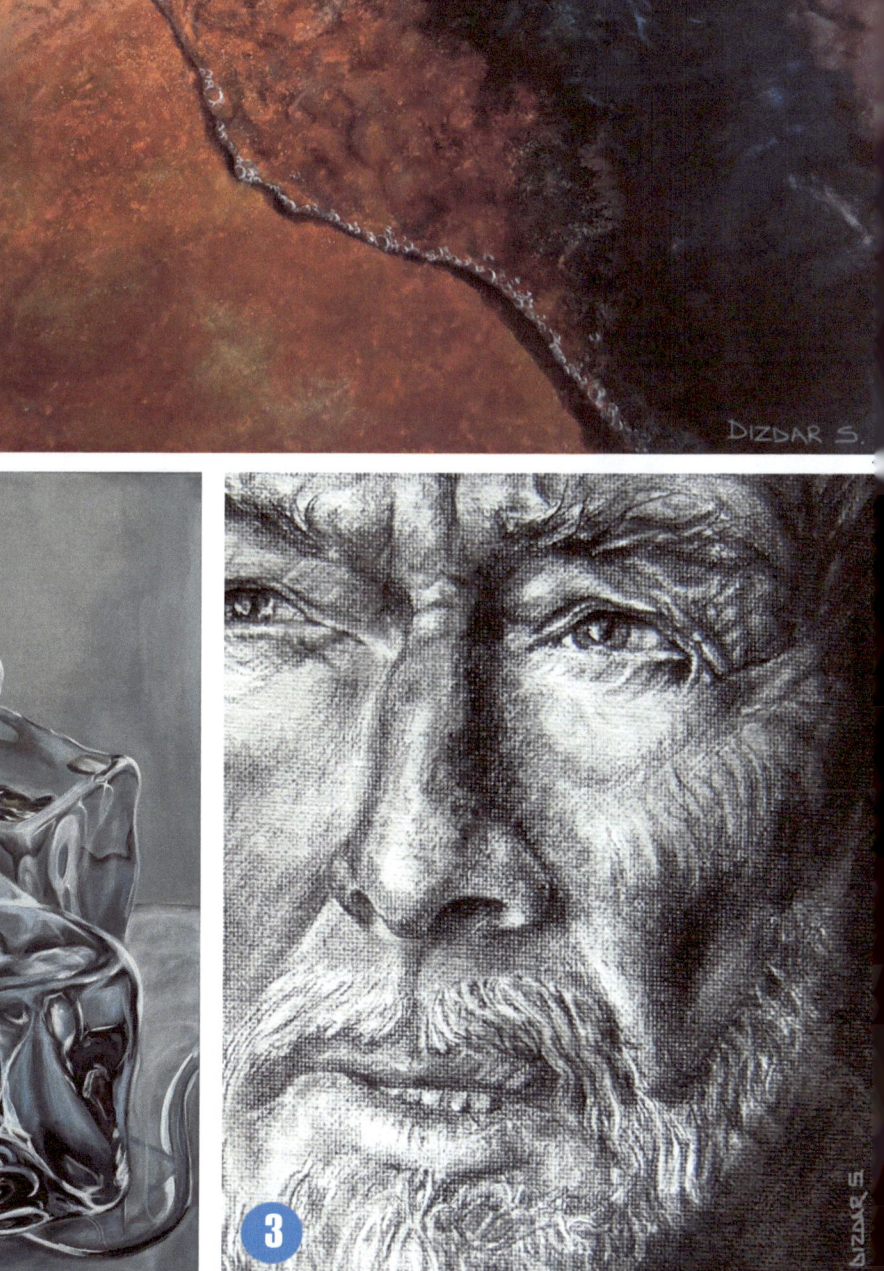

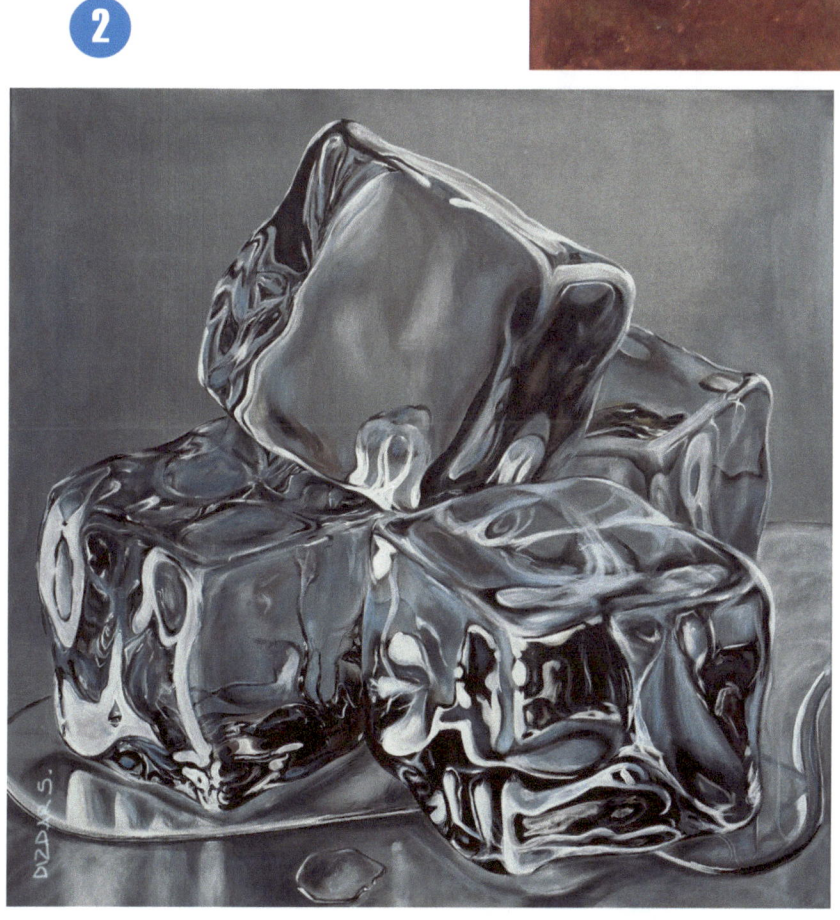

# ROSLYN RAMSAY
# VERITY

**LOCATION:** Kitchener
**WEB:** RoslynRamsay.com
**EMAIL:** Ramsay.verity@gmail.com

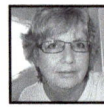

Roslyn is a Canadian visual artist experienced in portraiture, landscape and figurative paintings thorugh the media of watercolour, montage, acrylic, charcoal and pen & ink. Poetry and short story writing is another experimental venue she pursues. Portraits display her deep understanding of her subjects with over two hundred Portrait commisions in private and corporate collections.

**1** **Shattered** 16x20" Watercolour montage.

**2** **Olivia** 16x20" Charcoal pencil portrait.

**3** **Emotion - Dragonfly** 30x40"

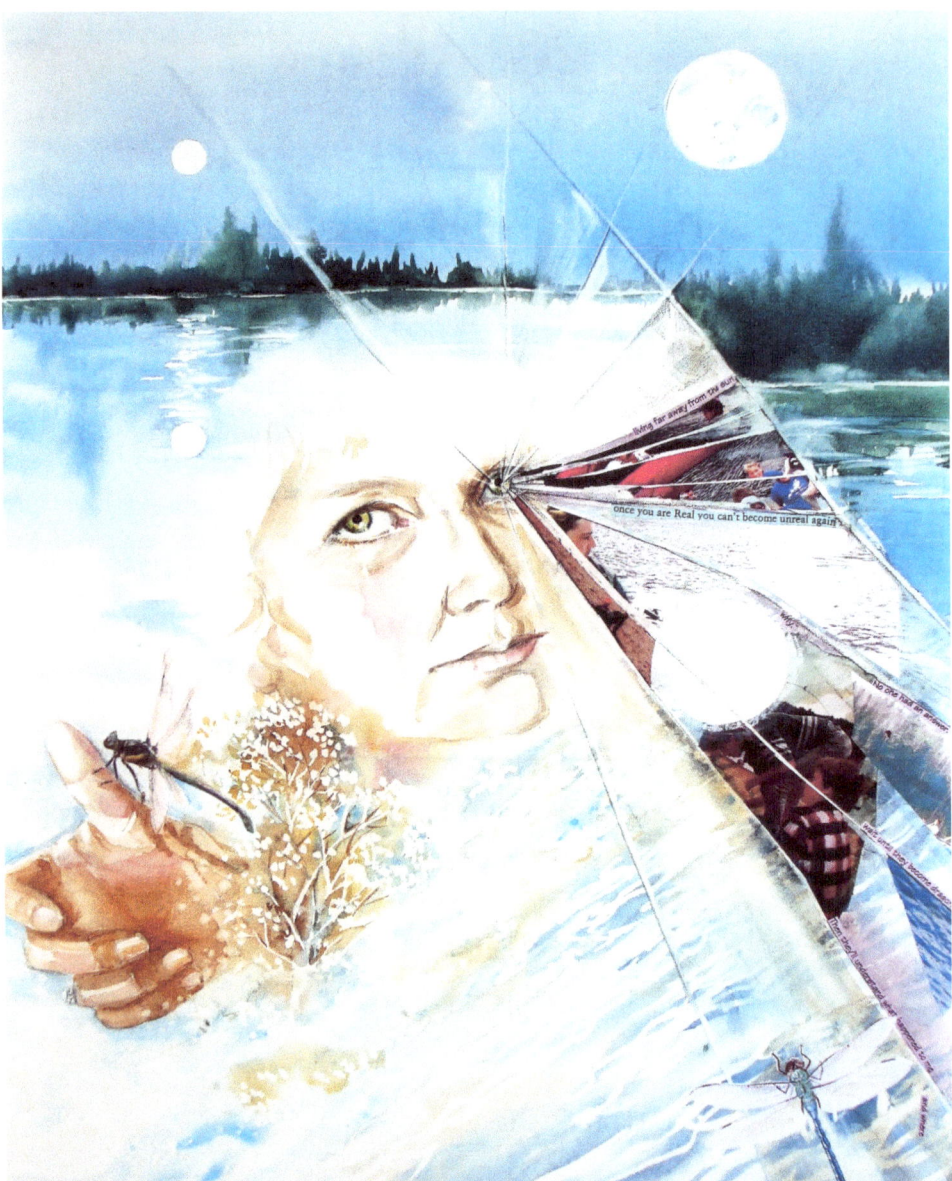

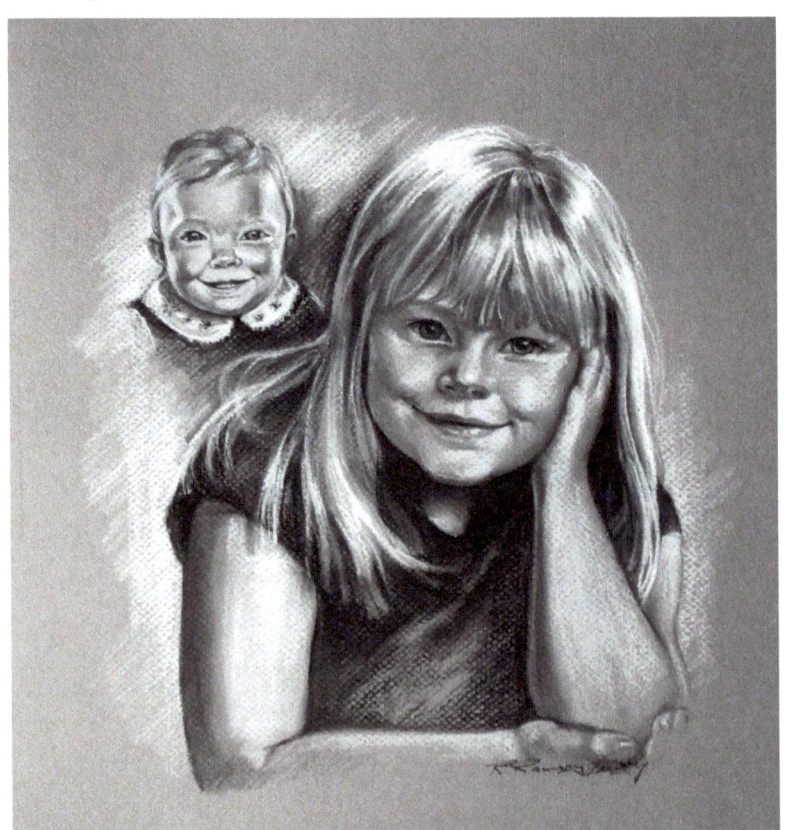

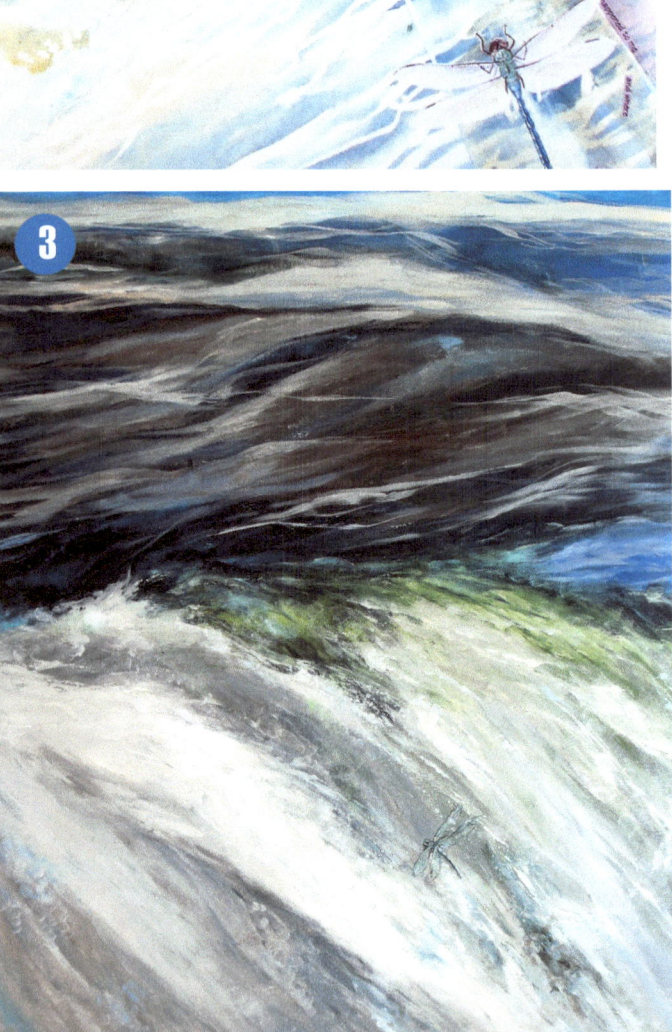

# DEBORAH PRYCE

**LOCATION:** Kitchener
**WEB:** uptowngallerywaterloo.com
gooseneckpress.ca
**EMAIL:** rdpryce@yaknet.ca

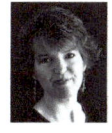

Deborah Pryce has enjoyed a varied career of designing trade show exhibits, creating architectural presentation drawings and house portraits, painting theatre sets, teaching, and illustrating children's books (The Cat and Going on a Lion Hunt). The artist's collective in Waterloo, UpTown Gallery, gives Deborah a great place to showcase her acrylics, mixed media and photography. She enjoys chatting about this increasingly vibrant artistic community and is challenged and inspired by its members.

**1 Security at Twilight** 36x36″ Acrylic on Canvas. I enjoyed choosing a slightly playful perspective for the Molson Bank that speaks of its stately, solid & slightly arrogant stature.

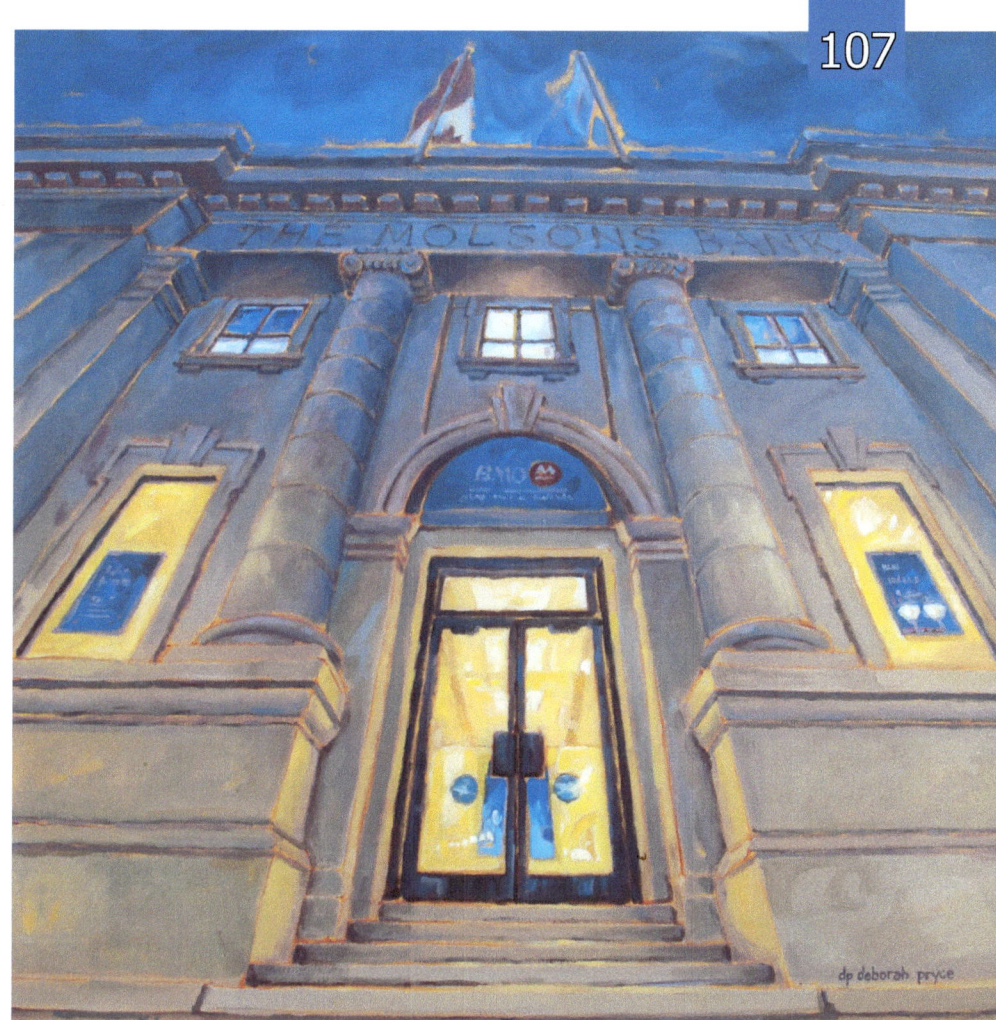

**2 Breaking out of the Box** 24x24″ Acrylic on Canvas. We all have areas in our lives where we need a chance to break from our routines that have become stagnant.

**3 Safety in the Storm** 18x18″ Mixed Media. This piece helped me express the wide variety of emotions I felt when hearing the stories of the protests in Egypt in early 2011.

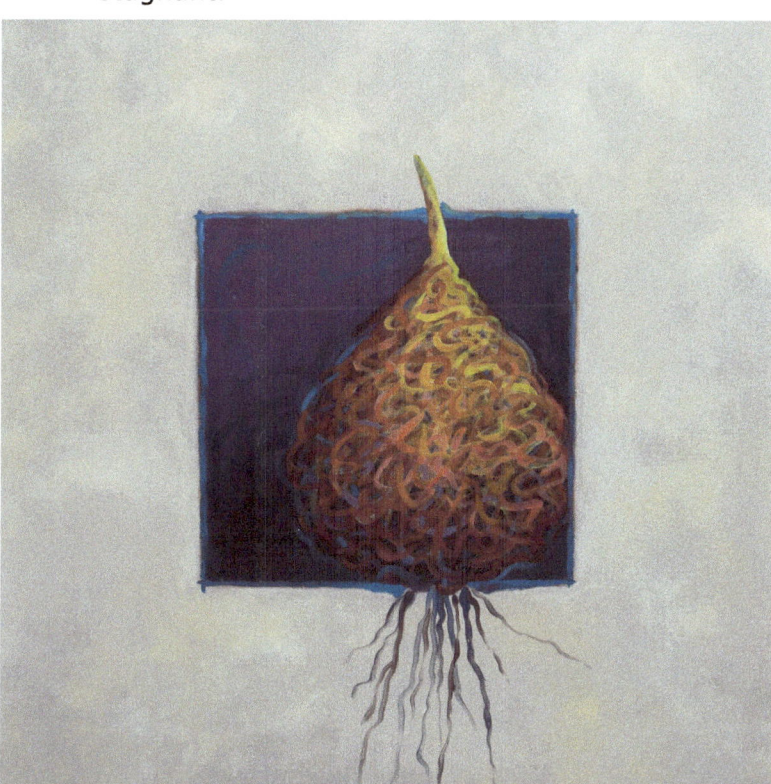

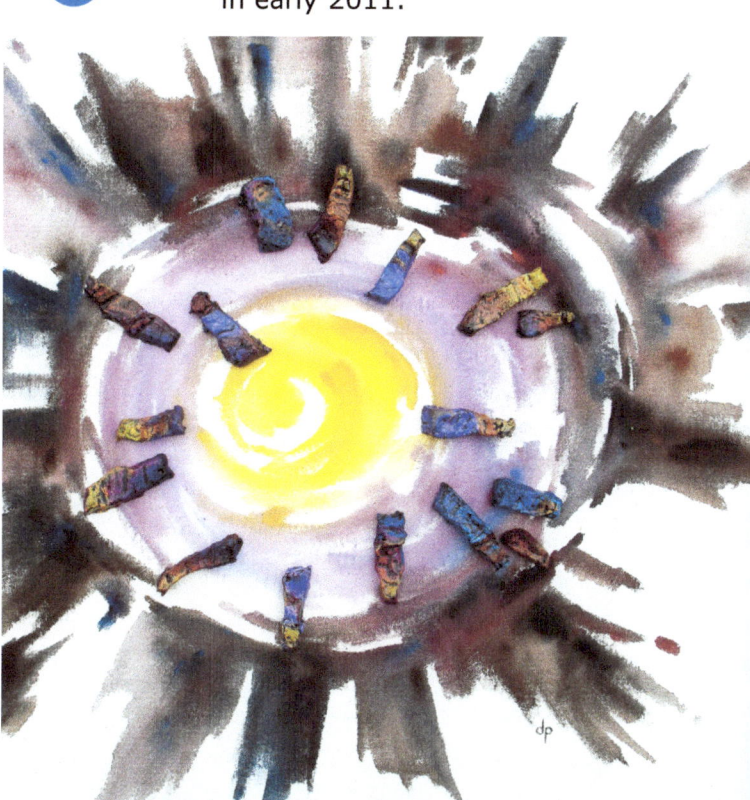

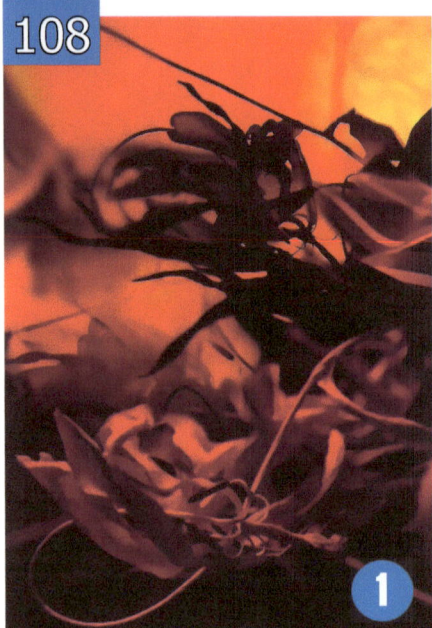

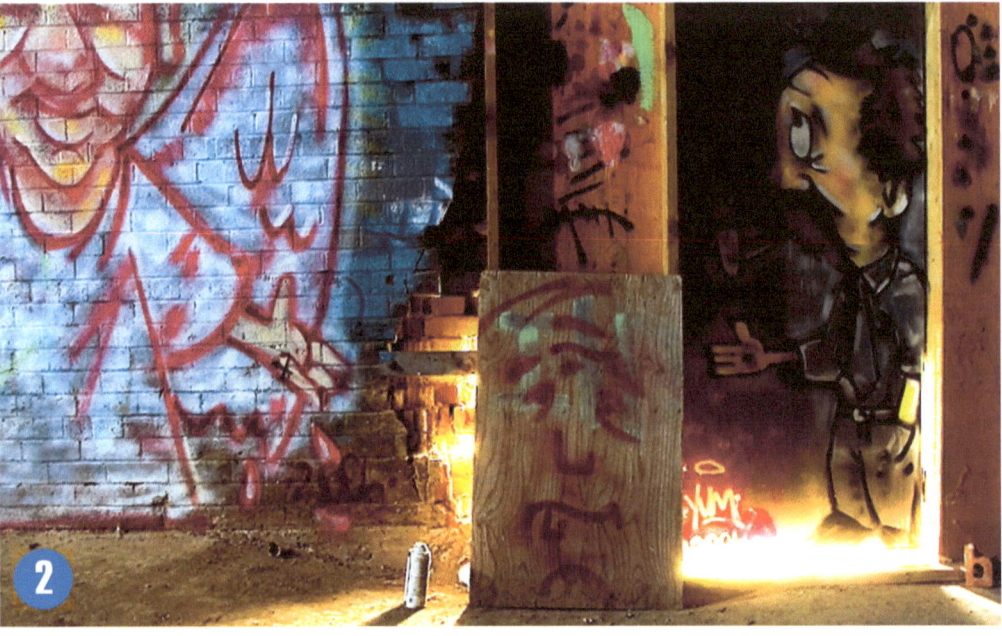

**1 Beautiful Death** Photo. A digital melding of 2 shots, both of dead gladiolas in front of a red rice paper lamp. The artist has always been fascinated by the beautiful lines of dead flowers.

**3 Cake Face 5** Photo. This image is part of an ongoing series exploring ordinary cake sprinkles as makeup. It has a darkly whimsical look inspired by the unique handmade wool scarf the model wears.

**2 Divine** Photo. The artist was struck by the ironic beauty of this graffiti wall and the light flooding through it."

# EMILY BEATTY IMAGERY

**LOCATION:** Belmont Village, Kitchener
**WEB:** emilybeatty.com
**EMAIL:** emilybeattyimagery@live.ca

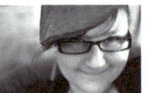

Emily has spent 22 of her 26 years in the KW area. The other 4 were spent in Toronto earning an Applied Media Studies degree from the University of Guelph and a Creative Photography diploma from Humber College. When she's not shooting artsy photos, Emily does traditional portraiture like wedding and boudoir photos and paints bright mixed media canvases. Her work attempts to bring viewers a sense of wonder and joy through bold, vibrant compositions; her goal is to get them asking questions about the boundaries between reality and artifice. She loves shooting vibrant colours, textures, and intriguing images of everyday items for local art shows and her business, Emily Beatty Imagery.

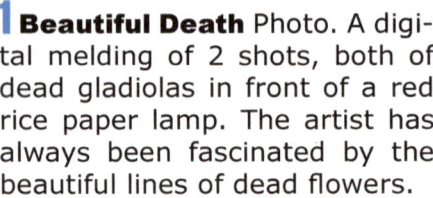

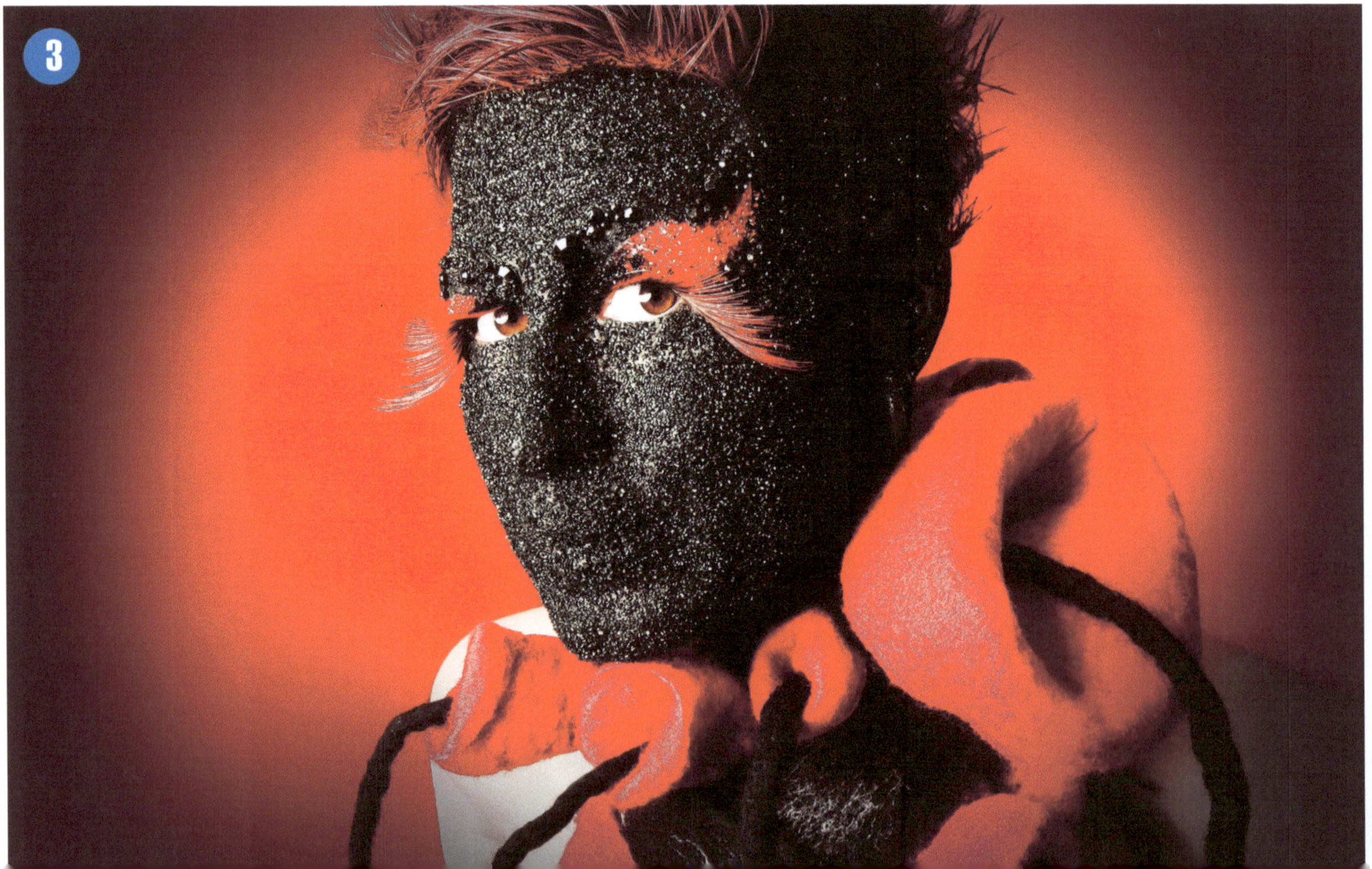

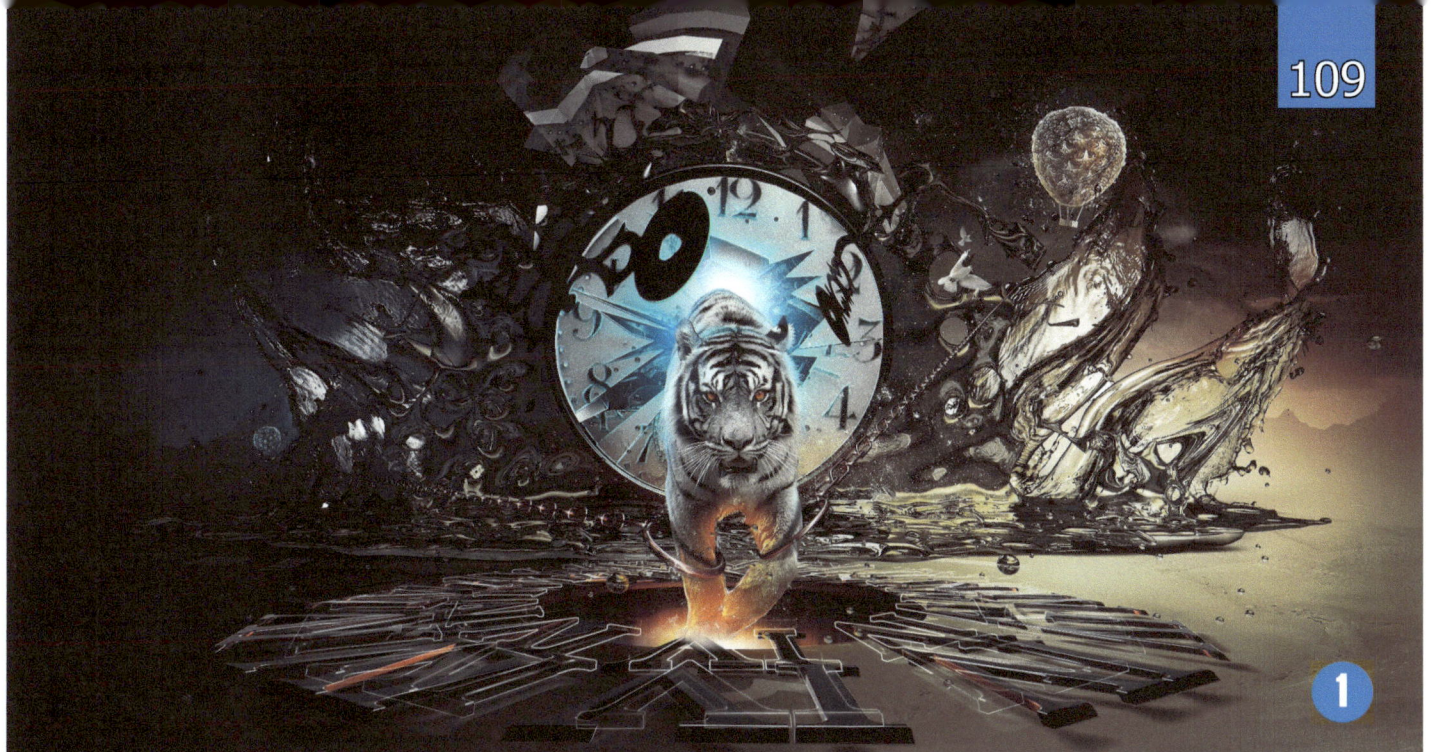

1

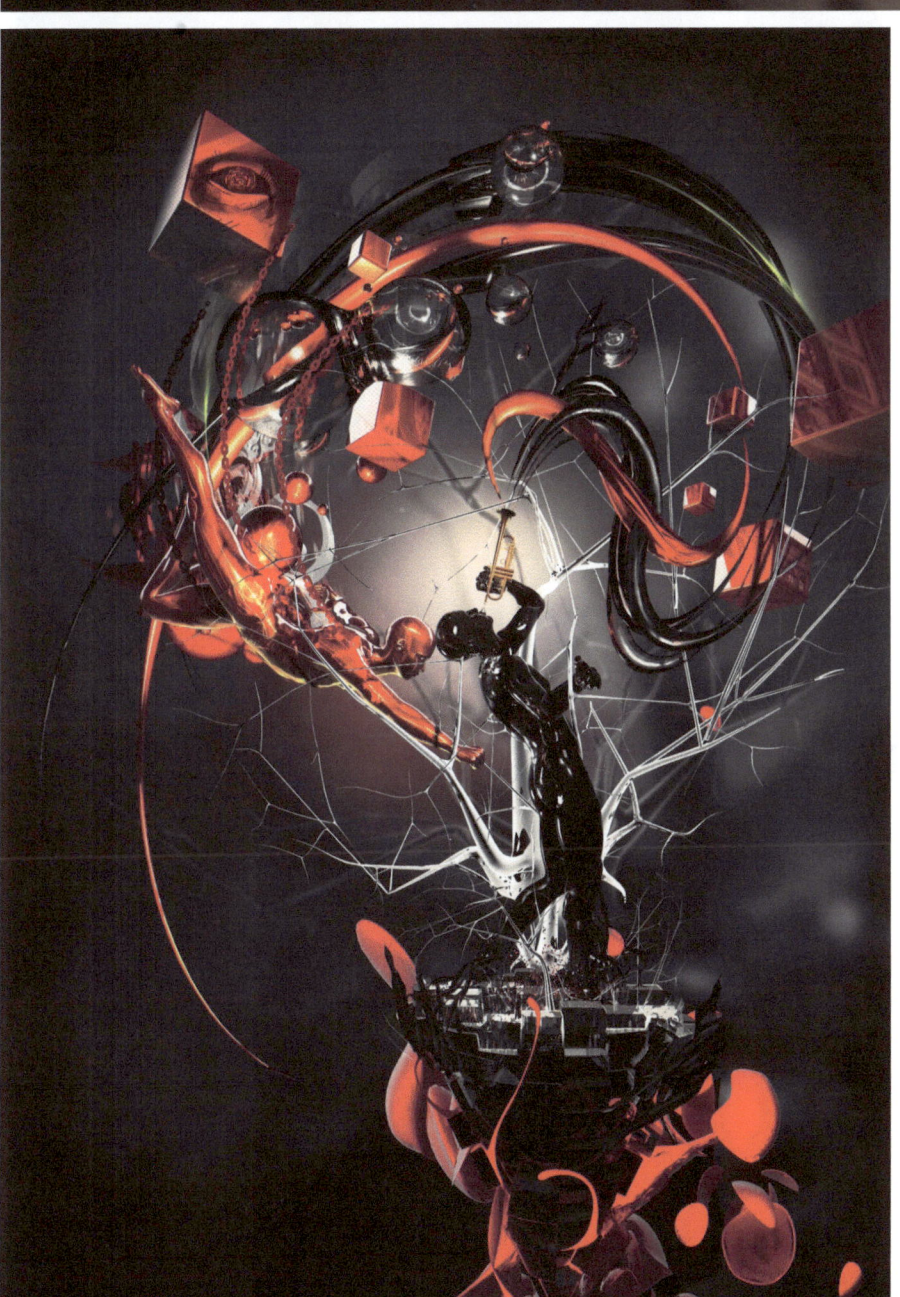

**1** **Atonal** Tension Digital. A personal experiment.

**2** **Beyond III** Digital. A collaboration effort initiated & directed by myself with: Nicolas Monin-Baroille, Roy Bourkel & Ola Gilen Rysamb for SlashThree's 15th exhibition: Paradigm Shift.

# JACOB BIAN

**LOCATION:** Kitchener
**WEB:** JakeBian.com
**EMAIL:** Canada1225@hotmail.com

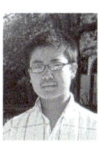

Jacob is a digital artist currently residing in Kitchener, Ontario. A proud member of the slashTHREE artist collective and currently ranked among the top three in the category of Digital Art in Ontario by the Behance Network. Believing that art is not limited to the canvas, he is a passionate musician in his time absent from the world of design. Music, nature, and culture are the main sources of his inspiration.

# MONTE WRIGHT

**LOCATION:** 13 Marketa Cres, Kitchener
**WEB:** MonteArtist.org
**EMAIL:** MonteArtist@rogers.com

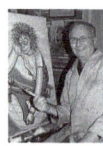

Monte Wright is an internationally recognized artist. In 2010 and 2011 his art has been shown in New York, N. Y.; Fort Lauderdale, Florida; Florence, Italy; London, England; and Argentina. His art may be seen in private collections both in Paris, France and Venice, Italy. Monte is a mixed-media artist from Kitchener, Ontario, Canada, who has shown his work for over four decades. He is well-known in Waterloo Region for his expansive murals and unique art forms. Often known for his Behind the Mask series Monte has also created action works that are objective expressions of humankind both globally and universally.

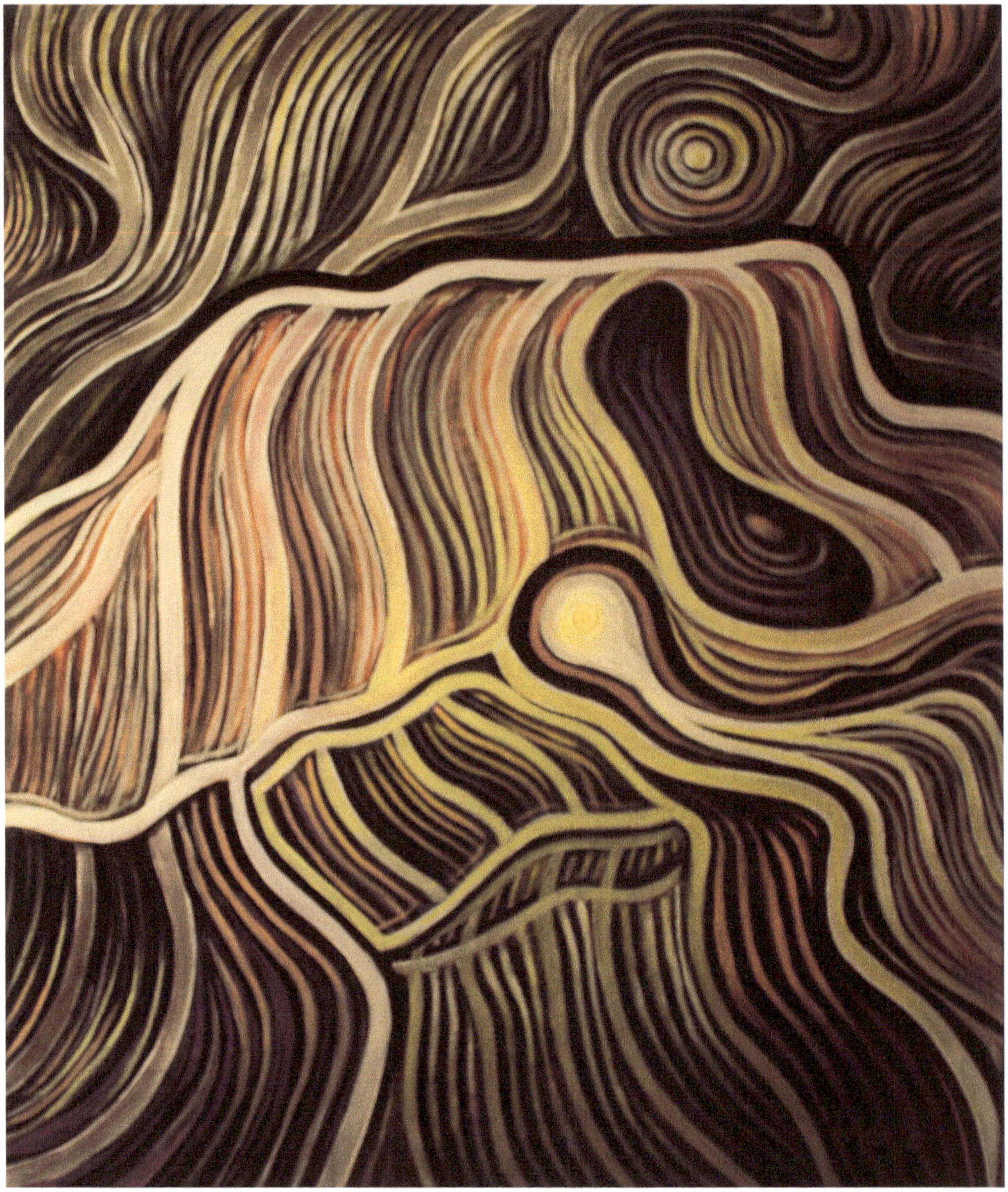

**1 Beneath The Surface 3**
30x36" Acrylic on canvas.

**2 Oneness** 26.5x26.5" Acrylic on canvas.

**3 Squeezeplay** 30" diameter. Mixed media on canvas.

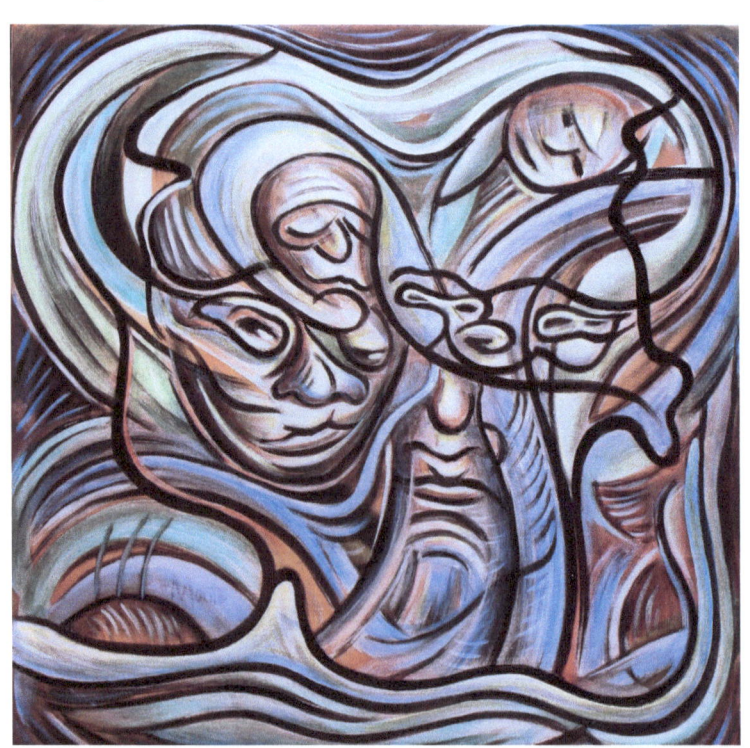

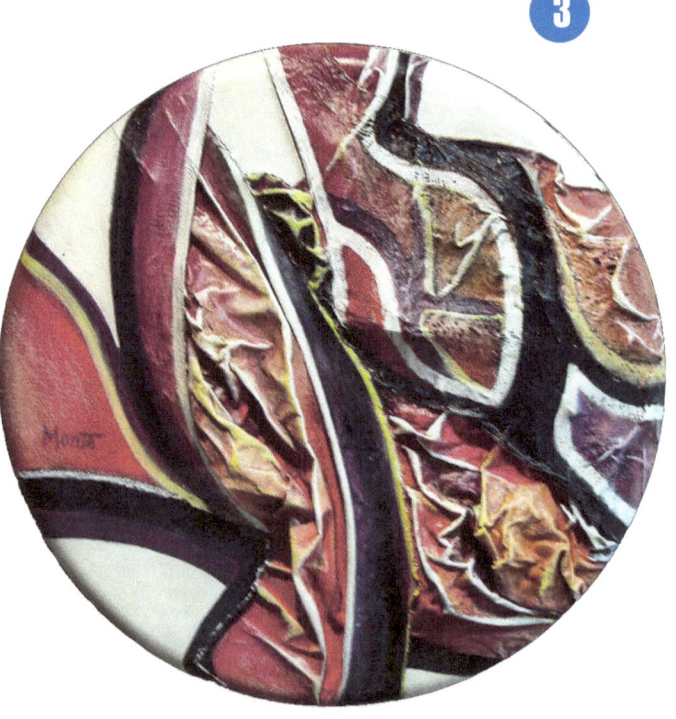

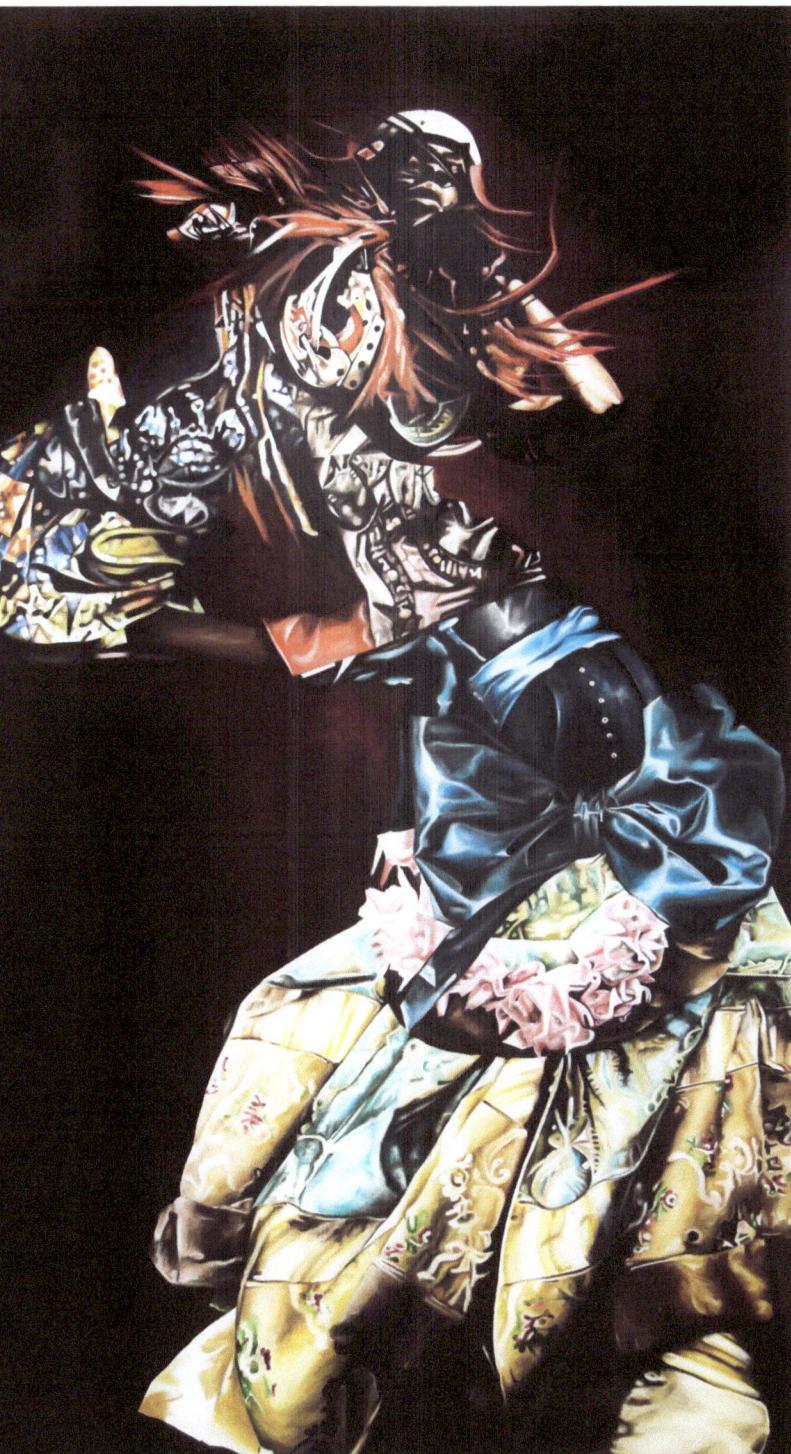

# NANA BEDIAKO

**LOCATION:** KW / Toronto
**WEB:** NanaBediako.tumblr.com
**EMAIL:** Gallerynana@gmail.com

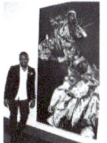

Bediako was born in Ghana and moved to Canada in 2005. He is a recent graduate from the University of Waterloo's Fine Arts program and is currently living in Toronto, Ontario where he is studying Fashion at the RCC Institute of Technology. Through his work, Bediako attempts to put on display all aspects of high fashion and the International fashion industry. His themes include glamour and beauty, as well as the ugly, unseen, and consumerist aspects of fashion. His paintings are meticulously executed and based on collages that the artist himself collected and assembled from International fashion magazines. Bediako's paintings are not portraits, rather the figures in his paintings are ambiguous and representational and are aimed at making the viewer question the role and position of the fashion industry.

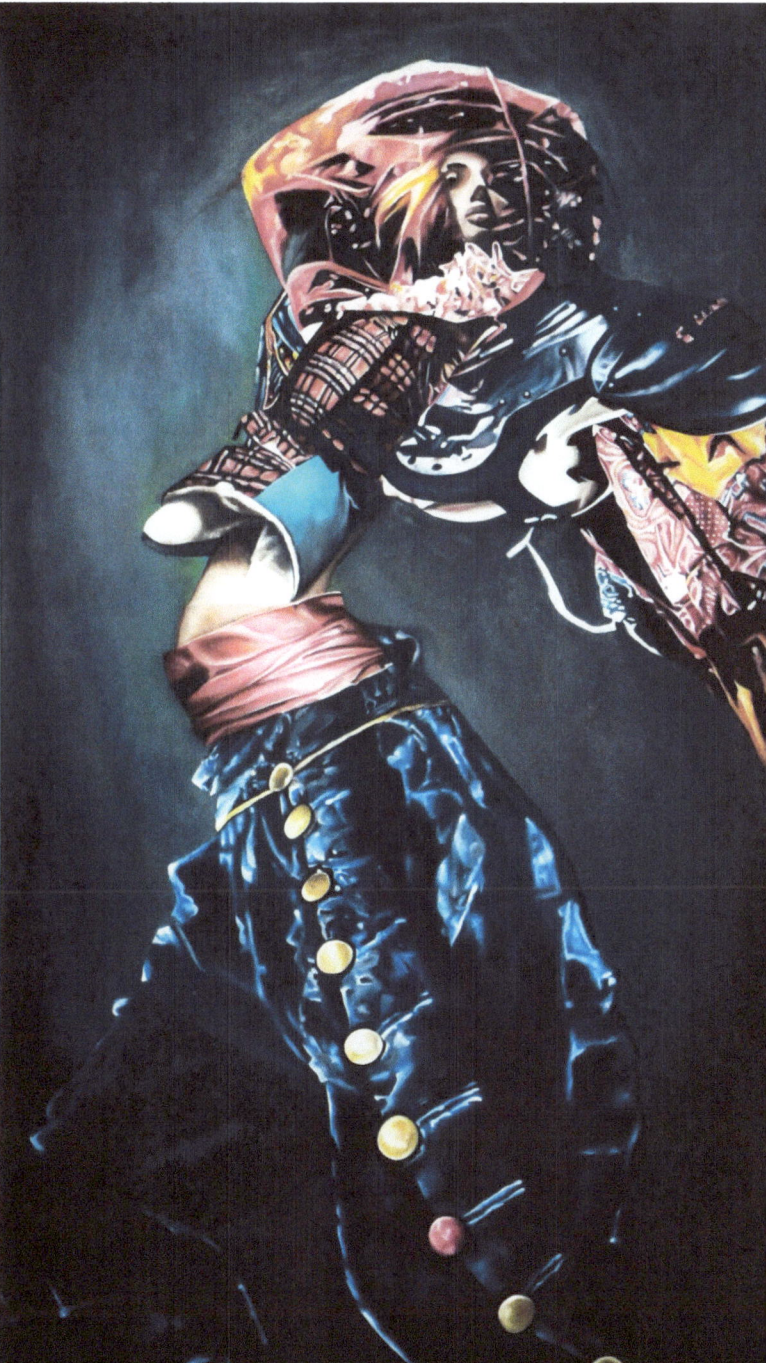

**1** **Wanton Behavior** 84x47" Oil on canvas. 2011.

**2** **I Want I Get** 84x47" Oil on canvas. 2011.

1

2

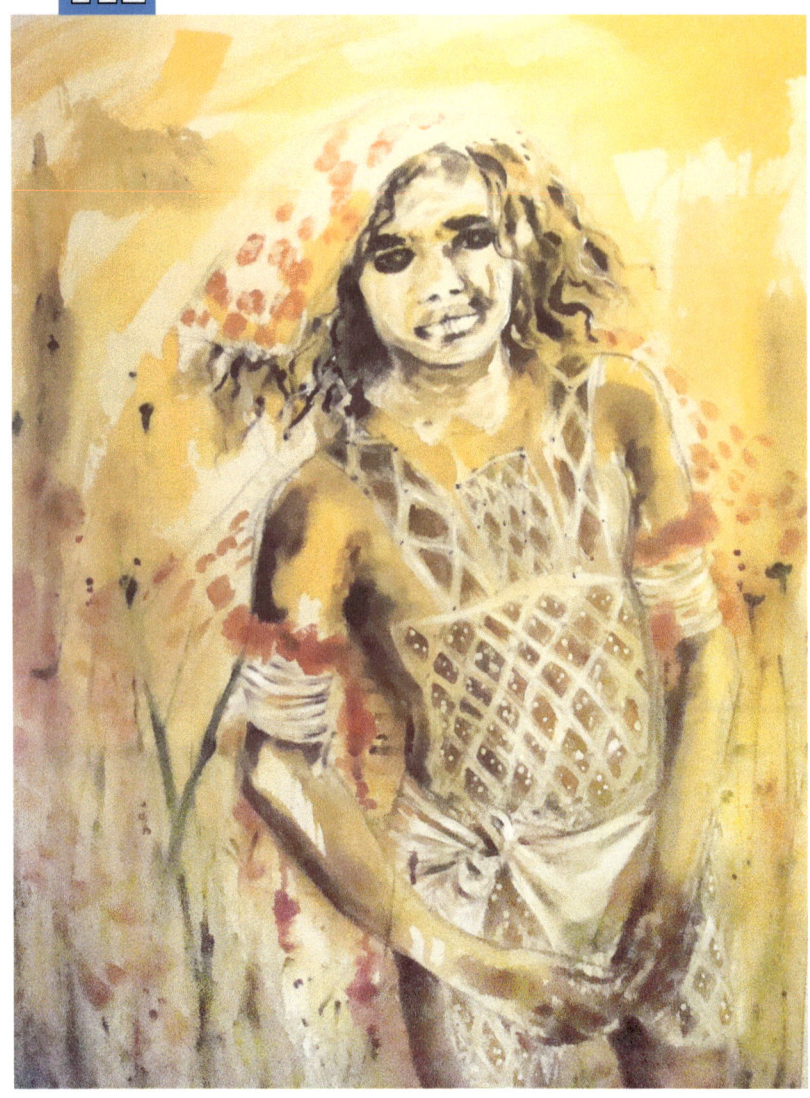

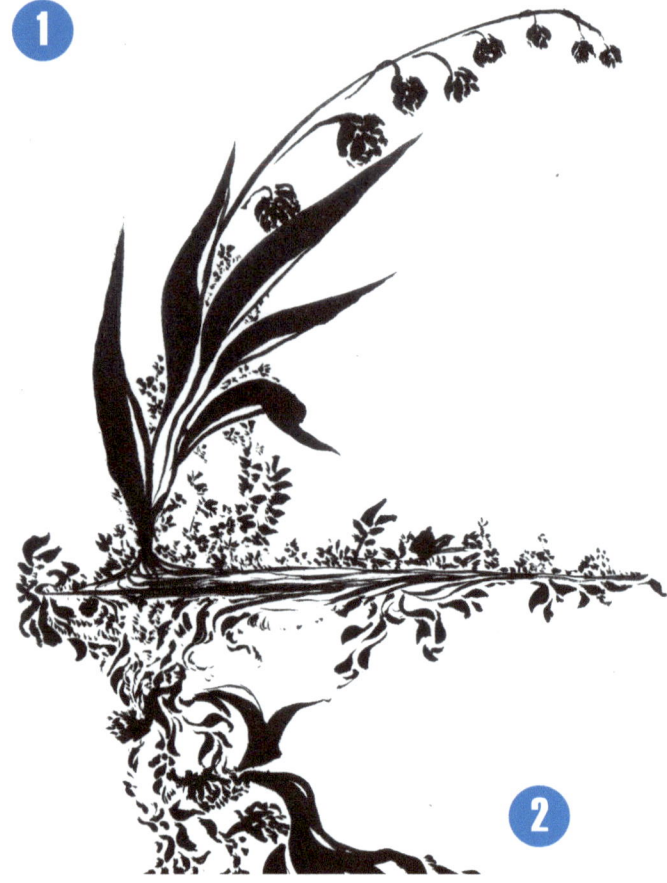

**2 Lilly of the Valley** 4x6" china ink on paper 2011.

**1 Yellow Sun** 3x4' Acrylic wash and charcoal on unprimed canvas 2007.

# STELA TOPOLCIC

**LOCATION:** Kitchener
**WEB:** Snowdrop.ca
**EMAIL:** Stelatop@gmail.com

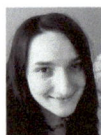

Stela likes to draw on napkins in coffee shops, and takes unabashed joy in complementary crayon sets from family restaurants. Her university of choice was The University of Waterloo from which she got her joint honours degree in Visual Arts and Rhetoric. After that she went to Western in London, Ontario and got her teaching degree, but moved back to Kitchener because it's geekier here. Stela loves painting spontaneously and putting her emotions on paper.

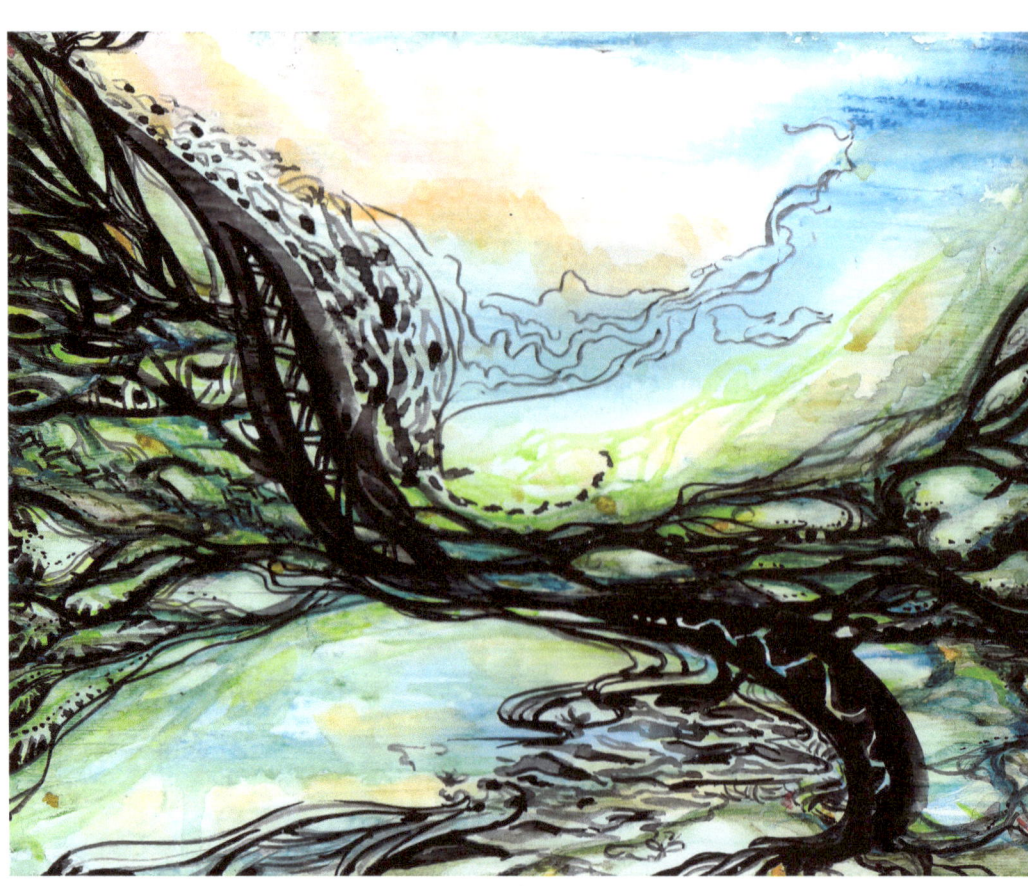

**3 Raphael** Raphael, the angel of healing. 8x10" watercolour and china ink on masonite 2010.

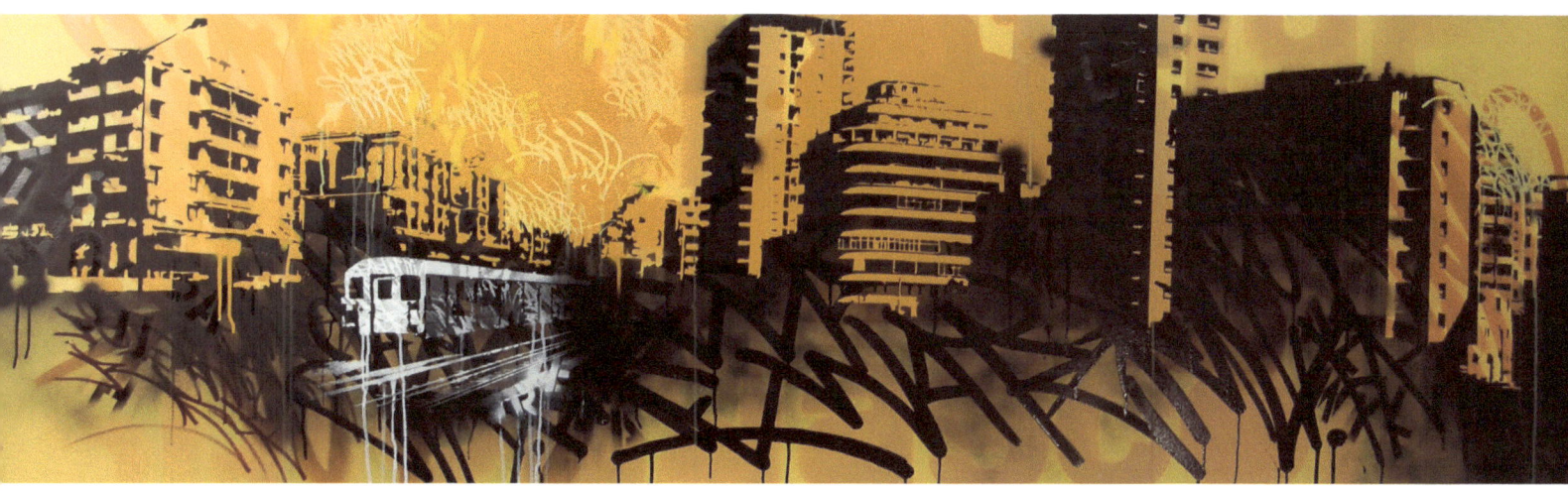

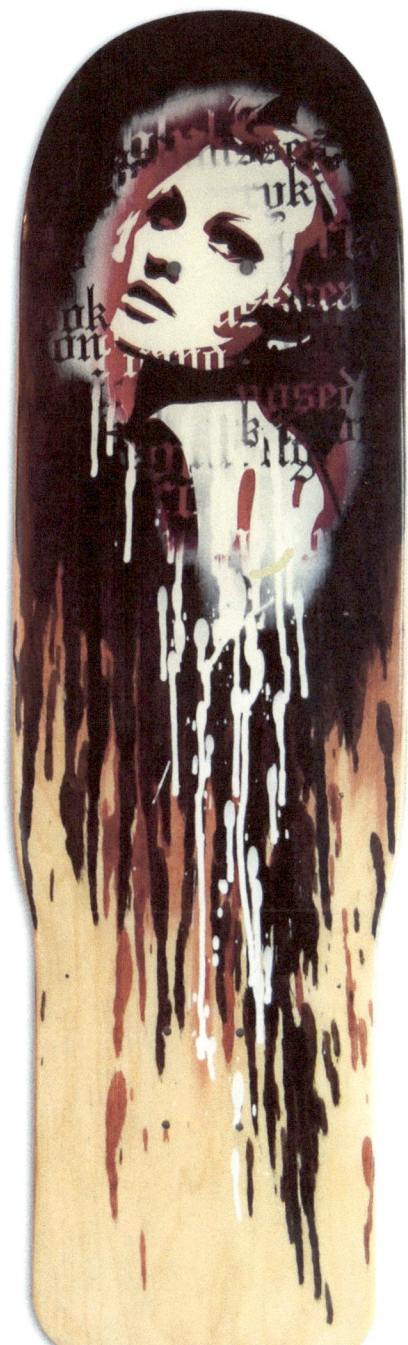

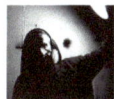

**1** **Summer Heat** 96x36x3" Oil, latex, spray paint, silk screen.

# KOSTA ONE

**LOCATION:** Kitchener
**WEB:** Kostaoner.blogspot.com/
**EMAIL:** Kostaoner@gmail.com

Kosta is an artist who grew up on street art. Falling in love with font and language started doing canvas work in his early 20s. Each canvas expresses another emotion, opinion, view or story from his daily experience.

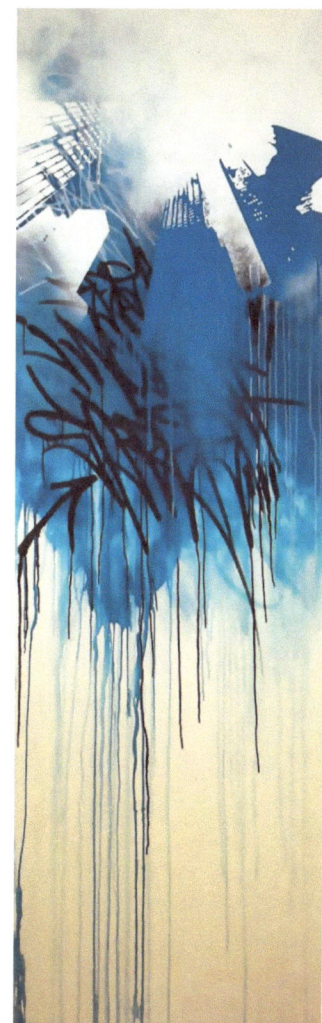

**2** **Break You Off (Skateboard: Pool shark)** 8 7/8x32¾ wheel base 15" Wood stain, lacquer, silk screen.

**3** **Tales Of The City Vol. 2** 30x30x1.5" Spray paint, oil, latex.

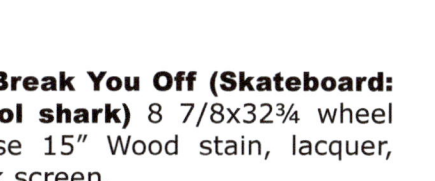

114

# MARGARET GISSING

**LOCATION:** Kitchener
**WEB:**
Wix.com/margaretgfreelance/portfolio
**EMAIL:** MargaretGissing@gmail.com

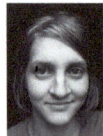

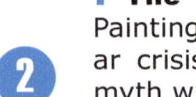

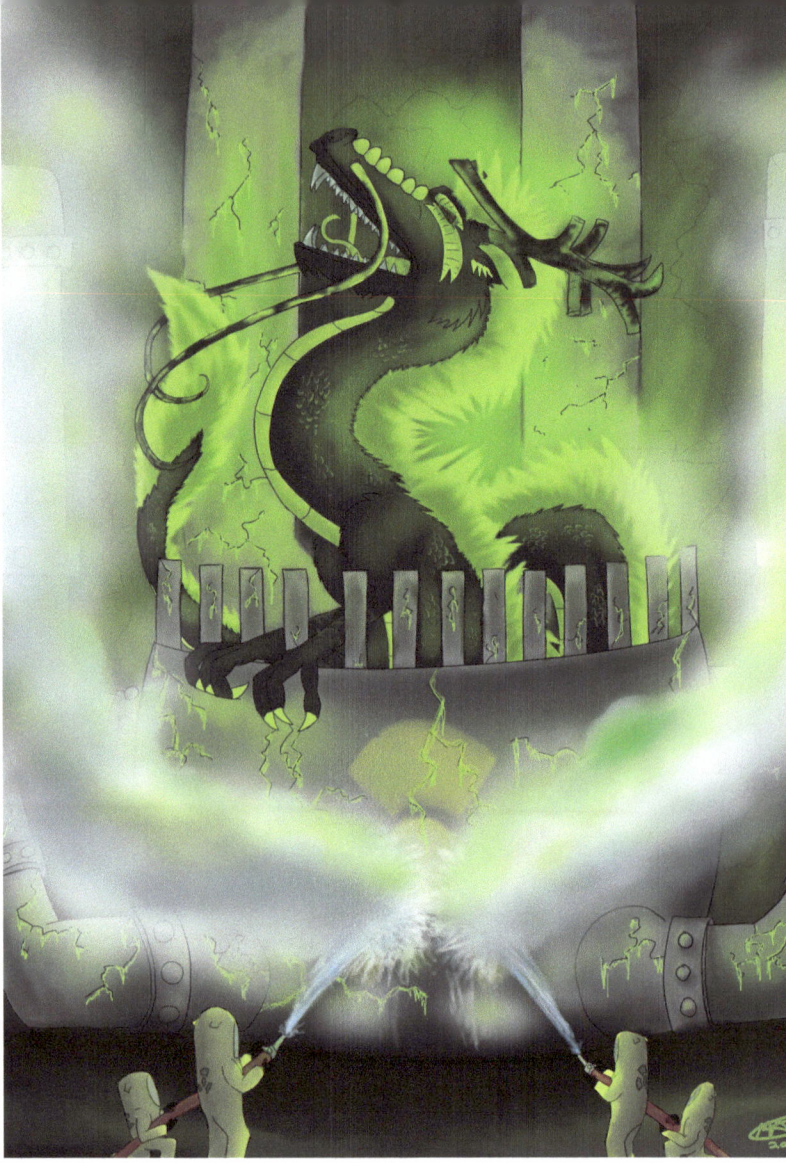

Margaret is the type of artist who can't remember a time when she wasn't creating. She enjoys working with all types of mediums such as sculpture, painting, graphic arts and textiles, but is strongest in the Digital Arts realm. Margaret makes sense of her world through art, and enjoys exploring human thought, nature, and fantasy elements through it.

**1 The Dragon of Fukushima** Digital Painting. In response to the Japan nuclear crisis, combining traditional Japanese myth with modern events.

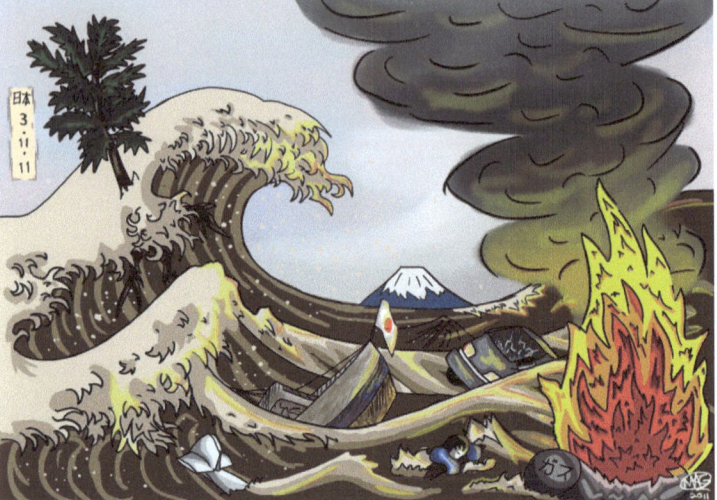

**2 Great Wave Over Japan** Digital Painting. Heavily inspired by "Great wave off Kanagawa" by Hokusai; to communicate the devastation of the Tsunami that hit Japan in March 2011.

**3 To Be or Not to Be** Digital Painting. A scene painted of an actor in the Royal Shakespeare Company's performance of Hamlet.

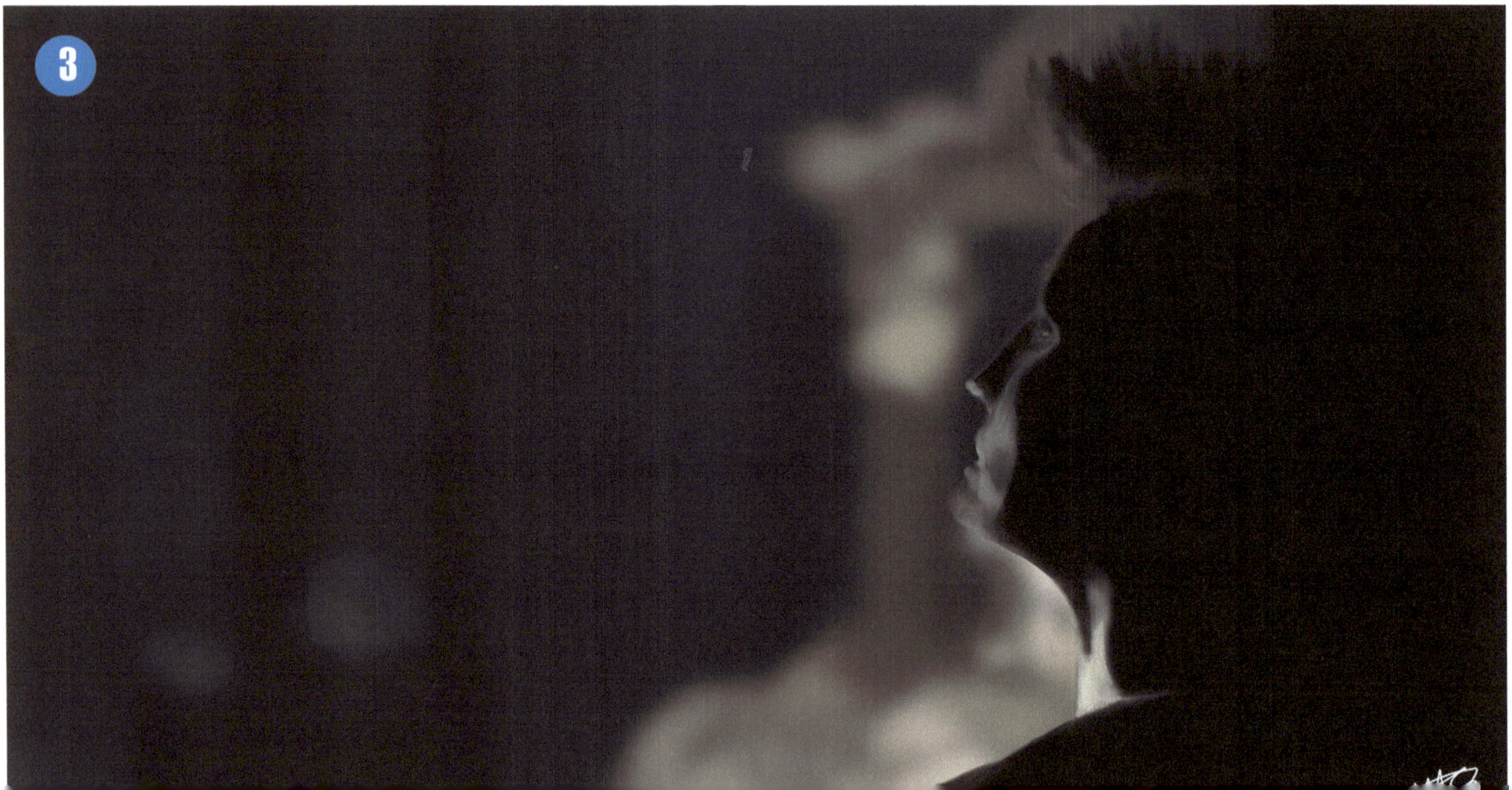

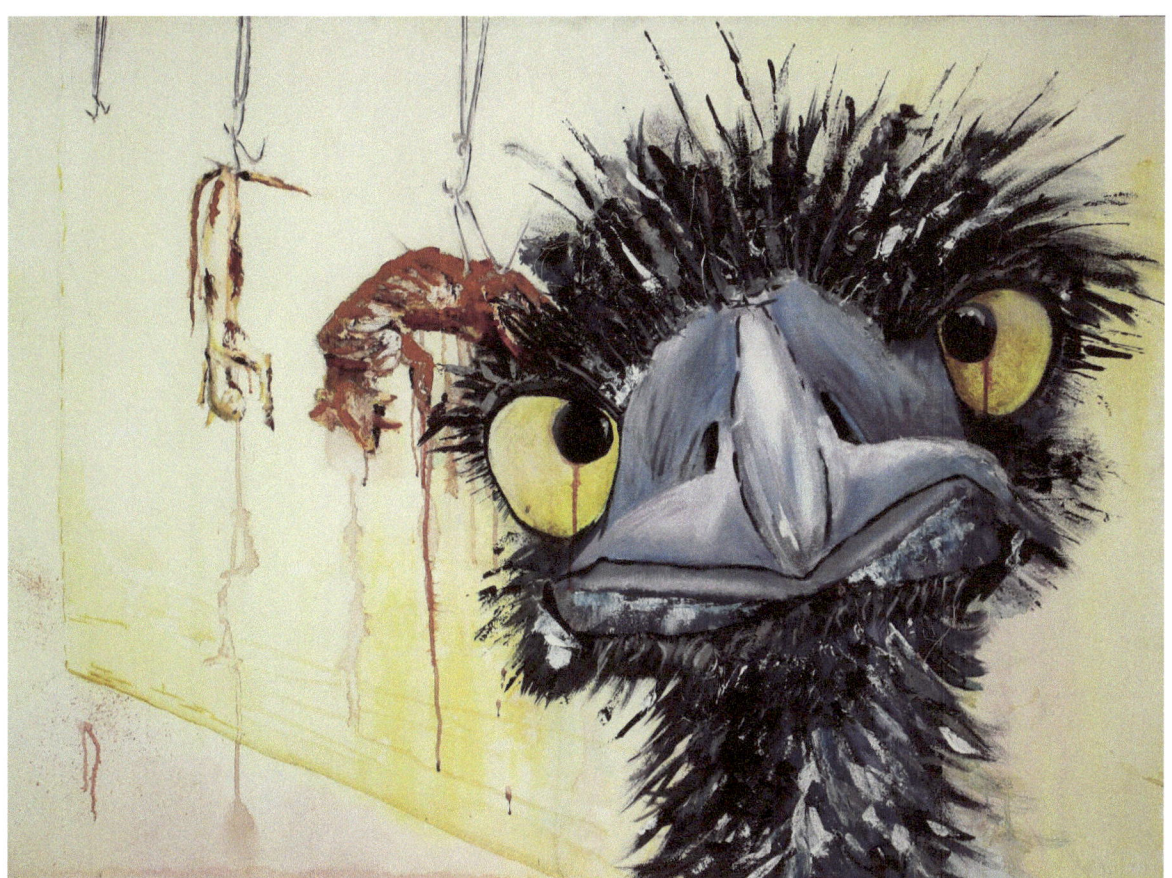

**1** **Eekel** 36x48" Acrylic and Oil on Canvas. 2009

# KEITH DE VRIES

**LOCATION:** Waterloo / Gowanstown
**WEB:** KeithdeVriesArt.com
**EMAIL:** KeithdeVries@hotmail.com

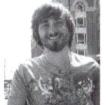 Keith loves to create. He studied art for four years at the University of Waterloo. In that time he painted, drew and sculpted but developed a love for sculpture and focuses lately on some costume making.

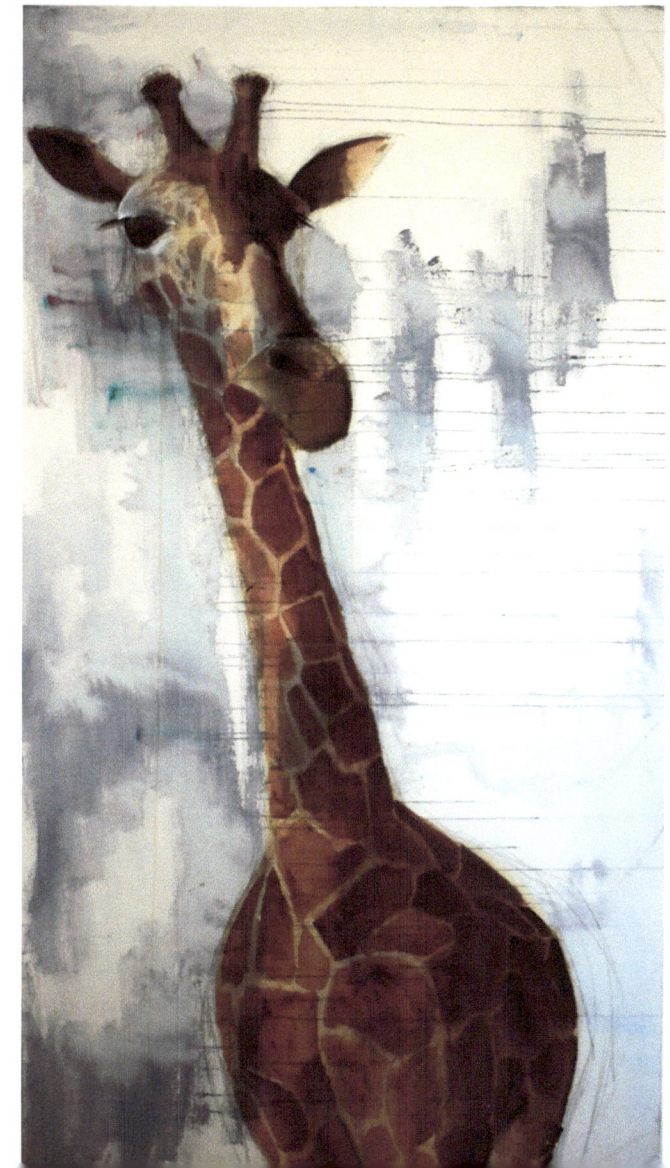

**2** **Giraffe** Acrylic on Canvas. 2010

# MARION R ANDERSON

**LOCATION:** New Dundee
**WEB:** MarionAnderson.ca
**EMAIL:** AlderCreekStudio1@sympatico.ca

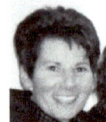

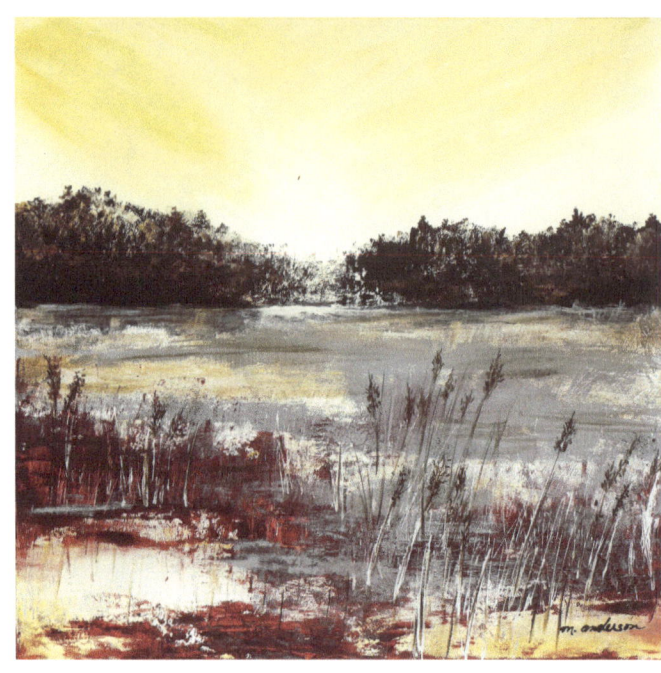

My work is based on lived-experience. This wetlands suite of large mixed media acrylic on canvas paintings features the Elsinore Swamp located just north of Southampton. My summers are spent teaching and plein air painting in this area. The marsh provides such a variety of texture that I find it necessary to use a limited palette for each piece as I attempt to capture a mood or temperature. As outdoor painters, our favourite saying is "if you don't like the weather, wait 20 minutes!"

**1** **Elsinore Evening** 36x36" Acrylic on canvas.

**2** **Marsh Multiples** 30x30" each. Mixed media acrylic on canvas.

**3** **Ripples & Reeds** 30x30" Acrylic on canvas.

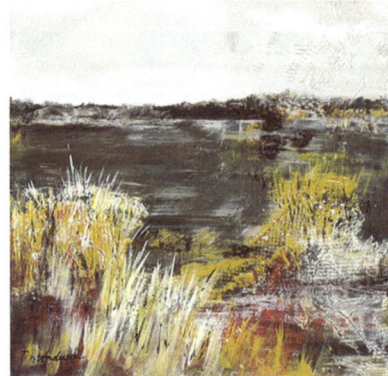
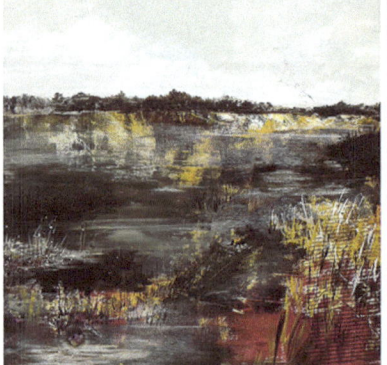
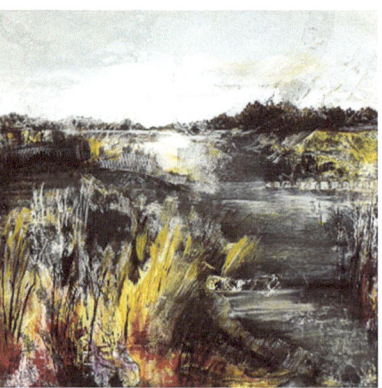

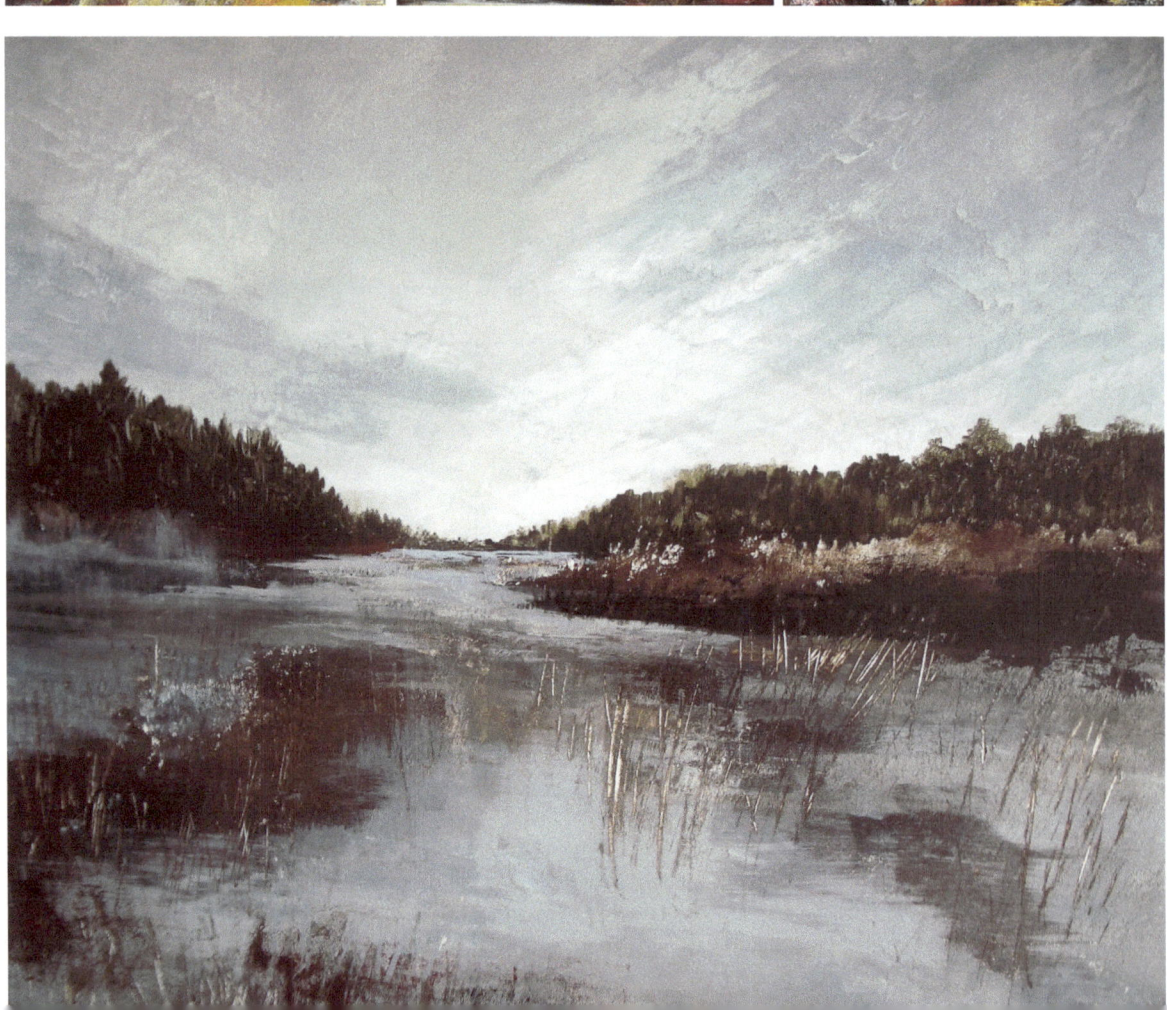

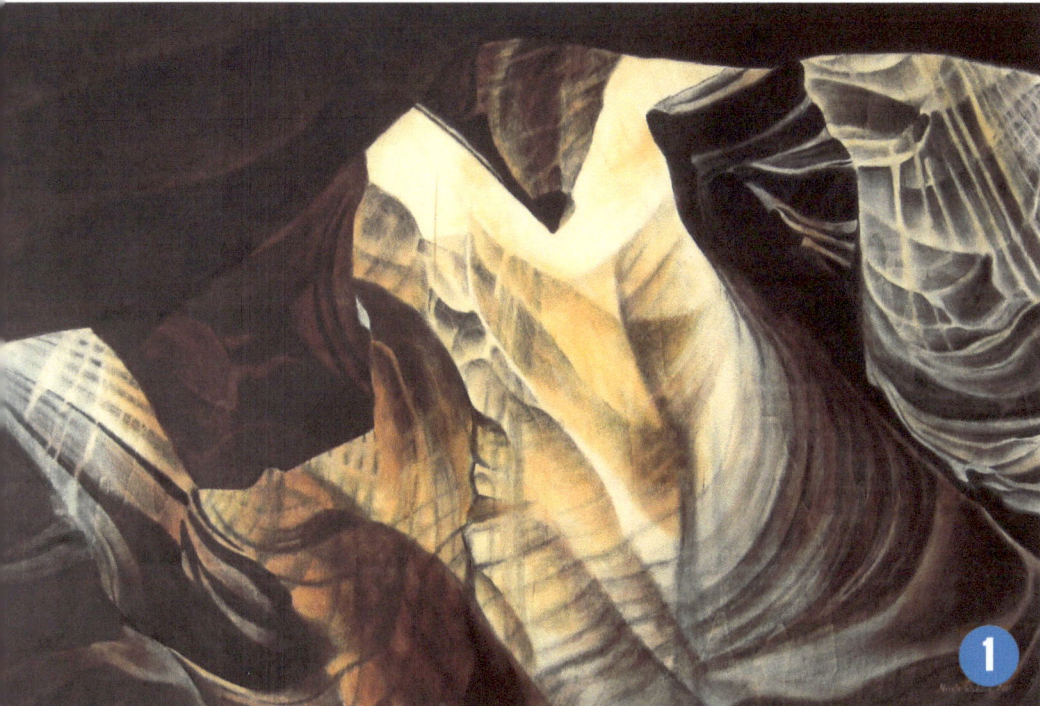

**1**

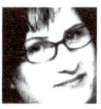

**2**

# NICOLE WADDICK

**LOCATION:** Waterloo
**WEB:** NicoleWaddick.ca
**EMAIL:** NWaddick@gmail.com

Nicole Waddick is a multi-disciplinary artist. She has a BA in Aesthetics and Cultural Studies from Carleton University. She studied painting at the Ontario College of Art and Design. In July 2011, she completed an artist residency in ceramics at Medalta in Alberta. Nicole is a member of UpTown Gallery and the Waterloo Potters' Workshop. She is an art instructor at the Button Factory and Cambridge Centre for the Arts. In May 2012, she will have a solo show at the Cambridge Centre for the Arts.

**1** **Antelope Canyon No. 10** 36x24" Charcoal and Acrylic on Wood 2011 Antelope Canyon is formed by windblown sand and flash floods. It is located in northern Arizona.

**2** **Slate by Oldman River No. 4** 30x36" Soft Pastel and Acrylic on Wood 2011.

**3** **Prairie Rotation** 6.5x16.5" Stoneware 2011.

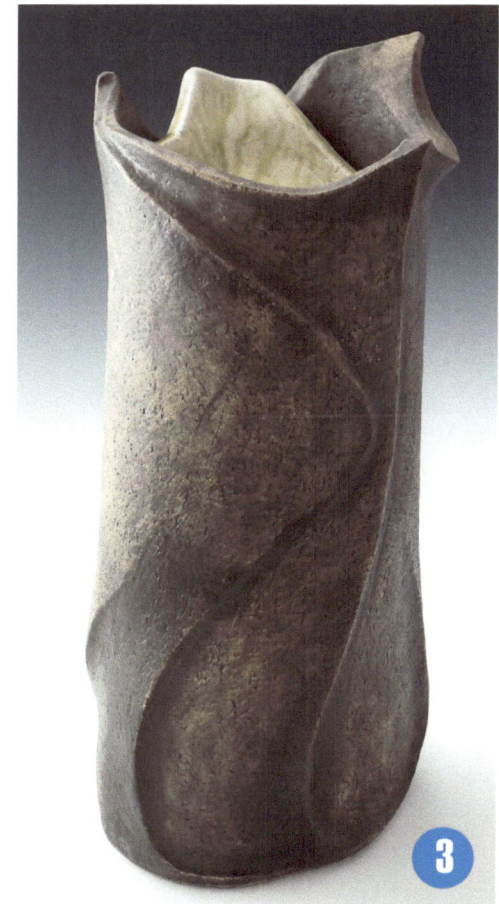

**3**

# RAEGAN LITTLE

**LOCATION:** Waterloo
**WEB:** RaeganLittlePhotography.com
**EMAIL:** Raeganlittle@rogers.com

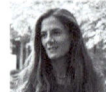

Having lived in Waterloo for 15 years, Raegan has been very involved in the community. She has served on a number of not-for-profit boards and committees, and in doing so has been fortunate enough to be involved in the local art scene in many ways. Raegan balances a busy family life with part-time photography work for a local furniture manufacturer.

**1 Tulips** Photograph.

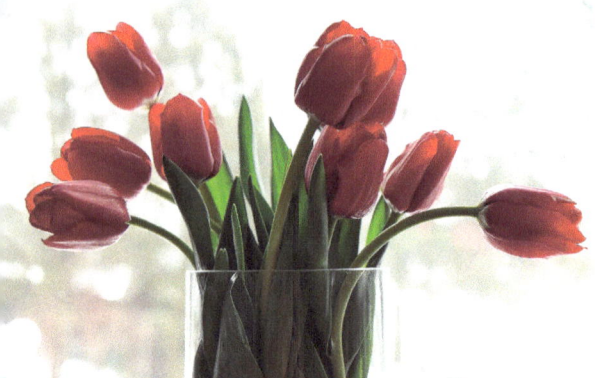

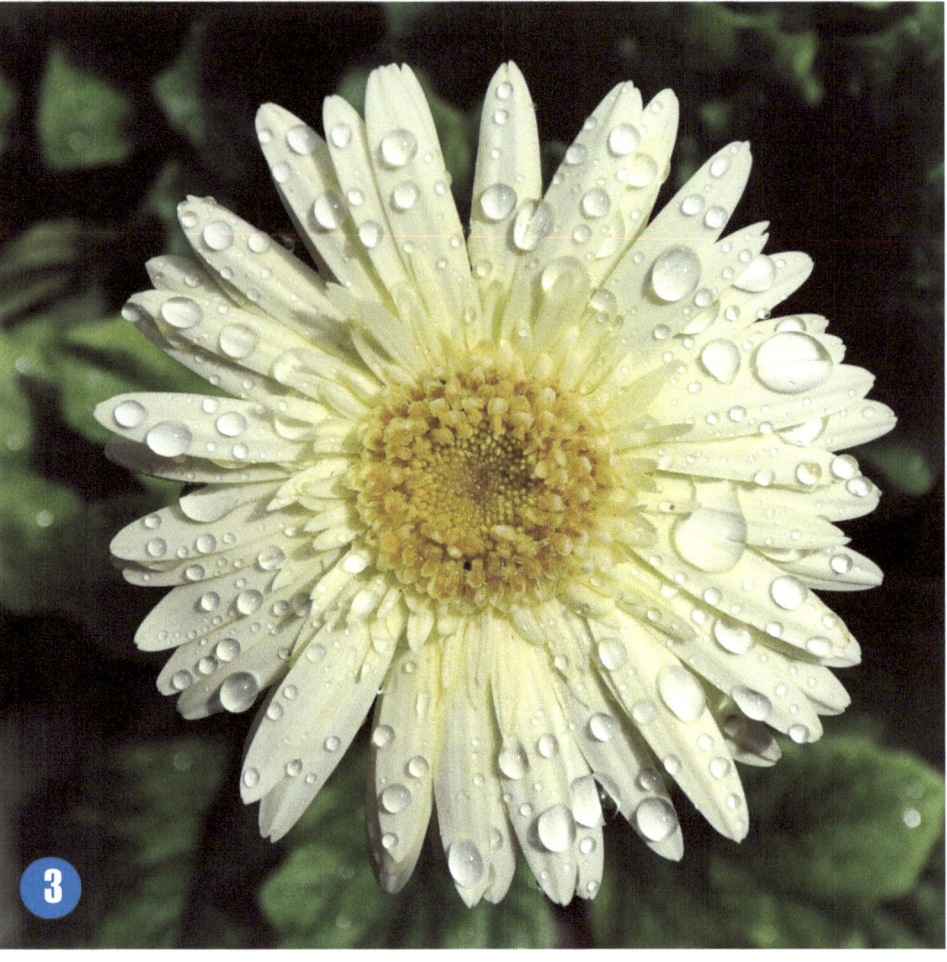

**2 Mike and Ike** Photograph.

**3 Gerbera with Raindrops** Photograph

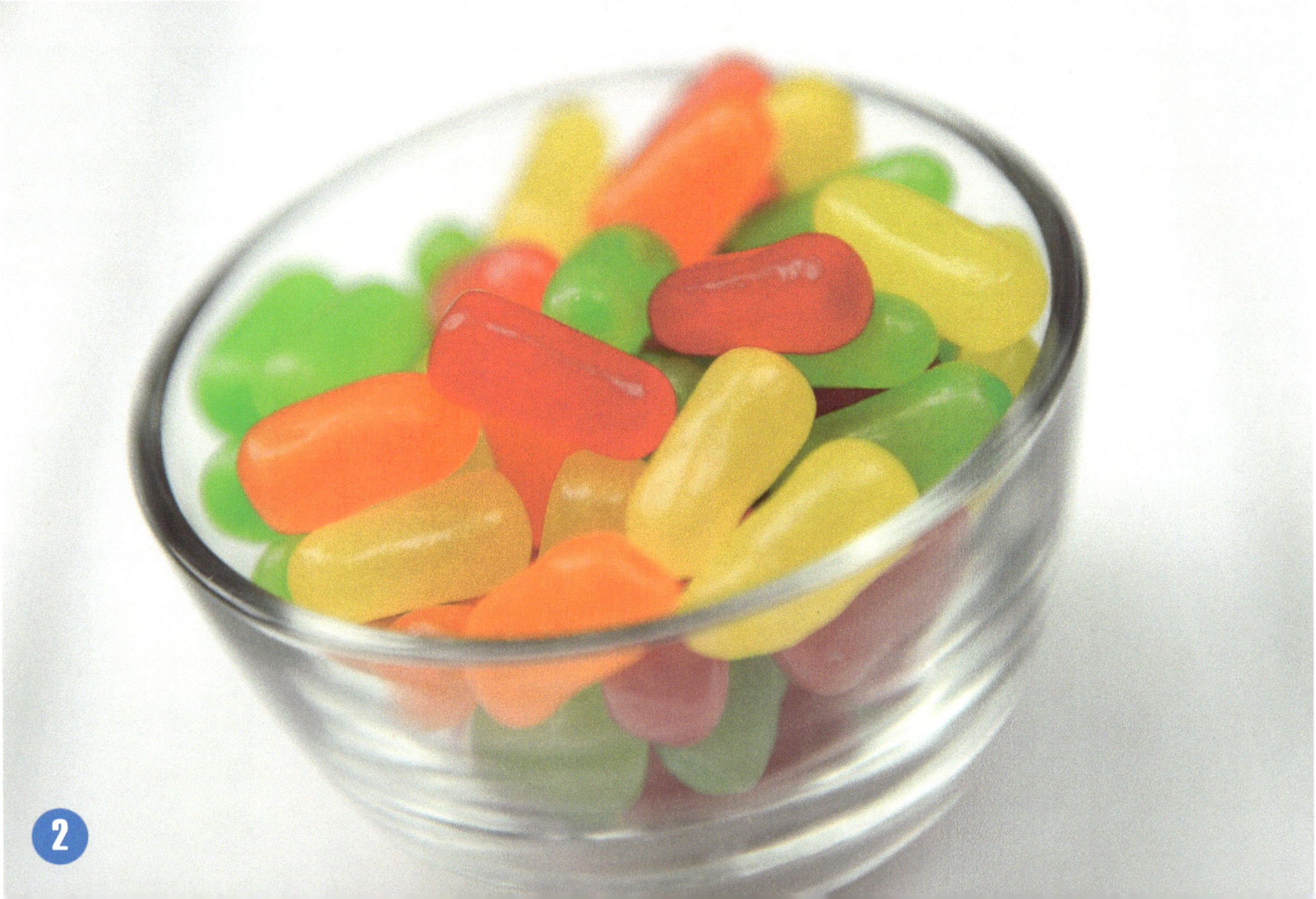

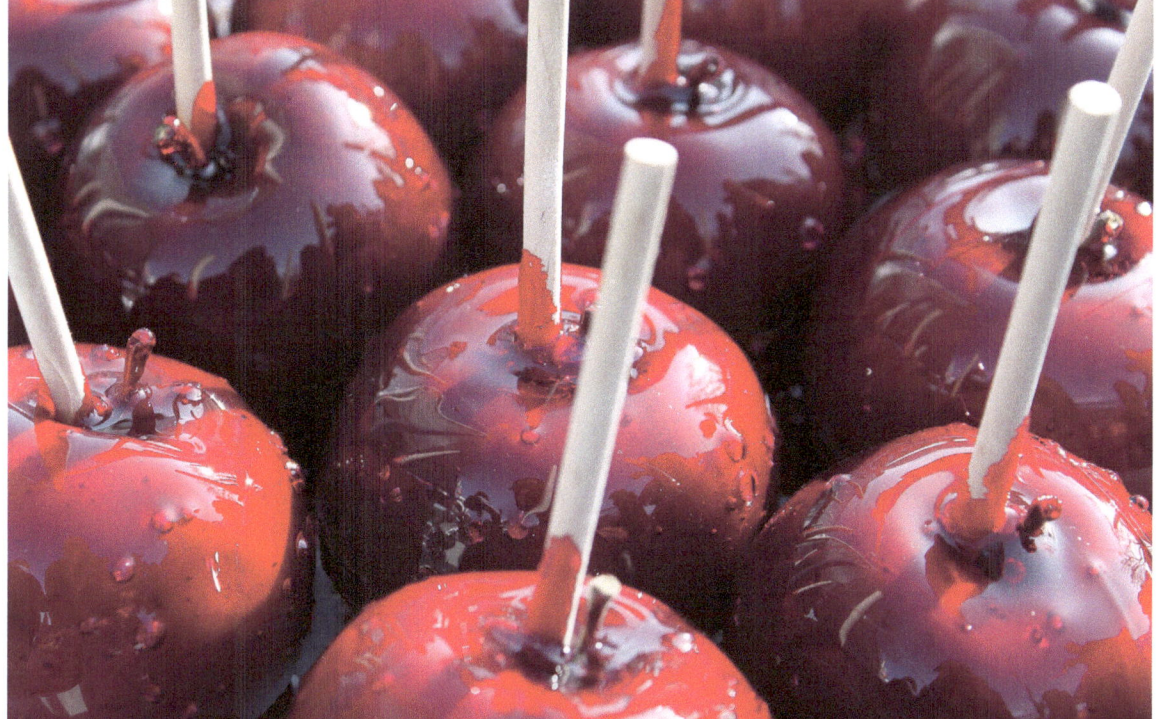

## JOHN-PAUL FILLION

**LOCATION:** Drayton
**WEB:**
Fineartamerica.com/profiles/johnpaul-fillion.html
**EMAIL:** Jpfillion@gmail.com

I've always had an interest in photography and have been told I have a "good eye". I won my first photography contest, which consisted of nearly a thousand entries, one year after I purchased my first SLR camera. Since then I have won several photography contests, sold pictures internationally and had my work put on display at city hall in downtown Kitchener. To me photography is a way of sharing with others what I see in the world around me.

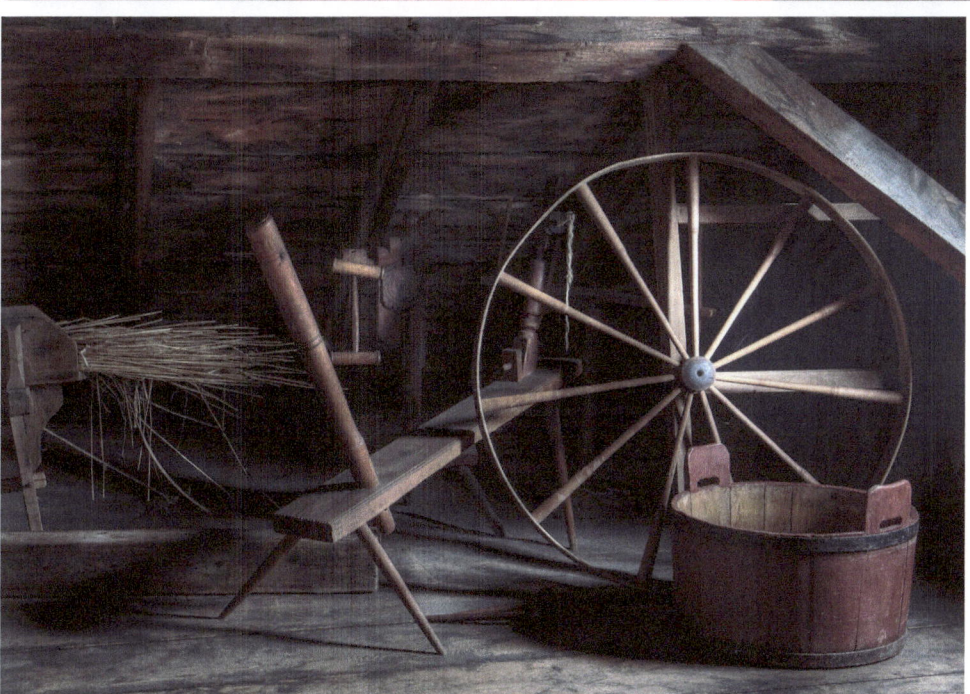

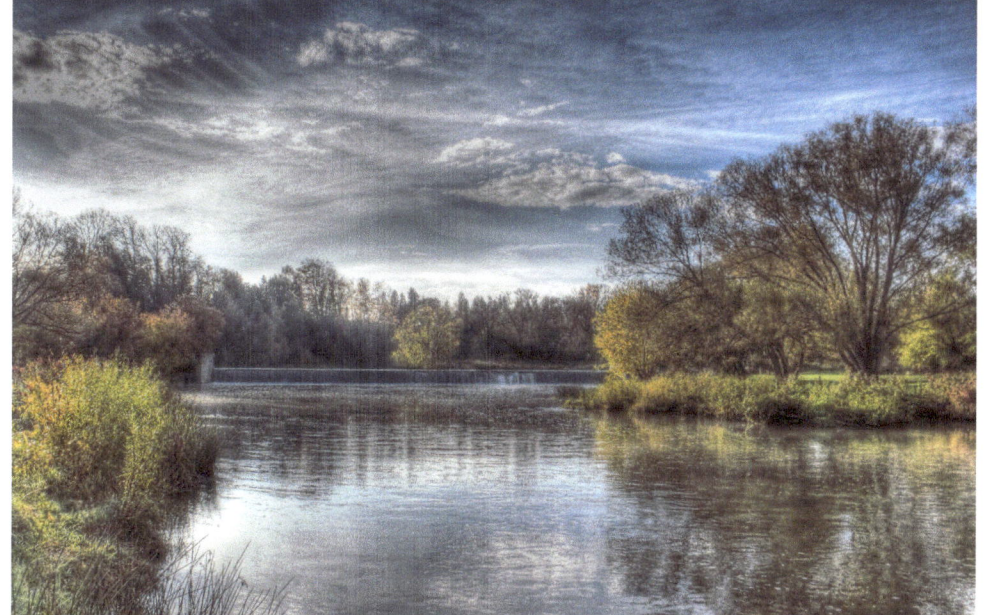

**1** **Elmira Maple Syrup Festival Candy Apples** Photo.

**2** **Joseph Schneider Haus Old Fashioned Spinning Wheel** Photo.

**3** **St. Jacobs Waterfall** Photo.

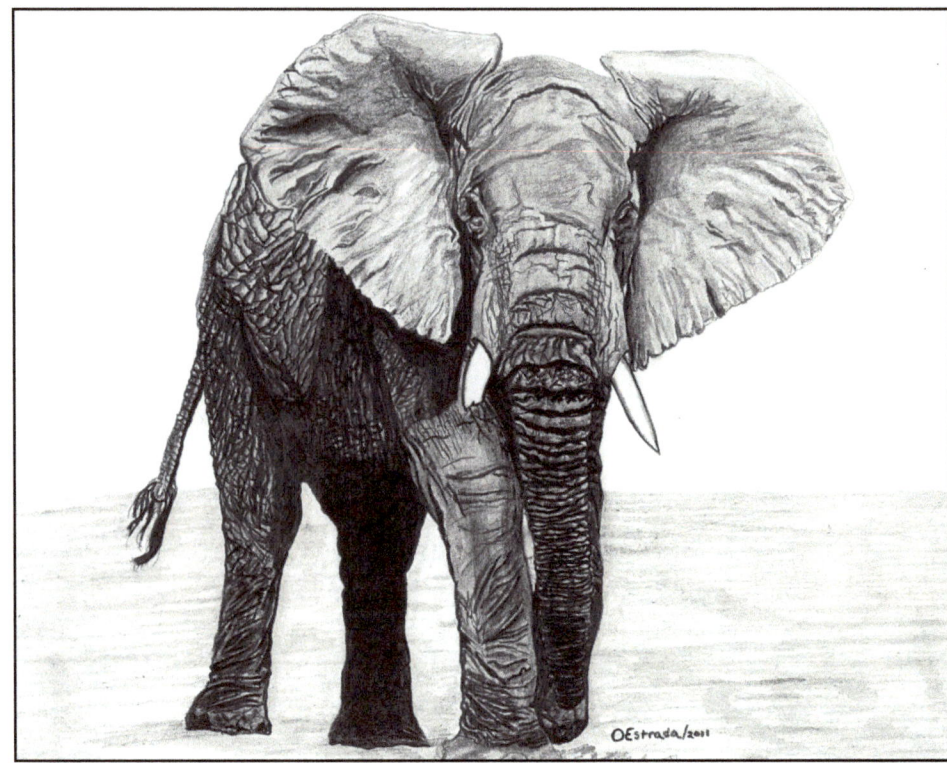

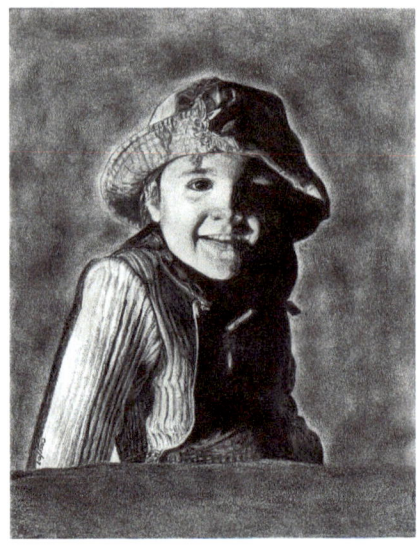

**Niece's Portrait** 8x10" Graphite sketch pencils.

# OSCARE ESTRADA

**LOCATION:** Kitchener
**WEB:** SketchsAndFrames.com
**EMAIL:** OscarEstrada74@rogers.com

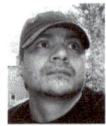

I discovered my talent at a very early age and Visual Art has been a passion ever since - my work was always in the hallways and main offices throughout my high school years. My attention to detail has always been noticed by the ones who appreciate my work. I focus on realistic art and portraits - If I see it I draw it. I like to create pencil sketches and coloured pencil drawings. Through my years of experience with coloured pencils I have taught myself how to blend the colours to create the proper shades and shadows. I focus on pencil sketches, but I also use acrylics and oils

**The Elephant** 8x10" Graphite sketch pencils.

**Snake Head** 8x10" Coloured pencils.

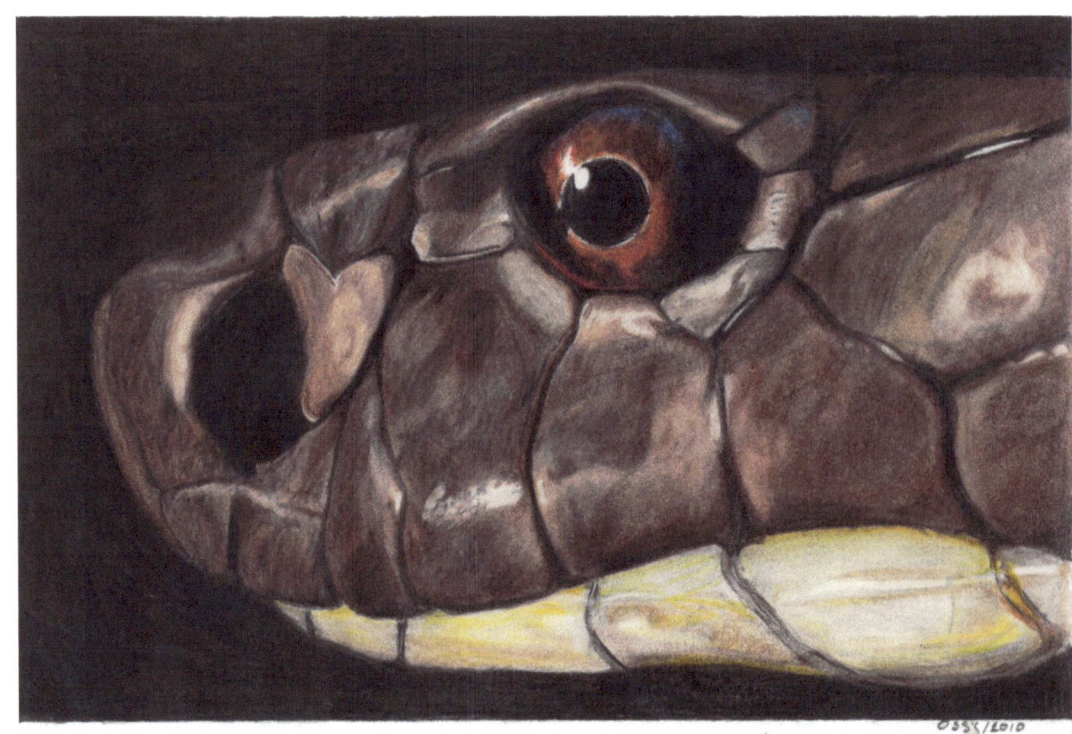

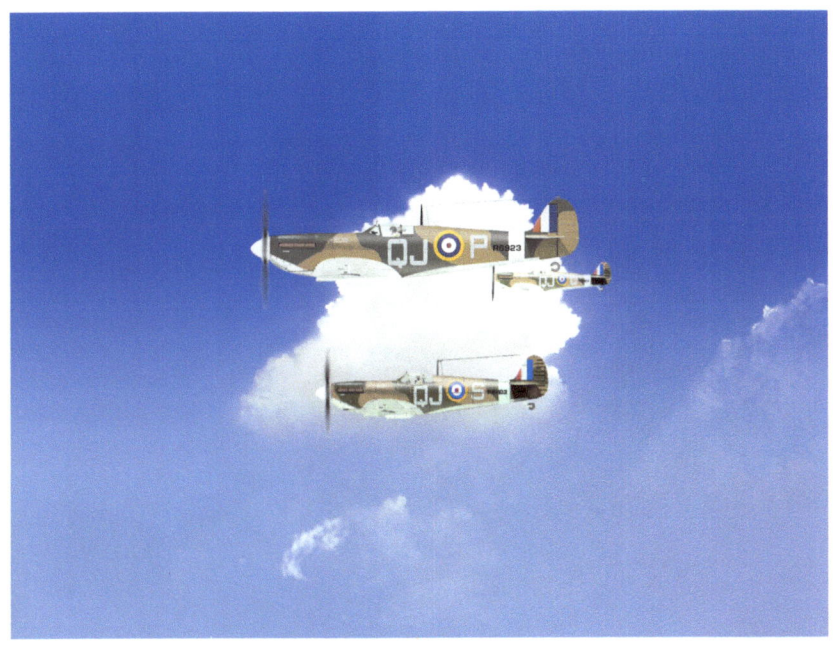

**1**

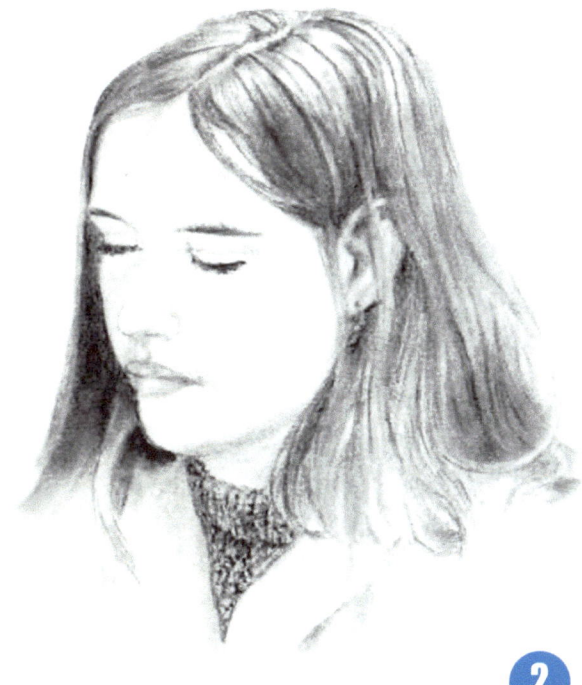

**2**

# GARY BABB

**LOCATION:** Kitchener Waterloo
**WEB:** (N/A)
**EMAIL:** Garybabb0b2@yahoo.ca

As a self-taught artist I may have had to take a different approach to learning about art as opposed to those with a formal education. However, I believe that all artists share a common love for art and an intense appreciation for all things around us. I can't remember when I picked up a pencil, but I do remember the immense pleasure it gave me to create. I was born in what was then known as Galt, now Cambridge and have spent the better part of my life in the area. Long walks absorbing the surrounding scenery have always been a source of relaxation and pleasure for me. Having an avid interest in developing my skills in different media I've been able to work in oils, pastels, pencil, charcoal and lately digital media.

**1 Thunder Head** Digital.

**2 Marie Older** Pencil.

**3 Lancasters** Pencil.

**3**

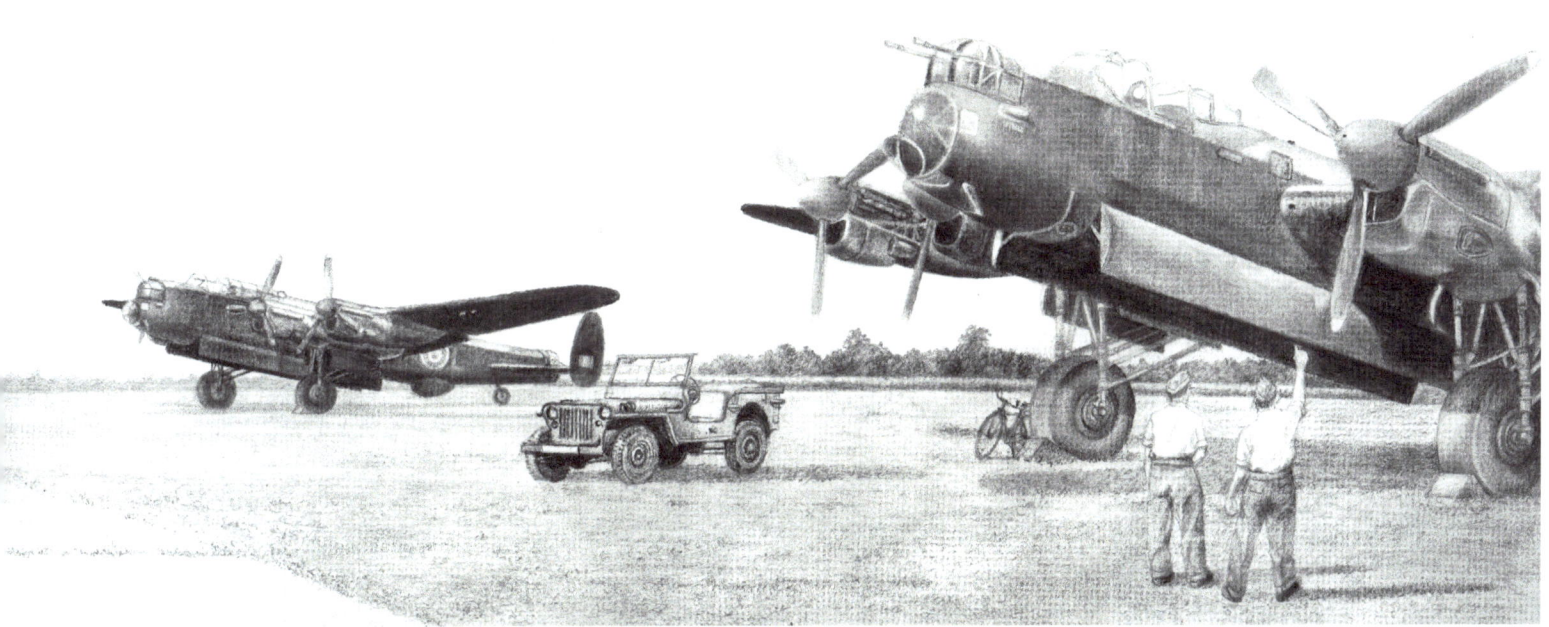

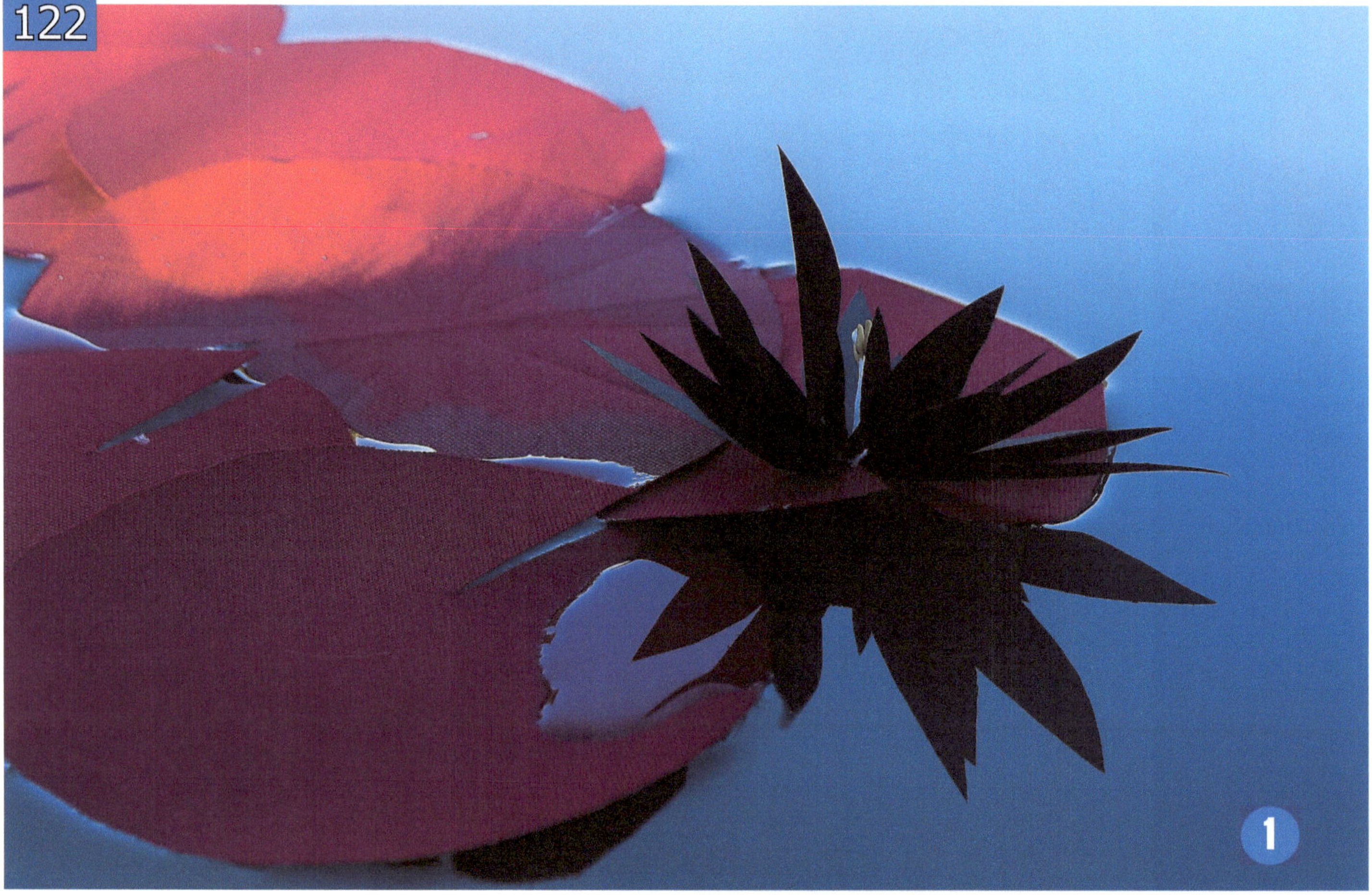

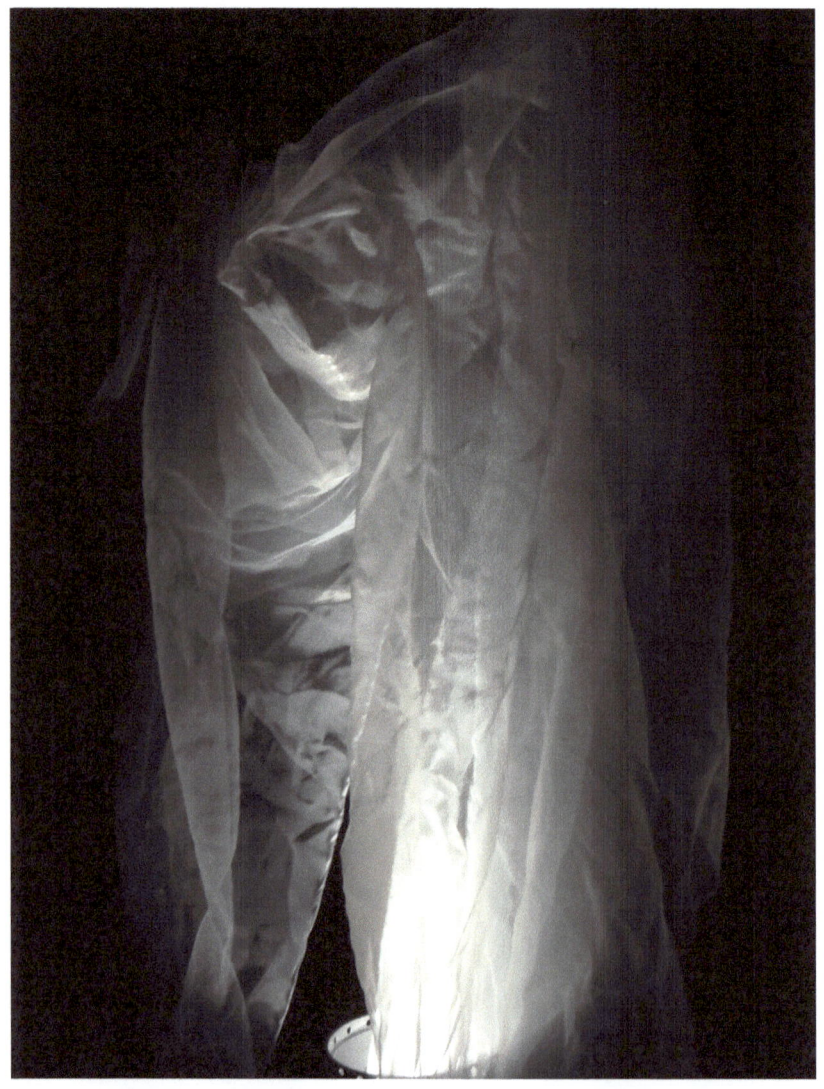

# REGINA-CONSTANZA SALAZAR

**LOCATION:** Kitchener
**WEB:** Http://rcsalazar.carbonmade.com
**EMAIL:** Rcdesalazar@gmail.com

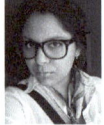

Constanza Salazar is a conceptual installation artist living in Kitchener, Ontario. She currently attends the University of Waterloo, focusing on her Honors Fine Arts and Philosophy. Constanza considers herself to be a sort of platonic artist, in that her whole work is comprised of materializing abstract forms. Her works have been described as ephemeral, ethereal and poetic.

**1** The Preconscious: The Bridge Between the Past and Present, Space and Time (series) Installation. Nylon Taslan Fabric, Sugar Floral Stamen, Cardstock Paper Taken from Freud's Iceberg illustration and study of the preconscious.

**2** The Ghost in the Machine (series) Figure 3 Installation. PETG transparent plastic sheets, shear voile fabric. Taken from Descartes' mind-body dualism in his work "Meditations".

# LEIGH SELLNER

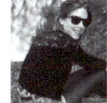

**LOCATION:** Kitchener
**WEB:** Flickr.com/photos/leighsellner
**EMAIL:** Leighsellner@gmail.com

Leigh was born in Kitchener, Ontario in 1993. She spent two years living in Daytona Beach, Florida (2007-2009) then moved back to Kitchener. Leigh has always enjoyed photography, always having a camera with her at all times. Her photographs focus primarily on portraiture, architecture and often are presented in black and white. Leigh hopes to go to Ryerson University in Toronto for photography in the fall of 2012.

**1 Domesticated Bliss** Photograph.

**2 Burrard Inlet** Photograph.

**3 Underwater** Photograph.

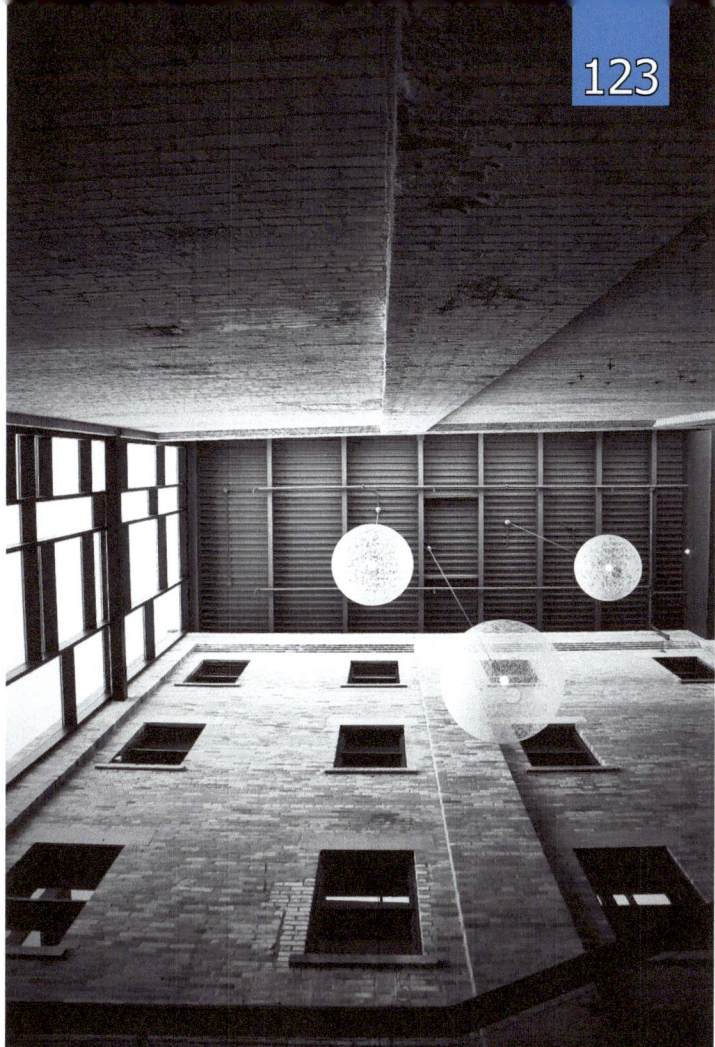

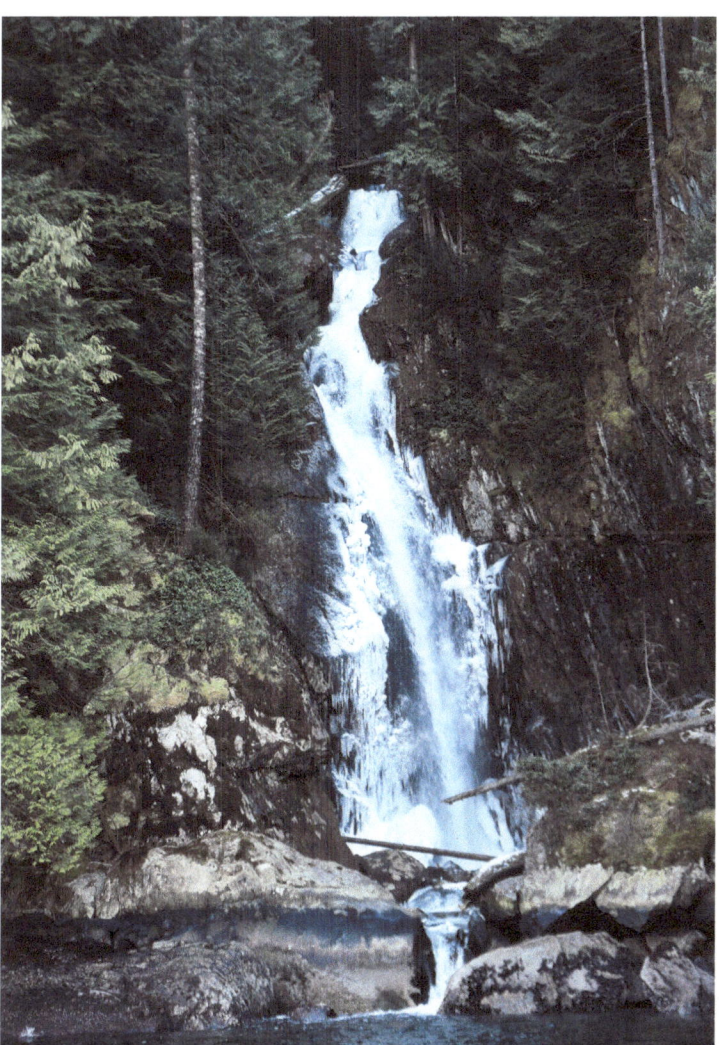

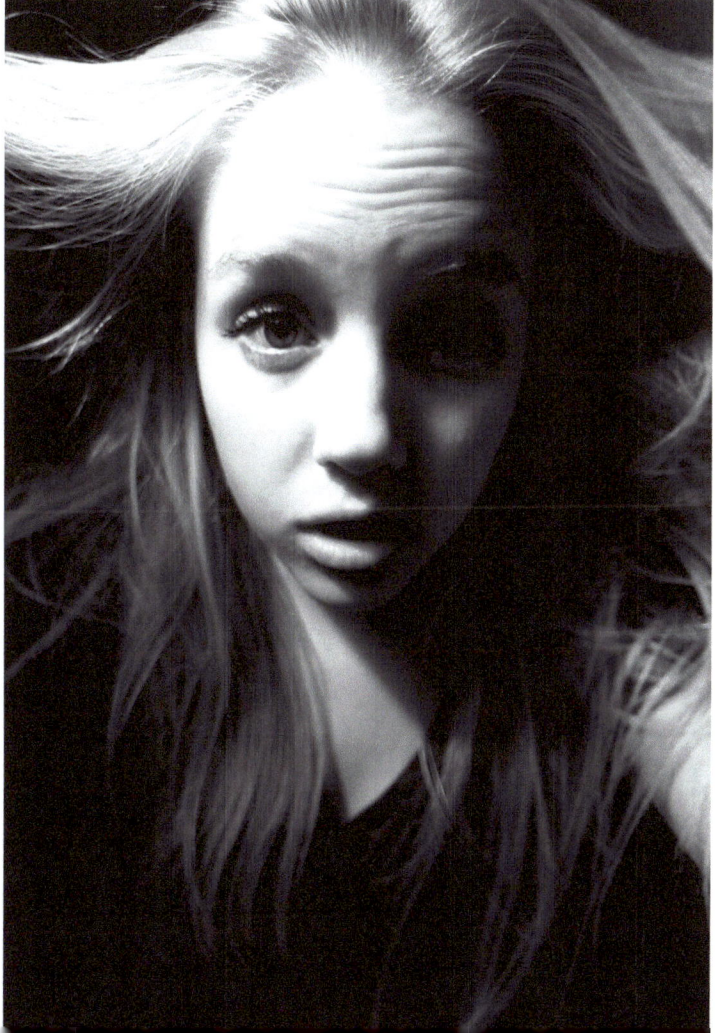

# ZAK WHITFORD

**LOCATION:** Fergus and Kitchener
**WEB:** TheWorldThroughMyLens.ca
**EMAIL:** Zak@theworldthroughmylens.ca

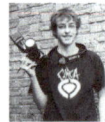

Zak started his photography business at the age of 16. Since then his work has been published in many magazines and newspapers. His goal is to keep his photography as authentic as possible making brilliant photos with minimal editing. He uses his skills as a photographer to create perfect photos with great attention to detail. Zak's services include commercial, real estate and outdoor portrait photography. He also uses his skills as a photographer to give back to his community and raises money for charity.

**1 Love** Photograph.

**2 Dancing Flame** Photograph.

**3 Rusty** Photograph.

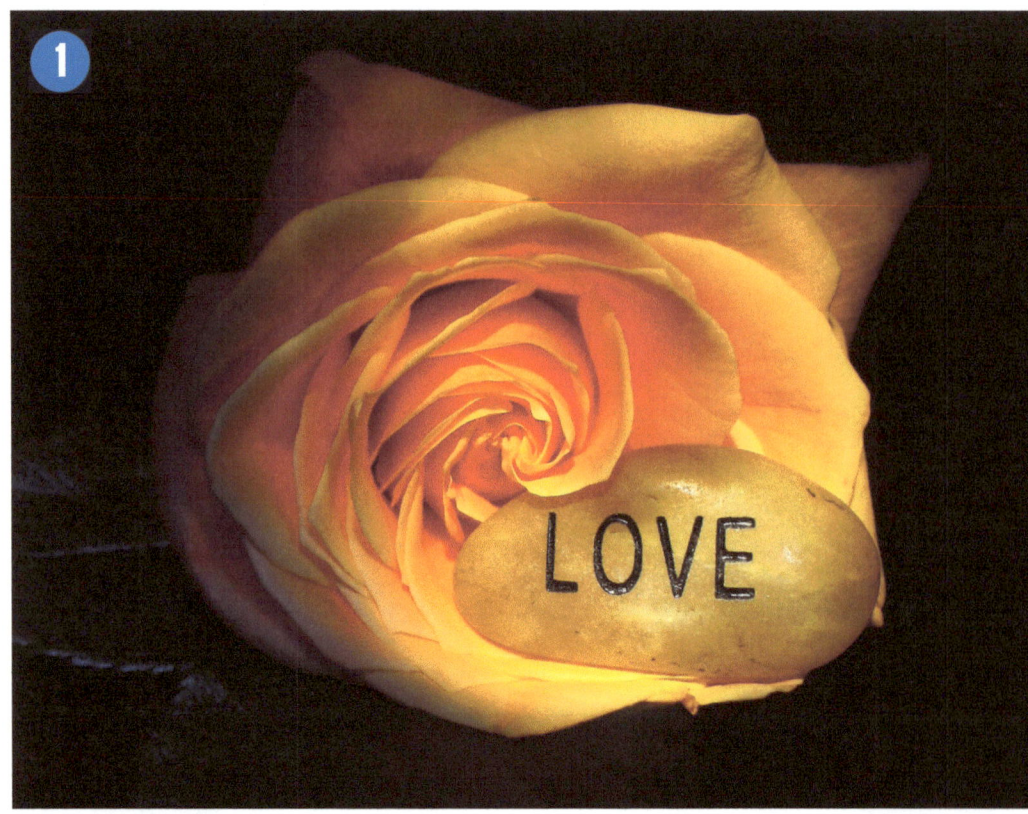

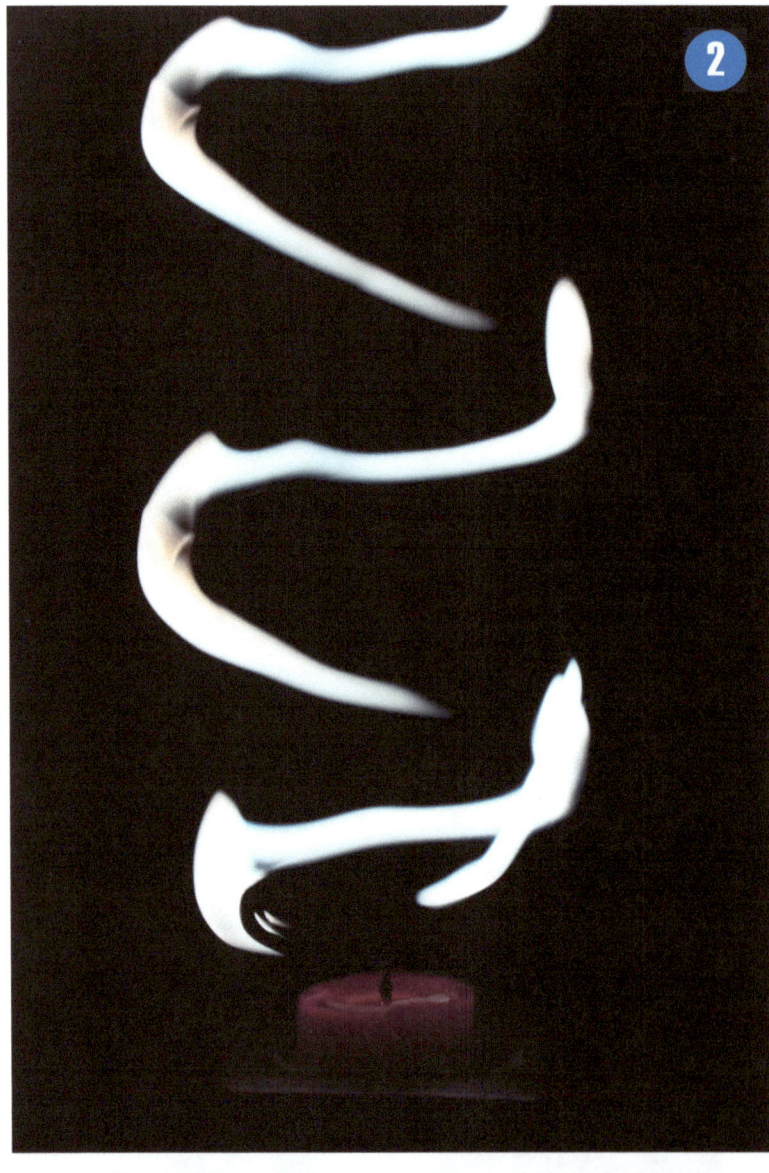

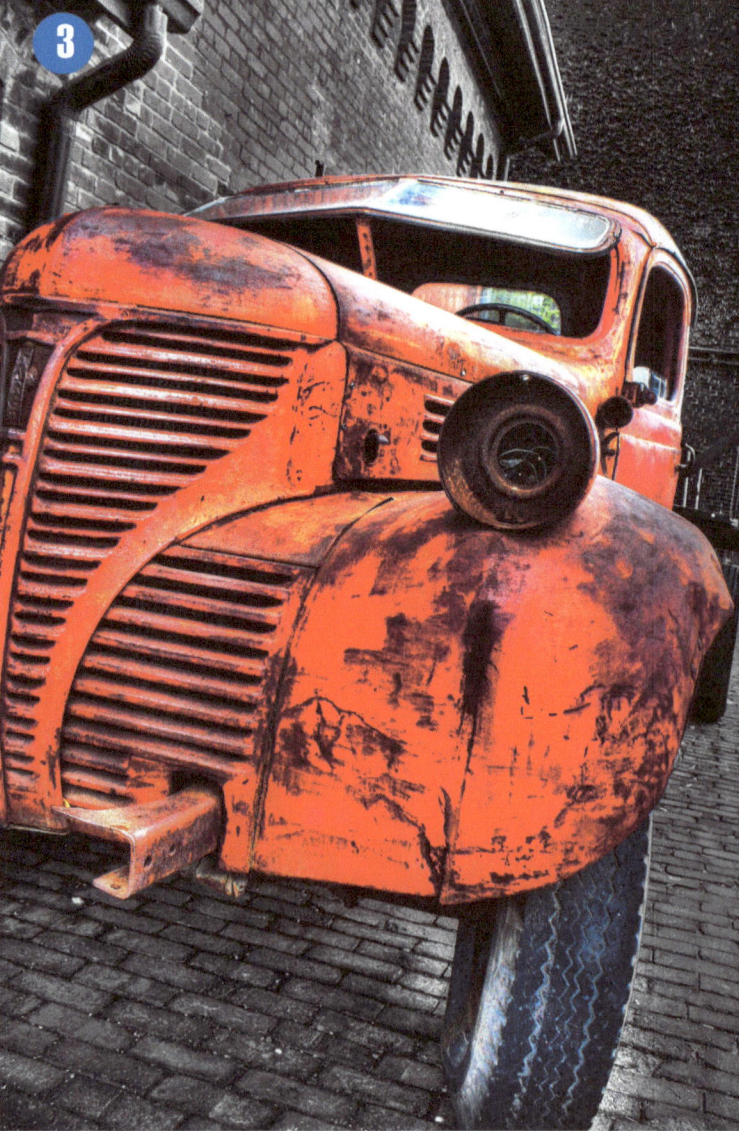

# SHIRLEY AL

**LOCATION:** Elora
**WEB:** ShirleyAl.com
**EMAIL:** Shirleyal@cogeco.ca

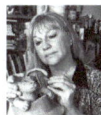

With a BFA from the University of Waterloo and an MA in Design from Stanford University, Shirley's exceptional creative skills are a result of many years of continuous study. Shirley is a graphic design professional. Her fine arts background lends a sophisticated flair to her graphic design and illustration work. She is well known in music circles for her collectible poster designs. Shirley brings an impeccable eye to her clay sculptures. Even with years of practice and technique, the uncertainties and mysteries of sculpture present absorbing paths for creativity. Uniquely hers, her sculptures reflect a play on the human form with elements of imbedded nature and organic movement. The result is whimsical yet richly enticing.

**1 Dreaming** 12x14" Raku fired clay.

**2 Dancer** 15x16" Raku fired clay.

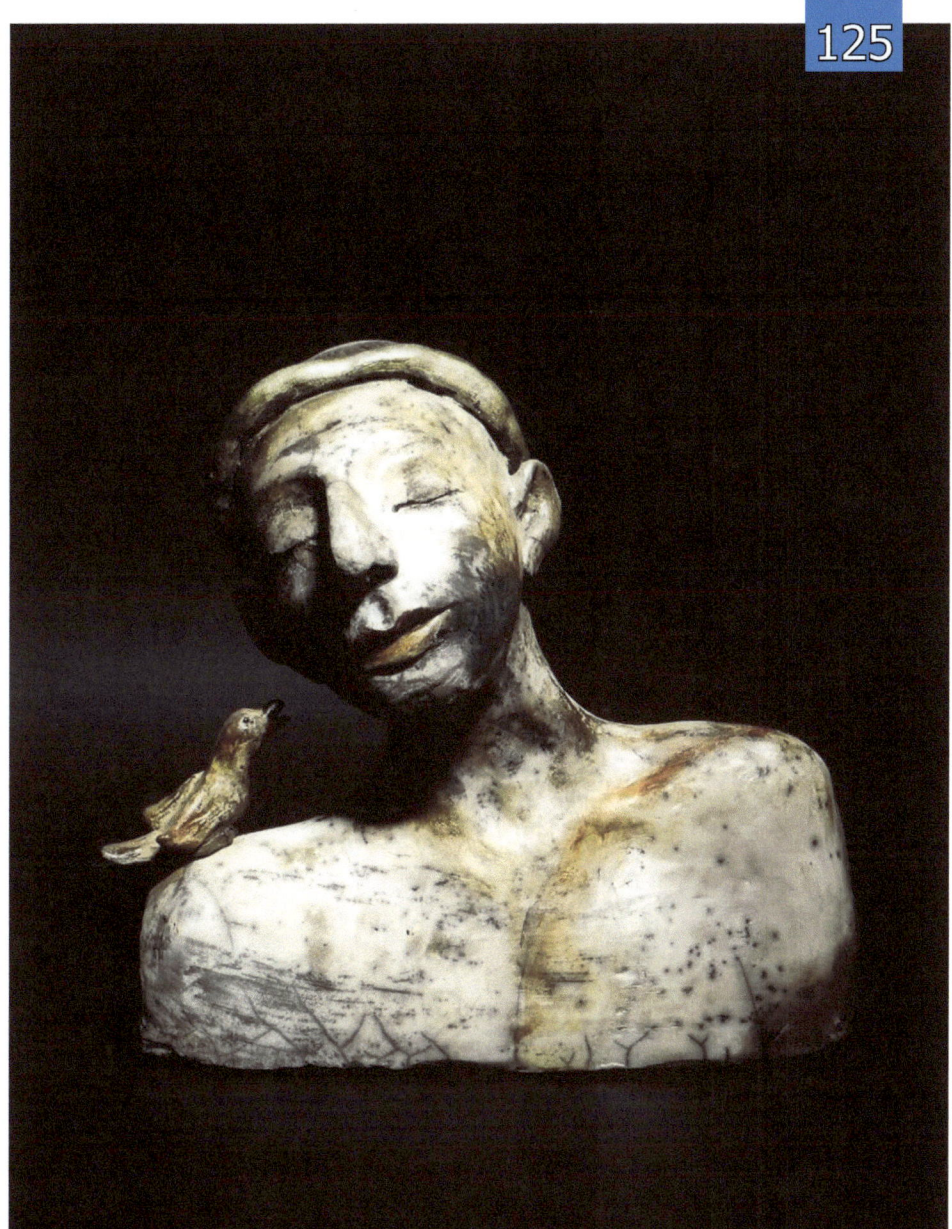

**3 Torso** 14x27" Red clay pit fired.

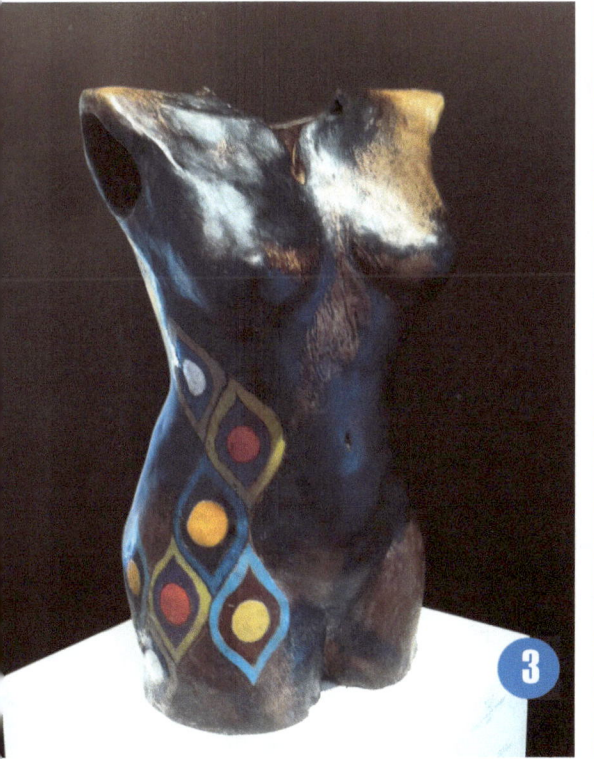

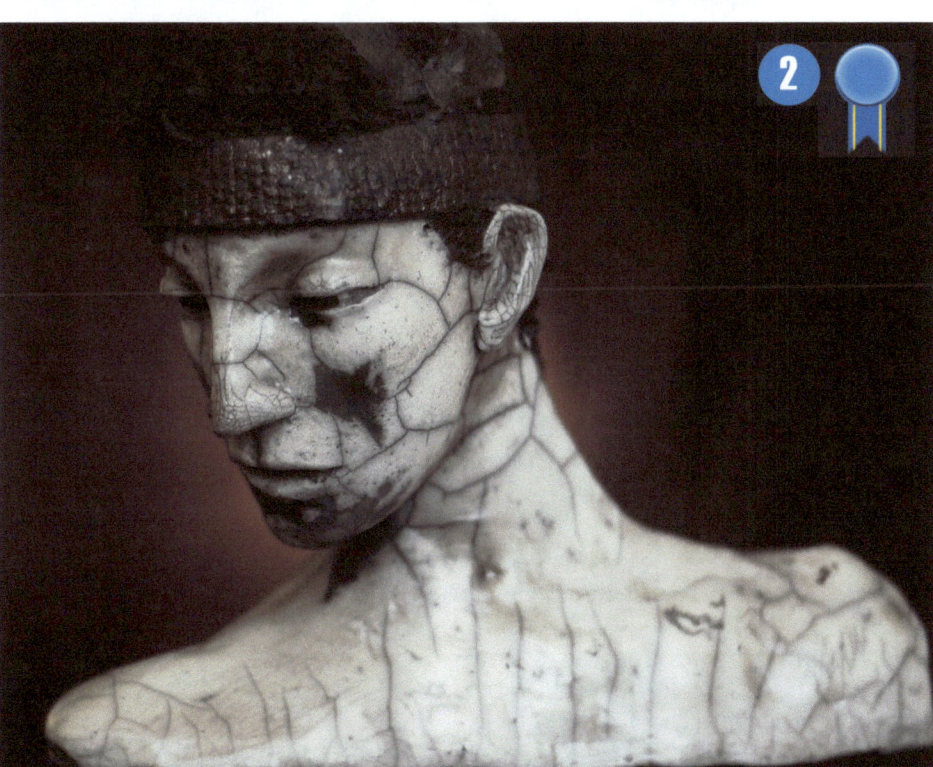

**1 Shark Attack** An HDR image of a rusty old car in a Southern Ontario wrecking yard as it is slowly being reclaimed back to the earth.

# KAREN
# VON KNOBLOCH

**LOCATION:** Kitchener
**WEB:** Flickr.com/photos/kvonk
**EMAIL:** Vonknobloch@rogers.com

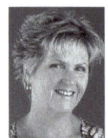

Karen von Knobloch started photography using a point and shoot camera 7 years ago to photograph the flowers in her garden. After joining a local photography club, her hobby quickly grew into a passion. Loving colour, texture, and nature, Karen loves to capture images of flowers, old rusty objects, wildlife and landscapes. Karen embraces the photographic process with creativity. She was recently Digital Photographer of the year and Photographer of the Year 2011 at GRIPS (Grand River Imaging and Photographic Society) and has won various awards in the KPL/KW Record Photography contest. She says… "Remember to look behind for the image you just walked past".

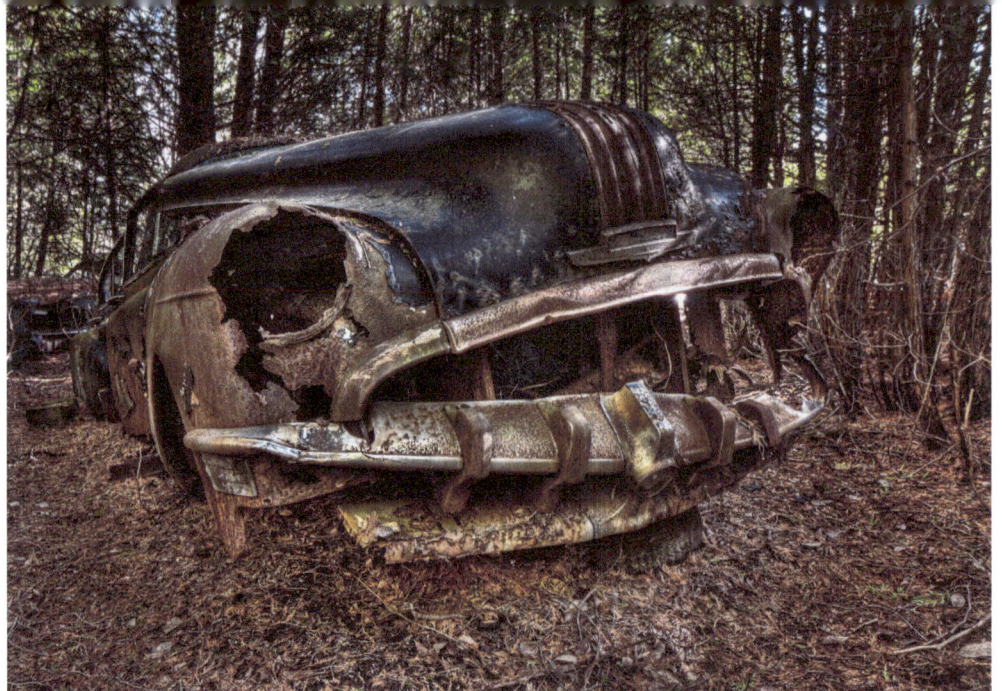

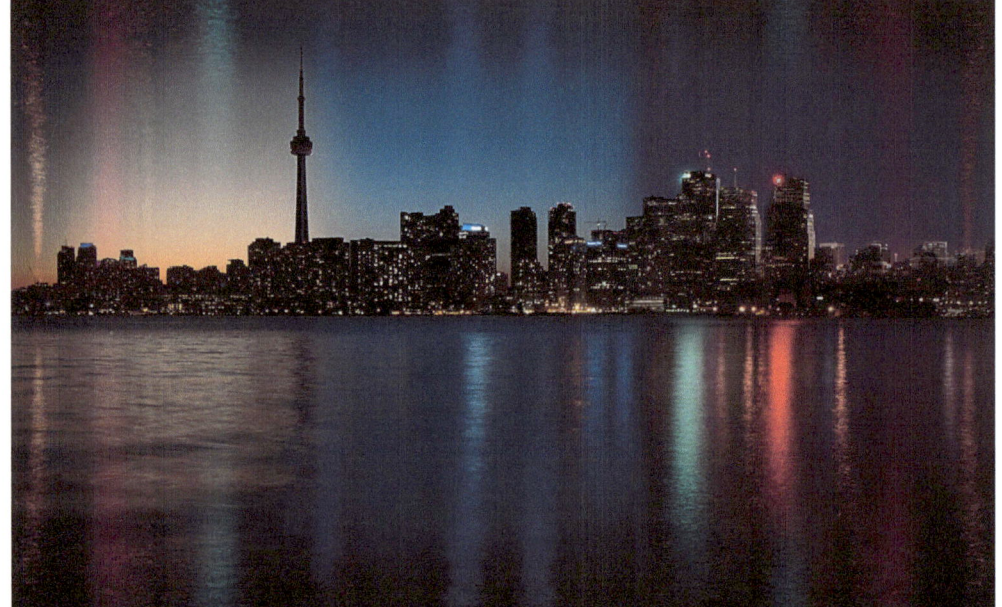

**2 Shades of Toronto** A composite of 4 images of the colours of the Toronto skyline during an evening at 25 minute intervals until the sky went black.

**3 Woodland Rendering** Out in the bush for a hike in the fall and saw these beautiful shadows and warm light along a trail creatively blurred for effect.

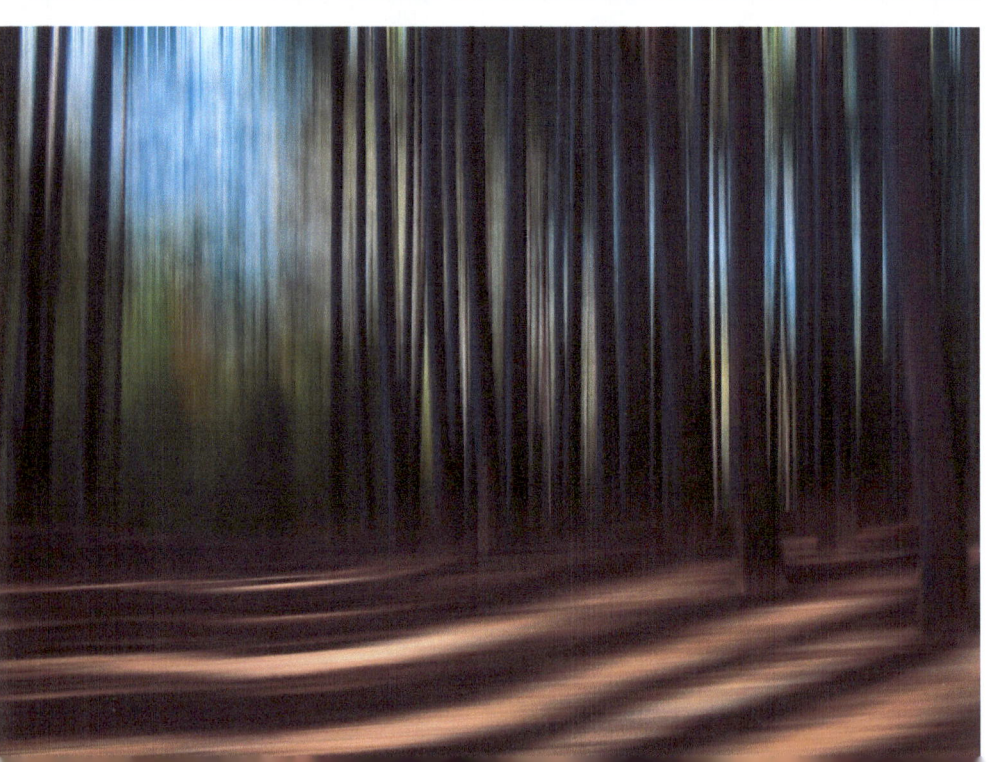

# LAURIE SPIEKER

**LOCATION:** Kitchener
**WEB:** GrandRiverGlassworks.com
**EMAIL:** Info@grandriverglassworks.com

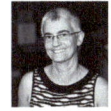

In 1996 Laurie Spieker, an avid enthusiast of stained glass, acquired a room of her own – a dedicated work space with a sturdy work bench. Here she learned that the "material teaches the artist". In 2007 she established Grand River Glassworks, KW's newest stained and fused glass teaching studio and retail store. Located inside her family-owned business, Fritz Electric, Laurie offers original glass art; quality instruction for all skill levels; art glass, tools, and supplies for sale; strong technique and product knowledge; and a warm smile. The studio is bright, the kiln is hot, and the atmosphere is welcoming.

**1** **Maple Leaf** 9x7" Stained Glass.

**2** **Dragonfly Pond** (Detail)15" diam. Stained glass.

**3** **Wetland Waterscape** 20x22.5" Stained Glass.

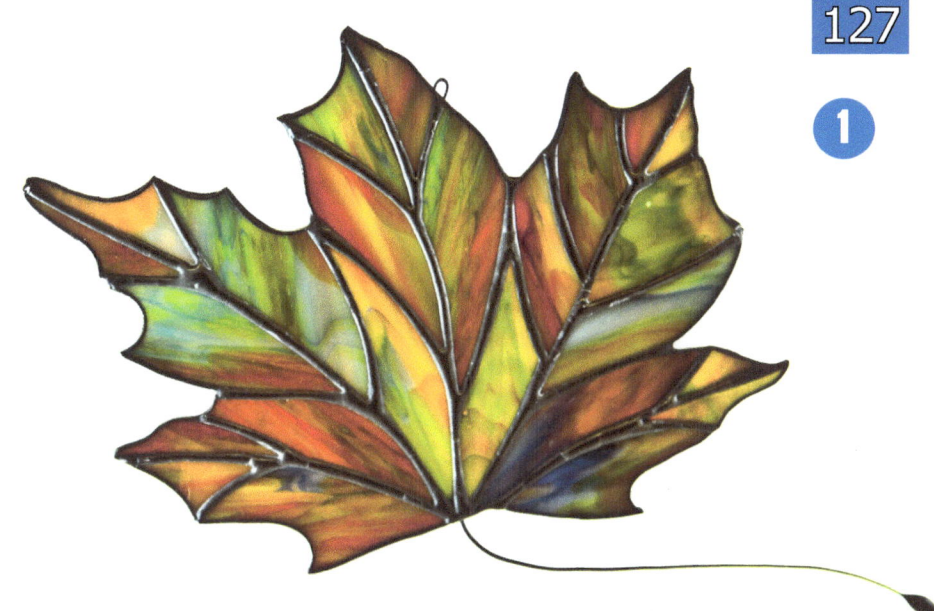

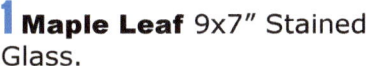

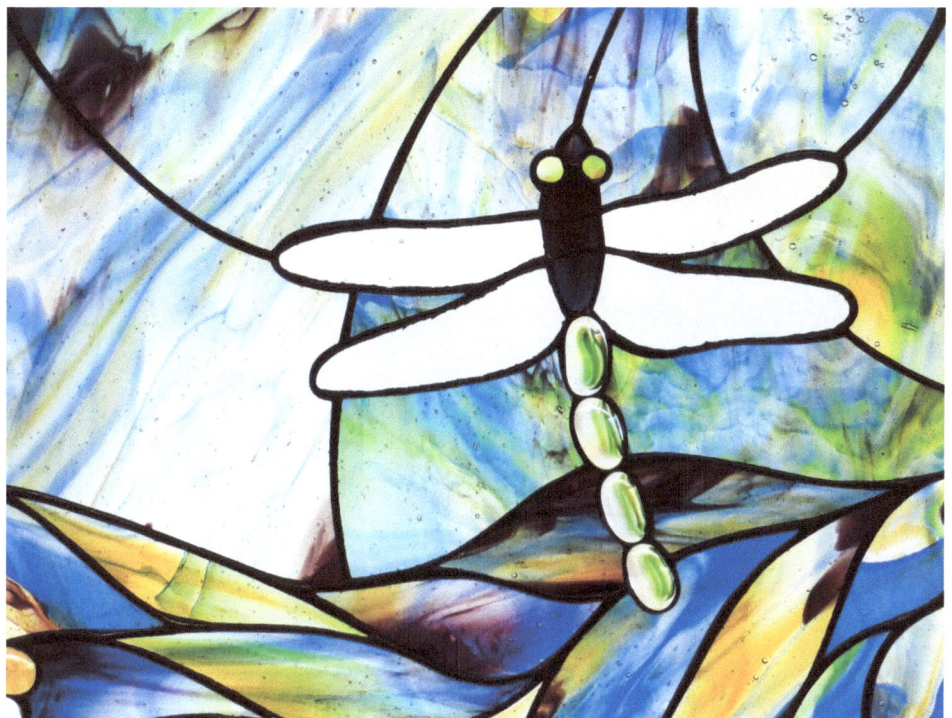

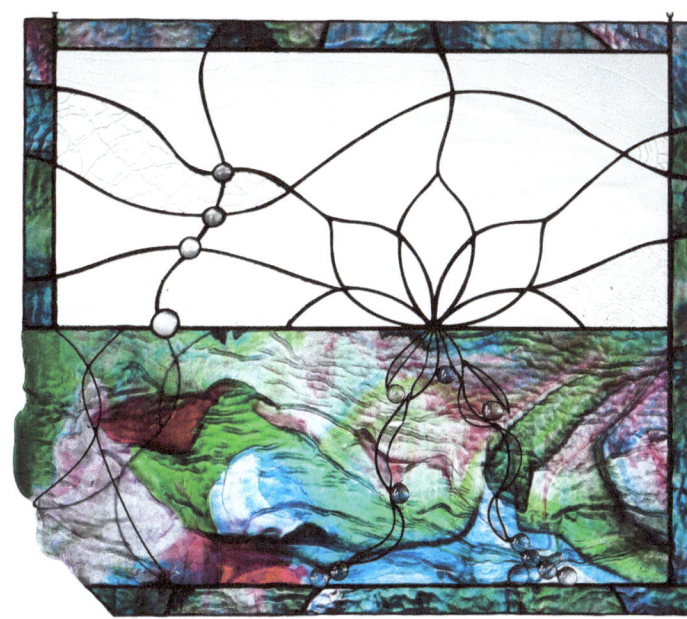

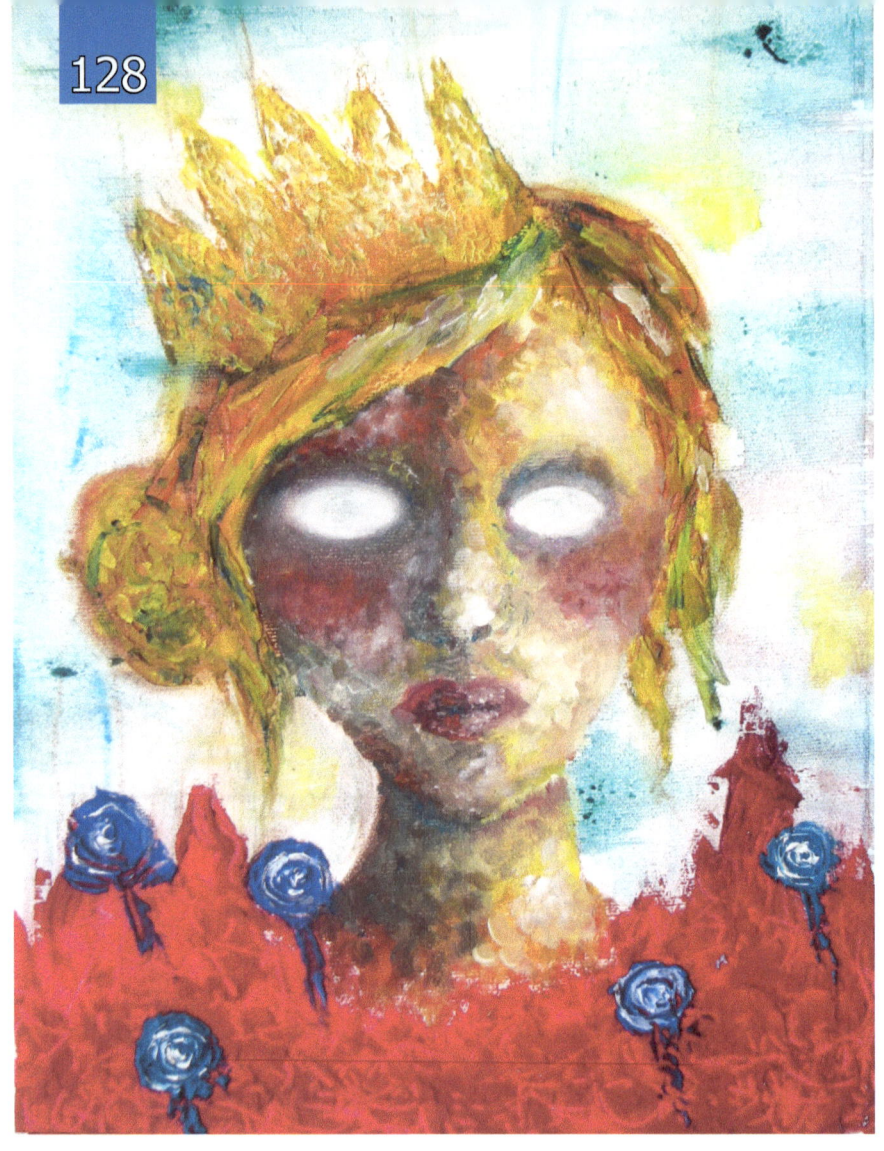

# SERENA LAWRENCE
**LOCATION:** Kitchener
**WEB:** (N/A)
**EMAIL:** Serena_Lawrence@hotmail.com

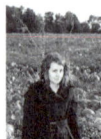

Serena Lawrence is interested in exploring relationships and her own encounters through different types of mediums and colours. She has a really mean (but cute) bunny and loves cupcakes.

**1** **Crown On The Ground** 12x9"
Oil colour and cold wax.

**2** **I Just Want To Be Your Friend** 3x4' Acrylic paint and raw canvas.

**3** **Deer** Lifesize. Sculpture of deer antlers.

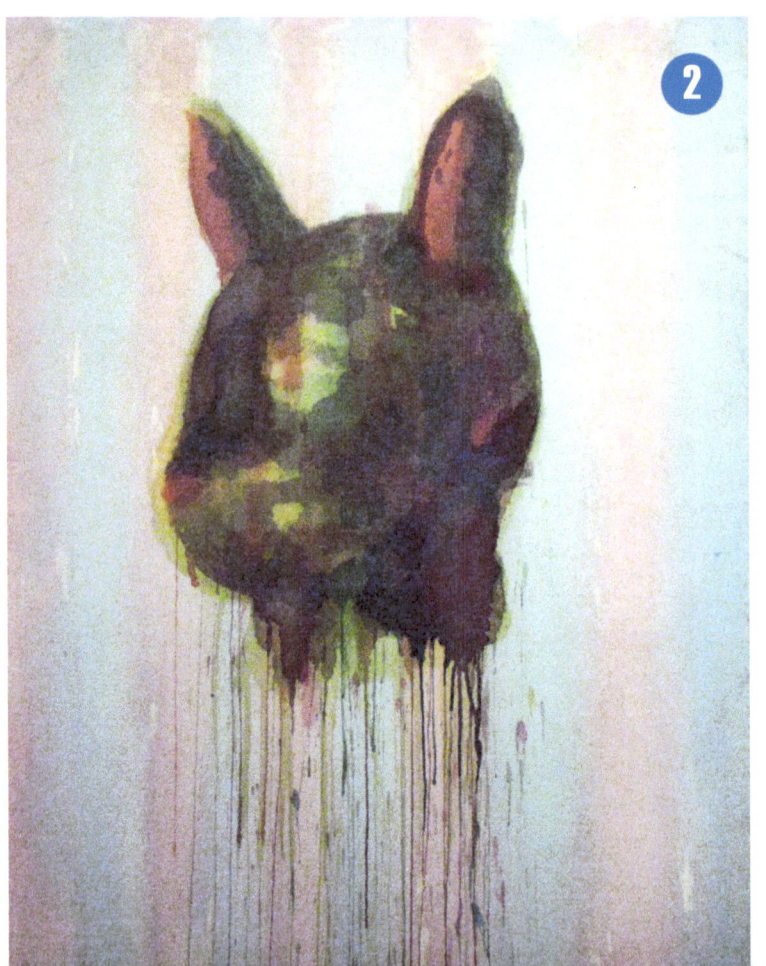

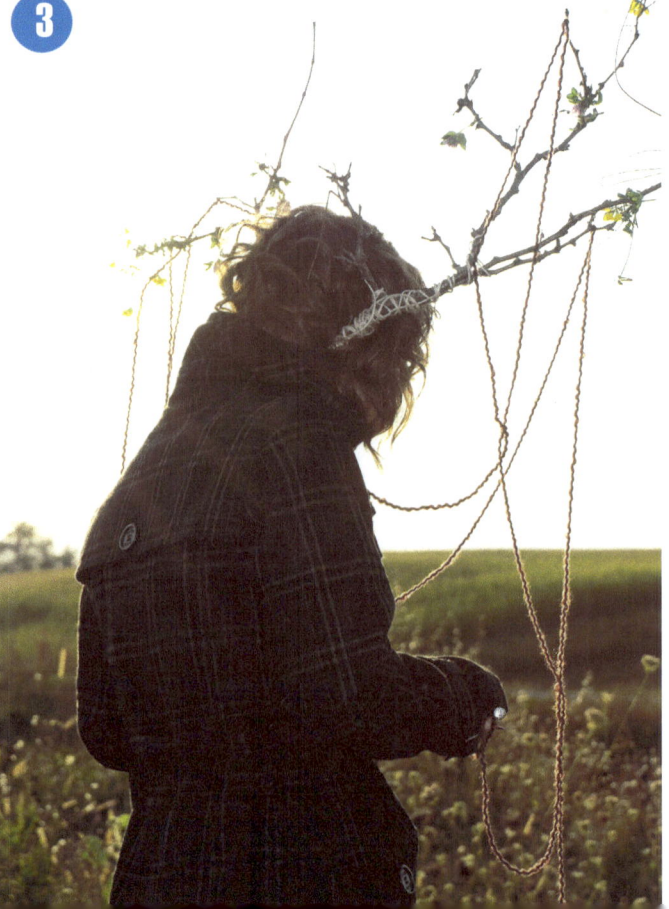

**1 Being Water** 8x10" Archival Photographic Print.

**2 Being Sky** 12x12" Archival Photographic Print.

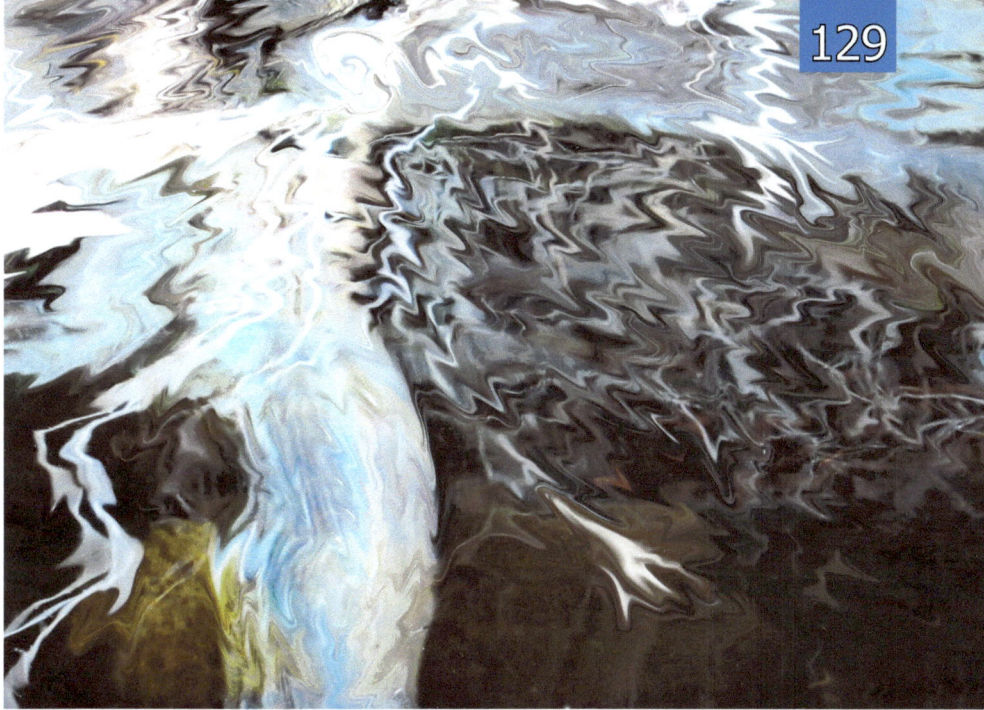

# LESLEY WALKER-FITZPATRICK

**LOCATION:** Stratford
**WEB:** mayafair.ca
**EMAIL:** lesley-maya@sympatico.ca

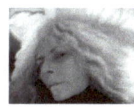
In the seminal spirituality of Nature I find my faith. In the current fragmented Eden on Earth I find pain, sorrow and fear. I seek the deep beauty of Earth's life mystery, the promise of Eden. In the sacredness of plants I discover my roots, expose my heart and flow with the current of the universal Mind. Born in Scotland, childhood in Guyana on the edge of the jungle, I planted my feet at the foot of the green goddess. I performed as Maya, the Goddess of Magic with magician Doug Henning at the Royal Alex Theatre and toured in Europe, the Middle East and Canada as a magician in my own right. I studied photography at the University of Rochester with William Giles and have worked on both sides of the lens. Amongst artists and photographers Edmund Soame (OCA), Richard Stodart (Open Line Studio), Dave Heath (Ryerson) and others, I sharpened my vision. I began by photographing my disabled brother as a young child. I used my camera to show the world his spirit and his humanity when most of the world saw only his disability.

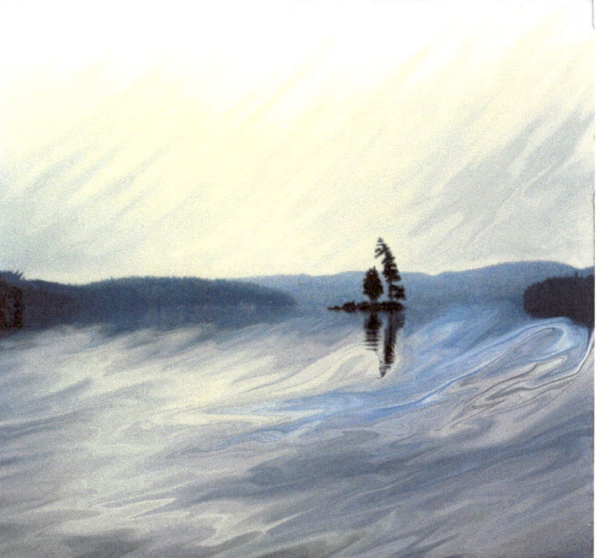

**3 Horizon** 12x12" Archival Photographic Print.

**1** **Convergence #2** 24x36" Mixed media and collage.

**2** **Earth Patterns** 28x22" Mixed media and collage.

**3** **Inspiration** 24x24" Mixed media and collage.

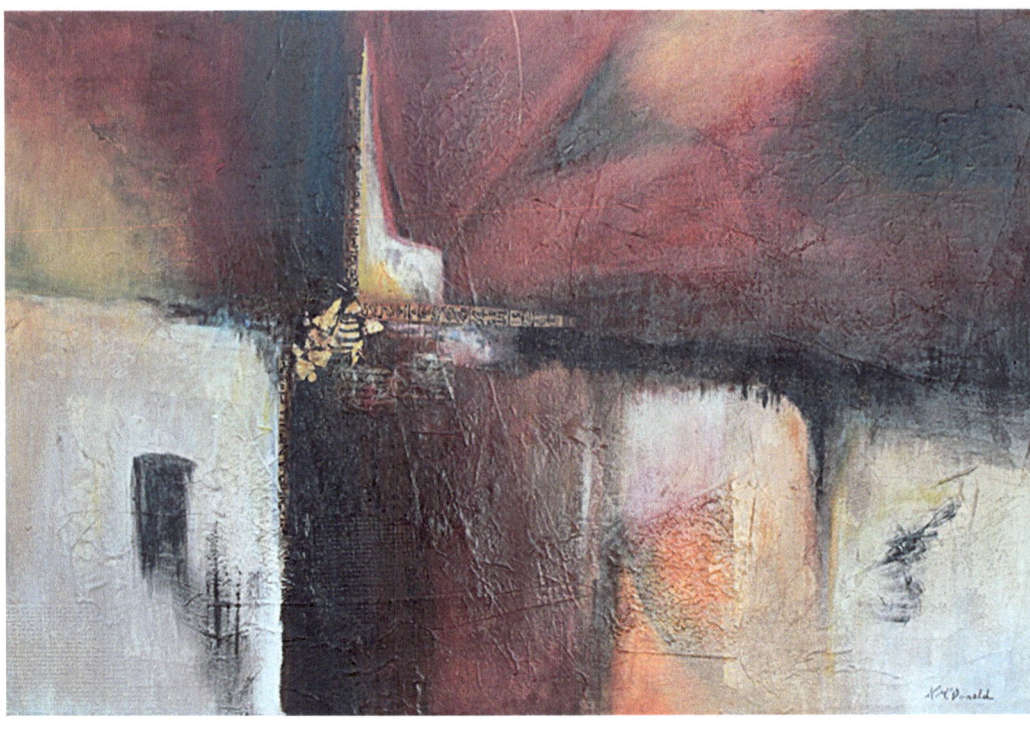

**1**

# NORMA MCDONALD

**LOCATION:** Waterloo
**WEB:** NormaMcdonald.com
**EMAIL:** Nor.mcdonald@gmail.com

An award winning mixed media and collage artist, Norma also utilizes acrylic, pastels, watercolour, papers and other media in her abstractions that are without reference to specific source material but derive mainly from memory and notes. Life's experiences, travel, an interest in ancient ruins and antiquities and a love of nature appear unexpectedly in her paintings. Norma prefers that people have the freedom to discover their own interpretations of her experimental abstract paintings. Filtered through unique eyes and life experiences, she is pleased when people see so many different colours, layers and techniques in her work that have resonated with them.

**2**

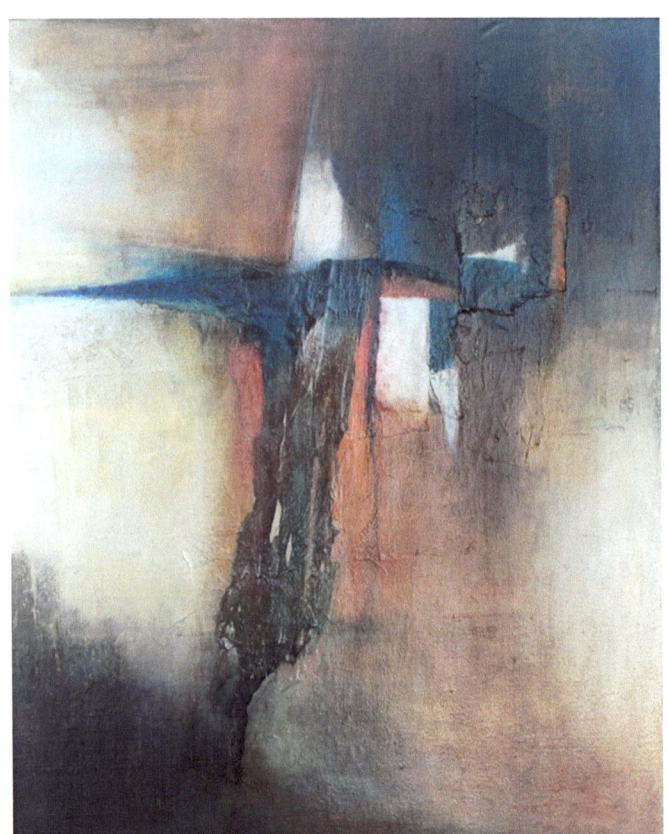

**3**

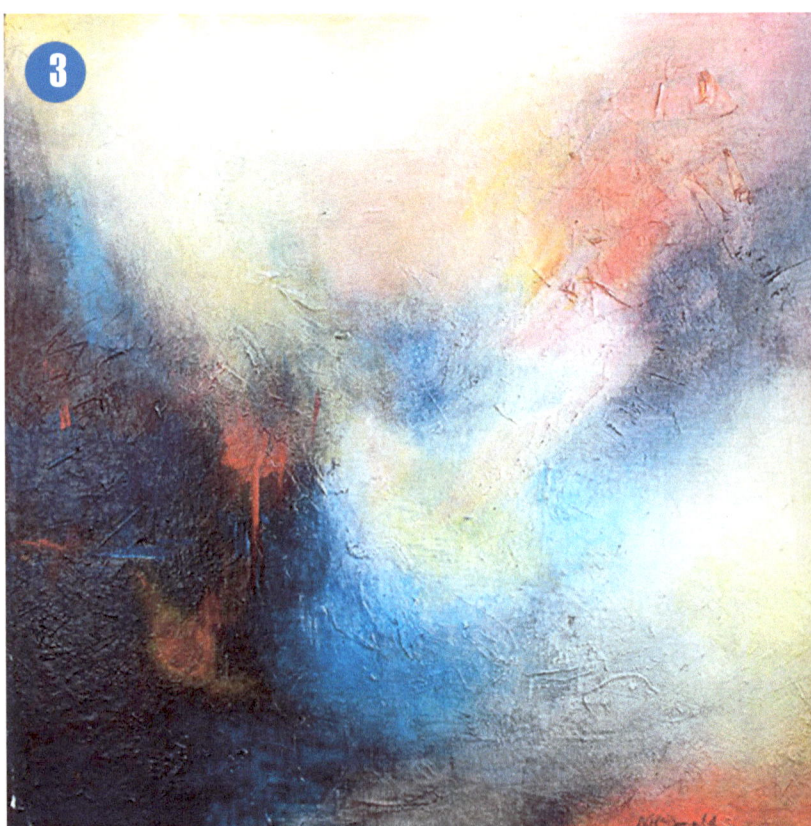

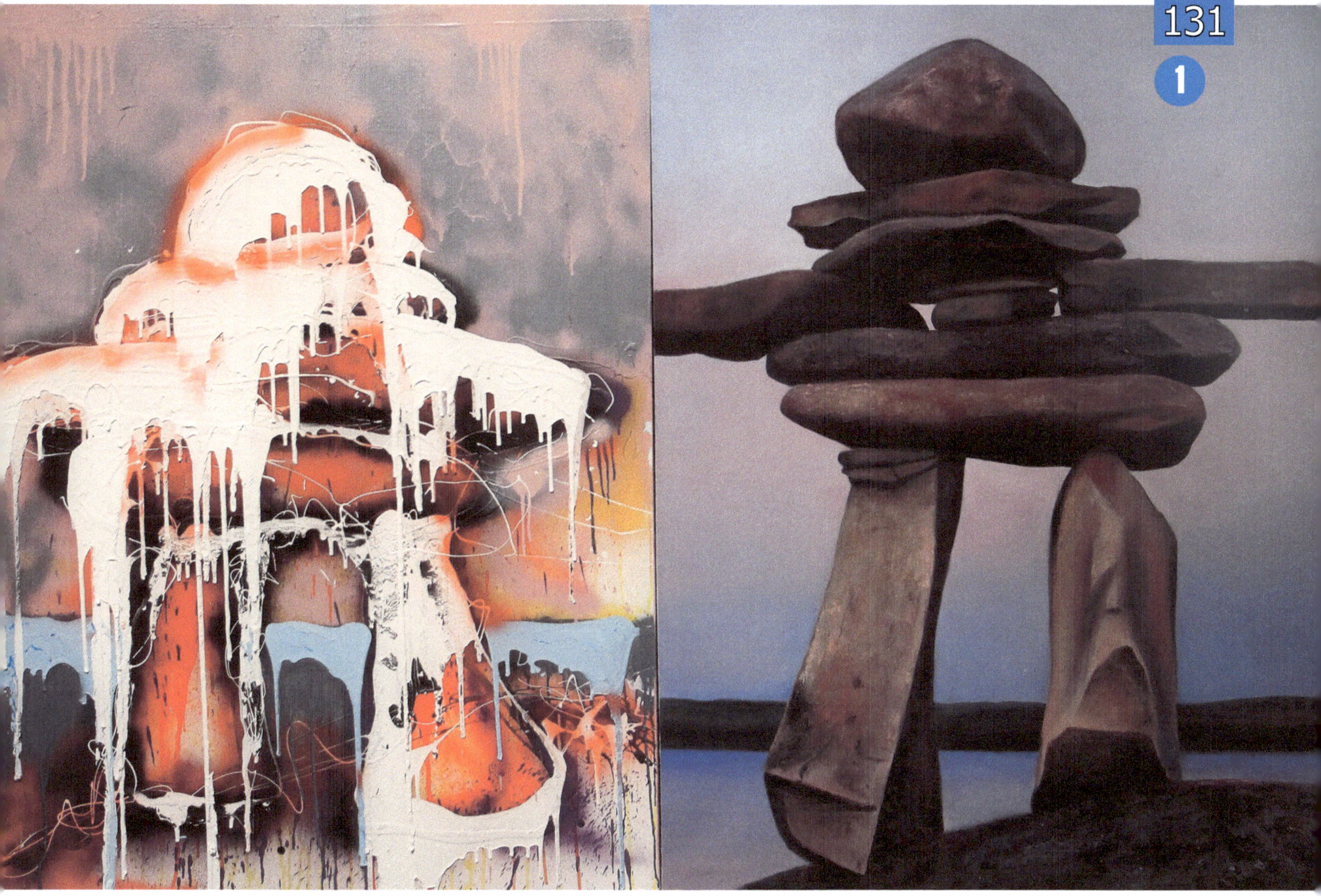

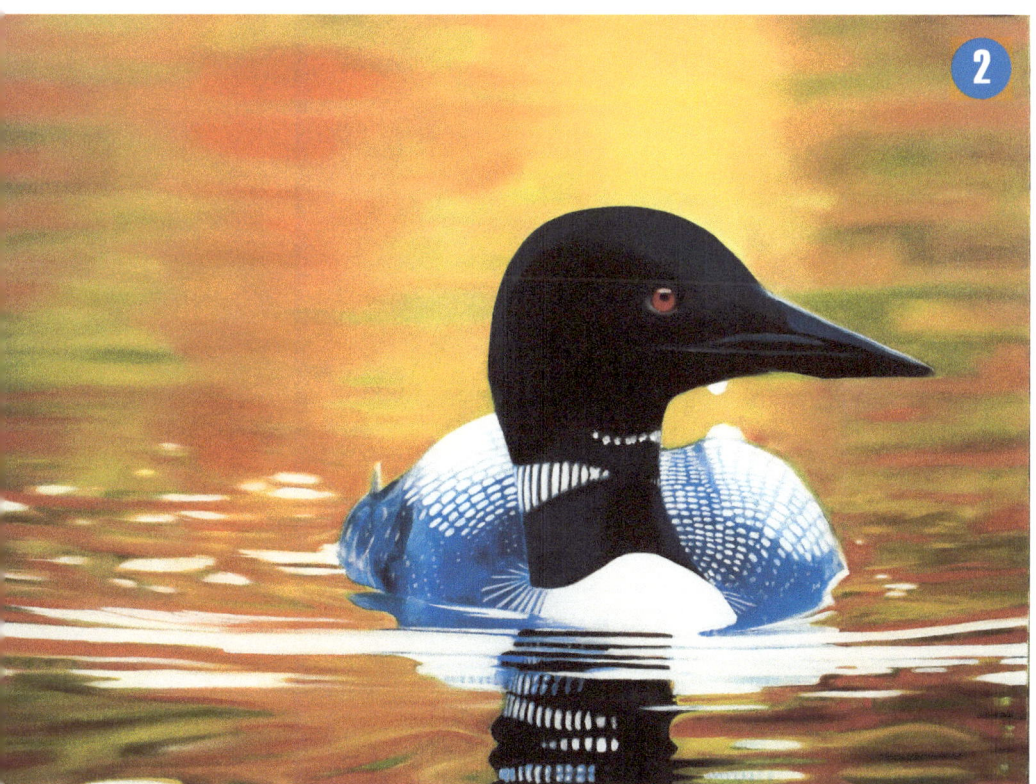

**1 Concrete vs. Fantasy Inukshuk** (2011) 36x48" Oil and mixed media on canvas. This diptych allows the viewer to gravitate towards the dominant side of their brain, making a conscious choice between right and left brain imagery.

**2 Distinct Loon** (2011) 22x30". Oil on canvas. An extremely realist representation of a loon on water, showcasing traits of the left side of the brain.

## HEATHER
## ELIZABETH HUGHES

**LOCATION:** Owen Sound
**WEB:** heatherehughes.com
**EMAIL:** heather.elizabeth.hughes@gmail.com

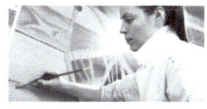

Heather Elizabeth Hughes graduated with an Honours Arts & Business degree from the University of Waterloo, Ontario, Canada specializing in studio painting. She simultaneously fulfilled the degree requirements for an art history specialization during her four years. Fresh out of school, Hughes continues the process of generating paintings of both a realist and abstract nature. It is her fascination with the duality of the human brain, the functioning of the right and left hemispheres, which continues her on a path of extremely diverse modes of painting.

# PHYLLIS DIDUR

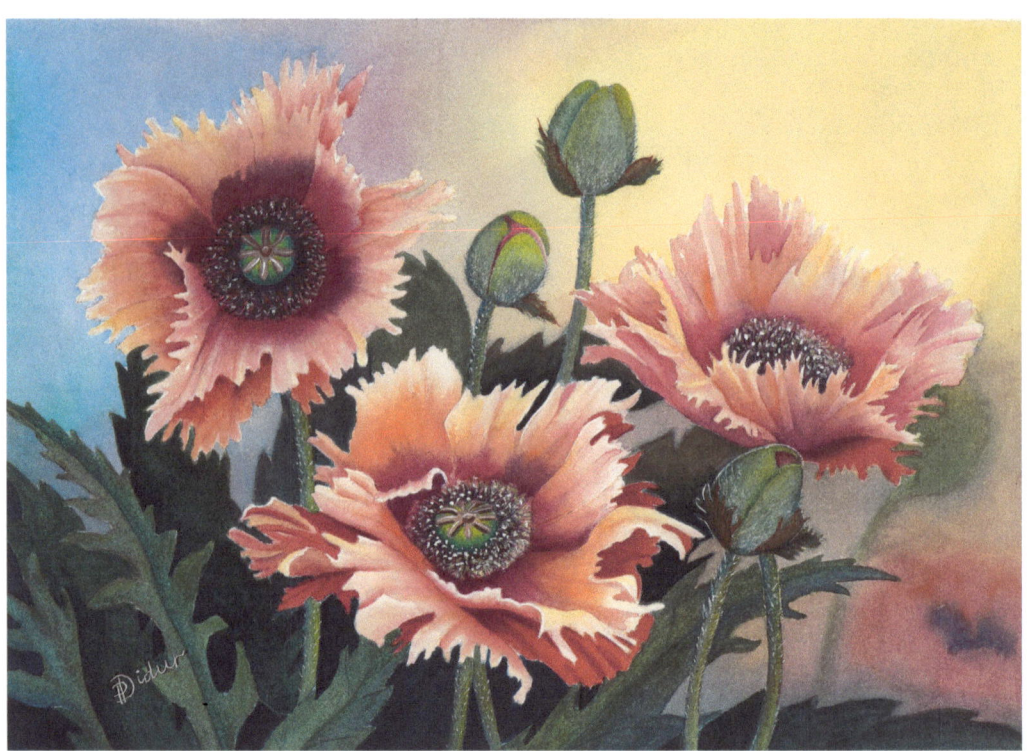

1

**LOCATION:** Waterloo
**WEB:**
www.Kwsa.ca/kwsa-members/Phyllis-Didur
**EMAIL:** PhyllisDidur@gmail.com

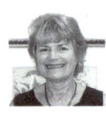

Phyllis is inspired by seasonal colours and the play of light and shadow on shapes found in nature. She enjoys painting flowers and landscapes. She sometimes uses watercolour paints or diluted acrylic paints on paper resulting in delicate or bold paintings, other times she uses oil and acrylic on canvas and both fused and traditional art glass. She has exhibited at WCAC, COAA, KWSA, KPL, Kuntz House, KOR Gallery, the Elora Art Centre and the Kitchener Law Library. Her paintings hang in private collections in Ontario, Manitoba, British Columbia, England and California. Her images have appeared on commercial greeting cards in Canada and in the US. Phyllis began painting after retiring from teaching. She has taken courses with painters in Canada and Europe. She served on the Gallery Committee at WCAC for several years, on the organizing committee for the juried show, "The Art of Cruickston" held at Homer Watson House and Gallery, and is past president of KWSA. She is an active member of WCAC, KWSA and Colour Wheel (5 local female painters).

**1 Pink Poppies** 16x20" framed. Watercolour on paper.

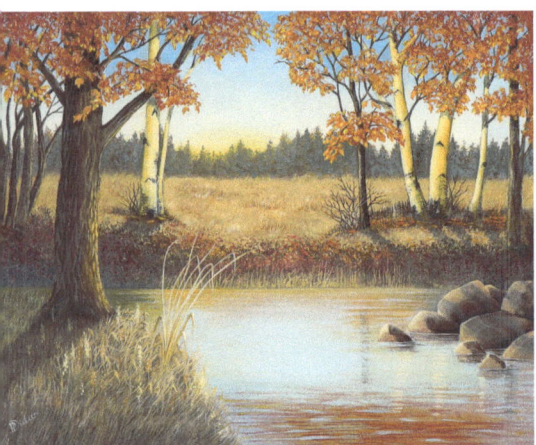

2

3

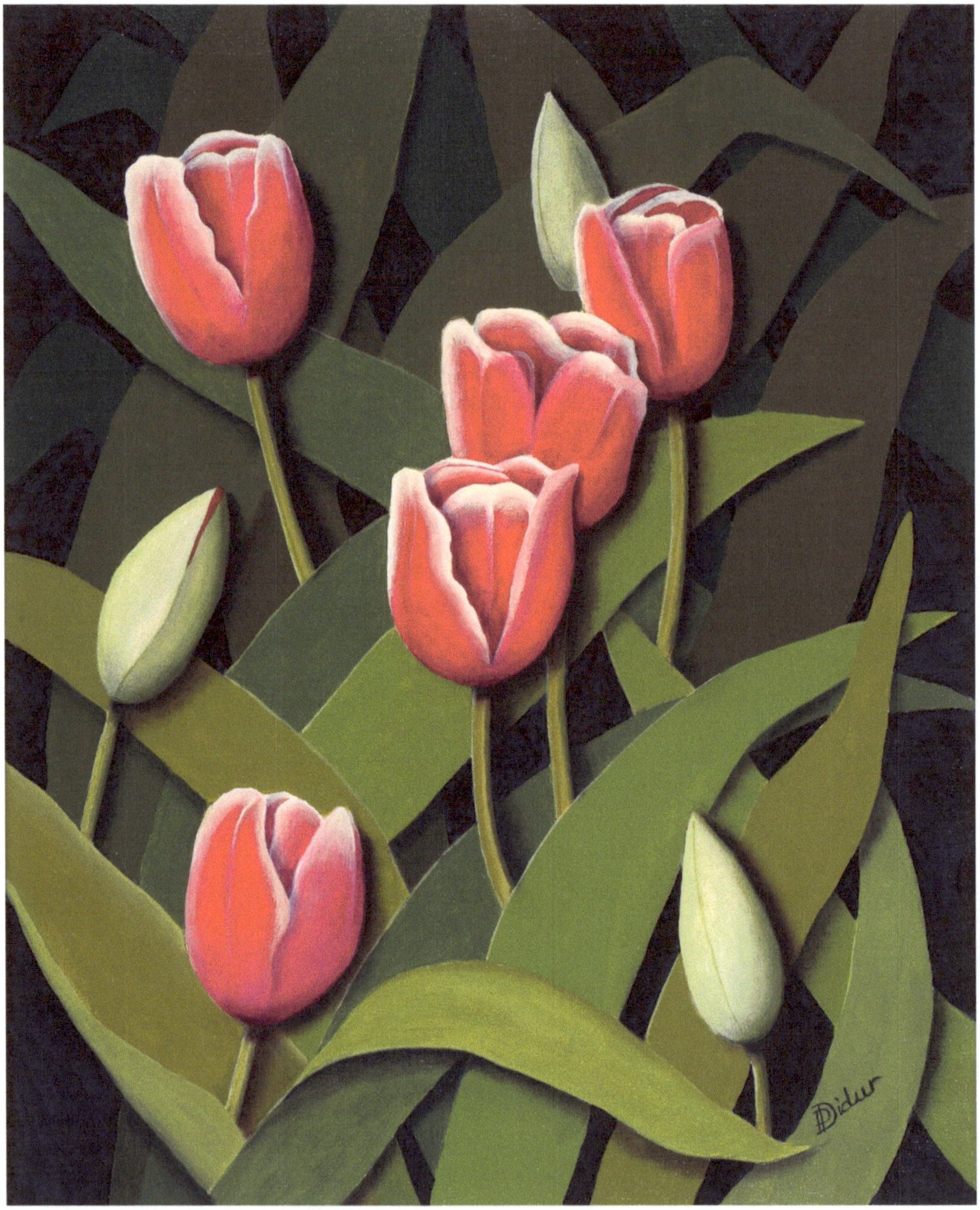

**2 Autumn Reverie** 16x20" Acrylic on canvas.

**3 Red Tulips** 16x20" Acrylic on canvas.

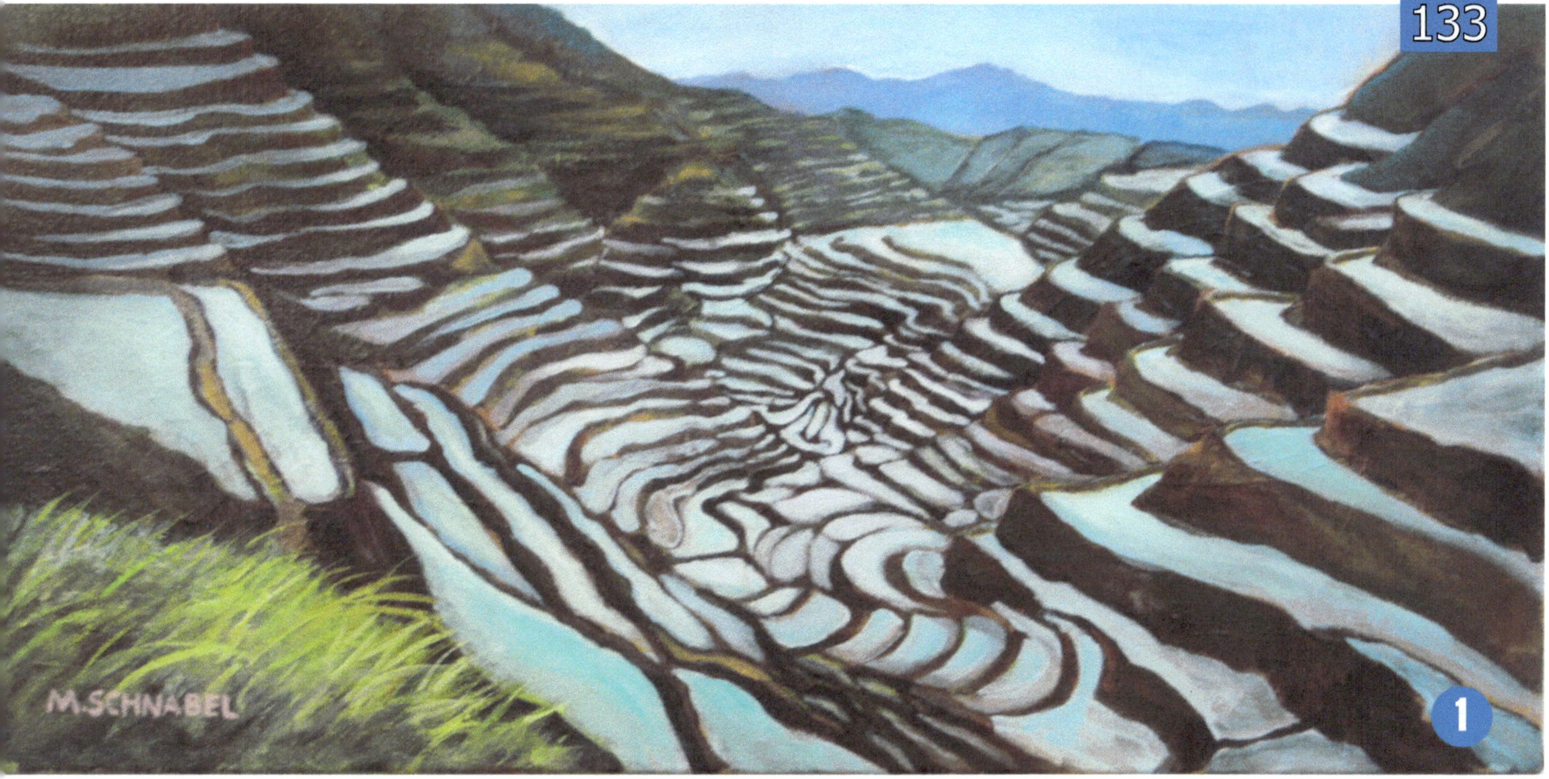

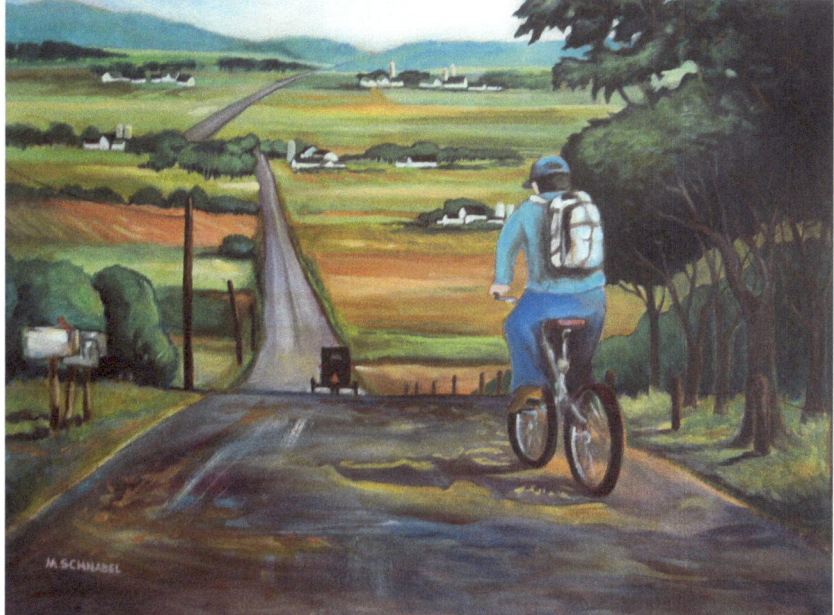

# MITZI SCHNABEL

**LOCATION:** Waterloo
**WEB:** MSchnabelDesigns.comxa.com
**EMAIL:** Mitzi@golden.net

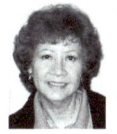

Mitzi's passion for art started at an early age. During 7th grade, she garnered the first prize in a national student art competition with a watercolor rendering of a typical Philippine village. She has maintained her lifelong interest in drawing & painting through many years by taking art classes with famous instructors in the numerous places where she has lived & worked e.g. Sydney (Australia), Los Angeles (California), Calgary (Alberta, Canada), and since the mid-80s in Waterloo (Ontario, Canada). Her avocation has also helped her develop her talents in other artistic areas, such as calligraphy, rubber stamp art, and web page design.

**1** **A Tribute to the Banaue Rice Terraces (Cordillera Region, Philippines)** 10x20" Acrylic on canvas.

**2** **Ang Dalaga (A Young Lady)** 12x16" Watercolour.

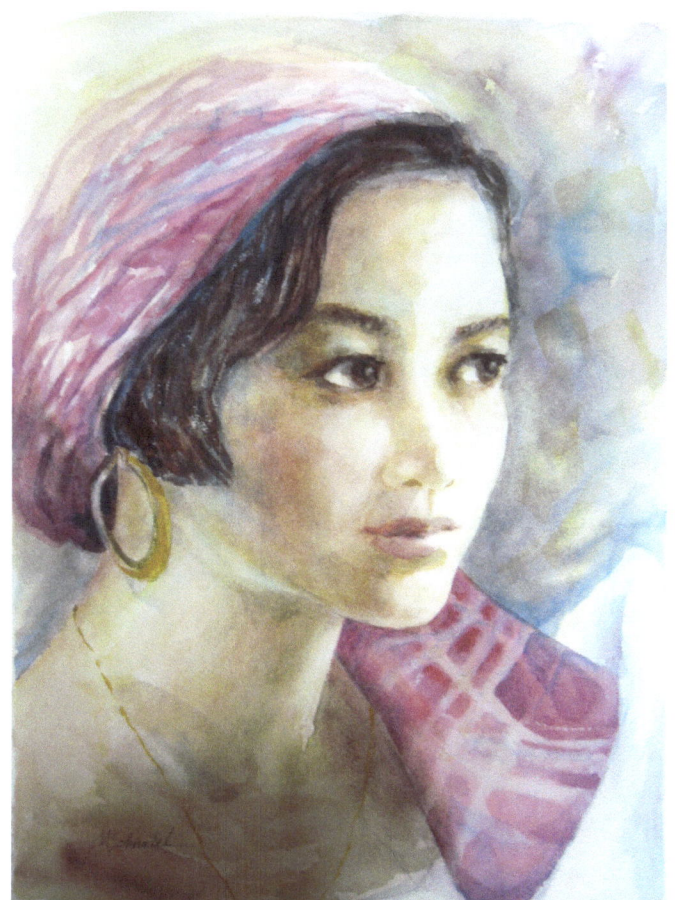

**3** **Country Cycling** 24x30" Acrylic on canvas. No Cars on this country road. What a marvelous experience!

**1 Doors of Opportunity** 16x20"
Acrylics on canvas.

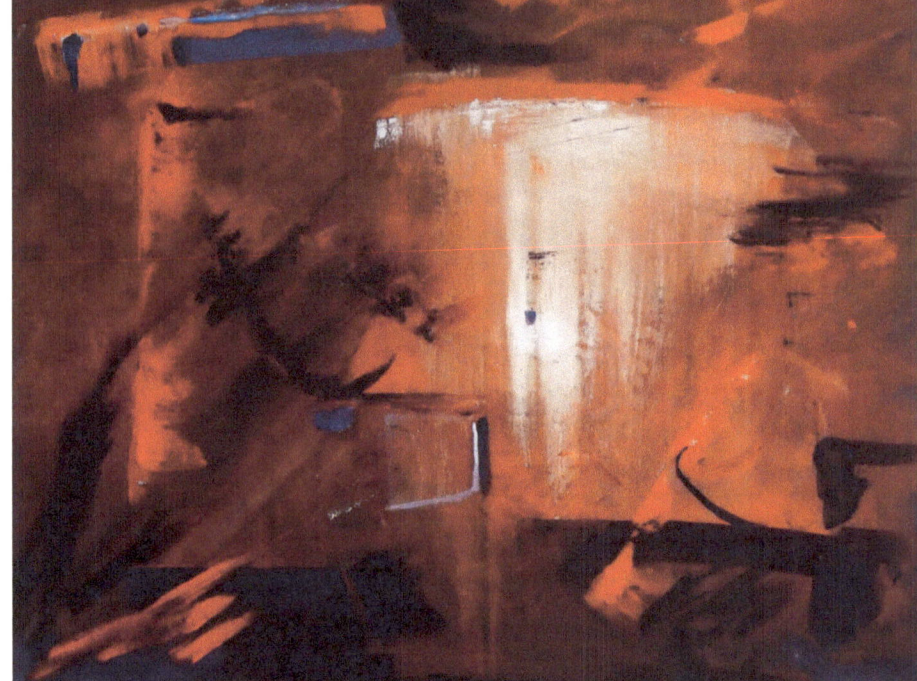

# SANDRA
# SCHIZKOSKE

**LOCATION:** Waterloo
**WEB:** (N/A)
**EMAIL:** Sandrasch@sympatico.ca

I love to paint!! I enjoy working with oils & acrylics due to the fact that I get to blend the colours with my fingertips or brushes; I love the feel of being closer to and becoming part of what I am creating. I hope not to lose that connection with my art, even when it's sold to an admirer.

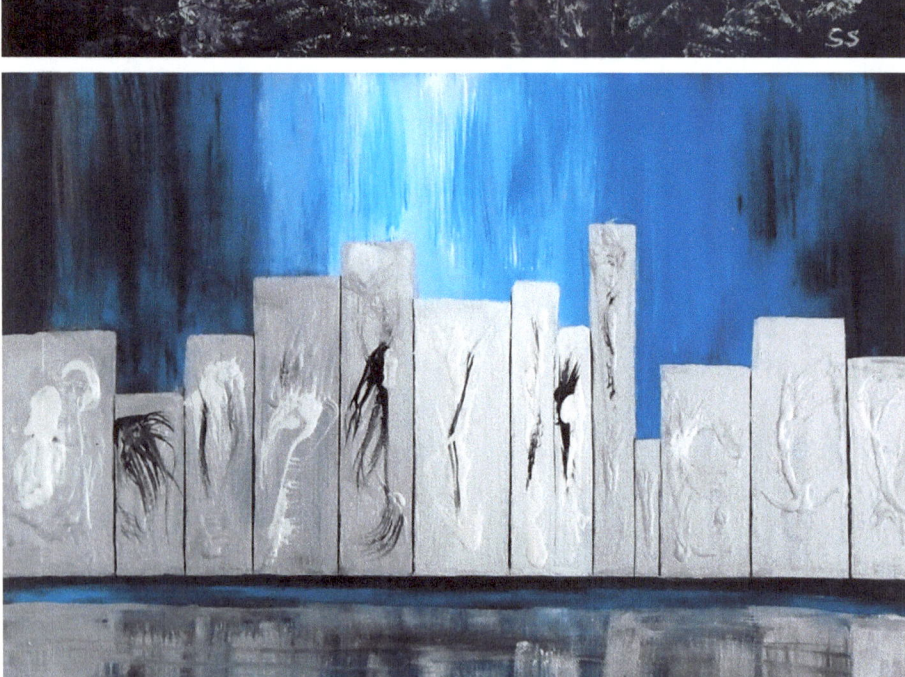

**2 A New World** 16x20" Oil on canvas.

**3 Secrets** 16x20" Acrylics on canvas my 1st abstract.

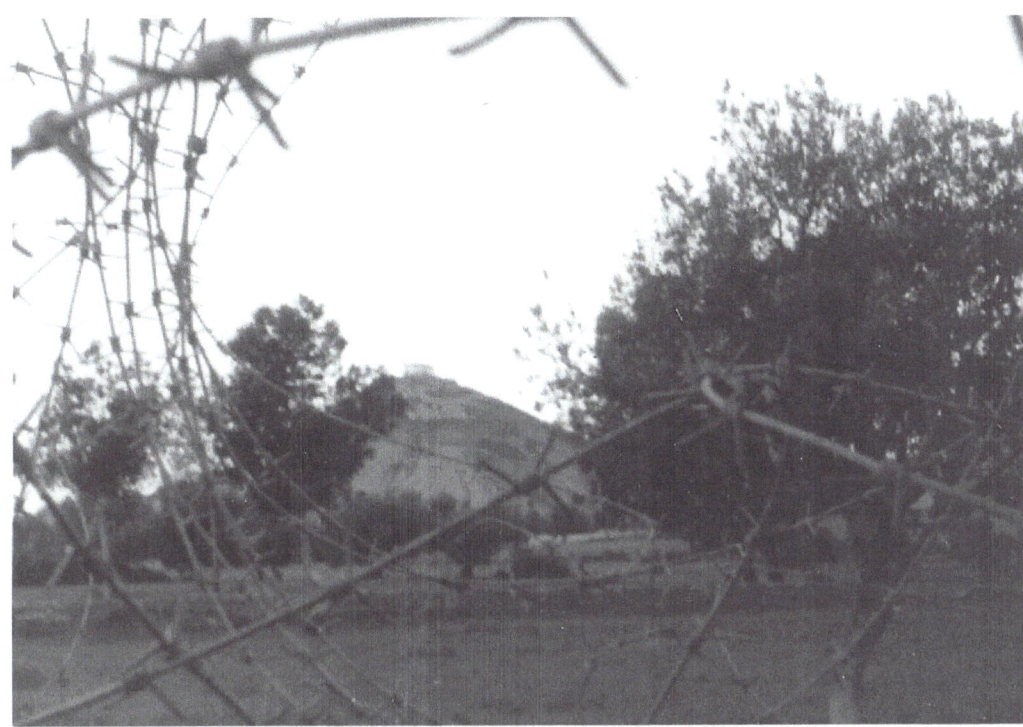

# FRANK REID

**LOCATION:** Waterloo
**WEB:** Artistsreids.ca
**EMAIL:** Frankwreid57@yahoo.com

Ex-Soldier & Peacekeeper, Adobe aficionado, Consultant, Public Speaker, Theatre Director/Producer/Writer, Photographer &, finally, book Author.

**1** **Barb** Photograph.

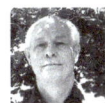

**2** **Commando Badge** 11x15" Photograph on laminate plastic.

**3** **The Ammo Box** 6x12" Photograph on laminate plastic.

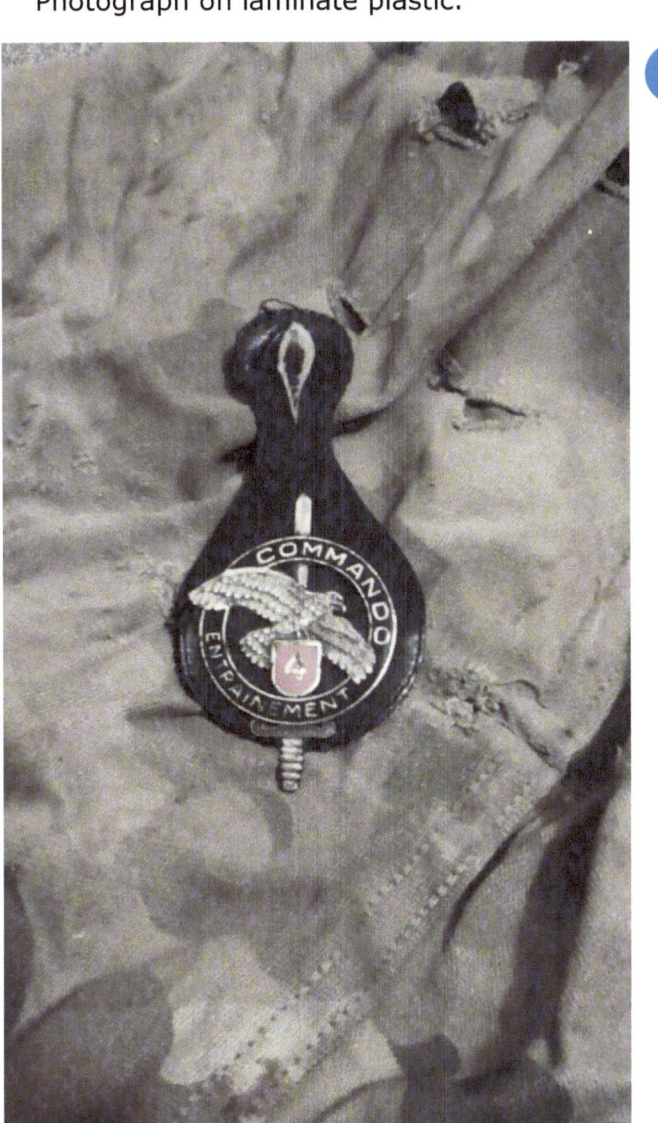

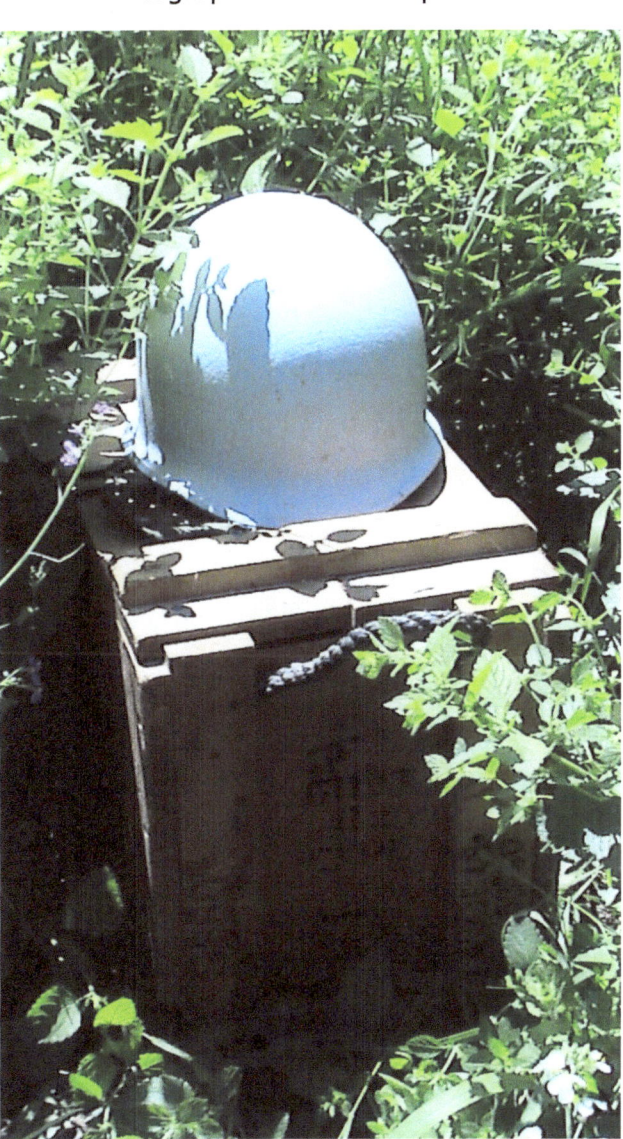

# VIRGINIA R. JOYES

**LOCATION:** St. Marys
**WEB:** VirginiaJoyes.ca
**EMAIL:** Virginia.Joyes@gmail.com

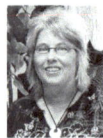

I am a sculpture artist using plaster and found objects. I grew up living in a scrapyard in Ellice township and found the most interesting objects to include in my artwork. I sign my artwork Virg and have been creating sculptures since the early 90's. All of my work has been exhibited at Gallery Stratford and once at London Regional Historical Art Gallery and Museum at one point in time. I recently joined Gallery 96 in Stratford. I helped to create the Tir Na Nog Garden steel gates in downtown Stratford learning to weld and use the plasma cutter on that project with the supervision of Mark Czajkowski. He also had me help to create the steel Rememberance archway located by the city hall in St. Marys. I am a graphic designer and recently graduated from Trios College taking Website Designer/ Developer program. I have lived in St. Marys for the past 16 years.

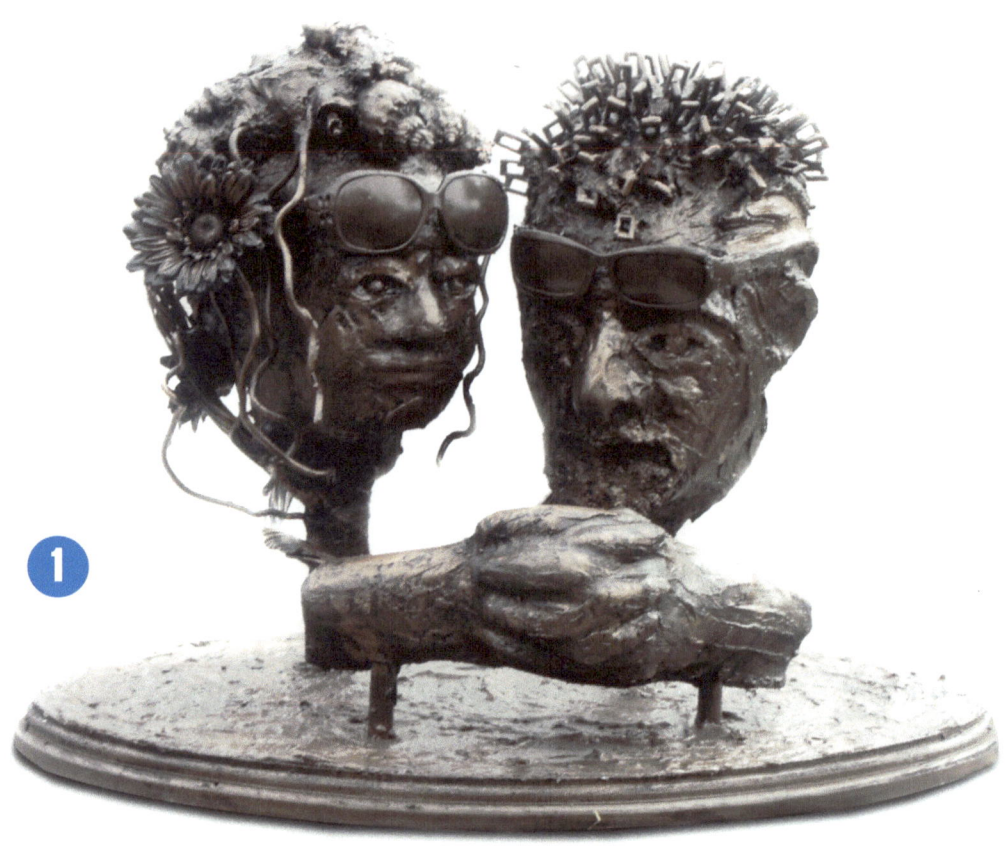

**1 Mark and Heike** Plaster and found objects.

# SOPHIA SOLARIS

**LOCATION:** Kitchener
**WEB:** SophiaSolaris.com
**EMAIL:** Info@sophiasolaris.com

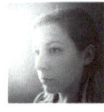

Sophia Solaris (born 1984) is an artist from Germany, living in Kitchener since Jan 2010. She received her final degree in July 2011 from the State Academy of Fine Arts, Karlsruhe, Germany. New to Canada Sophia Solaris' observations of North American culture lies in her wonderment of the overwhelming amount of waste that surrounds us. Fascinated with the wasteful nature of our environment she makes work that turns worthless pieces into something valuable.

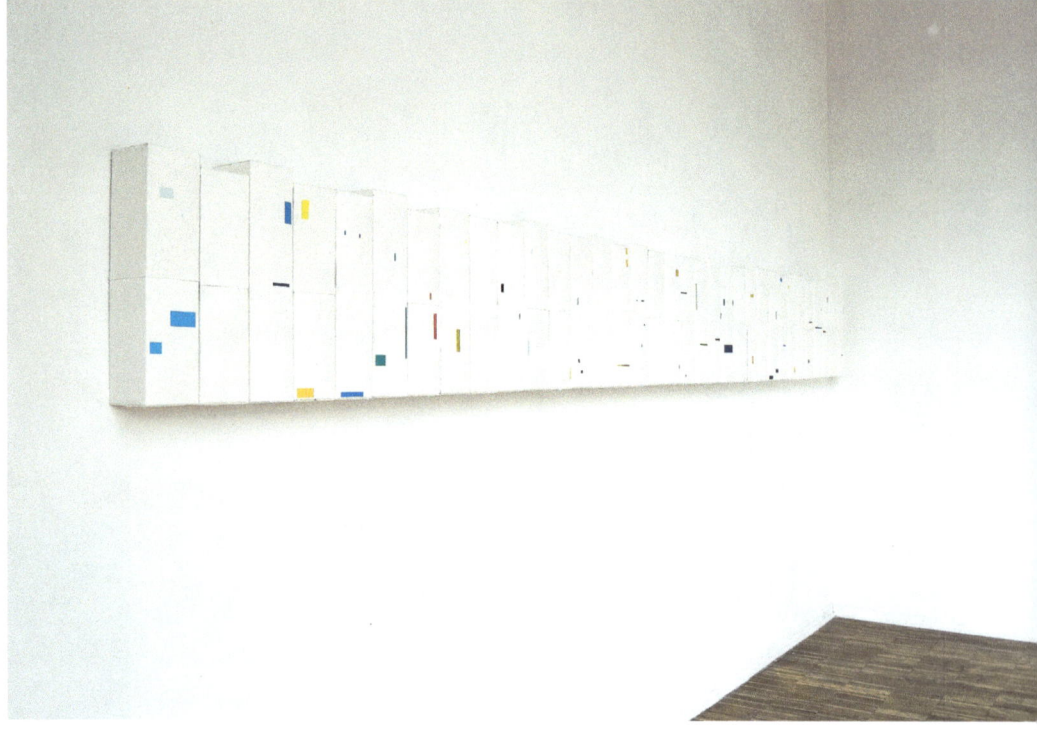

**1 White Hope** 142x16" Milk/ Juice Cartons. I peel the cartons and the color you can see is left from the label.

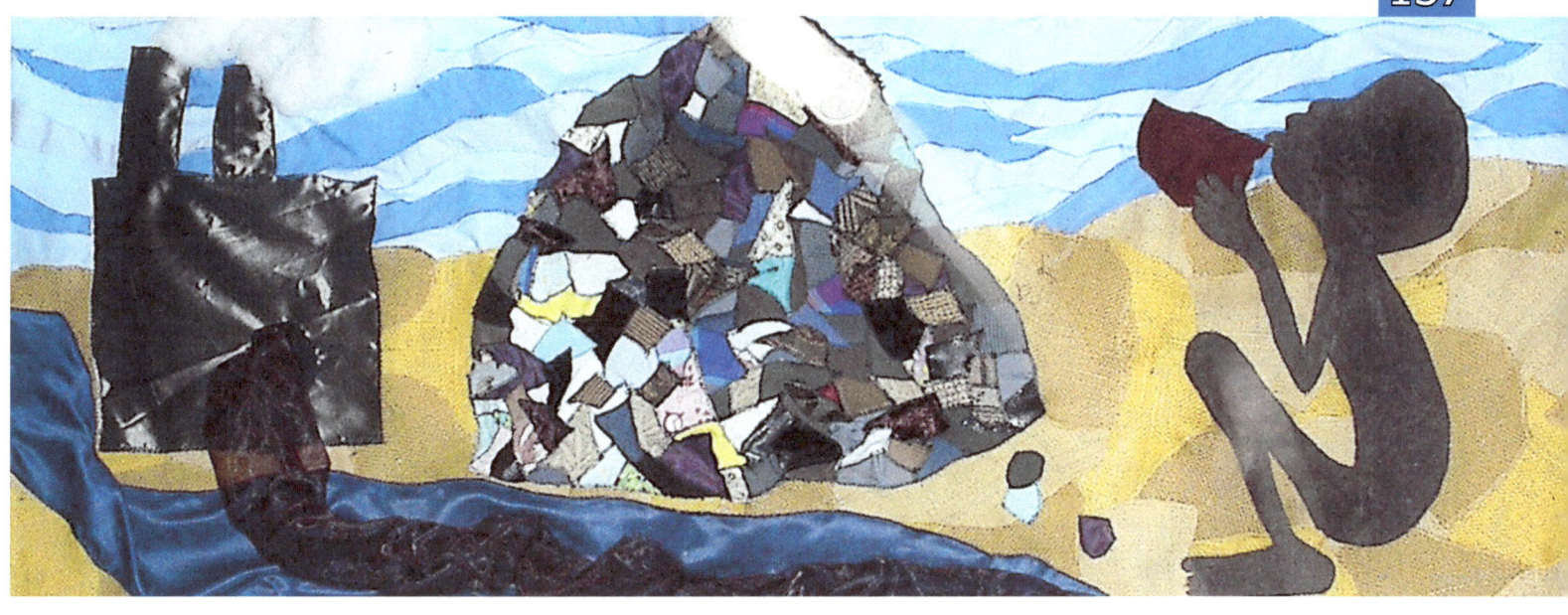

# CRYSTAL BRADFORD
# LIAM KIJEWSKI

**LOCATION:** Haysville
**WEB:** KWProcession.ca, TrashTheatre.ca
**EMAIL:** KWProcession@gmail.com

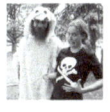 Deeply inspired by nature and our impact on it, Crystal utilizes waste in many of her pieces. She often works with textiles, making costumes and recycled prints. She has been taking her Trash Theatre project to schools and festivals in the region with Liam Kijewski. Together they also own Wildlife Gardening, a landscaping, restoration and native plant nursery. Working as an eco-arts instructor at the Button Factory, Crystal is an organizer for KW's Procession of the Species Celebration.

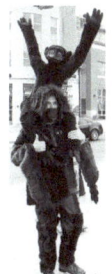 Working as an eco-arts instructor with the Button Factory, Liam co-ordinates KW's Procession of the Species Celebration with Crystal Bradford. Creating props and costumes for Trash Theatre he also enjoys drawing and printmaking. A graduate of OIART, Liam has recorded his rapping and playing with several projects, his latest being Rhythmic Recyclers. With Crystal he also owns Wildlife Gardening, a landscaping, restoration and native plant nursery business.

 **1 Poverty and Pollution** Appliqué with scrap materials.

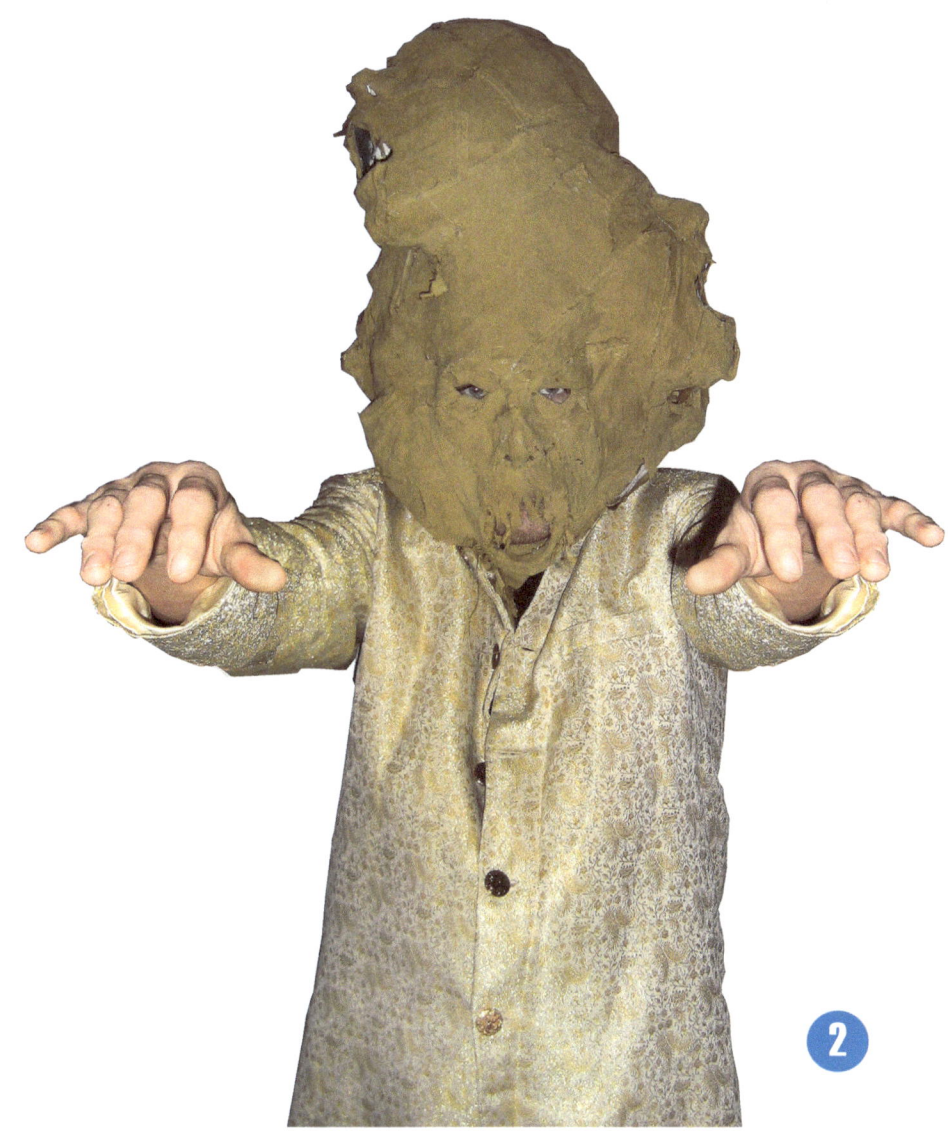

**2 Multi-headed Monster** Plaster Gauze, polyester shirt.

# BRENDA MILLION RADFORD

**LOCATION:** Stratford
**WEB:** RadfordStudio.com
**EMAIL:** Brenda@radfordstudio.com

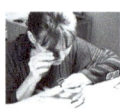 Brenda Million Radford is a Stratford Jewelry Design- er who loves working with people to create meaningful jewelry for them. Personal symbolism can be found in many of her custom pieces and it tells interesting stories about the people who commis- sion and wear her jewelry. Brenda spe- cializes in custom designed fine jewelry, limited edition collections and unique corporate designs

**1 Abstract Mask** 30x26 mm x18" Sterling Silver. Limited edi- tion collection.

**2 Dragon Ring** 15x20x20 mm Sterling Silver, custom designed.

**3 Family Ring** 10x23x26 mm Sterling Silver and gemstones. The ring is designed around her kids' initials.

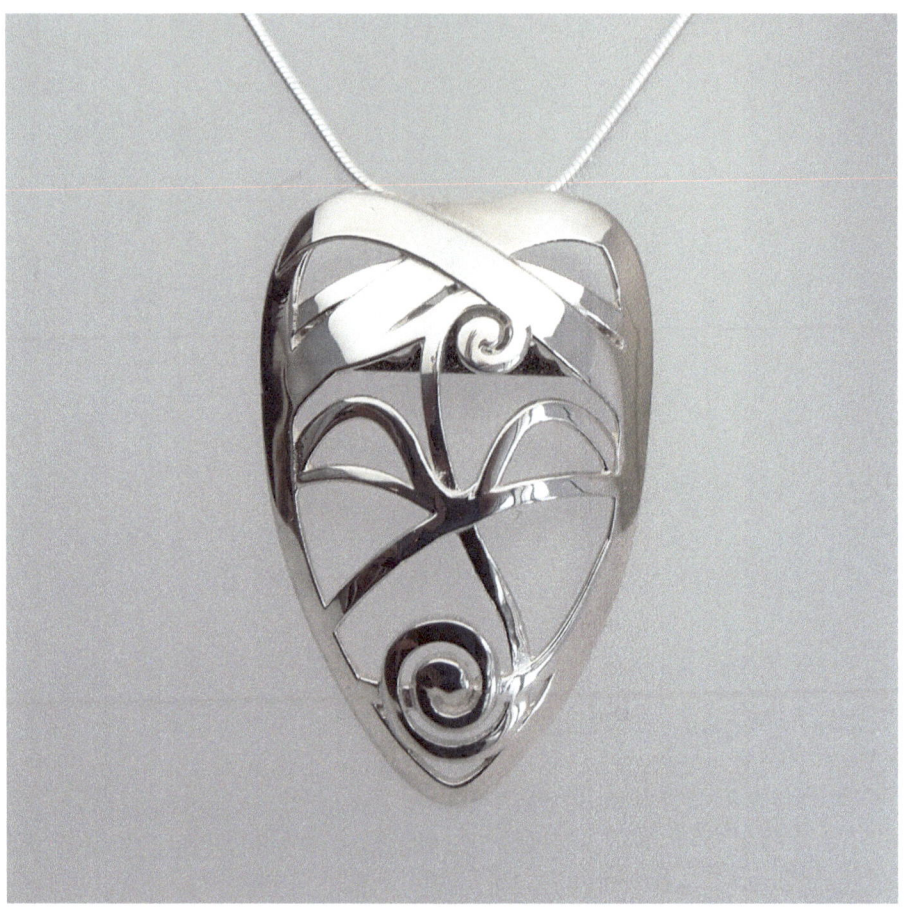

**1**

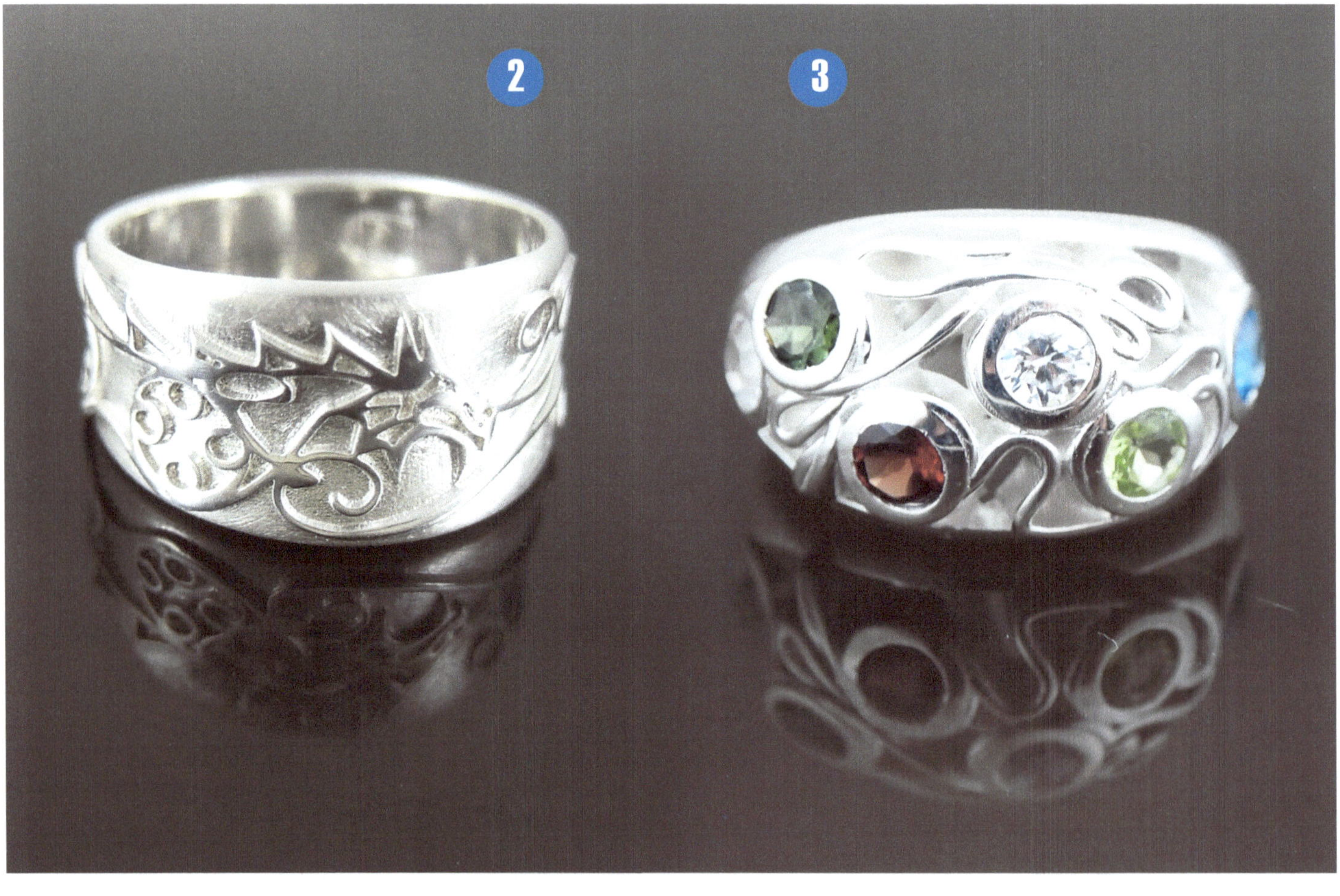

**2** **3**

# MARY ANN HELMOND

LOCATION: Kitchener
**WEB:** Mabeads.ca
**EMAIL:** Mabeads@rogers.com

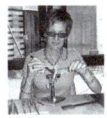

Working with hot glass is like sculpture and painting combined. Mary Ann's love of glass has become a passion for creating unique beads that are wearable works of art. Coloured rods of glass are melted, layered and manipulated in the flame of a torch and then annealed to strengthen the glass. The process involves careful planning and an eye for colour and design.

**1 Seahorse & Friends** (front and back views) 1.5x3.5 cm, effetre glass. Inspired by scuba diving in the Florida Keys.

**2 Art Nouveau Peacock** 3.1x3.1 cm effetre glass. Inspired by Art Nouveau and the peacocks in Waterloo Park: including an albino peacock! Collaboration with Roxann Blazetich-Ozols

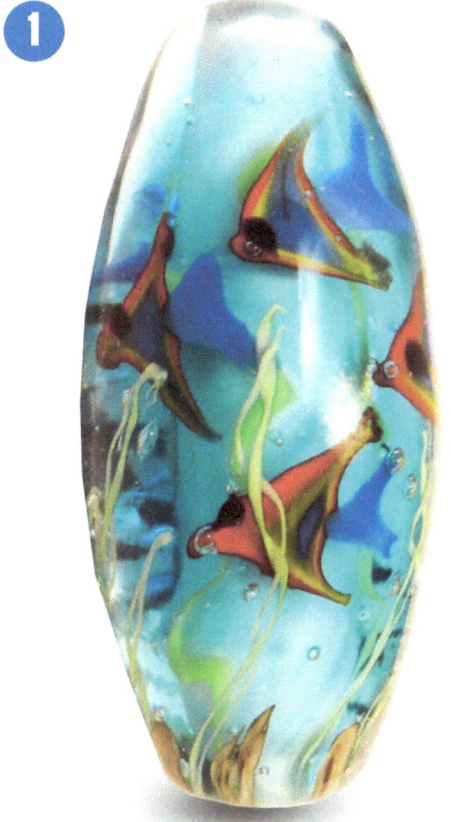

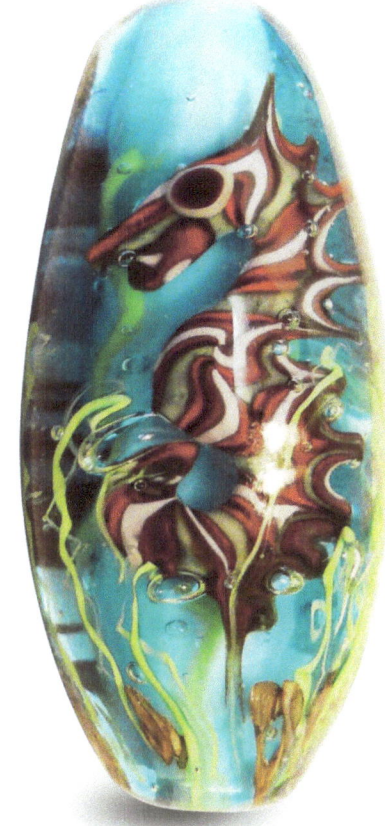

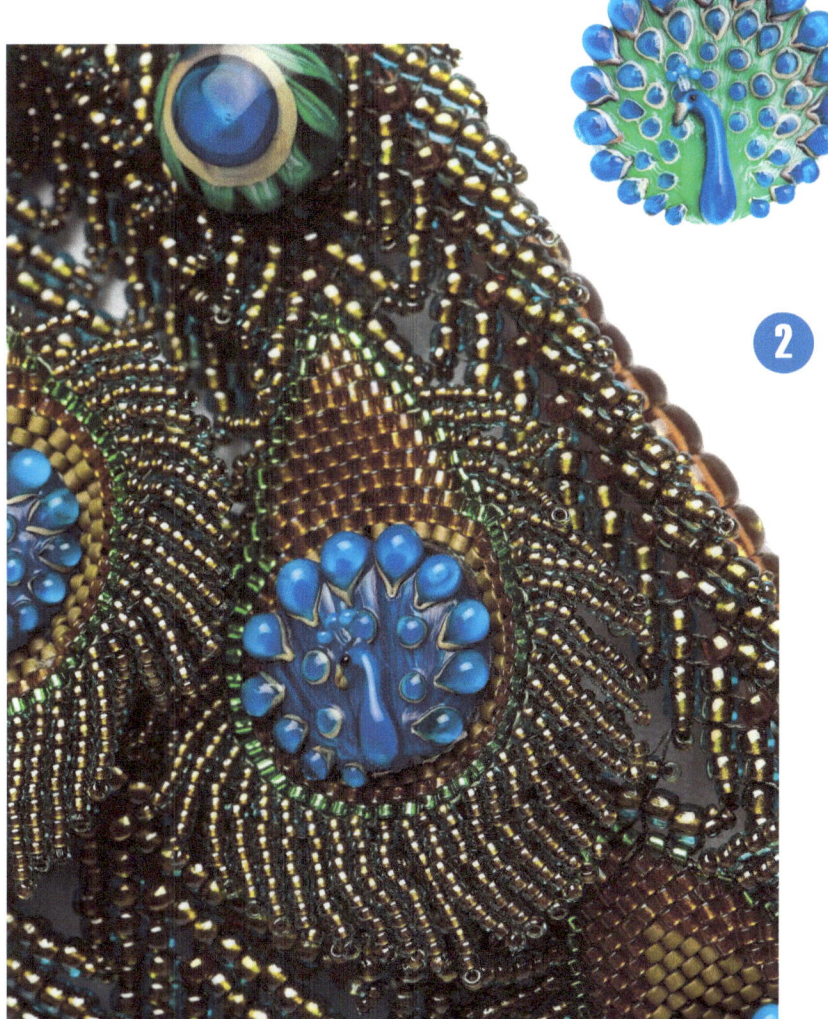

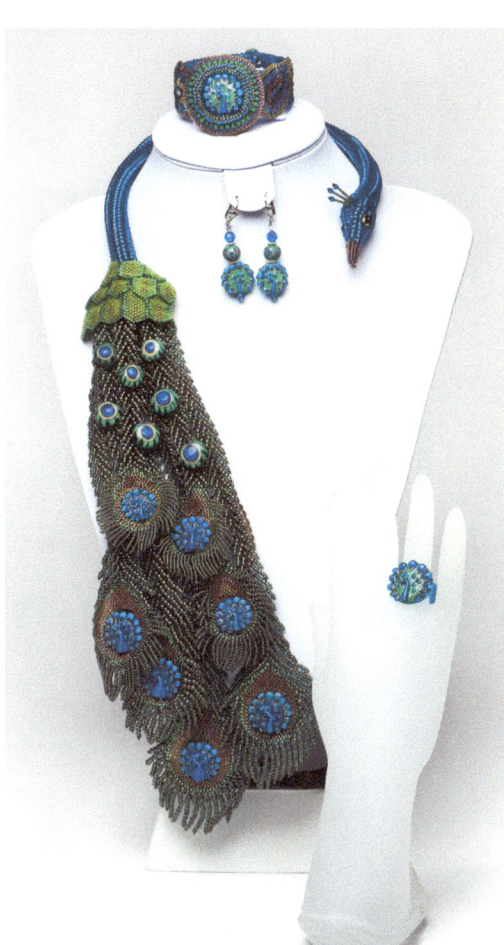

# SHEILA DIEMERT

**LOCATION:** Kitchener
**WEB:** SheilaDiemert.com
**EMAIL:** sdiemert@sympatico.ca

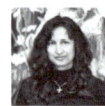

Spending a summer painting murals at a hostel in Tanzania, East Africa was a turning point for Sheila Diemert. That experience clearly illustrated the importance of art as a communication tool which can be both informative and uplifting. Her paintings capture and convey emotion, personality and spirit. In addition to installations in Tanzania, Sheila maintains a residence and studio in Kitchener-Waterloo.

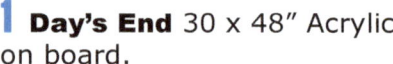

**1 Day's End** 30 x 48" Acrylic on board.

**2 Vying for Attention** 40 x 60" Acrylic on canvas.

**3 Country Drive** 40 x 60" Acrylic on canvas.

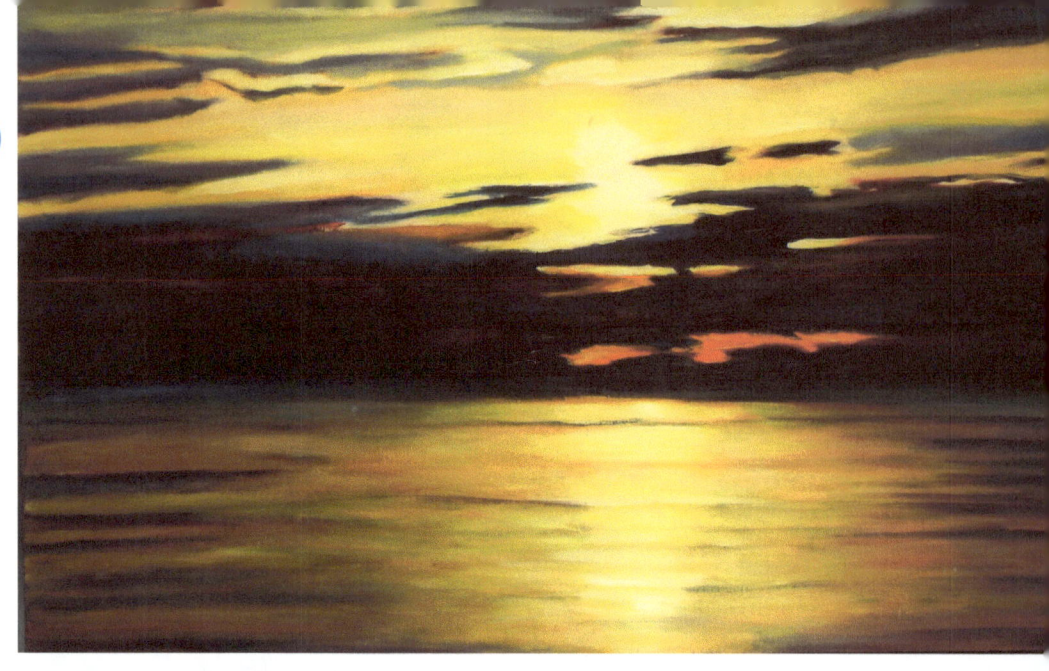

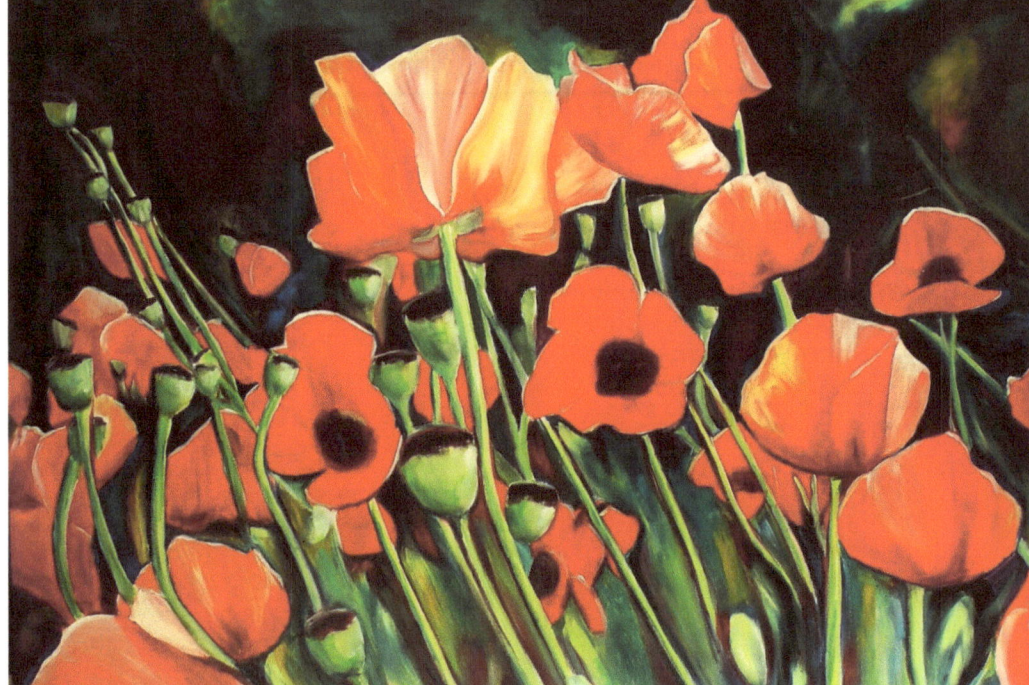

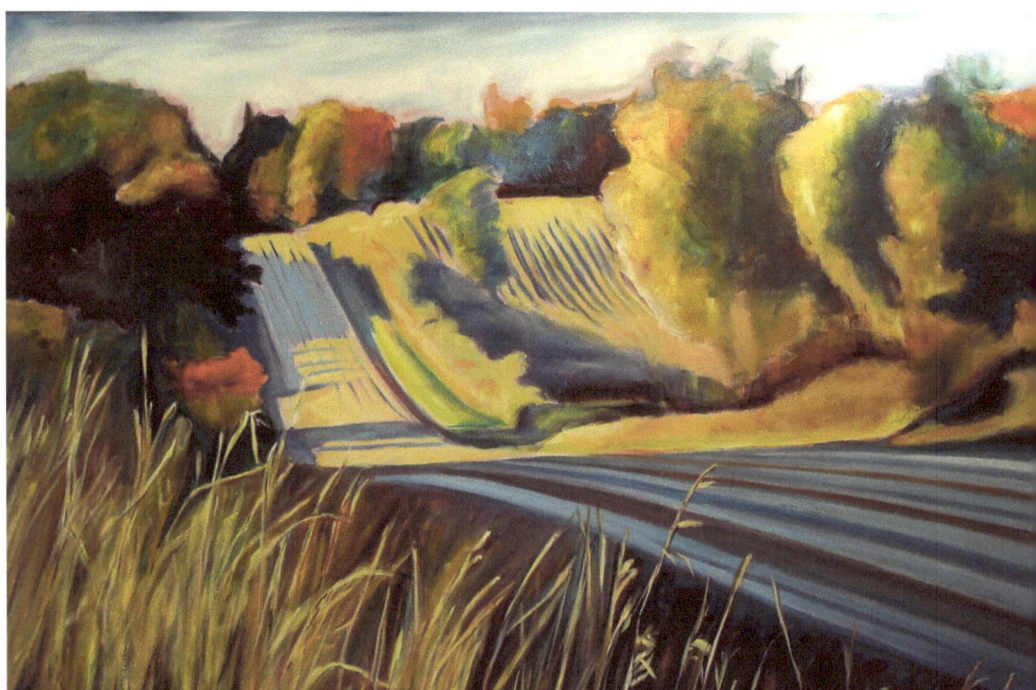

# DEBRA LENGYELL

**LOCATION:** Kitchener
**WEB:** (N/A)
**EMAIL:** Lengyell@sympatico.ca

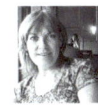 Debra Lengyell is an artist who works in acrylic, sculpture and pen. She began her career studying at Waterloo University and Mount Allison University where she majored in Fine Arts. Before taking an early retirement this fall to focus on her art, Debra was the art teacher at a local elementary school.

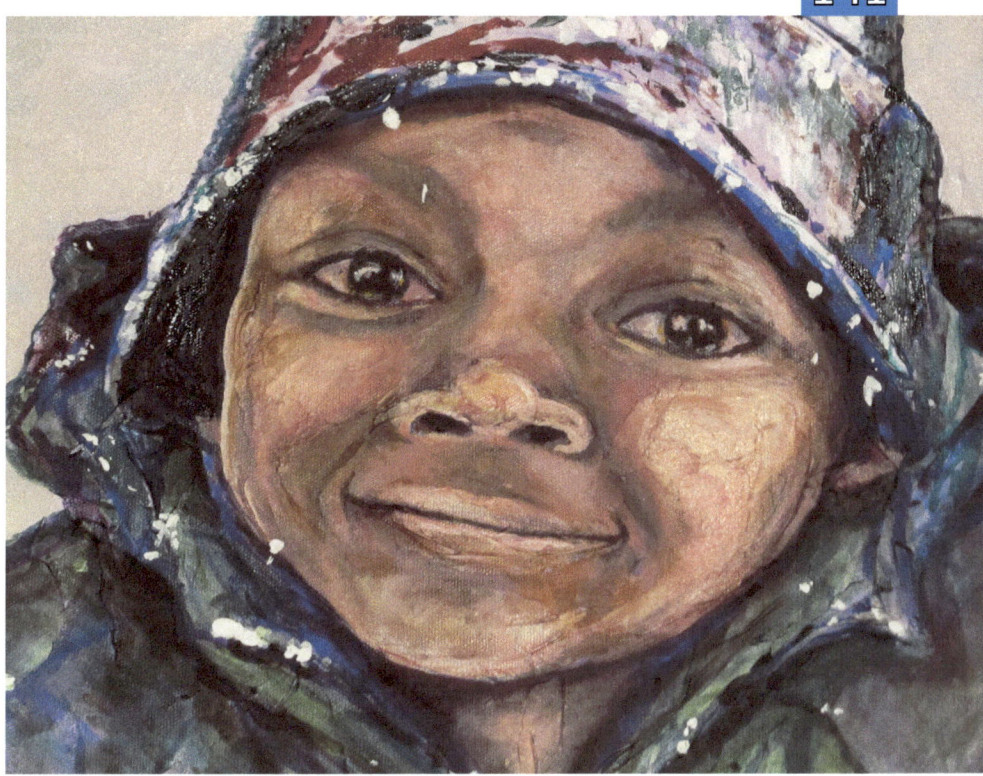

**1 Muku** 16x20" Acrylic on canvas.

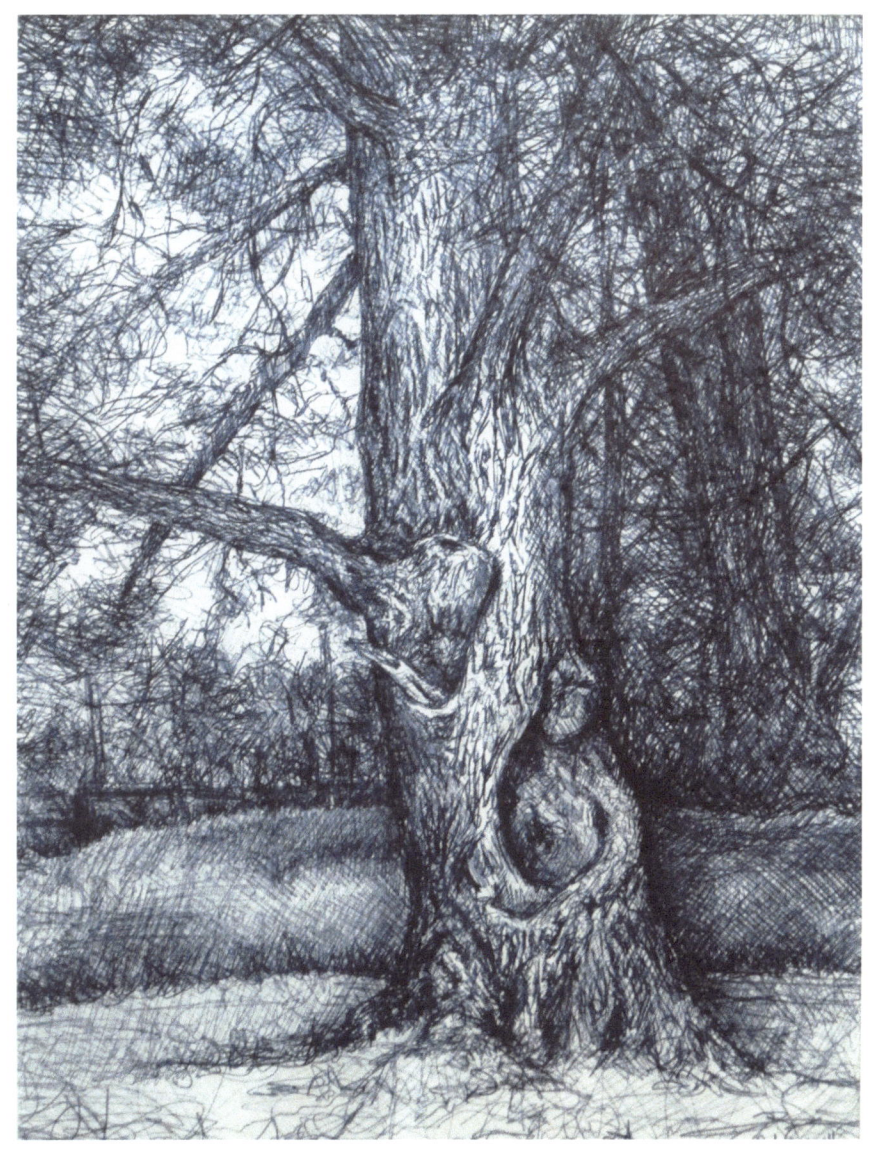

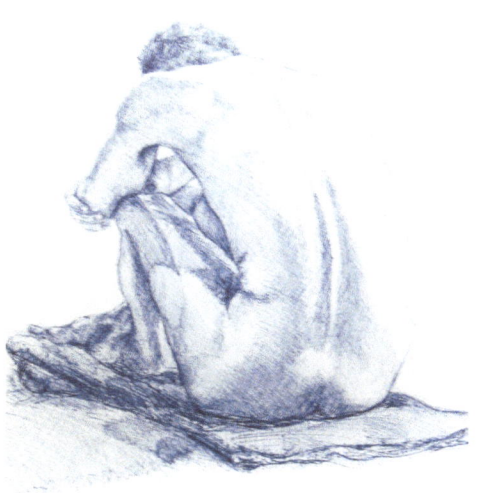

**2 The Back** 8x10" Ink on paper.

**3 Trees #1** 10x24" Ink on paper.

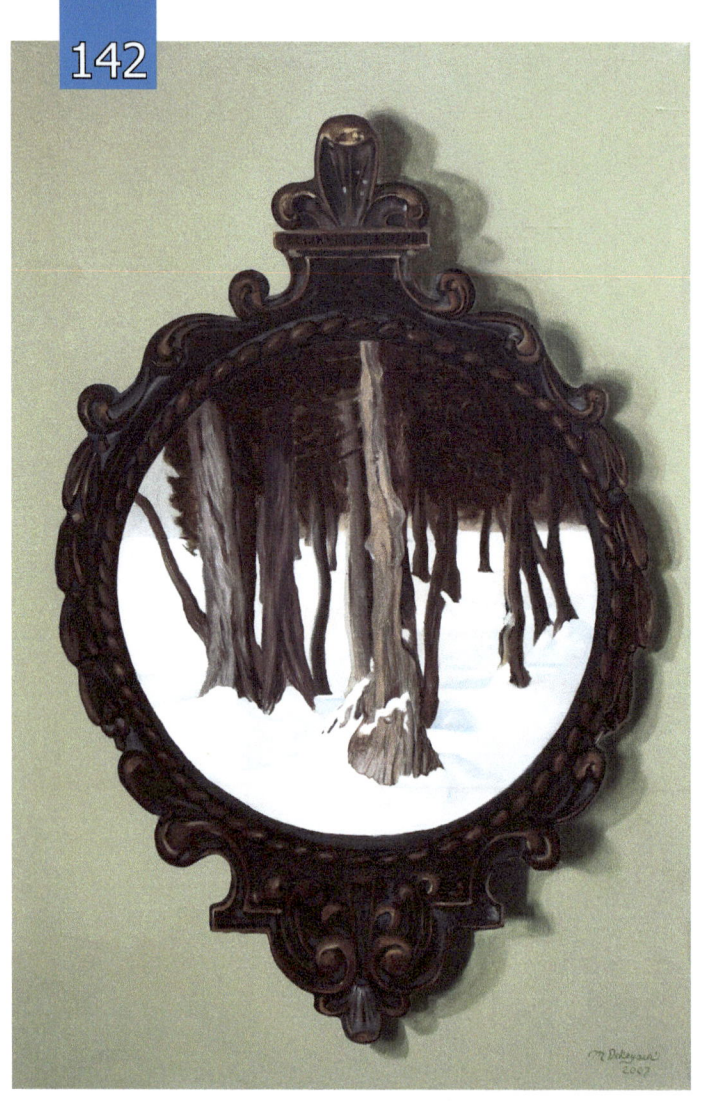

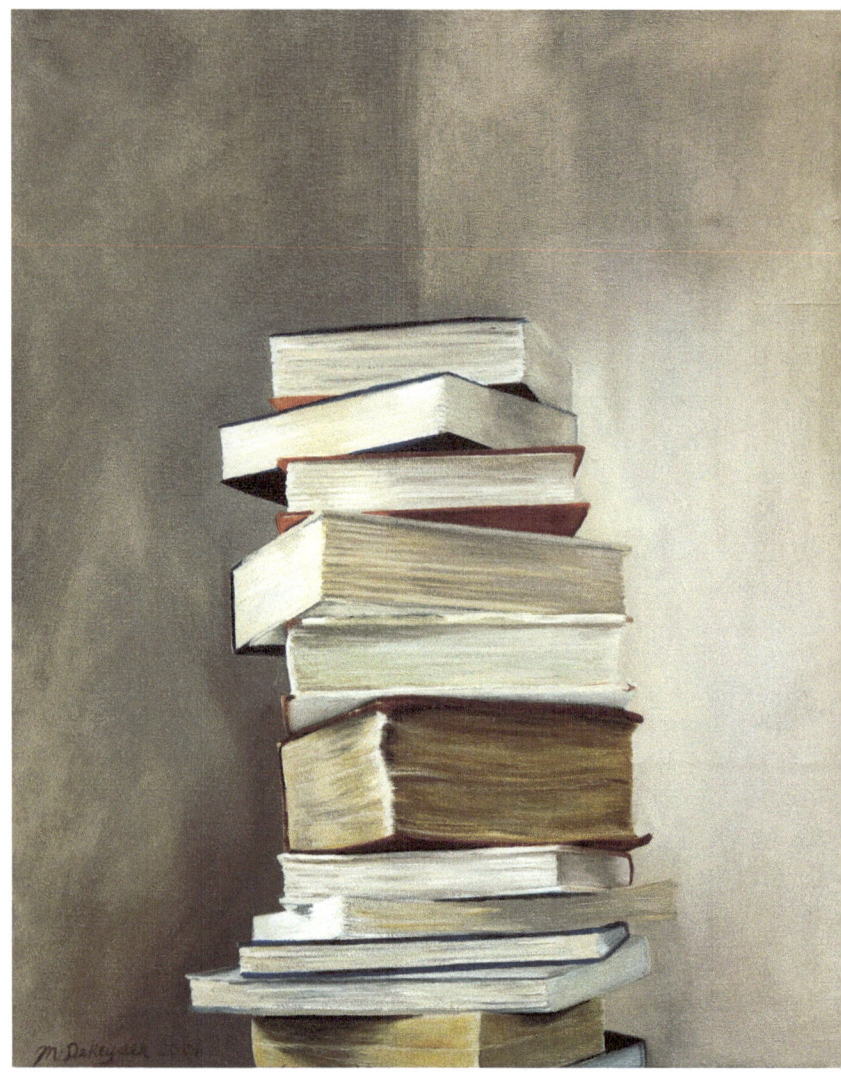

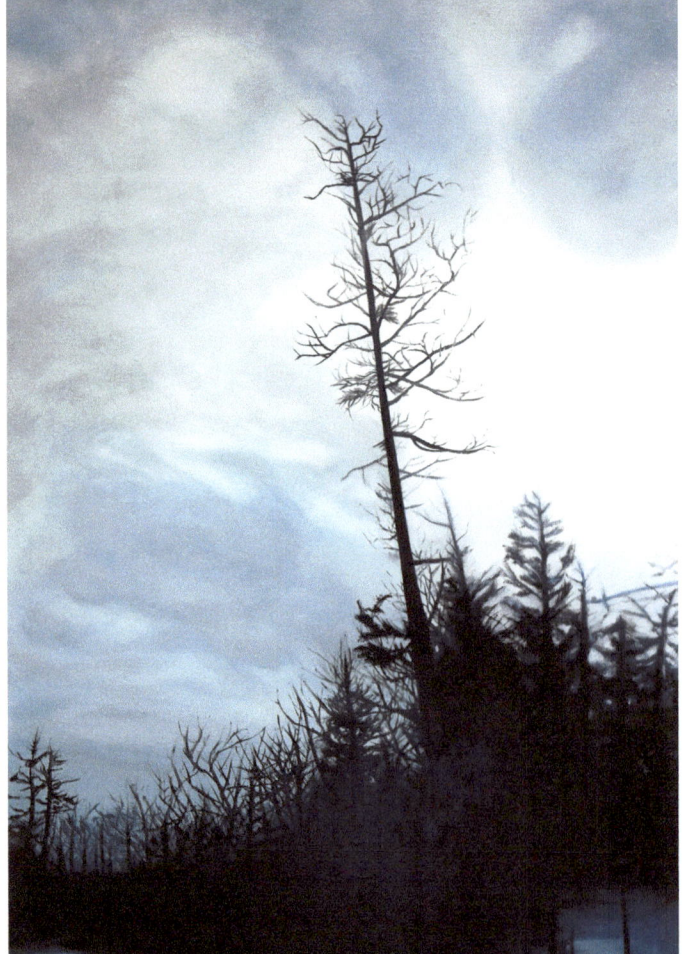

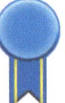

# MURRAY DEKEYSER

**LOCATION:** Waterloo
**WEB:** MurrayDekeyser.com
**EMAIL:** Murraydekeyser@hotmail.com

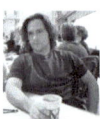

Murray Dekeyser was born in Kitchener, Ontario in 1977. He received his BFA (2000) from McMaster University and his MFA (2005) from the University of Waterloo. Dekeyser also attended the Dundas Valley School of Art for one year in the Advanced Studies program (2004). Dekeyser exhibited his work at the first ever Waterloo Arts Festival in Waterloo in 2006. Dekeyser is currently supply teaching for the Waterloo Region District School Board and painting and parenting whenever he can.

**1 Mirrorscape** 24x30" Oil on canvas.

**2 Tower of Books I** 24x30" Oil on canvas.

**3 Winter Tree** 24x36" Oil on canvas.

**I hope you enjoyed the show!**

**There are many other people who haven't been mentioned, that I would like to thank for either helping me out directly with advertising, recruiting, selling, exhibiting, just keeping me sane, or places that I just like. These are a few of them:**

**SiliconW.com**

**UptownGalleryWaterloo.com**

**Rarefunk.ca**

**StateOfTheArtSupplies.com**

**kwartzlab.ca**

**wpl.ca**

**TheArtStoreOfWaterloo.com**

**RoyalMedievalFaire.org**

**QueenOfHeartsCostumes.ca**

## INDEX OF ARTISTS

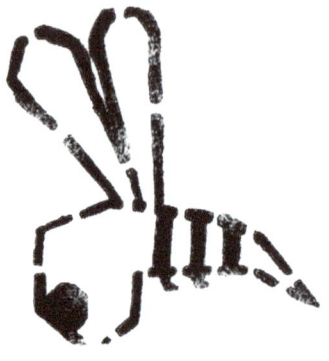

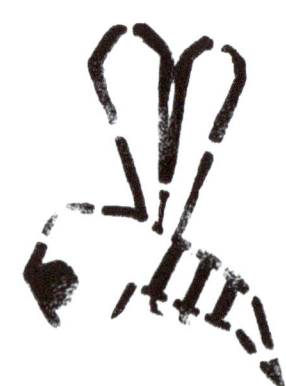

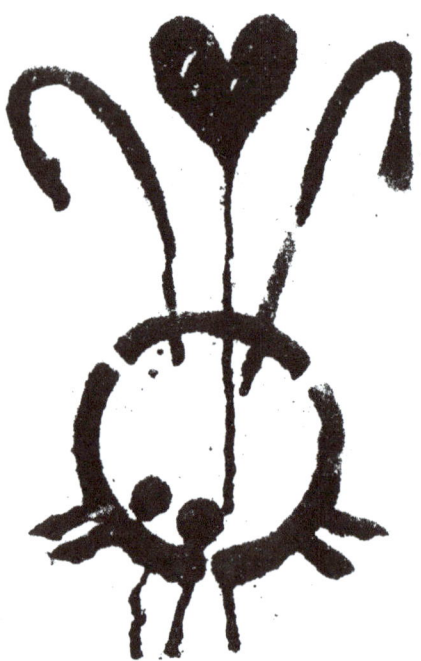

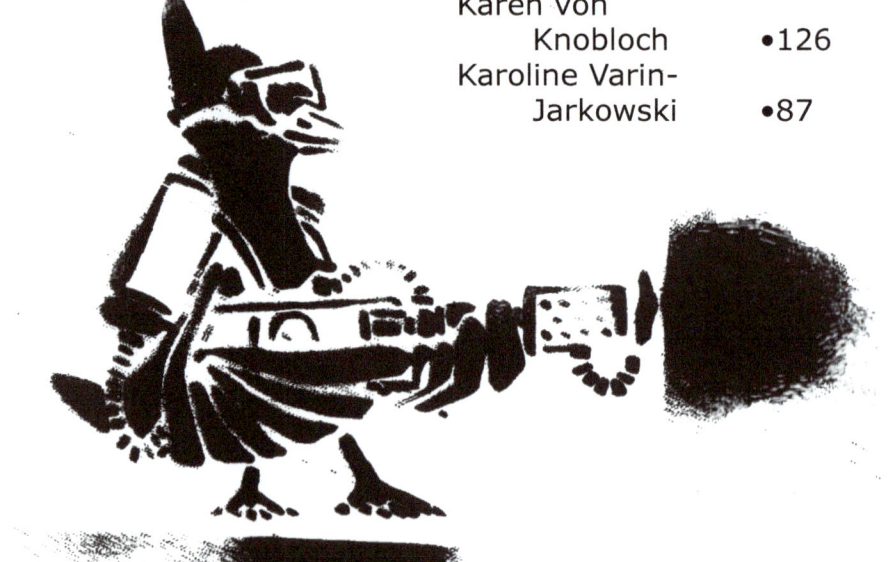

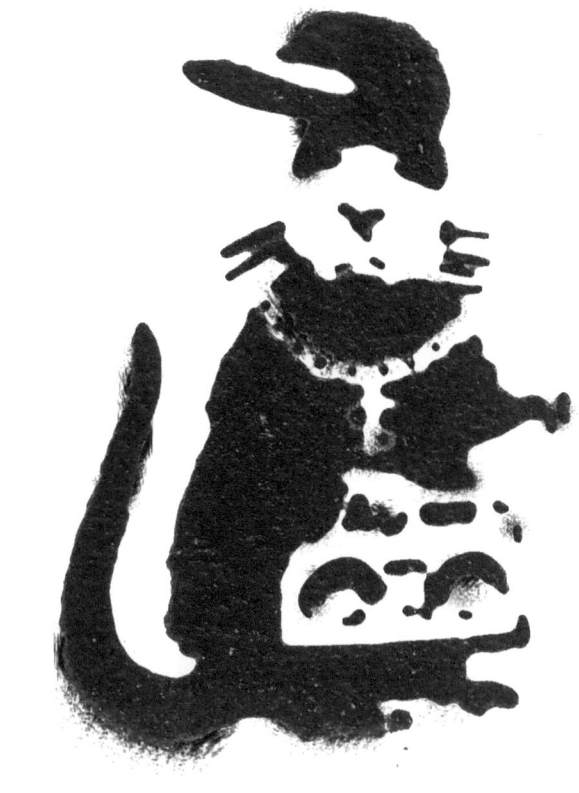

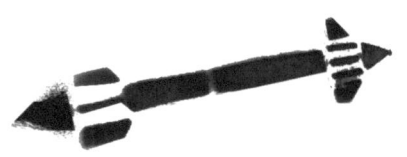

**Unauthorized Street Art** Most about 12" Spraypainted vandalism, various places in Waterloo.

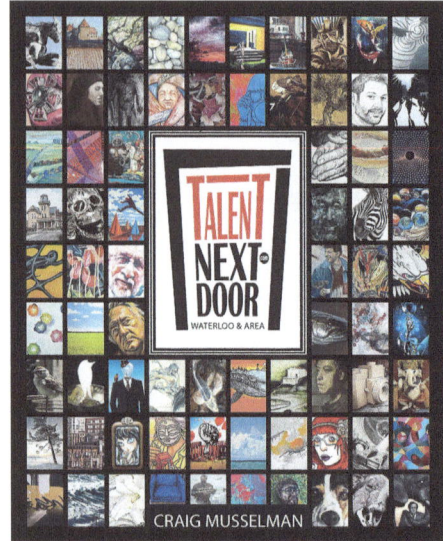

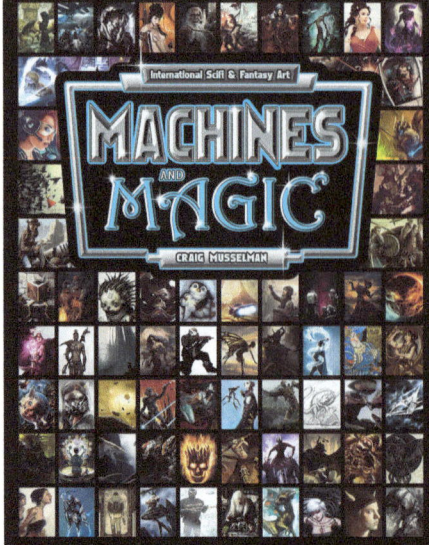

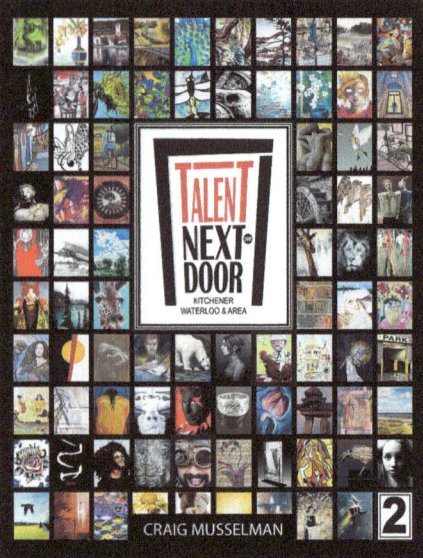

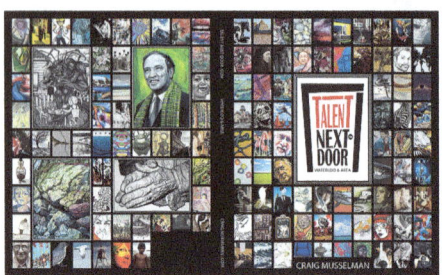

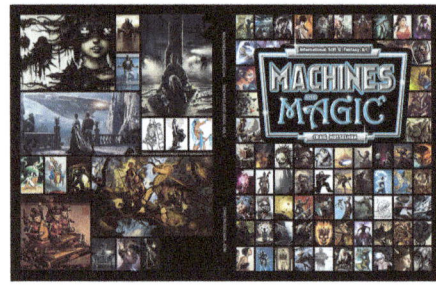

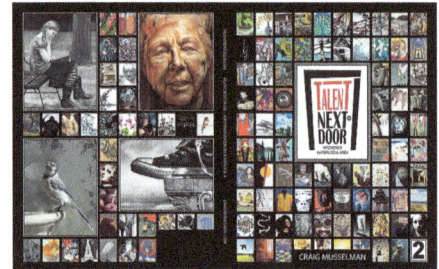

**Talent Next Door - Waterloo & Area Volume 1** 8x10" Featuring 142 top local artists from the Waterloo to Stratford region on 136 pages (2010) www.TalentNextDoor.com ISBN: 978-1453808061

**Machines and Magic Volume 1** 8.5x11" Outstanding Fantasy and Sci Fi art from every continent featuring 91 top artists on 156 colour pages. (2011) www.MachinesAndMagic.com ISBN 978-0987789501

**Talent Next Door - Waterloo & Area - Volume 2** 8.5x11" Featuring 139 top local artists from the Kitchener Waterloo region on 136 pages (2011) www.TalentNextDoor.com ISBN:978-0-9877895-1-8

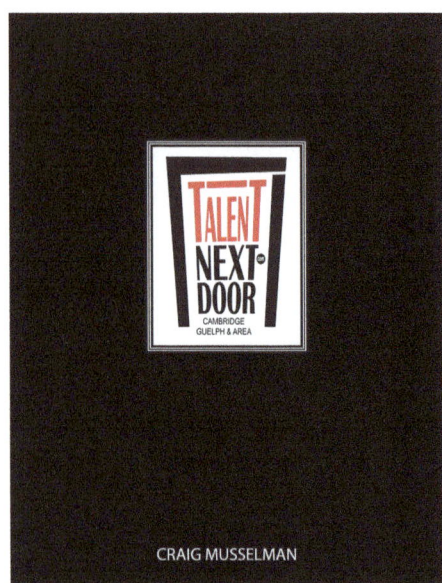

# ART BOOKS BY CRAIG MUSSELMAN

By 2011 Craig will have 4 books in print shown here, with several more planned for 2012. If you would like to participate, please visit the appropriate website for details or link through his portal at www.CraigMusselman.com. His books are printed by Createspace.com (an Amazon owned company) & are available through Createspace, Amazon & other online bookstores, but he usually has a few on hand for local pickup. He can be contacted at his business email CraigBMusselman@gmail.com or the email specific to each book.

**Steampunk Art** The best of steampunk art from around the world. Victorian Splendour of the future! Costumes, props, artefacts, and art. Recruiting submissions for 2012 www.SteampunkArt.ca

**Flower Reference** From my stock photo website a full colour book of hundreds of flower pictures to draw and paint. Featuring leaves, flowers and closeups. (spring 2012) www.ShootItFor.Me

**Talent Next Door - Cambridge / Guelph and Area Volume 1** 8.5x11" Featuring over 100 outstanding local artists from the Cambridge / Guelph region on over 100 pages (2011) www.TalentNextDoor.com

**Super Real Art** and **Black and White Drawings** one on realistic, "Wow how did you do that?" art the other drawings in black and white. Recruiting submissions for 2012/2013. www.RealisticArt.org

**Science Fiction / Fantasy Art Reference** From my stock photo website a full colour book featuring helpful references for all your fantasy/sci fi art needs. (planned for summer 2012) www.ShootItFor.Me

www.ingramcontent.com/pod-product-compliance
Lightning Source LLC
Chambersburg PA
CBHW050716180526
45159CB00003B/1049